PHYSIOLOGICAL
PSYCHOLOGY

McGraw-Hill Series in Psychology

HARRY F. HARLOW, *Consulting Editor*

John F. Dashiell was Consulting Editor of this series from its inception in 1931 until January 1, 1950. Clifford T. Morgan was Consulting Editor of this series from January 1, 1950, until January 1, 1959.

CLIFFORD T. MORGAN
University of California, Santa Barbara

McGRAW-HILL BOOK COMPANY
New York
St. Louis
San Francisco
Toronto
London

PHYSIOLOGICAL
PSYCHOLOGY
THIRD EDITION

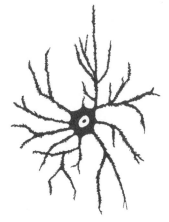

II

Preface to the Third Edition

THIS EDITION, like earlier ones, is intended to serve both as a textbook for undergraduate and graduate students preparing for psychology, physiology, and medicine and as a reference book for graduate students and other workers in these fields. To enable students of diverse backgrounds to study the book with less difficulty, the author has included the elementary facts of psychology, physiology, and anatomy as are necessary for the understanding of the main subject matter of physiological psychology. To make the book useful as a reference, original literature and other sources are frequently cited.

Bibliographic references are not, however, as complete as they were in earlier editions. This is because the research literature has had an enormous growth in the last twenty years, and there is simply not enough space to document thoroughly every topic covered. In fact, only with great effort was it possible to limit the bibliography to about the same size as it was in the two previous editions of this book. To do this, review articles, symposia, and other summaries have been cited frequently in place of more numerous references to original sources. Often only the more classical studies and the more recent articles have been mentioned, and in the case of more elementary background material, no reference to the research literature is made. Nevertheless, by going to the sources cited, the interested worker can usually construct a fairly complete picture of research to date.

Like the bibliography, the subject matter covered has had to be more selective than in previous editions. To stay within reasonable limits of space, the author has knowingly omitted the treatment of many topics and of literature relevant to the topics covered. No doubt he has also unknowingly omitted pertinent material, because the literature is now so enormous that no one person can keep abreast of all of it.

As in the past, the author's principal emphasis is on experimental research done with animal subjects rather than on human clinical studies. This is because the objective is to provide a knowledge of the physiological bases of normal animal and human behavior (see Introduction), not to offer professional clinical training. The latter is not needed or desired by many students, and in any case, if it is, it is better left to a more advanced level of training. Also, as in the past, the author has minimized "arm-chair" speculation and put the emphasis on the established facts without neglecting, he hopes, the problems and theories to which they relate.

The general sequence and organization is like that of earlier editions. Certain differences, however, should be noted. The coverage of both the senses and of motor functions has been condensed, in both cases with a reduction of two chapters, in order to provide for expanded treatment of the areas of motivation and learning, which have made great gains in recent years. The number of chapters on these latter topics remains the same, but they are now longer than they were.

Two kinds of bibliographic references are still provided. One is a set of general references to books and reviews. Because these often relate to two or more chapters, they have been grouped together near the end of the book rather than in individual chapters (see General References). The other set of references is a bibliography of the literature cited. Because each reference indicates the page in the text to which it applies, this bibliography also serves as an author index.

Thanks are due Miss Betty Borges and my wife, Jean S. Morgan, who did the lion's share of the work, for typing the manuscript. The authors and publishers who have kindly permitted the use of their illustrations are acknowledged in the legends of the respective illustrations.

CLIFFORD T. MORGAN

Contents

PHYSIOLOGICAL
PSYCHOLOGY

INTRODUCTION

PHYSIOLOGICAL PSYCHOLOGY may be defined as the study of the physiological basis of human and animal behavior. At present, it is primarily a fundamental or pure science, concerned with understanding the physiological events that underlie behavior.

Our task in this introduction is to present a preview of what is to come. First, we shall describe the organization of the book, how the subject matter is developed, and what the reader can expect to encounter. Then, in a second section, we shall review briefly the ways in which physiological psychology is studied.

THE BOOK AND ITS PROBLEMS

In order to get a bird's-eye view of our subject, let us consider its most general aspects. We shall do this by taking up the outline of the chapters and seeing what it means. There are, in all, 20 chapters. They fall into six main groups. Each group has a few central problems that run through its chapters. Let us see briefly what these problems are.

PHYSIOLOGICAL BACKGROUND

The first group of chapters covers the physiology of the organism as it pertains to our subject matter. Students of physiology would have to know their subject extremely well if they were to have at their command all the facts and concepts needed for the study of physiological psychology. Many who read this, however, will have had little or no physiology. Hence, to provide the proper physiological background for both the expert and the novice, we have tried to select and organize as briefly as possible the highlights of physiology needed for consideration of the main problems of the book. This is done in Chapters 1 through 4.

When we say "physiology," however, we speak loosely, for the next chapters have in them considerable material that is outside the bounds of physiology. It would be more correct to say that they contain the basic anatomy, physiology, and biochemistry for studying physiological psychology.

The events of the body with which we shall be most concerned take place in two general systems: the response mechanism and the internal environment. The response mechanism includes the sense organs, the nerves, the nervous system, and the various muscles and glands that are used when an organism makes a response. The internal environment, on the other hand, is the complex of substances—food materials, secretions of the glands, metabolic products of body functions—that circulate in the blood and lymph and make up an essentially chemical environment for the nervous system and other organs of the body.

Of the four chapters on physiological background, three are concerned with the response mechanism and a fourth with the internal environment. In the latter, we encounter a certain amount of endocrinology and biochemistry. What is said about the response mechanism, however, is partly anatomical and partly physiological. In order to understand function, one must first understand the structures in which the functions take place. Hence anatomy and physiology go hand in hand. Accordingly, in the first two chapters, the anatomy of the response mechanism is described; in the third one, its physiology is summarized; and in the last of this group, the nature of the internal environment is explained.

As we go along in the book, there will be more facts about anatomy, physiology, and biochemistry. These are introduced as they are needed to deal with each problem at hand. The first group of chapters therefore provides only a minimum background for launching into our subject.

SENSORY FUNCTIONS

In the second group of chapters, numbered from 5 to 9, we start to discuss the central problems of physiological psychology. This group concerns the senses. In earlier editions, this group was the largest in the book, for much more was known about sensory functions than about other areas of physiological psychology. This is probably still true, but in the meantime a great deal has been discovered in the areas of motivation and learning. For that reason, the chapters on sensory function have been condensed to make room for new knowledge in other areas.

When we study the senses, we shall follow the same general pattern for each sense. This is to begin with a description of the anatomy of the system so that we know its parts. Then we summarize the facts physiologists have provided about the events going on in the system. Finally, we correlate these facts with what is known of the psychological phenomena of sensory experience and perception.

In dealing with sensory phenomena, we consider them in four main classes: intensity, quality, space, and time. Relatively little is known about time perception, at least from the physiological point of view, and so our emphasis is on the other three. These represent three principal attributes of sensory experience in all senses. Our task is to find the physiological events that underlie them and explain their characteristics.

Let us make clear what is meant by *attribute*. A light seems bright or dim, a sound loud or faint, or a pain mild or strong. These are examples of the sensory attribute of *intensity*. Experience of various stimuli also has *quality*. Some lights are red and others green, we hear tones of high pitch or low pitch, and we feel a pinch on the arm as a pain or simply as a pressure. These are all qualitative differences. Thirdly, objects have a *spatial* aspect. Visual objects, for example, have shape, size, distance, and location—all spatial aspects. Even sounds seem big or small, near or far away; and most stimuli that are sensed with the skin have some size and shape. In each of these cases, we shall be concerned with the physiological mechanisms that enable us to perceive attributes in particular ways.

MOTOR FUNCTIONS

A great deal could be said about motor functions because both psychologists and physiologists, particularly the latter, have studied them extensively. For years, much of neurophysiology rested on the study of spinal reflexes. However, psychologists are not interested, nor do they have any important purpose, in the study of motor functions in great detail. Accordingly, we have condensed the available information into two chapters. This is enough to give a general picture of the motor systems and how they work.

The principal chapter is entitled Motor Functions. It is concerned with such activities as posture, balance, reflexes, coordination, and the execution of movement. The physiological basis of these activities is, in general, well understood. A second chapter, entitled Emotion, may be classified either as a chapter on motor functions or one on motivation, for it is both. Emotion involves the motor activities of both the skeletal musculature and the autonomic effectors such as the heart, blood vessels, and glands. Emotion also serves as motivation for other behavior, and some of the material to be considered concerns such motivation.

MOTIVATION

In addition to emotion, there are four chapters constituting a group on motivation. The first one, entitled Sleep, Arousal, and Activity, contains a brief treatment of attention, which is often considered to be associated with perception, but what is known about it physiologically is most closely related to sleep and activity. The other chapters in this group treat the physiological mechanisms of hunger and thirst, sexual behavior, and instinctive behavior. All of them describe the kinds of behavior in man and animals that are not merely responses to stimuli but are driven by some urge or impetus within the organism.

In the past, many psychologists and physiologists have thought of drives as internal stimuli. Sometimes drives are that, but usually they are more than that. Drives begin in the internal environment, and this environment in turn affects many organs of the body. It can excite such receptors as those in the stomach, heart, or blood vessels, and these can elicit experiences and responses. Or the internal environment may directly excite, or, if not that, sensitize, the nervous system so that motivated behavior is either emitted or elicited by stimuli that otherwise would have no effect on the organism. There are indeed many physiological factors at work in motivation. Our problem will be to put them together into a picture of a complex mechanism that explains basic motivations such as those for food, water, sex, and parental care.

LEARNING AND MEMORY

The fifth group of three chapters deals with learning and memory. In them we take up classical conditioning, avoidance conditioning, discriminative learning, maze learning, and more complicated kinds of problem solving. Throughout the chapters run two closely related problems. One is the problem of localization of function. Are different sorts of learning and memory localized in particular parts of the nervous system? To a certain extent they are, but on the whole one cannot identify their locus.

A second problem may be called the problem of recovery of function. This is involved in motor functions as well as in learning. When a person is paralyzed, e.g., by a "stroke" (i.e., a broken blood vessel in his brain), he usually improves over the course of time so that months after the injury he has shown considerable improvement. Similarly, organisms sometimes forget certain memories and habits after an injury to the brain, but they usually regain the habits or can relearn them if the injury has not been too severe. These are only two examples of recovery of function after brain injury. The phenomenon appears in many experiments on brain functions in learning.

MAN AND HIS DISORDERS

The last two chapters form a group that does not fit into the pattern of earlier chapters. In a sense they are miscellaneous. Much of the material in both chapters, however, deals with disorders that occur in man. The first one concerns disorders of the brain, mostly brain injury, and considers the relatively limited knowledge available so far of the way the human brain works in perception, motor functions, memory, and speech. The second and last chapter reviews what is known of the physiological basis of intelligence and personality disorders. This chapter also discusses biochemical theories of learning, since the most promising theories of the physiological basis of learning are biochemical, and a discussion of them fits most readily into the general topic of psychochemistry.

APPROACHES TO PHYSIOLOGICAL PSYCHOLOGY

We now have had a quick glimpse of the topics to be covered in the book. We ought also, however, to deal in this introduction with the way in which the various topics are studied. There are, in principle, several ways of studying the physiological mechanisms of behavior. The one we shall emphasize is experimental research in animals, but we should be aware of the others.

PHILOSOPHIC APPROACHES

To say that we are interested in the physiological events underlying behavior is to say, in other words, that we shall be dealing with the mind-body problem. This is as old as the ages. The founders of the world's religions, the philosophers, and almost all the intellects of the past have had something to say about it. Some of their beliefs were well founded; some were not. For example, the notion that the mentally ill are "possessed of demons," that the brain is a cooling device for the blood, or that the soul is located in the pineal gland are all ideas that were held at one time but do not survive in the light of modern scientific evidence.

The important point to be made here, however, is not whether such ideas are right or wrong; it is how conclusions about the relation of mind and body are reached. Philosophers put forth their ideas after reading other philosophers and gaining as much worldly knowledge as possible. This approach sometimes has merit, for often it is all that can be done. The mind-body problem, however, has been yielding to scientific treatment and has been taken out of the realm of philosophy. One cannot get very far by thinking about it. There are certain assertions often made by philosophers or those of religious persuasion about which science has nothing to say. Science, for example, has nothing to say about whether man has a soul. Yet, it is possible in science to understand how certain aspects of mental life are manifestations of underlying physiological processes.

CLINICAL APPROACHES

Another possible approach to the mind-body problem is through clinical experience with sick people. Medical men see many cases of people with some illness of the mind, the body, or both. By systematizing their clinical experience, they ought to be able to say something about how mind and body are related. They have. Medical clinicians, in fact, have a great deal to say about how mind and body are related in sick people. Their statements fall into two main categories.

One concerns the case in which mental events cause a disorder of the body. Many people going to practitioners are examples of this sort of relation. A branch of medicine—in fact, a specialty within psychiatry—known as psychosomatic medicine has grown up to deal with it. However, the field is still young, and not very many statements can be made with certainty. In any case, psychosomatic medicine is a branch of clinical medicine, not a basic science. Since we are concerned here with fundamental knowledge rather than with practical matters that are better learned at a later point in professional training, we shall have very little to say about psychosomatic medicine. Occasionally, however, we shall describe fundamental studies in animals that are related to the problems of psychosomatic medicine.

Somewhat the same reasoning applies to a second clinical approach to the mind-body problem. Here the problem is one of how disorders of the body affect mental and behavioral functions. Injuries to the brain and disorders of glands are the two principal areas in which such a relationship may be seen. Clinical neurologists deal with brain injuries, and specialists in internal medicine are concerned with glandular disorders. Because of limitations in ability to study these disorders systematically, there is not much of a fundamental nature to be learned from clinical experience with the disorders. Here and there throughout the book, however, and particularly in the chapter on brain disorders, we shall make use of knowledge gleaned in this way.

When we make reference to clinical material, it is well to keep in mind what its limitations are. In the first place, the clinician is not always sure what is wrong with a patient. The clinician may think he has a brain tumor when he really has an infection, or he may think the tumor is small when it actually is rather large. Because it is not always possible to be sure just what is wrong, where it is, and how bad it is, it is frequently not possible to be certain what it is in the function of the body that makes a difference in behavior. Secondly, one usually cannot use what the experimental scientist call "controls," i.e., see the patient's behavior when he was normal, and so cannot determine with any certainty that his physical disorder is the cause of what seems to be a behavior disorder. Thirdly, it is not possible to learn what one wants to know just when one wants to do so. People become ill as nature decrees, and they very often do not have the kind of illness, at the time when good use could be made of it, to answer scientific questions. For reasons such as these, clinical material does not provide a great deal of help in understanding the physiological underpinnings of behavior.

EXPERIMENTAL METHOD

In clinical studies it often would be helpful to know what would have happened "if"—if the patient had a different illness, if he had a higher intelligence, if he had been brought up in a different family, if any one of a number of factors had been different. In history and the social sciences, scholars would also give a great deal to know what would have happened "if—." Many of the sciences, however, particularly the natural sciences, are not under the shadow of this big "if." Researchers can find out, for they can *experiment*. They can set up the conditions just the way they want them, conduct their tests, and find out what lies behind the "if." It is largely for this reason that the natural sciences have made such great progress so rapidly.

Luckily, experiments in physiological psychology can be made, although not without troubles. Animals and people do not always behave as docilely as machines do, and experimenters must use their wits to set up just the kind of conditions desired. Experiments in this field are not nearly so neat and often not so clear-cut as they are in the natural sciences. But they are experiments, and they do answer questions, and by means of them steady progress is made.

Another handicap faced more in physiological psychology than in any other part of psychology is that usually experiments cannot be made on people. It is not safe to use many kinds of drugs and hormones with them, and it is not possible to remove various glands or parts of the nervous system at will. Researchers therefore must do the best they can, not with human beings, but with animals. For that reason, the greater part of this book is based on animals, not human beings. Fortunately, a good deal is known about evolution in behavior and in bodily form through the animals to man, and frequently very good deductions can be made from animal experiments to human beings, but this cannot always be done. It is necessary simply to recognize the limitation and make the best of it.

SCIENTIFIC INFERENCE

Experimental science is a complex process in which the "good" scientist indulges in a healthy mixture of experiments and hypotheses. From both his experiments and those of his comrades, he gets hunches, guesses, deductions, hypotheses, predictions—whatever one wants to call them—of what may happen under different circumstances, say of another experiment. He then proceeds to test his hypothesis with an experiment. Sometimes he is right and sometimes wrong, but in any event his new experiment produces ideas for more experiments, and he goes on around the cycle again. In the end, it is the experiments that are important and the facts that can be trusted, provided the experiments have been done properly, and the hypotheses, crucial as they are to inspiring the scientist and leading him to the more important experiments, are simply the means to the end.

The cycle of experiments and hypotheses goes on in physiological psychology as it does in other sciences. Each experiment suggests tentative conclusions or hypotheses that lead to other experiments. This process will show up again and again. We shall stress the experimental facts, but we shall try to show how one fact leads to the idea for the next experiment. In some places, too, where the experiments suggest an idea that has not been tested yet, we shall bring it out in the hope that some reader will see the way in which the next step may be taken or perhaps make the experiment himself. This way of writing may sometimes include details of the scientific process that one does not really need to understand the main points. Yet it keeps the facts and the theories straight, and it makes more vivid the steps investigators take in advancing knowledge and erasing the "ifs."

Not everyone makes a habit of going around the cycle of hypothesis and experiment. Some conduct experiments without any hypothesis in mind, and their experiments often do very little good because they do not concern any question of interest. For that reason, we shall say little or nothing about some experiments. Some scientists raise many interesting hypotheses but do very little experimenting. They call themselves theorists and have a place in the scheme of things. Where their ideas seem to be helpful, we shall explain them and use them. In general, however, we cannot devote much space to theories or hypotheses that have not been put to the experimental test. There are many such notions—one could devote a whole book to them—but they can be, and often are, wrong. The facts, however, seldom lie, and we shall give them most of our space and attention.

MEETING GROUND OF THE SCIENCES

Perhaps no subject draws upon so many different sciences and their methods as does physiological psychology. Every sort of pure and applied scientist—mathematician, physicist, chemist, physiologist, pharmacologist, anatomist, neurologist, psychiatrist, electrical engineer, as well as psychologist—has been taking part in our subject in one way or another. None can claim sole or even major rights to the subject, for each has contributed a share. There is no point in describing in detail what each of them has done and can do, but as one reads he may be able to see how the various sciences have met and joined hands to solve the mind-body problem.

1 THE PERIPHERAL RESPONSE MECHANISM

<hr>

T HE PHYSIOLOGICAL MACHINERY of behavior is exceedingly complex. In principle, however, it is simple. It consists of receptors, a central nervous system made up of brain and spinal cord enclosed in the bony cases of the head and spinal column, motor nerves carrying impulses outward from the central nervous system, and finally the various effectors of the body such as muscles and glands. These are the essential parts involved in the adjustments of men and animals to their environments.

In this chapter and the next these parts will be considered in some detail, in order to provide a general background of knowledge of the structures involved in behavior. Later on, in chapters that cover various aspects of behavior, additional details will be introduced as they are needed to deal with each particular problem. Here in these chapters we shall divide the summary into two parts: the peripheral response mechanism and the central nervous system. In this chapter we shall consider the receptors, the effectors, and the peripheral nerves going into and out of the nervous system.

THE FUNCTIONS OF CELLS

It was a discovery of great importance when Robert Hooke first observed (1665) that a very lowly organism, cork, is made up of cells. Subsequently many investigators observed cells in all kinds of tissues. Today it has been recognized that the *cell doctrine* (1838) applies to all animals and plants. *The cell is the fundamental unit of living organisms.* We must therefore look to the cell first to see what kinds of building blocks are used in the machinery of behavior.

It is almost always possible to distinguish three principal and important parts of a cell: the membrane, the cytoplasm, and the nucleus. These three parts are interrelated. What happens in one part affects events in the other parts. Each part, however, has an important role to play in the life of the cell. Each part is primarily responsible for certain properties of the cell (see Figure 1.1).

THE MEMBRANE

The membrane is the boundary of the cell. It keeps some things in, and some things out of, the cell. Because it is porous, however, it allows many things to pass through. The "things" in this case are chemical molecules or charged ions making up the positive or negative parts of molecules. The study of the membrane therefore can, and does, become a matter of physical and biological chemistry, which will be treated in Chapters 3 and 4.

One of the basic properties of the membrane is the maintenance of an equilibrium of pressures and of ions on the two sides of it. Some ions and molecules press from the outside inward; some, from the inside outward. Some pass in, and others pass out. The pressures and the movements, however, tend to remain in some kind of equilibrium. Those on one side tend to balance those on the other. From this general property of equilibrium derive some other important properties of the membrane.

Polarization is one of them. Some substances, called *electrolytes,* dissociate when they are dissolved in water, and there are many such substances in the body. The molecule bursts into two parts, one carrying a positive charge and the other a negative charge. Each part is called an *ion.* Because the membrane does not let everything through, it often happens that more positive ions collect on one side of the membrane than on the other, while an excess of negative ions collects on the other side. There may be an equilibrium of ions—the

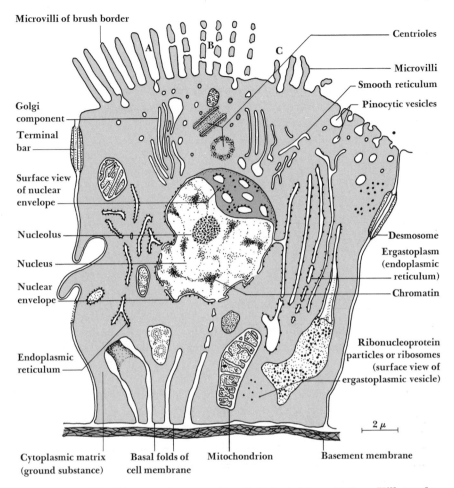

Microvilli of brush border

Golgi component

Terminal bar

Surface view of nuclear envelope

Nucleolus

Nucleus

Nuclear envelope

Endoplasmic reticulum

Centrioles

Microvilli

Smooth reticulum

Pinocytic vesicles

Desmosome

Ergastoplasm (endoplasmic reticulum)

Chromatin

Ribonucleoprotein particles or ribosomes (surface view of ergastoplasmic vesicle)

$2\,\mu$

Cytoplasmic matrix (ground substance)

Basal folds of cell membrane

Mitochondrion

Basement membrane

FIGURE 1.1—Diagram of a composite cell. (Adapted from *McGraw-Hill encyclopedia of science and technology*, vol. 2. New York: McGraw-Hill, 1960. P. 588. Used by permission.)

number of ions on the two sides may be equal—but one side may be more positive or more negative than the other. This state of affairs is called *polarization* of the membrane.

Related to polarization are two other important properties of cells that we shall later see emphasized in the cells of the nervous system. These are *irritability* and *conductivity*, properties that are always interlinked in cell functions. When a membrane is in equilibrium and when it is polarized, any loss of ions or change in the charges of ions on one side of the membrane breaks down or disturbs the equilibrium. A mechanical stimulus, for example, may knock off some of the ions on the outside of the membrane; or a chemical stimulus, made up, say, of negative ions, may neutralize positive ions; or an electrical stimulus, which may be negative or positive in charge, may neutralize ions. In these and other cases, the membrane equilibrium is disturbed.

Any such disturbance causes a counterreaction, because the membrane tends to maintain an equilibrium. Ions may move through the membrane or otherwise rearrange themselves on the membrane, because it has been thrown into disequilibrium. This property of the membrane is called *irritability*. Sometimes the counterreaction is not confined to the part of the membrane that has been disturbed. Ions and molecules move about in neighboring regions of the membrane to help restore the equilibrium in the irritated part. Thus the disturbance spreads to regions nearby. These, in turn, cause disturbances in their vicinity. As a result, the disturbance runs along the whole membrane from one point to the next. This is called *conduction,* a very important property of muscle and nerve cells.

CYTOPLASM

Cytoplasm is the main mass of the cell. It makes up the general area of the cell within the membrane and outside the nucleus. Cytoplasm varies enormously in its structure and chemical makeup. It may contain many granules and minute structures, some of which are a great aid to the anatomist and physiologist in distinguishing different kinds of cells and their state of health.

Generally speaking, two properties of the cytoplasm of cells are of special interest. One is *secretion*. The various chemical substances in the cytoplasm may so react with each other that they make new substances not found outside the cell. These may remain in the cell for internal use or they may pass out through the membrane and be circulated to other cells for their use. In the latter case, they are called *secretions*. There are also many substances that are made as waste products of the cell's chemistry and pass out of the membrane because the cell no longer "wants" them. These are *excretions.*

A second general property of the cytoplasm is *contractility*. This again is the product of some chemical reactions. When molecules change in shape or size or move about in a mass in such a way that the shape of the membrane and the cell is changed, this is called contraction or contractility. It is through such changes that cells can move themselves about or, in highly developed organisms, move other cells of the organism and thus move the organism as a whole.

A third general property of cytoplasm that is of interest to us is *metabolism*. This is the sum of the chemical reactions through which molecules of food stuffs are converted into various chemical forms for the storage and release of energy. Virtually all such chemical reactions take place in the cytoplasm, although they are influenced indirectly by conditions outside the cell and are often carried out under "instructions" brought by chemical messengers from the nucleus to the sites of metabolic activity in the cytoplasm. Two principal sites are the *mitochondria* and the *ergastoplasm* (Figure 1.1). The mitochondria are frequently referred to as the power plants of the cell, for in them takes place the oxidation of various food stuffs so that energy may be stored for later quick release in the form of phosphate bonds. This energy is used in various ways, but one of them is in the manufacture of proteins from amino acids, which is believed to take place in the ergastoplasm. Some of the details of these processes will be discussed in Chapter 4.

THE NUCLEUS

The nucleus of the cell is the locus of two important activities: the supervision of metabolic activities of the cytoplasm and the reproduction of cells. Both center around the chromosomes and their components, the genes. The latter consist of a complex substance, desoxyribonucleic acid (DNA), whose varied structure carries the genetic code. This code is carried through messenger RNA (ribonucleic acid) to the protein factories described above (see Chapter 4).

In the reproduction of a cell, the chromosomal material divides in two. When it does this, the rest of the nucleus, the cytoplasm, and the membrane usually split up too, each taking with it its share of the chromosomes. Two organisms are thus reproduced out of one. In sexual reproduction, two different cells must come together and their chromosomes interact with each other before the reproductive process begins. In any case, an important function of the nucleus and its chromosomes is the reproduction of the cell or cells that make up the organism.

In viewing the functions of the cell as a whole, we must note that the separation of properties of the membrane, cytoplasm, and nucleus is only a rough approximation. Actually, the activities of all parts of the cell are closely interrelated and are involved, directly or indirectly, in its various properties. Depolarization of the membrane may, for example, cause the cytoplasm to contract or to secrete, and chemical conditions in the cytoplasm naturally affect the equilibrium and exchange of materials at the membrane. The present summary, however, brings out the important features of the cell in which we shall later be interested.

THE RESPONSE MECHANISM

We have been discussing a "typical" cell, one that shows all the features of all the cells known in the human body. To a certain degree, all cells in an organism possess all the properties that we have described. However, by the time they may be seen in a grown animal or man, few, if any, cells show all these properties in equal degree. Instead, various cells have become highly specialized in their functions. They have undergone what the cell physiologist would call *differentiation*. One type of cell—the nerve cell—is so differentiated in structure and function that it specializes in irritability and conduction; another—the gland cell—in irritability and secretion; and so on. To get some appreciation of how this differentiation has taken place and what it has accomplished, let us look briefly at the scheme of cellular differentiation as seen in the evolution of organisms and in their embryological development.

CELLULAR DIFFERENTIATION

There are three classes of cells in which the physiological psychologist is most interested. They are the *receptors,* the *adjustor neurons,* and the *effectors.* Each class represents a high degree of specialization in one or more of the properties of cells just discussed. These classes are not rigidly defined, for neurons often serve the functions of receptors, but they will serve for our purposes.

These three classes made their appearance quite early in evolutionary history in very primitive multicellular organisms (see Figure 1.2), and they appear to have developed in a particular order (Parker, 1919). The first to be differentiated was the muscle effector cell; it specializes in irritability and contractility. An example of this first primitive effector is the common sponge. Later, the function of irritability was further specialized in a receptor cell, a cell whose principal function was to be excited by external stimuli and transmit the excitation to the effector. Such a receptor cell specialized in the property of irritability. Thus was differentiated a simple receptor-effector mechanism with which the organism could respond more effectively to its

FIGURE 1-2—Diagram of primitive response mechanisms. (Adapted from G. H. Parker. *The elementary nervous system.* Philadelphia: Lippincott, 1919. Pp. 200–202.)

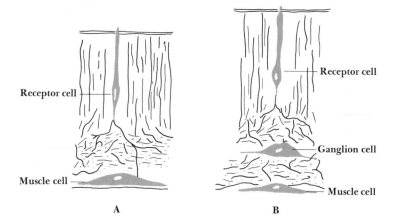

environment. Last to be developed was a third, eventually tremendously important class, the adjustor neurons. These became conductors between the receptors and the effectors. They are called adjustor neurons—although we usually shall refer to them simply as neurons—because they make possible a great variety of adjustive responses of the organism to the stimuli of its environment. They serve their purpose because they have specialized in conduction.

All three types of cells—the receptors, adjustor neurons, and effectors—have changed greatly in evolution and are found in many shapes and forms throughout the evolutionary series. Their forms in mammals and man, however, are the forms of greatest interest to us and will be described in the next sections.

THE RECEPTORS

Mammalian receptors are specialized to respond to four different types of stimuli: thermal, mechanical, chemical, and light stimuli. The thermal receptors are the cold and warm receptors of the skin. The mechanical receptors include those for hearing, balance, and touch. The chemical receptors are those for taste, smell, and chemical sensitivity of the skin. And, of course, the light receptors are those in the eye.

Such specialization according to stimulus sensitivity is relative rather than absolute. A light receptor in the eye responds to thermal or chemical stimuli if they are intense enough, and a mechanical receptor responds similarly to intense chemical stimuli. Moreover, all receptors have retained their ability to respond to electrical stimuli. This fact is convenient for the experimenter because such stimuli are easily produced and controlled. Hence they are frequently used in experimentation. As a consequence of this specialization in two directions, there are, altogether, three varieties of receptors: the unspecialized neuron, the specialized epithelial cell-neuron combination, and the specialized neuron.

Each kind of receptor is employed in more than one sense. The specialized neuron is found in vision and smell. The structure combining a neuron and specialized epithelial cell is encountered in hearing, balance, taste, touch, and probably also in the thermal senses. The unspecialized receptor serves in touch, pain, thermal sensitivity, and perhaps also in chemical sensitivity of the skin, although the latter is still in some doubt.

Along with specialization in sensitivity goes specialization of structure, but one cannot always tell the function of a receptor merely by looking at its structure. Specialization of form or structure has taken two general directions (see Figure 1.3). One is the "adoption" of an epithelial cell by a neuron to form a receptor structure. The other is the "migration" of neurons into the position of a receptor and the development of sensitive hairs on them for initiating responses to stimuli.

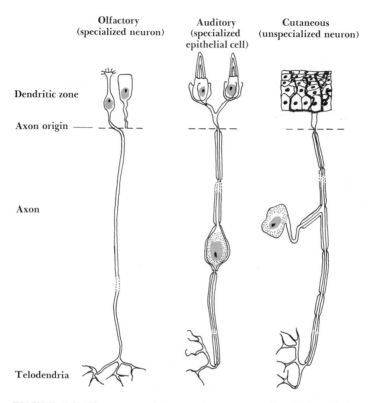

Olfactory
(specialized neuron)

Auditory
(specialized
epithelial cell)

Cutaneous
(unspecialized neuron)

Dendritic zone

Axon origin

Axon

Telodendria

FIGURE 1.3—Three general types of receptor cells. (Adapted from D. Bodian. The generalized vertebrate neuron. *Science,* **August 3, 1962, 137, 325. Adapted from** *Science* **by permission.)**

NEURONS

Although, as we have just seen, neurons are parts of receptor structures, by far the greatest number of them are found in that great adjustor mechanism, the nervous system, which connects receptors and effectors. Ordinarily, therefore, when we speak of a neuron without further qualification, we shall be referring to the adjustor neurons of the nervous system.

STRUCTURE—As can be seen in Figure 1.4, the neuron has three parts: the dendrites, the cell body, and the axon. The cell body is frequently called the *soma,* meaning body. The dendrite or the axon may be referred to as a *fiber* without distinguishing whether an axon or a dendrite is meant.

The dendrites and axons, in turn, have their separate features and can be distinguished on three different counts. (*1*) The dendrites are to be found in positions where they can be excited by environmental stimuli or by the activities of other cells, either sensory epithelial cells or other neurons. Thus the dendrite is the "receiving" end of the neuron. The axon, on the other hand, is connected to effectors or to other neurons to which it "delivers" the nervous impulses carried by it. (2) The dendrite tapers off in size as it leaves the cell body so that one can hardly tell where the cell body ends and the dendrite begins. However, the place where the axon leaves the soma is plainly marked by a small elevation in the soma from which the nerve cylinder extends outward with uniform size. (3) A neuron usually has several dendrites branching much like a tree; there is, on the other hand, only one axon leaving the soma, even though this axon may send off collaterals or branches, and it may have several endings known as telodendria.

TYPES OF NEURONS—Neurons come in many sizes and shapes. Microanatomists have studied them meticulously, classified them, and given them names. In Figure 1.5 are examples of commonly encountered neurons that illustrate various possible arrangements. One is a motoneuron of the type serving various muscles of the body; its cell body is in the spinal cord of the lower

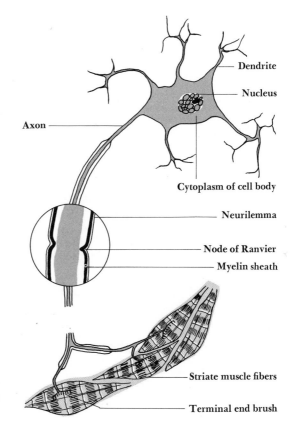

FIGURE 1.4—Diagrammatic drawing of a neuron.

Dendrite

Nucleus

Axon

Cytoplasm of cell body

Neurilemma

Node of Ranvier

Myelin sheath

Striate muscle fibers

Terminal end brush

part of the brain, and its fibers occur in motor nerves. Other neurons that look somewhat like that one form long connecting lines in sensory or motor pathways. The other neurons in Figure 1.5 are interneurons, that is, adjustor neurons. One of these, the giant pyramidal neuron, has its cell body in a motor area of the brain and sends its long fiber (not shown) downward to connect with motoneurons. Another is a short connecting interneuron with many ramifications to hook up many neurons with each other, usually in the brain. Still a third, the bushy one, illustrates another interneuron in which the dendrites "collect" from many different sources but deliver impulses to another point over a single axon.

FIGURE 1.5—Different types of neurons in the nervous system. A, motor neuron of the spinal cord similar to that in Figure 1.4; B, neuron of the motor area of the brain; C, short connecting neuron called Golgi type II; D, a bushy cell found in networks of neurons; E, bipolar neuron of sensory nerves. (Adapted from C. L. Evans. *Starling's principles of human physiology.* 9th ed. Philadelphia: Lea & Febiger, 1945. P. 192. By permission of J. & A. Churchill Ltd.)

A   B   C

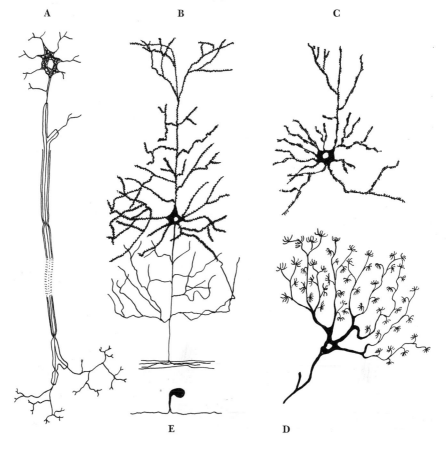

E   D

OTHER TYPES OF CELLS—It should be noted in Figure 1.4 that the axon has a covering. In fact, it has two coverings: a thin membrane on the outside, called *neurilemma,* and between it and the fiber a fatty sheath called the *myelin sheath.*

The neurilemma is found almost exclusively on axons outside the central nervous system. It takes part in the regeneration of axons when they have been injured or severed. Hence, generally speaking, axons outside the central nervous system can regenerate whereas those inside the central nervous system do not.

The *myelin sheath* is found both inside and outside the central nervous system. In fact, it is generally found on axons larger than 1 micron in diameter. Axons that have it are called *myelinated fibers.* The smaller ones that do not have it are called *unmyelinated fibers.* The myelin sheath, it will be noted in Figure 1.4, is segmented. It is interrupted at regular intervals by nodes called *nodes of Ranvier.* These nodes have been thought to be important in the conduction of nervous impulses in myelinated fibers and will be discussed further in Chapter 3.

Although the neurilemma is not found in the central nervous system—either in the brain or spinal cord—another kind of related cell is. This is the *neuroglia,* or merely *glia,* cell. Actually there are many kinds of neuroglia, though that fact need not concern us. Neuroglia cells are also quite numerous. Indeed, they are far more numerous than neurons. They have generally been regarded as supporting cells—cells that hold together and keep in place the neurons—for they generally weave around and intertwine among nerve cells and the blood vessels that serve them. Some investigators, however, suggest that they may also be important in the excitation and conduction of nerve impulses and hence even in such activities as learning (Galambos, 1961). And recently it has been shown that electrical potentials can be recorded from glia cells (Tasaki and Chang, 1958). Beyond this, however, very little is known about the role of glia cells in nervous functioning except that they are a common source of tumors.

THE EFFECTORS

The effectors are the means by which an organism responds to its world. Effector cells, like other kinds of cells, have differentiated in both structure and function. In vertebrate animals there are two main classes of effectors, the muscles and the glands.

MUSCLES—Muscles are of three varieties (see Figure 1.6): One, the most primitive and least differentiated, is the nonstriated or *smooth* muscle cell. In the typical case it is spindle-shaped. It contains within it strands of a special substance, the *fibrillae,* whose change in shape is what makes the muscle contract. *Striated* muscles, a second class, are more elaborate in form. They

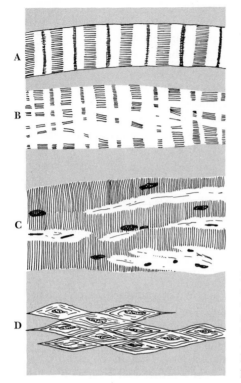

FIGURE 1.6—Types of muscle cells. A and B are striated muscle fibers; C shows the muscle fibers of the heart; and D is a sketch of some smooth muscle fibers. (Adapted from M. F. Guyer. *Animal biology.* 3d ed. New York: Harper & Row, 1941. P. 405. By permission of the publishers.)

are much more elongated than are smooth muscle cells, and they are enclosed in a special elastic membrane, the sarcolemma. Within this membrane are the fibrillae that contract, and these are differentiated into two substances, one darker than the other. Because the fibrillae are regularly alternated throughout the muscle cell, they give the muscle a striped, or striated, appearance under the microscope. Finally, there is a third kind of muscle, *cardiac* muscle, that is really just a special kind of striated muscle. Its chief distinction is that its fibers are not arranged in parallel, as are the striated muscle cells, nor are they enclosed in a membrane, but they branch and unite in a network, or syncytium.

GLANDS—In most instances, but not all, glands receive effector neurons from the nervous system, and they therefore rate as a class of effectors. Their function usually is to secrete chemical substances that are important to the life of the organism. Thus glands make adjustments of the internal environment just as muscle effectors make adjustment in and to the external environment.

There are many different glands, and we shall consider some of them later. Here we should recognize two major classes of glands, the duct and the ductless. The *duct* glands empty their secretions into the cavities of the body, e.g., the duct glands of the digestive tract, whereas the ductless glands put their secretions directly into the blood. Because they are circulated in the blood, secretions of ductless glands have a more profound effect on the body as a whole and on nervous activity in particular. We therefore shall later become most interested in them.

THE PERIPHERAL NERVOUS SYSTEM

Later on, when we take up each of the senses in turn, there will be a detailed description of the anatomy and physiology of each of the receptor organs of the body. Similarly, when we come to motor functions, there will be more discussion of the effectors, how they are constructed and how they work. For the present, however, we need not discuss further the receptors and effectors. The peripheral nervous system, on the other hand, being so elaborate and being involved in all the receptors and effectors, requires fairly detailed description.

GENERAL ORGANIZATION

In this section, the terminology used in describing the nervous system and the classification of its parts into divisions will be described.

DEFINITION OF TERMS—To present even the most general aspects of neuro-anatomy is no simple matter. We certainly need every aid to understanding that we can grasp. One of these is a system of terminology that has been developed for dealing with the central and peripheral nervous system. The terminology uses the brain and spinal cord as its point of reference, but it is necessary and useful in dealing with the peripheral nervous system as well. It is illustrated in Figure 1.7.

The terms *anterior* and *posterior*, better limited to the brain only, refer to the front and back of the head, respectively. *Rostral* and *caudal*, on the other hand, mean headward and tailward, respectively. *Dorsal* refers to the top of the head or to the back of the spinal cord, whereas *ventral* is used to indicate the bottom of the brain and the side of the spinal cord nearest the abdominal cavity. *Medial* is in the direction of the midline of the body, and *lateral*, away from it. Finally, *proximal* and *distal* indicate what is near to and far from some given position, respectively. All these terms indicate direction or relative position and do not in any way refer to a specific locus.

GRAY MATTER AND WHITE MATTER—There is another general feature of the nervous system that is convenient to know and use, its color. Neurons are naturally gray in appearance. Many nerve fibers, however, have a cover on them, the *myelin sheath*, mentioned above, which is white. Whenever a part of the nervous system looks white, it is known immediately that it is made up,

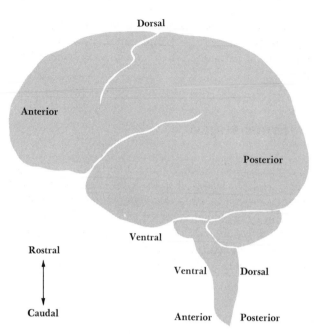

FIGURE 1.7—Side view of the human brain, illustrating the various terms used in neurology to denote direction or position.

in whole or in part, of myelinated fibers. The cell bodies of neurons, on the other hand, are never covered with myelin, and they consequently are always gray. Thus when gray matter is seen in the nervous system, this means that it consists of cell bodies. Gray matter and white matter, therefore, are convenient terms for distinguishing the clumps of cell bodies from tracts or nerves made up of fibers.

CENTERS AND PATHWAYS—There are other terms that will be used frequently in the pages ahead. These, too, apply to cell bodies and fibers. Fortunately for the student, the nervous system frequently has cell bodies and nerve fibers in separate places. A clump of cell bodies is called either a *ganglion* or a *nucleus*. In general, when the clump is outside the brain or spinal cord it has the name ganglion, and usually, but not always, a clump within the central nervous system is called a nucleus. On the other hand, nerve fibers when gathered together in a bundle may be called *nerves* or *tracts*. The term nerve is used for such bundles outside the central nervous system, and the term tract refers to such bundles within the brain or spinal cord. These terms— ganglia, nuclei, tracts, and nerves—are not the only ones used for clumps of cell bodies and nerve fibers, but they are the most common ones and will do for most of what we have to say in this book.

DIVISIONS OF THE NERVOUS SYSTEM—Now, with these terms in mind, we can consider the nervous system, particularly the peripheral nervous system. To do that, we need to consider first the general divisions of the nervous system.

There are two principal ways in which the nervous system may be divided. According to one, the brain and spinal cord together constitute the *central* nervous system as distinguished from the *peripheral* nervous system, which includes all the ganglia (groups of cell bodies) and nerves (nerve fibers) outside the brain and spinal cord. In classifying them in another way, we may distinguish between the *somatic* and *autonomic* nervous systems. Each has peripheral and central components, but their distinguishing feature is the part of the body with which they are concerned. Included in the autonomic system are those parts of the central nervous system and those nerves of the peripheral nervous system involved with the responses of (1) the smooth muscles of the intestines, urogenital tract, and blood vessels; (2) the muscles of the heart; and (3) those endocrine glands that receive a nervous supply. In general, the autonomic system controls the internal environment. In the somatic nervous system are included all those parts of the central and peripheral nervous system that convey impulses from the sense organs, organize them in the brain, and deliver motor impulses to the striated skeletal musculature of the body and limbs.

Although the peripheral endings of the autonomic and somatic nervous systems are quite distinct, there is no clear separation of them in the central nervous system or even in the main trunks of peripheral nerves. In the latter, the autonomic and somatic fibers can be sorted out, to some extent, on the basis of known differences in fiber types and by tracing the fibers to their terminations. Some centers of the central nervous system, on the other hand, are concerned principally either with autonomic functions or with somatic activities. But such divisions of function are always a matter of degree, and autonomic and somatic processes are always closely coordinated. That is to be expected, because adjustments of the internal environment of the nervous system are always essential to somatic adjustments, and vice versa, and the two mechanisms therefore must be thoroughly interlinked.

So much for the general organization of the nervous system. Now let us consider some of the details. The rest of this chapter deals with the peripheral nervous system, first the peripheral somatic system and then the peripheral autonomic system.

THE PERIPHERAL SOMATIC SYSTEM

This system is made up of nerves and ganglia. It is usually considered in two parts, cranial and spinal, depending on the part of the central nervous system from which the nerves and ganglia take origin. Motor fibers of both cranial and spinal nerves have their cell bodies within the central nervous system, usually in the ventral region nearest the point of exit of the fibers. Sensory fibers, on the other hand, nearly always have their cell bodies in ganglia outside the central nervous system. Cranial ganglia are to be found here and there in the recesses of the skull near the several small holes in the skull that serve as entrances and exits for nerve fibers. The spinal ganglia are arranged much more regularly along the spinal column.

THE CRANIAL NERVES—One ordinarily distinguishes 12 sets of cranial nerves. Their names and functions are summarized in Table 1.1, and their arrangement is illustrated in Figure 1.8. The first two nerves, the olfactory and the optic, are purely sensory in function. Neither of them is a true nerve, however, in the sense that nerves ordinarily consist only of fibers pushed out from the nervous system. Instead, these nerves represent portions of brain tissue that have migrated from the central nervous system to form the retina of the eye and the olfactory membrane but that, nevertheless, have maintained their connections with the brain. Three other nerves, the IIIrd, IVth, and VIth, are made up entirely of motor fibers innervating the muscles of the eye and con-

TABLE 1.1—The names, functions, and origins of the cranial nerves

NUMBER	NAME	FUNCTIONS	ORIGIN OR END IN THE BRAIN
I	Olfactory	(s) Smell	Cerebral hemispheres (ventral part)
II	Optic	(s) Vision	Thalamus
III	Oculomotor	(m) Eye movement	Midbrain
IV	Trochlear	(m) Eye movement	Midbrain
V	Trigeminal	(m) Masticatory movements	Midbrain and pons
		(s) Sensitivity of face and tongue	Medulla
VI	Abducens	(m) Eye movement	Medulla
VII	Facial	(m) Facial movement	Medulla
VIII	Auditory vestibular	(s) Hearing	Medulla
IX	Glossopharyngeal	(s) Tongue and (m) pharynx	Medulla
X	Vagus	(s) Heart, blood (m) vessels, viscera	Medulla
XI	Spinal accessory	(m) Neck muscles and viscera	Medulla
XII	Hypoglossal	(m) Tongue muscles	Medulla

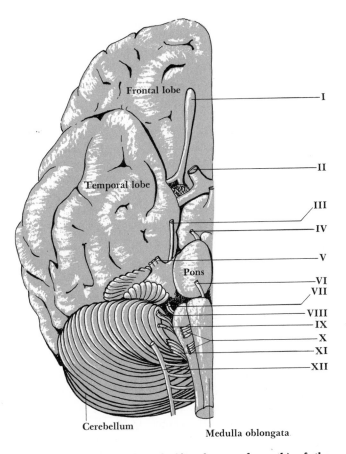

FIGURE 1.8—A ventral view (looking from underneath) of the brain, showing the cranial nerves. (Adapted from C. H. Best and N. B. Taylor. *The living body.* 2d ed. New York: Holt, 1944. P. 451. By permission of the publishers)

cerned with its movement. The central nuclei of these nerves constitute an important center for the control of eye movements.

The Vth cranial nerve, the *trigeminal,* is the nerve that is most important for sensations and movements of the mouth. It carries tactile sensations from the face, tongue, and mouth, and it is the principal motor nerve concerned with chewing. Its motor functions in chewing, tongue movement, and swallowing are augmented, however, with the services of two other nerves, the *glossopharyngeal* (IXth) and *hypoglossal* (XIIth). Then, too, in the trigeminal's control of facial movements the facial (VIIth) nerve takes a part. Certain of these nerves are also involved in taste reception. Of these, the most important is the facial (VIIth), which serves about two-thirds of the tongue, but the glossopharyngeal (IXth) and the *vagus* (Xth) also help by innervating the taste buds of the back part of the tongue and throat. The vagus nerve is mentioned here only in passing, but we shall see later on that it is quite important in the autonomic functions. To make the list complete, let us note that the VIIIth nerve is a purely sensory nerve carrying auditory and vestibular impulses from the internal ear.

THE SPINAL SOMATIC NERVES—These are more regularly arranged and more uniform in their function than the cranial nerves. There are 31 pairs of them (in man) disposed at regular intervals along the spinal cord. They enter and leave the cord through spaces between the spinal vertebrae. They may be classified into five groups, according to the part of the cord with which they are associated (see Table 1.2).

Just before entering the vertebral column, the spinal nerves divide into two roots (see Figure 1.9). Of these, the dorsal root is sensory in function, and the ventral root is motor (although there are exceptions). On each dorsal root there is a marked swelling, the *dorsal* spinal *ganglion,* that contains the cell bodies of the sensory fibers passing through it from the sense organs into the spinal cord. It is within the spinal cord itself, however, that the cell bodies of the motor fibers are to be found. Because these cell bodies form a mass of gray matter, resembling a horn, in the ventral part of the cord, they are frequently spoken of as the *ventral horn cells.*

The sensory portions of the spinal nerves come from the tactual, thermal, and pain receptors of the skin; from the receptors in the blood vessels; from pressure and pain receptors in the muscles, tendons, and joints; and to some extent from the internal receptors in the digestive tract and body cavities. As this list plainly indicates, the sensory roots of the nerves mediate sensitivity of most of the body except the face. Similarly, although each nerve has its distribution confined to a relatively small area of the body (dermatome, see Chap. 9), the motor portions of the spinal nerves control all the striated muscles of the arms, legs, and body except for those of the head and neck.

TABLE 1.2—*The name, number, and position of the spinal nerves in man*

NAME	NUMBER	POSITION
Cervical	8	Neck
Thoracic	12	Chest
Lumbar	5	Loin
Sacral	5	End of spinal column
Coccygeal	1	End of spinal column

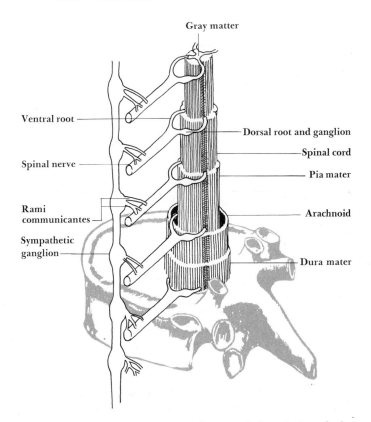

Gray matter

Ventral root

Spinal nerve

Rami
communicantes

Sympathetic
ganglion

Dorsal root and ganglion

Spinal cord

Pia mater

Arachnoid

Dura mater

FIGURE 1.9—A three-dimensional diagram of the spinal cord, the spinal nerves, and the bony case of the spinal cord. (Adapted from E. Gardner. *Fundamentals of neurology*. Philadelphia: Saunders, 1947. P. 34. By permission of the publishers.)

THE PERIPHERAL AUTONOMIC SYSTEM

As we have already said, the autonomic system is concerned principally with internal adjustments of the organism, whereas the somatic system is concerned with adjustments between the external world and the organism. Correlated with the different roles played by these two systems are certain differences in their structure and activities. (1) The somatic system embraces both sensory and motor activities, but the autonomic is considered only as a motor system. There are, however, sensory fibers innervating the viscera, called visceral afferents, that are plainly concerned with autonomic functions. (2) All the connections of the somatic system, except for the special cases of the retina and olfactory bulb, are to be found within the central nervous system; on the other hand, it is signally characteristic of the autonomic system that many of its synapses and its ganglia lie outside the central nervous system. (3) In respect to organization of functions, the two systems differ in that the autonomic tends to function more as a whole and is less differentiated than the somatic system. (4) They differ also in distribution of fibers, for, as we have already seen, the autonomic system innervates the glands and smooth muscles of the viscera and blood vessels, whereas the motor somatic system is distributed to the striated muscles of the skeleton.

DIVISIONS OF THE AUTONOMIC SYSTEM—We distinguish two channels of outflow of nervous activity in the autonomic nervous system (see Figure 1.10): (1) The *sympathetic* outflow takes place through the *thoracic* and *lumbar* regions of the spinal cord, and for this reason it is sometimes referred to as the thoracicolumbar system; (2) the *parasympathetic* division takes its origin in the *cranial* and *sacral* regions of the central nervous system, and it may accordingly be called the *craniosacral system.*

The sympathetic and parasympathetic divisions are largely, although not completely, antagonistic in their effects. In general, the sympathetic system *mobilizes* the resources of the body for use in work and special emergencies, whereas the parasympathetic system *conserves* and stores bodily resources. In other words, the first helps to *spend* bodily resources and the second helps to *save* them. This statement, although true in general, does not hold in certain specific instances. Naturally, too, these two systems never act independently of each other but are brought into correlated activity in varying degrees, depending upon the demands made on the organism by the external world. Through their antagonistic yet coordinated action, a comparatively stable equilibrium of the internal environment is maintained under many different conditions of work and rest. How that is done will be illustrated in the more detailed treatment of the two systems that follows.

THE SYMPATHETIC SYSTEM—Spinal paths of conduction exist for the autonomic system just as in the somatic motor system. The motor cells of the autonomic system tend, however, to be found in the lateral parts of the spinal gray matter rather than in the ventral horns, as are the somatic motor neurons. In the thoracicolumbar segments of the spinal cord, the axons of autonomic cells pass through the ventral roots with the somatic motor axons and make up part of the ventral roots. Just outside the spinal cord, however, these sympathetic axons leave the main nerve root and enter a *sympathetic ganglion,* where they end upon the cell bodies of other neurons.

There are 22 sympathetic ganglia (in man), arranged regularly along the spinal cord and constituting the so-called "sympathetic chain," or ganglionic cord. In the ganglia of this cord terminate the fibers originating in the spinal cord as just described. These fibers are called *preganglionic* fibers. Because they are mostly myelinated, the bundle they form as they leave the spinal nerve is called the *white ramus.* The cell bodies in the ganglion send axonal

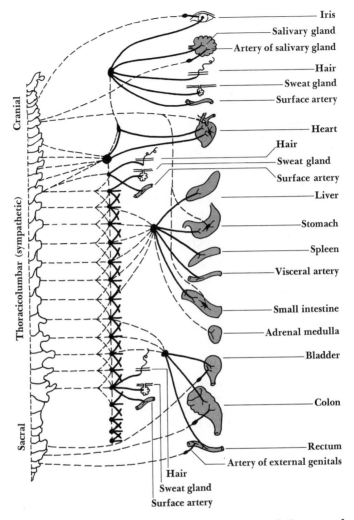

Iris
Salivary gland
Artery of salivary gland
Hair
Sweat gland
Surface artery
Heart
Hair
Sweat gland
Surface artery
Liver
Stomach
Spleen
Visceral artery
Small intestine
Adrenal medulla
Bladder
Colon
Rectum
Artery of external genitals
Hair
Sweat gland
Surface artery

Cranial
Thoracicolumbar (sympathetic)
Sacral

FIGURE 1.10—Diagram of the autonomic system and the parts of the body that it serves. (Adapted from **W. B. Cannon**. *Bodily changes in pain, hunger, fear, and rage*. 2d ed. New York: Appleton-Century-Crofts, 1929. P. 23. By permission of the publishers.)

fibers back to the spinal nerves, as shown in Figure 1.11, and because they are unmyelinated they are known as the *gray ramus*. Fibers in this ramus are called *postganglionic* fibers.

Not all the fibers leaving the sympathetic ganglion go back to the spinal nerve, nor do all the preganglionic fibers from the spinal cord terminate in the nearest ganglion of the sympathetic cord. As shown in Figure 1.11, they may pursue any one of three courses: (1) They may end upon the cell bodies in the nearest sympathetic ganglion, as described above; (2) they may pass through that ganglion into the bundles of fibers that connect the various sympathetic ganglia with each other, thus forming a cord, in which case they end finally upon the cell bodies of ganglia above or below the segment from which they came; (3) they may pass out through the sympathetic ganglion in an autonomic nerve to the distal part of the body and there end in *collateral ganglia* located in the vicinity of the muscles or glands that are to be innervated. These collateral ganglia are another part of the autonomic system not yet mentioned and are peripheral centers for the distribution of sympathetic effects, although, as we shall see below, they receive some parasympathetic innervation.

A final aspect of the structure of the peripheral sympathetic system to be noted is that, although preganglionic fibers leave the spinal cord only in the thoracic and lumbar regions, sympathetic ganglia are to be found in the cervical regions as well. The cervical sympathetic ganglia are three in number: superior, middle, and inferior (see Figure 1.10). These receive their fibers by way of connecting pathways to the thoracic and lumbar sympathetic chain. Thus for a preganglionic fiber to reach the cervical ganglia it must leave the spinal cord in the thoracic region and enter the thoracic sympathetic cord and then turn upward to the cervical ganglia.

FIGURE 1.11—Diagram of the relations of autonomic ganglia, spinal cord, and peripheral nerves in the sympathetic system (thoracicolumbar outflow). (Adapted from L. Edinger. In J. F. Fulton, *Physiology of the nervous system.* Fairlawn, N.J.: Oxford University Press, 1938. P. 208. By permission of the publishers.)

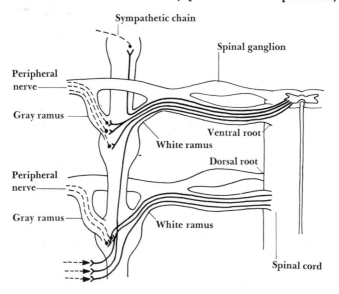

Despite this somewhat roundabout way in which preganglionic fibers reach them, the cervical ganglia are the most important in the sympathetic chain. Their postganglionic fibers innervate the blood vessels and sweat glands of the head, the dilator fibers of the pupils, the blood vessels of the heart, and the heart itself. The principal control of the blood supply of the brain is, in fact, vested in the sympathetic outflow of the cervical ganglia, although there is in this respect an antagonistic action of the parasympathetic system (see below).

The distribution of both the cervical and the thoracicolumbar divisions of the sympathetic cord is summarized in Table 1.3. From this and Figure 1.10 it can be seen that the thoracicolumbar chain innervates all the other organs of the viscera below the heart: the liver, stomach, intestines, bladder, urogenital organs, and adrenal glands. In the vicinity of these organs are three ganglia bearing the names of, and distributed to, the organs indicated in the figure.

Turning now to the more functional aspects of the sympathetic system, we may refer again to the general fact that the sympathetic system mobilizes rather diffusely the resources of the organism. Because this is of particular importance when the organism is threatened with danger and has strenuous work to do, the sympathetic system has been thought of as subserving *emergency* functions. In the light of this generalization, the significance of the principal effects of sympathetic activity becomes clear: widening of the pupils constriction of visceral blood vessels so that blood is directed to the muscles and brain, acceleration of the rate of heartbeat, inhibition of intestinal and gastric activity, secretion of adrenalin with the result that blood sugar is raised and tissue metabolism increased—all these effects prepare the organism to deal with an emergency situation. Further details concerning the sympathetic system and its functions may be found in Table 1.3.

THE PARASYMPATHETIC SYSTEM—As we have already seen, the sympathetic system has ganglia either in the region of the spinal cord or in the vicinity of the organs that it innervates. Only in the latter situation, however, are there the ganglia of the parasympathetic division. This has long preganglionic fibers arising either in the brain or in the sacral division of the spinal cord and extending to the parasympathetic ganglia, which are always close by the tissues to which their fibers are distributed. Thus there is no chain of parasympathetic ganglia by which nervous effects can be interrelated. From such a structural difference in the two systems one may surmise a characteristic functional difference, viz., that the sympathetic division tends to act more diffusely and as a whole, whereas the parasympathetic division is a more highly differentiated system that is more capable of independent activity in each of its parts.

Because the parasympathetic division is fairly specific in its various functions, neurologists have been able to distinguish several subdivisions which

TABLE 1.3—*Autonomic pathways and their functions*

ORGAN	ORIGIN	NERVE	EFFECTOR	FUNCTION
Eye:				
Para	Midbrain	III (Oculomotor)	Ciliary muscle	Accommodation
			Iris	Contraction
Ortho	Spinal cord	Ciliary nerve	Eyeball	Exophthalmos
			Iris	Dilation
Cerebral arteries:				
Para	Medulla	VII (Facial)	Carotid artery and blood vessels of brain	Dilation
Ortho	Spinal cord	Various		Contraction
Heart:				
Para	Medulla	X (Vagus)	Heart and coronary vessels	Inhibition and coronary constriction
Ortho	Spinal cord	Various	Heart and coronary vessels	Acceleration and dilation
Stomach and small intestine:				
Para	Medulla	X (Vagus)	Gastric musculature	Contraction and secretion
Ortho	Spinal cord	Splanchnic	Gastric muscles and glands	Inhibition of contraction and secretion
Genitourinary tract:				
Para	Spinal cord	Sacral	Genitourinary muscles and blood vessels	Urination, defecation, vasodilation, erection
Ortho	Spinal cord	Hypogastric	Genitourinary muscles and blood vessels	Contraction of sphincters, prostate, and seminal vesicles, inhibition of rectum and bladder
Arteries of body:				
Para	Spinal cord	Various	Blood vessels	Dilation
Ortho	Spinal cord	Various	Blood vessels	Contraction

have their respective duties. It will serve no purpose, however, to go into such details. Only two general subdivisions are worth noting. These are the cranial and sacral parts of the parasympathetic division. The cranial part consists of all the nerves and outlets that are associated with the brain and the head. This part serves, among other things, the iris of the eye, the salivary glands, and the heart. The sacral part comes from the extreme lower end of the spinal cord. It serves the bladder, the colon, the rectum, and the arteries of the genitals.

As was said above, the general functions of the parasympathetic system are those of conservation of bodily resources and building up of the body. Thus the parasympathetic outflow causes constriction of the pupil, a response that serves to protect the eye from excessive light. It inhibits the heartbeat and causes vasodilation, in this way lowering blood pressure, which reduces the utilization of fuels throughout the body. It participates in digestion, definitely a constructive process, in several ways: by increasing the rate and amount of salivary secretion, by increasing contractions of the stomach, by causing digestive juices to be secreted into the stomach. Through the sacral outflow, moreover, the parasympathetic division frees the body of unwanted, and perhaps even poisonous, materials by causing the bladder and the colon to empty.

2 THE CENTRAL NERVOUS SYSTEM

As we have noted previously, the central nervous system is the organ that is housed in the bony case of the skull and the spinal column. It can be subdivided and named in a variety of ways, depending on the particular grouping of structures to which one wishes to refer. The gross division, which is easy to see, is into *brain* and *spinal cord*. The brain may be divided into three parts: the *forebrain,* which in mammals, and particularly in man, is by far the largest part; the *midbrain;* and the *hindbrain.* The midbrain and hindbrain, taken together, comprise most of the so-called *brain stem* because they form a sort of stem for the forebrain.

There are other ways of subdividing the brain, and they will be introduced as needed, but the parts named here will serve as the major headings of the outline of this chapter. Here, specifically, we shall discuss the spinal cord, the brain stem, and forebrain. A last section of the chapter will describe briefly the evolution of the brain.

THE SPINAL CORD

One of the chief functions of the spinal cord is to conduct impulses to and from the brain. Although impulses enter and leave the brain through the cranial nerves, sensory impulses from all over the body except the head go to the brain through the spinal cord. Likewise, the control of the actions of the body, except the face and neck, is exercised by the brain through conduction paths that lead through and out of the spinal cord. In the spinal cord, therefore, are to be found great conduction paths proceeding upward and downward between the brain and the various exits and entrances of the spinal nerves. Conduction is thus the first important function of the spinal cord. In addition, however, the spinal cord serves as an integrating center of its own and mediates, as we shall see in later chapters, many complex reflex actions without much help from the brain. But with this brief comment concerning its general function, let us consider the essential anatomy of the spinal cord.

GENERAL FEATURES

The internal structure of the spinal cord is much simpler and more uniform throughout its various parts than is that of the brain. No matter where it is sectioned, it presents the same essential appearance. The interior is gray matter (cell bodies), so distributed as to present the picture of a butterfly whose essential form is the letter H (see Figure 2.1). Outside the gray matter are great columns of white matter making up various fiber tracts passing up and down the cord. Dividing the cord into symmetrical halves are two median clefts, the dorsal and ventral fissures. Between them, in the central part of the cord, are two commissures joining the two halves of the cord; one is the crossbar of the H, composed of gray matter and called the *gray commissure;* ventral to it is the *white commissure,* which consists of fibers passing from one side to the other.

GRAY MATTER

The central parts of the gray matter are concerned mainly with impulses crossing the midline in the commissural fibers, for there are fibers as well as cell bodies in the gray matter. The cell bodies of the more peripheral gray matter are concerned, on the other hand, with sensory or motor functions or with projection functions. Thus the dorsal horns of gray matter extend out-

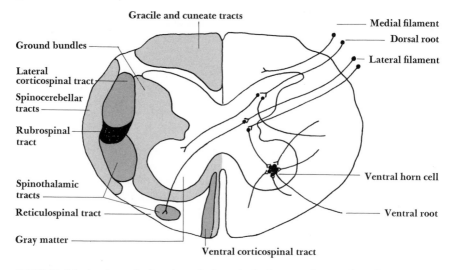

Gracile and cuneate tracts

Medial filament

Dorsal root

Lateral filament

Ground bundles

Lateral
corticospinal tract

Spinocerebellar
tracts

Rubrospinal
tract

Spinothalamic
tracts

Reticulospinal tract

Gray matter

Ventral horn cell

Ventral root

Ventral corticospinal tract

FIGURE 2.1—A schematic drawing of the principal connections and pathways
of the spinal cord.

ward toward the edge of the cord to the point where the fibers of the dorsal
sensory ganglion pass into the cord by way of the *dorsal root.* The dorsal
horn is, therefore, in great part sensory in function. Although the ventral
horn is not so near the surface of the cord, it is plain that its functions are
mostly motor, for from it stream fibers that emerge from the cord in the
ventral roots and form the motor portion of the spinal nerves. Finally, the
more lateral portions of the gray matter contain cell bodies whose fibers are
found in the conduction paths of the spinal cord. One must remember, however, that such statements as these, and those which follow, are necessarily
schematic.

CONDUCTION PATHS

The white matter of the cord is divided into three pairs of columns by the
median clefts and the dorsal and sensory roots. Between the dorsal roots and
the dorsal fissure are the dorsal columns (or fasciculi); between the dorsal
and ventral roots are the lateral columns; in the ventral region marked off by
the ventral roots and the ventral fissure are the ventral columns. In general,
the dorsal columns conduct impulses brainward and are, therefore, sensory or
afferent; the ventral columns carry impulses downward and are motor or
efferent; the lateral columns are mixed.

A further distinction between pathways may be made on the basis of their
length. Long tracts connect centers of the brain and the spinal cord, whereas
the short ones, sometimes known as *ground bundles* or *intersegmental tracts,*
only connect different levels of the spinal cord. Long tracts tend to be located,
as Figure 2.1 shows, in the peripheral part of the cord, whereas the ground

bundles are nearer the cell bodies of the gray matter, which they must connect at different levels.

To understand the way in which these long tracts are named will make reference to them later more convenient. In conventional nomenclature, the name of each tract includes first the name of the center from which it arises and in which cell bodies of its fibers are usually located and then the name of the place in which the fibers of the tract end. There are a few exceptions to this rule; tracts are sometimes assigned special names according to their significance or according to the persons who first described them. Some of the more important tracts are named and related to each other in Figure 2.1. These tracts will be referred to from time to time in later chapters, and the illustration accordingly deserves special attention. There is, however, no need for further description at this point.

THE BRAIN STEM

Now we shall proceed upward through the main divisions of the brain. We have already named them briefly at the beginning of the chapter. The brain stem, as we indicated, consists of the hindbrain and the midbrain. One structure that runs through both the hindbrain and midbrain, and indeed into the forebrain, will be considered separately; this is the reticular formation.

HINDBRAIN

The principal parts of the hindbrain are the medulla, pons, cerebellum, and a portion of the fourth ventricle (see Figure 2.2). The medulla (adjectival form is bulbar) joins the spinal cord to higher parts of the brain. It is important as the place of exit and entrance of the majority of cranial nerves (see Figure 1.8). As one might suspect, it contains several nuclei of cell bodies associated with these nerves. In addition, however, it contains autonomic nuclei concerned with breathing, heartbeat, and blood pressure. For this reason, the medulla is sometimes called the vital center of the brain. Without it the fundamental processes of breathing and heart action could not go on. Finally, the medulla contains many tracts passing through it, which conduct impulses upward and downward between the cord and the higher centers of the brain. Later in this chapter, when we compare the brains of different animals, some of the functions of the medulla will be described in more detail.

Upward from the medulla, the second division of the hindbrain consists of the cerebellum, the pons, and a part of the fourth ventricle. The cerebellum is a structure that resembles the cerebral hemispheres, in that gray matter forms its outer surface, and white matter, together with certain nuclei, makes up its interior. For purposes of brief description, the cerebellum may be said

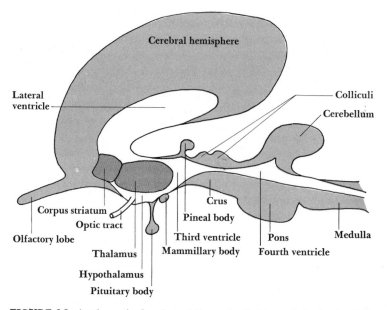

FIGURE 2.2—A schematic drawing of the main divisions of the brain. (Adapted from J. D. Lickley. *The nervous system.* New York: Longmans, 1919. P. 20.)

to be divided into four parts: a *ventral* portion, receiving fibers that have been relayed from the sense organs of equilibration, the semicircular canals, utricle, and saccule (see Chapter 10); the *anterior* and *posterior* portions, which are supplied chiefly with sensory fibers from the spinal cord; and a dorsal portion, otherwise known as the *neocerebellum*, which has extensive connections with the nuclei of the pons (see below) and also with the frontal lobes of the cerebral cortex. The principal role played by the cerebellum is a smoothing and coordinating of impulses leading to muscular movements; it is to be regarded, therefore, primarily as an organ of motor coordination.

Forming the ventral portion of the hindbrain in this region is the *pons*. It consists of (1) transverse fibers emerging from one side of the cerebellum and traversing the ventral surface of the hindbrain to reenter the cerebellum on the opposite side; (2) a complex of nuclei, the *pontine nuclei*, within this band of transverse fibers; and (3) fiber tracts ascending and descending to various levels of the central nervous system. In the pons, also, are to be found the nuclei of the trigeminal nerve (Vth), which is so important in sensations and movement of the mouth and face.

MIDBRAIN

The *midbrain* is relatively small and forms a bridge or stalk connecting the forebrain and hindbrain. The main parts of the midbrain that interest us are the *tectum* (which means "roof") and the floor.

The floor is mainly a passageway between higher and lower parts of the nervous system. Sensory tracts run upward in it, and the motor tracts course downward. Also in the floor of the midbrain are some motor reflex centers that we shall consider at a later time.

The tectum of the midbrain, on the other hand, has sensory duties. The tectum is divided into two pairs of sensory centers—four in all. Each one is called a *colliculus*. One pair of such centers, called the *superior colliculi,* makes "bumps" that lie a little above and ahead (anterior) of the other pair. The superior colliculi are primitive visual centers. The other pair of colliculi are called the *inferior colliculi* because they lie a little behind and below the level of the superior colliculi. The inferior colliculi are lower centers for hearing.

RETICULAR FORMATION

Largely within the hindbrain but also extending into the midbrain and the hypothalamus of the forebrain (see below) is a structure known as the *reticular formation* (Magoun, 1963). Because it is intimately related to sleep, arousal, and attention, it is also called the *reticular activating system* (RAS). It has the name reticular because under the light microscope it is seen as a network of fibers and cell bodies. The RAS constitutes one of two general routes traveled by sensory impulses on the way to the cerebral cortex (see Figure 2.3). The other route, described below in connection with the thalamus, is the direct one. The reticular system provides an indirect route. It is also a relatively diffuse one. Although there appears to be some specificity according to sense in the reticular formation, the various sensory inputs and their outputs upward are not clearly segregated, as they are in the direct sensory pathways.

The part of the RAS that relays sensory impulses to the cerebral cortex is called the *ascending* reticular system, and this will later be of the greatest interest to us. Another part, a *descending* system, sends impulses downward to the spinal cord. Besides sending impulses upward to the cortex, the RAS also receives impulses from the cortex. Thus the RAS and the cerebral cortex form a closed loop in which impulses in the RAS arouse the cerebral cortex, but those in the cortex in turn arouse the RAS. We shall see later the part played by the RAS in sleep and arousal (Chapter 12).

THE FOREBRAIN

To the psychologist, the forebrain is the most important part of the brain for it possesses virtually all the parts concerned in sensation and perception and in the coordination of behavior patterns, including those of emotion, motivation, learning, language, and thinking. We shall therefore give the greatest attention to its anatomical structure.

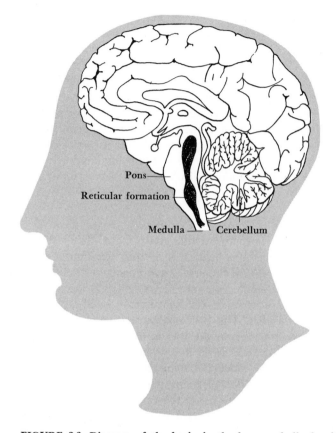

Pons

Reticular formation

Medulla   Cerebellum

FIGURE 2.3—Diagram of the brain in the human skull, showing
the position of the reticular formation. (Adapted from J. D. French.
The reticular formation. *Scient. American,* 1957, 196, 55. Reprinted
by permission. Copyright © 1957 by Scientific American, Inc. All
rights reserved.)

The neuroanatomist usually distinguishes two major parts of the forebrain:
the *telencephalon* and *diencephalon.* These represent further steps in the
differentiation of the forebrain. We occasionally, but not often, shall refer to
these major parts, and so it is useful to indicate briefly what they include
(see Figure 2.2). The *diencephalon* consists of the *thalamus, optic tracts* and
the *retinas* of the eyes, the *pituitary body,* the *mammillary bodies,* the *hypothalamus,* and the *third ventricle.* Of these parts, the thalamus and hypothalamus will be discussed here and the third ventricle a little later in this
chapter. The other parts will be considered at the appropriate places later in
the book. The *telencephalon* consists of the *olfactory bulb* and *olfactory tracts,*
the *cerebral hemispheres,* and the *basal ganglia.* The latter two structures are

described below, but the olfactory tracts are treated in the chapter on the chemical senses (Chapter 5).

THE THALAMUS

The thalamus is the great relay station of the brain. It consists of many nuclei connected with each other, with the lower centers of the brain and spinal cord, and with the cerebral hemispheres of the telencephalon above it. The structure and interrelationships of these nuclei are most difficult to visualize. We can give only the most general impression of them at this point. It is impossible to discuss the thalamus without also referring to the lobes and parts of the cerebral cortex lying above it. The explanation of these references will be given later when we discuss the cerebral hemispheres in the section following this one.

SUBCORTICAL NUCLEI—The nuclei of the thalamus can be divided into three main groups. Nuclei with only subcortical connections are disposed mainly along the midline of the thalamus and in the anteroventral part; they connect in some cases with the basal ganglia or with other parts of the thalamus, but so far as is known they do not send any fibers to or receive any fibers from the cerebral cortex. They are of little significance to us.

RELAY NUCLEI—A second group of nuclei, the thalamocortical projection nuclei, otherwise known as the *sensory relay nuclei,* are of the greatest importance (see Figures 2.4 and 2.5). Of this group we need mention only the ones with which we shall come in contact most often. The *lateroventral nucleus,* lying in a position indicated by its name, receives fibers from the cerebellum and sends projections to the frontal lobe (see Figure 2.7), particularly the precentral gyrus (see Figure 2.8). It functions, as one might suspect from its anatomical connections, in the coordination of the activities of the cerebellum and the frontal lobe in controlling muscular movements. The *posteroventral nucleus,* situated close to the lateroventral, is the major relay station for sensory fibers representing the skin and muscle senses and sends projections to the cortex, particularly to the postcentral gyrus, which is employed in somesthetic sensory activities. Besides these two parts of the ventral nucleus, there are two other thalamic relay nuclei of note, the *lateral* and *medial geniculate bodies,* which are slight enlargements on the lateral surface of the thalamus. The former is the station through which impulses from the eyes are relayed to the cortex and to other visual centers, whereas the latter exercises a similar function in hearing. Of these two centers more will be said later.

ASSOCIATION NUCLEI—The third group of thalamic nuclei are the "association" nuclei, which receive their impulses from within the thalamus but send

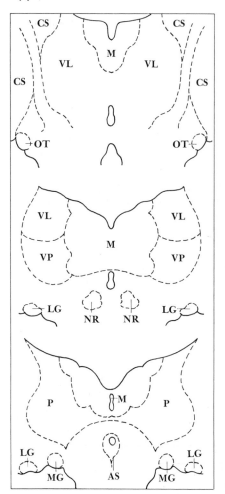

FIGURE 2.4—Three diagrammatic cross sections of the thalamus showing its principal nuclei. Upper section: anterior thalamus; middle section: middle thalamus; and lower section: posterior thalamus. The main nuclei of the thalamus are: M, medial group; VL, lateroventral nucleus; VP, posteroventral nucleus; P, posterior group; LG, lateral geniculate bodies; and MG, medial geniculate bodies. Other structures, not part of the thalamus, are: CS, corpus striatum; OT, optic tracts; NR, red nucleus; and AS, aqueduct of Sylvius. (Adapted from J. F. Fulton. *Physiology of the nervous system.* 2d ed. Fairlawn, N.J.: Oxford University Press, 1943; A. E. Walker. *The primate thalamus.* Chicago: University of Chicago Press, 1938.)

projections to the cerebral cortex (see Figures 2.4 and 2.5). In general, nuclei of this type send their thalamocortical fibers either to the anterior part or to the posterior part of the cortex. The particular areas that they serve can be understood only by knowing something about the organization of the cortex, which we have not yet considered.

THE HYPOTHALAMUS

The other principal part of the diencephalon is the hypothalamus and its associated structures. These, as we shall see, have some important and unusual functions connected with the peripheral autonomic system. These functions set them apart from the other structures of the brain that we have been discussing.

AUTONOMIC NUCLEI—Primary control of autonomic functions is vested in the hypothalamus. It is there that differentiation and organization of different patterns of autonomic reaction take place. As one can see in Figures 2.2 and 2.6, this center is rather clearly set off from the rest of the brain, lying in the ventral and medial part of the diencephalon. Associated with the hypothalamus are the pituitary gland and its stalk, the infundibulum, which projects from the floor of the hypothalamus (see Figure 2.6). Also protruding from the floor of the hypothalamus are the paired *mammillary bodies.* The rest of the hypothalamus proper is made up of several nuclei, which we may consider in two main groups: (*1*) the posterior and lateral nuclei and (*2*) the medial and anterior nuclei. The function of the former is primarily sympathetic, whereas the latter organize, for the most part, parasympathetic functions.

If one stimulates the first, or posterior, group electrically, all the effects of sympathetic discharge are obtained: The pupils dilate, the heart is accelerated, blood pressure is elevated, stomach contractions and intestinal activity are halted. Removal of this group of nuclei presents all the symptoms of lessened activity of the sympathetic system and of a resulting dominance of parasympathetic activity: The pupils contract, the heart beats more slowly, the blood pressure drops.

FIGURE 2.5—Some projections of thalamic nuclei to the cerebral cortex. (Based on work of A. E. Walker and W. E. L. Clark. After T. C. Ruch and S. C. Kasdon, unpublished.)

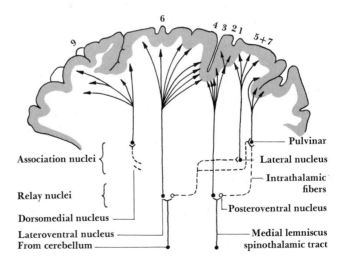

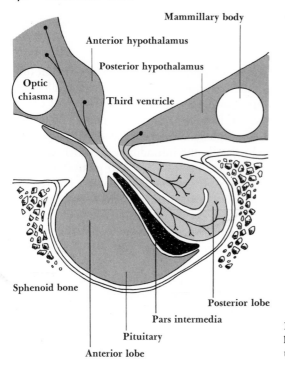

Mammillary body

Anterior hypothalamus

Posterior hypothalamus

Optic chiasma

Third ventricle

Sphenoid bone

Posterior lobe

Pars intermedia

Pituitary

Anterior lobe

FIGURE 2.6—A sketch of the hypothalamus and the pituitary body.

The anterior and medial group of hypothalamic nuclei is predominantly parasympathetic in function. If it is stimulated electrically, the heart is slowed, blood sugar is lowered, and various other parasympathetic phenomena appear. To destroy the anterior group is to bring about an increase in blood sugar, a rise in heartbeat and blood pressure, vasoconstriction, and general sympathetic effects. These are the results to be expected if the sympathetic system is left without the antagonistic effect of the parasympathetic division.

GENERAL FUNCTIONS—All the individual autonomic effects that can be produced by hypothalamic activity are controlled also by lower centers in the medulla and spinal cord. The distinctive importance of the hypothalamus is not in producing these autonomic effects but in *integrating* them into patterns of activity that adjust the internal environment of the organism.

Such integrating functions of the hypothalamus are related to various neural and endocrine mechanisms for regulating the internal environment. Receiving fibers from the cerebral cortex, it adjusts autonomic responses to the cortical events mediating somatic behavior. It sends efferent projection fibers downward to the bulbar mechanisms of respiration, heartbeat, and glandular regulation. Such projection fibers also extend even farther downward to the preganglionic neurons of the spinal cord, thus regulating autonomic adjustments. Finally, the hypothalamus sends nerve fibers to the pituitary gland with which it is so closely associated. In this way, it controls certain of the activities of the pituitary gland and, because of the pituitary's control of other glands, hormonal secretions in general.

We may note in passing some of the general functions that the hypothalamus is able to subserve by these various means. Body temperature is crucially dependent upon this center. Whenever it is necessary for the body to lose heat, the hypothalamus causes vasodilation, increased sweating, increased respiration, and a lowering of metabolism. Through converse effects, it causes heat to be conserved and, in addition, by inducing shivering, the body temperature to be raised. As the primary neural center regulating endocrine secretions, the hypothalamus plays a major role in regulating metabolism, particularly of fats, carbohydrates, and water. It is there, too, that the control of blood pressure and thus of the distribution of blood to the brain is mainly, though not exclusively, vested. Sexual functions, which include complex autonomic effects as well as certain somatic reactions, depend upon the hypothalamus. Furthermore, physiological conditions associated with hunger and thirst are dependent in an important degree upon the activity of the hypothalamus. It is also a center for emotional behavior. All those behavioral functions of the hypothalamus will be considered in detail in later chapters.

CEREBRAL HEMISPHERES

We shall move on now to the telencephalon, of which the principal part is the *cerebral hemispheres.* These consist of the *cerebral cortex* (cortex means "rind" or "covering"), which is gray matter; the *corpus striatum* enveloped by the cortex and consisting both of nuclear masses and of white fiber tracts passing to and from the cortex; and the *corpus callosum,* which consists of fiber tracts passing between the cortices of the two cerebral hemispheres.

CEREBRAL CORTEX—Of these, the cerebral cortex will receive a large measure of our attention, for in it reside the complex psychological functions that distinguish man. In birds and lower animals the cortex is not very important; only the first signs of its development are present. In mammals, however, the cortex undergoes a great development compared with changes in the rest of the nervous system. Indeed, in man the cerebral cortex is about one-half the weight of the entire nervous system, and it has so expanded into its allotted space in the skull that it shows many invaginations and ridges which thus greatly enlarge the amount of cortex. An invagination has the name *sulcus* or *fissure,* and the ridge between two of them is known as a *gyrus.*

To indicate various parts of the cerebral cortex, one makes use of certain sulci and gyri as landmarks, the most important being described here. The cortex is divided into symmetrical halves, or hemispheres, by the deep *longi-*

tudinal fissure that runs along the midline. On the dorsal surface of the cortex and somewhat posterior to the center is the central sulcus, a deep furrow that runs laterally and slightly anteriorly from the median longitudinal fissure (see Figure 2.7). On the lateral surface of the cortex the *lateral fissure* may be seen running posteriorly and dorsally.

On the basis of these three principal fissures, one may mark off four pairs of lobes in the cerebral cortex (see Figure 2.7). The *frontal lobes* include all the cortex anterior to the central sulcus. The *parietal lobes*, occupying the dorsal surface of the hemisphere, extend posteriorly from the central sulcus and laterally to the lateral fissure. Lateral and ventral to the lateral fissure, one finds the *temporal lobes*. A fourth pair of lobes, the *occipital*, are also distinguished, but they are not marked off by any major fissures (Figure 2.7).

ARCHITECTONIC STRUCTURE—The cerebral cortex can also be described in terms of its histological, or cellular, structure. Although the cortex is really a great ganglion, it is unlike most ganglia found elsewhere in the nervous system in that, possessing as it does a great many connections between its various cells, it also contains a great number of nerve fibers. A large proportion of the cortical cells, in fact, possess comparatively short and greatly branched fibers that connect only with other cells within the cortex. Moreover, there are different kinds of cells, as well as connections, and the study

FIGURE 2.7—Side view of the human brain, showing lobes and principal fissures used to describe the various areas of the cerebral cortex. (Adapted from A. Kuntz. *A textbook of neuroanatomy.* 4th ed. Philadelphia: Lea & Febiger, 1945. P. 335. By permission of the publishers.)

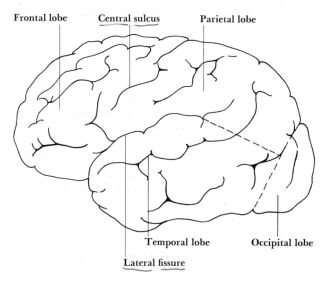

Frontal lobe   Central sulcus   Parietal lobe

Temporal lobe   Occipital lobe

Lateral fissure

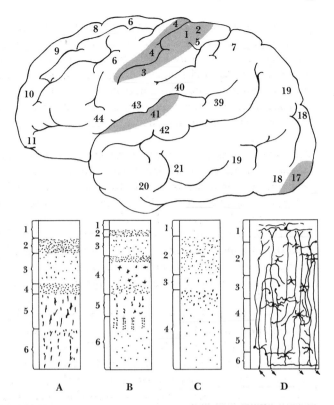

FIGURE 2.8—A schematic drawing of Brodmann's areas of the cortex and the cellular layers of different areas. The numbers on the brain are those assigned in the Brodmann system; those below are layers of the cortex. A, cross section from area 4, the motor cortex; B, from area 17, the visual cortex; C, temporal lobe; and D, synaptic relations in area 4 as seen by special staining techniques. (Adapted from S. Cobb. *Foundations of psychiatry.* Baltimore: Williams & Wilkins, 1941. P. 72. By permission of the publishers.)

of these, by means of appropriate histological techniques, brings out systematic differences in the organization of cells in different cortical areas.

Such a study of cytoarchitecture has yielded several facts of importance (see Figure 2.8). First of all, cortex can be old, new, or intermediate in phylogenetic age. Most of the cerebral cortex seen in vertebrates is *neocortex*, meaning new cortex, for it begins in reptiles but becomes most prominent in the mammals. Neocortex is composed of six fundamental layers. Within these layers there may be subgroups, and some layers are more or less prominent in certain areas, but all neocortex has the same essential structure in this respect. On the other hand, *paleocortex*, meaning old cortex, consists mostly of cortex on the ventral surface of the brain, including structures in the limbic system discussed below. It is old because it has three or four layers and is more primitive in structure. It is found in all vertebrates, being the only cortex in fishes and the lower vertebrates. In between paleocortex and neocortex is some cortex called *transitional cortex* because its structure is intermediate between the other two. The cingulate gyrus lying in the wall of the longitudinal fissure (see below) and certain parts of the temporal and frontal lobe consist of such transitional cortex.

ARCHITECTONIC AREAS—On the basis of cytoarchitectural differences, it is possible to divide the cortex into many different architectonic areas, meaning areas differing in cellular architecture. A widely used system, developed years ago by Brodmann, provides a different number as a label for each of these distinguishable areas. In recent years, it has become apparent that architectonic areas frequently do not correspond to functional areas, as established by means of lesions or by electrical mapping. Consequently, the Brodmann system has declined in usefulness. However, some of the more frequently used nomenclature in the Brodmann system is as follows (see Figure 2.8).

Within the frontal lobes, three general areas may be distinguished. (*1*) The *precentral area,* Brodmann's area 4, lies immediately in front of the central sulcus. When stimulated electrically, this region yields movements of various parts of the body (see Chapter 10) and for this reason is also called the *motor area.* (*2*) Immediately in front of the precentral area is the *intermediate precentral area,* sometimes called the *premotor area* or *Brodmann's area 6,* which is intimately concerned in motor functions (again see Chapter 10). (*3*) In the larger and anterior part of the frontal lobe and including several architectonic areas are the *prefrontal areas,* sometimes referred to as the *frontal "association" areas* because they have some special functions in integrating mental activity (see Chapter 18). Within the prefrontal area and just anterior to the intermediate precentral area are the *frontal eye fields,* so called because stimulation of this region causes eye movements; this area corresponds to Brodmann's area 8.

In the parietal lobe there is first the *postcentral area,* Brodmann's 3–1–2, which lies immediately posterior to the central sulcus. This is a sensory area, concerned primarily in sensations of touch and taste. Behind it are several areas, which for our purposes may be considered together as the *posterior parietal area* (Brodmann's 5 to 7). It receives fibers related indirectly to touch and kinesthetic functions and is of proved importance in them.

In the occipital lobes, the area of principal importance is area 17, the *striate area,* which is the primary cortical center for vision. Closely associated with it is the *prestriate area,* Brodmann's 18 and 19. It is regarded as a visual "association" center.

Regarding the temporal lobes, for the present we shall note only that they contain a primary sensory area for hearing and other areas concerned in visual discrimination. The latter do not fit with the Brodmann map and will require detailed consideration elsewhere (Chapter 17). The hearing areas, or more specifically auditory cortex, are, in the case of man, fairly well buried in the walls of the lateral fissure. In less invaginated brains, such as the cat's or dog's, they lie in more accessible positions on the temporal surface.

PROJECTION AREAS—Brodmann's architectonic system is frequently a convenient system for referencing cortical areas, but it is only one system and it is limited in its usefulness. Another system is based on electrical methods of mapping cortical projection areas. This is applicable to those areas of the cortex in which an evoked electrical response can be obtained upon stimulation of a sense organ.

It happens that the projection of each sense on the cerebral cortex is topographically organized. That is to say, for each point on the sensory surface there is a corresponding point in the cortical area to which the sense projects. Hence, a cortical projection area is a map, albeit sometimes a distorted one, of the sense it represents.

Each sense has more than one projection area in the cortex. Typically, it has two, and occasionally it has three. Such maps can be distinguished because each is a complete map of the sense represented, and, moreover, the two maps may be mirror images of each other or at least have a different orientation on the surface of the brain. One of these maps in each sense corresponds well with a Brodmann area and with the known thalamic projections of the sense to the cortex. This map is given the number I. Thus there are Visual I, Auditory I, and Somatic I as primary cortical projection areas for the respective senses. A second area usually does not correspond very well with Brodmann nomenclature or, as yet, with known anatomical projections. It is given the number II. Hence there are also Visual II, Auditory II, and Somatic II. The maps obtained for the rabbit, the cat, and the monkey are shown in Figure 2.10. We shall discuss them again below in connection with the evolution of the brain.

FIBERS OF THE CEREBRAL HEMISPHERES—Below the cerebral cortex is a great mass of nerve fibers of which a large part is myelinated, therefore constituting white matter. These fibers are of three kinds: commissural, association, and projection fibers. Those of the first type have their cell bodies in the cortex of one hemisphere and pass in a great white sheet to the other hemisphere. These fibers make up the corpus callosum, which is the principal connection between the two hemispheres and forms the floor of the median longitudinal fissure as well as the roof of the lateral ventricles (see below). Besides the corpus callosum, there are other commissural fibers passing between the two hemispheres, but they are of little concern to us. "Association fibers" are those which connect one part of the cortex to another. They were formerly thought to play a large part in the integration of activities of the cortex, but it now appears that they do not extend very far from their points of origin, and it is more probable that the relation of various areas to each other is conducted directly through the cortex or by way of the thalamus, more often the latter.

Of greatest functional importance are the projection fibers by which impulses reach and leave the cortex. Projection fibers are classified as *afferent* or *corticopetal* (those radiating upward from the thalamus and other subcortical centers to the cortex) and *efferent* or *corticofugal* (those projecting downward to various subcortical centers). The latter fibers may end at any one of several points: the basal ganglia, thalamus, midbrain, hindbrain, or ventral horn cells of the spinal cord. Corticopetal fibers, on the other hand, have their origin almost without exception in the nuclei of the thalamus. These have been described briefly above in connection with the relay and association nuclei of the thalamus.

THE BASAL GANGLIA

The phylogenetically oldest parts of the telencephalon are the basal ganglia. These are a mass of gray matter lying below the cortex and, for the most part, above the thalamus or diencephalon, although certain small but important parts of them are lodged between the diencephalon and mesencephalon (midbrain). The latter (Chapter 10) are significant in maintaining the posture of the organism and in certain aspects of the coordination of movement. Although properly a part of the cerebral hemispheres, they appear to have migrated, in phylogenesis, away from the main portion of the basal ganglia, which is the *corpus striatum*. This term means "striped body" and has its origin in the fact that projection fibers passing upward and downward between the cortex and thalamus are interspersed among the cell bodies of the corpus striatum, thus giving it its striped appearance. The corpus striatum is a fairly complex as well as important structure, but its further description is not necessary for the present purposes (see Chapter 10).

THE LIMBIC SYSTEM

In recent years, it has become apparent that a complex system involving the cerebral cortex, certain subcortical structures, and the hypothalamus is important in emotion and related activities. This system has been called the *limbic system* (McLean, 1958). "Limbic" means border, and the system has been given this name because in many respects, particularly because it involves parts of the brain that are relatively old in an evolutionary sense, it is a borderline system. It is also a complex system, and only the parts to which we shall later refer in behavioral experiments will be described.

The cortical part of the limbic system is the *cingulate gyrus*, which lies in the longitudinal fissure just above the corpus callosum (see Figure 2.9). The principal parts of the subcortical limbic system are the *septal area*, lying just

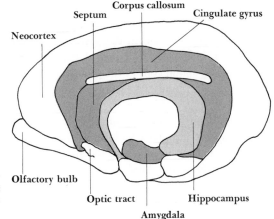

FIGURE 2.9—Semidiagrammatic drawing of the limbic system, which is represented by shading.

under the forward end of the corpus callosum; the *amygdaloid complex,* or amygdala, which lies in the ventral surface of the brain not far from the temporal lobe; and the *hippocampus,* a structure shaped somewhat like a horse's tail—hence its name—beginning near the amygdala and swerving upward in the brain. These various parts are interconnected with each other and with both the hypothalamus and mammillary bodies, but further description of the system will be left to the chapter in which emotion is discussed in detail (Chapter 11).

VENTRICULAR SYSTEM

In discussing the various parts of the brain above, we have frequently mentioned the ventricles. A word is in order about what these are, how they are arranged, and what they contain.

All organs of the body are supplied with blood in greater or lesser amounts, and the nervous system, because of its crucial importance in the economy of the body, receives much more than most other organs. Peculiar to the nervous system, however, is another type of fluid supply, the cerebrospinal fluid. This is to be found in the *ventricular* and *subarachnoid* cavities of the brain and spinal cord. The ventricular system is within the brain and spinal cord; the subarachnoid spaces are in the external linings.

The ventricular system consists of four ventricles in the brain and a spinal canal in the spinal cord. Two ventricles, ordinarily called the *lateral ventricles,* are found in the cerebral hemispheres in a position indicated in Figure 2.2. These communicate with each other and with the third ventricle, which is located in the midline in the thalamus and hypothalamus. By means of the Sylvian aqueduct which passes through the midbrain, separating it into a floor and a roof, the third ventricle is connected with the fourth ventricle contained within the posterior pons and anterior medulla. This narrows down in the posterior part of the medulla to a small canal that runs the length of the spinal cord in the gray commissure.

The subarachnoid spaces are between layers of the external lining of the brain (meninges). One of them comes into close proximity with the fourth ventricle, being separated from it only by a thin membrane, which has small openings in it through which fluid from the ventricular system can communicate with that in the subarachnoid spaces.

The cerebrospinal fluid is an almost colorless liquid very much like the blood in composition except that it has no red or white corpuscles and contains no blood proteins. Indeed, it appears to be rich in the food materials of the blood. Its function with respect to the nervous system is not clearly understood, although it is clear that it is partly nutritive. It is believed that this fluid is secreted or filtered from the blood in networks of arterial blood vessels (choroid plexi) found in the ventricles, and it appears to be absorbed by a similar net of venous vessels (arachnoid villi) in the subarachnoid spaces (Livingston, 1960).

EVOLUTION OF THE BRAIN

We have now discussed briefly the main parts of the central nervous system, with some mention of the function of these parts. There will be considerably more detail later in connection with specific topics. We have been describing a typical brain of one of the higher mammals, such as a monkey or ape or man. Actually, the description would apply, for the most part, to the cat or the dog. The essential structure of the central nervous system, however, began in the lower vertebrates, and this in turn had its origins in invertebrate evolution. It will help us, therefore, to understand some of the functions of the parts of the nervous system, as well as to fix more clearly in mind what we have already discussed, if we summarize some of the principal features of the evolution of the central nervous system.

A great deal is known about the evolution of the nervous system in the invertebrates (see Dethier and Stellar, 1961), but we shall not go into that here since we shall be concerned almost exclusively with the vertebrates, and particularly with the mammals. Hence, we take each of the principal parts of the central nervous system that have been described and trace the changes that take place in it through vertebrate evolution. In that way we can summarize earlier sections of this chapter and be prepared later for certain differences to be found in various species used in psychophysiological experiments.

THE SPINAL CORD

Throughout phylogeny the spinal cord remains a structure with relatively fixed capacities and functions. Its own rather independent part in behavior is as a center for reflex behavior; its relation to the brain is one of conducting impulses between the brain and the peripheral sense organs and muscles. However, insofar as the functions of the brain change, so does the spinal cord undergo change. Of these changes, two are most important: the formation of the autonomic system and the changes in the termination of the spinal cord. (1) In even the lowest fishes the spinal nerves have the structure typical of higher animals, but these must also mediate autonomic functions, and it is only in the higher fishes that sympathetic ganglia together with a distinct autonomic system are formed. (2) All connections between the spinal cord and the higher centers of the brain are, in fishes and amphibia, relayed by way of the medulla. Some are so relayed even in man (e.g., the dorsal columns), but it is in the reptiles that the first direct connections become established between the spinal cord and the thalamus. Moreover, only in mammals does the coordination between the brain and spinal cord entail direct tracts between the spinal cord and the cortex. This, we shall see, is related to the fact that only in mammals does the cerebral cortex take on general sensory and motor functions.

MEDULLA

Quite uniform throughout all vertebrates are the general functions of the medulla. It contains the centers for respiration, cardiac activity, and gastrointestinal functions. In it also are the principal centers of the special mechanoreceptors, viz., the lateral line organs of fishes, vestibular receptors, and auditory receptors. The amount of the medulla given over to these centers at different phylogenetic levels is proportional to their importance. The lateral line organs diminish in size and are lost in higher amphibia. There is very little change in the vestibular receptors in vertebrate evolution, and while the auditory receptors have no independent status in fishes, appearing only in amphibia and reptiles, they become a fully developed mechanism in birds and mammals. Paralleling these various changes in sensory structure are corresponding enlargements or recessions in the size and importance of bulbar nuclei.

One of the most striking phylogenetic changes in the medulla is associated with the diminishing size and importance of the gustatory receptor system. Taste buds are distributed all over the body of many fishes and are of prime importance in the determination of their behavior. The nuclei for taste in the medulla are accordingly enormously expanded, so much so that they form large evaginations called the *vagal lobes*—"vagal" because they represent primarily the enlargement of the nuclei of the vagus nerve. The taste receptors are curtailed, however, in further evolution, and in mammals they are limited to the tongue and a small part of the internal surfaces of the mouth. With this recession of taste goes a diminution in the vagal lobes, until in man, for example, the gustatory nucleus becomes a comparatively inconspicuous center in the medulla.

CEREBELLUM

The first structure of the nervous system to be specialized for the coordination of sensory and motor impulses was the cerebellum (Figure 2.10). It was apparently developed in connection with the vestibular and lateral line systems which are so important in the lower vertebrates, but even in cyclostomes, prevertebrate organisms lower than the fishes, where the cerebellum is first seen, it has connections with the frontal and spinal portions of the nervous system. Much of its later development involves the extension and increase in the number of these connections. The cerebellum achieves its greatest importance in birds, where it reaches its largest size in relation to the rest of the brain and where it is an important organ for coordinating the sensory and motor impulses involved in flying. The cerebellum, as it is seen in birds and lower forms, is known as the *paleocerebellum*, which means "old cerebellum."

In mammals, the most important changes in the nervous system are related to the formation of the cerebral cortex and the large cerebral hemispheres. Associated with this development appear new cerebellar structures, which constitute the *neocerebellum*. These are the cerebellar hemispheres, and they are concerned primarily with the coordination of impulses that are delivered to, and distributed from, the cerebral cortex.

MIDBRAIN

The principal functions of the midbrain throughout the evolutionary series are audition, vision, and the conduction of impulses between the higher and lower centers of the nervous system. In fishes some of the midbrain is concerned with the lateral line organs, but when these organs disappear in higher animals the associated midbrain centers also disappear. In inframammalian forms the colliculi are the principal sensory centers for vision and audition, but as encephalization proceeds and the cerebral hemispheres are developed, the importance of the midbrain in these sensory functions diminishes.

THALAMUS

In the lower vertebrates the thalamus constitutes almost the entire forebrain, and it is concerned principally with vision, forming relay stations between the eyes and the midbrain. It subsequently enlarges to include centers for hear-

DOGFISH   SALMON   ALLIGATOR

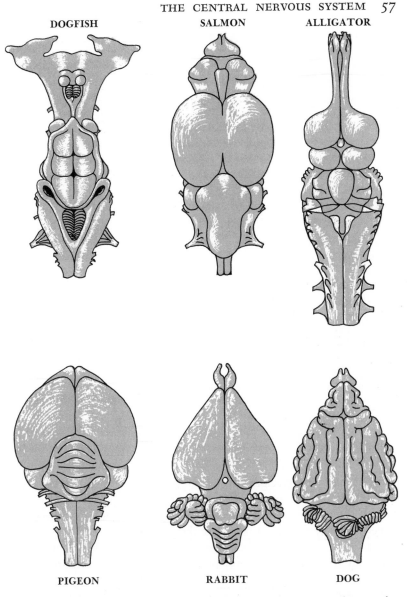

PIGEON   RABBIT   DOG

FIGURE 2.10—Comparative development of the brain in the vertebrate series. The dogfish and the salmon have no true cerebral hemispheres, but the highly developed midbrain in the latter looks like hemispheres. The alligator has cerebral hemispheres, but they are paleocortex (old cortex) and relatively small. In the pigeon we see further development of cortex, but only in mammals like the rabbit do the hemispheres constitute the major portion of the brain and consist largely of neocortex (new cortex). In the dog, the hemispheres are still larger and begin to fold in convolutions. (Adapted from P. H. Mitchell. *General physiology*. 5th ed. New York: McGraw-Hill, 1956. P. 155. By permission of the publishers.)

ing, pressure, pain, and temperature. As the cerebral cortex grows in mammalian forms, the thalamus becomes for the most part a great relay station between the cortex and lower centers, but it also probably serves very important functions as a coordinator of sensory impulses and of impulses traveling between it and the cortex. In warm-blooded animals, birds and mammals, the hypothalamus is differentiated from the main body of the thalamus and becomes an important center of integration for the autonomic system.

CORPUS STRIATUM

This is established as a motor center in fishes. It expands greatly in amphibia and reptiles and reaches its greatest development in birds. The cerebral cortex of the mammal takes over many of the functions of the corpus striatum, and as a result the latter becomes relatively less important in the later stages of phylogenesis.

THE CEREBRAL CORTEX

In fishes there exists no cerebral cortex; only the olfactory bulbs and a primitive forebrain, made up of thalamus and corpus striatum, are present. In amphibia and reptiles, however, a primitive cortex appears in the form of a nucleus of cell bodies interposed between the olfactory bulb and the rest of the forebrain; this first cortex is plainly concerned only with olfactory functions. Later on, in birds, is laid down the first cortex having nonolfactory functions, but only in mammals does it become a true cortex with a definite cortical structure as well as important functions. Such a "somatic" cortex is sometimes called *neocortex* because of its more recent phylogenetic development. Even in mammals one can distinguish it from the old cortex, or *paleocortex*, which has olfactory functions. As olfaction recedes in importance in the adjustments of the animal and as various other sensory and motor functions become corticalized, the neocortex comes, in mammals, to constitute the larger and more significant portion of the cerebrum.

But above and beyond these basic stages in the evolution of the cerebral cortex are other important developments in the somatic cortex itself. Chief of these are the enormous growth and convolution of the cortex and the special prominence given to frontal-lobe development; these begin with the rat and reach their peak in man (see Figure 2.10). The rat, for instance, has a very simple cortex with no convolutions, but in carnivora (e.g., cats and dogs) one can observe clearly the principal fissures, the central and lateral, and the beginnings of others. In the primates and man, many fissures are present, forming numerous gyri by means of which one can denote rather precisely various parts of the cortex. The emergence and growth of a convoluted cortex go hand in hand with increasing mass and with differentiation of both structure and function.

Worthy of special note is the development of neocortex not concerned in sensory or motor functions (see Figure 2.11). In the rabbit, virtually all the cortex is accounted for by sensory projection areas, motor cortex, or limbic (transitional) cortex. As one goes up the mammalian series, however, areas not accounted for in this way grow relatively larger. Such areas are loosely

FIGURE 2.11—Maps of sensory, motor, and association (unshaded) areas of the cerebral cortex. (Adapted from C. N. Woolsey. Patterns of sensory representation in the cerebral cortex. *Fed. Proc.*, 1947, 6, 438, Fig. 1.)

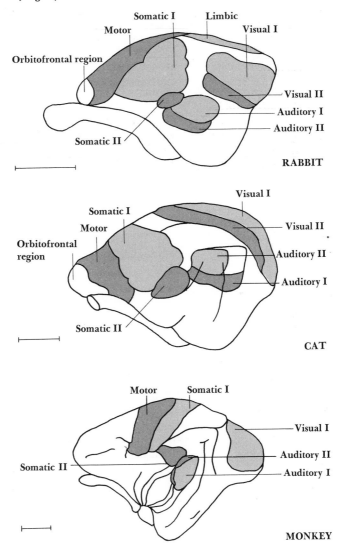

called "association" areas because they are related to learned behavior and complex processes. In the frontal lobe, this trend takes the form of increasingly larger prefrontal areas. In the posterior parts of the cerebral cortex, it is seen in increasingly larger parietal and temporal areas outside the known sensory areas.

BRAIN WEIGHT AND BEHAVIOR

In closing this section on the evolution of the brain, we may note that the relative size of the brain is correlated with the general intelligence of animals (Witherspoon, 1960). In order to express brain weight in relative terms, it is ordinarily related to body weight by some equation. Several equations have been proposed, but one that seems most satisfactory is of the form

$$E = kP^{0.67}$$

where E is brain weight, P is body weight, and k is the constant of proportionality indicating relative size of brain (Jerison, 1961). This constant k increases considerably throughout the vertebrate series, and it takes a relatively large jump from the anthropoid apes to man. The ratio of brain weight to body weight in man is, indeed, three to four times that of the apes. This corresponds to a comparable difference in intellectual capacity.

3 NEURONAL PHYSIOLOGY

THE TWO PRECEDING CHAPTERS dealt primarily with the structure of the organs important in behavior. Only incidentally, to help with the exposition, were some functions described. This chapter and the next one deal primarily with function, that is, with the physiology of the organs previously described. This chapter presents a brief summary of neuron physiology; the next one, a summary of biochemical factors affecting the nervous system.

Neuron physiology has for some years been one of the most active subjects of research in physiology. Hundreds of papers about it are published every year. Although much progress has been made, many problems are still unsolved. In a brief chapter about such a large and changing subject, we cannot present a completely accurate picture of its present status nor one with which every neurophysiologist would agree. We can provide only a sketch that includes the principles most widely accepted at the present time.

POTENTIALS IN NEURONS

The typical structure of the neuron has already been described. It has a cell body (soma), one or more dendrites, and an axon. It has a membrane, and sometimes, but not always, a myelin sheath surrounds its fibers. As we shall see in this chapter, there are some differences in the physiology of the cell body, dendrites, and axon. In the case of all three, however, the key to the understanding of their functions lies in the *cell membrane* (see Eccles, 1959).

RESTING POTENTIAL

The membranes of cells, we saw in Chapter 1, may become polarized. That is to say, there may be more ions of a particular kind, positive or negative, on one side of the membrane than on the other side. When that happens, an *electrochemical potential* is set up.

This is the case with the membrane of neurons. In its resting state, there is an electrochemical-potential difference between the two sides of the membrane. This is called the *resting potential.* Typically, it is −50 to −100 millivolts, although it may be smaller. The minus signs indicate that the resting potential is *negative* if the inside of the membrane is taken as a reference. Put another way, the outside of the membrane has an excess of positive ions over negative ones; the inside, an excess of negative ions over positive ones. The situation is represented in Figure 3.1.

That illustration also gives a hint of how the experiment is made in which such a potential is measured. A nerve or nerve fiber is cut, and a voltmeter of

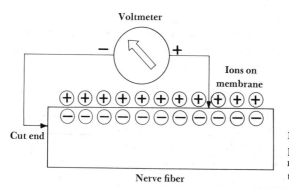

FIGURE 3.1—Diagram of a polarized membrane and measurement of resting potential.

some kind is arranged in a circuit so that one electrode is placed on the out-side of the nerve (or neuron) and the other either against the cut end of the nerve or inside a neuron. In modern experiments, it has been possible to insert an extremely small electrode well into the axon of a relatively large neuron. Whether done in this precise way or more crudely, the voltmeter indicates that the outside of the membrane is positive and the inside negative.

Why is there a resting potential, and why is it such that the inside of the membrane is negative with respect to the outside? Physiologists have puzzled over this and experimented vigorously to answer it. The most widely accepted theory is the sodium theory. In this, it is assumed that the membrane, in its resting state but not in all states, is relatively impermeable to sodium, while being permeable to most other ions, such as potassium (K^+) and chloride (Cl^-) ions. Since it is known that there is a large excess of sodium ions on the outside compared with the inside of the membrane during the resting state, it is assumed that this excess is responsible for the polarization of the membrane and hence for the resting potential (see Eccles, 1959).

SPIKE POTENTIAL

Until relatively recently, the only other potential given much attention by psychologists and physiologists was the spike potential or, more loosely, the nervous impulse. Nowadays the term spike potential or merely spike is pre-ferred, for there are other kinds of potential that are also of considerable im-portance in the functioning of the nervous system. These are described below.

The spike potential is really a very rapid change of potential, first in one direction and then in the reverse direction, eventually returning to the resting level. It is so rapid that in larger fibers it goes through its complete swing in less than one millisecond. If one is recording a resting potential of, say, −70 millivolts and then electrically stimulates a fiber with a sufficiently intense stimulus, the voltmeter quickly swings from −70 millivolts toward zero and typically past it to, say, +30 millivolts, and then returns to the resting level (Cole and Curtis, 1939). A typical spike potential is shown in Figure 3.2, although, as we shall see, a record is seldom as simple as this one.

IONIC CHANGES—For a long time, it was thought that the spike potential was merely the momentary abolition of the resting potential. If this were so, the spike potential should stop at zero and not overshoot. Yet careful measure-ments of spikes shows that such overshooting to a positive potential is typical. An extension of the sodium theory mentioned above has been used to explain this apparent mystery. According to the theory, during the spike potential the membrane is made permeable to sodium, and sodium ions rush through the membrane to the inside. If this happened only to the extent necessary to equalize concentration on the two sides, the spike would stop at zero. Instead, however, it overshoots by momentarily building up a larger concentration on

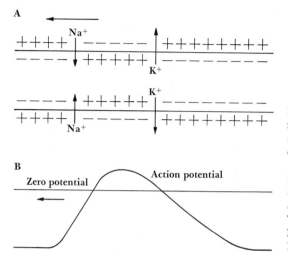

FIGURE 3.2—Diagram of a nervous impulse advancing along a membrane in the direction of the arrow. (Adapted from J. C. Eccles. In J. Field, H. W. Magoun, and V. E. Hall (Eds.), *Handbook of physiology*, vol. 1. Washington, D.C.: American Physiological Society, 1959. P. 64.)

the inside than on the outside, thus making the inside swing positive. There is indirect evidence that this may take place.

Why the sodium quickly passes back through the membrane and establishes a resting potential again is still largely a mystery. Somehow, metabolic processes within the neuron supply energy for an "ionic pump" to pump the sodium ions back. Equally mysterious is why the membrane suddenly but briefly becomes permeable to the sodium ions. It is as though stimulation opened some valves in the membrane, the sodium ions rushed through only to be forced out by a pump inside the membrane, and the valves again closed. That is the generally accepted picture, but that is also about as much as is known about it.

ALL-OR-NONE LAW—One of the now well-established principles of spike activity is that spikes obey an *all-or-none law*. Actually, the law does not always hold, and, even when it does, some qualifications must be attached to it, but it is nevertheless an important feature of spike potentials. The all-or-none law refers to the *ungraded* size of the potential. Either it takes place at the largest size possible under the circumstances or it does not occur at all. The "largest size possible" depends on the size of the fiber in which the spike takes place and on chemical conditions surrounding the fiber, for example, on the relative amount of sodium present. Given a certain fiber size and these other conditions, however, the spike is all-or-none in size.

AFTERPOTENTIALS—In some cases, but not in all, the declining spike potential does not return immediately to the prespike resting level. Instead, it may undershoot, that is, fall short of the resting level, or it may overshoot to a level above the resting level. It may do first one, then the other (see Figure 3.3). The undershooting is associated with an increased sensitivity of the neuron to stimulation; the overshooting, with a subnormal phase of sensitivity. Neither the causes nor the significance of these afterpotentials is very well understood, but since they sometimes appear in records along with the spike potential, they have been mentioned in passing.

GRADED POTENTIALS

The ungraded all-or-none spike potential has been known for fifty years (Adrian, 1914). Somewhat later the existence of *graded potentials* in neurons was discovered (Gasser and Graham, 1933). By "graded potentials" is meant potentials that are not all-or-none; they can be of any size. Such graded potentials are now known to be of critical importance in nervous functions. Indeed, they are necessary events in evoking spike potentials in the *normal* functioning of cells. Three kinds of graded potentials may be distinguished.

RECEPTOR OR GENERATOR POTENTIALS—Receptors, we have seen earlier, may be either neurons specialized to respond to a particular kind of stimulation or specialized epithelial cells innervated by nerve fibers. Graded receptor potentials have been found in all specialized receptors so far investigated

FIGURE 3.3—The composite action potential and excitability cycle of neurons.

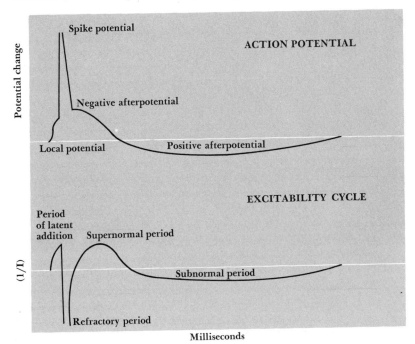

(see Gray, 1959). These are potentials that are roughly proportional in size to the stimulus evoking them. Although they die away after stimulation ceases, their time constants are such that they build up relatively slowly as compared with spike potentials. Consequently, they show summation or facilitation. That is to say, the effects of a series of stimuli can be additive. One brief stimulus evokes a potential, but if another stimulus is applied before the effects of the first have dissipated, the second stimulus builds more potential on top of the first. This is illustrated in Figure 3.4.

Besides being graded in size, receptor potentials can be distinguished from spike potentials in two other ways.

First, spike potentials can be elicited by electrical stimulation. In fact, that is the way experimenters typically evoke them and probably the only way in which they are normally tripped off in the nervous system. There will be more on this later. A receptor potential, on the other hand, is elicited by a very specific kind of stimuli, the kind for which the particular receptor has been specialized. In other words, a receptor potential has a *specific excitant*. All the evidence points to the conclusion that it cannot be evoked by electrical stimuli but rather only by a specific excitant.

Secondly, receptor potentials are aroused in different parts of the neuron, and sometimes in entirely different neurons, than are spike potentials. In the case of the Pacinian corpuscle, which is a pressure receptor, a graded receptor potential arises at the end of the fiber most directly affected by the compression of the receptor. The spike potential separately arises through the action of the receptor potential at a point half way along the fiber's length within the corpuscle. In the case of the visual receptors, it now seems certain that the potentials arising in the rods and cones are exclusively receptor graded potentials. Thus in this case the whole receptor neuron is reserved for receptor potentials, the spike potential arising under the influence of this potential in the horizontal or bipolar cells (see Chapter 6).

Because the receptor potential is clearly a link between stimulation and the spike potential, thus generating the spike potential, it is sometimes called the *generator potential*. This is the terminology used in vision.

2. POSTSYNAPTIC POTENTIAL—As we shall see later on, neurons do not directly connect with one another anatomically. Each is its individual cell with its own membrane. At their terminals, however, neurons come very close together (100 angstroms), and their junction is called a *synapse*. Synapses typically consist of one or more axon terminals delivering excitation to the dendrites or to the soma of a neighboring neuron.

The potential that arises in the somadendritic structure is called a postsynaptic potential and is conventionally abbreviated as PSP (see Grundfest, 1959). It is very much like a receptor potential in being a graded potential that can build up with repeated excitation or with excitation arriving simultaneously from different axon terminals. It is also like the receptor potential in requiring a *specific excitant*. In this case, the excitant is always a chemical

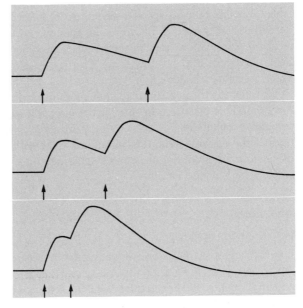

FIGURE 3.4—Summation of receptor potentials with different intervals between stimuli. (Adapted from J. A. B. Gray. In J. Field, H. W. Magoun, and V. E. Hall (Eds.), *Handbook of physiology*, vol. 1. Washington, D.C.: American Physiological Society, 1959. P. 135.)

molecule, whereas in the case of receptors other kinds of energy, photic or mechanical, may also serve as specific excitants. Later in the chapter we shall discuss these excitants. For the present, the point is that receptor and postsynaptic potentials are alike in being graded and in requiring specific excitants.

SUBTHRESHOLD POTENTIAL—A third kind of graded potential may arise in connection with electrical or other stimulation of a fiber. If an electrical stimulus that is not quite strong enough to elicit an all-or-none spike is applied to an axon, a graded potential may be recorded that is more or less proportional to the intensity of the stimulation (see Figure 3.3). This is called a subthreshold response or potential, or sometimes a local response or potential. Both are appropriate because this potential does not propagate down an axon as does the spike potential; hence it is local. It is subthreshold, because the moment it becomes strong enough to cross the threshold, it trips off the full-blown all-or-none spike. This point is regarded as the threshold of propagation.

EXCITATION AND CONDUCTION

As a result of the research of recent years, it is now widely accepted that there are two kinds of neuronal membranes (see Grundfest, 1959). One is electrically stimulable; the other is not. The kind that is not electrically stimulable responds only to specific excitants. This second kind is found in the dendrites and somas of neurons—in general, at the points in the neuron receiving stimulation from the external environment or from other neurons. Some receptors, and possibly some neurons, possess only this kind of membrane (see Bullock, 1959).

This nonelectrically stimulable membrane gives only a graded electrical potential. This potential, in turn, is the electrical stimulus for the electrically stimulable membrane, which is found in axons and the longer conducting lines of the nervous system. If stimulated sufficiently, this electrically stimulable membrane gives the all-or-none spike response that propagates along the whole length of the neuron.

THRESHOLD

Because the explosive propagated spike is an all-or-none potential and because it is the largest of the potentials measured, it becomes a convenient signal to use in studying the excitability of neurons. The transition from a graded potential to the spike potential may be considered a *threshold* because it occurs so suddenly and so definitely. The amount of stimulus required to produce the spike potential is called the critical level of potential or, more frequently, the threshold stimulus. By measuring the value of the threshold stimulus, under various conditions, one can learn a great deal about the excitability of the neuron and factors affecting it (see Figure 3.3).

Other terms related to the concept of the threshold are as follows: *Excitability* refers to the strength of stimulus required to produce a spike potential and is usually expressed as the reciprocal of the threshold. When excitability is high, the threshold is low, and vice versa. *Subliminal stimulation* refers to stimulation that is below the threshold intensity, and similarly *subliminal excitation* refers to the excitation of graded potentials that are too weak to trip off a spike potential.

LATENT ADDITION

There is a very brief period, often not more than 0.5 millisecond, following the application of a subliminal stimulus, when a second stimulus, if applied, will add to the effects of the first one. It is a period in which the effects of successive stimuli can summate in increasing the graded potential to the threshold level for eliciting a spike. As one might expect, this period of latent addition corresponds to the time that it takes a graded potential to die away. This varies considerably with the size of the fiber or with the structure of synapses in the nervous system.

The concept of latent addition applies not only to repeated brief stimuli but also to stimuli that are relatively long, say several milliseconds in duration. In this case, the effects of the continued stimulation summate over time to generate one spike and then, after recovery from this, another spike, and so on, depending on the intensity and duration of the stimulus.

REFRACTORY PERIOD

Following the period of latent addition, there is typically a short period of depression. If the stimulus that aroused the graded potential is subthreshold, the depression is only a minor one; a stimulus slightly more intense than normal may elicit a spike. If, however, a spike potential has been tripped off by the first stimulus, the depression will be complete. No stimulus, no matter how intense, can arouse a response in the fiber. This complete depression is known as the *absolutely refractory period* (see Figure 3.3). Following this, there is always a gradual return to normal sensitivity, in which relatively intense stimuli can excite the fiber. This part of the depressed period is called the *relatively refractory period*.

These refractory periods are the really large and significant changes in excitability correlated with the evocation of spike potentials. In some cases, however, it is possible to record either or both of two other periods of changed excitability (see Figure 3.3). One is a *supernormal period*. This may occur immediately after the relatively refractory period and appears to represent an overshooting of the resting potential. During this period, excitability is slightly greater than normal. After the supernormal period or, in some cases, following the relatively refractory period, there is a *subnormal period* during which excitability is slightly less than normal. These periods, when they are measured, are considerably longer relatively than the absolutely and relatively refractory periods. The latter are typically finished in one millisecond, whereas the supernormal and subnormal periods may take fifteen or twenty milliseconds, and in some cases hundreds of milliseconds, to run their course.

CHANGES IN POLARIZATION

All the potentials and changes in excitability we have been discussing can be understood in terms of underlying changes in the polarization of the neuron's membrane. The resting potential represents a steady level of polarization. A stimulus evoking a graded response changes this level of polarization; ordinarily it does this by partially *depolarizing* the membrane. Such partial depolarization changes the level of potential, and this results in a current flow (see Figure 3.5). Sodium ions are conducted inward through the membrane, and potassium ions outward through it. If this current flow reaches a critical level, there is a sudden complete depolarization and even a reversal of polarization of the membrane. These are the refractory period and the period of the spike potential. During the period of repolarization, excitability is less than normal, and the membrane is relatively refractory. A similar reasoning applies to the afterpotentials and to subnormal and supernormal periods.

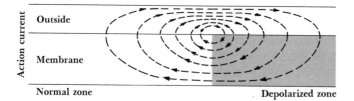

FIGURE 3.5—Diagram of the currents in and along the neuronal membrane when it is depolarized.

Any excitant or stimulus that reduces the resting potential may be regarded as *depolarizing*. Most of the conditions discussed so far are in that category. On the other hand, any condition that increases the membrane potential to a higher value than the resting potential may be regarded as *hyperpolarizing*. There are, as we shall see, situations both in receptors and in postsynaptic areas where hyperpolarization takes place, and these are important in understanding nervous function, particularly the phenomenon of inhibition. Any condition that hyperpolarizes a membrane works against, or is opposite to, the excitants and stimuli causing the graded depolarizing potentials necessary to reach the threshold of the spike potential. Thus, whenever hyperpolarization takes place, the threshold for obtaining a spike potential is increased, and excitability is decreased. Hence hyperpolarization may reduce or eliminate the production of spikes.

PROPAGATION OF SPIKE POTENTIALS

Let us now consider the case of an electrical stimulus applied to an electrically stimulable membrane. This is shown in Figure 3.6. Let us assume that two electrodes are used, each on a different part of the membrane. In such a situation, when a direct current from a battery is used, one electrode is called the cathode, the other an anode. At the anode, electrons are flowing into the membrane; at the cathode, electrons are flowing out.

If, while stimulating in this way, one also has some means of recording from the neighborhood of the electrodes, the following is found: At the cathode, a graded potential builds up, if the electrical stimulus is subthreshold; the membrane becomes partially depolarized. At the anode, the opposite happens; the membrane becomes hyperpolarized. If the intensity of the stimulus is increased to threshold value, it can be concluded that outward-flowing currents are depolarizing, while inward-flowing currents are hyperpolarizing.

Now let us see what kinds of electrical circuits are involved and how these are related to the propagation of the spike potential. At first, the membrane is merely a link in an external circuit formed by the battery and the two electrodes. If the depolarizing cathodal current is strong enough, however, it undermines the membrane and totally depolarizes it. Then a new circuit is set up, one that is independent of the electrodes. It involves the external fluid medium of the membrane, the membrane itself, and the protoplasm within the neuron (see Figure 3.5). Currents flowing from the depolarized region inside the membrane move ahead of the electrode and, by flowing outward, depolarize the region ahead. As this becomes depolarized, current flows inward in the zone of depolarization and then ahead to excite and depolarize the region ahead of it. And so on it goes. In this way, the spike potential propagates itself down the length of a fiber. The critical event in all this is a large enough depolarization to set up a current that is sufficient in intensity to break down completely the adjacent region.

It has long been a question whether conduction is the same in myelinated fibers as in unmyelinated fibers. The myelin sheath covering the myelinated fiber consists of a fatty substance that has a relatively high resistance. The sheath is interrupted at intervals by a node of Ranvier. It has been hypothesized that conduction in myelinated fibers is *saltatory*, that is, tends to die under the sheath but to build up again at the nodes (see Tasaki, 1959). The latest evidence would appear to rule this out, for when the density of membrane current is measured at points along a fiber, conduction of action potentials is a continuous process (Lorente de No, 1963).

SYNAPTIC TRANSMISSION

Probably no aspect of nervous function has received more attention than the question of synaptic transmission. In Sherrington's early work on spinal reflexes (1906), it became apparent that there is something different about synapses that is not evident in the activity of axons. And research and theory

FIGURE 3.6—Diagram of current flow in and along the membrane of a neuron when an electrical stimulus is applied.

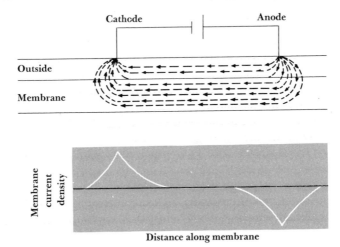

since then have been directed toward explaining these differences, often with considerable divergence of views.

The chief differences are as follows: (1) Synapses interpose a delay in the transmission process. Although the synaptic gap is of the order of 100 angstroms (10^{-8} meter), the delay between the arrival of an impulse at an axon terminal and the initiation of the postsynaptic impulse is of the order of 0.5 to 1.0 millisecond. During that time an impulse could be traveling a meter in a fiber. (2) Inhibition of spikes, as well as their excitation, is found at the synapse. On the other hand, electrically stimulable fibers may show "fatigue" but never outright inhibition as such. (3) Inhibitory and excitatory conditions at the synapse may persist over relatively long times (hundreds of milliseconds). The period of latent addition for electrically stimulable membranes is less than one millisecond.

CHEMICAL TRANSMITTERS

It is now generally agreed among investigators in the field that the above differences are to be accounted for by a different means of transmission at synapses (see Eccles, 1959; Gray, 1959). The messenger at the synapse is *chemical*, whereas that in an electrically stimulable membrane is *electrical*. No one knows just how many kinds of chemical transmitters there are nor exactly which synapses involve which transmitter. Two transmitters that have been identified, however, are *acetylcholine* and a substance closely related to epinephrine, the hormone of the adrenal medulla. This substance is called *norepinephrine* (see Chapter 4). Synapses employing acetylcholine as a transmitter are called *cholinergic*; those employing norepinephrine are called *adrenergic* (see von Euler, 1959). Transmission at the junction of motor axons and striped muscles is definitely cholinergic; so is transmission at many of the synapses of the central nervous system as well as some of those of the autonomic system. Adrenergic transmission by means of norepinephrine is characteristic of certain synapses in the autonomic system.

SYNAPTIC VESICLES—All the evidence is that the chemical transmitters are synthesized and stored in the terminals of axons. There are some definite ideas of how they are synthesized, but we need not go into them here (see von Euler, 1959). As to storage, the electron microscope has recently revealed the presence of *synaptic vesicles* in the presynaptic axon terminals (Eccles, 1959), and acetylcholine has been highly concentrated in subfractions of neurons containing synaptic vesicles (De Robertis et al., 1963). Various ways in which synaptic junctions are made, as seen under the electron microscope, are shown in Figure 3.7.

SYNAPTIC DELAY—It takes time for these transmitters to be secreted by the action of the spike potential arriving at the presynaptic terminals. It also

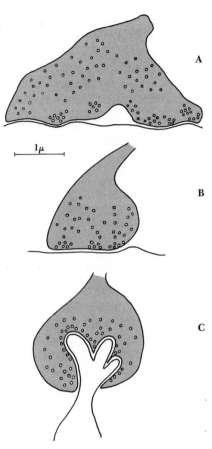

1μ

FIGURE 3.7—Types of synaptic junctions revealed by electron microscopy. (Adapted from J. C. Eccles. In J. Field, H. W. Magoun, and V. E. Hall (Eds.), *Handbook of physiology*, vol. 1. Washington, D.C.: American Physiological Society, 1959. P. 61.)

takes time for them to diffuse across the synaptic gap and then to interact chemically with the postsynaptic membrane to build up a postsynaptic potential (PSP). These delays, it would appear, are the cause of synaptic delay noted in reflex or other activities involving synapses.

FACILITATION—Chemical transmitters may accumulate briefly in the synaptic space and slowly (relatively) build up a graded postsynaptic potential. This accounts for the relatively long persistence of synaptic events. A series of impulses arriving at synaptic terminals may cause spikes to be generated postsynaptically for a period after the initial series has ended. This phenomenon is known as *facilitation*.

Chemical transmitters, however, cannot accumulate indefinitely. If they are not utilized rather rapidly, they are either destroyed or carried away in the blood stream. In the case of the cholinergic transmitter, acetylcholine, this is destroyed at the synapse by an enzyme known as cholinesterase.

POSTSYNAPTIC POTENTIALS

Postsynaptic potentials have already been mentioned, but the whole story about them has not been told. The *specific excitants* required to arouse them, it is now clear, are the chemical transmitters. Another significant fact about them is that they may be either excitatory or inhibitory (see Eccles, 1959). An excitatory potential, called an EPSP, is a *depolarizing* potential. An inhibitory potential, called IPSP, is a *hyperpolarizing* potential. Hyperpolarizing potentials, obviously, offset depolarizing potentials and can, if sizable, prevent the depolarization of a membrane to the critical level required for a spike potential. Herein lies the mechanism of inhibition in synaptic nervous systems.

It is not known exactly what determines whether a PSP will be excitatory (depolarizing) or inhibitory (hyperpolarizing). It is probably *not* the nature of the chemical transmitter, for the same transmitter may be excitatory at one set of synapses and inhibitory at another. That leaves two other possibilities: (1) The difference may depend on the anatomical arrangement of the presynaptic and postsynaptic membranes, and schemes explaining inhibition in this way have been proposed. (2) Or, alternatively, postsynaptic membranes may differ chemically so that one membrane, or part of a membrane, reacts to a transmitter with an IPSP, and another membrane, or part of a membrane, reacts to a transmitter with an EPSP. The answer may be some combination of these.

In actual fact, all combinations of inhibition and excitation seem to exist. Some neurons exercise only an inhibitory influence over other cells. This is the case in the stretch reflex when sensory stimulation of a muscle-spindle receptor by the stretch of a muscle causes the direct inhibition (relaxation) of the opposing muscle, a reaction discussed in more detail in Chapter 10 in relation to *reciprocal inhibition.* Some believe that such direct inhibition usually involves a short neuron of the Golgi II type (see page 20), although not all agree. Some neurons, for example, the motoneuron in the stretch reflex just mentioned, can be inhibited by one neuron and excited by another. Some neurons, conversely, inhibit certain neurons while exciting certain others. Probably some neurons are excited only by other neurons and are excitatory only in their action on others. If so, that makes all possible combinations.

NEUROEFFECTOR TRANSMISSION

It will be remembered from Chapter 1 that two general types of effectors may be distinguished: muscles and glands. Muscle effectors may be further subdivided into three kinds: striped, cardiac, and smooth; glands into two kinds: endocrine and exocrine. These distinctions should be kept in mind for the next few pages.

SKELETAL MUSCLES—Transmission at the synapse of an axon and a striped muscle is very much like that at synapses in the central nervous system (see Fatt, 1959). The transmitter is acetylcholine secreted by the axon terminals. The terminals are roughly circular in shape and have diameters of 25 to 70 microns. They are called *end plates*. The terminal is the part of the muscle fiber that is distinctively different from the rest of the fiber, both in appearance and, more important, in its excitability. Like the postsynaptic areas of neurons, the area *is not* electrically stimulable. It is responsive only to the specific excitant of acetylcholine. When so excited, it builds up a local potential, like the postsynaptic potential of neurons, which must reach a critical size (about 10 millivolts in mammalian striped muscles) to trip off the all-or-none spike potential of the muscle fiber. This spike potential is associated with the contraction of the muscle fiber. The muscle fiber, like an axon, has a resting potential (about 70 millivolts) and is electrically stimulable. Thus events in the axon and muscle fiber closely parallel those in the neurons we have described above.

AUTONOMIC SYSTEM—If we turn now to smooth muscle, however, we encounter a quite different situation (von Euler, 1959). First, whereas every striped-muscle fiber is innervated by axons, and reactions are limited specifically to the fibers stimulated by the transmitter released at a particular end plate, the vast majority of smooth-muscle fibers (probably about 99 in 100) are *not* innervated. Yet they contract. They do this because the chemical transmitter emitted at the endings of the few cells that are innervated seeps over to them and excites them.

To explain further their action, we should recall that neurons of the autonomic system usually synapse in ganglia located outside the brain and spinal cord. Chemical transmission at this synapse is by acetylcholine, as it is in other central synapses. With certain exceptions, *postganglionic* neurons innervate the smooth muscles of the autonomic system.

The chemical transmitter that does this is different for the sympathetic and parasympathetic systems. The parasympathetic system, like the central nervous system, employs acetylcholine. In the sympathetic system, however, the transmitter is a substance known as *norepinephrine*, a close relative (nonmethylated) of the hormone *epinephrine* secreted by the adrenal medulla (see Chapter 4). There is a question whether epinephrine may sometimes be a synaptic transmitter, but the weight of the evidence seems to be against that.

Epinephrine, however, definitely plays a role in exciting smooth muscle, and its role is very much like that of a chemical transmitter. The adrenal gland is analogous to postganglionic fibers in an autonomic ganglion, for it receives preganglionic fibers. These fibers transmit excitation to the secretory cells of the gland via acetylcholine. The resulting epinephrine goes directly into the blood and circulates to other glands and to smooth muscles. There, in certain instances, it directly excites smooth muscles.

The potencies of norepinephrine and epinephrine are, however, quite different at different sites. In some cases, norepinephrine is many times more powerful in exciting a muscle or gland than epinephrine. In other cases, it is quite the reverse (see Chapter 11).

Thus there are as "transmitters" in the autonomic system three different substances: acetylcholine, norepinephrine, and epinephrine. But only the first two appear to be true synaptic transmitters. Epinephrine, it is believed, has its effect solely by circulating from the adrenal gland to its various sites of action. Neither norepinephrine nor epinephrine is as quickly destroyed by enzymes as is acetylcholine. The latter, it will be recalled, is destroyed so quickly after secretion into synaptic spaces that its action is effectively limited to the particular postsynaptic membrane it first contacts. The relatively long life of norepinephrine and epinephrine, on the other hand, enables them to excite muscles (and glands) some distance away from the point of secretion.

It is interesting to note in passing that most smooth muscle is not electrically stimulable. In this respect, the whole muscle fiber is like the postsynaptic sites of central neurons and striped-muscle fibers.

OTHER NEURONAL PHENOMENA

There are still other phenomena of receptor and neuron function that we should consider here, because they will be referred to at various points in subsequent chapters. These phenomena, and the terminology that goes with them, will be described briefly in this section. In later chapters, details will be added as needed to treat adequately specific topics.

COMPOUND ACTION POTENTIAL

About the oldest method of studying the electrical activity of the nervous system consists of placing one (the active) electrode on a nerve and another electrode somewhere else on the body (neutral or ground) and then recording from this arrangement while the nerve is excited in some way. The record thus made is called a compound action potential because it is made up of many action potentials (usually spikes) in the fibers making up the nerve.

Most nerves consist of fibers that differ in size from relatively small to relatively large. The size of the fiber determines two important characteristics of the fiber's spike potential: size of the spike and speed of conduction. The general rule is that the size of the spike potential is proportional to the square of the diameter of the fiber. Similarly, the larger the fiber, the faster the conduction of the spike.

As a consequence of these relations, a compound action potential recorded some distance from the point where a nerve is set into action, say by a brief electrical pulse, will consist of activity extending over a rather long time. If there are groups of fibers of different sizes, humps will be seen in the compound action potential (see Figure 3.8). These represent spikes traveling at different speeds.

Two or more humps are typical of action potentials recorded from sensory nerves. Figure 3.8 gives an example from a cutaneous nerve of a frog. The figure schematizes a record made at four different distances from a stimulating electrode giving rise to a compound action potential. Close to the point of stimulation, the potential appears to consist of a single hump. A little farther away, however, two humps begin to be distinguishable. In the fourth record, still farther away, two humps are even more clearly seen.

The meaning of the record is this: The first, tall hump represents large fibers carrying impulses at high speed. The second hump reflects a group of smaller fibers carrying smaller impulses at slower speed. By noting which humps appear under different stimulating conditions, it is often possible to infer what fibers are or are not responding. The greater the distance between the stimulating electrode and the recording electrode, the more a compound action potential is spread out in time and usually the easier it is to determine the humps in the potential.

EVOKED POTENTIALS

When one makes essentially the same recording as just described but does it in the central nervous system, say at some point on the cerebral cortex, the resulting potential is called an *evoked potential.* Such potentials are ordinarily employed in the study of sensory pathways, by using either normal sensory stimuli or electrical stimulation of nerve, but they may be recorded at many points in the nervous system (see Chang, 1959).

The evoked potential typically consists of an initial positive deflection followed by a negative deflection and possibly other waves, depending on what is being recorded. Of these, the positive deflection represents presynaptic potentials in the terminals of the fibers bringing the messages to the site of recording, and other potentials usually represent postsynaptic activities or even activities in neighboring neurons. Since one is usually interested in tracking signals between the points of stimulation and recording, the initial positive deflection is the part of the potential of greatest significance to the experimenter.

Evoked potentials have been employed on a large scale in the past few years to "map" sensory projections. Various areas of the cortex, as well as those in lower centers, subserving different sensory function have been mapped in this way.

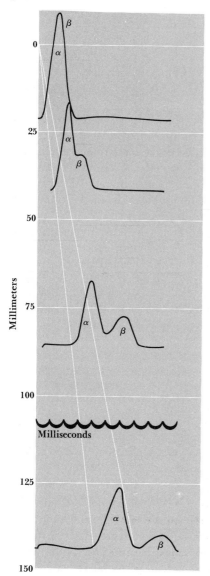

FIGURE 3.8—Propagation of an action potential in a nerve containing fibers of two different sizes. (Adapted from H. S. Gasser and J. Erlanger. *Electrical signs of nervous action.* Philadelphia: University of Pennsylvania Press, 1937. P. 77.)

MICROELECTRODE RECORDING

The two kinds of recording just described give crude, overall measures of activity in large groups of fibers. However, fibers having rather different functions are freely mixed in various nerves and pathways of the nervous system. In order to answer some of the most basic questions of psychological (and physiological) significance, it is desirable to know precisely what is going on in a particular fiber (see Frank, 1959).

One way of determining this, the first one developed, is to dissect three or four fibers away from their neighbors and place them under a recording electrode. Then, when any or all of these fibers are activated, one can see in the records a limited number of identifiable spikes. Because fibers differ characteristically in size and hence in the height of their spikes, it is usually possible to distinguish the spikes of different fibers by their height.

This method of recording from individual fibers has its uses, but for many purposes it is desirable to obtain records from single units and to do this without dissecting or otherwise disturbing the nervous system. For this purpose, several different types of microelectrodes have been developed. One consists of a wire filed down to needle point and then covered with insulation almost to its tip. Another employs glass tubing drawn out to a pointed tip through which either a saline solution or a fine wire may serve as an electrode. Whatever the particular method, the resulting electrode is of the order of 1 micron, which is as small or smaller than the fibers from which records are made.

With such electrodes it is possible to record a spike or series of spikes in a single neuron and to study the behavior of this neuron under various conditions of stimulation or of a changing environment. This method, as we shall see, has given a definite answer to some of the most perplexing questions in physiological psychology.

RECEPTOR FIELDS

One of the things such a method permits is to determine the receptor field of an individual sensory neuron. By *receptor field* is meant the area of the surface of a sense organ served by a particular nerve fiber. Because some sensory neurons have many dendritic branches spreading out on the sensory surface, while others serve a single cell or spot, the size of receptive fields varies enormously. Some in the skin of the cat are as large as 9 by 5 centimeters, that is, 45 square centimeters.

The concept of a receptor field is not limited to the peripheral sensory neuron. It can be applied to, say, the third-order neuron of the optic nerve or even higher-order neurons in the nervous system. By studying receptive fields farther upstream, one can see precisely how receptor surfaces are represented in the sensory pathways of the brain.

ADAPTATION—In the study of the activity of single units, the phenomenon of adaptation is frequently encountered. A stimulus which at first evokes activity becomes less effective as it is repeated time after time. This adaptation may be reflected either in an augmented threshold, in which case the intensity of the stimulus must be increased in order to elicit the same number of impulses, or, if the stimulus intensity remains the same, in a smaller number of impulses.

Units vary widely, however, in the degree to which they adapt. Some show hardly any adaptation, whereas others give only an initial burst of impulses and stop responding altogether despite continuing stimulation. Generally speaking, units may be divided into two classes, depending on their rate of adaptation. *Tonic* units are those that show little or no adaptation and that continue to respond during steady or repeated stimulation. *Phasic* units are those that adapt rapidly.

"ON" AND "OFF" RESPONSES—In units of the phasic variety, another phenomenon is frequently encountered. When a stimulus starts, it fires an initial burst of impulses and then falls silent during the course of stimulation. The initial burst is an *on response*. However, when the stimulus is turned off, it gives forth another burst of impulses. The latter is called an *off response*, for it is a reaction to the cessation of stimulation rather than to its onset. In complex synaptic networks, usually in the sensory synapses of the nervous system, units may be found that give only "on" responses, some may give on-off responses, and others only "off" responses. Typically, however, which way a unit responds is not a characteristic of the unit itself but depends on how the sense organ, one or more synapses upstream, is being stimulated. One condition of stimulation may cause "on" responses, another "off" responses. This point will be elaborated in our discussion of vision (Chapter 6).

SPONTANEOUS ACTIVITY—If one searches for different units in the nervous system, he is likely to come upon units that are "spontaneously" firing. The term "spontaneously" must be put in quotes because about all one can be sure of in most instances is that there is no knowledge of any particular stimulus that would be the cause of their firing. One cannot always be sure that they are firing without any help from neighboring neurons or other environmental influences.

In some cases, the cause of the "spontaneous" activity may be the "spontaneous" secretion of transmitter substance at the synapse. It is known that this happens on a small scale at some neuromuscular junctions (see Fatt, 1959). The end plates of axons emit small quantities of acetylcholine in random fashion, and this is reflected in very small variations in the postsynaptic end-plate potential called *miniature end-plate potentials*. In other cases, there may be a spontaneous variation in the postsynaptic potential of a neuron; if the amount required to set off a spike is relatively small compared with the PSP, the result is a "spontaneous" spike potential. Another possible cause is given in the next section dealing with recurrent nervous circuits.

Whatever the cause, the fact is that some units in the nervous system characteristically give spontaneous spikes. For the investigator, this is con-

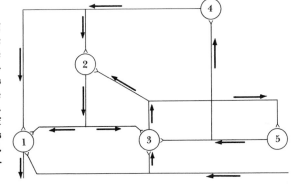

FIGURE 3.9—Diagram of neurons and their synaptic connections illustrating the principle of recurrent, reverberatory nerve circuits as seen in the IIIrd nerve nucleus. (Adapted from R. Lorente de No. Analysis of the activity of the chains of internuncial neurons. *J. Neurophysiol.*, 1938, 1, 207–244.)

venient because it permits him to study the phenomenon of inhibition. He can find certain stimulating conditions that inhibit the spontaneous firing, as well as conditions that increase the rate of such firing.

RECURRENT NERVOUS CIRCUITS

Sometimes the cause of so-called spontaneous activity is a circular synaptic network forming a recurrent nervous circuit. In such a network, neurons are so arranged and connected with one another that, once an impulse is started, it can travel in a circular path and, in principle, go on around it forever. Such a circular network is diagramed in Figure 3.9. That particular network is in the IIIrd nerve nucleus of the midbrain, but reverberatory circuits probably exist in many parts of the brain, and certainly in the cerebral cortex, where there are very many interneurons.

It should be noted that reverberatory circuits can influence neighboring neurons as well as their own neurons. Collateral axons from the circuit impinging on other neurons not in the circuit may be stimulated. Hence, some units that are not in a reverberatory circuit may be firing, apparently spontaneously, because they are being excited by collaterals from the circuit.

4 THE INTERNAL ENVIRONMENT

T HE CONCEPT of the *internal environment* was formulated more than a century ago by the physiologist Claude Bernard. The concept refers to all those chemical, thermal, and stimulus conditions within the body that form an environment for its organs. For the most part, such an internal environment consists of the blood, its chemical makeup and its chemical relations with various tissues. The concept contrasts with that of the external environment, which consists of all the external conditions acting upon the body. It happens that some, but by no means all, conditions in the internal environment profoundly affect behavior. Hence it is necessary to consider, at least in brief outline, the general characteristics of the internal environment.

Our treatment will proceed in four sections: (1) the *metabolic machinery*, in which we shall outline the basic steps in the regulation of metabolism; (2) the *hormones*, their identity and general functions; (3) *homeostasis*, its nature and influence in the regulation of behavior; and finally (4) *psychoactive drugs*. The latter, of course, are not normally a part of the internal environment, but their action, when they are taken into the body, is exerted through the bloodstream and thus through the internal environment.

METABOLIC MACHINERY

Man and animals, of course, get their food supplies from the outside environment in the form of carbohydrates, fats, and proteins. These materials are first eaten, and then in the alimentary tract they are broken down to a form in which they can be absorbed into the bloodstream from the walls of the intestine. After that, they are distributed to different parts of the body. In the liver and other tissues, complex materials are further broken down to simpler compounds that can be used in chemical reactions by the cells of the body as a source of energy. At the same time, these simpler compounds may be used as building blocks to make various complex substances that the body requires. These processes of breakdown and rebuilding are the major aspects of metabolism with which we shall be concerned.

DIETARY ESSENTIALS

Although the organism can build up many of the materials that it needs, it must have certain compounds as building blocks to carry on its synthesizing activities. There is consequently a rather large list of dietary essentials without which most higher animals cannot exist. This list includes ten essential amino acids, three indispensable fatty acids, all the vitamins, and certain inorganic elements.

CARBOHYDRATE METABOLISM

Because there are three kinds of food stuffs—carbohydrates, proteins, and fats—there are three kinds of metabolism to consider. Of the three, however, carbohydrate metabolism is the central one in two respects: First, it is the primary source of energy for the body as a whole and particularly for the brain and muscles with which we are most concerned; secondly, as we shall see later, the products of protein and fat metabolism find their way back into the chains involved in carbohydrate metabolism. For that reason, we shall begin with, and emphasize, carbohydrate metabolism.

The sources of carbohydrate in food ordinarily consist of starches and complex sugars. However, these are not in a form suitable for absorption and use in the bloodstream. They are reduced to such form by being broken down in the digestive tract with the aid of enzymes (see below) into glucose, which is a simple sugar and a member of the general class of hexose sugars ($C_6H_{12}O_6$). In this form (see Figure 4.1), it passes into the bloodstream where it circulates and is ordinarily kept at a relatively constant level (40 to 90 milligrams per milliliter of blood). From the blood—or rather the plasma, since this part of the blood, which excludes corpuscles, is the part concerned— glucose is circulated to various organs of the body where it is used.

Aside from the blood plasma, two organs are of particular interest. They are the *liver* and *muscle*, for in these sugar may be deposited in the form of glycogen, which is a polymer of glucose of unknown size $(C_6H_{12}O_6)^n$. The deposits in muscle are relatively small and are only sufficient for the intermittent work that muscle may be called upon to do. Those in the liver are the principal resources that may be tapped when more sugar is needed. As can be seen in Figure 4.1, when glycogen is burned, say in muscles, the by-products of its breakdown are lactic acid and pyruvic acid. Although these substances may be rebuilt into glycogen or further broken down into acetate

FIGURE 4.1—Diagram of interchanges of glucose and lactic and pyruvic acids between plasma and the organs that take part in carbohydrate metabolism. (Adapted from T. C. Ruch and J. F. Fulton. *Medical physiology and biophysics.* 18th ed. Philadelphia: Saunders, 1960. P. 1016.)

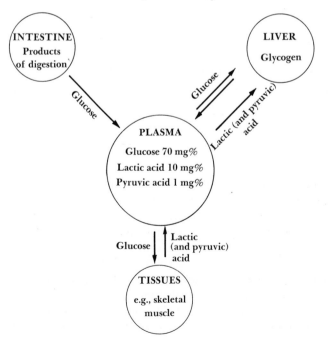

or carbon dioxide, small amounts of them move into the bloodstream and normally circulate there.

ENERGY STORAGE

In reactions outside the body, the oxidation of a substance containing carbon and hydrogen breaks down the substance eventually to carbon dioxide and water and at the same time releases energy. Usually this energy is in the form of heat. That is what happens when wood is burned. The same thing happens to some extent when carbohydrates are oxidized within the body. The body is heated by the burning of carbohydrates.

However, other kinds of work, besides the liberation of heat, must be done in the body and done quickly. In muscles, this work is mechanical; the muscle contracts. In the nervous system, the work is electrical and chemical; nervous impulses transmit messages along and between neurons. And both kinds of events are extremely rapid.

To perform these kinds of work, the body has an intermediate step that involves a compound known as *adenosine triphosphate, or ATP* for short. This compound is formed of adenylic acid and inorganic phosphate by the breakdown of glucose and other carbohydrates. Its important characteristic is that it contains two unusually *energy-rich phosphate* bonds. In these bonds is stored the energy released in carbohydrate (and other forms) of metabolism, and this energy is available for "instant" release when needed. For that reason, ATP is referred to as the body's "storehouse of energy" (see Stumpf, 1953).

The ATP can react quickly with a great many compounds to release this energy. When it does so, it breaks down either into an intermediate compound, adenosine diphosphate (ADP), or back to adenylic acid and an inorganic phosphate. From these stages, it can be built up again, through carbohydrate metabolism, to be ready again to supply instant energy when needed. In this way, the relatively slow breakdown of carbohydrate stores energy in ATP that can be quickly released in muscle contraction or in nervous impulses. Later in this section we shall see how this is done in the case of the nervous impulse.

It may be noted in passing that energy is required to build up glycogen from glucose. This energy also comes from ATP which got it previously from the breakdown of glucose, lactic acid, pyruvic acid, or one of the other steps in metabolism.

ENZYMES

The steps involved in metabolism are enormously complex. There are literally thousands of them. These many steps are continually being carried out in an orderly and rapid fashion. Involved in virtually every step is a material called an *enzyme*. This is a biological catalyst—a substance that accelerates a chemical reaction. If it were not for the aid of enzymes, the chemical steps in metabolism would be slowed to a snail's pace, and some would not take place at all.

Enzymes are made by the body from material synthesized from food stuffs. An enzyme is often, if not always, made up of two distinct parts. The larger part, because it consists of a giant protein molecule, is known as the *apoenzyme*. This by itself is incapable of catalytic activity. To endow it with this ability, that is, to activate it, another part called a *coenzyme* and having relatively low molecular weight is required. This must be combined with the apoenzyme to form an enzyme with catalytic properties.

Because ATP, ADP, and adenylic acid are constantly interconverted, they participate in many metabolic reactions, and they are among the most important coenzymes in metabolism. As we shall see below, vitamins are also coenzymes.

Figure 4.2 gives a scheme of the behavior of an enzyme system. In the typical case, the enzyme combines with its *substrate*, the compound whose reaction it catalyzes. Apparently the shape of the complex protein molecules accounts for the very remarkable *specificity* that enzymes show in their ability to direct biochemical reactions in an orderly fashion. Some enzymes appear to catalyze the reactions of only single compounds and then in only one of several possible directions. In such cases, if the structure of the substrate molecule changes even a little, the catalytic effect is lost. This notion, known as the *lock-and-key theory*, suggests that the enzyme must fit its substrate in such a way that it strains certain of the bonds of its molecules, thus allowing them to be more readily broken or replaced.

The activity of an enzyme is measured by the amount of chemical change it catalyzes under given conditions. This activity is affected by a number of factors. (1) Within a certain range, the amount of reaction that takes place initially is directly proportional to the *concentration of the enzyme*. (2) With a given amount of enzyme, the initial rate of reaction increases up to a maximum point as the *substrate concentration* is increased, but then no further increase occurs and the rate may fall off somewhat. (3) Most reactions require an *optimal* pH, i.e., an optimal degree of acidity or alkalinity of the medium in which the reaction takes place. Different enzyme systems have different optimal pH's, and this optimal pH may vary with such other factors as the temperature, the concentration of salts, etc. (4) Enzyme activity also is affected by temperature, and under specified conditions there is usually a specific *optimal temperature*. Up to a certain point, the rate of reaction is increased exponentially as the temperature increases, but then the enzyme is adversely affected by further temperature increases and the rate diminishes. (5) The effectiveness of enzyme action is influenced by such factors as visible light, X rays, and other types of radiant energy, which may actually destroy or inactivate the enzyme irreversibly. In the normal course of chemical re-

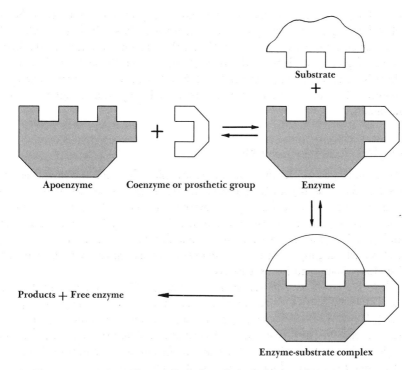

FIGURE 4.2—A schematic representation of the behavior of an enzyme system. (Adapted from W. D. McElroy. The mechanism of inhibition of cellular activity by narcotics. *Quart. Rev. Biol.*, 1947, 22, 26.)

actions within the organism, many of these factors operate at once. The substrate may be used up temporarily. Or the reaction and other reactions going on simultaneously may change the pH or temperature of the medium.

Although we have covered quite a list of factors affecting enzyme activity, there is still another important factor to add to the list: *inhibition of enzyme action.* There are certain relatively inactive compounds in the body that can compete with any of the components of the enzyme system and by their competition inhibit the enzyme system. Some compounds, for example, are so similar to the substrate in structure that they can "take over" some of the enzyme molecules. Thus they reduce the supplies of enzyme that are needed for the substrate. In a similar way, compounds related in shape to the co-enzymes may inhibit total catalytic activity. All such compounds that interfere with the combination of substrate and parts of the enzyme system are *inhibitors.*

The reason for explaining so fully what enzymes are and what affects them is that they are the governors of almost every step in intermediary metabolism. Enzymes set the rate of reactions and let them take place rapidly at ordinary body temperatures. For example, the rate of conversion of glucose to hexose phosphate (glucose-6-phosphate; see Figure 4.3) is set in large measure by an enzyme known as *hexokinase*. When this enzyme is inhibited, the breakdown of glucose and its synthesis to glycogen is partly stopped. As a result, there is an excess of sugar in the blood. Similarly, specific enzyme systems are required for many other processes that make up the essential links in metabolism.

FAT AND PROTEIN METABOLISM

As we indicated above, there are interconversions between the three classes of food stuffs. This is shown in Figure 4.3 where it can be seen that both fats and proteins can enter the steps in carbohydrate metabolism at various points. Moreover, substances in carbohydrate metabolism may be converted into fats and proteins. The essential point is that fats and proteins serve as storage systems which can, when needed, deliver materials into carbohydrate metabolism for oxidation and energy release.

Fats are very concentrated sources of energy. Ounce for ounce, they contain more energy than carbohydrates or proteins. This energy is typically used, in the well-fed organism, as a reserve system. Fat entering the bloodstream from the digestive tract is deposited in adipose tissue in subcutaneous regions. There it remains until needed. If the energy expenditure of the body is greater than that which can be supplied by carbohydrates, it is called out and utilized in the manner indicated in Figure 4.3. Because of the interconversion of food stuffs, some of the fat stored in subcutaneous tissues may be derived from carbohydrate and protein metabolism. Incidentally, it has been recently demonstrated (Correll, 1963) that the liberation of fatty acids from adipose tissue is under nervous control.

The proteins eaten in food have a different history. First, under the influence of enzymes in the digestive tract they are all broken down into twenty or so different amino acids. Of those, about ten are essential in that the body cannot make them and they must be present in the proteins eaten for the body to get them. The others can be manufactured by the body from essential amino acids. Once in the blood plasma, amino acids are recombined to make the various proteins involved in chemical reactions of the body, or they are put away in storage. Proteins may be stored in various places but the principal depots are the liver and muscle. In these places, they may be called upon for energy as required. This they furnish via the amino acids, as indicated in Figure 4.3.

GENES AND ENYZMES

As is now well known, genes are the basic units of heredity. They determine the structure of an organism and, in large part, the various activities taking place in it. Recently it has become clear that genes play their part by means

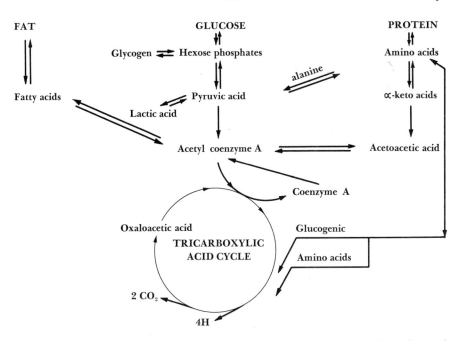

FAT   GLUCOSE   PROTEIN

FIGURE 4.3—Diagram to illustrate interconversions among the three classes of food stuffs. (Adapted from T. C. Ruch and J. F. Fulton. *Medical physiology and biophysics.* 18th ed. Philadelphia: Saunders, 1960. P. 1021.)

of enzymes controlling, as we have seen, the chemical reactions going on in the body. There is a very close biochemical link between genes and enzymes, and genes frequently carry hereditary characteristics by affecting enzyme systems. (For more details of the relation between genes and protein metabolism, see Chapter 20.)

Biochemists tell us that the color of flowers, the color of a fly's eye, and the light from luminescent bacteria are all the results of enzyme-controlled reactions. Moreover, these complex features of the individual can be changed by gene mutations that bring about changes in enzyme systems, which in turn block the appropriate reactions. And there are naturally occurring hereditary defects in enzyme systems that have been discovered and studied. One that is of particular significance to psychologists is *phenylpyruvic oligophrenia.*

Phenylpyruvic oligophrenia is a relatively rare type of inherited mental defect. It is due to a single mutant recessive gene. This gene causes to be lacking a liver enzyme required to metabolize an amino acid, phenylalanine. Hence this amino acid is not metabolized (to tyrosine) in the normal way. Instead, it is converted to phenylpyruvic acid. Certain metabolites of this substance are accumulated in excess and appear in the urine. For this reason, a simple urine test can be used to determine the presence of the condition.

For the present purpose, the point is that one particular mental defect is the result of an enzyme defect which in turn is linked to a gene defect (also see Chapter 20).

VITAMINS

Vitamins are chemical compounds that are essential for proper growth and other life processes. That is why they are called vitamins. And the reason that they are so "vital" is that they function as coenzymes—the active part of an enzyme—in the catalysis of enzyme-controlled reactions. Consequently, when individual vitamins are lacking in the diet, the enzyme-controlled reactions for which they are essential are blocked, thereby causing some derangement of metabolism. This blockage always causes some characteristic *deficiency symptoms*.

Because vitamins are chemically unrelated to one another, they are not easily classified. The usual way of classifying them is into *fat-soluble* and *water-soluble* vitamins. The fat-soluble vitamins are A, D, E, and K. The water-soluble substances are the B vitamins, which include thiamine, riboflavin, nicotinic acid, B_6, pantothenic acid, biotin, folic acid, B_{12}, *p*-aminobenzoic acid, inositol, choline, and the C vitamin, ascorbic acid.

In recent years, substances known as *antivitamins* have been discovered and used experimentally, instead of vitamin-deficient diets, to produce the symptoms of vitamin deficiency. Antivitamins inhibit the activity of specific vitamins. When an antivitamin is fed to an animal whose diet is complete in all the vitamins and other dietary essentials, it will develop symptoms of vitamin deficiency. Pyrithiamin, for example, is an antivitamin for thiamin, a member of the B group. When less than a milligram of pyrithiamin is added to the diet of mice, symptoms of thiamin deficiency arise faster and in more complete form than they do when the diet is made deficient in thiamin. In this and similar cases, however, the effects of the antivitamin can usually be overcome by feeding very large amounts of the vitamin.

Antivitamins behave as inhibitors because they compete with the vitamin for the apoenzyme, yet are themselves inactive. Pyrithiamin, for example, is very similar in chemical structure to the vitamin thiamin, whose action it inhibits. It has an affinity for the apoenzyme of thiamin and takes thiamin's place in forming the enzyme, but since it does not have the activating properties of a vitamin it prevents the enzyme from doing its work.

ACETYLCHOLINE METABOLISM

In Chapter 3 we saw that acetylcholine is intimately related to nervous and neuromuscular events. It is the chemical transmitter at neuromuscular junctures and at cholinergic synapses of the central and parasympathetic nervous systems. Its metabolism—formation and breakdown—has been studied in considerable detail and is a part of the metabolic cycles discussed above. Put very briefly and simply, the acetylcholine cycle is depicted in Figure 4.4.

In the presence of an enzyme *choline acetylase,* acetylcholine is synthesized from choline, one of the B vitamins, and acetyl coenzyme A. The latter is formed from coenzyme A and acetyl phosphate. Acetyl phosphate is an energy-rich phosphate whose energy is obtained from ATP. Coenzyme A is a complex molecule containing another B vitamin, pantothenic acid. Thus acetylcholine is built up from energy stored in energy-rich phosphates originally obtained from glucose metabolism.

Acetylcholine is stored, as we have seen, in vesicles in neurons (also see De Robertis et al., 1963). One might say that it is kept in protective custody, for as soon as it is secreted by nervous activity, it is immediately attacked and broken down by an enzyme known as *cholinesterase.* That fact, indicated in Chapter 3, accounts for the high specificity of synaptic junctions in the nervous system. It means that very quickly after acetylcholine is released it is broken down and hence it cannot diffuse to, or have any effect on, areas other than those in which it is released.

HORMONES

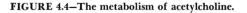

Hormones are substances secreted by the various glands of internal secretion, the *endocrine glands.* The term "hormone" is coined from a Greek word meaning to arouse or to set in motion, and that describes, at least roughly, what a hormone does. Like an enzyme or vitamin, it is required in very small

FIGURE 4.4—The metabolism of acetylcholine.

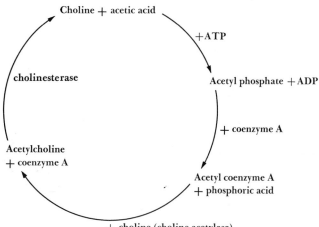

amounts, and it serves as a regulator of certain rather specific metabolic activities. Exactly how it carries out its regulating function is not clear. It undoubtedly influences the effectiveness of one or a few enzyme systems, but it probably does not function directly as a catalyzer in the sense that an enzyme does. In any case, the hormones are important regulators of rates of activities and in many instances have an important bearing on behavior.

The endocrine glands consist of the hypophysis (or pituitary), the thyroid, parathyroid, adrenal, pancreas, ovary, and testis. Some of these consist of more than one part having different secretory functions, but such subdivisions will be described as we discuss the glands in turn. Figure 4.5 shows the location in the body of the various glands.

HYPOPHYSIS

The hypophysis is located at the base of the brain connected to the hypothalamus by a stalk known as the *infundibulum*. Although several parts may be distinguished, for all practical purposes the gland may be divided into two parts: an anterior part called the *adenohypophysis,* or glandular hypophysis, and a posterior part, the *neurohypophysis.* Actually both parts secrete hormones, but the anterior part is not connected with the brain nor does it have

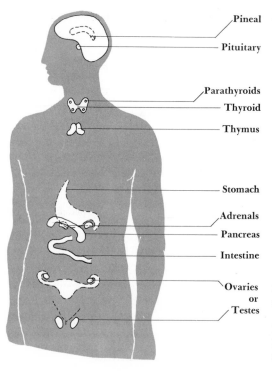

Pineal

Pituitary

Parathyroids

Thyroid

Thymus

Stomach

Adrenals

Pancreas

Intestine

Ovaries or Testes

FIGURE 4.5—Silhouette of the human figure, showing the location of the endocrine organs. (Adapted from R. G. Hoskins. *Tides of life.* New York: W. W. Norton, 1933. P. 19. By permission of the publishers.)

any innervation, whereas the neurohypophysis is served by a pathway from the hypothalamus reaching it through the infundibular stalk. Although the adenohypophysis is largely controlled by hormones circulating in the blood, some of its activities can be explained only by assuming that it somehow is under nervous control. Therefore it is assumed that secretions of the neurohypophysis, liberated under nervous control, may reach the anterior hypophysis by means of a plexus of blood vessels serving both parts of the gland. We shall now consider the two parts separately.

ADENOHYPOPHYSIS—The anterior pituitary gland secretes six known hormones. Most of these are *trophic* hormones in that they promote the activity of other specific endocrine glands.

Three of them are *gonadotrophic hormones,* meaning that they promote the activity of the gonads, particularly that of the female ovaries: (*1*) follicle-stimulating hormone (FSH); (*2*) the luteinizing hormone (LH), which is also called the interstitial-cell-stimulating hormone (ICSH); and (*3*) the lactogenic hormone, also called prolactin. Each takes part in a particular phase of the ovarian cycle (see Chapter 14). The FSH brings the follicle to maturity, at which point LH causes it to rupture, releasing its ovum, and stimulates it to produce estrogenic hormones and to form a corpus luteum (see below). The latter is brought to maturity by the lactogenic hormone, which for this purpose is called the luteotrophic hormone (LTH). The lactogenic hormone also stimulates development and milk production of the mammary glands and for that purpose is called the mammotrophic hormone (MH) or, more commonly, prolactin.

Of the other three hormones of the anterior pituitary, two are trophic hormones for particular glands. The *thyrotrophic hormone,* or thyrotrophin, regulates activity of the thyroid gland. An *adrenotrophic hormone,* otherwise called adrenotrophin or adrenocorticotrophic hormone (ACTH), stimulates one part of the adrenal gland, the adrenal cortex. A sixth hormone, the growth hormone or *somatotrophin,* promotes general bodily growth. The latter is partly under the control of blood sugar (Roth et al., 1963).

NEUROHYPOPHYSIS—An extract of the posterior pituitary or neurohypophysis is called *pituitrin.* This substance has three effects: (*1*) It has the pressor effect of raising blood pressure by constricting blood vessels leading from the arteries, (*2*) it stimulates smooth muscles and particularly those of the uterus, and (*3*) it has an antidiuretic effect of inhibiting the excretion of urine through the kidneys. In recent years, two distinct hormones have been separated from pituitrin and synthesized: *vasopressin* and *oxytocin.* These have overlapping effects, doing to a certain extent the same things. However, vasopressin is largely responsible for the pressor and antidiuretic effects and for this reason is also called antidiuretic hormone (ADH), whereas oxytocin is principally responsible for the smooth-muscle stimulating effects. Of these two hormones, the antidiuretic hormone will later be of interest to us in connection with thirst, and oxytocin is involved in mammary reflexes in nursing.

ADRENAL GLAND

The adrenal gland, located on the kidneys, has two parts, each secreting its own family of hormones: (1) the adrenal *cortex* or outer part and (2) the adrenal *medulla* or inner core of the gland.

ADRENAL CORTEX—The adrenal cortex is essential to life. If it is removed, an animal becomes weak, loses its appetite, and gradually dies. However, life may often be prolonged by feeding excess quantities of sodium chloride. Specific physiological measurements reveal a great many changes resulting from adrenal insufficiency, but the chief ones are two: (1) a disturbance of sodium-potassium balance in which excessive sodium is excreted by the kidneys, while more potassium is retained than is normal; (2) carbohydrate metabolism is altered, and in particular the deposition of glycogen in the liver is reduced. Put another way, there are two principal functions of the adrenocortical hormones: maintenance of sodium and electrolytic balance and the deposition of glycogen in the liver.

Biochemical research of recent years has produced more than thirty different extractable materials from the adrenal cortex. All are of a chemical structure known as *steroids.* Of all these, however, only a half dozen are biologically active, and three are the most active: *cortisol* (á close relative of, but more potent than, cortisone), *corticosterone,* and *aldosterone.* These, like the hormones of the neurohypophysis, have overlapping functions, but aldosterone is by far the most potent in promoting sodium retention and electrolyte balance, while cortisol is the most active in carbohydrate metabolism. Corticosterone lies in between in its potency in both functions.

ADRENAL MEDULLA—The adrenal medulla secretes two closely related hormones: *epinephrine* and *norepinephrine.* These are also called adrenalin and noradrenalin, respectively. The difference between these is that norepinephrine lacks a methyl group (CH_3) found in epinephrine. Taken together, these hormones are called *catechol amines* or catechol hormones. The precursor of the catechol amines in their manufacture in the adrenal gland is phenylalanine, the amino acid mentioned above in connection with phenylpyruvic oligophrenia (see Figure 4.6).

Epinephrine and norepinephrine were discussed in the preceding chapter in connection with chemical transmission of nerve impulses. It was seen there that norepinephrine is secreted by adrenergic nerve endings of sympathetic nerve fibers.

The general effects of the catechol amine hormones are often similar though not always exactly the same. Both raise blood pressure, but epineph-

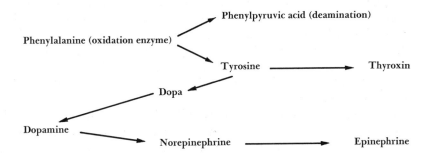

FIGURE 4.6—Phenylalanine, an amino acid, is metabolized to three different hormones: thyroxin, norephinephrine, and epinephrine, as well as to phenyl-pyruvic acid.

rine does it by increasing cardiac output, whereas norepinephrine does it by general vasoconstriction (see Chapter 11). Both raise blood-sugar levels, having a direct effect on the release of glycogen from the liver, but epineph-rine is much more effective in this respect than norepinephrine.

BIOGENIC AMINES—At this point we should mention another substance having functions related to the catechol amines and having some similarity to them chemically. This is *serotonin* which is an indole amine rather than a catechol amine. The two catechol amines together with serotonin are sometimes re-ferred to as the biogenic amines (Himwich, 1958).

Serotonin is rather unique in acting like a hormone but yet not being secreted by an endocrine gland. It is produced in certain cells of the gastro-intestinal mucosa and passes from these cells into the blood plasma. There it is taken up by blood platelets and circulated around the body. If tissue is damaged, it is liberated from the blood platelets and has both a local and a general effect circulating in the blood. It is a powerful local vasoconstrictor, thus reducing hemorrhage, but it is also a general hypotensive. That is to say, it lowers blood pressure and indirectly reduces hemorrhage. Serotonin is found in small amounts in the brain.

PARATHYROID GLANDS

The parathyroid glands are very small organs, weighing in man about 0.1 gram; they are found in the vicinity of the thyroid gland. Their number and position vary considerably between species and among individuals of the same species. In man, they most often form two pairs. Although the hormone, *parathormone,* has been extracted and purified, its exact chemical structure is not known.

Parathormone controls calcium and phosphate levels in the blood. When the parathormone level is high, the calcium level is high and the phosphate level low, and vice versa. Under normal circumstances, there appears to be a simple feedback between hormone output on the one hand and the calcium-phosphate balance on the other. A lowering of blood calcium increases parathormone output which in turn mobilizes calcium from bone where it is deposited and stored. Then increased blood calcium reduces the level of parathormone output.

This mechanism obviously controls indirectly the amount of calcium deposited in bone, but it has another, more important effect on nervous activity. The level of blood calcium directly affects the excitability of nerve tissue. The lower the calcium level, the more irritable is the nervous tissue. Hence, the principal symptom of parathyroid insufficiency is general irritability. There is a tendency for muscles to twitch and for reflexes to be hypersensitive. If the insufficiency is severe, general tetany, muscle spasms, and convulsions develop.

THYROID GLAND

The thyroid gland consists of two lobes located respectively on the two sides of the windpipe. Its general function is to regulate metabolism. It apparently does this in diverse ways, affecting other glands, the activity of enzyme systems involved in metabolism, and virtually all aspects of energy expenditure in the body. It seems to have no specific target organs, but it affects the way cells function in carbohydrate utilization and protein synthesis (Weiss and Sokoloff, 1963).

Since growth as well as the normal functioning of an organism depends on metabolism, deficiency of thyroid secretion in the young or growing organism stunts growth. Among human beings, an organism suffering such a deficiency early in life is called a *cretin*. If, on the other hand, deficiency occurs in adulthood, the condition is known as *myxedema*. The person suffering mxyedema has a lowered metabolism, and this results in almost everything else being below normal: heart rate, circulation, body temperature, and general activity level.

The principal hormone of the thyroid gland is *thyroxin*. Recently another hormone, present in much smaller quantities but more active in promoting metabolism, has been isolated. The two hormones are closely related chemically and have the same functions in promoting metabolism. Like the catechol amines, they are manufactured from the amino acid tyrosine which in turn comes from phenylalanine (see Figure 4.6). In fact, thyroxin may be made in the laboratory by mixing iodine with any tyrosine-containing protein, e.g., casein. In the body, the tyrosine is stored in a more complex form in the gland, and at the same time the gland traps iodine entering the blood along with food stuffs. Then the thyroxin is made by the gland, as needed, at the time it is secreted into the blood.

As indicated earlier, thyroid production is under the control of the thyrotrophic hormone of the anterior pituitary. The two glands form a feedback loop. As thyroxin concentration in the blood rises, the output of thyrotrophic hormone decreases, and vice versa. In this way an equilibrium is maintained.

PANCREAS

The pancreas, lying below the stomach, is both an exocrine gland and an endocrine gland. As an exocrine gland, it delivers pancreatic juice into the small intestine where its enzymes assist in the breakdown of proteins and fats. As an endocrine gland, it secretes two hormones, *insulin* and *glucagon*. These are secreted by two different kinds of cells, the beta and alpha cells, respectively, located in structures known as the *islands of Langerhans*.

INSULIN—Insulin is the best known of the two hormones of the pancreas. Its function is to lower the level of blood sugar. It is not certain how it does this, but it is believed that it acts on the permeability to blood glucose of the cells of the body. In any case, the effect of insulin is to put more glucose into the various tissues of the body, and this is the reason, wholly or in part, why it lowers blood sugar.

Insulin production is controlled by the level of blood sugar. Hence a feedback loop, like that of the parathyroid glands, is formed by the hormone and its effect on the blood. In this case, however, the more blood sugar, the more insulin; and the less blood sugar, the less insulin. Because the amount of sugar passing into the blood, as well as its utilization by tissues such as muscle, varies widely from time to time—with eating and exercise—the output of insulin undoubtedly varies widely, but through its action the level of blood sugar is maintained within rather narrow limits.

A chronic insufficiency of insulin is known as *diabetes mellitus*. In this condition, a high blood-sugar level causes sugar to be excreted in the urine, which is the basis of the common urine test for diabetes. To excrete this sugar, the kidney "pumps" out more water than usual, and this takes other body minerals such as salt with it. Hence the diabetic is dehydrated and unusually thirsty. Since his tissues are unable to secure sufficient supplies of glucose, his body relies on an excessive metabolism of proteins and fats in place of sugar. These, however, are incompletely metabolized and waste products, called ketone bodies, accumulate. These are in effect poisonous and cause shortness of breath, coma, and, in severe cases, death.

GLUCAGON—Glucagon, the second hormone of the pancreas, has an effect opposite to that of insulin. It increases blood sugar. However, its activity is short-lived so that an injection of pancreatic extract containing both insulin and glucagon causes first a brief increase in blood sugar and then a longer-lasting lowering of blood sugar.

Glucagon's mechanism of action is on the liver where it mobilizes glucose. It does this by enhancing the enzyme activity through which liver glycogen is converted to glucose. In this respect, it behaves exactly like epinephrine, except that epinephrine also promotes the metabolism of glucose in muscle.

The relation of glucagon to blood sugar is a feedback loop opposite to that of insulin and sugar. When blood sugar falls, the secretion of glucagon is stimulated while the secretion of insulin is decreased. Together, insulin and glucagon maintain blood-sugar level in balance.

GONADS

The gonads, or sex glands, consist of the ovaries in the female and the testes in the male. The hormones secreted by these organs are, collectively, the gonadal or sex hormones. Actually, these hormones, or some of them, are also secreted by the adrenal cortex and by the placenta (in the case of the pregnant female). The gonadal hormones, from the chemical point of view, are all members of the same general class, the *steroids*, as the hormones of the adrenal cortex.

Gonadal hormones fall into three general classes: the *progestins*, the *androgens*, and the *estrogens*. All these hormones are secreted in varying amounts in four different places: ovaries, testes, adrenal cortex, and placenta. The principal places of production, however, are androgens in the testes, estrogens in the ovaries and placenta, and the progestins in the corpus luteum (ovary) and in the placenta of the pregnant female. The three groups of hormones are closely related chemically in such a way that the estrogens are derived from the androgens and the androgens from the progestins.

As in the case of several other glands, each type of secretion consists of several hormones of slightly different structure and varying degrees of potency. The primary member of the progestins and the one from which others are derived through metabolism is *progesterone*. This substance is a key intermediate in the manufacture of the androgens, estrogens, and adrenocortical hormones. The two most active androgens are *testosterone* and *androsterone*. The two most active estrogens are *estradiol* and *estrone*.

The functions of these hormones and their relationships with the three gonadotrophic hormones of the pituitary are complex. Some of their functions will be detailed later in connection with sexual and maternal behavior. Here we may simply note that the progestins promote physiological conditions for the maintenance of pregnancy, the androgens promote and maintain various secondary sex characteristics in the male, and the estrogens have a similar function in the female. This is an oversimplification, but it will serve for the present.

HORMONE INHIBITORS

Like enzymes and vitamins, the hormones may be inhibited by specific chemical substances. Sometimes the inhibitors damage the cells that make the hormone, sometimes they block the enzyme system needed to make the hormone, and in still other cases they seem to work by blocking the action of a hormone in the metabolic steps in which it is concerned. Some examples of hormone inhibitors of these various types are worth considering briefly.

Alloxan is an inhibitor of insulin. Injection of alloxan into an animal is followed by diabetes and all the symptoms of insulin deficiency. If, afterward, a histologist looks at the pancreas of the animal, he can see that alloxan does its deadly work by attacking the beta cells, the specific cells that produce insulin. Now it is interesting that hormones of the anterior pituitary gland normally inhibit in the same way as alloxan; at least, repeated large doses of anterior pituitary extract have this result. The effect, however, is not nearly so great and, in the normal individual, it does not harm beta cells as much as does alloxan. Nevertheless, the pituitary—the master gland—normally masters other glands partly by loosing hormone inhibitors to work on them.

Another somewhat different example of hormone inhibitors concerns the thyroid gland. This gland's secretion can be inhibited by several substances; among them are *thiouracil*, sulfaguanadine, and a number of other sulfa compounds. In this case, however, no harm to the cells of the thyroid is apparent. The inhibitors seem to work by directly blocking the production of hormone. Thiouracil, regularly administered to an animal, results in all the symptoms of thyroidectomy. Moreover, the thyroid greatly increases in size with only a week of thiouracil administration. This result apparently can be laid at the door of the pituitary, for the inhibition of thyroid secretion seems to stimulate the pituitary to put out more of the thyrotrophic hormone that normally steps up activity in the thyroid gland—another nice example of the complex links between glands.

There are still other examples of a third kind of hormone inhibition: direct interference with the effects of hormones. Estradiol and testosterone are two sex hormones that are very much alike chemically. It is known that estradiol will inhibit the action of testosterone. The explanation of this effect seems to be the same as that for enzyme inhibitors and antivitamins: Because the molecules of the two substances have much the same shape, they compete for the same substrate in metabolic reactions.

HOMEOSTASIS

The main emphasis so far in this chapter has been on intermediary metabolism and on how complex compounds are formed in the body and energy is stored and set free. Much is to be gained by such an approach. It is also desirable, however, to look at the larger aspects of the internal environment and to see how it is so organized as to provide a favorable medium in which the various cells of the body can carry out their normal duties.

CONCEPT OF HOMEOSTASIS

All cells must have a favorable equilibrium between them and their environment. On the one hand, most of the metabolic reactions that occur in the cells demand a constant supply of materials. On the other hand, these reactions themselves produce variations in the temperature, pH, osmotic pressure, etc., of the internal medium that would be detrimental to cell function unless checked or counteracted. Most cells of the body, however, lost some of their ability to maintain an equilibrium with the environment when they differentiated to perform special functions. As a consequence, few cells can maintain a favorable internal equilibrium all by themselves. They have had to collaborate and to some extent specialize so that their environment is maintained relatively constant under a wide variety of conditions.

Physiologists use the term *homeostasis* to refer to this constancy of the internal environment or, more strictly speaking, the maintenance of the internal environment within the rather narrow limits conducive to normal cell function. Their studies show that the typical warm-blooded animal maintains a constant body temperature, pH, blood pressure and heart rate, blood-sugar level, salt and water balance, calcium and phosphorus balance, etc. Indeed, the number of factors that are relatively constant in the body is remarkable.

There are several different but interrelated factors in this homeostatic equilibrium. The hormones are one. There is a long list of others: the lungs, through which carbon dioxide is excreted and oxygen taken in; the circulatory system, which controls the distribution of blood to the various tissues; the kidneys, through which various products of metabolism, particularly those from the breakdown of proteins, are excreted; the digestive tract, by means of which essential materials are brought into the body; and finally, the nervous system, which takes part, directly or indirectly, in regulating the other homeostatic mechanisms. Of particular importance to us are the mechanisms that regulate blood-sugar level, hydrogen-ion concentration, and oxygen supply, for the functioning of the nervous system, and thus behavior, crucially depends on their being kept uniform within very narrow limits of variation.

BLOOD–SUGAR LEVEL

In most mammals, the concentration of sugar (glucose) in the blood stays between 60 and 90 milligrams per 100 cubic centimeters of whole blood. *Hypoglycemia*, or depression of the blood sugar below this lower limit, deprives the cells of the carbohydrate they need, because the rate at which glucose can get into cells depends in part on how much is in the blood stream. Most tissues of the body can function adequately for fairly long periods of time at low blood-sugar levels, but the nervous system is especially dependent upon steady supplies of glucose. It can store very little carbohydrate, and it cannot readily make use of other materials for its metabolic functions. As a result, when an animal has hypoglycemia it will go into a coma and die if something is not done to rectify it.

The converse situation, *hyperglycemia,* i.e., elevation of blood sugar above the upper limit of normal concentration, has a less dramatic effect on the nervous system and cell functions in general. Nevertheless, prolonged and severe hyperglycemia can lead to widespread metabolic derangements and specifically to the symptoms of the disease diabetes.

LIVER FUNCTION—A central factor in keeping blood sugar at the right level is the activity of the liver (Figure 4.7). In the first place, the liver can store fairly large amounts of carbohydrate in the form of glycogen. Secondly, under appropriate stimulation it can either convert glycogen and secrete it into the blood in the form of glucose or it can remove glucose from the blood and store it as glycogen. Both these activities depend on specific endocrine influences and on how much carbohydrate is available to the liver. With normal food intake, most of the glycogen in the liver comes from carbohydrate absorbed through the intestine. But the liver can also convert fats and proteins into carbohydrates, a process regulated by the hormones of the adrenal cortex, the anterior pituitary, and the thyroid gland.

CARBOHYDRATE UTILIZATION—Blood-sugar level also depends on two other major factors: the rate of intestinal absorption of sugar and the rate at which the tissues use carbohydrate. How much carbohydrate is absorbed in the intestine depends, of course, on how much the animal is eating. But the hormones of the adrenal cortex and thyroid gland also make a difference in the rate of intestinal absorption.

The rate at which carbohydrate is used depends largely on the muscular activity of the animal. In addition, however, the hormone of the thyroid gland can speed up carbohydrate utilization, whereas the hormones of the anterior pituitary, on the other hand, seem to depress it. The reason is that the anterior pituitary hormones can inhibit one of the enzymes involved in glucose breakdown. Insulin offsets to some degree this inhibitory effect of the anterior pituitary hormones, and it increases the rate of carbohydrate breakdown. Moreover, it increases the rate at which blood sugar, at a given concentration, enters the cells of the body where it can be used.

HYDROGEN–ION CONCENTRATION

Many of the metabolic reactions that take place in the body produce relatively strong acids and bases. The dissociation of acids and bases in water gives rise to hydrogen ions (H^+) and hydroxyl ions (OH^-), respectively, and an excess of one or the other makes the medium acidic or alkaline. It is customary to refer to the acidity or alkalinity of a medium in terms of its

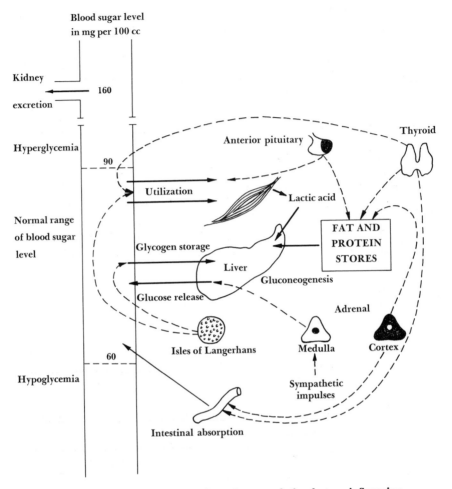

FIGURE 4.7—A schematic representation of some of the factors influencing blood-sugar level. (Adapted from M. Bodansky. *Introduction to physiological chemistry.* 4th ed. New York: Wiley, 1938. P. 318. By permission of the publishers.)

hydrogen-ion concentration, or pH. The values of pH are designated on a logarithmic scale in which low values represent acidity and high values alkalinity. The neutral point on this scale is 7.0, and it is interesting to note that the normal pH of the blood is about 7.4, i.e., slightly alkaline. The extreme limits of variation of the pH of the blood are 7.8 to 6.8. Above or below these values, cell functions, particularly those of the nervous system, are so disturbed that death results. Thus it is essential that the hydrogen-ion concentration of the internal environment remain stable.

The body has three ways of keeping the pH stable. One is a set of *buffers* in the blood. These are chemical materials that can "bind," or take up, acid ions. A second is by the excretion of acids from the kidneys. Such acids are buffered temporarily in the blood and then excreted by the kidneys. Finally, there are the lungs, through which carbon dioxide escapes. Carbon dioxide in solution is acidic, and it is the ultimate product of carbohydrate metabolism.

There is a little more to say on this last point. If carbonic acid in the blood becomes too high, there are two ways of speeding its escape through the lungs. One is by increasing the rate of breathing. The other is by increasing the circulation of blood through the lungs. There are neural mechanisms for doing both these things. In one case, carbonic acid in the blood excites the "breathing center" in the hind part of the brain to speed up breathing. In the other, carbon dioxide in the blood excites vasomotor centers so that blood vessels are constricted, blood pressure is increased, and blood courses more rapidly through the arterioles of the lungs. This is a good example of the interrelation between the nervous system and the internal environment to keep the latter as constant as possible.

OXYGEN

Oxygen, of course, is needed directly or indirectly for the oxidation reactions in intermediary metabolism. All needed oxygen must enter the body through the lungs. There it is absorbed into the blood through arterioles, where it combines immediately with the hemoglobin of the red corpuscles. When the amount of oxygen in the air is normal and when breathing is also normal, the red corpuscles absorb about 95 percent of the oxygen they could possibly carry. If, however, the amount of oxygen entering the lungs is less than it should be, the oxygen saturation of the blood is cut down—a condition called *anoxemia*.

Oxygen is carried from the lungs to the tissues by the red corpuscles. This transport must go on at a normal rate or there are dire results. A balance in oxygen transport is held, it is interesting to note, not by any direct reactions to oxygen deficiency but rather by the pH of the blood, especially the pH changes that come about from too much carbon dioxide or lactic acid. Thus there is a common method for keeping both the pH and the oxygen supply on an even keel in the internal environment. This single mechanism for regulating the two factors is effective because an excess of carbon dioxide and a deficiency of oxygen usually appear together in the body's metabolism. Breathing increases oxygen supplies and decreases carbon dioxide in the blood. Similarly, an increase in blood supply to the tissues carries away more carbon dioxide and brings up more oxygen. That is why pH generally and carbon dioxide specifically can serve to regulate both carbon dioxide and oxygen supply.

REGULATORY BEHAVIOR

So far, we have discussed only the relatively automatic physiological mechanisms that maintain the constancy of the internal environment. As we shall see in later chapters, the behavior of an organism can also contribute to homeostasis. In such cases, the behavior is called *regulatory behavior*, for it is initiated by some adverse condition of the internal environment and it serves to bring about beneficial physiological changes. We cannot go into details at this point, but one illustration will serve to show what is meant.

Birds and mammals maintain their body temperature within very narrow limits. If the temperature outside a warm-blooded animal gets colder, a number of changes take place to keep the animal's body at the same temperature. In the first place, the rate of heat production in the body increases. This comes about through stepped-up thyroid function, which improves the general metabolic rate through quickened heart rate and heightened muscular activity. In addition, the animal may increase its heat production by shivering. Secondly, changes take place that reduce the rate of heat loss from the body. The superficial blood vessels constrict; the hair of the body erects, forming a good insulating coat in the case of certain furry animals; and the animal may roll into a ball, exposing only a minimum of body surface. At the same time, the animal may behave in such a way as to reduce the heat loss and increase heat production. If possible, it will move to a warmer area of the environment. Given access to building materials and a variety of foods, it will build a nest, hoard large stores of food, increase its food intake, and select a diet of high caloric value (see Chapters 13 and 15).

A great deal is known about behavior of this sort, and we shall have more to say about it later. The important fact to remember here is that the coordinated activity of the nervous system is an important factor in keeping the internal environment constant.

PSYCHOACTIVE DRUGS

Drugs are chemical substances that may be administered for some beneficial effect on man or animals. Chemical substances that have harmful effects are called *poisons*. Virtually all drugs, however, have poisonous effects when administered in large enough doses. Drugs may be naturally occurring substances in minerals or plants, or they may be synthesized substances. In recent years, an increasing proportion of the drugs that are being used are synthetics because it has frequently been found that synthetic substances, which can more easily be prepared in pure form, can be more potent and have fewer undesirable side effects than naturally occurring drugs.

Until recently, almost all drugs were administered to combat disease or to alleviate some biological condition not related to state of mind or anything psychological. In recent years, however, *psychoactive drugs*—drugs used for the specific purpose of modifying psychological conditions—have come into increasing use. Other names for psychoactive drugs are psychotropic drugs, psychopharmacological agents, or neuropharmacological agents. The term *psychopharmacology* covers the general field of psychoactive drugs.

Psychoactive drugs, once introduced into the body, become a part of the internal environment, circulating in the blood and acting on certain organs of the body. Psychoactive drugs act primarily on the nervous system or on certain pathways and connections within it. For that reason, it is logical to discuss them here so that we may refer to them as necessary in later chapters concerned with sensory and behavioral topics.

The psychoactive drugs may be considered under four main headings: (1) sedatives, (2) tranquilizers, (3) activators, and (4) psychomimetic drugs.

SEDATIVES

Sedatives are drugs that, given in sufficient doses, produce sleep. Sometimes they are called *hypnotics*. The most commonly employed sedatives are barbiturates, such as sodium amytal and pentobarbital (Nembutal). Another sedative frequently used which is not a barbiturate is glutethimide (Doriden). Because sedatives in mild doses make a person somewhat less "inhibited," they are sometimes used in psychotherapy to enable a patient to express himself with less restraint, but otherwise the sedatives are not very interesting psychologically. The sedatives generally depress the threshold of neurons and thus reduce nervous activity. For that reason, they have long been used as anticonvulsants in the case of epilepsy or to combat the effects of convulsant drugs. It appears that the sedatives have a specific depressing effect on the reticular system and hence on cortical arousal.

TRANQUILIZERS

The tranquilizing drugs have evoked the most interest in recent years both among the general public and among scientists studying psychoactive-drug effects. They are drugs that have a calming effect without putting a person to sleep or without seriously interfering with normal mental functioning. They are sometimes called *ataraxic*, implying peace of mind, or *neuroleptic*, which refers to the quieting of the nervous system. They may be divided on the basis of chemical structure into four main groups (see Berger, 1960).

DIPHENYLMETHANES—Members of this group are so named because they have in common the diphenylmethane structure. Many of them are closely related to the antihistamines. Two representatives of the group are benactyzine (Deprol, Suavitil) and hydroxyaine (Atarax, Vistaril). Like the phenothiazines and Rauwolfia alkaloids (see below), these drugs stimulate the hypo-thalamus and slightly depress the reticular formation. Unlike them, however, they have no effect on the limbic system and they slightly depress the cerebral cortex,

PHENOTHIAZINE DERIVATIVES—The parent compound of this group of drugs, *phenothiazine*, was for a time used as a tranquilizer, but because it had cer-tain toxic effects, particularly on the liver, its use was abandoned. More than twenty closely related derivatives have been prepared and employed in medi-cine. Of these about a dozen have been used as tranquilizers. Two that are most often used in the treatment of patients and in psychopharmacological research are chlorpromazine (Thorazine) and prochlorperazine (Compazine, Stemetil).

Drugs in this group have a variety of effects. One is to block the adrenergic nervous system. They also stimulate the hypothalamus and the limbic system but slightly depress the reticular formation.

RAUWOLFIA ALKALOIDS—Drugs in this category are derived from the *Rau-wolfia* root, an herb medicine long used in India. Three members of this group have been isolated and used effectively as tranquilizers: reserpine (Serpasil), deserpidine (Harmonyl), and rescinnamine (Moderil).

Drugs in this category have the effect of releasing serotonin stored in the brain (see above) and hence of increasing the number of breakdown prod-ucts of serotonin in the urine. They stimulate the limbic system and the hypothalamus but depress slightly the reticular formation.

PROPANEDIOLS—The original member of this group, mephenesin (Tolserol, Mephate), was first used as a muscle relaxant but was found to have a tran-quilizing effect. The molecule was modified chemically to eliminate certain undesirable effects, and in this way several other compounds were made. Probably the best known of this group is meprobamate (Miltown, Equanil).

Members of this group, unlike the phenothiazines and Rauwolfia alkaloids, do not affect the autonomic nervous system. They do reduce conductivity in long interneuronal pathways and thus reduce muscle tension and spasm. They have no depressing effect on the reticular formation (but may possibly stimulate it); they stimulate the hypothalamus and cerebral cortex. They depress somewhat the limbic system.

ACTIVATORS

A class of drugs receiving increasing attention in recent years includes those that, in general, have effects opposite to the tranquilizers. They are variously called stimulants, activators, psychic energizers, or antidepressants, although these terms are not always exactly synonymous. They may be divided into three general classes: analeptics, monoaminoxidase inhibitors, and cholinergic drugs.

ANALEPTICS—The term analeptic means antidepressive. The characteristic of drugs in this class is that they antagonize the action of drugs that depress the central nervous system. They generally produce hyperexcitability of the nervous system. The drugs of this class that are best known are amphetamine (Benzedrine) and dextroamphetamine (Dexedrine). These have an adrenergic action. Other stimulants in this class that lack such action are pipradrol (Meratran) and phenidylate (Ritalin).

MONOAMINOXIDASE INHIBITORS—Monoaminoxidase (MAO) is an enzyme that is widely distributed in the body, and it is probably important in some way in the metabolism of catechol amines (epinephrine and norepinephrine) and serotonin. The administration of monoaminoxidase inhibitors (MAOI) causes the level of serotonin and catechol amines to rise in the brain and liver. One of the first and best known of the agents in this class is iproniazid (Marsalid). Other compounds that have a greater potency are nialamide (Niamid), isocarboxazid (Marplan), and tranylcyprozine.

CHOLINERGIC DRUGS—As used here, the term cholinergic drug refers to any substance that tends to increase the level of acetylcholine in the brain and nervous system. Generally speaking, these may be called activators, although in certain instances and in certain doses, their effects may not be particularly activating. Substances that tend to increase acetylcholine may be divided into three categories: acetylcholine itself, acetylcholine precursors, and anticholinesterases.

Acetylcholine (ACh) when injected into the blood or when liberated in normal nervous function is, as we indicated earlier, rapidly disposed of by the enzyme cholinesterase. If, therefore, it is desired to increase the concentration of ACh, some way around this must be found. One such measure is to inject ACh directly into the ventricles of the brain. This has been done in both human beings and animals but more often in animals. It is also possible to apply ACh directly to the surface of the cortex or to some brain area and observe for a time the effects of increasing its concentration.

Another way to increase ACh is to administer substances from which it can be made—the precursors of ACh. One such drug is diethylaminoethanol (Deaner). A chemical pathway exists for the formation of ACh from this substance. Given in sufficiently large doses, this appears to have caused some remissions of schizophrenics (Berger, 1960).

Still a third way of increasing ACh levels is to use an anticholinesterase—a substance that inactivates the cholinesterase enzyme. In this way, the breakdown of ACh is inhibited. There are several such inhibitors. One is eserine. Another is diisopropyl fluorophosphate (DFP).

PSYCHOTOMIMETIC DRUGS

A psychotomimetic drug is one that produces in some degree some of the symptoms of a psychosis. Two naturally occurring drugs in this category are mescaline and hashish. Introspective reports of their effects have been in the literature for years, and mescaline in particular has had some thorough study. In more recent years, the psychotomimetic drug paid the greatest attention is *lysergic acid diethylamide,* or more briefly LSD-25 (see Chapter 20). Another drug that may produce symptoms somewhat like those found in catatonic schizophrenia is *bulbocapnine.* This has been used in both animals and people to produce "experimental catatonia." Similar catatonic symptoms may be produced by the injection of acetylcholine into the ventricles of the brain and by the anticholinesterases described above.

Besides LSD-25 and bulbocapnine, there are a large number of drugs for which psychotomimetic effects have been reported (see Clark, 1963). Some of them have been prepared and consumed for centuries by primitive peoples. Those that have been studied in recent years include compounds that are anticholinergic in action (atropine and hyoscine), some that are related to the metabolism of the biogenic amines (bufotenine, adrenochrome, and psilocybin), and mescaline (also called peyotl), a substance prepared from certain cactus plants and formerly used by Mexican and American Indians in ritualistic ceremonies.

5 THE CHEMICAL SENSES

IT IS CUSTOMARY TO DISTINGUISH three chemical senses: taste, smell, and common chemical sensitivity. Hence, these are the senses we shall study in this chapter. Less is known about them, particularly smell and common chemical sensitivity, than is now known about the other senses. Consequently the chapter will be relatively brief.

The structural differences in the three types of sense organs have already been described briefly in Chapter 1 (see Figure 1.3). They were used as illustrations of the three ways in which receptors may differentiate to perform their functions. The common chemical receptor is a relatively undifferentiated free nerve ending; the smell receptor is a highly specialized neuron; and the taste receptor consists of a specialized epithelial cell served by a neuronal fiber. Further details will be brought out below in connection with the individual senses.

COMMON CHEMICAL SENSITIVITY

The common chemical receptors are more widely distributed in the body than the other chemical receptors. The chief problem, in fact, is to distinguish them from the receptors for pressure and pain, which are also liberally distributed throughout the skin.

RECEPTORS

Free nerve endings associated with epithelial cells can subserve either pain or pressure or common chemical reception. But even though one cannot tell the difference with the naked eye, it is probable that common chemical receptors are different from the other two (Crozier, 1916; Moncrieff, 1944). With cocaine one can anesthetize the touch and pain receptors, but after sensitivity to touch and pain are gone, the application of an acid—a stimulus for the common chemical receptor—can still be felt. Conversely, after the common chemical receptors have become adapted to stimulation by acids, one can feel pressure or pain. Not everyone, however, is satisfied with these experiments, and the distinction between common chemical sensitivity and pain sensitivity has been questioned (Jones, 1954; Pfaffmann, 1951).

NEURAL PATHWAYS

Common chemical receptors are widely distributed throughout the body, especially in exposed moist surfaces such as those of the mouth and throat. They are served by fibers from various cranial and spinal nerves, but they do not seem to be represented in the central nervous system by any special pathways or centers. They seem to run along with the fibers for taste or the skin senses. However, more research is needed on this point.

APPROPRIATE STIMULI

The most effective stimuli for the common chemical receptors are dilute solutions of acids, alkalis, and salts, or, in general, any substances that ionize well or tend to dehydrate tissues. The threshold concentration of hydrochloric acid and of sodium hydroxide, for example, is about 0.01 N (normal). (A normal solution is one in which 1 mole of a substance divided by the valence of the ions into which it dissociates is dissolved in 1 liter of water. A mole is the molecular weight of a substance in grams.) The threshold for alcohol, which is relatively nonionizable, is about 3 N. Compared with the thresholds of taste or smell, these are very high; this fact reflects the relatively primitive nature of the common chemical receptors.

TASTE

Let us turn now to taste or gustation, both of which terms will be employed. In taking up this sense, we shall cover quickly, or omit altogether, points on which there are confusion and controversy and put the greatest emphasis on those facts and experiments that seem to help most in understanding the physiological basis of taste.

TASTE RECEPTORS

It was noted above that the taste receptors, in contrast to those of smell, make use of a specialized epithelial cell supplied with nerve endings. This cell is called a *taste receptor cell* or merely a *taste cell*. Such cells are located in a more complex structure of cells called a taste bud. Such a structure, shown in Figure 5.1, is a flask- or bud-shaped cluster of cells embedded in the ridges (papillae) of the tongue. Many of the cells of the taste bud seem to be there to support the sensory taste cells. These supporting cells, however, may only "be different stages in the age or functional state of but a single type" (Pfaff-mann, 1959) for there seems to be a continuous process of atrophy and growth going on among the receptor cells. Taste cells are stimulated when chemical solutions penetrate a pore in the taste bud and the spaces among the taste cells.

It is significant that the integrity of the taste cell depends upon the neuron that serves it. In the embryonic development of the individual, it is the sensory neuron that causes the epithelial cell to differentiate into a taste cell. Moreover, the process is reversible, for sectioning the taste nerves after differentiation has taken place causes the taste cells to change "backward" toward more primitive epithelial cells (Olmsted, 1921). This phenomenon indicates,

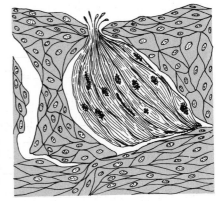

FIGURE 5.1—Structure of the taste bud. (Adapted from P. H. Mitchell. *Textbook of general physiology.* 4th ed. New York: McGraw-Hill, 1948, P. 189. By permission of the publishers.)

perhaps, that there are some chemical influences or neurohumors of the primary neuron that induce the specific changes in the epithelial cells.

GUSTATORY SENSITIVITY

Even a casual observation of the structure of taste buds makes it clear that there must be two stages in the process of exciting taste receptors. One is penetration of the taste bud by the chemical stimulus. The second is the chemical reaction, presumably, through which nerve impulses are set off. Both are important in taste sensitivity.

Penetration is a factor in the time required for appreciating gustatory stimuli. It usually takes some time to sense taste stimuli. If, for example, one applies a salt solution of 3 N concentration, it will be about ten seconds before the sensation of salt reaches a maximum of intensity. Penetration is an important factor in this delay. It also accounts in part for sensitivity to different kinds of substances.

A second factor determining taste sensitivity seems to be the different types of taste receptors that exist for different stimuli. This point, however, is better considered under the general topic of taste qualities.

TASTE QUALITIES

As in smell, vision, hearing, and the skin senses, many theorists and investigators have attempted to apply the classic doctrine of specific nerve energies to the problem of taste sensation (see Boring, 1950). They have supposed that there are a few basic qualities of taste sensation of which all other sensations are mixtures and that these qualities depend on a corresponding number of specific taste receptors.

It has long been well agreed, with considerable evidence to support it, that there are four fundamental taste qualities. The names for the four experiences are sour, salt, sweet, and bitter. There are six different lines of evidence, which we can cover quickly, that indicate that these four are the correct ones: (1) Qualitative differences in subjective experience fall rather definitely into four such categories. (2) Experiences that cannot be so classified can be explained in terms of the stimulation of tactual or common chemical receptors. (3) Individual papillae can be found on the tongue that give rise, when stimulated, to a single quality of experience, at least at low intensities of stimulation. (4) The areas of the tongue in which each quality may be aroused are not coextensive but fall into four rather distinct zones (see Figure 5.2). (5) Some drugs, applied to the tongue, eliminate one quality of experience while leaving the others relatively unaffected. (6) One can reproduce fairly accurately the taste of any substance by mixing typical sweet, bitter, salt, and sour stimuli in appropriate proportions.

—— encloses region lacking sweet
· · · · encloses region lacking bitter
- - - - encloses region lacking salty
• • • encloses region lacking sour
⊙ ⊙ circumvallate papillae

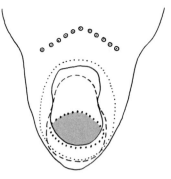

FIGURE 5.2—Regions of the tongue in which sweet, bitter, salty, or sour sensitivity is lacking. (Adapted from R. S. Woodworth and H. Schlosberg. *Experimental psychology.* Rev. ed. New York: Holt, 1954. P. 300. By permission of the publishers.)

THE CHEMICAL BASIS OF THE QUALITIES—Considerable effort has been expended to determine precisely what groups of chemicals are correlated with the qualities of taste experience (see Moncrieff, 1944; Pfaffmann, 1959). The unanimity of many investigators in finding the hydrogen ion (H^+) of acids to elicit "sour" leaves little question about its importance in this taste quality.

"Salt," however, is not so simple, for more than one ion or atom is able to elicit it. In general, the inorganic salts, particularly the halides (chlorine, iodine, and bromine) of sodium, potassium, ammonium, lithium, and magnesium are most effective, and it has been suggested that the halides, in ionized form, are responsible for "salt." Not in accord with this generalization, however, is the fact that the nitrates (NO_3^-) and sulfates (SO_4^-) also are capable of evoking "salt." Perhaps it is better to say that the negative ion (anion) is the chemical basis of "salt," but this statement, too, has some exceptions, and it is not known whether they can be accounted for in terms of the factors of penetrability noted above.

"Bitter" is closely allied with a family of complex chemical substances known as the alkaloids. Their basic properties appear to be due to amino groups (NH_2) or to trivalent nitrogen atoms (N^{3-}). Many substances, on the other hand, which are not alkaloids and which may be quite unrelated to them chemically, evoke "bitter." Some of the inorganic salts are examples. No simple chemical property, therefore, can be said to be the basis of "bitter."

Much the same statements apply to "sweet," although the sugars are the class of substances most notable for their sweetness.

Complicating things still further is the fact that the same substance in different concentration may taste both sweet and salty. This is true of both sodium and potassium chloride, as can be seen in Table 5.1.

TABLE 5.1—The taste of salts at different concentrations

CONCENTRATION (M)	NaCl	KCl
0.009	No taste	Sweet
0.010	Weak sweet	Strong, sweet
0.02	Sweet	Sweet, perhaps bitter
0.03	Sweet	Bitter
0.04	Salt, slightly sweet	Bitter
0.05	Salty	Bitter, salty
0.1	Salty	Bitter, salty
0.2	Pure salty	Salty, bitter, sour
1.0	Pure salty	Salty, bitter, sour

SOURCE: C. Pfaffmann. The sense of taste. In J. Field, H. W. Magoun, and V. E. Hall (Eds.), *Handbook of physiology*, vol. 1. Washington, D.C.: American Physiological Society, 1959. P. 514.

The failure so far to find a limited number of chemical properties correlated with sensory qualities should not cause dismay, for knowledge of what are the receptive substances in the taste cells is also needed. As we shall see below, there is evidence that taste receptors, indeed, even certain portions of their membranes, have specific chemical sensitivities. Until more is known about these specificities, one cannot expect to understand very well the properties of chemical stimuli, for these must be determined by the chemical nature of the receptive substances in the receptors.

SPECIFIC FIBERS FOR TASTE—Although it may not be known exactly what chemical groupings are related to the four basic taste qualities, there is now some idea of how the different receptors sort out different stimuli. This idea comes largely from the work of Pfaffmann (1959) with electrical responses in individual fibers of the taste nerves. Pfaffmann's basic technique consists of locating a single unit under his electrode and then testing the response of the unit to a series of stimuli representing the four taste qualities. In Figure 5.3 are the results he obtained with a sample of nine different elements studied in the rat.

On the left are three elements that respond most vigorously to salt. Two of these, however, are moderately responsive to acid. One in the center column responds quite selectively to sugar, whereas two others are fairly insensitive to any stimulus. On the right are three elements that are all insensitive to sugar. All three are also sensitive to salt and sour, but one of these also responds to "bitter" (quinine) whereas two do not do so very significantly. From this sort of data, one can see that individual nerve fibers in the taste nerve have different sensitivities to different stimuli but that there is no simple relation to the four basic qualities.

Since the records of Figure 5.3 were taken from nerve fibers rather than from taste receptor cells, one may ask whether one fiber serves several receptor cells representing different qualities. Anatomically, this might be possible, for two or three fibers typically serve one taste bud and may synapse with more than one receptor cell. However, the same kind of experiment described above has been made with micropipettes thrust into individual receptor cells with the same results (Kimura and Beidler, 1956). Hence the patterns of sensitivity depicted in Figure 5.3 are no doubt representative of receptor cells themselves.

How then can taste quality be signaled to the brain? A cue is provided by another experiment with two units of the taste nerve (Pfaffmann, 1955). In this experiment, illustrated in Figure 5.4, the frequency of spikes was counted as a function of the stimulus intensity of two substances, sodium chloride and sucrose (table sugar). One fiber showed much greater sensitivity to sodium chloride than to sucrose; the second fiber was more sensitive to sucrose than

FIGURE 5.3—The frequency of response of nine different single-fiber preparations to five standard taste solutions. For elements D and I, the sucrose concentration was .3 molar; otherwise it was 1.0 M. (Adapted from C. Pfaffmann. Gustatory nerve impulses in rat, cat, and rabbit. *J. Neurophysiol.*, 1955, 18, 429–440.)

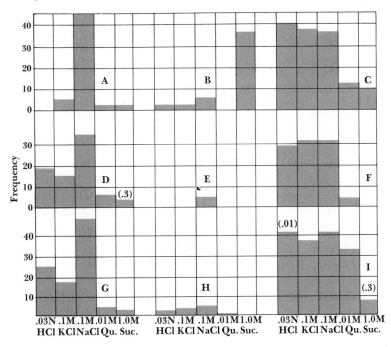

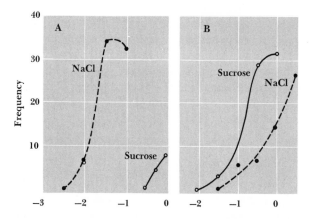

FIGURE 5.4—Relative specificities of two different elements in the rat. Each is sensitive to NaCl and sucrose, as well as to other stimuli; but element A is relatively more sensitive to NaCl, and element B is relatively more sensitive to sucrose. Frequency is number of impulses during the first second of discharge. (Adapted from C. Pfaffmann. Gustatory nerve impulses in rat, cat, and rabbit. *J. Neurophysiol.*, 1955, 18, 429–440.)

to sodium chloride. This arrangement, as Pfaffmann (1959, pp. 512–513) explains, provides for the required "signals":

> The two fibers, A and B . . . , respond to both sodium chloride and sucrose, but A is more reactive to sodium chloride and B is more reactive to sucrose. At all concentrations of sodium chloride, the frequencies in A are higher than that in B; at all concentrations of sucrose, B is greater than A. Such a two-fiber system, therefore, signals sodium chloride when A is greater than B and sucrose when B is greater than A. Thus different information may be conveyed by the same nerve fiber depending upon the activity in a second parallel afferent fiber. . . . Intensity would be correlated with an increase in overall frequency of discharge. Such a model may be expanded by adding more fibers to provide a greater variety of combinations of discharge pattern. If sensory quality depends upon such patterns, we might expect quality of sensation to change as the afferent population is reduced, for example when the stimulus concentration approaches threshold. Such changes in quality are well known [see Table 5.1].

ADAPTATION AND INTERACTION

Something more can be learned about the mechanism of signaling from studies of adaptation and of interaction between stimuli of different kinds.

If the tongue is continuously stimulated with a particular stimulus, two effects may be observed: (1) The absolute threshold for stimuli interspersed among, or immediately following, the continuous stimulation is elevated. And it is generally elevated in proportion to the intensity of the adapting stimulus (see Figure 5.5; Hahn, 1934). (2) The subjective intensity of the adapting stimulus lessens. In other words, a stimulus does not taste as strong after it is experienced for some time as when first tasted. Each of these two effects may be used to measure adaptation.

In some of the senses, e.g., somatic and visual, adaptation of this kind can be largely or entirely ascribed to changes taking place in receptor cells. Presumably, as in vision, some substance involved in the receptor's response to a stimulus is exhausted during continued stimulation. One way of checking this hypothesis in taste is to determine the cross effects of adapting with stimuli representing the same taste quality, e.g., two kinds of salt such as sodium chloride and calcium chloride. If adaptation to one salt causes adaptation to another, it may be assumed that the site of adaptation is the receptor cell. If it does not, then the adaptation must be more central.

This kind of experiment produces mixed results (Hahn, 1949). In the case of acid (sour), adaptation is fairly general. Adaptation to one acid also causes adaptation to another. In the case of bitter and sweet stimuli, this sometimes happens and sometimes does not, depending upon the combination of stimuli employed. In the case of salt, however, there is no cross adaptation;

FIGURE 5.5—Adaptation and recovery curves for NaCl. The ordinate gives threshold concentrations during a thirty-second period of adaptation to 5, 10 or 15 percent NaCl and then during a thirty-second period of recovery. (Adapted from H. Hahn. Die Adaptation des Geschmackssinnes. Z. Sinnesphysiol., 1934, 65, 105–145.)

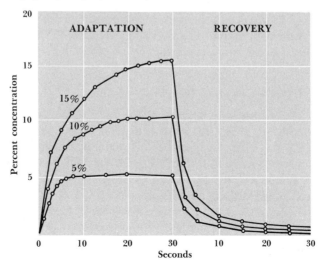

adaptation to one salt does not affect the threshold to other salts. This psychological fact has been checked by electrophysiological means, and both action potentials and responses of individual units in the taste nerves also show no cross adaptation (see Pfaffmann, 1959).

There is another respect, however, in which electrophysiological results do not confirm the psychological data. Continuous stimulation with sodium chloride yields a fairly steady discharge of impulses in the taste nerves even though subjective intensity in man diminishes under such conditions (Beidler, 1957). This, at least in the case of salt, points to central adaptation rather than to peripheral adaptation.

A related observation concerns the masking of one stimulus by another. A well-known case of such masking is the "covering" of a sour taste by a sweet taste. In everyday life the sourness of, say, lemonade may be cut by adding sugar. Such masking is not seen in the action potential of taste fibers. If the response of the fibers to 10 percent sucrose alone and of pH 2.5 alone is compared with the response to a mixture of these two concentrations, the nerve response *increases* rather than decreases as one might expect from the subjective experience of cross masking. Hence such masking would appear to be central rather than peripheral in origin (Andersson et al., 1950).

RECEPTOR MECHANISMS

The present view of the receptor mechanism of taste, based on the kind of research described above, is this: Each cell has areas of its membrane that are differentially sensitive to certain kinds of chemical stimuli. In some cases, the cell possesses only one kind of sensitivity, but more frequently, there are two or three kinds of sensitivity. Usually, however, a cell is markedly more sensitive to certain substances than to others. Hence, a signal from a combination of fibers indicates fairly well the kind of chemical substance stimulating the cells. In some cases, one substance may adapt a cell so that it does not respond to certain other substances. Frequently, however, any adaptation or masking effects of one stimulus on another is a central rather than a peripheral matter.

NEURAL CENTERS AND PATHWAYS

We can turn now to some of the higher centers of the taste system (see Pfaffmann, 1959). Branches of three different cranial nerves serve the taste buds: the VIIth, IXth, and Xth. In most of the experiments discussed above, the records were made from fibers of the VIIth nerve, since the taste portion of this nerve, the *chorda tympani*, passes through the middle ear and is readily accessible to the experimenter. All three nerves, after passing through their respective cranial ganglia, terminate in the medulla or pons of the brain (see Figure 5.6). Here the fibers are collected in a tract, the *solitary tract*, which runs a short distance posteriorly and ends upon the second-order neurons of the *solitary nucleus*.

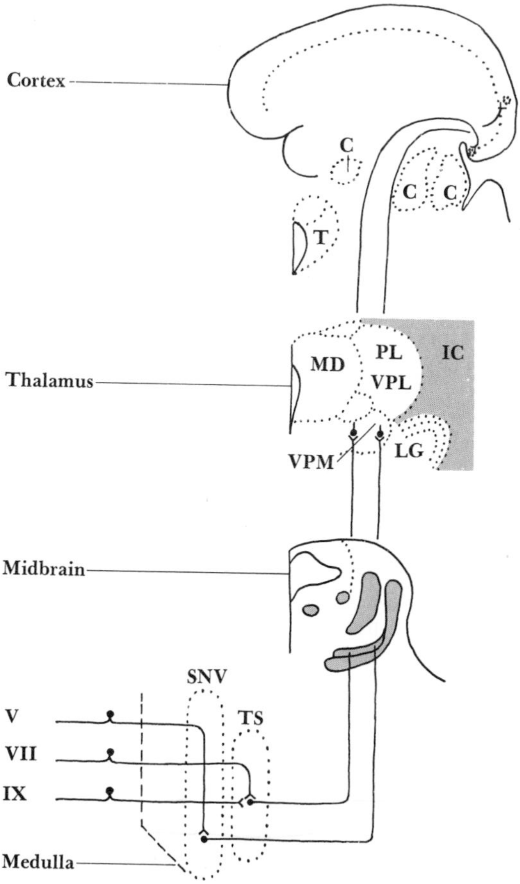

FIGURE 5.6—Schematic diagram of taste and somatosensory pathways from the face. At the level of the medulla, SNV is spinal nucleus of the Vth nerve; TS, nucleus of the solitary tract. In the thalamus, LG, lateral geniculate nucleus; MD, dorsomedial nucleus; PL, posterolateral nucleus; VP, posteroventral nucleus. At level of the cortex, C, corpus striatum; T, thalamus. (Adapted from H. D. Patton. In T. C. Ruch and J. F. Fulton (Eds.), *Medical physiology and biophysics.* 18th ed. Philadelphia: Saunders, 1960. P. 372.)

It is interesting to note that the solitary tract and nucleus, although relatively small in man, are extremely large in some fishes—so large, in fact, that they form large lateral lobes, called *vagal lobes,* on the medulla. In these fishes, taste is quite important. Indeed, the taste buds are not limited to the tongue and mouth but are distributed liberally over most of the body surface. This distribution correlates with the large size of the bulbar centers for taste.

SUBCORTICAL PATHWAYS—From the solitary nucleus, fibers run forward in the brain in a tract called the *medial lemniscus.* It is easy to lose track of these fibers when purely anatomical methods are used, and it was thought for a long time that they terminated in some regions associated with the olfactory system. This theory, however, neglected the fact that taste is more closely allied with the skin senses than with smell, at least in embryological and evolutionary development. It is now known that this relationship is preserved in the higher centers of the brain and that taste pathways from the medulla terminate in the posteroventral nucleus of the thalamus (see page 43), the same nucleus concerned with the skin senses. The projections for taste then continue with those from the skin and the face and mouth to the cerebral cortex. There appears, however, to be some separation of taste and tactual functions in the posteroventral nucleus (Benjamin and Akert, 1959).

Even though it is known that the taste pathways end in the face somatic area of the cortex, it is difficult for some reason to obtain gross evoked potentials from that area when taste stimuli are applied to the tongue. Potentials may indeed be obtained on such stimulation, but control stimulation by tactile stimuli shows that they are of tactile origin (Patton and Amassian, 1952). On the other hand, fortunately, with very small microelectrodes embedded in the tongue-face somatic area, responses from individual units can be obtained. Some of the units respond only to taste stimuli and not to tactile or temperature stimuli. Other units respond to all three kinds of stimulation, showing convergence of activity on these units (cf. Somatic Senses, Chapter 9). Even the "pure" taste units, however, show some convergence for they tend to respond to all types of chemical stimulation and are far less specific in their response than the taste nerve fibers described previously (Cohen et al., 1957).

CORTICAL FUNCTIONS IN DISCRIMINATION—Before much of the above became known, the first important clue to the close identity of the somatic and taste cortical areas came from human clinical cases in which tumors or lesions of the areas caused some disturbance of taste sensation (Börnstein, 1940). Through such clues it was possible to draw the schematic diagram of Figure 5.7. It is now known that the taste area overlaps the masticatory area labeled in that figure as "chewing."

From this lead, other investigators proceeded to make experimental lesions and to test their effects on taste discrimination in the corresponding portion of the thalamus of monkeys (Patton et al., 1944). Monkeys, like human beings, do not like quinine and react to it as though it were bitter. Hence

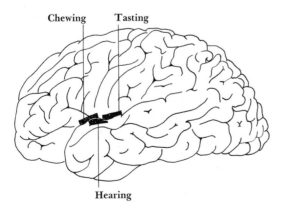

Chewing   Tasting

Hearing

FIGURE 5.7—The approximate position of the cortical area for taste and its relation to the areas for chewing and hearing. (Adapted from W. S. Börnstein. Cortical representation of taste in man and monkey. *Yale J. Biol. Med.*, 1940, 6, 732. By permission of Yale University Press.)

monkeys were presented, preoperatively, with containers of water with graded amounts of quinine in it (Patton and Ruch, 1944). By determining the concentration of quinine that they could "discriminate" just well enough to avoid, thresholds for bitter were determined. Two examples of such thresholds are shown in Figure 5.8. When the threshold determinations were complete, lesions were made in the posteroventral nucleus (see page 43) which projects to the cortical area concerned in sensations of the mouth and face. In the inset of Figure 5.8 one can see the place of such lesions in the thalamus. After operation, the thresholds were measured again. In Figure 5.8, at the extreme right, are data for one such case. The thresholds, as determined by this method, are considerably elevated by the thalamic lesions.

In the paragraph above, the word discriminate was put in quotes and a qualification was put on thresholds "determined by this method." It now appears that a distinction must be made between "discrimination" and "prefer-

FIGURE 5.8—Taste discrimination of quinine before and after injury to the facial portions of the posteroventral nucleus of the thalamus. For the meaning of the letters, see Figures 2.4 and 5.6 (Based on work of H. D. Patton, T. C. Ruch, and A. E. Walker. Experimental hypogeusia from Horsley-Clarke lesions of the thalamus in Macaca mulatta. *J. Neurophysiol.*, 1944, 7, 171–184. Courtesy of T. C. Ruch.)

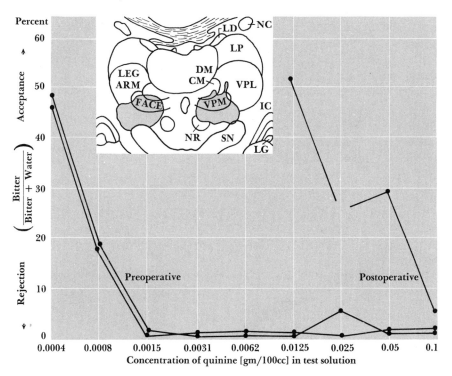

ence." In an experiment with rats, the taste area of the cortex was located by using evoked potentials in conjunction with electrical stimulation of the taste section of the VIIth as well as the IXth cranial nerve (Benjamin and Pfaffmann, 1955). This area was then ablated and preoperative and postoperative tests made of the rats' reactions to quinine. When tested postoperatively and ad libitum in a two-bottle preference situation these rats showed deficits in discrimination similar to those reported for monkeys (Benjamin, 1955a). However, if the rats were tested when very thirsty and compared with normal but also thirsty rats, they showed no difference from the normal rat (Benjamin, 1955b). Both were less discriminating.

In other experiments with monkeys, it has been shown that lesions limited to the face area of the somatic cortex do not produce taste deficits in preference tests (Patton and Ruch, 1946). To produce substantial deficits with cortical lesions, it is necessary to invade a relatively large area including not only the face area but some of the insular and anterior temporal cortex as well (Bagshaw and Pribram, 1953). This situation is comparable to that encountered in hearing (Chapter 8) and the somatic senses (Chapter 9). Only a lesion larger than the primary receiving area will cause significant deficits in ability to discriminate.

THALAMIC FUNCTIONS IN DISCRIMINATION—More clear-cut results are obtained if, instead of destroying cortex, lesions are made in the posteroventral nucleus of the thalamus from which fibers project to the cortex. Several experiments of this kind have been made (see Oakley and Pfaffmann, 1962). Discriminative ability was measured preoperatively and postoperatively with a two-bottle preference technique. The experiments agreed in finding that taste-preference thresholds are altered by lesions made in the thalamic relay nucleus. The rejection threshold for quinine is significantly elevated, and preferences for certain concentrations of sucrose and sodium chloride become less marked. The animals, however, are not completely ageusic. Hence it appears that information projected to the cortex is necessary for making the most acute discriminations, but some ability to discriminate remains after interruption of the projections and, presumably, is mediated at a subcortical level.

SMELL

Probably less is known about the sense of smell than about any other sense. In part, this is because it has received comparatively less attention from experimenters. In part, it is because smell has proved to be a difficult sense with which to work.

THEORIES OF RECEPTOR FUNCTION

As is often the case when a field yields very few facts or facts that make little sense, the field of smell is one that abounds with theories. There are literally dozens of theories designed in some way to account for the manner in which olfactory stimuli activate receptors and give rise to experience. In general, the theories divide into two different, but related, groups: those concerned with the qualities of experience and the theories of the mechanism of receptor stimulation. Since no theory is very satisfactory, we shall not present them in detail but only indicate generally what they are (see Crozier, 1934; Moncrieff, 1944; Adey, 1959).

QUALITIES OF EXPERIENCE—Psychophysicists have long assumed that there are a limited number of qualities of experience in each sense. In most senses, this is true, and there is fairly general agreement on what the primary qualities are. This is not so in olfaction. No classification of smells seems to fit all circumstances. One classification provides for nine basic smell qualities; another for six, and another for four. Each has its merits and its drawbacks, but none is generally acceptable.

STIMULUS PROPERTIES—Closely related to the problem of classification of odors is the question of how stimuli excite the olfactory receptors. Presumably there is some connection between the two. Substances of a given chemical structure should, in theory, give rise to a certain kind of experience. We found above that in taste such a relation is not very satisfactory in that modality. It is no better, if not worse, in smell.

We shall indicate briefly some of the theories that have been proposed. As one might expect, the preferred theory of stimulation has been chemical. It assumes that certain classes of compounds react with certain substances in the receptors to initiate impulses. Problems have developed, however, when there are frequently no apparent rules for the grouping of compounds according to their stimulating abilities. A recent variation of this theory is an enzyme theory (Kistiakowsky, 1950) in which it is proposed that odors somehow inhibit reactions that involve enzymatic catalysts (see page 86). In this theory, a substance would be odorous and have a particular quality because it changed the concentration of certain reaction products in the receptors. This theory, like most, has been criticized on several grounds (Adey, 1959).

Other theories assume some one aspect of olfactory stimuli to be critical in the activation of receptors: In vibrational theories, molecular structure and activity are considered important; the infrared theory holds that absorption of the invisible infrared rays is the significant property; another makes a similar assumption about ultraviolet absorption; and another theory considers an optical property of substances, the Raman shift, to be critical. The plain fact is that what happens is not known. Let us now look at the known anatomical and physiological facts of olfactory function.

OLFACTORY ORGAN

The olfactory receptors are tucked away in alcoves at the roof of the nasal cavities (see Figure 5.9). To reach the receptors, gases must make their way through the nostrils of the nose and be reflected upward to the olfactory region by the bones (conchae) projected into the cavities in Figure 5.9. Only a small part of the gases and air going into the nose ever reaches the olfactory receptors. This fact has been the bane of research workers in the field, and they have resorted to all sorts of contrivances to get olfactory stimuli to the receptors in known quantities.

Usually about 500 square millimeters in size, the olfactory epithelium (Figure 5.10) in man can be distinguished by the sharp, although irregular, boundary that it makes with the adjacent epithelium and by its typically yellowish or (in some animals) brownish color. It is composed of three types of cells: (1) the pigmented *columnar* cells, which are sandwiched between the olfactory cells and whose function is plainly one of support; (2) the *basal* cells, which are blocklike in form and are located on the innermost surface of the epithelium, thereby providing the groundwork to which the rest of the epithelium is attached; and (3) the more numerous *olfactory* cells proper. The outer portion of these olfactory neurons consists of fine filaments, or

FIGURE 5.9—The nasal cavity and olfactory structures. (Adapted from E. Gardner. *Fundamentals of neurology*. Philadelphia: Saunders, 1947. P. 204. By permission of the publishers.)

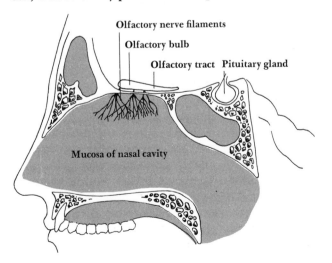

Olfactory nerve filaments

Olfactory bulb

Olfactory tract   Pituitary gland

Mucosa of nasal cavity

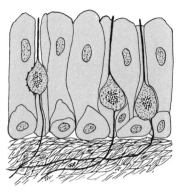

FIGURE 5.10—The olfactory epithelium, or membrane. At the bottom are basal cells. Standing upright are the supporting sustentacular (columnar) cells. The olfactory receptor cells are the oval ones with the lone hairs. (Adapted from H. L. Wieman. *General zoology.* New York: McGraw-Hill, 1925. P. 221. By permission of the publishers.)

"hairs"; the middle portion is the cell body; and the inner part tapers off into axons conducting excitation away from the epithelium. Passing upward through the bony *cribriform* plate, from which the epithelium hangs, these fibers end upon the second-order neurons of the olfactory bulb. This structure lies just above the cribriform plate.

The outer surface of the epithelium is bathed in a mucous fluid secreted by the epithelial cells of the nasal cavities. It seems quite probable that all gases must be soluble in this fluid to be able to excite olfactory receptors and that excitation takes place in the hairs of these receptors.

NEURAL CENTERS AND PATHWAYS

As was indicated above, axons from the olfactory epithelium pass through the cribriform plate to the olfactory bulb. This bulb, an extension of the brain, is itself rather complex. One of its chief features is the *glomeruli*, which are bushy networks of fibers going into the brain. Another feature of the bulb is its networks of reverberatory circuits. Axons from one neuron stimulate a second neuron, which in turn excites the first neuron. This reverberatory system, like similar systems elsewhere in the brain and spinal cord (see page 81), allows impulses to continue after a stimulus has ceased. It also provides a sort of amplifying system which probably increases the sensitivity of the organism to olfactory stimuli.

From the olfactory bulb, fibers pass toward the brain in the *olfactory tract*. From this point on, things become very complicated indeed. The primary olfactory cortex, as determined by electrical tracking of impulses in the system, probably consists of a frontal prepyriform area, a temporal prepyriform area, part of the amygdala, and, in some animals, the olfactory tubercle. All are structures on or near the ventral surface of the brain and are referred to as the ventral olfactory cortex. As shown in Figure 5.11, the region given over to primary olfactory function varies in different animals and is smaller in monkeys and man than in many lower animals.

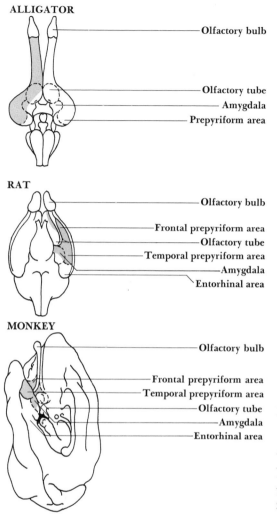

FIGURE 5.11—The comparative extent of primary olfactory cortex in alligator, rat, and monkey. (Adapted from A. C. Allison. Morphology of the olfactory system in vertebrates. *Biol. Rev.*, 1953, 28, 220.)

By electrophysiological methods it is possible to trace impulses originating in the olfactory bulb and tract to several other structures in the brain. One or more synapses are involved, and the routes are often circuitous. These structures are schematized in Figure 5.12. The principal ones to note there are the hippocampus, the fornix, and the septum, all of which were mentioned in Chapter 2. They will also be discussed more extensively later, in the chapter on emotion (Chapter 11). They are not regarded as being primarily olfactory in function but rather as structures whose activity is influenced by olfactory impulses.

ELECTROPHYSIOLOGICAL FUNCTIONS

There have been numerous studies of electrical activity in the olfactory system, beginning with the olfactory bulb and extending throughout the structures described above. Some have been instrumental in determining which structures are primary and which are secondary in the olfactory system. Few of them, however, appear to be especially significant for psychological problems.

One such study concerned unit activity in the olfactory bulb under different conditions of olfactory stimulation (Adrian, 1954). If stimulation is sufficiently intense, each unit appears to respond to almost any kind of stimulation. In this respect, units of the olfactory bulb appear to be like those of the taste nerve. However, when the stimulus intensity is near threshold, units respond to only one class of stimuli. By employing a number of different stimuli and grouping together those that, near threshold, excite a particular

FIGURE 5.12—Diagram of the relations of the olfactory cortex with other structures of the brain. (Adapted from W. R. Adey. In J. Field, H. W. Magoun, and V. E. Hall (Eds.), *Handbook of physiology*, vol. 1. Washington, D.C.: American Physiological Society, 1959. P. 546.)

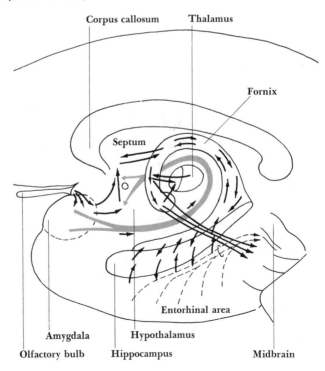

unit, substances have been grouped into four classes: (*1*) acetones, including amyl and ethyl acetate; (*2*) aromatic hydrocarbons, e.g., benzene; (*3*) paraffin hydrocarbons and heavy oils, e.g., octane; and (*4*) terpenes and related compounds such as dipentane, cedarwood oil, and eucalyptus oil. Work of this sort should be repeated and extended before it can be determined if there is any basis for deciding whether four fundamental qualities of smell have been discovered in this way.

BEHAVIORAL MEASURES

There are relatively few experiments in which olfactory sensitivity and discrimination have been studied in relation to the function of different parts of the brain. Two techniques have been used: conditioning and discrimination. Two animals have been used as subjects: rats and dogs. Rats were used in discrimination experiments; dogs, in conditioning experiments.

DISCRIMINATION STUDIES—In early experiments with rats (Swann, 1934), lesions were made in various structures then thought to be part of the olfactory system and still known to be connected with it. These included the septum, the hippocampus, the fornix, the amygdala, and the pyriform lobe (see Figures 5.11 and 5.12). The rats had previously been trained to discriminate between wood shavings scented with anise and wood shavings scented with creosote. The lesions had no effect on the discrimination.

In another experiment (Brown and Ghiselli, 1938), a variety of subcortical lesions were made, mostly in the thalamus, in rats that had been trained on an olfactory discrimination. No impairment resulted. In a related experiment, the radiations from the anterior group of thalamic nuclei suspected of being concerned in olfactory functions were severed in the rat (Lashley and Sperry, 1943). Again, no deficit in discrimination followed. Such experiments have fairly well ruled out the limbic, thalamic, and neocortical areas as important in olfaction.

CONDITIONING STUDIES

Conditioning experiments with dogs have dealt with the pyriform area, the amygdala, and the hippocampus. Dogs were conditioned to raise their foreleg in response to certain stimuli and not to raise it in response to other stimuli. Thus a conditioned discrimination was set up. Combined lesions in the pyriform and the amygdala abolished the discrimination to the extent that the dogs now reacted to all stimuli by raising the foreleg (Allen, 1941). However, neither this lesion nor a lesion of the hippocampus, made either separately or in combination with the other, had any effect on the basic conditioned response (Allen, 1940).

6 THE VISUAL SYSTEM

O F ALL THE SENSES, vision has been the most thoroughly studied. Not only are its centers and pathways well known, but its neurons and synaptic connections have been described in accurate detail. In addition, modern physiological methods, particularly those of electrical recording, have provided much information about the physiological events taking place in the visual system. Moreover, ability to control various aspects of visual stimulation has permitted gathering a vast body of strictly quantitative information concerning visual perception. Then, finally, the method of extirpation of parts of the brain, used in animals, has provided in several instances direct means of discovering the centers of the nervous system concerned in visual perception.

To summarize the knowledge of the physiological mechanisms of vision requires two chapters. The present chapter will be devoted primarily to the anatomy and physiology of the visual system, although we shall occasionally refer to the facts of visual perception in order to point out the relevance of some of the material treated. The following chapter will deal with the physiological mechanisms of visual sensation and perception.

THE EYE

The chief feature of the anatomy of the eye is that it is so constructed as to be able to perform the functions of a camera (see Figure 6.1). Inside the eye is its photosensitive plate, the *retina*, and protecting this plate from stray light is a pigmented *choroid* coat of tissue, which surrounds the eye except in front, where the transparent *cornea* admits light. Such light must pass, as must the light entering a camera, through a small aperture, the *pupil*, and then through a *lens*, which by means of its curved surfaces so bends light that it is brought to a focus on the photosensitive retina. Unlike the arrangement in a camera, however, is the fact that the light, in its course from the cornea to the retina, passes through a semifluid, but transparent, *humor*. The eye, moreover, is more adaptable than a camera, for muscular regulation of the size of the pupil and the curvature of the lens controls the amount of

FIGURE 6.1—A diagram of the eye. (Adapted from **H. C. Warren and L. Carmichael.** *Elements of human psychology.* **Boston: Houghton Mifflin, 1930. P. 80. By permission of the publishers.)**

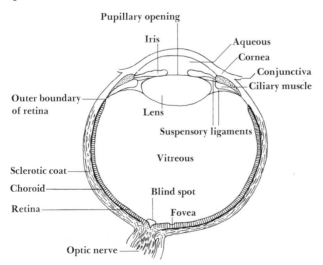

Pupillary opening

Iris

Aqueous

Cornea

Conjunctiva

Ciliary muscle

Outer boundary of retina

Lens

Suspensory ligaments

Vitreous

Sclerotic coat

Choroid

Blind spot

Retina

Fovea

Optic nerve

light admitted to the eye and the clearness of the retinal image, whether the object it views is near or far.

RETINAL LAYERS

There will be more discussion later about the effect of light in the eye, but the structure of the retina may be considered first (Figure 6.2). It is made up of supporting cells and of neurons, but only the neurons are of importance to us. There are three main groups of neurons, arranged in three layers. The first group is a row of primary receptive neurons, the sense cells, facing toward the outside of the eyeball; their receptive portions have taken the highly specialized forms of *rods* and *cones* in which are contained the chemical materials responsive to light. Making synapse with such sensory neurons are the *bipolar* neurons of the second layer, and these bring impulses to neurons of the third group, the *ganglion* cells. The axons of these cells extend

FIGURE 6.2—Diagram of the cellular relations in the retina. Numbers refer to layers of the retina. (Adapted from J. F. Fulton (Ed.). *A textbook of physiology.* 16th ed. Philadelphia: Saunders, 1949. P. 438. By permission of the publishers.)

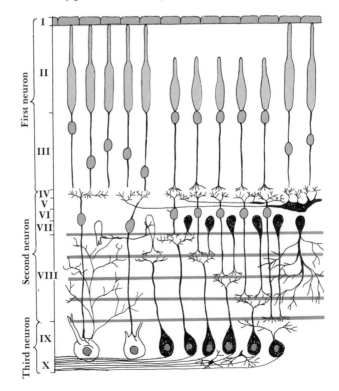

over the inner surface of the retina and are collected at one point, the *blind spot*, somewhat medial to the center of the retina, where they leave the eyeball and proceed as the optic nerve to the visual centers of the thalamus and midbrain. Thus the visual organ is made up, essentially, of photoreceptor neurons, intervening bipolar cells, and ganglion cells, with the latter transmitting messages directly to the brain.

LATERAL NEURONS—Knowledge of other details of retinal structure is also necessary for understanding visual functions. The retina, we have noted before, is an outgrowth of the brain, and a careful study of its structure has shown that it fully demonstrates this kinship (Polyak, 1941). All the cells of the retina, described above, are true neurons, and their various synaptic connections appear to be as complex as many in the brain. First of all, the bipolar cells often collect from several rods and cones, and these also impinge upon a number of bipolar cells; thus neural effects arising in the rods and cones both diverge and converge in their transmission from receptor cells to ganglion cells. There are, moreover, at least two types of "association" cells that serve further to interconnect the activity of receptor cells: *Horizontal* cells pick up from some receptor cells and deliver to others; and in the inner part of the retina *amacrine* cells spread effects aroused by bipolar cells to several ganglion cells or, in some instances, return excitation from bipolar elements to the receptors. The functional system set up by these various interconnections, as the reader can see, permits all sorts of mutual influences between various layers and adjacent parts of the retina. In this respect, the retina appears to be very much like the brain.

RODS AND CONES—Going on to other details of the retina, we may note that the rods and cones constitute two types of receptor cells. Their connections with bipolar and horizontal cells, however, clearly indicate that they do not form two distinct systems, as has frequently been assumed (Polyak, 1941). Bipolar cells often collect from both rods and cones, and so also do horizontal cells (see Figure 6.2). It may be expected, therefore, that the activities of rods and cones will be intimately related in visual functions.

Although in many vertebrate eyes the difference between rods and cones is quite clear, this is not always the case. There is, in fact, considerable variation in the structure of rods and cones in the eyes of man and other vertebrates. In Figure 6.3, for example, are drawings of the photoreceptors of four different vertebrate animals. The photoreceptors of the frog divide themselves fairly well into cones and rods. They resemble their names, the cones being short and pointed and the rods being long and cylindrical. The rods and cones of the house sparrow again seem to be fairly well distinguished, but the cones look a little more like rods, and one kind of rod (3) comes fairly close to looking like a cone. In the receptors of man, the situation becomes even less clear. To be sure, there are many cones from the various regions of the

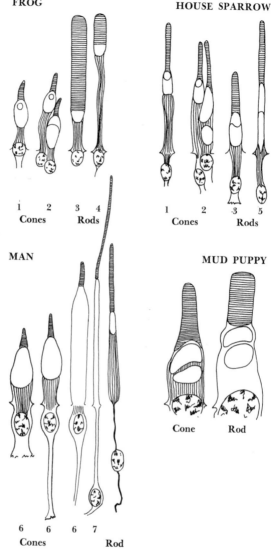

FIGURE 6.3—Drawings of rods and cones found in the eyes of different vertebrates. (Based on the work of L. B. Arey and G. L. Walls. Adapted from E. N. Willmer. *Retinal structure and colour vision.* New York: Cambridge, 1946. P. 2. By permission of the publishers.)

peripheral retina (6) that look like cones, and the rod looks like a rod. But the "cone" found in the *fovea centralis,* the all-cone area of the fovea (7), outdoes the rods in being long, cylindrical, and rodlike. Another comparison of rod and cone is given for the mud puppy (an amphibian). Here the so-called rods very much resemble cones, although they can still be distinguished.

These are just examples of what one encounters in the retinas of various vertebrates. Histologists (Walls, 1942; Willmer, 1946) who have carefully studied these retinas conclude that the differentiation between rods and cones is by no means clear-cut and that each may have the properties, or take on the properties, of the other. It even seems possible that certain eyes, e.g., that of the lizard (gecko), which seem to have all rods, actually are cone eyes in which the cones have come to look like rods (see Walls, 1942). In the human retina, too, as we have just pointed out, there is a region in the fovea centralis that resembles rods but behaves like cones.

DUPLICITY THEORY

The reason for stressing the problem of distinguishing rods and cones is that such a distinction is a basic point in the duplicity theory. This theory, put forth at the end of the nineteenth century by von Kries and now widely accepted, assumes that there are two types of receptors making up two systems in vision, each with its own properties. The rods are assumed to function in night vision at low illuminations; they are much more sensitive than the cones and are used when there is little light. The cones are regarded as daylight receptors, operating when illumination is high. The cones see color; the rods, only shades of black and white. The rods are most sensitive in the greenish part of the spectrum; the cones are most sensitive in the yellowish part. The cones are most numerous in the central part of the eye, their connections with the neurons of the visual system are more point-to-point, and the cones thus are most involved in space perception and visual acuity. The rods, on the other hand, are more numerous in the periphery of the eye, great numbers of them converging on a small number of ganglion cells of the retina, and the rods thus are specialized, not for spatial vision but for intensity vision and for sensitivity to very weak stimuli.

All these statements are part of the general statement of the duplicity theory. All of them are to some extent true, but there are enough exceptions to some of them to make one doubt that the duplicity theory in this simple, straightforward form is true. Some of the exceptions will be cited in this and the next chapter.

VISUAL STIMULUS

Although the stimulus for vision, light, can be regarded as corpuscles, or quanta, it is usually more useful to think of it as vibratory energy. All the various kinds of light, moreover, may be specified in terms of two variables: the amplitude of the vibration, or the *intensity*, and the frequency of vibrations or its inverse, *wavelength*, derived by dividing the speed of light by its frequency. Most light stimulating the eye does not, of course, consist of a single wavelength but of many. The light, however, can always be specified, if the appropriate equipment for analysis is available, in terms of the intensity and wavelength of the respective components, which together make up the *composition* of the light.

The unit commonly employed for the designation of wavelength is the millimicron. A micron is one millionth of a meter; it is the unit used throughout this and the next chapter. Generally speaking, the vertebrate eye is sensitive to wavelengths between 380 and 760 millimicrons. At extremely high intensities, however, the visible spectrum widens, and there is also some variation among different species. At the short end of the spectrum, the blue end, the lens and optic media are limiting factors in sensitivity for they filter out much of the blue light.

THE MEASUREMENT OF LIGHT—Scales that are practical for the measurement of light are based upon an arbitrary unit, the *international candle,* which is approximately equivalent to the total amount of light emitted by an ordinary candle having a flame about 1 inch in height. One is usually interested, however, not in the total intensity emitted by a light source but in the amount of light falling upon an object. That is *illumination,* and the unit of it is the *footcandle:* the light falling upon 1 square foot of area placed at a 1 foot distance from an international candle. Sometimes, however, it would be preferable to know how much light is reflected by an object. This is *luminance,* and one of the most commonly used units of luminance is the *millilambert:* the light reflected by a perfectly diffusing and reflecting surface 1 foot square and illuminated by 0.93 *footcandle.* Much of the time it is permissible to state the comparative amount of light entering the eye in terms of the luminance of the object viewed. Retinal illumination depends upon the size of the pupil through which light enters the eye, and this in turn depends upon retinal illumination, because the regulation of the size of the pupil is a reflex affair.

THE RETINAL IMAGE—The eye, we have seen, functions like a camera and is so constructed that an image of external objects is formed on the retina. The retinal image, moreover, is kept in focus when objects are far or near, bright or dim, a feat that is accomplished by two mechanisms, the pupil and the lens. As in a camera, so in the eye: the narrower the aperture, the sharper the focus of the retinal image. The focus, accordingly, is best when the illumination is high and the pupil contracted as a result. To adjust the image for best focus according to the distance of the viewed object, it is necessary that the curvature of the lens be changed.

Even with these devices for adjusting the focus of the retinal image, it is by no means so nearly perfect as it might be. There are at least three principal ways in which an otherwise well-focused image will be blurred by the scattering of light (Figure 6.4). (*1*) The internal media of the eye diffract light, even as moisture in the air distorts and makes the appearance of objects hazy. (*2*) The retina and internal surface of the eye are light in color and can reflect light to other parts of the eyeball. (*3*) Some light can penetrate into the eye through its walls. Consequently, there is always a good deal of

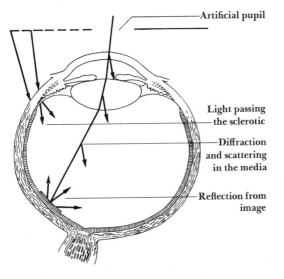

Artificial pupil

Light passing
the sclerotic

Diffraction
and scattering
in the media

Reflection from
image

FIGURE 6.4—Points in the eye
from which light may scatter.
(Adapted from S. H. Bartley.
Vision. Princeton, N.J.: Van
Nostrand, 1941. P. 58. By per-
mission of the publishers.)

stray light in the eye, which affects unfavorably the clearness of the retinal
image. In some cases the "unilluminated" part of the retina may be about
3 percent as bright as the bright part of the image (Bartley, 1941).

PHYSIOLOGY OF THE RETINA

Why does light striking the eye give rise to a visual sensation? Why do we
see light? The most general answer is that nerve impulses are excited in the
retina and these travel to the brain, just as all sense organs initiate impulses
that act as messages or signals. In addition, however, between the moment a
stimulus impinges on a receptor and the initiation of nerve impulses, there is
usually one or more intervening events. In vision, one of these is a photochemical event. Besides that, there are several kinds of electrical events that
can be measured. In this section, we shall consider first the photochemistry
of the retina and then several aspects of the electrical activity of the retina.

PHOTOCHEMISTRY

The fact that a photosensitive pigment is involved in vision was first discovered by Franz Boll in 1876. He noticed that the dark-adapted eye of the
frog had a reddish-purple color but that when the eye was exposed to light
the pigment bleached to a yellowish color. For that reason, the photosensitive
substance was first called "visual purple," and the substance it became after
exposure to light was called "visual yellow." Nowadays, as will be seen, there
are different, more technical names for these substances.

Today, it is known, largely through the research of Wald (1959) and his collaborators, that in one species of animal or another there are four different photosensitive pigments. Two are found in the rods; two in the cones. The substances are very similar, each being a slight chemical variant of the other. Different substances occur in different species of animals, depending upon whether they live on land or in water, whether they are predominantly nocturnal animals with rod eyes or diurnal animals with cone eyes, or whether they have mixed eyes as many animals do. All the substances, however, behave in essentially the same way. For that reason, we can take one substance as a model. This will be the one originally discovered by Boll as "visual purple" and now called rhodopsin. After discussing it at length, we can show briefly how the other substances differ from it.

RHODOPSIN AND PORPHYROPSIN—The most thoroughly investigated substance, *rhodopsin*, is found in the rods of most vertebrate animals. When struck by light, it breaks down into *retinene* and *opsin* (see Figure 6.5). Actually, there are three steps between rhodopsin and these products, all ordinarily taking place extremely rapidly in the retina. The very first step depends only on light, for light supplies the energy for the breakdown.

The second step depends on temperature; it will not take place at temperatures below $-20°C$. The third one involves water and takes place only if the preparation is wet. These facts have been determined by exposing rhodopsin in a test tube or on "film strips" outside the eye. Although the intervening steps are of interest to biochemists, it is the breakdown to retinene and opsin that is important in understanding normal visual sensitivity.

Retinene in the eye does not remain very long as retinene. Either it joins spontaneously and rapidly with opsin to re-form rhodopsin or it is converted to vitamin A. The first is always occurring, and if the light decomposing rhodopsin is either not very intense or not very prolonged, it is the principal reaction. However, under continuous, intense exposure to light that produces a considerable amount of retinene, the second reaction occurs. Retinene is an aldehyde of vitamin A, which is a complex alcohol. The conversion of retinene to vitamin A is a reduction reaction in which hydrogen is taken on by the molecule.

The conversion of vitamin A and opsin to retinene is a reverse process—an oxidative reaction requiring energy. (Oxidation in chemistry may be either the addition of oxygen or the removal of hydrogen. In most biochemical reactions, it is usually the latter.) Because the spontaneous formation of rhodopsin from retinene and opsin is energy-yielding, this energy is available to convert vitamin A and opsin back to retinene so long as there is some opsin available to trap the vitamin A. Thus, in the dark, all the retinene is converted to rhodopsin either directly or after being first converted to vitamin A. In the light, an equilibrium is set up in which, depending on the intensity of

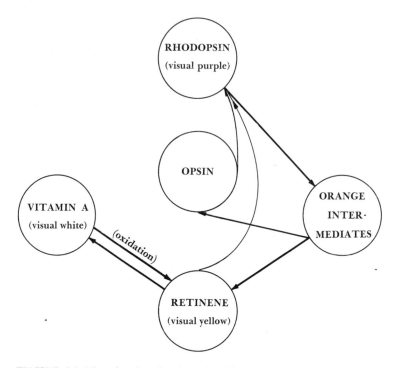

FIGURE 6.5—The visual cycle through which rhodopsin is broken down by light and resynthesized. (Adapted from G. Wald. In J. Field, H. W. Magoun, and V. E. Hall (Eds.), *Handbook of physiology,* vol. 1. Washington, D.C.: American Physiological Society, 1959. P. 679.)

light and hence on the rate of decomposition of rhodopsin, two cycles go on simultaneously:

$$\left\{ \begin{array}{l} \text{Rhodopsin} \xrightleftharpoons{\text{light}} \text{retinene + opsin} \\ \text{Retinene + opsin} \underset{+O_2}{\overset{+H^+}{\rightleftarrows}} \text{vitamin A + opsin} \end{array} \right\}$$

Enzymes are involved in the second reaction but not in the first.

Porphyropsin differs from rhodopsin in only one respect: It contains a slightly different vitamin A. In porphyropsin, the vitamin A contains an additional double bond in its carbon ring as compared with the vitamin A in rhodopsin. To denote this difference, the vitamin A and retinene in rhodopsin are called vitamin A_1 and retinene$_1$, whereas those in porphyropsin are called vitamin A_2 and retinene$_2$.

IODOPSIN AND CYANOPSIN—In mixed eyes containing both rods and cones, the rods usually outnumber the cones by a very considerable margin. For that reason, rhodopsin (or porphyropsin) is the photosensitive pigment present in greatest concentration and most easily extracted. To obtain the photosensitive pigment of the cones requires that one use an eye that is made up primarily of cones. Even then, fairly involved procedures are required. Such a substance has been obtained from the chicken retina and called iodopsin. It is presumed, for reasons that will develop, that a similar substance is the photosensitive material in the cones of man. Iodopsin is very probably a mixture of substances, or it is accompanied by other similar substances. Otherwise there is difficulty explaining human color vision. In any case, it is identifiably different from rhodopsin.

The two are different in two ways: First of all, iodopsin resynthesizes from its retinene and opsin, after decomposition by light, at a much more rapid rate than rhodopsin resynthesizes. When the two substances are allowed to resynthesize in extracts in the dark, iodopsin is almost completely resynthesized when only a small percentage of rhodopsin has been re-formed. Secondly, the spectral-absorption curves of the two substances are different. This will be explained in the next section.

It has been learned by appropriate experiments that these two differences are to be accounted for by the protein portion of the molecule, the opsin. Rhodopsin and iodopsin share exactly the same retinene and hence, after reduction, the same vitamin. It is the opsins that are different. The opsin in rhodopsin is called a scotopsin and that in iodopsin a photopsin. Scotopsins are found in rods; photopsins in cones.

The three substances discussed so far—rhodopsin, porphyropsin, and iodopsin—were all first discovered by preparing extracts of retinas. When it became clear that the difference between the two scotopsins is in the vitamin A or retinene portion of the molecule and that the difference between scotopsin and photopsin is in the opsin portion, it could be deduced that there ought to be a fourth substance incorporating the $retinene_2$ of the porphyropsin system and the cone opsin (photopsin) of the iodopsin system. To check this deduction, the appropriate materials were mixed in the laboratory, and, as predicted, a fourth pigment was synthesized. This was called cyanopsin. Since this substance consists of photopsin and $retinene_2$, it was logical to look for it in the cones of fresh-water animals known to possess vitamin A_2. By measurement of the spectral absorption of such cones (described below), it was established that the cones of these animals do indeed contain cyanopsin.

SPECTRAL ABSORPTION—All chemical substances absorb light in varying degrees in different parts of the spectrum. To measure such absorption, it is customary to pass lights of relatively pure wavelengths through a solution of the substance and to measure the percentage of light absorbed. When this is done repeatedly throughout the spectrum from ultraviolet to infrared light, a curve can be drawn showing the spectral absorption of the substance.

In the case of photosensitive materials, this same principle of measurement can be used, but in a slightly different and simpler way. In this case, the interest is in the photosensitivity of the material and hence in the degree to which different wavelengths of light cause the material to decompose. To measure this, the amount of decomposition of materials is compared. The curve constructed in this way is comparable to the spectral-absorption curve, only in this case it may be called the *spectral sensitivity* of the substance.

In biochemistry and indeed in many fields of chemistry, spectral-absorption curves prove exceedingly useful as means of identifying otherwise unknown substances. Each substance has its own characteristic curve of absorption or of spectral sensitivity. In particular, the wavelength of greatest (or peak) sensitivity usually serves as a unique characteristic identifying the substance.

In Figure 6.6 are the spectral sensitivities (within the visible spectrum) for the four photosensitive pigments described above. It will be seen that the peak of sensitivity for rhodopsin is about 500 millimicrons; that for iodopsin, about 560 millimicrons. For the substances found in fresh-water animals, the peak of porphyropsin is about 520 millimicrons; for cyanopsin, it is about 610 millimicrons.

To interpret a spectral-sensitivity curve, one must be careful to know and understand the physical conditions under which it is measured. Factors other than the sensitivity of the chemical substance may enter into, and modify, the final result. For example, the lens and optic media of the eye strongly absorb light in the blue region of the spectrum. Hence, any measurement of spectral sensitivity made in the intact human eye with these "filters" in place reflects this absorption as well as the sensitivity of photosensitive materials. Similarly, pigments of the retina in the neighborhood of the photoreceptors may selectively absorb or reflect light, thus modifying any measured spectral sensitivity. To equate sensitivities measured under different conditions, or to interpret sensitivity curves measured where modifying conditions are present, one must make an appropriate correction for the characteristics of the measuring conditions. This point will arise later when we discuss the relation of spectral-sensitivity curves and the measured properties of human and animal vision.

ELECTRORETINOGRAM

We turn now to the electrical events that can be measured in the retina. These are of four kinds. First, and of little interest to us here, is a resting *corneoretinal potential*. This is a potential that can be measured between the front and the back of the eye and is generated somewhere in the retina, probably across the choroid membrane. This potential is employed chiefly to record eye movements, for as the eyes move, the axis of this potential moves; this can be measured if electrodes are affixed to a point to the side of the eyes, usually at the edge of the eye socket. Secondly, there is a phasic change of potential that occurs when the eye is illuminated by light; this is the *electroretinogram*. Thirdly, there are *nerve impulses*—unit responses—that can be

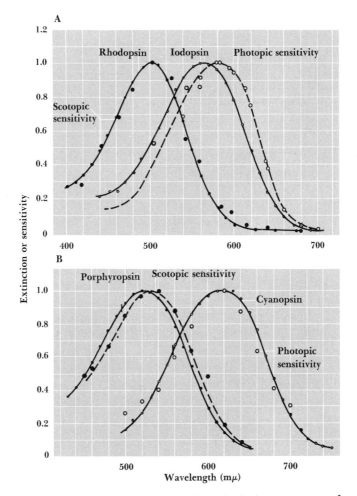

FIGURE 6.6—Absorption spectra of four visual pigments compared with scotopic and photopic sensitivity. (A) Chicken visual pigment versus pigeon retinal sensitivity. (Adapted from G. Wald, P. K. Brown, and P. H. Smith. *J. gen. Physiol.*, 1955, 38, 675. By permission of The Rockefeller Institute Press.) (B) Porphyropsin, cyanopsin, and spectral sensitivity of the tench. (Adapted from G. Wald. In J. Field, H. W. Magoun, and V. E. Hall (Eds.), *Handbook of physiology*, vol. 1. Washington, D.C.: American Physiological Society, 1959. P. 684.)

recorded from ganglion cells or their fibers in the optic nerve. Finally, there are direct current or *graded potentials* that can be recorded from electrodes appropriately placed in the layers of the retina. These last three will be discussed here in some detail.

The electroretinogram, abbreviated ERG, is best recorded by placing one electrode upon the cornea and another at the back of the eye. From such electrode placements, one picks up the overall electrical changes that occur in the retina when it is stimulated by light. The typical course of the ERG is shown in Figure 6.7. It consists of four phases (see Granit, 1959): First, when the light is flashed on there is a slight negative electrical change, the A wave. Secondly, this is followed shortly by a substantial positive change (B wave), and then thirdly, by a smaller and longer-persisting positive wave, the C wave. If now, fourthly, the light is turned off, there is a slight positive hump, the D wave, and then a slow return to normal resting state.

These are the typical electrical effects seen in visual stimulation. They vary considerably, however, with the intensity and duration of the stimulus. With weak light, the A wave may be weak or not seen at all, and with very short flashes none but the A and B waves may be seen. Both the latency and height of the B wave, on the other hand, vary with the intensity of light, and this fact has been employed to measure the effectiveness of visual stimulation.

ANALYSIS OF THE ERG—The ERG, everyone agrees, is the composite of several different electrical effects, although exactly how it is made up is not certain. The analysis that has been fairly well accepted for some years is that suggested by Granit (1947) and shown in Figure 6.7. The initial A and B waves are regarded as relatively rapid and opposing processes made up largely of the components PIII and PII, respectively. A sluggish component, PI, is a large part of the C wave, although PI and PIII are also included. The hump identified as the D wave, in this system, is analyzed as mainly an off effect of

FIGURE 6.7—The electroretinogram (ERG) and its analysis into components. (A) first negative wave; (B) first positive wave; (C) slow positive wave; and (D) positive wave when stimulus goes off. The three components, PI, PII, and PIII, are presumed to account for the shape of the ERG. (Adapted from S. H. Bartley. Some factors in brightness discrimination. *Psychol. Rev.,* 1939, 46, 347.)

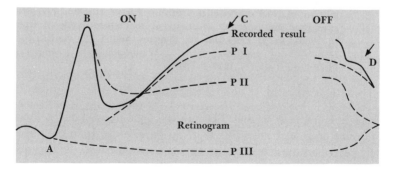

the B wave. Other investigators (Johnson, 1958) suggest that the D wave is a mirror image of the A wave.

Of the four waves labeled in Figure 6.7, the first two, the A and B waves, have received the greatest attention in research. The B wave has been used more than any other as an index of visual sensitivity, but the A wave in recent years has received increasing attention.

It is now quite clear that each A and B wave is not a single wave but rather two waves (Johnson, 1958). Each has an early component identified with photopic receptors (cones) and a somewhat slower wave associated with scotopic receptors (rods). Since the rods are considerably more sensitive than the cones, when allowed to adapt in the dark, scotopic components are prominent in the dark-adapted eye. In fact, at levels of stimulation well below those required to activate cones, the scotopic components are the only ones appearing in the record. Conversely, at high levels of illumination, when a flash of light is superimposed on an otherwise well-illuminated eye, the scotopic component becomes very small and the A and B waves that can be seen are those connected with the photopic receptors.

There are two or three different ways of demonstrating separate photopic and scotopic components of the A and B waves, but we shall not discuss them here (see Johnson, 1958). The method of most interest to us is one in which they are employed as a measure of spectral sensitivity. It is similar to the method of determining the spectral sensitivities of photochemical substances, except in this case the A or B wave, rather than spectral absorption, is the measure of sensitivity. Usually a given voltage of, say, 25, 50, or 100 microvolts is arbitrarily taken as a threshold; then the intensity of a light of a given wavelength required to produce this voltage is determined.

SPECTRAL SENSITIVITY—If the spectral sensitivity of the human eye or of other mixed rod-and-cone eyes is measured in this way, sensitivity curves corresponding to photopic or scotopic systems may be obtained, depending on whether the measurements are made at high or at low levels of illumination. Moreover, the peaks of the curves obtained in this way correspond fairly well with those secured photochemically from the rhodopsin and iodopsin systems. However, there is usually a discrepancy in the blue end of the spectrum. Here the curve as obtained from the ERG is higher, that is, indicates better sensitivity, than that obtained for rhodopsin or iodopsin. The difference, it is now generally believed (Riggs, 1958), is related to the scattering of blue light. The ERG is a composite response of the whole retina, not just one region. If a light is focused on one region, there still is considerable light scattered around and stimulating other parts of the retina. The optic media are so constituted that they scatter blue light more than red light or lights of longer wavelength. Hence, more of the retina is stimulated. This explanation is bolstered by the fact that one can obtain a very nice ERG when a stimulus is applied to the blind spot (Boynton and Riggs, 1951; Asher, 1951). In this case, the entire ERG must arise from the scattering of stimulus light since the blind spot is insensitive to stimuli.

GANGLION–CELL RESPONSES

The ERG is an overall response of the retina. By appropriate recording techniques, one can look at the "fine grain" of retinal processes. One way of doing this is to place very small electrodes, capable of reflecting the activity of individual cells, on either ganglion cells or fibers of the optic nerve. Whichever is the site of recording, the responses of ganglion cells may be recorded.

Over a period of years, the Swedish physiologist Granit (1959) has studied the responses of ganglion cells in a great many different eyes. When he first began, it was not clear just what cells were under his electrodes, for he simply inserted his electrode into the retina and recorded from electrode positions that gave him nerve impulses when the eye was stimulated by light. It now seems clear, however, that all his records are from ganglion cells, for neither the receptor cells nor the bipolars appear to produce nervous impulses (see below).

Granit's principal interest was in determining the spectral sensitivity of the units from which he was recording. To do this, once his electrode was placed on an active unit, he simply flashed a light of a particular wavelength and recorded the number of impulses the flash set off in the unit. By varying the intensity of the light, he could find some small number of impulses, for example, four, that could easily be counted. The intensity of light that produced this number of impulses was then regarded as the absolute threshold of the unit. In the use of this method, the number of impulses counted is not important so long as it is kept the same throughout any given set of measurements. By varying the wavelength of the light flash and obtaining a threshold at each wavelength, Granit could obtain curves of spectral sensitivity comparable (*1*) to the spectral-sensitivity curves of photochemical substances, (*2*) to the curves obtained with the ERG, or (*3*) to the visibility curves of the human eye, which we shall discuss in the next chapter.

In employing this method, the experimenter, having measured the spectral sensitivity of one unit, can move the position of his electrode and record from another unit. In this way, he can explore the retina and measure the spectral sensitivity of a large sample of units in one eye. If the retina contains units of different spectral sensitivities, he should find that some units give one curve and other units give other curves. The eyes of many different animals have been studied in this way.

What were the results? Generally speaking, two kinds of units have been found. *Dominators* and *modulators* are the names Granit gave to them. Dominators are units with broad spectral sensitivity. Although they have peaks of sensitivity, they respond in some degree to much of the visible spectrum. Modulators are units with narrow spectral sensitivity; they respond only in a restricted part of the visible spectrum.

DOMINATORS—Many of Granit's measurements were made before the existence of the four types of photosensitive materials had been discovered. In fact, at the beginning of his work, only the rhodopsin system was known, although the iodopsin system was strongly suspected on the basis of studies of human photopic vision.

Now that the evidence is relatively complete from both photochemical and electrophysiological fields of research, the agreement between the two is rather good. The dominators Granit found in one eye or another correspond fairly well with Wald's four photosensitive materials. In the typical vertebrate eye, Granit found two dominators, one with a peak of sensitivity around 500, which he called the scotopic dominator, and the other around 560, the photopic dominator. These dominators, as can be seen in Figure 6.8 (Wald et al., 1955), agree acceptably well with the curves of spectral sensitivity measured by Wald for rhodopsin and iodopsin, respectively.

Similarly, curves of scotopic and photopic dominators secured from the eye of the fresh-water fish tench agree fairly well with Wald's spectral-sensitivity curves for porphyropsin and cyanopsin. The correspondence for the photopic curve and cyanopsin is quite good, while there is a discrepancy of about 10 microns for the scotopic curve and porphyropsin. There are, however, many factors, including the kind of solution a photosensitive pigment is in (Wald and Brown, 1956), that can account for minor discrepancies. The correspondence is close enough to indicate that the dominators measured electrophysiologically correspond to the photochemical substances studied in test tubes.

MODULATORS—Modulators are units whose sensitivity lies in a narrow spectral band, as shown in Figure 6.9. A modulator can be named and distinguished according to the wavelength at which it has its peak of sensitivity. Distinguished in this way, many different modulators have been found, if one con-

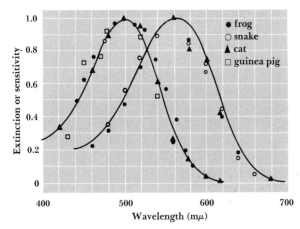

FIGURE 6.8—The absorption spectra of rhodopsin and iodopsin compared with those of dominator elements. (Adapted from G. Wald, P. K. Brown, and P. H. Smith. Synthesis and bleaching of rhodopsin. *J. gen. Physiol.*, 1955, 38, 676. By permission of The Rockefeller Institute Press.)

siders the dozens of animals that have been studied. Usually, however, no more than three or four different ones are found in any one eye, and often there is only one or two. This is to be expected in view of the fact that color vision apparently varies widely in animals. Some have none at all; some have a little and are comparable to a partially color-blind person.

Several animals have mixed eyes like man, although the relative number of rods and cones and their distribution in the retina vary. One mixed eye, in which dominators have been studied and which may be like man's eye, is the eye of the frog. Modulators distinguished in this eye are shown in Figure 6.9. Altogether there are four. A "blue" modulator has a peak at around 475 millimicrons. Then there is a "green" unit peaked at about 530 millimicrons. And close together are two modulators, a "yellow" one at about 580 millimicrons and a "red" one at about 600 millimicrons.

Because of the experimental error inherent in all measurements, one cannot say with certainty that the "yellow" unit at 580 is truly different from the "red" one at 600. The assumption that the two are different, however, fits in with other facts about human color vision, which we shall discuss in the next

FIGURE 6.9—Spectral sensitivity of the modulators found in the mixed eye of the frog. (A) Separate modulators; (B) coupled modulators. (Adapted from F. Granit. Color receptors of the frog's retina. *Acta Physiol. Scand.*, 1941, 3, 137–151.)

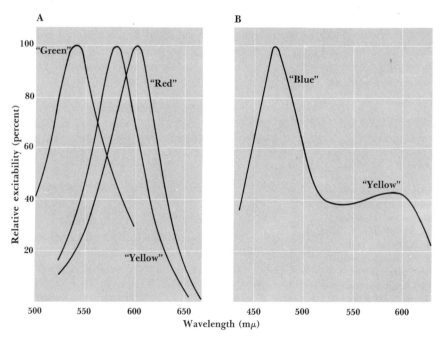

chapter. The "blue," "green," and "red" receptors appear quite regularly in experiments with many different eyes.

COUPLING—The curves shown on the left of Figure 6.9 have been selected from many that are available to represent units having a single peak. One of the interesting things, however, about experiments of this sort is that "coupled" units occur rather frequently. That is to say, many units show two or more peaks, as though they represented the coupling of two or more different receptors. One example is given on the right of Figure 6.9. This is not unexpected since, except for the fovea of man, more than one receptor is frequently connected via bipolar cells to a given ganglion cell, and records of the sort we have been discussing undoubtedly come from ganglion cells.

The coupling of receptors to ganglion cells, as seen in these experiments, may be of many different sorts. Sometimes, as in the eye of the rat, which is predominantly a rod eye, a "red" receptor is coupled with a scotopic dominator. The same kind of coupling is seen in the guinea pig (rod?) eye. In addition, in this eye a "blue" receptor is usually coupled with a "green" one. In the pure cone retina of the snake, no "blue" modulators have been found, while "green" and "red" receptors may appear either separately or coupled together. In the mixed eye of the frog, illustrated above, a "blue" modulator sometimes appears, which incidentally behaves in many ways like a rod. When it does, it is usually coupled with a "yellow" modulator.

These modulators are significant in color vision. We shall see this in the next chapter when we discuss visual perception.

RECEPTOR FIELDS

The responses we have been describing are those of the ganglion cells of the retina. Because the axons of these ganglion cells make up the fibers of the optic nerve, it would make no difference in principle whether the recording were done from optic-nerve fibers or from the ganglion cell bodies. The cells would be the same, and the responses would be the same. Historically, it has been simply a matter of convenience, or of the suitability of a technique of recording, that determined whether electrodes have been placed on the cell bodies or the optic-nerve fibers. This fact should be kept in mind during the following discussion.

FIBER RESPONSES—In 1938, Hartline, working with the optic nerve of the frog, discovered three "types" of fibers (see Figure 6.10). One "type" of fiber fired its spikes when a light illuminated the retina. That is what would be expected. Not expected, however, was a "type" of fiber in which there was no response during retinal illumination but which gave a burst of impulses when the illumination was turned off. This he called an "off" fiber. Still a third "type" of fiber responded in both ways; it gave an "on" response with

| Maintained | On-Off | Off |
| X type | Y type | Z type |

FIGURE 6.10—Diagram of the activity of three types of ganglion cells distinguished in the vertebrate eye by Hartline. (Adapted from S. H. Bartley. Some factors in brightness discrimination. *Psychol. Rev.*, 1939, 46, 340.)

the beginning of retinal illumination, then stopped firing, but gave an "off" response upon cessation of illumination. Thus, Hartline established the three kinds of responses in fibers: "on" responses, "off" responses, and "on-off" responses.

RETINAL FIELDS—The word "type" used above has been placed in quotes because actually there are no fiber types. The particular response given by a fiber is not a fixed characteristic of the fiber but rather of the conditions of stimulation. The same fiber can give either an "on" response, "off" response, or "on-off" response, depending on the part of the retina illuminated and the wavelength of light used for a stimulus.

The dependence of the response on retinal position has been demonstrated by taking a spot of light and systematically exploring an area of the retina (Kuffler, 1953). When this is done, maps like that in Figure 6.11 are constructed. The map typically has a center area in which a fiber consistently fires with *either* an "on" or an "off" response and a peripheral area in which it consistently fires in the opposite way. If the center gives "on" responses, the periphery gives "off" responses, and vice versa. In between is a transition zone, in which the fiber gives both "on" and "off" responses.

Obviously this kind of field represents a complex interplay of receptors converging through bipolars on the particular ganglion cell from which the record is made. It is quite clear that the "on" effect represents excitation from the receptors in the "on" area. For that reason the area is called an excitatory area. It is similarly clear that the "off" area represents inhibitory influences from the receptors in the "off" or inhibitory area. The transition zone is one in which some receptors are excitatory and others inhibitory.

The exact map obtained of a receptor field depends upon a number of stimulus conditions (Granit, 1959). The principal ones are background illumination, i.e., general state of adaptation of the eye; the intensity of the stimulus spot; the area or size of the spot; and the wavelength used. These will be discussed in turn, the first three briefly and the last one at some length.

In general, if the background illumination is increased, the size of the receptor field decreases. Moreover, the response of the peripheral area, be it "off" or "on," tends to decrease, and the response of the center area, be it "off" or "on," tends to become more prominent.

The effects of stimulus intensity and size are less predictable. Increasing intensity may convert a receptor field into a single "on-off" zone (Kuffler, 1953). The same effect, incidentally, may be obtained by *decreasing* the background illumination. In general, if an "on" response has been most prominent, reducing stimulus intensity causes the "off" response to disappear, leaving the "on" response little affected. And either increasing the background illumination or reducing the area of the spot will produce the same result. Such results indicate clearly the interplay of excitatory and inhibitory processes in the retina.

WAVELENGTH—One of the most significant factors affecting "on" and "off" responses is the wavelength of the stimulus light used. Many of the ganglion cells, especially in such animals as the goldfish, appear to be "color-coded" (Wagner et al., 1963). That is to say, whether they give an "on" response or an "off" response depends in part on wavelength. This can be demonstrated by plotting the spectral sensitivity of an "on" response obtained from a ganglion cell while stimulating a particular spot on the retina and then similarly plotting spectral sensitivity for the "off" response. Such a diagram, obtained from a cell of the goldfish retina, is shown in Figure 6.12. In this case, the "on" response shows something of a peak of sensitivity in the region of 500 millimicrons; the "off" response, another peak in the region of 700 millimicrons. Similar differences in the spectral sensitivity of "on" and "off" responses have been obtained for many color-coded cells with peaks in other regions of the visible spectrum.

Not all ganglion cells, however, are color-coded in this way. In Figure 6.12 is another unit having both "on" and "off" responses of about the same spectral sensitivity. The peak in this case was about 600 millimicrons. The center of the receptive field gives "on" responses; the periphery, "off" responses. It

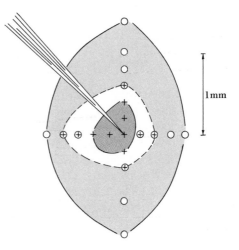

FIGURE 6.11—Distribution of discharge patterns within the receptive field of a ganglion cell located at the tip of the electrode. (Adapted from S. W. Kuffler. Discharge patterns and functional organization of mammalian retina. *J. Neurophysiol.*, 1953, 16, 49.)

1mm

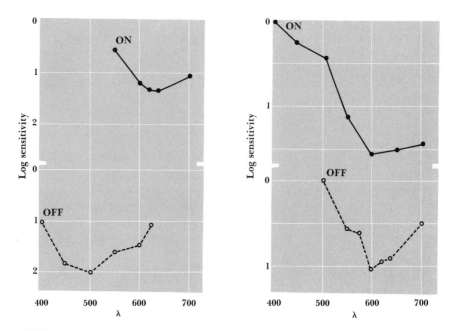

FIGURE 6.12—"On" and "off" responses as a function of wavelength. (Adapted from H. G. Wagner, E. F. MacNichol, Jr., and M. L. Wolbarsht. Function basis for "on"-center and "off"-center receptive fields in the retina. *J. Opt. Soc. Amer.*, 1963, 53, 69.)

would appear that the number of such non-color-coded cells as compared with color-coded cells varies with the animal being used. There seem to be more of them in the goldfish eye than in the eye of the cat or frog. Possibly this is because of differences in color vision. This is not known.

More research will be needed before the meaning of these facts can be stated explicitly. It is certainly clear at the present time that there are both excitatory and inhibitory influences playing on the ganglion cells and that the precise balance between them depends on wavelength, on intensity, and on spatial relations within the retina.

DIRECTIONAL SENSITIVITY—Closely related to "on" and "off" responses of the retina is the fact that some of the ganglion cells of the retina respond only to moving stimuli. Indeed, many respond only to stimuli moved in a particular direction. This has been established in the rabbit (Barlow and Hill, 1963) and in the pigeon (Maturana and Frank, 1963). No doubt it will prove to be a general characteristic of vertebrate eyes. This directional sensitivity appears to be a consequence of excitatory and inhibitory influences canceling each other except when a certain set of cells are stimulated in a particular order.

GRADED PHOTOPIC RESPONSES

We have now seen that the "on" and "off" *spike* potentials of ganglion cells are a consequence of excitatory and inhibitory influences originating somewhere between the light stimulus impinging on the receptors and the ganglion cells themselves. The next question to ask, naturally, is what these influences are, how they are generated, and where. On the basis of recent research, the answer seems to be that they arise in the vicinity of the horizontal and bipolar cells situated between the receptors (rods and cones) and the ganglion cells. They consist of graded potentials, not spike potentials. Because, as we shall see, they are correlated with spectral sensitivities of cones, some workers (MacNichol and Svaetichin, 1958) call them graded photopic responses (GPR); others (Tomita, 1963) call them S potentials because they are slow and graded rather than rapid spike potentials. Svaetichin (1953), when he first observed them, thought they arose from the cones and called them cone potentials. Later work (see Tomita, 1963) shows that they do not originate in the cones; hence that designation has been dropped.

In working with graded responses, the procedure is to put a microelectrode in a given position in the retina and then stimulate the retina with lights of different wavelengths, all the while recording the amount and direction of potential generated in this way. Once the spectral sensitivity of the "unit" has been determined, the electrode is moved to a new position and the procedure repeated. After a number of "units" have been measured at different positions, the spectral sensitivities of the various units are compared to determine how many different responses there are. In addition, in some experiments the eye is selectively adapted with a light of a particular wavelength to see whether a response can be altered by such adaptation.

Altogether, three types of responses have been identified: (1) an L response, meaning a luminosity response; (2) an R-G response, for red-green response; and (3) a Y-B response, for yellow-blue. In records of these responses, values above the base line are positive potentials, indicating depolarization, and values below the base line are negative, indicating hyperpolarization (see page 70).

LUMINOSITY RESPONSE—In Figure 6.13 are two examples of L responses obtained from the eyes of fishes. The amplitude of the potential at different wavelengths presents a picture much like that of spectral-sensitivity curves of photochemical materials. The one on the left having a peak around 500 millimicrons was taken from a deep salt-water fish (see MacNichol and Svaetichin, 1958), which incidentally showed no other kind of graded response. The other, with a peak varying from 560 to 600 millimicrons, depending on the species of fish used, was obtained in shallow-water fishes.

The distinguishing thing about an L response is that its shape cannot be altered by selective adaptation. Adaptation to any kind of light, whether it be

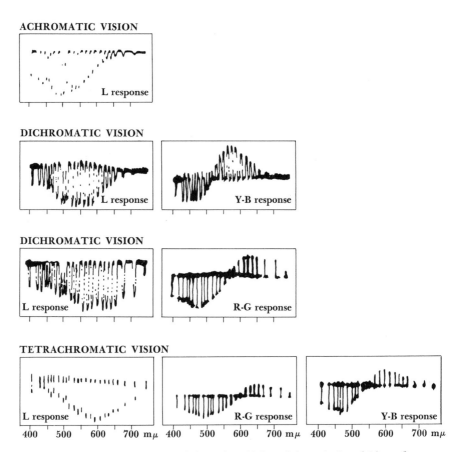

FIGURE 6.13—Graded responses of the retina. (Adapted from G. Svaetichin and E. F. MacNichol, Jr. Retinal mechanisms for chromatic and achromatic vision. *Ann. N.Y. Acad. Sci.*, 1958, 74, 388.)

blue, green, or red, will decrease the size of the response but only in proportion to the sensitivity of the eye to the wavelength. And the whole response adapts together, so that the response maintains its shape throughout the spectrum. This implies a unitary receptor mechanism, not color-coded, and hence one that is "signaling" general luminosity.

R-G AND Y-B RESPONSES—Two other kinds of responses, the R-G and Y-B, are different in two respects (see Figure 6.13). One is that they are diphasic. In each case, the response at the shorter end of the spectrum (blue or green) is negative, and that toward the longer end of the spectrum (yellow or red) is positive. The other difference is in the negative and positive components of the response. The negative limb can be diminished or made virtually to disappear by selectively adapting with blue light (447 millimicrons). Similarly, adapting with red light (710 millimicrons) makes the positive R component of the response disappear. Thus it is plain that each limb of the diphasic response represents a different and separable receptor process.

The examples just given are all from the eyes of fishes. Similar responses, though not identical in every detail, have been found in other cold-blooded animals and also in the cat. Thus they appear to be common in all vertebrates (Tomita, 1963).

Now it should be clear where part, if not all, of the excitatory and inhibitory influences arise. They represent color receptors of different spectral sensitivities generating graded potentials of positive (excitatory) and negative (inhibitory) sign. It is thought that these potentials arise in the extraneuronal spaces—spaces between neurons—from horizontal and similar cells of glia origin (see page 21). Hence, it appears that they are the result of some interaction between receptor-bipolar neurons and the glial cells packed around them.

THE CENTRAL VISUAL SYSTEM

Knowledge of the anatomy of a system is frequently ahead of the physiological information concerning it. This was once true of the retina. It was studied anatomically in great detail before modern biochemical and electrophysiological methods of studying it were well developed. It is not, however, true of the central visual system. Although some of its anatomical connections are known and known well, by electrophysiological means, connections have been found for which there are not as yet established anatomical pathways. In such cases, there is no choice but to presume that the anatomical pathways exist. For this reason, the physiological and anatomical data concerning the visual system will be discussed together. But first we shall have a preview.

GENERAL VIEW

The two optic nerves, one from each eye, are made up of the axons of ganglion cells of the two retinas (see Figure 6.14). Directed backward and medially, the two nerves meet in the optic chiasm at the base of the brain just anterior to the stalk of the pituitary body. In animals below the mammals, all fibers cross at the chiasm and terminate in the sides of the thalamus or midbrain opposite to the eye of their origin. In mammals, however, the fibers from the more lateral parts of the retina remain uncrossed; since the number of uncrossed fibers in the higher mammals is about equal to that of the crossed fibers, the lateral half of the retina is represented in the same side

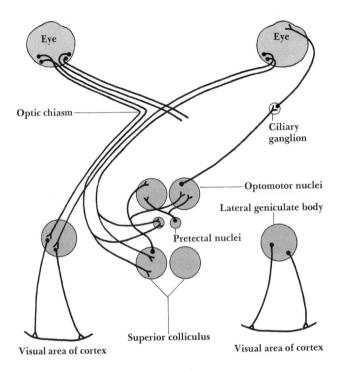

Eye

Eye

Optic chiasm

Ciliary
ganglion

Optomotor nuclei

Lateral geniculate body

Pretectal nuclei

Superior colliculus

Visual area of cortex

Visual area of cortex

**FIGURE 6.14—Diagram of the centers and pathways of the visual
system.**

of the brain, whereas the medial half projects to structures of the opposite
side.

The principal places of termination of the fibers of the optic nerve are the
lateral geniculate nuclei of the thalamus (LGN), the superior colliculi (SC)
of the midbrain, and the pretectal nuclei lying just in front of the colliculi.
There is undoubtedly some segregation of fibers such that different fibers go
to each of these subcortical stations. On the other hand, substantial numbers
of those going to the colliculi also have collaterals serving the lateral geniculate nuclei (LGN) and the pretectal nuclei.

From these various subcortical stations, higher-order neurons project to
different parts of the brain. The best-known projection is from the LGN to
the *striate area* of the cortex, otherwise known as the primary visual area of
the cortex. The superior colliculus sends fibers to the optomotor nuclei of the
brain stem involved in the control of eye movements. Where else the colliculus sends fibers is not known, but it may very well have other connections.
It is also presumed that the LGN sends fibers to association nuclei of the
thalamus, particularly to the pulvinar and to the lateral nucleus of the
thalamus (see page 44). Otherwise it is difficult to explain the fact that

responses to visual stimulation can be picked up in the lateral nucleus and in the posterior parietal cortex to which both the lateral nucleus and pulvinar project. There will be more on this later.

At the level of the cerebral cortex, four areas are to be considered. The first is the striate cortex of the occipital lobe, the primary visual area mentioned above. The second is a region in front of and peripheral to the striate cortex, known as the *prestriate cortex*. These two areas are presumed to be the same as Visual I and Visual II, respectively, which have been delineated by the method of evoked potentials, although that may not be the case (Bard, 1956; see Hubel, 1963). A third area, also identified by evoked potentials in the cat, has been called Visual III. It is located in the parietal-temporal region overlapping the auditory projection areas (see below and Chapter 3). In the monkey, a fourth area on the inferior surface of the temporal lobe has an identified visual function because lesions made in it interfere with learned visual discriminations (see Chapter 17).

With this outline of the centers and pathways of the visual system, we are now prepared to take each way station separately and to understand better what the facts in each case mean.

OPTIC NERVE

Research on the optic nerve, as distinguished from retinal ganglion cells, has been pursued mainly with the use of gross evoked potentials. These have been called "mass recording" (Bartley and Nelson, 1963), in contrast to the microelectrode technique. Relatively large electrodes are placed on the optic nerve and records made of the consequences of light stimulation of the retina or, in some cases, of electrical stimulation of the retina or optic nerve. Of the various facts emerging from research with this method, three will be described here: (1) on-off effects, (2) fiber groupings in the optic nerve, and (3) endings of fibers in more central visual stations. Other points are better brought out in the next chapter in connection with visual perception.

ON-OFF EFFECTS—On-off effects are seen in the optic nerve, just as they are in retinal ganglion cells and, as we shall see below, in the lateral geniculate nucleus. At very weak intensities, or very brief flashes of light, the only wave seen in the optic-nerve recording is an "on" response. With increased intensity or duration, a second wave, an "off" response, follows the end of the light stimulus. At medium levels of intensity, a second component, not seen in the "off" response, appears in the "on" response. In other words, in this case, there are two "on" responses of different latencies, and one "off" response. This fact has usually been taken to mean that there are two populations of receptors giving rise to the two "on" responses, each with its own level of sensitivity and latency. Since conduction velocity varies with fiber size (page 64), the fact that there are two "on" responses also means that there are two groups of fibers in the optic nerve that differ in size.

FIBER GROUPINGS—In some animals, but not in all, it is possible to distinguish more than two different fiber groupings. Four have been found in the rabbit; three in the cat. However, the fact that a grouping is not found does not mean that it is not there. The amplitude of waves may be too small, or the waves may merge or overlap so as not to be distinguishable. Hence it has been concluded that there are, in general, four different fiber groupings even though they have not been distinguished in all eyes studied (see Bartley, 1959).

The general rule seems to be that conduction rates of the four groups step down by halves (Bartley, 1959). The second group conducts half as fast as the first, and so on. Similarly, the size of the waves produced in each group steps down. Smaller fibers not only conduct more slowly; they also produce smaller spike potentials. And the threshold of excitation of each group is also different. In the case of the first two groups, which are most readily studied, the threshold for eliciting a response in the second group is 2½ times as high as the threshold for the first group.

CENTRAL TERMINATION—The different fiber groupings end at different points in the brain (see Bartley, 1959). The first and fastest group terminates in the lateral geniculate body and then, by means of relays, conducts impulses to the striate cortex. The second group also ends in the lateral geniculate body, but it synapses there with neurons that relay to the lateral nucleus of the thalamus. The third group terminates in the pretectal area; the fourth and slowest group, in the superior colliculus. In view of the fact that many fibers passing to the superior colliculus have collaterals terminating in the lateral geniculate body, the separation into fiber groups is not a clean one. Nevertheless, it appears to exist.

LATERAL GENICULATE NUCLEUS

To be accurate, we should point out that it is the *dorsal* nucleus of the lateral geniculate body that projects to the primary visual cortex (striate area). For brevity, however, we shall refer to it as the lateral geniculate nucleus or even more briefly as LGN.

TOPOGRAPHICAL ORGANIZATION—The anatomy of the LGN has been studied principally by the method of secondary degeneration, which will be explained below. In addition, some electrical studies to be considered below throw some light on its fine structure. Degeneration experiments are particularly informative in this case because of the synapses made in the LGN by optic fibers and by LGN cells projecting to the visual cortex. By making lesions in the cortex or cutting the radiations to it, LGN cells are caused to degenerate. In this way, one can determine the points on the cortex to which points in the LGN project (Lashley, 1941). Similarly, by making lesions in the LGN, fibers of the optic nerve are cut, and this causes degeneration of ganglion cells in the retina. Thus the projection of the retina on the LGN can be mapped.

We see, then, that there is a high degree of point-to-point projection of the retina upon the LGN and of the LGN upon the striate cortex. We must say "high degree," for there is evidence of convergence, divergence, and lateral spread of activity in the LGN (see below). Nevertheless, the point-to-point, "straight-through" arrangement is a conspicuous feature of the LGN.

This means, then, that the LGN is topographically organized. Corresponding to each point on the retina, there is a point in the LGN and another in the striate cortex. This topographical organization, as in the case of other senses, is not maintained at a constant size. The maps at each level are distorted in the relative sizes of the parts (cf. somesthesis, Chapter 9). The central retinal field in the higher primates, where detail vision is considerably better than it is in the periphery, is represented by relatively larger areas of the LGN and striate cortex. Nevertheless, the basic spatial relations are kept intact.

In many animals, particularly the higher primates, this organization is carried even further. The LGN is divided into a number of distinct layers, each of which is topographically organized and each of which is in register with the other (see Bartley, 1959). In the monkey and in man, there are six such layers; in the cat, only three. Moreover, in each case, the layers are served alternately by the two eyes. In the cat, the outer and inner layers receive fibers from the eye on the opposite side; the middle layer, fibers from the eye on the same side. In the six-layered LGN of man and the monkey, there is similarly alternate representation of the two eyes, except in this case three represent one side and three the other.

Besides fibers from the optic tract, the LGN undoubtedly receives fibers from other sources. Little is known about them, but a topographically organized projection from the visual cortex back to the LGN has been demonstrated in the rat (Nauta and Bucher, 1954) and in the cat (Beresford, 1961). The LGN may also be served by the reticular formation, for the RF affects its activity, but, on the other hand, the RF may do this only by way of the striate cortex and its downward projection to the LGN.

ELECTRICAL ACTIVITY—The rest of our discussion of the LGN in this section will be based on studies of electrical activity. From such studies, something has been learned about (*1*) binocular interaction, (*2*) "on" and "off" responses, (*3*) receptive fields, and (*4*) wavelength responses. Each will be discussed in turn, but first it is necessary to make some statements about the electrical events taking place in the LGN.

The LGN, like other stations of the visual system, has been studied both by mass recording and by microelectrode techniques (see Hubel, 1963). Both are useful, but the most interesting data come from recent studies with microelectrodes in which the behavior of individual units is observed. Both will be referred to as necessary in what follows.

Some cells in the LGN are fired by a single impulse from an optic fiber (Bishop et al., 1958). This is exactly what one would expect from a one-to-one system. For many units, however, this is not the case. Instead, a single optic-fiber impulse causes only a graded postsynaptic potential (page 66) without a spike. To produce a spike, impulses from several optic fibers must impinge on the cell. This shows that convergence and summation of impulses are sometimes necessary and hence that there is interaction in the LGN.

Some cells in the LGN are spontaneously active while the eyes are in darkness, although it is not exactly clear how many there are (DeValois et al., 1962; Hubel, 1960; Erulkar and Fillenz, 1960). Spontaneously firing neurons have turned up in most sensory systems, and they are nice candidates for inhibition by the onset of stimulation as well as for "off" units that fire on the cessation of stimulation.

With long-continued, repetitive stimulation, the responses of LGN cells tend to decline (Mancia et al., 1959). This has been called habituation because it is like the general phenomenon of habituation. Conversely, when the organism is aroused by some other form of stimulation, e.g., olfactory, or by electrical stimulation of the reticular formation, the LGN responses to repetitive visual stimulation return. This is called dishabituation. Reticular activation also increases the rate of spontaneous discharge of LGN neurons (Ogawa, 1963). These findings indicate that the reticular formation directly or indirectly exercises some control over the level of firing in the LGN.

/ BINOCULAR INTERACTION—We stated above that the layers of the LGN are alternately served by optic fibers of the two eyes. This statement is true of the vast majority of cells of the LGN. It implies that the impulses from the two eyes are, to a very large degree, kept separate at the level of the LGN and that much of the superimposition of the information from the two eyes must occur at the cortical level.

There are, on the other hand, a small number of cells of the LGN that can be fired by optic-nerve fibers from either eye. At least, in one study of the cat, about 8 percent of more than one hundred different LGN cells could be fired in this way (Bishop et al., 1959). The precise nature of the binocular interaction was not studied, but it seemed clear that in some cells interaction was possible and that impulses arriving from one eye could affect responses to those arriving from the other eye.

2. "ON" AND "OFF" RESPONSES—"On" and "off" responses can be demonstrated in the LGN by either the mass-recording technique or the microelectrode technique. Using mass-recording techniques, one simply notes the appearance of waves in the record obtained from the LGN in relation to turning on and off a visual stimulus. Three distinct "on" responses can be seen at latencies of

30, 140, and 380 milliseconds if the light stimulus is sufficiently bright (see Bartley and Nelson, 1963). Similarly, two distinct peaks of "off" responses at latencies of 30 and 170 milliseconds can be seen after turning the stimulus off. The exact meaning of these various peaks is open to question, but they certainly indicate the presence of "on" and "off" responses in the LGN.

RECEPTIVE FIELDS—These "on" and "off" responses may be used to plot the 3. receptive fields of cells in the LGN in the same way that the receptive fields of optic-nerve fibers may be plotted. Once a microelectrode has been placed on an individual unit, all that is necessary is to flash a spot of light on different points of the retina and map the locations at which a response, either "on" or "off," is evoked in the LGN unit.

In general, the results obtained are similar to those found for the retina (Hubel and Wiesel, 1961). Two kinds of units are found: those with centers giving "on" responses and peripheries giving "off" responses, and those with centers giving "off" responses and peripheries giving "on" responses. In between are zones of "on-off" responses.

Other characteristics of the receptive fields of LGN neurons are similar to those of ganglion cells. The shapes are similar in that both sets of fields are concentric. (We shall see below that this is not the case in the visual cortex.) If large spots of light are used, including quite diffuse light, "on" and "off" responses tend to cancel out. In some cases, geniculate cells would not respond to diffuse light at any intensity. Without going into details, one may conclude that LGN cells have receptive fields generally like those of retinal ganglion cells (see Hubel, 1963).

WAVELENGTH RESPONSES—In the case of the retina, we found that for many, 4. but not all, of the cells a unit may or may not give an "on" response or an "off" response, and whether or not it does so depends upon the wavelength of the stimulating light. The same thing is true for cells of the lateral geniculate nucleus (Hill, 1962; DeValois, 1960).

The results of one study are summarized in Figure 6.15 (Hill, 1962). In it, seven types of units were found, using the peak of spectral sensitivity as the criterion. Two of these peaks were inhibitory; that is, they represented "off" responses. These were at about 450 and 500, although most were around 500 to 510. Five were excitatory; they represented "on" responses. The best-defined peak was at 500 millimicrons or a little above; another prominent one was at 435. Three other peaks that were occasionally found were at 460, 580, and 635 millimicrons.

The different peaks of response occurred in several combinations. That is to say, a given unit had one or more peaks representing "on" and/or "off" responses, each having a different peak of sensitivity. As illustrated in Figure 6.15, the "on" responses would have a peak at one wavelength, in this case about 450 millimicrons, and the "off" responses would peak at another,

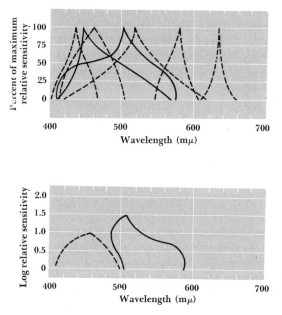

FIGURE 6.15—Sensitivity curves of lateral geniculate cells. (Adapted from R. M. Hill. Unit responses of the rabbit lateral geniculate nucleus to monochromatic light on the retina. *Science*, January 12, 1962, 135, 99. Adapted from *Science* by permission.)

in this case about 500. Obviously, this represents some interaction of excitatory and inhibitory influences.

Studies of the LGN of the monkey give results that are similar, although they differ in detail (DeValois, 1960). Some LGN units were found that gave only "on" responses. These had a single peak and appeared to be comparable to the luminosity receptors of the goldfish (page 151). Also comparable to the graded responses of the goldfish were two sets of units that could be labeled R-G and B-Y units on the basis of the peaks of their sensitivity. The R-G units gave "on" responses in the red region and "off" responses in the green region of the spectrum; the B-Y units gave "on" responses in the blue and "off" responses in the yellow regions of the spectrum. It is interesting that these units gave virtually no responses at all to white light. White light, covering all regions of the visible spectrum, caused the "on" and "off" responses to cancel out.

The significance of these data for color vision will be discussed in the next chapter.

CEREBRAL CORTEX

From an anatomical point of view, there is only one area of the cortex clearly associated with the visual system. This is the so-called primary visual cortex or *striate cortex* (so named from the striped appearance of the cortex in this region) to which the lateral geniculate nucleus projects (Doty, 1958). The method of evoked potentials, used to map cortical areas giving responses to light stimuli, confirms expectations from anatomy that this is indeed the "primary" visual cortex. It has been called Visual I. In addition, the method of evoked potentials brings out the existence of another area lateral to it in such animals (cat, rabbit, and monkey) as have been studied with the method. The latter area, roughly coextensive with areas anatomists call the prestriate area (Lashley and Clark, 1946), has been called Visual II.

In the cat, still a third area, Visual III, can be distinguished by the aid of evoked potentials (Thompson et al., 1950). This is in the vicinity of, and overlaps, areas concerned with hearing. Whether it exists in the monkey is questionable. Even the presence of Visual II in the monkey is difficult to demonstrate (Doty, 1958), although it does exist (Hubel and Wiesel, 1962). There are thus some differences between cat and monkey; what they mean is not at present clear.

By behavioral methods, it has been established that a fourth area in the temporal lobe of the monkey is somehow concerned with vision. It seems, however, to be concerned with the learning and retention of visual habits, not with sensory affairs, and so it will not be discussed until later when visual discrimination learning is covered (Chapter 17).

EVOKED POTENTIALS—Most of the work discussed here will consist of studies with evoked potentials, either with mass recording or microelectrode recording. Hence, a word is in order about the general characteristics of these potentials before considering more specific phenomena. Most of the work, too, is based on the cat, unless a specific statement is made otherwise.

If the retina is stimulated either with a light or an electrical stimulus, the record of activity in the cerebral cortex is always complex. There is usually an initial positive deflection, but after that there may be other negative and positive waves, depending on the animal used and the conditions of stimulation. Investigators are still trying to determine just what each deflection in this complex record means (Doty, 1958), but until they do, it will not be known what, if any, significance it has for psychological functions. At present, about all that is worth saying is that the evoked potential in the cortex can be divided into a "fast" response and a "slow" response (Doty and Grimm, 1962). The fast response is clearly the consequence of retinal activity and represents the first group of impulses seen in the optic nerve (Bartley and Nelson, 1963). The slow response is most probably elaborated in the network of cells in the cortex, but it may also have components directly aroused by messages arriving from the retina (Doty and Grimm, 1962).

TOPOGRAPHICAL ORGANIZATION—Both Visual I and Visual II are topographically organized. That is to say, each point on the retina is represented doubly on the cortex, once by a point in Visual I and again by a point in Visual II.

This has been established both by "mass-recording" techniques (Thompson et al., 1950) and by studies of single cortical units (Hubel and Wiesel, 1962). Thus two maps lie adjacent to each other, separated by a line that represents the vertical meridian.

In contrast to the lateral geniculate nucleus, the organization of cortical cells is *binocular*. Whereas the LGN has alternating layers representing the two eyes, there is no such segregation of binocular events in the cortex. Instead, the great majority (about 85 percent in the cat) of cortical cells receiving LGN inputs are activated by stimuli to either eye (Hubel and Wiesel, 1962). Hence the bulk of binocular mixing of visual impulses takes place at the cortical level.

ON-OFF UNITS—As might be expected, investigators have examined cortical cells to see whether they, like their counterparts in the retina and LGN, exhibit on-off behavior and have receptive fields. They do, but with a remarkable difference. In no case is the field concentric, as it is in the retina and LGN. The areas giving "on" and "off" responses are not separated by circles but rather by straight lines (see Hubel, 1963). One cell, for example, may have an "on" retinal area that is a straight line flanked on either side by "off" lines or bars. Another cell may have the reverse. Other cells may have receptive areas consisting of one excitatory line (on) and one inhibitory line (off) next to it.

Because of the summation that takes place, this arrangement means that cortical units are exceedingly sensitive to the orientation of a retinal stimulus. If a bar of light or darkness—something with an edge—falls on the retina in the correct orientation to match the receptive field of a cortical unit, it will excite or inhibit the cortical unit. But it will do only one or the other, depending on whether it is in the "on" field or the "off" field. If both are stimulated simultaneously, as when a bar of light is perpendicular to the axis of the receptive field, the effects tend to cancel so that the cortical unit does not fire. Consequently, the cortical cell responds only when a retinal stimulus with an "edge" appears on the "right" part of the retina and in the "right" orientation.

The retinal fields, or more properly the retinal axes, of cortical units vary from unit to unit. The axis of one cell may be horizontal, that of another vertical, that of another oblique, and so on. Its axis may have any angle. Hence, various cells of the cortex are uniquely sensitive to stimuli having edges at the appropriate points and in the appropriate orientations in the visual field.

RETINAL STIMULI—All this means that the topographical organization of the cortex, although existing, may have little significance. The cortex does not respond to retinal stimulation as though it were the film in a camera. Rather, it performs a translation—and a radical one at that—of the information received from the retina. It "abstracts" certain properties of the stimulus and responds only to these. Cells that do this have been called complex cells; others that respond to stimulation on a strictly topographical basis are called simple cells (Hubel, 1963).

Two other facts fit in with this conception of complex cells performing a translating or abstracting function. One is the magnitude of the cortical response to diffuse stimulation. The maximum evoked response to such stimulation is *outside* the striate area. Even the responses obtained in the striate area are not maximum in the area representing central vision but rather peripheral to it (Doty, 1958). In other words, the cells representing fine, detail vision in the cortex do not respond to gross illumination of the retina.

The other fact is that complex cells of the striate cortex, though relatively insensitive to a spot of light or diffuse illumination, are unusually sensitive to movement. Moving a stimulus through the visual field is the very best way to get them to fire. This is because such movement alternately stimulates the "on" and the "off" segments of the visual cortex so that the "on" response reinforces the "on" response rather than canceling, as is the case with simultaneous stimulation (Hubel, 1963).

Some of these points will be put to use in the next chapter when we consider specifically how physiological processes account for some of the phenomena of visual perception.

SUPERIOR COLLICULUS

Although the superior colliculus sits at a position low in the brain and is phylogenetically older than the cerebral cortex, it will be mentioned last simply because it will now be easier to understand what there is to say about it.

The superior colliculus (SC), like the lateral geniculate, is a structure precisely ordered along topographical lines. It is also organized into layers but in a different way. In the frog, which has no striate cortex and whose LGN is not layered, the SC is arranged in four layers. All four layers faithfully represent the retina in a topographical order, and all four are in register. Microelectrode studies, however, show that the layers respond in different ways to stimuli (Maturana et al., 1959). The first and second layers receive optic-nerve fibers that give "on" responses; the third layer receives on-off fibers from the optic nerve; and the fourth layer receives "off" fibers. The first and second layers are distinguished in their response to stimuli. The first one responds to stimuli that are moving or where the contrast is maintained. The second responds only to edges that are curved and does not respond to straight-edged stimuli.

7 VISUAL PERCEPTION

THE PRECEDING CHAPTER dealt with the anatomy and physiology of the visual system. It presented those facts that appear to be especially relevant to understanding the mechanisms of visual perception, which is our subject in this chapter. As the occasion arises, we shall refer to points made there, and in addition some physiological facts will be introduced as they fit our purpose.

The term "perception" is being used in its broadest sense to include both sensation and perception. More specifically, it will cover the following topics, each constituting a major section of the chapter: luminosity, color vision, adaptation, flicker vision, spatial vision, and brightness vision. Because the facts of visual perception are treated extensively in other handbooks (Stevens, 1951) and textbooks (Geldard, 1953), they will not be detailed here except as they are especially relevant to our interest in studying physiological mechanisms. On the other hand, there is a great deal of physiology also covered extensively elsewhere (Field, 1959) which will be treated here only when it appears relevant to perception.

LUMINOSITY

If one measures the sensitivity of any photosensitive material or organ at different wavelengths, determining the energy at each wavelength that is required to produce some constant response, the curve obtained is called a curve of *spectral sensitivity*. As we have seen, curves of this sort have been measured for the four visual pigments: rhodopsin, iodopsin, porphyropsin, and cyanopsin. The same thing can be done, and has been done many times, for the human eye and the eyes of other animals. In this case, by convention, the curve obtained is a *luminosity function*. This is the same thing, by another name, as a spectral-sensitivity curve.

METHODS OF MEASUREMENT

Luminosity functions may be measured in either of two general ways: electrophysiologically and psychophysically.

ELECTROPHYSIOLOGICAL METHODS—In the preceding chapter we discussed two different ways of determining the spectral sensitivity of the eye, both employing methods of electrical recording. The first made use of the electroretinogram (ERG), the electrical change recorded from the surface of the eyeball when the eye is stimulated with a light. As indicated there, both the A wave and the B wave of the ERG vary with the sensitivity of the eye, but the B wave is usually more prominent, especially at low intensities of illumination, and so the B wave has been most often used to obtain a spectral-sensitivity, or luminosity, function.

The second method was also discussed. This is the microelectrode method of recording from individual ganglion cells. In this case, some particular number of impulses is arbitrarily taken as the constant response while wavelength and intensity are varied. The various "dominator" and "modulator" curves obtained by this method in different animals are spectral-sensitivity curves. However, because the modulators are related to color sensitivity and discrimination, whereas the dominators appear to reflect overall luminosity, only the curves for the dominators are regarded as luminosity functions.

PSYCHOPHYSICAL METHODS—A psychophysical method is one in which the organism makes some response indicating its sensitivity to a stimulus. In man this is usually a verbal report of "I see it" or of two stimuli being matched in perceived intensity. In animals, it may be some response such as pushing a lever, pecking at a disk, or something indicating a reaction to a stimulus. Behavioral methods in animals are quite laborious; consequently, few luminosity functions have been measured psychophysically in animals.

In man or animals, there are several different "constant responses" that may be employed. The simplest one is a *threshold* of seeing. The intensity of the stimulus light is varied until the weakest intensity that can just be seen is found and recorded. This method limits one to weak intensities or at least to the weakest intensities that will activate the receptors being stimulated.

To obtain luminosity functions at higher intensities, a method of *increments* or a method of *matching* is used. In the method of increments, a steady light is used as a background stimulus. Then an increment is added to that, and the size of the increment is varied until a differential threshold is found such that the observer can just detect the increment. In matching methods, a standard light is matched with a comparison light. Usually the first is white, and the second colored. The intensity of the colored light is varied until the observer judges it to match the standard light in intensity. In another variation, the two lights are flickered alternately, and the intensity of the comparison light is adjusted to the value that makes the flicker disappear. Since lights of different subjective brightness, when alternated, are perceived as flickering, the intensities at which flicker disappears are those of equal luminosity.

Data obtained by these various methods will be referred to in this chapter.

LUMINOSITY FUNCTIONS

The thesis on which investigators have been working for nearly a hundred years is, very simply, that luminosity functions are identical with spectral-absorption curves of photosensitive substances found in the rods and cones. Hence the aim has been to compare luminosity functions obtained in a particular eye with the spectral sensitivities of photochemical substances known to exist in the same eye. To do this, allowance must be made for any other pigments in the eye that might alter an organism's luminosity function. The lens and optic media, for example, are slightly yellowish, thus absorbing some blue light passing through them. Hence, for a fair comparison, a luminosity function must be measured in an aphakic (lensless) eye or a computational correction must be made. In animals, the lens can be removed; in man, fortunately for these experiments, there are some individuals without lenses on which measurements can be made. In some animals, there is also some pigmentation in the retina, which must be reckoned with. In pigeons and chickens, for example, there are some brightly colored oil globules that are in a position to act as color filters.

SCOTOPIC FUNCTIONS—In general, the fit of spectral-absorption curves of rhodopsin and porphyropsin to scotopic (rod) luminosity functions has been good. Some of these fits were shown in Figures 6.6 and 6.8. In Figure 6.8, the curve for rhodopsin was superimposed on measurements of luminosity for several different animals. All the measurements in animals (frog, snake, cat, and guinea pig) were obtained by the microelectrode method and represent the dominators found in these eyes, all having peaks around 500 millimicrons. In Figure 7.1, a comparison is made between rhodopsin and the human psychophysical threshold measured in the aphakic (lensless) eye. The fit, except for the little leg in the luminosity function of man, is very good and well within the limits of experimental error. Even the minor discrepancy in man is known to be due to transmission losses in the media of the eye. There is no doubt that the dark-adapted eye of man and animals containing rhodopsin has a sensitivity at different wavelengths entirely determined by the absorption characteristics of the eye and of rhodopsin.

There are, as one might expect, fewer data for the relatively rare animals having the porphyropsin system in place of the rhodopsin system. The freshwater fish tench is one such animal. In the two curves at the right of Figure 6.6, the spectral sensitivity of porphyropsin is compared with the tench's scotopic sensitivity as measured by the microelectrode method. The two are close but not identical. The scotopic luminosity curve is displaced about 10 millimicrons toward the red end of the spectrum. The reason for the dis-

FIGURE 7.1—Absorption spectra of chicken rhodopsin and iodopsin compared with the spectral sensitivity of human rod and cone vision. (Adapted from G. Wald, P. K. Brown, and P. H. Smith. Synthesis and bleaching of rhodopsin. *J. gen. Physiol.*, 1955, 38, 677. By permission of The Rockefeller Institute Press.)

—— absorption spectra of chicken - - - human lensless peripheral vision
 ○ iodopsin △ cones
 ● rhodopsin ▲ rods
 --●--●--●- mutual sensitivity of rhodopsin (chicken) and human rod vision

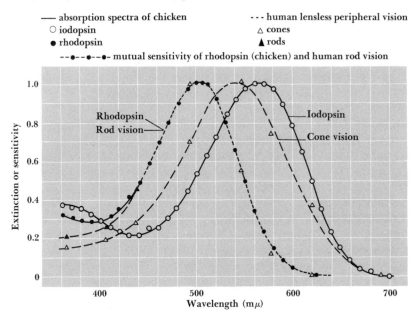

crepancy is not known; it may be due to some pigment in the fish's eye at the time of measurement. The correspondence is good enough, however, to believe that an explanation for the slight discrepancy will be found.

PHOTOPIC FUNCTIONS—When an attempt is made to fit together the data for the light-adapted eye just as was done for the dark-adapted eye, some very good fits and also some poor ones are obtained. For most animals, the visual pigment involved is iodopsin and the corresponding function is the photopic luminosity function.

In Figure 6.8 are curves of photochemical spectral sensitivity and experimental points for photopic luminosity functions. As before, there is an acceptable fit for the photopic dominators of the frog, snake, cat, and guinea pig. There is a discrepancy, however, for the bird (Figure 6.6). Photopic sensitivity is displaced about 20 millimicrons toward the red from the curve for iodopsin. It happens that iodopsin has been extracted from the eye of the chicken, whereas dominator measurements were made in the pigeon. The retinas of both animals contain oil globules functioning as filters, although the color and disposition of the globules in the two animals are somewhat different. In any case, the explanation for the discrepancy would appear to be that the photopic dominators measured in the pigeon were displaced toward the red by the action of red retinal filters. This may also be the explanation for the discrepancy between chicken iodopsin and the human photopic function (Figure 7.1).

For the porphyropsin-cyanopsin system, there are only the data of the fresh-water fish tench, as was the case also for scotopic luminosity (Figure 6.6). The experimental points again are microelectrode data. These, as can be seen, probably include sizable experimental error, but the fit between the luminosity function and the photochemical data appears to be satisfactory.

As we shall see in the next section on color vision, things are not so simple as they might appear from the facts given so far. We shall there have to contend with the function of modulators as specific color receptors. However, it appears that the shape and position of the luminosity functions, both scotopic and photopic, of the vertebrate eye are explained by the spectral-sensitivity curves of the extractable visual pigments, plus some correction for the transmission characteristics of the optic media and, in some animals, for special filtering structures in the retina.

COLOR VISION

We now take up the topic of color vision because many of the data, as well as the methods by which they are obtained, are quite similar to those for luminosity. First, however, it is necessary to review briefly the theories of vision that are related to the problem of color vision.

THEORY OF COLOR VISION

There are two general sets of theories about the eye's function in color vision. One concerns the respective activities of the rods and cones and is called the *duplicity* (or *duplexity*) *theory*. This was explained in the preceding chapter. The other consists of theories about the kinds of receptors taking part in color vision. It is usually assumed that the cones are the color receptors. The question dealt with is how many different kinds there are and how their sensitivities are distributed. This question has led to all kinds of theorizing, but the range of possibilities has been narrowed considerably in recent years, and now there are only two serious candidates: the trichromatic theory and the opponent-process theory.

TRICHROMATIC THEORY—The most favored theory, and probably the one still receiving the most votes among visual theorists, is a trichromatic theory. This assumes that there are three, and only three, kinds of cones, one more sensitive in the blue, another more sensitive in the green, and a third more sensitive in the red region of the spectrum. For simplicity, they are referred to as B, G, and R receptors.

The phrase *more sensitive* is deliberately used here in contrast to *most sensitive* because it is not necessary, in order to have a workable system, that the sensitivities of the three receptors be very different (Hurvich and Jameson, 1957). Their spectral sensitivities might be rather close together, and they might all have their maximum sensitivities in the greenish-yellow portion of the spectrum, where, in fact, the peak of iodopsin is found. For the cones to provide a color-discriminating mechanism, it is only necessary that the R receptor be more sensitive in the red than the other two, the G more sensitive in the green than the other two, and similarly with the B receptor.

In the trichromatic theory there is no separate luminosity receptor—no receptor that signals only white or black—except, of course, the rods. The perception of white is assumed to come about by the simple addition of the outputs of the three color receptors. When these outputs are about equal, the organism sees white. This is an important difference, and probably rather crucial, between trichromatic theory and opponent-process theory.

OPPONENT-PROCESS THEORY—As originally put forth, the opponent-process theory also assumed three sets of cones. In this case, however, one set consisted of luminosity receptors which functioned only on the black-white continuum. The other two sets were color receptors. One set provided the basis for yellow and blue perception, the other set for red and green. Each receptor was assumed to function in two ways, delivering one kind of message for one of its colors, say yellow, and another kind of message for the other member of the pair, say blue.

In its modern form, the idea of two kinds of messages from receptors has been abandoned. In its place, it has been assumed that there are two pairs of units, making four in all, located somewhere in the retina and so arranged that one opposes the action of the other in its effect on bipolar cells or at least on neurons upstream from the receptors. Thus a yellow receptor would oppose the influence of the blue receptor, and the red would oppose the influence of the green receptor, in some final common path upon which the two members of each pair would converge.

Two different models for an opponent process have been entertained (Hurvich and Jameson, 1957). One (see Figure 7.2) is something of a tour de force to compromise with the trichromatic theory. It assumes that there are only three different cones with their respective differences in spectral sensitivity. These are regarded as being linked with units in such a way as to provide two opposing pairs of activities. As can be seen in Figure 7.2, this requires a complicated linkage in which each of the three color receptors is linked to two members of the two pairs of opposing units. A second model is simpler. It assumes that there are four different cones with their respective spectral sensitivities and that these at some point converge in such a way as to form opposing pairs.

We shall now consider the data bearing on these theories. There are many such data, and to cite them all would make a book by itself. We shall confine ourselves only to the most salient of them.

COLOR MIXTURE

One of the most convincing arguments for opponent-process theory, at least subjectively, is the fact that the colors we perceive seem to fall naturally into two pairs of opposites. First of all, most people judge that there are four

FIGURE 7.2—Two alternative mechanisms in opponent-process theory. (Adapted from L. M. Hurvich and D. Jameson. An opponent-process theory of color vision. *Psychol. Rev.*, 1957, 64, 388.)

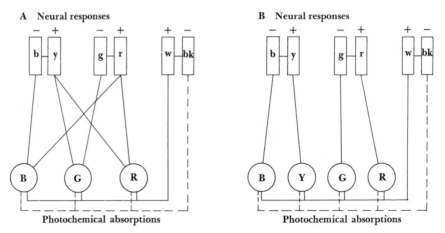

psychologically unique colors: blue, green, yellow, and red. The points in the spectrum yielding these perceived colors have been measured carefully, with the result that the perceived hues are seen at approximately the following wavelengths (Dimmick and Hubbard, 1939):

Blue	476
Green	515
Yellow	582
Red	494c

The "c" for red means "complementary of." It is necessary to specify red by its complementary because unique red is extraspectral. That is to say, at the red end of the spectrum pure wavelengths are never completely free of a yellowish tinge. To get rid of this, one must add a little blue to cancel out the yellow. The complementary of the remaining unique red is a bluish-green wavelength of 494.

SIMILARITY ANALYSIS—The position in the spectrum of unique colors has been studied in another way, namely, by the method of similarity analysis (Ekman, 1954). This method is as follows: A subject is presented with stimuli two at a time. He is asked to rate on a suitable scale the subjective similarity of the two stimuli. Many different pairs from all parts of the visible spectrum are presented, and a matrix of similarity judgments is thus set up. This matrix is subjected to factor analysis—a correlational analysis—which yields "loadings" indicating the relative contributions of factors to the perception of any given stimulus. In the case of color vision, the loadings at each wavelength appear to indicate the relative contributions of basic color experiences.

In Figure 7.3 one can see the results of such an analysis. It yields *five* curves, each having the appearance of a modulator or narrow-band unit measured physiologically (see page 146). The B (blue) curve peaks at about 475; the G (green) at about 530; the Y (yellow) at 580 to 600; the R (red) at 640 to 650. The fifth peak of the V (violet) curve is at about 440 millimicrons. The existence of the V curve represents a well-known fact, that, at very short wavelengths below unique blue, colors appear as a reddish-blue which is violet. The method by which these data were obtained probably explains the position of the V and R peaks, but we shall discuss this later in the present section.

THE COMPLEMENTARY COLORS—The phenomenon of complementary colors, just mentioned, has been another argument in favor of the opponent-process theory. The basic phenomenon is that, perceptually, yellow cancels out blue, and vice versa, to yield a gray or white. Similarly, red and green cancel to a perceived gray or white—a light with luminosity but no color. This phenomenon is often represented by a color circle in which points of the spectrum opposite each other on the circle are complementary to one another.

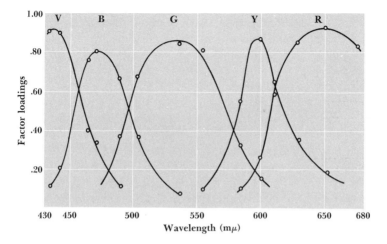

FIGURE 7.3—Curves of spectral sensitivity of the color receptors inferred by similarity analysis. (Adapted from G. Ekman. Dimensions of color vision. *J. Psychol.*, 1954, 38, 472.)

The amount of light of one hue required to cancel its complementary can be, and has been, measured quite precisely. The resulting curves are shown in Figure 7.4. The dashed line is for blue-yellow and shows the amount of blue that must be added at each wavelength given on the abscissa to cancel out the yellow of a light of constant energy. The curve could have been plotted upside down, and it would make no difference. The same statements hold for the solid line representing green-red. These curves have a remarkable similarity to the direct-current slow potentials recorded in the retina of the goldfish (see page 152). The other curve given in the figure is simply a photopic luminosity function showing the relative sensitivities of the cones, independent of any color sensation, when measured at photopic levels of illumination.

These facts of unique and complementary colors make it seem natural to suppose that the retinal color mechanism involves opposing processes. But they do not prove it, and it is possible with some gyrations—mainly by assuming that red and green mixtures produce yellow as well as white—to devise an explanation based on trichromatic theory.

TRISTIMULUS MIXTURE—On the side of trichromatic theory is a fact that is sometimes referred to as the *trichromatic law of color vision*. This law says that any perceived color can be duplicated by using only three appropriately chosen wavelengths. By choosing a wavelength somewhere in the blue region of the spectrum, another somewhere in the green, and a third in the red region, and varying the mixture of the three, one can match the hue of any color seen by man. This fact happens to provide a very convenient method of specifying colors. It also seems to argue that there need be only three different color receptors in the human retina. The argument, however, is somewhat specious for there could very well be several different color receptors, all having overlapping spectral sensitivities, such that any particular wavelength used in color mixture could stimulate—and undoubtedly does—two or more receptors. Nevertheless, the simple idea that only three stimuli, ergo three receptors, are all that is required for human color vision has had wide appeal.

LUMINOSITY FUNCTIONS

Up to this point, luminosity functions have always been depicted as smooth curves that might imply underlying unitary visual pigments. This is the true state of affairs for scotopic luminosity functions. Measurements of these functions uniformly yield smooth curves. It is not true, however, of photopic functions. These have a fine grain, consisting of small "humps" on the curve. Such humps can be clearly seen if the measurements are sufficiently accurate and made under the appropriate conditions.

A *mesopic* luminosity function is one made at an intermediate level of adaptation involving both rods and cones. Such functions can be obtained in

FIGURE 7.4—Chromatic response functions. (Adapted from L. M. Hurvich and D. Jameson. An opponent-process theory of color vision. *Psychol. Rev.*, 1957, 64, 389.)

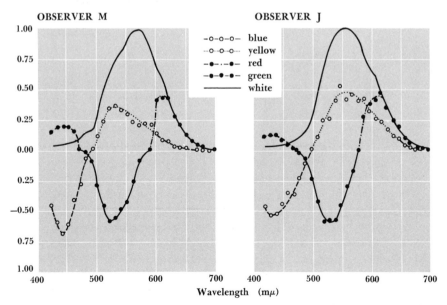

a variety of ways but, in the data about to be presented, the method was to have the observer match the brightness at a given wavelength to the brightness of a standard patch. The data are given in Figure 7.5 (Kinney, 1955).

The smooth curve in Figure 7.5 is a scotopic luminosity function, secured by obtaining thresholds at a point somewhat outside the fovea. It is always such a smooth curve. As one moves into the mesopic range of illuminations, however, humps begin to appear superimposed on the scotopic function. The first one to appear is a red hump at about 610 millimicrons. At somewhat higher brightness, two additional humps appear, one in the blue at about 470, and another in the yellow-green region around 530. The receptor involved in the red hump has a different and greater sensitivity than those in the blue and green regions. This particular experiment was limited to mesopic levels of brightness and thus missed two other humps.

The other humps were seen in an experiment (Figure 7.6) at higher brightness using a surround of the test patch presented to the light-adapted eye (Sperling and Jolliffe, 1962). One hump, at around 550, was to be expected. It is about where the peak of the photopic-luminosity curve is supposed to be. The other one, however, is in the yellow region around 580. In this region, at mesopic levels, is a notch formed by the red hump and the scotopic curve. But as brightness increases, the notch is filled in and replaced by a hump.

It is tempting to think of the humps as peaks of sensitivity for the different

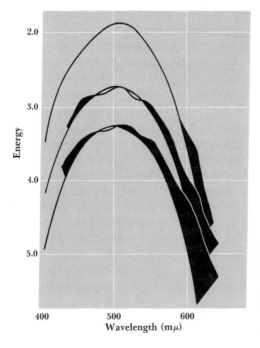

FIGURE 7.5—Mesopic luminosity functions compared with the scotopic function. (Adapted from J. A. S. Kinney. Sensitivity of the eye to spectral radiation at scotopic and mesopic intensity levels. *J. Opt. Soc. Amer.*, 1955, 45, 513.)

color receptors. We have seen above, however, that a model can be constructed in which three color receptors feed into two opposing pairs of units farther along the visual pathway. In any case, the possibilities of interaction must be taken into account, and the perception of color undoubtedly reflects such interaction.

COLOR BLINDNESS

Some degree of color blindness in man is reasonably common, being found in about 6 percent of males and 0.5 percent of females. It is probably also quite common in animals, as judged by human standards, but knowledge of color vision in animals is extremely limited. Color blindness has been studied extensively in the hope of gleaning clues to the physiological mechanism of color. And certainly any theory of the mechanism must account for color blindness as well as for normal color vision.

Color blindness may be classified in a number of ways. The most usual classification is on the basis of tristimulus color mixture. Normal people require three wavelengths to provide matches of all the colors they can see; hence they are *trichromats*. The most common type of color-blind individual is called a *dichromat*, for in his case only two wavelengths are required to match all the colors he can see. The relatively rare person (0.003 percent) who is totally color-blind (sees no color at all) is named a *monochromat*. Each kind of color blindness provides some information relevant to the physiological mechanism of color vision.

DICHROMATISM—Dichromats have been classified into four varieties. Two of these are red-green blind; they confuse reds with greens. Two are yellow-blue blind; they confuse yellows and blues. Red-green-blind individuals are considerably more common than yellow-blue individuals and thus have been studied more thoroughly.

The two varieties of red-green-blind individuals are known as *protonopes* and *deuteranopes*, respectively. Once it has been established that a person is red-green blind, the way to determine his subclassification is to measure his photopic luminosity function. If his luminosity function is shortened in the red region—in other words, if he is relatively insensitive in the red, as compared with a normal individual—he is classified as a *protonope*. Because of his deficiency in the red, the protonope has long been regarded as missing a red receptor or at least as missing a receptor process in the red region of the spectrum.

On superficial inspection, the luminosity function of the deuteranope appears to be normal. For that reason, it has been thought that there is nothing missing in the deuteranope. Rather, the defect should be in the connections. More specifically, it would appear that the inputs from red processes are fused with those of the green process (Boynton et al., 1959).

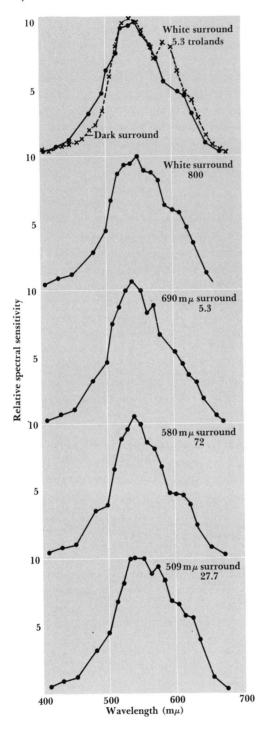

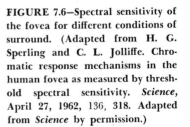

FIGURE 7.6—Spectral sensitivity of the fovea for different conditions of surround. (Adapted from **H. G. Sperling and C. L. Jolliffe.** Chromatic response mechanisms in the human fovea as measured by threshold spectral sensitivity. *Science*, April 27, 1962, 136, 318. Adapted from *Science* by permission.)

There is, however, some difference of opinion on this matter. Two careful investigators who have measured luminosity curves in deuteranopes (Graham and Hsia, 1958) find that there is a loss in the blue-green region of the spectrum. They are bolstered in their position by having a subject who is normal in one eye and deuteranopic in the other and who shows such a comparative loss. Their method is to measure the absolute photopic threshold in the fovea. On the other hand, when measurements are made by matching methods, at higher levels of brightness (Heath, 1958) an actual enhancement, rather than a loss, is found in the blue-green region. At this writing, the reason for the difference between the two methods has not been resolved. Hence no conclusions can be drawn about the physiological mechanism of deuteranopia.

One significant finding, however, comes from the study of the subject who is normal in one eye and deuteranopic in the other (Graham and Hsia, 1958). Such a subject, knowing what normal color vision is, can say how things appear to her in her color-blind eye. The results are represented in the color-matching diagram of Figure 7.7. This shows the wavelength she chooses in her normal eye to match the color of wavelengths seen in her color-blind eye. Notice that all the wavelengths below 500 are matched to about 470, the unique or pure blue. Similarly, all the wavelengths above 500 are matched to about 670, which is yellow. In other words, in her deuteranopic eye she sees all colors as either blue or yellow. No red or green is seen.

Yellow-blue blindness is much rarer than red-green blindness. As far as is known, its two varieties are parallel to those of protonopic and deuteranopic red-green blindness. These varieties have been named *tritanopia* and *tetartanopia*. The latter appears to have a normal luminosity function but to have merged or confused connections of the yellow and blue processes (Hurvich and Jameson, 1957). The tritanope, on the other hand, suffers some loss of luminosity in the blue region and hence appears to be deficient in blue pigment (Wright, 1952).

MONOCHROMATISM—The totally color-blind individual sees only white, black, and shades of gray. The significant thing about his color vision, from the standpoint of physiological theory, is that he has an approximately normal luminosity function. It does not have the humps that can be found in normal individuals, but its overall appearance is that of a photopic luminosity function. This argues against the assertion of trichromatic theory that perception of white comes about through addition of the activities of three color receptors. On the other hand, by assuming that the three color receptors are there but simply misconnected so that their individual contributions cannot be perceived, the trichromatic theorist can argue his way out of this objection. But, taken at face value, the fact of photopic luminosity in monochromats appears to favor an opponent-process theory in which a separate luminosity process is assumed.

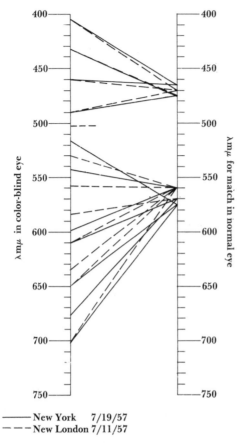

FIGURE 7.7—Binocular color matching by a subject color-blind in one eye. (Adapted from C. H. Graham and Y. Hsia. Color defect and color theory. *Science,* March 12, 1958, 127, 679. Adapted from *Science* by permission.)

ADAPTATION

If the eye is exposed to light, it is being light-adapted. In general, such light adaptation causes the sensitivity of the eye to decrease; more light is required to be seen. Conversely, after exposure to light, if the light is turned off and the eye left in darkness, it is dark-adapted. Such dark adaptation causes the sensitivity of the eye to increase; gradually, the eye can see lights of weaker and weaker intensity. The question is, What is the physiological mechanism of such light adaptation and dark adaptation?

DUPLICITY

In Figure 7.8 is a series of curves of dark adaptation (Hecht et al., 1937). The curves show the course of adaptation in the human eye following different intensities of exposure of the light adaptation preceding dark adaptation. Two features of the curves are noteworthy. First, all the curves, except the lowest one, have two sections. The first section, representing quite rapid adaptation ending briefly on a plateau, has been called a cone section because it appears to represent the dark adaptation of the cones. The second section, which requires a much longer time and represents a slower process of adaptation, is called the rod section because it appears to represent rod activity.

The two sections of the dark-adaptation curve and the more rapid adaptation of the first section can be easily explained. The cones generally have a higher threshold, so that weak adapting lights hardly involve them at all. Their relatively rapid adaptation, if they have been light-adapted, is explained by the fact that the photopic visual pigment (iodopsin) regenerates much more rapidly than the scotopic pigment. This has been demonstrated in test-tube experiments (see Wald, 1959).

LIGHT ADAPTATION

The second noteworthy point about Figure 7.8 is the difference in dark adaptation caused by the amount of previous light adaptation. The dark-adaptation curves that follow adaptation to bright lights start at a higher point and require a longer time to flatten out at maximum sensitivity. They also

FIGURE 7.8—Curves of dark adaptation following light exposures of different intensities. (Adapted from S. Hecht, C. Haig, and A. M. Chase. The influence of light adaptation on subsequent dark adaptation of the eye. *J. gen. Physiol.*, 1937, 20, 837. By permission of The Rockefeller Institute Press.)

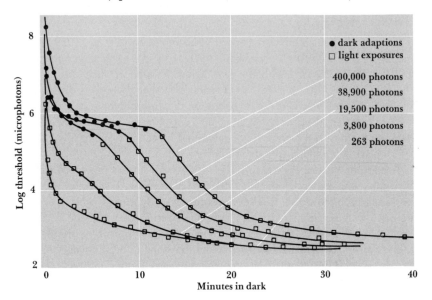

show best the difference between the cone and rod sections. The dark-adaptation curves following relatively weak preadapting lights begin at a lower point and reach their asymptotes more rapidly. They also show less of the cone-rod break.

The fact that a high degree of light adaptation is followed by a slower dark adaptation than is a low degree of adaptation is explained by another photochemical fact. It will be recalled (page 138) that rhodopsin (or iodopsin) can be regenerated from its breakdown products at two different rates, depending on the chemical reactions involved. The fast rate occurs when rhodopsin is regenerated directly from its breakdown products, retinene and opsin. The slow rate occurs when it must be regenerated from vitamin A and opsin. The concentration of these products depends upon how much retinene and opsin accumulate. In high light adaptation or long light adaptation, more retinene is produced, and this produces more vitamin A, causing the regeneration of rhodopsin to be slower.

It may be concluded, then, that the general course of light and dark adaptation is determined by the breakdown and regeneration of visual pigment. Then it may be asked just how precise the relationship is. Do the breakdown and buildup of visual pigment fully explain adaptation?

If one looks closely at the curves in Figure 7.8, particularly those following high light adaptation, one may wonder whether the rhodopsin limb of the curve begins early enough. In other words, it might appear that this limb does not begin until after a delay of several minutes. What is going on during this delay? Presumably rhodopsin is regenerating. If so, why does not sensitivity begin to return more quickly?

PHOTOCHEMISTRY

This question has an answer. Several years ago (Granit et al., 1939) measurements of dark adaptation were made in the frog eye by means of the B wave, and this was compared with the rate of regeneration of visual purple, also in the frog's eye. This showed (see Figure 7.9) that there is a discrepancy in the early phases between the regeneration of visual pigment and the curve of dark adaptation. Regeneration goes on continuously from the beginning of dark adaptation, but sensitivity as measured by the B wave hardly changes at all for a while and begins to recover after a delay.

Recent measurements clear up this mystery. By a most ingenious technique, Rushton and his colleagues (1961) have measured directly the bleaching and regeneration of rhodopsin—and also iodopsin (Rushton, 1957)—so that this may be compared with changing sensitivity in light and dark adaptation. They found that the concentration of visual purple is proportional to the *logarithm* of visual sensitivity, which happens to be the way sensitivity is usually plotted but is not what one would expect. Rather, a direct relationship between visual pigment and sensitivity is more logical.

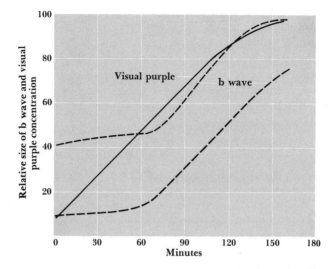

FIGURE 7.9—Comparison of the regeneration of visual purple with dark adaptation measured from the B wave of the electroretinogram of the frog. (Adapted from R. Granit, A. Munsterhjelm, and M. Zewi. The relation between concentration of visual purple and retinal sensitivity to light during dark adaptation. *J. Physiol.*, 1939, 96, 31–44.)

The discrepancy is explained by a theory, almost certainly true, of the structure of the rods (Wald, 1959). Rods are regarded as compartmentalized structures. Each compartment contains many molecules of pigment, but when only one molecule has been bleached by one quantum of light the compartment is no longer capable of excitation. When the several compartments of a rod have thus been inactivated, the rod no longer is excited. However, the molecules in the interior of the compartments can go on bleaching. Thus, a rod is light-adapted when only a small part of its material is bleached. Conversely, regeneration must proceed almost to completion before it is reflected in increasing sensitivity. Put quantitatively, the greatest part of light adaptation occurs in the bleaching of the first 10 percent of rhodopsin, and similarly the greatest part of dark adaptation occurs during the regeneration of the last 10 percent of rhodopsin (Rushton, 1961). When these principles are put in mathematical form, the relationship between concentration of visual pigment and sensitivity is logarithmic.

This leads, then, to the conclusion that the bleaching and regeneration of visual pigments, when understood in detail, fully explain the changes in visual sensitivity taking place in light and dark adaptation. This is not to say that neural interaction in the retina plays no part. It does. There is a precise relationship, for example, between area and visual threshold (Wald, 1938).

The larger the area, the better is the sensitivity. This relationship indicates summation of activity in neighboring areas of the retina. There is also binocular summation (Crozier and Holway, 1939). The sensitivity is better when two eyes are stimulated as compared with one, and this summation must take place in the brain. Summation of this sort, however, is a parametric effect. It determines the general level of sensitivity but, with summation held constant, changes in sensitivity depend on the photochemistry of the visual pigments.

FLICKER DISCRIMINATION

The term flicker discrimination refers to the perception of a change in brightness in the alternation of visual stimulation. At low rates of flicker, a person sees the light as flickering, although the subjective rate is not always the same as the objective rate. As the flicker rate is increased, some point is reached at which the light is no longer perceived as flickering; instead it now appears steady. The rate at which this happens is called the *critical flicker frequency* (CFF) or sometimes the *fusion frequency*. It is this that is measured in most experiments on flicker discrimination.

Early experiments on flicker discrimination were done with an episcotister. This is much like a fan except its blades are flat. The whirling blades interrupt a beam of light seen by the subject in the intervals between the blades. Recent experiments have more often used electronic devices in which pulses of light are switched on and off by electrical circuits. This method affords precise control over a number of variables, including the pulse-to-cycle ratio (the percentage of time the light is on).

FLICKER FUNCTIONS

Perhaps no other visual function has been so often and so accurately measured as the relation of flicker discrimination to visual intensity. Many of the lower animals give reflex movements of the head, eyes, or body to flickering stimuli, and these movements can be used for measuring CFF under many different circumstances in many different animals. In Figure 7.10 is a typical flicker function for the human observer. It indicates that the CFF varies from 2 or 3 cycles per second at very low intensities to about 60 cycles per second at high intensities. The curve also shows a clear division into a rod segment at low intensities and a cone segment at high intensities. This is typical of the shape of curves found in all eyes possessing both rods and cones.

As has been mentioned before, some animals possess all-rod eyes, others all-cone eyes. The flicker functions measured in such animals are of some interest because they show exactly how to break down the duplex function in Fig-

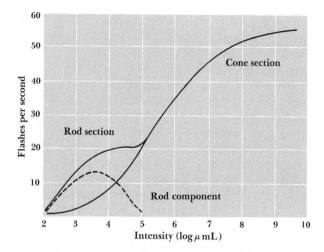

FIGURE 7.10—Analysis of the curve for flicker discrimination. (Adapted from W. J. Crozier and E. Wolf. Theory and measurement of visual mechanisms. IV. Critical intensities for visual flicker, monocular and binocular. *J. gen. Physiol.*, 1941, 24, 505–534. By permission of The Rockefeller Institute Press.)

ure 7.10. As one might expect, flicker functions in pure-cone or pure-rod eyes are simple, continuous functions, not broken into segments. They are sigmoid in shape and are fitted by a probability integral. This implies a normal (Gaussian) distribution, in terms of log sensitivity, of the characteristics of the visual system that are important in flicker discrimination, although it is not clear just what these characteristics are.

If one subtracts the cone section of the lower part of the curve, as obtained from pure-cone eyes, from the rod section, the rod contribution to the curve at first increases; then as intensity is further increased, it decreases again, so that at higher intensities only the cones are contributing to the result (Crozier and Wolf, 1941). This has been interpreted to mean that the rods are inhibited by the cones when cone activity is sufficiently intense. Whether or not this is correct, it is clear that rods are significant in flicker discrimination only at relatively low intensities and hence at relatively low flicker rates.

NEURAL RESPONSES

Three kinds of electrical responses relevant to flicker discrimination have been recorded along the optic pathway: (*1*) the electroretinogram (ERG), (*2*) evoked potentials, and (*3*) the electroencephalogram (EEG). All these show oscillations in size correlated with a flickering light up to some combination of intensity and flicker rate. Presumably the neural mechanism of flicker discrimination is one of detecting differences in the peaks and troughs of such oscillations. When these differences diminish to some critical value, the brain can no longer detect them, and the perception of fusion should result. Not knowing what this critical value is nor how faithfully electrical records reflect it, one can only look for differences in the records that the *experimenter* can detect.

ELECTRORETINOGRAM—As in the case of other visual functions, one can use the B wave of the ERG as a response of the retina to pulsating light. At relatively slow rates of flicker, one can detect repetitions of the B wave following the flashes of light presented to the retina (Granit and Therman, 1935). However, the ability of the ERG to follow visual flicker is limited, for the ERG becomes fused well before the CFF is reached. The maximum rate of flicker for fusion in the ERG varies between 20 and 40 cycles per second for different eyes, yet the CFF goes up to 60 cycles or higher. This fact is not surprising, however, because the ERG is a kind of summed average of activity in the retina and does not reflect the behavior of individual units or even of small groups of units in the retina. It simply means that the ERG is of little help in this particular instance.

EVOKED POTENTIALS—Records of evoked potentials may be taken at several points along the optic pathway while the organism is being stimulated with flickering light. The records may be either of the mass-recording type, in which many impulses make up the record, or of the microelectrode variety. Most data obtained have been with mass recording (see Bartley and Nelson, 1963).

Evoked potentials have been studied under two different conditions of stimulation. One is the flicker method, which amounts to repetitive stimulation of the retina and pathway. The other is with pairs of stimuli separated by varying intervals of time. The second is more interesting because it provides information about the channel capacity of the system, whereas the first merely confirms what is already known, namely, that the optic pathways must somehow follow the flash rate up to CFF.

From studies of the response to the second flash delivered at some interval after the first, it becomes quite clear that no *individual* neurons along the optic pathways can follow flash rates as high as the flicker fusion frequency. The thesholds and latencies of retinal neurons, as seen in optic-nerve fibers, vary considerably from one neuron to another, but the refractory periods are such that they can fire only 5 to 20 times a second. The same is true of neurons farther along the pathway in, say, the lateral geniculate body. If a shock is delivered to the stump of the optic nerve (Bartley, 1936) and the cortical response recorded, an interval of about 200 milliseconds (in the rabbit) must elapse before a second full-sized response can be elicited from the cortex. The interval is undoubtedly less than that in man, but, even so, the neurons in the system are incapable of firing oftener than 5 to 20 times a second. The significance of this will be brought out below.

ELECTROENCEPHALOGRAM—The electroencephalogram (EEG) of man has a natural rhythm, the *alpha rhythm*, of about 10 cycles per second. (Frequencies between 8 and 13 cycles are usually called alpha.) The rabbit, on which considerable work relevant to flicker discrimination has been done, has a dominant rhythm of about 5 per second. Different animals very somewhat in the rate of this dominant rhythm, and allowances for that have to be made in extrapolating from animals to man. The alpha rhythm undoubtedly determines the excitability of the cortex and the ease with which it accepts trains of impulses from below. In one phase of the rhythm, stimuli must be stronger than in another phase to evoke a response in the EEG.

In flicker stimulation, this rhythm is modified within rather broad limits. Indeed, it conforms or follows the rate of flicker. And, in man, it does this up to 55 to 60 cycles per second if the intensity of light is high, and this is about the upper limit of flicker discrimination. Thus one can see in the EEG record of man a following that corresponds roughly to the perception of fusion (Jasper, 1937).

As the EEG follows flicker to higher frequencies, the amplitude of the recorded waves gradually becomes smaller. And it does this in an interesting way. At 20 flashes per second, the amplitude is about half what it is at 10 flashes, and at 40 it is about half the amplitude of 20 flashes. It is as though all the fibers contributing to the evoked potential could not keep up with the flicker rate and, at the higher rates, were firing only some of the time but in volleys.

ALTERNATION-OF-RESPONSE THEORY

The idea just expressed has been put forward by Bartley (1959; also Bartley and Nelson, 1963) in a theory called the alternation-of-response theory. This theory seems to account nicely for just about all the known facts about flicker vision—more than will be recounted here. In essence, it is a volley theory of activity in the optic pathway. Individudal fibers are assumed to have low limiting rates of firing, of, say, 5 to 20 times per second. However, some fire on one flash of light, while others fire on another, so that successive volleys of impulses keep up with the flickering light up to about 60 flashes of light at high intensities, when individual volleys could not keep up with more than 10 flashes per second.

This theory not only takes account of the known limitations of the optic pathway but is confirmed by both subjective measurements and evoked-potential measurements from the visual cortex (Bartley, 1959). The record of Figure 7.11, a schematic EEG record from the rabbit, shows the first few cycles beginning with the onset of a flickering stimulus. Notice that at first the record is irregular; the waves are not all of the same amplitude and they are irregularly spaced. After a few flashes, however, they begin to follow the flicker at regular intervals and with uniform amplitude. This is exactly what one would expect from the alternation-of-response theory. At the very first flash of light, most elements in the pathway discharge and then become refractory for the second flash. Sooner or later, though, because of varying periods of refractoriness, the cortex becomes "reorganized," so that responses to light are evenly distributed among the contributing units.

BRIGHTNESS ENHANCEMENT

When dealing with the effect of a flickering light upon a photosensitive plate, one must somehow evaluate the intensity of a steady light that is equivalent to the flickering light. This is usually done by assuming Talbot's law. According to this law, the effective intensity of a flickering light is the product of the intensity of the flash and the fraction of the light-dark cycle it requires. If this is 50 percent, as is typically the case, a flickering light should be half as bright as a steady light of the same intensity.

This law holds well for rather high rates of flicker, and for that reason flicker photometry for measuring brightness and luminosities is possible. However, at rather low flicker rates up to 16 or 20 flashes a second, it does not hold if the light is fairly intense. On the contrary, such a flickering light is brighter than it should be by Talbot's law. At 10 cycles per second, it may be four times as bright subjectively as Talbot's law would predict. This effect is called *brightness enhancement.* (Bartley, 1959) and is illustrated in Figure 7.12.

The explanation of brightness enhancement seems quite clear (Bartley, 1959). It depends on the dominant alpha rhythm of the electroencephalogram. This rhythm represents a waxing and waning of excitability of the cortex and particularly of the occipital cortex. Impulses arriving at the cortex have a greater effect when they are in step with the more excitable phase of

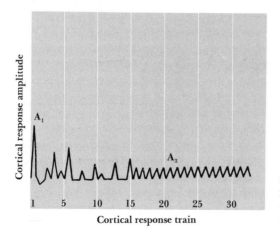

FIGURE 7.11—The typical response of the visual cortex of the rabbit to flashes at a frequency greater than that to which any single channel can respond. (Adapted from S. H. Bartley and T. M. Nelson. Some relations between sensory end results and neural activity in the optic pathway. *J. Psychol.*, 1963, 55, 134.)

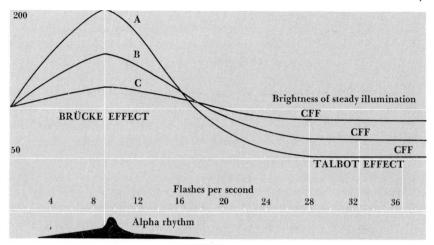

FIGURE 7.12—The brightness of a flickering light relative to a steady light at different flicker frequencies. A, light-dark ratio of 1 : 1; B, 7 : 2; and C, 8 : 1. (Adapted from S. H. Bartley. Some factors in brightness discrimination. *Psychol. Rev.*, 1939, 46, 344.)

the alpha rhythm than when they are not. Hence brightness enhancement is greatest at a flicker rate that is the same as that of alpha. It happens too that there is an interaction between flicker and the alpha wave so that the alpha can be "driven" by flickering light within certain limits of flicker rate (Halstead et al., 1942). The flickering light changes the alpha rate, and the alpha rate influences the effectiveness of flickering light.

"ON" AND "OFF" RESPONSES

As we have seen earlier, short flashes of light of the kind encountered in flicker discrimination produce both "on" responses and "off" responses in the optic pathway. One may ask how these responses are related to flicker discrimination. Is it an "on" response, an "off" response, or some combination of them that is responsible for flicker perception? There is no direct answer to this question, but experiments on pulse-to-cycle fraction (PCF) have a bearing on it (Bartley and Nelson, 1961).

With the appropriate electronic apparatus, flicker may be maintained at a constant rate while the length of the light flash is varied. This procedure changes the pulse-to-cycle fraction while leaving the repetition rate unchanged. The effect of doing this has been studied in man for PCFs as little as 0.02 and as high as 0.98 (Bartley and Nelson, 1961). The typical result is that the perception at low PCF is one of fusion, at moderate PCFs the effect is flicker, and then again at a higher PCF the effect is fusion.

The neurophysiological theory proposed for this effect is as follows: Very short pulses elicit only weak "on" responses, not "off" responses. These are insufficient to cause flicker. As the pulses are lengthened, "off" responses are produced, and these produce flicker. However, as PCF is lengthened, the dark interval is shortened, and the "off" response of one cycle is followed quickly by the "on" response of the next cycle. This causes the "off" response to be inhibited by the "on" response, and the consequence of this again is fusion. In essence, this theory says that the flicker ordinarily perceived is to be explained by the "off" responses, or at least by "off" responses alternating with "on" responses, in the optic pathway. It seems plausible, but it has not been directly confirmed.

PHOSPHENES

A phenomenon related to flicker has attracted the interest of a few investigators and deserves a brief description. This is the *phosphene*. A phosphene is a visual sensation evoked by stimuli other than light. Pressure on the eyeball will produce a phosphene; so will electrical stimulation. The latter is more easily controlled and has been used in systematic investigations of phosphenes and their behavior (Motokawa, 1949; Gebhard, 1952, 1953; Clausen, 1955). The literature is at times contradictory, but the following main points are well established (Clausen, 1955).

The electrical threshold for a phosphene varies with frequency. In the light-adapted eye, it is at a minimum with an alternating-current rate of 20 cycles per second. The phosphenes seen at this frequency are in the central visual field. At about 35 cycles per second there is another minimum of sensitivity which is correlated with phosphenes seen in the more peripheral retina. In the dark-adapted eye, another minimum at about 6 cycles per second appears. Aside from these minima, two other points are worth noting: (1) During dark adaptation, the threshold at first decreases and then later increases. The net effect is an increase, which is quite the opposite, of course, from what happens to the light threshold. (2) There is no fusion for alternating currents; at rates as high as 70 cycles per second flicker is still perceived.

How these facts are to be interpreted physiologically is not entirely clear. It would seem, however, that electrical stimulation bypasses the photochemical apparatus and directly stimulates neural elements in the retina.

SPATIAL VISION

The term spatial vision refers to the perception of patterns and details in the visual world. Other terms have been used, and some will be used here to refer to one or another aspect of spatial vision. These are detail vision, visual acuity, pattern discrimination, object vision, and movement discrimination. Detail vision is practically synonymous with spatial vision; it refers to perceiving objects, contours, or other spatial aspects of a stimulus. Visual acuity refers to the threshold of detail vision—to the smallest objects or separation between objects that can be seen. Pattern discrimination and object vision refer to the perception of shapes. Movement discrimination, as is obvious, refers to the perception of motion in the visual environment. The latter, incidentally, may occur when the organism is relatively incapable of perceiving the object that is moving.

With these terms of reference in mind, we shall discuss the physiological mechanisms of spatial vision under four main headings: measures of spatial vision, spatial vision in man, pattern vision in animals, and movement perception.

MEASURES OF SPATIAL VISION

In studies of human and animal perception, a great many different methods have been used. When, however, only studies in which physiological mechanisms are considered, the number of methods narrow considerably. In fact, they fall pretty well into two main classes: object visibility and pattern discrimination.

OBJECT VISIBILITY—An organism can be presented with an object and asked, Do you see it or not? With an animal, the test is whether or not the animal reacts to objects in its environment. Does the animal move about normally without bumping into things? Can it pick up objects without fumbling? Can it jump accurately from one platform to another over an intervening gap? In the case of people, the person may be shown a hair or wire and asked whether he sees it or not. The smallest line he can see then becomes a measure of his visual acuity. Or a dot may be moved around in the visual field, and the person asked to say when he does or does not see it. This kind of measurement is called *perimetry* and is used to map the field of a person suffering from a visual defect.

PATTERN DISCRIMINATION—In tests of pattern discrimination, two or more objects are presented to the organism, and it must somehow indicate that it can tell the difference between them. This is the method routinely employed in testing animals. However, the animal must be trained. He is rewarded for reacting to one stimulus and sometimes is also punished for reacting to the other. Because training is involved, it is sometimes difficult to tell, in cases of impairment of ability to discriminate, whether the difficulty lies in the realm of learning and retention or whether it represents merely a loss of sensory capacity. It is the latter in which we are interested here; when does an animal have or not have the sheer sensory capacity for making a discrimination, quite apart from his ability to learn and remember? We shall defer the discussion of the learning and retention of pattern discriminations to a later chapter (Chapter 17).

SPATIAL VISION IN MAN

The ability to study the physiological mechanisms of spatial vision in man is distinctly limited. Since direct intervention in the visual system is not feasible, very little can be learned from electrical methods of recording or from experimental lesions. There are left the measurements that can be made in individuals suffering accidental injuries, and in these cases it is not known precisely where the lesion is. Certain inferences can also be made from the experimental psychology of vision, but these are risky. The few statements that can be made will be treated under three main headings: visual acuity, perimetry, and hidden figures.

VISUAL ACUITY—There have been two established methods for measuring visual acuity: the minimum separable method and the minimum visible method. In the first method, the observer's task is to detect a gap between two lines or between two parts of a figure. In the minimum visible method, a dark line on a light background, or vice versa, is presented, and the smallest width of line that can be seen is measured. The two methods give results that, in general, are comparable. However, the minimum visible method ordinarily gives a considerably better value for visual acuity than does the minimum separable method.

A typical curve relating visual acuity to intensity of illumination is given in Figure 7.13. That curve is for man, but curves like it may be obtained from animals by taking advantage of the fact that many animals reflexly follow moving stripes in the visual field (see Optokinetic Reactions below). In mixed eyes, the curve usually has a barely detectable separation into two limbs representing rods and cones. The rod section, however, does not amount to much; it is a short, relatively flat limb at the lower intensities. That means that there is relatively little visual acuity or object vision afforded by the rods. The bulk of the curve, including all medium to high values of visual acuity, represents cone activity.

The cone section of the curve has a sigmoid shape much like that found for curves of flicker discrimination. This particular shape is well fitted by a probability integral. For that reason, it is assumed that visual acuity increases with intensity because the thresholds of receptors are normally distributed in terms of log sensitivity (Crozier, 1940). This is probably correct, but it is an inference without direct verification.

STABILIZED IMAGES—Although visual acuity depends on intensity and hence, probably, on the distribution of receptor thresholds, it also depends on another factor, the involuntary movements of the eyes. Such movements are rapid and small, though detectable, tremors of the eyes that occur constantly in fixating a visual object.

Although the existence of these involuntary movements has been known

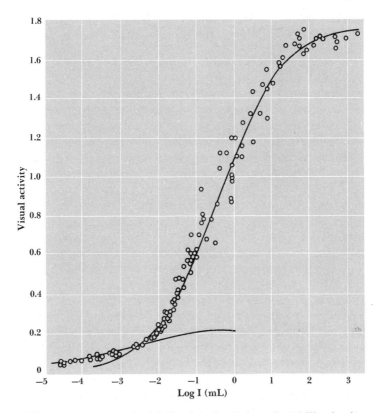

FIGURE 7.13—The relation of visual acuity to intensity of illumination in the human eye. Adapted from S. Hecht. Vision. II. The nature of the photoreceptor process. In C. Murchison (Ed.), *A handbook of general experimental psychology.* Worcester, Mass.: Clark University Press, 1934. P. 774. By permission of the publishers.)

for a long time, it was only in the past few years that it has become possible to measure their role in visual acuity and object perception. This was accomplished by an ingenious method of stabilizing the retinal image and thus making it independent of tremor (Riggs et al., 1953). The method consists of mounting a mirror on the cornea of the eye and putting the image viewed by the observer through an optical system involving the mirror in such a way that the movement of the eye causes a compensatory movement of the image. Thus, so far as the retina is concerned, the image remains motionless.

When the retinal image is stabilized in this way, an interesting thing happens. The contours of an object gradually fade, and, in some cases, the object disappears altogether. In other words, there is an adaptation for visual objects.

This phenomenon immediately suggests that perhaps movement is required for object vision. Such a suggestion might seem particularly plausible in view of the finding (see page 163) that some cells in the visual cortex seem to be particularly responsive, or perhaps solely responsive, to movement. Such an interpretation, however, is clearly not correct. During the first few moments of inspection of a stabilized image, it is seen just as clearly as in normal vision. The difference is that the image later begins to fade. Hence motion is not necessary for object perception. It is, however, necessary for the maintenance of responses in the interacting elements of the system. Cells in the system evidently need the brief rests afforded by the oscillation of images caused by eye tremor.

The exact location of the cells that are involved in this adaptation has not been established. Possibly all the cells along the line to the brain behave in this way. On the other hand, it is plausible that the effect is entirely retinal (Riggs et al., 1961).

PERIMETRY—We turn now to the question of how the human brain functions in object perception. Although there is a vast amount of clinical literature on this question, there are no definitive answers. In general, the topographical projection of the retina to the visual cortex has been the focus of attention. From such a projection, which is well established even though there appears also to be nontopographical projection (see page 163), one might believe that objects are perceived because they have a mirrorlike counterpart in the visual cortex. That has been the dominant view (Doty, 1961). Some of the available facts fit with it, and some do not, as we shall see.

It is generally agreed that a man deprived of his geniculostriate projection cannot see patterns at all (Teuber, 1960). He is object-blind. This is true whether the loss is a total destruction of the striate cortex or an interruption of the projections to the striate cortex. It is also true that subtotal injuries to the striate cortex cause more restricted losses of object vision, leaving some object vision intact. In Figure 7.14 are two cases mapped by methods of perimetry. These are extreme cases. One has lost virtually all peripheral vision, but central "tunnel" vision is intact. The other has lost a large area of central vision but has some peripheral vision intact. The areas of visual loss as mapped by perimetry are known as *scotomata.*

OBJECT VISION—From maps like these, one might conclude that object vision in man is determined by a point-to-point topographical projection of the retina on the visual cortex. Indeed, there is some such relationship. There are, however, other aspects of the visual defect that do not fit in with this simple view. Two relevant phenomena encountered in such defects are *completion* and *extinction* of visual patterns.

One of the characteristics and interesting things about people with subtotal visual-field defects is their ability to recognize shapes (Teuber et al., 1960). Indeed, their shape recognition is not what one would expect from perimetry. The second case in Figure 7.14, for example, could easily recognize large forms, such as triangles, circles, and squares, even when a large part of the

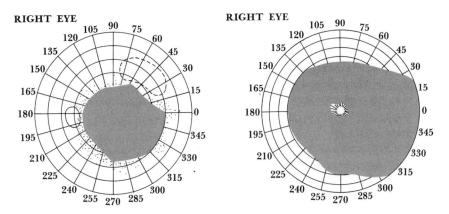

FIGURE 7.14—Two cases of visual scotomata incurred by damage to the visual cortex. (Adapted from H.-L. Teuber, W. S. Battersby, and M. B. Bender. *Visual field defects after penetrating missile wounds of the brain.* Cambridge: Harvard University Press, 1960. Pp. 20 and 28. Reprinted by permission of the publishers and The Commonwealth Fund.)

form fell in the area of visual defect. This ability is called filling in or *completion.* The person completes the pattern without any apparent difficulty even though from perimetry it appears not to be seen. This is normally done for the blind spot in the retina, but this is small and, moreover, it is "filled in" in the cortex. It is surprising that it occurs for large "blind spots" caused by injury to the cortex.

Another surprising phenomenon is the *extinction* of objects (Bender, 1952). This is a fading, somewhat akin to the fading of stabilized images, that may occur in areas of mild defect when normal areas are at the same time stimulated. For example, a patient may see a pattern presented in a defective portion of his field, so long as it is on a fairly homogeneous background. Then, if a pattern of any kind is presented in the "good" part of his visual field, the first pattern becomes much less distinct or may fade out entirely. If the pattern in the "good" part is taken away, he can immediately see the pattern in the "bad" part of his visual field. Obviously, the defect is not all-or-none, and there is some interaction between the defective and normal parts of the visual field.

HIDDEN FIGURES—Another kind of difficulty is regularly seen in patients with visual-field defects. This is a difficulty in perceiving hidden figures embedded in more complex figures of interlocking contours (see Figure 7.15, page 195). Such a test of hidden figures has existed in many forms, but the one most standardized today is known as the Bender-Gestalt. The subject is required to find, by tracing, a figure shown in isolation in each of a set of more complex figures.

The interesting fact about performance on this test is that it is impaired by injuries almost anywhere in the cerebral cortex. Impairment may accompany specific visual-field defects, but it may be seen in cases of injury completely outside the striate cortex where there is no scotomata. Aphasic patients— patients suffering impairment of language abilities (see Chapter 19) and who usually have injuries in the lateral portion of the brain rather than the occipital—do the worst on hidden-figure tests. But although aphasics are the worst, any sort of brain injury causes significant impairment on this task. Why this is so is not known. It merely indicates that some aspects of pattern perception in man depend on areas of the cortex other than the striate cortex.

We may summarize by saying (1) that total destruction of the visual cortex in man causes a complete loss of *pattern vision*, (2) that subtotal losses cause specific scotomata but these are not all-or-none, for in scotomatous areas, there is some completion of patterns as well as some extinction of them, and (3) that pattern perception depends in part on cortical areas outside the primary visual cortex.

PATTERN VISION IN ANIMALS

It is generally believed that there is a progressive corticalization of function in the vertebrate series (Marquis, 1935). That is to say, functions are gradually transferred from lower centers of the brain to the cortical level. Within limits, this is undoubtedly true, for lower vertebrates have little neocortex as it is seen in mammals, and even the bird appears to have little visual function depending on the cortex (Layman, 1936). But how far this holds in the mammalian series is open to question. It would appear that there is more corticalization of visual function in man than in monkeys, cats, dogs, and rats, but whether or not there are systematic differences among the mammals below man is not known. It is simply a possibility that must be kept in mind.

VISUAL CORTEX—Until recently the same flat statement could be made about the other mammals as was made about man: Cats, rats, and monkeys have no pattern vision after their visual cortex is destroyed. All the experiments, however, on which this statement was based had been done with adult animals. The usual procedure was to train the animal to make a pattern discrimination, then remove the striate cortex, and retest long enough to establish both that the animal had lost the habit it had previously acquired and that, given a long period of training, was incapable of acquiring it. Such was the typical result (rat, Lashley and Frank, 1934; cat, Smith, 1938; monkey, Klüver, 1937). Such animals also indicated a lack of pattern vision in obvious ways: they bumped into objects and did not seem to see objects in their environment.

More recently, however, it has been shown that, if the striate area is destroyed in newborn animals (cat), loss of pattern vision does not result (Doty, 1961). Such animals, tested as adults, appear to an observer to have normal

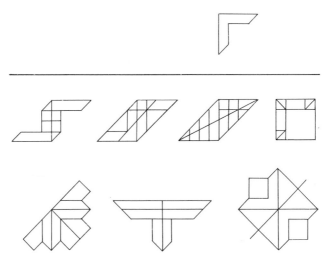

FIGURE 7.15—Sample from a hidden-figure test. (Adapted from H.-L. Teuber and S. Weinstein. Ability to discover hidden figures after cerebral lesion. *Arch. Neurol. Psychiat.*, 1956, 76, 369.)

visual abilities in every respect. Also, when trained on a shape discrimination, they perform as well as normals. It appears from histological studies of the brains at the end of the experiment that these cats had no remaining striate cortex.

It must be concluded that, while pattern vision normally requires the striate cortex, it is not necessary if its destruction occurs early in life. Some areas, cortical or subcortical, outside the geniculostriate system then subserve the pattern-vision function. This effect, though somewhat surprising in the case of pattern vision, is not an isolated one. We shall see at other points in this book that functions normally carried out by certain parts of the brain can be taken over by others, especially if the destruction occurs at an early age.

There have been a number of studies of the effects of subtotal destruction of the striate cortex. In general, the results are similar to those reported for man, although in animals one is not so sure just what the animal is seeing. Moreover, there are no tests for completion and extinction. In the case of the rat (Lashley, 1939), there are instances in which animals with some striate cortex remaining failed pattern-vision tests. There are still others in which good pattern vision remains with very small remnants of the striate cortex functioning, in one case with as little as 700 intact cells projecting to the striate area. Thus the animals seem able either to "fill in" the scotomata or in some way to make use of their residual visual field for discriminating patterns.

In other experiments (Sperry and Miner, 1955; Sperry et al., 1955), the striate cortex has been riddled with knife cuts, wires, and interruptions of the visual cortex, so that connections within the cortex are broken up and many areas of the striate cortex are isolated from each other. The effects of all this are essentially nil (in the cat). The subjects can pass quite nicely a battery of tests for form or pattern discrimination. This result, together with the studies of people with occipital injuries, makes it apear that the topographical arrangement of the striate cortex is of little significance in pattern vision (see Doty, 1961).

SUBCORTICAL CENTERS—If there is a corticalization of functions in the mammal, one would expect the transfer of functions in evolution to be from the superior colliculus to the striate cortex. The superior colliculus appears to be *the* visual center in lower vertebrates like the fish and frog. Moreover, the superior colliculus maintains a very precise topographical arrangement parallel to that of the lateral geniculate body and the striate cortex (Maturana et al., 1959). Indeed, a large share of the cells of the geniculate are served by collaterals of fibers on their way from the retina to the superior colliculus. It is therefore interesting to inquire what function the colliculus has in vision. Unfortunately, there is relatively little work on this question.

In one experiment with cats (Blake, 1959), the colliculi appeared to play a crucial role in pattern vision. After removal of the colliculi the cats showed typical symptoms of object blindness. They did not recognize previously familiar objects, and, more significantly, they were unable to pass a test of pattern discrimination that they had learned prior to operation or to learn again to pass it. These animals also showed, as might be expected, defects of eye movements and in orientation toward objects. It is possible, therefore, that the defect encountered here is different in nature from the object blindness seen in striate cats. It may be due to oculomotor defects that interfere with looking at visual patterns. More research on the superior colliculus is needed before firm conclusions can be drawn.

MOVEMENT PERCEPTION

The perception of motion is an aspect of spatial vision. It involves the displacement of objects in space, Not very much is known about it from a physiological point of view, but this will summarize what is known.

HUMAN SCOTOMA—The motion perception of individuals suffering subtotal injuries to the striate area have been studied (Bay, 1953; Teuber, 1960). In the field of the scotoma, patients sometimes see movement, or a moving object, when they cannot see a stationary object. Movement also frequently prevents the fading or extinction of objects that otherwise may occur in the scotomatous area. In both cases, it would appear that the movement provides more stimulation than a stationary object. In any case, it is not uncommon in clinical reports to find motion perception in scotomatous areas. This probably does not mean that movement perception depends on some other part of the brain. Rather, movement perception may be partially spared because it involves more interaction and more stimulation of different parts of the total visual field than stationary objects do. This is not known.

DISCRIMINATION—In lower animals there are two experiments, both on cats, concerning the discrimination of real movement in the absence of the striate cortex. Neither experiment was particularly thorough or satisfactory. In one, animals were trained to distinguish between a stationary spot and a spot moving in a circle (Kennedy, 1939). In the other, cats had to discriminate between two sets of stripes, one moving and the other stationary (Morgan, 1937). Both experiments demonstrated that cats without the striate cortex can discriminate real movement. They agreed, however, in finding that the rate of movement required for such discrimination was considerably higher after cortical destruction than before. Moreover, the performance of the animals was so unstable as to prevent the measurement of postoperative thresholds of movement. Thus it is clear that movement perception is radically impaired, though not abolished, in the absence of the striate cortex.

OPTOKINETIC REACTIONS IN ANIMALS—Movement perception of a sort has been studied in another way, by means of *optokinetic reactions* (Smith, 1937). These reactions are movements of the eyes or head, depending on the species used, that follow vertical stripes moving horizontally in the visual field (see Figure 7.16). Such a following reaction is a reflexive response that

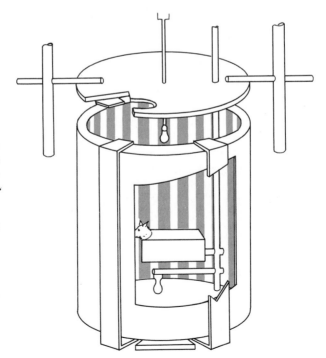

FIGURE 7.16—
Schematic side view of apparatus for the study of optokinetic reactions in animals. (Adapted from K. U. Smith. The postoperative effects of removal of the striate cortex upon certain unlearned visually controlled reactions in the cat. *J. genet. Psychol.*, 1937, 50, 145. By permission of the Journal Press.)

occurs when the animal is totally immersed in the field and can see no stationary objects or background, only the moving stripes. This technique, incidentally, has been used to measure visual acuity, as well as flicker discrimination, in various normal animals.

Movement vision, measured in this way, has also been studied in the cat after removal of its striate cortex. There is no impairment at all. If anything, the reflex optokinetic reactions to moving stripes become somewhat more stable and dependable after removal of the visual cortex than they are in the normal animal. And when the stripes are reduced in size to the point at which the reactions disappear, thus giving a threshold of visual acuity, the visual acuity of the cat is just as good without the visual cortex as with it. It cannot be concluded from this that movement "perception" is normal, for it has been shown above that this is not the case. It does show that reflex reactions to movement are intact after removal of the striate cortex.

BRIGHTNESS DISCRIMINATION

We turn now, in this last section, to the topic of brightness discrimination. Brightness discrimination is the detection of a difference in the intensities of two lights or surfaces. In the simple case, it is merely the perception of the presence or absence of light in the visual field. When the smallest difference in brightness that can be detected is measured precisely, it is customary to express this difference in terms of $\Delta I/I$, in which I stands for the standard intensity of light and ΔI is the increment of intensity that is just discriminable.

BRIGHTNESS THRESHOLDS

In Figure 7.17 there is a characteristic set of curves for brightness discrimination as a function of intensity. Wavelength is the parameter for the different curves, which have been displaced arbitrarily for clarity. In these functions, as in most discrimination functions for the human eye, the presence of two limbs representing rod and cone functions can be seen. The break is clearer for the short wavelengths—the blue end of the spectrum—than it is for the long wavelengths. This is because rods are relatively more sensitive than cones in the blue whereas in the far red, beyond 600, virtually all the curve is determined by cones.

RETINAL PROCESSES

Electrical methods of measuring effects in the retina corresponding to brightness differences have not been extensively used. In one case, however, the eye of *Limulus* (Riggs and Graham, 1945) was adapted to a given intensity of illumination I and then exposed to an increment of illumination ΔI. The

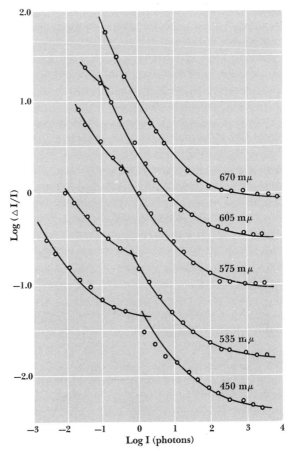

FIGURE 7.17—Brightness discrimination at different intensities and wavelengths of light. (Adapted from S. Hecht, J. C. Peskin, and M. Patt. Intensity discrimination in the human eye. II. The relation between $\triangle I/I$ and intensity for different parts of the spectrum. *J. gen. Physiol.*, 1938, 22, 15. By permission of The Rockefeller Institute Press.)

value of $\triangle I$ required to elicit a constant increase of the number of nerve impulses in the optic nerve was taken as the brightness threshold. The results are shown in Figure 7.18. The invertebrate eye of *Limulus* contains only one type of receptor, not two, and it therefore gives a single unbroken function. In general, however, the function is similar to, although not so steep as, the psychological data for human brightness discrimination.

It is probable that the general form of the brightness-discrimination function, including the rod-cone break and the spectral effects just mentioned, is determined in the retina. The nervous system ought also to be involved, but its contribution has not been studied in any precise way.

CEREBRAL CORTEX

There are a good many experiments on the role of the visual cortex in brightness discrimination in animals. All mammalian animals studied, except possibly man, seem able to discriminate brightness after removal of the visual

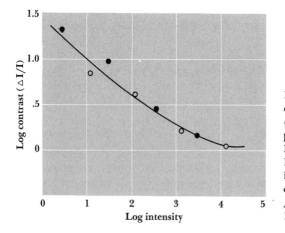

FIGURE 7.18—Intensity discrimination of the horseshoe crab (Limulus) measured electrophysiologically. (Adapted from L. A. Riggs and C. H. Graham. Effects due to variations in light intensity on the excitability cycle of the single visual-sense cell. *J. cell. comp. Physiol.*, 1945, 26, 1–13.)

cortex. Whether human beings with total destruction of the striate cortex can see light or not still is a question that, strangely, has not been clearly determined, and there are different opinions on it (see Neff, 1960; Teuber, 1960). But in animals, even though they can see lights after striate removal, there is no doubt that there are some interesting problems of *memory* for brightness-discrimination habits following such an operation (see Chapter 17). It may be concluded that the visual cortex is not necessary for brightness discrimination in animals.

There are, however, some losses in brightness discrimination after striate destruction. When careful measurements are made of the thresholds $(\Delta I/I)$, there is a sizable impairment in brightness discrimination. Experiments in cats demonstrate this quite clearly (Mead, 1939; see also Bridgman and Smith, 1942). The whole curve is shifted upward about a logarithmic unit, that is to say, by a factor of 10. Apparently, then, the visual cortex is involved in good brightness discrimination but shares this function with subcortical centers.

SUBCORTICAL CENTERS

Here, as elsewhere, little work has been done on subcortical centers. In an old series of experiments (Ghiselli, 1938), lesions were made in the superior colliculi of rats. These, by themselves, had no effect; brightness discrimination was unimpaired by bilateral removal of these structures. If, on the other hand, the colliculi were destroyed after the striate cortex had also been removed, there was an amnesia for the habit. The animals did not remember the discrimination learned preoperatively. This result, however, was in some way concerned with memory, not capacity, for the animals were fully capable of relearning the discrimination.

These facts, taken at face value, seem to mean that the superior colliculus is normally not involved in brightness discrimination but that, in the absence of the visual cortex, it may become so. In no case, however, does it seem to be crucial. In the absence of both the striate cortex and the superior colliculi, animals are capable of learning a brightness discrimination. The structure, then, that mediates this function under these circumstances is not known.

Recent experiments on the learning and retention of brightness-discrimination habits implicate some of the pretectal nuclei lying just in front of the colliculi (Thompson and Rich, 1961). These seem, however, to be entirely concerned with memory functions rather than sensory capacity and will be discussed at a later point in the book (Chapter 17).

8 HEARING

P
ROGRESS IN UNDERSTANDING the sensory functions is dependent to a large extent upon the ability to control precisely, at the experimental level, the physical aspects of stimuli. That ability has been acquired in audition largely because of the immense strides that have taken place within the field of electronics, most particularly, in the development of oscillators, amplifiers, and various timing devices. These instruments now make it possible to produce known acoustic stimuli as well as to analyze and record various physiological aspects of hearing. As a consequence, considerable headway has been made in both the psychology and physiology of hearing during the span of the past thirty years.

AUDITORY STIMULATION

Sound waves are the stimuli for hearing. There are many sorts of sound waves. Some are simple and relatively pure, like the note of a piano or violin. Some are extremely complex, like speech or the sound of a gun. To give a complete physical description of the nature of all these sounds would become rather complicated. To serve our purposes here, however, it is necessary to know only a few basic points about sound.

THE NATURE OF SOUND

One is that sound is the vibration of an elastic medium. Sound waves are like the vibration of a car or of any solid object, except that they take place in air and fluid media as well. Also, they can be of much higher frequency than ordinary mechanical vibrations. In air or in water, the sound wave is first a compression of the medium, then an expansion, taking place in the molecules of the medium, progressing in air at about 1,000 feet per second (760 miles per hour) until it gradually dies out.

Another basic point about sound is that, no matter how complex it may be, it can always be analyzed into simple components. This analysis can be made mathematically, if the precise shape of the sound wave is known, by the aid of a formula known as Fourier's theorem. In practice, engineers and research workers have special devices that can be used for performing the analysis. In any event, the simple sound wave, into which all complex waves can be analyzed, is a *sine wave*. Some examples of sine waves are shown in Figure 8.1, page 205. These waves represent the compression and expansion of the particles of air. The compression becomes greater and greater until a peak is reached and then subsides smoothly. But like a pendulum, it overshoots the mark, expanding to a maximum and then returning again toward zero. Every sine wave has two aspects, intensity and frequency, which are what are used to measure and characterize sounds.

INTENSITY

Intensity corresponds to the magnitude of the swing of the sine wave. Waves with high peaks are very intense; those with small swings are weak. This aspect of a sine wave can be stated in two way. One is in terms of pressure. The distance from any point on the graph of a sine wave to the base line represents the pressure in the particles of air at that particular instant. The pressure is canstantly changing, of course, throughout the duration of the sine wave, for that is what sound is: rapidly changing pressure. If one wanted to measure the intensity of a sound wave in terms of pressure, he would take the peak of the wave; that would be the maximum pressure. There are meters, called sound-pressure meters, that measure these peaks, and they are used in auditory research.

ENERGY—Basically, however, interest is not just in the peak of a sound wave but in the whole wave. Thus it would be helpful to add up all the various pressures in the sound wave for a given period of time. Such an integration of pressures represents the total energy in a sound wave. And it is energy that acoustical engineers and research workers use as their reference in talking about the intensity of sounds. Pure sine waves, however, always have the same shape—by definition—and there is a constant relation between pressure and energy measurements of sine waves. This constant can be used to convert measures of sound pressure into sound energy.

DECIBELS—For a number of reasons, which we do not need to go into here, a logarithmic scale is used for measuring sound intensities. Such a scale is more useful not only in acoustical engineering but in understanding the mechanisms of hearing as well. A logarithmic scale, of course, is set up according to the exponents of a base number, usually taken as 10. Thus a sound that is 10 times would have a value of 2; one that is 1,000, a value of 3; and so on. The unit of this logarithmic scale of intensities of sound has a name, the *bel*. A bel is the logarithm of a ratio of 10. In most work with hearing, however, the bel is too big a unit. A finer one is needed. The bel is therefore split into ten parts, called *decibels*. A decibel is one-tenth of a bel.

We should notice one final point about these units of intensity. They are *ratios*. In hearing one is seldom concerned about the absolute energy of the stimulus sound waves. What is wanted is to know how much more intense or less intense one sound is than another. Therefore there is always some reference intensity. Sometimes this is known; sometimes it is not. Very often the reference intensity is some arbitrary reading, such as the number of volts of electricity applied to the loudspeaker used in the experiments. It matters little what the reference intensity is, so long as it is known. Given a reference intensity, it is a simple matter to describe all the sound stimuli used as some number of decibels above or below this intensity.

FREQUENCY

The second important aspect of a sine wave that must be known to describe it precisely is its frequency. The alternations of pressure that make up sine waves can be very slow, even as little as two or three per second, or they may be rapid alternations of several hundred thousand per second. But a pure sine wave always has a frequency, which must be known. The frequencies or sound waves that are involved in human hearing are between 20 and 20,000 cycles per second. Some of the animals have hearing for higher or lower frequencies than this.

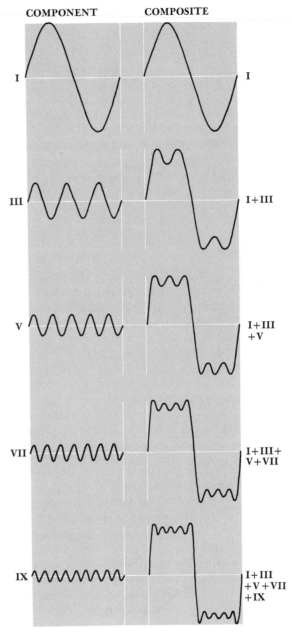

COMPONENT   COMPOSITE

I   I

III   I+III

V   I+III +V

VII   I+III+ V+VII

IX   I+III +V+VII +IX

FIGURE 8.1—Sine waves and the way they add up to a complex wave. On the left are sine waves of different frequency, the top one being a low frequency and the bottom one a high frequency. On the right are complex tones made by adding together different components of pure sine waves. The reverse also works. Any complex sound can be analyzed into some number of sine waves of different intensities. (Adapted from E. G. Boring, H. S. Langfeld, and H. P. Weld (Eds.). *Foundations of psychology.* New York: Wiley, 1948. P. 316. By permission of the publishers.)

With frequency and intensity, all sounds can be specified, whether they are simple or complex. The complex sounds consist of many different frequencies occurring together, but it is possible to describe them by naming each of the component sine-wave frequencies and giving the intensity of each component. Actually, in everyday life pure sine waves are seldom encountered, although they are produced in a laboratory for precise scientific purposes. In most of the experiments to be described here, pure sine waves were used and their frequencies were known. Where this was not the case, the experimenter had some good reason for using a noise or other complex sound without caring about its exact composition.

AUDITORY MEASUREMENTS

In this chapter, as in others, most of the experiments to be discussed were done with animals. Although human beings can make all sorts of judgments about auditory stimuli, animals are more limited. Even so, methods have been devised for measuring in animals reactions that parallel most of the reactions by people. The following are the kinds of stimulus situations to be discussed in this chapter (see Neff, 1961).

CLICK STIMULI—In hearing, as in the other senses, electrical methods of recording, both gross and microelectrode, have been employed to track and to map auditory responses in the brain. For this purpose, a click stimulus has frequently been used, because such a brief, sudden stimulus evokes the most clear-cut electrical responses in the brain. Such a stimulus is inherently noisy, meaning that it is composed of a mixture of frequencies. However, it can be tailored, if desired, so that its principal component is a particular frequency.

ON-OFF STIMULATION—If one wishes to know whether or not an organism can hear, one can choose a reasonably intense stimulus, turn it on and off, and see whether there is any response to such a stimulus. Such on-off stimulation has been frequently used both in electrical studies of neural responses and in trained animals. In the latter case, the animal is usually conditioned to make a simple response, such as lifting its paw, running in a wheel, or shuttling from one side of a box to the other in response to a sound coming on. In the typical experiment, this method is combined with the ablation of some part of the brain to determine whether the ablation makes a difference in the animal's hearing.

By decreasing the intensity of the stimulus to the point at which the animal ceases responding, this method can be extended to provide a measure of the *absolute threshold*. Then, by comparing the absolute threshold, say, before and after a brain lesion, the amount of *hearing loss* expressed in decibels occasioned by the lesion can be measured. By obtaining the absolute threshold at different frequencies throughout the animal's range of hearing, an *audiogram* is obtained. Sometimes in an experiment there is a hearing loss at certain frequencies but not at others.

INTENSITY DISCRIMINATION—If an organism is given a pair of tones or clicks, one at a higher intensity than the other, and the organism can tell the difference, this is a measure of an intensity discrimination. In work with animals, they usually are trained to make a response indicating whether the second member of a pair is more intense than the first and to make no response when both members of the pair are the same. This means that the animal must learn *not* to respond to "same" and to respond to "different."

FREQUENCY DISCRIMINATION—Exactly the same method, with one slight change, can be used to measure a frequency discrimination. The change is to make the two members of the pair different, when they are different, in frequency rather than in intensity. In the case of both intensity and frequency discrimination, *differential thresholds* can be measured by narrowing the differences to the point at which the discrimination breaks down. Although this is occasionally done, it is more common to present reasonably large differences and to see merely whether the animal can or cannot make the discrimination.

PATTERN DISCRIMINATION—A special kind of frequency discrimination, but one that is more difficult than that just described, is a *pattern discrimination*. In this a pair of tones is on one occasion presented in the sequence high-low-high and on another occasion in the sequence low-high-low. The animal is then trained, say, to respond positively to the high-low-high sequence but not to respond to low-high-low.

SOUND LOCALIZATION—Both human beings and most laboratory animals are relatively good at localizing the direction of a sound source. Such sound localization can be measured experimentally by training an animal to go (for food) to one of two boxes, depending on the location of a buzzer. The sound can be varied randomly from trial to trial between the two boxes. By moving the boxes closer and closer together until the discrimination breaks down, one can measure just how acute a discrimination can be made.

The tests we have just described can be grouped together under one or another of three headings. Those for frequency and pattern discrimination are related to the *pitch* perception of the organism; those for on-off discrimination and intensity discrimination are in the domain of *loudness* perception. In a third category by itself is *sound localization*. These three kinds of perception will constitute three of the sections of this chapter. Before considering them, however, we must first study the anatomy and physiology of the auditory system.

AUDITORY SYSTEM

It is only with the greatest difficulty that man has been able to devise instruments for the analysis of sound. Yet the human ear is a mechanism that performs such an analysis with great, although not perfect, precision. Concerned in this analysis are the intricate structures of the external, the middle, and the inner ear, and giving it meaning in human experience are the various auditory centers and pathways of the brain. In this section we shall describe the principal features of these structures. Then in later sections we shall try to see how they are concerned in auditory experience.

EXTERNAL EAR

What most of us commonly call the ear is to the anatomist only the *pinna* of the external ear. In animals like the dog the pinna is of some use, for it can be pointed in different directions to help "collect" sound waves somewhat more efficiently than people do. For human beings, however, the pinna is little more than a decoration showing where the real ears are hidden. Aside from the pinna, there are two important parts of the external ear. One is the *external meatus,* the canal that runs from the pinna inward; the other is the *tympanic membrane* located at the end of the external meatus and marking the inner boundary of the external ear. It is through these parts of the external ear that sounds are conducted to the middle and inner ears (Figure 8.2).

MIDDLE EAR

Placed obliquely across the end of the external meatus, the tympanic membrane is a cone whose apex points inward (see Figure 8.2). Firmly attached to this apex is the *malleus,* one of three ossicles (bones) of the middle ear. Joined by tight ligaments to the malleus is the *incus,* the second of the three ossicles. This articulates in turn with the *stapes,* the third of the middle-ear bones. Finally, the stapes is attached to the oval window (see below) of the inner ear. It is through this series of bones that sounds are conducted from the external to the inner ear.

Associated with the ossicles are two muscles, the *stapedius* and the *tensor tympani.* The latter is attached to the malleus in such a way that, when it contracts, tension is put upon the tympanic membrane. The stapedius muscle, on the other hand, is attached to the stapes near its joint with the incus, and its contraction so dampens the movement of the bony stapes that the amplitude of vibration of the stapes is reduced, or attenuated.

Surrounding the ossicles of the middle ear is an air-filled cavity. Air pressure in this cavity is ordinarily maintained at the same level as the outside air by means of the *Eustachian tube* connecting it with the mouth cavity, although when air pressure changes rapidly, the Eustachian tube sometimes becomes clogged and the middle-ear pressure is not equalized with the pressure of the outside air. The cavity of the middle ear is contained in the temporal bone of the skull, which makes up part of the wall of the cavity. Also bounding the middle-ear cavity is the tympanic membrane, which has already been mentioned, and two other membranes, the *oval* and *round* windows leading into the inner ear.

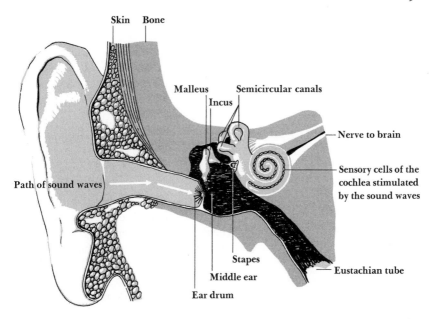

Skin   Bone

Malleus   Semicircular canals

Incus

Nerve to brain

Path of sound waves

Sensory cells of the cochlea stimulated by the sound waves

Stapes

Middle ear

Ear drum

Eustachian tube

FIGURE 8.2—A schematic drawing of the ear. (Adapted from H. Davis (Ed.). *Hearing and deafness.* New York: Holt, 1947. P. 110. By permission of the publishers.)

COCHLEA

The inner ear is part of a system of intercommunicating cavities in a bony labyrinth. Composing it are the cochlea, the semicircular canals, and the vestibular sacs. The latter two structures are of no importance in hearing but will be discussed later in another connection. The cochlea, however, is the primary receptor organ of hearing (see Figure 8.2). It gets its name from its coiled structure. In man, the cochlea has 2¾ turns. In lower animals it may have more or less than that number of turns. The broader end of the cochlea is its *base;* it becomes smaller as it coils and terminates finally in its apex.

The bony cavity of the cochlea is divided into three canals: *scala vestibuli, scala media,* and *scala tympani.* Each of these runs virtually the entire length of the cochlea. Separating the scala vestibuli and scala media is a thin cellular membrane, known as *Reissner's membrane,* and between the scala media and scala tympani is the *basilar membrane.* At the base of the scala vestibuli is the *oval window,* to which is attached the stapes of the middle ear, as has already been mentioned. At the base of the scala tympani is the *round window,* facing into the cavity of the middle ear near the opening of the Eustachian tube. All three canals are filled with fluid. Also to be noted is the fact that the scala vestibuli and tympani communicate with each other at the apex of the cochlea through an opening called the *helicotrema.*

BASILAR MEMBRANE—Reissner's membrane forms one wall of the middle canal of the cochlea; the basilar membrane forms the other. Sitting on the basilar membrane near its inner edge and toward the axis of the coil of the cochlea is a complex cell formation called the *organ of Corti* (Figure 8.3). Although there are many supporting cells in the organ of Corti, the important cells in it are the *hair cells,* for these initiate the physiological response to an acoustic stimulus. The hair cells are arranged throughout the cochlea, from its base to its apex, in two groups. One group is a single row of *internal hair cells.* The other consists of three or four rows of *external hair cells.* Dividing them are the rods and tunnel of Corti. An important accessory structure to the hair cells is the *tectorial membrane* in which the hairs of the cells are embedded. Beneath the hair cells are the endings of the fibers of the auditory portion of the VIIIth nerve (see page 26). The hair cells and the nerve endings that serve them make up the primary receptor apparatus.

The most significant structural property of the basilar membrane is its variation in width from one end of the cochlea to the other. Its width varies in exactly the opposite way from the size of the cochlea within which it lies. The basilar membrane is narrowest at the cochlear base where sound enters,

FIGURE 8.3—The organ of Corti in the human ear. (Adapted from J. D. Lickley. *The nervous system.* New York: Longmans, 1919. P. 107. By permission of the publishers.)

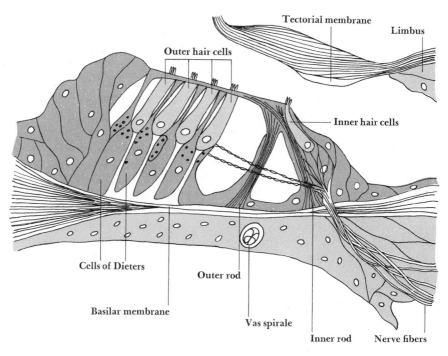

and it is widest at the apex. This variation in width means that it also varies in both stiffness and mass, and these characteristics, particularly that of stiffness, permit it to function as an acoustic frequency analyzer (see below).

TRAVELING WAVES—Thanks to the brilliant work of Von Békésy (1960), there is now available some precise knowledge of what happens in the cochlea during acoustic stimulation. Von Békésy has actually measured pressure changes in the cochlea during such stimulation. These pressure changes take the form of a *traveling wave* or bulge. The following is a brief description of the events producing the traveling wave and of its action in the cochlea.

Sound pressure is transmitted to the cochlea by way of the footplate of the stapes of the middle ear on the oval window. A sound wave reaching this point sends a wave of pressure up the scala vestibuli. This pressure wave causes a net movement of the canal formed by the Reissner and basilar membranes in the direction of the scala tympani. This is possible because this canal is bounded by the *round window*, which is flexible, and can move in and out in response to pressure on the *oval window*. Otherwise said, the pressure on the oval window causes a bulging inside the cochlea toward the round window.

This bulging does not take place all at one instant nor all in one place in the cochlea. Because the basilar membrane varies in stiffness, its narrower basal portion being stiffer than its wider apical region, the wave entering the cochlea at first causes relatively little bulge. As it travels up the cochlea to points of less stiffness, the magnitude of the bulge increases until at some point it reaches a maximum. Thereafter, its energy having been transmitted across the cochlea to the scala tympani canal, it rapidly dies out.

That is the general picture of the traveling wave. The exact pattern of travel, however, depends on frequency. A wave of low frequency travels farther than one of high frequency. The high-frequency wave need travel only a short distance before its amplitude reaches a maximum and then dies out. The low-frequency wave travels to a point where the basilar membrane is wider before it peaks and dies. This is illustrated in Figure 8.4 where it can be seen that waves of higher frequency have a position of maximum displacement nearer the base of the cochlea than those of lower frequency. It is this difference in travel for various frequencies that enables the cochlea to be a frequency analyzer and thus forms the basis, at least in part, for pitch perception.

COCHLEAR MICROPHONICS—Several different potentials and potential changes have been distinguished in electrical recordings from the cochlea (see Davis, 1959). The interior of the scala media is electrically positive with respect to the outside and other tissues; this potential has been called the endocochlear or *endolymphatic potential*. Its origin is in the stria vascularis of the outside wall of the canal. *Summating potentials,* so called because they are relatively

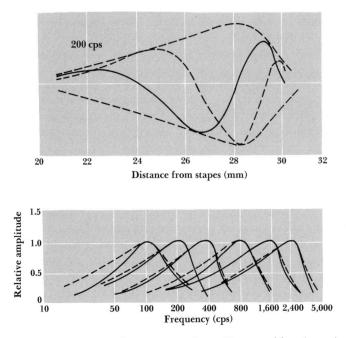

FIGURE 8.4—A traveling wave on the cochlear partition (upper) and a series of displacement curves for six points on the basilar membrane (lower). (Adapted from G. von Békésy. The variation of phase along the basilar membrane with sinusoidal vibrations. *J. Acoust. Soc. Amer.*, 1947, 19, 452–460.)

slow to build up and persist beyond the precise moment of acoustic stimulation, have also been identified.

The most important potential in understanding auditory stimulation is the *cochlear microphonic*. This originates in the hairs of the hair cells, and it serves as the "generator potential" (page 65) for the excitation of auditory nerve fibers ending on the hair cells. Up to relatively high intensities of stimulation, the cochlear microphonic reproduces faithfully the wave form of the stimulus. And it has no threshold other than the ability of an instrument to record it. Hence it is very much like the electrical record one might get from a microphone; that is why it is called a microphonic.

AUDITORY NERVE

The nerve fibers that innervate the hair cells have their cell bodies in the *spiral ganglion*, which is located in the inner wall of the cochlea between its axis and the organ of Corti (see Figure 8.2). Axons from this ganglion collect at the base of the cochlea and pass out the bottom of the coil as the auditory branch of the VIIIth nerve. Just outside the cochlea the auditory branch of the VIIIth nerve is joined by the vestibular branch from the semicircular canals, utricle, and saccule. The two branches divide again, however, just before they reach the medulla. Moreover, the auditory portion itself divides into *dorsal* and *ventral* branches, which end in corresponding nuclei of the medulla. Here are located the cell bodies of second-order auditory neurons.

The VIIIth nerve, like the cochlea, gives an electrical potential when the ear is stimulated by sound. Unlike the cochlear microphonic, however, the auditory nerve potential is an *action potential*. It consists of nerve impulses in neurons triggered by the cochlear microphonic. These nerve impulses have been studied by means both of click stimuli and of pure-tone stimuli of varying frequencies.

If a single click of fairly high intensity is sounded, the response in the auditory nerve consists first of a well-synchronized volley of impulses, called the N_1 response, followed by two smaller waves called the N_2 and N_3 responses. How many of these responses are recorded depends on the intensity of the stimulus; with a weak click, only N_1 is seen; with a moderately intense stimulus, only N_1 and N_2. The responses following the N_1 response are due mostly to repetitive firing of auditory neurons following the initial click stimulation. The different responses are spaced about 1 millisecond apart, and this signifies a refractory period in the neurons of about this value. Such a refractory period means that the auditory nerve fibers cannot "follow" frequencies above 1,000 cycles per second.

This point is brought out more clearly by using steady tones of different frequencies from low to high. If the tone is of 1,000 cycles or less, one sees a fairly regular burst of impulses on every cycle of the tone. Above 1,000 cycles, and particularly between 2,000 and 4,000 cycles, the action potential follows rather clearly the frequency of the stimulus, but the volleys of impulses become smaller in magnitude. This means that individual fibers are skipping some cycles and responding only every second, third, or nth cycle of the stimulus. Since the skips are more or less random, the following of the stimulus occurs through volleys of staggered impulses. No one fiber follows every time, but together they follow by staggering their responses. This principle is known as the "volley principle" (Wever, 1949), and we shall refer to it again later (cf. Alternation-of-response Theory, Chapter 7).

Although nerve impulses can stay in step up to a point, the latency with which they respond is variable. As the frequency of the stimulus is raised, this variability means that impulses, even when staggered, are less well synchronized. Consequently, above about 4,000 cycles per second, following of any kind breaks down. No synchronization can then be detected in the impulses of the auditory nerve fibers. In neurons of a higher order in the brain, synchronized following of a stimulus is even less good and breaks down at lower frequencies.

BRAIN-STEM PATHWAYS

A schematic diagram of the projection of the auditory system from the cochlea through the brain stem to the thalamus and cortex is shown in Figure 8.5. For the present, we shall look only at the left-hand side of this diagram. As can be seen in the diagram, the projection is rather more complicated than is that of the visual or somesthetic pathways. There are more centers involved and, in most cases, more synaptic links. There are so many links, in fact, that, even though first-order neurons from the cochlea reach the brain stem, most of the activity reaching the cerebral cortex is by way of fourth-order neurons. Some may even involve more neurons. The numbers in the diagram represent the order of the neurons, whether first, second, and so on.

Some second-order neurons have been reported as embedded in auditory nerve (Harrison et al., 1962). Whether these are typical of very many animals is not known. Certainly the principal locus of second-order neurons is in the cochlear nuclei of the medulla. Actually, there are two pairs of cochlear

FIGURE 8.5—Diagram of the auditory pathways in a typical mammalian brain. Numbers refer to first-order neuron, second-order neuron, etc. (Adapted from R. Galambos. Some recent experiments on the neurophysiology of hearing. *Ann. Otol. Rhinol. Laryngol.*, 1956, 65, 1053–1059.)

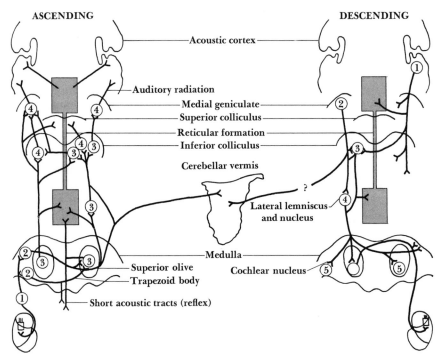

nuclei, one dorsal and the other ventral. These are served by two branches of the auditory nerve carrying the terminations of fibers arriving from the cochlea.

Some of the second-order neurons of the cochlear nuclei remain on the same side, while some cross the midline and make connections with other bulbar nuclei or proceed upward before synapsing with third-order neurons. The principal terminations of second-order neurons are in the trapezoid body, located along the midline of the lower pons, and the superior olive, placed more laterally at about the same level. From these nuclei, neurons originate that course upward in the *lateral lemniscus* to the *inferior colliculi*. In the lateral lemniscus, however, there are also intervening neurons. These are collectively called the nucleus of the lateral lemniscus even though they are not compactly organized. Collaterals of second- and third-order neurons from the cochlear nuclei and the superior olive are given off to the reticular formation. The pathway formed in this way, and perhaps other indirect fibers not in the lateral lemniscus, constitutes an *extralemniscal pathway* (Galambos et al., 1961). Those in the lemniscus constitute the classical, direct sensory pathway, sometimes referred to as the *lemniscal pathway*.

Most of the fibers in the lemniscal pathway end in the inferior colliculus, so that the colliculus is a principal relay station on the way to the medial geniculate body. Some fibers, however, bypass the colliculi and terminate directly in the medial geniculate body. So far as is known, all direct projections to the auditory cortex are relayed in the medial geniculate body so that the geniculate is to be regarded primarily as a relay station. The inferior colliculus, on the other hand, although it does relay to the geniculate, is so highly organized and has enough connections of its own that it must be regarded as something more than a relay nucleus. At least, as we shall see later, certain perceptual capacities are retained in the absence of the pathway to the cortex as long as the superior colliculus is intact.

AUDITORY CORTEX

Attempts to delimit the cortical areas involved in hearing have a long and sometimes confusing history. Most of this work has been done on the cat because this animal has been the most convenient one to use for various experiments, behavioral, physiological, and anatomical. What has proved most confusing is that the medial geniculate body does not show degeneration from cortical lesions in the same straightforward way that the lateral geniculate body does. One area (AI in Figure 8.6) causes considerable degeneration in the medial geniculate (Rose and Woolsey, 1949), and this is now regarded as the primary projection area. For more extensive or complete degeneration, however, it is necessary to include the additional areas shown in Figure 8.6. Attempts to settle the matter by methods of electrical mapping were at first hampered by limitations in recording methods, but these eventually delimited AII and a third area which is more or less coextensive with the second somatic area and hence is called SII or sometimes AIII.

Without going into the details of the methods of establishing the auditory cortex, let us note that the map in Figure 8.6 shows all those areas in the cat's cortex now known to have an auditory function (see Ades, 1959). This is a composite map based on many different studies using different techniques. The AI is the most essential area, but to affect seriously cortical auditory functions, lesions must include areas other than AI. In the next section, we shall indicate some of the properties of the various auditory areas of the cortex.

EFFERENT CONNECTIONS

On the right-hand side of Figure 8.5 is a diagram of the *descending* pathways of the auditory system. Certain of the pathways, including fibers descending from the cortex and some running out to the ear itself, have been demonstrated either by histological or physiological techniques. Some of the others are inferred. It now seems well established that all sensory systems possess efferent fiber systems backtracking on the sensory pathways (Livingston, 1959). They appear to have inhibiting or suppressor functions that selectively affect the sensory input, in this way having a sharpening effect on sensory transmission. This point will be illustrated later.

PITCH AND FREQUENCY

From this point on, we shall consider some of the psychological aspects of hearing and the pysiological mechanisms that underlie them. First we shall consider pitch, for some of the findings on this subject form a better basis for a later discussion of loudness.

It should be recalled from more elementary courses in psychology that psychologists distinguish between characteristics of a *stimulus* and attributes of sensation or *experience*. Intensity and frequency are characteristics of an auditory stimulus; loudness and pitch are attributes of auditory experience. In general, the frequency of a stimulus is the most important determinant of the pitch attribute, but the correlation is not one-to-one for there are other factors besides frequency that affect perceived pitch. But so far as physiological studies are concerned, they have been limited to observing the correlates of frequency in the cochlea and the nervous system.

THEORIES OF PITCH

For a long time in the history of hearing, there have been rival theories of the mechanism of pitch. One theory, formerly called telephone theory but now more often termed *periodicity theory*, attributes to the frequency of im-

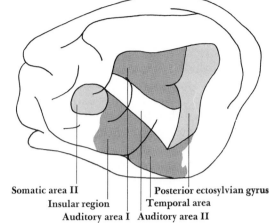

FIGURE 8.6—Composite view of all areas of the cat brain showing auditory function. (Adapted from H. W. Ades. In J. Field, H. W. Magoun, and V. E. Hall (Eds.), *Handbook of physiology*, vol. 1. Washington, D.C.: American Physiological Society, 1959. P. 597.)

Somatic area II   Posterior ectosylvian gyrus
Insular region   Temporal area
Auditory area I   Auditory area II

pulses in the auditory system the essential cue for pitch perception. A second theory, long called resonance theory but now more commonly referred to as *place theory*, attributes to the place of stimulation on the basilar membrane and later the place of activity in auditory pathways the essential cue for pitch perception. Both theories have been modified in the light of modern findings so that no one believes the telephone or the resonance theories in their original forms.

There is general agreement today (Davis, 1959) that pitch has a *duplex* basis. At low frequencies, where auditory nerve fibers can follow the frequency of a stimulus, either faithfully or in volleys, frequency would appear to be important. At higher frequencies, where such following breaks down, a place theory of pitch is generally accepted. The reasons for this will become apparent in what follows.

COCHLEAR ANALYSIS

We have already seen that impulses in the auditory nerve follow the frequency of a stimulus up to about 1,000 cycles per second and then by volleying keep up reasonably well into the region of 2,000 to 4,000 cycles per second. This fact, ascribed to the refractory properties of auditory neurons, might be disregarded as an incidental feature of neurons if the alternative explanation in terms of place of cochlear stimulation were completely satisfactory. But it is not, as we shall see.

From measurements of traveling waves in the cochlea, the ear appears to be a good acoustic analyzer by place of excitation for tones of high frequency but not for tones of low frequency. As we indicated above, the cochlear bulge for high tones travels a short distance, peaks, and dies out. For lower and lower tones, the bulge travels farther and farther before doing this. And one can map a different peak for different frequencies. However, as the tone becomes lower in frequency, two things happen: (1) More and more of the cochlea is stimulated by the bulge so that for low tones virtually all of it is subject to excitation. (2) The peak becomes less and less sharp; consequently the peaks for low tones are so flattened that it is hard to tell the difference between two tones of slightly different frequency. Yet the human ear can distinguish such tones. It is this apparent failure of the ear as an analyzer at low frequencies that has led people to accept *periodicity* as an alternate mechanism of pitch perception at low frequencies.

Perhaps, though, experimenters have given up too easily on the place theory at low frequencies. As a way of checking the reasoning, experiments have been made in which the skin of the forearm is exposed to a traveling bulge mimicking the characteristics of the cochlear bulge (Von Békésy, 1962). In this case, the subject reports a sharp localization of sensation and can discriminate well changes in frequency on the basis of changes in the location of the peak of the traveling bulge. Thus, the timing sequence of the stimulation of points on the skin suffices for good discrimination. Apparently, there is some way of sharpening the effects of excitation in neighboring afferent neurons. One possible mechanism of sharpening, as we shall see, is inhibition. In the skin, there is strong inhibition around the region receiving maximal stimulation. Inhibition has been demonstrated in neurons of the auditory system. This inhibition, rather than a duplex mechanism involving periodicity, may eventually show the way to a simpler, all-place mechanism of hearing.

INHIBITION

Inhibition in the auditory system is more than an inference from a cutaneous model of the ear. It has been directly demonstrated at all levels of the auditory system. In two experiments, inhibition was studied by stimulating the *olivocochlear* bundle. This bundle is part of the descending pathways and extends from the superior olive in the brain stem to the cochlea. It terminates in or near the hair cells of the cochlea.

In one experiment (Galambos, 1956), weak or moderate stimulation of the olivocochlear bundle was paired with an acoustic click to the ear of cats while records were at the same time being made of the action potentials of the cochlea. Without olivocochlear stimulation, a click normally evokes the N_1 and N_2 responses described above. With such stimulation, however, these responses were either greatly reduced or abolished. In another experiment, records were made not only of N_1 and N_2 responses of the VIIIth nerve but also from the inferior colliculus, medial geniculate body, and auditory cortex (Ruben and Sekula, 1960). This study showed that responses higher up in the auditory system are more sensitive to inhibition by olivocochlear stimulation than those lower down. Weak olivocochlear stimulation abolished cortical responses to the click while leaving intact responses at levels below the cortex. With increasing stimulation, the responses at thalamic and midbrain levels dropped out, and finally at the highest intensities of stimulation, the N_1 and N_2 responses in the cochlea were abolished.

It remains to be seen exactly how inhibition operates in the auditory function, but some hints are provided in the work to be described below on individual fibers in the auditory system.

RESPONSE AREAS

A place theory of pitch perception calls not only for an acoustic analysis in the cochlea according to place but also for a similar coding of information according to place in the auditory system. In other words, the separation according to frequency performed in the cochlea must be maintained throughout the system, at least to the point where it is utilized in pitch perception. From this reasoning, one would expect that certain fibers in the auditory system would be more responsive to some frequencies, and that other fibers would be more responsive to other frequencies, of acoustic stimuli. This in fact happens.

Historically, the first recording from individual neurons of the auditory system was done in the cochlear nucleus of the medulla. We shall, however, begin with the auditory nerve. The basic technique in all instances is to sink microelectrodes into a group of neurons and to "isolate a unit" by stopping the electrode at a point where one sees spike potentials occurring in response to an acoustic stimulus. Once a unit is located, the threshold of the unit at different frequencies can be determined by changing both intensity and frequency until one obtains a minimum response of the unit, usually one or more spikes. The plot made of the results of such measurements gives the so-called *response area* of a unit.

AUDITORY NERVE—In Figure 8.7 is the response area of a fiber in the auditory nerve (Tasaki, 1954). The shape of this area is typical. Sensitivity is relatively better at low tones than at high ones. It increases gradually with increasing frequency to a point where it is best. This point can be used to name the fiber as, say, a 7,000-cycle fiber. Above the peak sensitivity, the curve falls off sharply so that the unit is said to have a sharp high-frequency cutoff. The unit in Figure 8.7 is only one example. By probing, it is possible to locate different units with different peak sensitivities. It is typical of all such experiments, whether in the auditory nerve or farther upstream, that most of the units found are high-frequency units. Their peaks usually lie above 1,000 cycles per second. On the other hand, in this experiment as in others, a few units with peaks as low as a few hundred cycles are found.

In all experiments with individual units in the nervous system, it is common to encounter units that fire "spontaneously." By this term is meant only

Response area of a single auditory nerve fiber

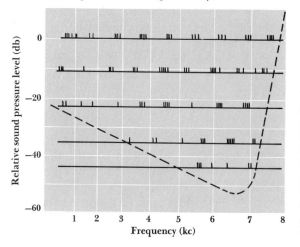

FIGURE 8.7—Spike responses of a single auditory fiber to tone bursts of different frequencies and intensities. (Adapted from I. Tasaki. Nerve impulses in individual auditory nerve fibers of guinea pig. *J. Neurophysiol.*, 1954, 17, 97.)

that the unit fires without a specific stimulus controlled by the experimenter. Whether or not the firing occurs because of stimulation arriving from other sources in the nervous system is not known. Such spontaneously firing units were found in the auditory nerve. Sometimes these units could be made to fire more rapidly by acoustic stimulation. In the case of auditory-nerve units, such spontaneous activity was not inhibited by acoustic stimulation, but a different picture is presented when the same kind of experiment is made in the central nervous system.

COCHLEAR NUCLEUS—In Figure 8.8 are results obtained in the cochlear nucleus of the cat. These were the first experiments with individual auditory units (Galambos and Davis, 1943, 1948). The shapes are similar to those found in first-order neurons of the auditory nerve. Sensitivity increases gradually up to a peak and then cuts off abruptly. The three curves in this figure are for three different units and illustrate the fact that units with different peak sensitivities are found in the medulla as well as in first-order neurons.

INHIBITORY AREAS—Units found in the cochlear nucleus frequently display not only response areas of excitation but also the phenomenon of inhibition. In other words, under certain circumstances, acoustic stimuli inhibit rather than excite the unit. This phenomenon of inhibition was demonstrated in two different ways.

One was to stop the firing of spontaneously discharging fibers. Two such cases of inhibition are shown in Figure 8.9. The response area, depicted in solid lines, was separately mapped. In the course of doing this with a spontaneously firing unit, one inhibitory area was found at frequencies below the response area; tones of low frequency would inhibit the spontaneous activity of the unit, while tones of higher frequency (about 1,400 cycles per second) would cause the activity to increase. In the second case, the inhibitory area was above the response area; the neuron was most sensitive to a frequency of about 1,400 cycles per second, but its spontaneous activity could be arrested by tones in the neighborhood of 2,000 cycles per second.

A second way of demonstrating inhibition was to sound two tones at once. The experimenters would first find the response area for the particular neuron under the microelectrode. Knowing the response area, they could choose a test tone that would excite the fiber. Then they would sound a second tone, changing its frequency from time to time, and find the frequencies that would inhibit firing of the neuron to the first tone. In this way they could find frequencies at certain intensities that would inhibit a neuron excited by another tone. Figure 8.9 illustrates the kinds of results obtained. Sometimes the inhibitory areas mapped in this way lay to one side or the other of the response areas; sometimes they overlapped the response areas.

The important conclusion from this work for understanding the physiological mechanism of pitch is that a particular sound frequency not only excites certain neurons of the auditory system more than others but also inhibits certain units. The inhibitory effect thus provides a mechanism for "sharpen-

FIGURE 8.8—Thresholds of response at different frequencies for individual, second-order neurons of the auditory system. (Adapted from R. Galambos and H. Davis. The response of single auditory-nerve fibers to acoustic stimulation. *J. Neurophysiol.*, 1943, 6, 45.)

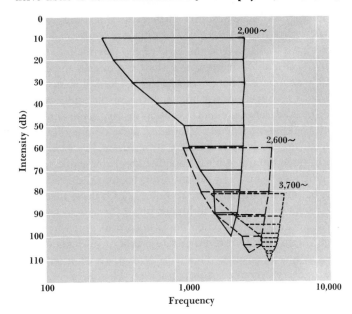

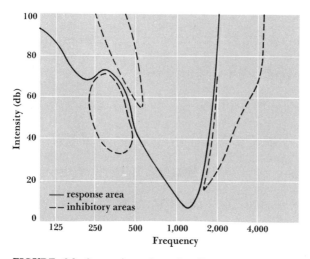

FIGURE 8.9—Composite schematic diagram of inhibitory areas. (Adapted from R. Galambos and H. Davis. Inhibition of activity in single auditory-nerve fibers by acoustic stimulation. *J. Neurophysiol.*, 1944, 7, 287–304).

ing" the differential effects of acoustic frequency. What starts out in the cochlea as the excitation of a relatively large group of receptors can be narrowed down to a smaller group of neurons by the inhibition of units that also respond otherwise to other frequencies.

If we now look at units farther up the auditory system, we find that expectations based on this reasoning are confirmed. Studies of individual units have been made at the level of the inferior colliculus, medial geniculate body, and auditory cortex. We shall not discuss these individually but shall simply summarize them (Ades, 1959). The following are the most important points: (*1*) Some units at higher levels of the auditory system are frequency-specific and some are not. That is to say, some units have response areas with peaks at a particular frequency; some do not. Those that do not may not respond to any kind of auditory stimulation. (*2*) Many units respond only to clicks or to stimuli with a complex spectrum while remaining unresponsive to pure-tone stimuli. (*3*) Many units spontaneously fire, and these sometimes can be inhibited by acoustic stimuli. (*4*) Of those that are frequency-specific, the response areas of those higher up in the system tend to be narrower than those lower down. In other words, a cortical unit when stimulated at a fairly high intensity may not respond to a much wider band of frequencies than it does at low intensities. This is in contrast to what we have seen for units in the auditory nerve or cochlear nucleus. Thus there is an actual sharpening of response in frequency-specific elements at higher levels of the auditory system.

TONOTOPIC ORGANIZATION

From all that has been said so far, it would be natural to expect that the auditory system would be tonotopically organized. That is to say, there should be an orderly arrangement of centers and pathways such that responsiveness to different frequencies would be arranged in a manner somewhat like the map of the cochlea. Put another way, one might expect the cochlea to be unrolled at different points in the auditory system. Otherwise the cochlear map would be wasted. More important, it would not be possible to have orderly arrangements of both excitation and inhibition in the auditory pathway. As expected, there is at least a reasonable tonotopic projection in the system.

Such a projection has been demonstrated at several levels: in the cochlea nuclei, where there is one unrolling of the cochlea for the dorsal nuclei and two more in different parts of the ventral nuclei (Rose et al., 1959); in the trapezoid body and inferior colliculus (Sumi et al., 1956); and in the auditory cortex (Hind, 1953). In the latter case, the studies are too numerous to mention and unfortunately do not always agree with each other in detail (Ades, 1959). It does appear, however, that at the cortical level the cochlea is unrolled twice, once in AI and once in AII. And the two maps are the reverse of one another. In AI the area representing the basal cochlea lies next to the area for the apical cochlea in AII; and vice versa. Actually, evoked potentials may be recorded in all the areas marked in Figure 8.6, which includes some of the primary somesthetic area as well as SII, but the degree of tonotopic organization in areas outside AI and AII is not entirely clear.

FREQUENCY DISCRIMINATION

We come now to behavioral experiments in which animals are taught a discrimination and then, after a lesion has been made, are tested for their ability to perform the discrimination. In this situation, it must be remembered, we should distinguish between retention and capacity. It very frequently happens in lesions of the nervous system (see Chapter 17) that preoperative habits are lost; yet after sufficient retraining, they may be relearned. This shows that it was the habit, not the capacity, that was affected by the lesion. In nearly all lesions of the auditory system, there is some interference with preoperatively acquired habits, but at this point we are not interested in that fact. All we are concerned with is capacity.

The method of measuring frequency discrimination in animals was described earlier in this chapter. We must speak of frequency discrimination because it is a change in frequency that is presented to the animal. Since, however, frequency is the main determinant of pitch perception, and one can be quite sure the animal is not reacting to other cues such as intensity, one is by inference dealing with pitch perception.

AUDITORY CORTEX—In Figure 8.6 are various cortical areas known to have auditory function. The question is in what way, if any, these areas are involved in an animal's capacity to discriminate pitch. There are a number of experiments on this question, and some of the early ones were confusing in giving superficially different results (Ades, 1959). It now seems quite clear that the following conclusions can be drawn (see Goldberg and Neff, 1961; Neff, 1961): No subarea, nor indeed the auditory area as a whole, is re quired for gross frequency discrimination. After lesions of any or all of these areas, the discrimination habit may be lost but, with retraining, it can be relearned. Thresholds of frequency discrimination have not been measured carefully, so that it is possible that there is some loss in capacity for making fine discriminations. But the fact remains that large discriminations can still be made.

This fact established, experimenters have turned their attention to points lower in the auditory pathway. One such point is the brachium of the inferior colliculus (BIC). This is a bundle passing between the inferior colliculus and the medial geniculate and regarded, on the basis of anatomical studies, as carrying the classical, direct auditory pathway. It is easily transected. Curiously, however, transection of the BIC does not eliminate evoked potentials from the auditory cortex. These can still be recorded to clicks after BIC section (Galambos et al., 1961). For this reason it is concluded that there is an extralemniscal auditory pathway to the cortex. This conclusion is supported by the fact that transections of the BIC that extend well beyond the limits of the BIC, especially toward the midline, can abolish evoked auditory potentials in the cortex.

The latter experimental fact correlates with the capacity of cats to perform a frequency discrimination (Goldberg and Neff, 1961). Transection of the BIC in cats caused them to lose postoperatively their previously learned frequency discrimination, just as if the auditory cortex had been ablated. In both cases, however, the cats were able to relearn the discrimination. But when the extralemniscal pathway was sectioned by extensive transection of the BIC and structures medial to it, so that evoked potentials in the auditory cortex were abolished, the animals were unable to learn the frequency discrimination after prolonged training. It appears, then, that the extralemniscal transection abolished the capacity for frequency discrimination. Since the nature of the extralemniscal pathway is not clear, just what this result means is not yet understood.

PATTERN DISCRIMINATION

From the findings with frequency discrimination, one would conclude that the auditory cortex has little or no role in pitch perception. As we shall see later, the same is true of intensity discrimination. What importance, then, does the auditory cortex have? Experiments so far show that it is important in two perceptual capacities: pattern discrimination and sound localization. We shall consider sound localization later.

A pattern discrimination, as we have previously described it, is really a temporal frequency discrimination. Animals must distinguish tones varying in frequency so that they can tell the difference between low-high-low and high-low-high. To do this, they must discriminate not only the frequency difference but the order in which the difference takes place. This is apparently the crucial difference, for the capacity to make a tonal-pattern discrimination, unlike frequency discrimination, depends on the auditory cortex. In this case, it is not necessary for all the auditory cortex to be destroyed for the capacity to be lost. Either one of two combinations will have that result: After complete extirpation of AI, AII, and EP (Figure 8.6), the capacity is lost (Diamond and Neff, 1957). It also is lost when there is a complete extirpation of the combination of the insular (I) and temporal (T) regions (see Goldberg and Neff, 1961). From this it is concluded that the auditory cortex is important in discriminations involving time or temporal sequences.

LOUDNESS AND INTENSITY

In man, it is relatively easy to measure the relation of loudness and intensity in three different ways: (1) "Zero loudness" may be measured by determining the weakest intensity that can be heard. When this intensity is plotted for different frequencies of the audible spectrum, one has an *audiogram*. (2) By asking an observer to judge when a tone is twice as loud as some other tone or half way between two tones in loudness, one can construct a *loudness scale*. (3) By presenting two tones of different intensities, an *intensity discrimination* can be measured, and by narrowing the difference to the smallest one that is detectable, a *differential threshold* is obtained.

In work with animals, using behavioral measures, it is not practicable to obtain a loudness scale, but *audiograms* and *intensity discriminations* are readily measured. Using electrical or other physiological measures, one also can obtain differences in the *amplitude* of response that may be construed as reflecting differences in perceived loudness. These, then, are the measures with which we shall be concerned here.

MIDDLE EAR

Sounds reaching the inner ear must be transmitted to that point by way of the tympanic membrane, ossicles of the middle ear, and the oval window. These ossicles comprise a series of levers. To them are attached two muscles, the tensor tympani and stapedius muscles, whose contraction can affect the operation of the ossicular levers. It is of interest to ask what this middle-ear mechanism contributes to loudness.

LEVER ACTION—It was once thought that the bones of the middle ear could act like mechanical amplifiers, increasing the effective intensity of sound transmitted to the oval window (Stevens and Davis, 1938). This now appears not to be so (Davis, 1959). The area of the human tympanic membrane is relatively large (50 to 90 square millimeters), while that of the oval window is small (about 3.2 square millimeters). However, the amplitude of movement at the center of each is about the same and hence there is no mechanical advantage. But since the force at the oval window is applied to a much smaller area, the pressure applied is greater. This difference is about what is required to drive the fluid of the cochlea as compared with air. Hence, the middle-ear bones form what physicists would call an impedance-matching device. This permits a transfer of energy from air to fluid with very little loss. Thus the middle ear, as a lever system, subtracts nothing nor adds anything to the effective intensity of sound in the inner ear.

CONDUCTION DEAFNESS—For this last statement to be true, however, the lever action must be unimpeded. It is possible for the movement of the ossicles to be hampered or even frozen by diseases of the middle ear. One, such as otitis media, fills up the ear with foreign material, thus impeding ossicular movement. Another consists of hardening or calcifying processes that freeze the three bones together. In all such cases, a mild deafness called *conduction deafness* is caused, changing the audiogram and also the loudness of all sounds heard, by amounts up to 40 or 50 decibels.

TYMPANIC REFLEX—The muscles of the middle ear contract reflexly in response to a moderately loud sound. This action is called the *tympanic reflex* or sometimes the *acoustic reflex*. The effect of this reflex on the intensity of sounds reaching the middle ear has been studied several times, but one of the most recent and definitive experiments is as follows (Galambos and Rupert, 1959):

Wire electrodes are permanently implanted on the round window of the cochlea in cats. From such an electrode, a record can be made that shows both the cochlear microphonic and the N_1 response of the auditory nerve. And this can be done in the otherwise normal, freely moving animal. The intensities of sound required at different frequencies for producing microphonic and N_1 responses of given amplitudes are measured. Then, in a second operation, the tensor tympani and stapedius muscles of the middle ear can be cut separately or together, and measurements of the microphonic and N_1 responses again made.

Such an experiment shows clearly that the tympanic reflex attenuates sound. The difference in intensities, in this experiment, runs up to 20 decibels. All this difference is due to the stapedius muscle; cutting the tensor tympani has little or no effect. It happens that recording from the round window is not a good way to tell whether different frequencies of sound make any difference (Davis, 1957). However, there is reason to believe from other experiments that the effect is greatest at low frequencies and becomes progressively weaker at high frequencies.

This reflex undoubtedly has a protective function. The number of decibels that it attenuates a sound may not be great, but it is great enough to reduce markedly the hazards of damaging the internal ear. As we shall see below, it is only at extremely high intensities that exposure to sound causes cochlear damage, and a reduction of a few decibels ordinarily prevents such damage (see Galambos and Rupert, 1959). Incidentally, it is an easy matter to condition the tympanic reflex in 20 or 30 trials to some other signal such as a weak light (Simmons et al., 1959).

COCHLEA

The contribution of the cochlea to the audiogram and to the perception of loudness may be studied in a number of ways. Among them are (*1*) acoustical resonance of the cochlea and middle ear, (*2*) study of the cochlear microphonics, (*3*) exposure deafness, and (*4*) experimental lesions of the organ of Corti. The first three of these give about the same results; the last does not, but for reasons that are explicable.

ACOUSTICAL RESONANCE—By physical means, one can determine the amplitude of vibration of a structure at various frequencies. This has been done for the middle-ear bones and for the scala vestibuli of the cochlea (Davis, 1959). The peak of response, that is, the frequency at which a structure vibrates most, is referred to as the resonant frequency of the structure.

In the middle ear of man, the resonant frequency is about 1,700 cycles per second, but the peak is not sharp. Rather, it slopes off gradually on either side. The resonant frequency in the cochlea is about 4,000 cycles per second, again sloping off gradually on either side but more sharply on the high-frequency side. The two curves of resonance combine to yield an overall frequency response that has a relatively broad maximum of 800 to 6,000 cycles, falling off rapidly above that but less rapidly below 800. This curve looks very much like the human audiogram, leading to the conclusion that the audiogram is largely determined by the combined acoustic resonance of the middle ear and cochlea (Figure 8.10).

The audiograms of animals other than man have about the same shape as man's, but the position of the curve, including the position of maximum sensitivity, varies from animal to animal. In the cat, for example, it is somewhat higher (Neff, 1947), and in small animals like the rat (Gould and Morgan, 1942) and bat (Galambos and Griffin, 1942) it is displaced several octaves toward the higher frequencies.

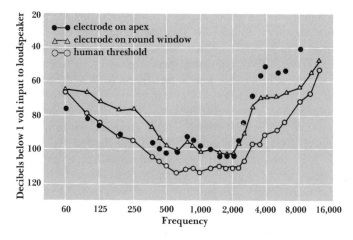

FIGURE 8.10—The cochleogram and the audiogram. (Adapted from S. S. Stevens, H. Davis, and M. H. Lurie. The localization of pitch perception on the basilar membrane. *J. gen. Psychol.*, 1935, 13, 209.)

COCHLEOGRAM—The cochlear microphonic, it will be recalled, has no true threshold. The limit for recording it is set by the conditions of recording and auditory stimulation. However, an arbitrary voltage may be set as the threshold and this used to measure the sensitivity of the ear to different frequencies. A curve representing such measurements is called a cochleogram because it is parallel in meaning to an audiogram.

The exact shape of the cochleogram depends on the positions from which it is recorded. It is best to record from many positions on the cochlea, using the best values obtained at each position (Lempert et al., 1947; Davis et al., 1953). It is clear that the cochlear microphonic reflects reasonably well, just as acoustical resonance does, the characteristics of hearing as measured by the audiogram (Figure 8.10). This is to be expected because the microphonic originates in the hair cells of the organ of Corti and faithfully reproduces within rather wide limits the wave form of the acoustic energy reaching the hair cells.

EXPOSURE DEAFNESS—If a man or an animal is exposed to a loud sound for a period of time, he becomes deaf. How deaf depends on the loudness of the sound, the frequency composition of the sound, and the period of exposure. If this combination is not too severe, the deafness is temporary, lasting a few minutes or hours (Davis et al., 1950). With more damaging combinations, the deafness may be permanent (see Davis, 1957). Needless to say, permanently damaging exposures are avoided in experiments with man, but they have been used in animals.

In permanent injuries caused by exposure in animals, the damage done to the ears has been studied (see Davis, 1957). The damage is usually limited to the organ of Corti. If not too great, only the hair cells may be destroyed; in more severe cases, the supporting cells of the organ of Corti may also be destroyed. Because, in this kind of injury, damage is limited to the organ of Corti, it is of interest to determine its effects on hearing.

In general, the effects that have been found correlate fairly well with what one would expect from a knowledge of the cochlea as an acoustic analyzer, although there are differences. High tones are more damaging than low tones, although the effects of low tones are more widespread and affect more frequencies than high tones. And high tones have more specific effects, causing hearing losses in a narrower band of frequencies than low tones. These effects fit with the conception of low tones stimulating more of the cochlea than high tones and of localization in the cochlea being better for high tones than for low ones.

COCHLEAR LESIONS—Another approach to determining the contribution of the cochlea to loudness perception is to make lesions in the organ of Corti (Schuknecht, 1953; Schuknecht and Neff, 1952; Schuknecht and Sutton, 1953). This may be done by drilling appropriate holes in the cochlea and in other ways. Following such lesions, audiograms may be measured by conditioning techniques. One shortcoming of the method is that injury may also be done to the terminals of the auditory nerve fibers. To separate the effects of injury to the hair cells from that to nerve fibers, it is necessary to make post-mortem histological analyses and then to pay particular attention to those animals in which injuries to hair cells occur with appreciable involvement of nerve fibers. Selected cases (cats) of this sort are presented in Figure 8.11.

The results show that restricted injuries to the hair cells cause mild hearing losses. And the hearing losses correlate with the position of the injury in the cochlea. High-tone losses occur with basal injuries; low-tone losses with apical injuries. High-tone losses, however, are sharper and more severe. With a basal lesion, hearing at the high frequencies drops off sharply and is severely impaired. With low tones, on the other hand, the effects are more widespread, even though they are limited to the low tones, and they are less severe. Again, all this fits with what is known of the acoustics of the cochlea.

In summary, then, by whatever method is used, it is found that the characteristics of the audiogram, and thus of the absolute threshold at various frequencies, are largely, if not completely, determined by the characteristics of the middle and inner ear. The resonant characteristics of these structures determine the place and the amount of acoustical stimulation of the hair cells. These respond with a generator potential, which in turn activates nerve fibers, reflecting the effective mechanical stimulation brought to bear on them.

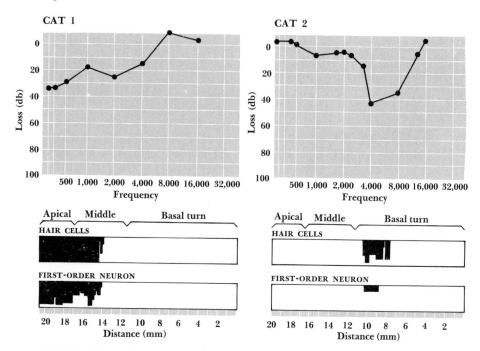

FIGURE 8.11—Audiograms and charts of cochlear damage in two cats. In lower part, dark areas are those damaged. (Adapted from H. F. Schuknecht and S. Sutton. Hearing losses after experimental lesions in basal coil of cochlea. *AMA Arch. Otolaryngol.*, 1953, 57, 129–142.)

AUDITORY NERVE

The fibers of the auditory nerve that innervate the hair cells are arranged in an orderly way but not in such a way that they are easy to work with surgically. They approximate the form of twisted rope. Those from the basal quarter of the cochlea form the core of the nerve, and around them twist in one direction fibers from the apex and in the opposite direction fibers from the middle region of the cochlea (see Stevens and Davis, 1938). This fact has a bearing on the effects of injury to the auditory nerve.

NERVE DEAFNESS—Clinical otologists have long distinguished two types of deafness (see Davis, 1947). One, *conductive deafness,* which has already been mentioned, is caused by a loss in the conduction of sound to the inner ear. Audiograms of people with conductive deafness typically show a rather uniform loss of sensitivity at all frequencies. The other type, called *nerve deafness,* is caused by some damage to the receptor mechanism or to the auditory nerve. Cases of nerve deafness typically show either losses of sensitivity in a restricted range of frequencies or losses at high frequencies. The restricted losses are called *tonal gaps;* the losses in the high frequencies are called *high-tone deafness.*

NERVE SECTION—As an experimental study of nerve deafness, one can partially section the auditory nerve and measure the effect on thresholds of hearing. Naturally, such experiments are with partial sections, for, as one might expect, total sections make the organism completely deaf. There are two sets of experiments employing such partial sections.

Representative results of the first experiments are shown in Figure 8.12 (Neff, 1947; Wever and Neff, 1947). With some partial sections, nothing at all happened to the audiogram; the cat's hearing remained quite normal. With relatively severe sections, as judged by the amount of degeneration of fibers and their ganglion cells, high-tone deafnesses were produced. Sensitivity in the low frequencies was preserved but, somewhere in the middle range of frequencies, sensitivity dropped off rapidly, and above that point the animal was completely deaf to high tones. The remarkable thing about these experi-

FIGURE 8.12—Examples of audiograms and damage to first-order auditory neurons (ganglion cells) after partial section of the VIIIth nerve. On the left, white areas represent fibers and cells destroyed. (Adapted from W. D. Neff. The effects of partial section of the auditory nerve. *J. comp. physiol. Psychol.,* 1947, 40, 203–216; and E. G. Wever and W. D. Neff. A further study of the effects of partial section of the auditory nerve. *J. comp. physiol. Psychol.,* 1947, 40, 217–226.)

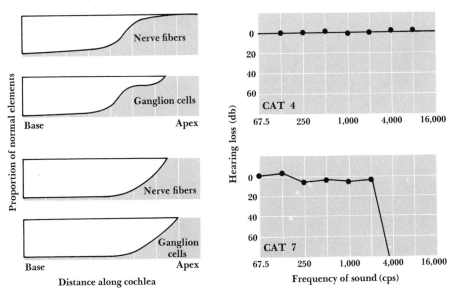

ments is how few fibers are required to preserve normal hearing. One must section more than half the auditory nerve to measure an effect on hearing, and then, so long as any hearing is left, the low tones are preserved.

From what has been said earlier, one might expect hearing losses for low tones to be less sharp and less severe than those for high tones. However, in this experiment, no such low-tone losses were observed. The reasons might be: (1) There are no fibers in the auditory nerve that are frequency-specific for low tones and (2) the section of the auditory nerve was made in such a way as to spare such fibers.

Another, later experiment tested these possibilities by using a different surgical approach in sectioning the auditory nerve—an approach designed to include fibers from the apical end of the cochlea, which is the "low-tone end" (Schuknecht and Woellner, 1953). In the case of two cats, this was successful. These cats showed moderately severe, even if widespread, hearing losses for low tones whereas hearing at the high frequencies was spared. It may therefore be concluded that hearing losses due to partial injury of the auditory nerve are much like the losses incurred after injury to the hair cells of the cochlea.

ACTION POTENTIALS

We shall now turn our attention briefly to the question of how the magnitude of neural responses in the auditory system correlates with intensity of stimulation. This is of interest because it has long been classical theory (Adrian, 1928) that the perception of physical intensity by an organism depends on the frequency of sensory impulses or, more generally, on the magnitude of neural effects in a given sense. In general, this theory is confirmed by the experimental facts, but it sometimes needs qualifying.

AUDITORY-NERVE UNITS—The magnitude of the N_1 response of auditory nerve fibers in the vicinity of the cochlea has been measured as a function of the varying intensity of acoustic clicks presented to the ear of a guinea pig or cat (see Davis, 1959). The size of the N_1 response increases along a sigmoid curve, which fits fairly well with classical theory. However, after reaching a plateau on this curve, further increases in intensity cause the curve to rise again fairly rapidly. Such a break does not fit either with theory or with the known characteristics of loudness. In this case, however, it appears that units tend to group into those either with low-intensity thresholds or with high-intensity thresholds; hence the break may have been an artifact of the units involved in the N_1 response.

COCHLEAR-NUCLEUS UNITS—Data more in accord with classical theory have been obtained from individual units of the cochlear nucleus (Galambos and Davis, 1943). In this case, the number of impulses discharged is related to the intensity of the acoustic stimulus to the ear. Curves like those shown in

Figure 8.13 for three different units typically are sigmoid with a slight curvature at the lower intensities and a marked flattening off at higher intensities. Curves of this shape are, in fact, very much like the loudness function obtained for human observers, except that the human loudness function extends over a much wider range of intensities (Stevens and Davis, 1938). It is to be expected, however, that overall perception will depend on the composite action of many different fibers with widely varying thresholds.

Individual units have been studied at other points in the auditory system (see Galambos et al., 1952). Many of them are like those found in the cochlear nucleus and illustrated in Figure 8.13. Some, however, are not. In fact, some fibers in the medial geniculate body react in the opposite fashion. They are most active at low intensities and, as intensity is increased, the frequency of their discharge falls. This phenomenon, however, fits in with what one would expect from inhibitory processes in the system. Presumably fibers that decrease their activity with increasing stimulation are being affected by inhibitory units acting upon them or are themselves inhibitory in function.

AUDITORY CORTEX

We shall discuss finally, in connection with the mechanisms of loudness and intensity, behavioral studies designed to determine the role of the auditory cortex, and indirectly subcortical structures, on the perception of intensity.

FIGURE 8.13—The frequency of impulses in individual elements of the auditory system. Fibers are labled according to the frequency at which they respond best. (Adapted from R. Galambos and H. Davis. The response of single auditory-nerve fibers to acoustic stimulation. *J. Neurophysiol.*, 1943, 6, 39–57.)

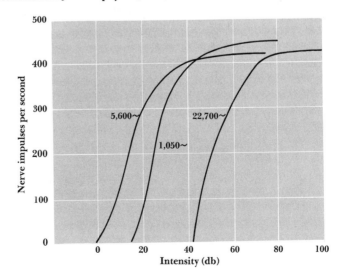

Two kinds of experiments have been carried out: (*1*) measurements of the absolute threshold or audiogram and (*2*) measurements of intensity discrimination.

ABSOLUTE THRESHOLD—In the 1930s and 1940s, there were a great many experiments on the effect of various cortical lesions on auditory sensitivity, as measured by the threshold of audibility for pure tones (see Ades, 1959). It at first appeared that substantial deficits were caused by cortical lesions of reasonable size and located in the auditory region. But there were many discrepancies among the results, depending on the method used, the size and location of the lesion, and the amount of time allowed for recovery after operation. The latter proved to be an important factor, even though it is not yet understood exactly why (Girden, 1942).

It has subsequently been established that, when allowance is made for recovery and when adequate testing procedures are employed, there is no appreciable effect of cortical lesions on the absolute threshold for pure tones (Kryter and Ades, 1943). This is true even though bilateral cortical lesions are so extensive that they include all auditory cortex. Ability to hear tones, then, is simply not dependent on the auditory cortex, at least in the cat, and probably not in man either (Landau et al., 1960).

One set of experiments carried on the search at subcortical levels (Kryter and Ades, 1943). The inferior colliculi were removed on both sides. This caused a loss of about 15 decibels in auditory sensitivity, but that is not very great. Also, the medial geniculate—and sometimes also the auditory cortex, but this made little difference—was destroyed in addition to the inferior colliculus. Thus the entire auditory system from the midbrain up was destroyed. This caused a loss of about 40 decibels. Such a hearing loss is appreciable, but it still is not great when the range of normal hearing includes more than another 60 decibels. It was concluded, then, that the most important contribution to auditory sensitivity is made at the brain-stem level below the inferior colliculi.

INTENSITY DISCRIMINATION—Almost the same conclusion can be drawn about the capacity to discriminate differences in intensity (see Neff, 1961). After all the cortical areas shown in Figure 8.6 are removed bilaterally, the capacity of a cat to discriminate differences in intensity remains unchanged. The capacity decreases somewhat, but it is still relatively good after transection of the classical auditory pathway at the level of the brachium of the inferior colliculi (BIC). The capacity diminishes even more, but the discrimination of large intensity differences can still be made after a transection of both the extralemniscal and the lemniscal pathways at the level of BIC. Thus the capacity to make intensity discriminations, as well as to hear the presence of a sound, resides to a considerable extent at the level of the midbrain or lower. The auditory cortex is not concerned in any significant degree.

As we have seen, this conclusion does not apply to the discrimination of tonal patterns. Neither does it hold for sound localization, which is the next and last subject to consider.

SOUND LOCALIZATION

Both human beings and many animals can localize the direction of a sound with a high degree of accuracy. This capacity is called *sound localization*. It is a binaural phenomenon, depending on differences in the characteristics of a sound arriving separately at the two ears. Let us see what is known about the physiological basis of this phenomenon. To approach the topic, we should first review briefly the auditory cues involved.

CUES TO LOCALIZATION

For many years it has been recognized that there are three different types of binaural cues, at least in theory, that may serve in the localization of sounds: (1) intensity, (2) phase, and (3) time of arrival (Woodworth and Schlosberg, 1954).

INTENSITY—If two sounds differ only in intensity but separately stimulate the two ears, the observer will perceive a single sound coming from a particular direction. The direction of the sound, which in this case is imaginary because it is presented to the ears by means of earphones, is judged to be on the side of the greater intensity. In real life, single sounds arriving at the two ears generally do not differ appreciably in intensity unless the frequency is high, say above 1,000 or more cycles per second. That is because low frequencies bend well around the head; only at higher frequencies does the head throw enough of a sound shadow to create a binaural difference in intensity. Under these circumstances, intensity may serve as a cue to direction (Pieron, 1952).

PHASE—In theory, differences in phase may serve as a cue to the direction of a sound. However, this could and does occur only at relatively low frequencies, say below 800 cycles per second (see Garner, 1949). Physical calculations show that, at greater frequencies, phase differences between the two ears can be more than 180°, and the observer cannot appreciate which is leading and which is lagging. At low frequencies of stimulation, binaural phase differences reduce, so far as the ear is concerned, to differences in time of arrival, which is the third cue for sound localization.

TIME—Many sounds that we localize are impulsive. We hear them start and stop. In this case, a sound that is off to one side arrives at one ear before it arrives at the other. Like phase, this time difference could start impulses in one ear before those in the other and thus serve as a cue to localization. Actually, differences in intensity also cause differences in latency of neural responses, so that the time of starting a neural response in the auditory system is common to all three possible physical cues to sound localization.

With these points as background, let us see what features of neural function are significant in sound localization.

LATERALITY OF PROJECTION

The auditory system is distinctively different from other sensory systems in its bilateral duplication of signals arriving from the two ears (see Ades, 1959). Crossing occurs in the system at virtually the first opportunity, which is the medulla. Here some of the fibers from the cochlear nucleus cross over to the superior olive (SO) of the opposite side. This, as we shall see, appears to be significant. Crossing may also occur in the lateral lemniscus just below the inferior colliculi and then again between the colliculi. As in the case of other senses, there is also ample communication between the two cortices by way of the corpus callosum. Whether these various crossings above the superior olive mean anything or not is not yet known. The general point, though, is that information from the two ears can interact all along the auditory pathway from the medulla to the cortex.

Let us look now at each point in the pathway from the cochlea to the cortex.

COCHLEA

In the early experiments on individual units of the cochlear nucleus, there was one in which the microphonic potential of the cochlea was recorded at the same time as impulses were being picked up in the nucleus (Galambos and Davis, 1943). In this experiment, in fact, individual spikes were recorded in superimposition on the cochlea potential. As can be seen in Figure 8.14, the phase of the generator cochlear potential correlates well with the time of origin of impulses in the individual units. The units always fire in a definite part of the cycle. And the variability in this respect is quite small. If it is assumed that this information is preserved farther along the pathway, sound localization based on arrival times differing by a fraction of a millisecond should be possible. In actual fact, numerous experiments with human observers show that a time difference of the order of 0.03 to 0.3 millisecond, depending on the individual, can serve as a localization cue (Woodworth and Schlosberg, 1954).

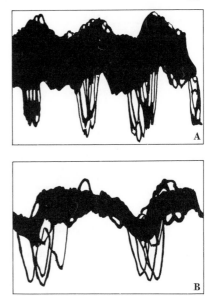

FIGURE 8.14—Nerve responses occurring in a constant phase of the cochlear microphonic waves. A, 1,050 cps stimulus; B, 550 cps stimulus. (Adapted from R. Galambos and H. Davis. The response of single auditory-nerve fibers to acoustic stimulation. *J. Neurophysiol.*, 1943, 6, 51.)

SUPERIOR OLIVE

Perhaps the most interesting physiological data on sound localization come from studies of the superior olive of the cat. This is the structure in the medulla receiving fibers from the two ears. Studies of individual units in this structure have been made in experiments in which clicks were presented at slightly different times, through earphones, to the separate ears of the cat (Galambos et al., 1959).

As we have indicated previously, some units found in experiments of this kind are insensitive to clicks, whereas other units are sensitive only to clicks. In other words, some tone-sensitive units respond to certain frequencies more than to others, whereas others are activated only by impulsive clicks. We shall discuss here only click-sensitive units.

If a stimulus is presented to only one ear at a time, some of the click units in the superior olive respond only to stimulation of the one ear and not to the other. In other words, their response is limited to only one of the two ears. This, however, does not mean that they are impervious to binaural stimulation. In fact, if the stimulation is dichotic, that is, comes from two ears at a time or in close succession, their behavior depends on the time interval between the two clicks to the two ears (see Figure 8.15). In this case, when the left ear led the right ear, it always responded; so did it also when the left led the right by 1.5 milliseconds or more. However, in between, when the right-ear click led the left-ear click by 0.5 to 1.0 millisecond, the response of

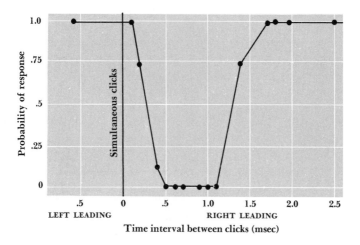

FIGURE 8.15—Effect of time difference in clicks delivered to the two ears on the probability of a response in a unit in the superior olivary nucleus of the medulla. (Adapted from R. Galambos, J. Schwartzkopff, and A. Rupert. Microelectrode study of superior olivary nuclei. *Amer. J. Physiol.*, 1959, 197, 527–536.)

the unit was completely suppressed. As the authors observed, such units are "exquisitely sensitive to whether the right ear or the left was stimulated first by a pair of clicks. . . ." It is interesting that the time differences observed here accord almost exactly with the time difference of 0.65 millisecond in the human ear at which a sound is localized as being close to one ear (see Woodworth and Schlosberg, 1954, p. 355).

It appears, then, that at the first point of bilateral mixing of binaural information, a mechanism has been found for discriminating time differences in the stimulation of the two ears. Of course, it is necessary that this information somehow be transmitted to those structures where the organism uses it in sound localization.

AUDITORY CORTEX

Experiments performed on the auditory cortex with time differences in the stimulation of the two ears, though not so precise as those with units in the superior olive, nevertheless fit in with the general picture (Rosenzweig, 1954). In this case, gross evoked responses were recorded from the auditory cortices of the cat. If the two hemispheres are compared with monaural stimuli, the evoked response is somewhat greater in the contralateral cortex than on the ipsilateral side. If, now, the two ears are stimulated at exactly the same time, the response is greater in each cortex. In other words, there is binaural summation. As a time difference is introduced, the side of greater response shifts gradually, depending on which ear is leading. And the ratio of the responses in the two hemispheres increases up to a difference of about one millisecond, or slightly more, where it flattens out and becomes little different from that if only one ear were stimulated.

Here we are dealing with the time interval over which the stimulation of the two ears summates in the evoked potential of one cortex. What this summation indicates about underlying activity is not known. However, the time interval involved is of the correct order of magnitude.

To be described now are experiments on auditory localization in which lesions have been made in the auditory cortex or below. The cortical level proves to be most crucial for this function (see Neff, 1961). If incomplete lesions of the auditory cortex are made, cats that previously learned to localize sound partially or completely lose the habit. They are, however, able to relearn it. If, on the other hand, bilateral lesions are made in all cortical areas in which evoked responses to acoustical stimuli may be recorded (AI, AII, EP, I-T, SII, and SS), cats completely lose the capacity for sound localization and are unable to reacquire it. Hence sound localization appears to be cortically bound. It is not surprising, then, that complete bilateral transection of the auditory pathways at the brachium of the inferior colliculus also produces a complete and permanent loss of localizing capacity.

9 THE SOMATIC SENSES

IN THE 1830s, JOHANNES MÜLLER enunciated the doctrine of specific nerve energies. This is the doctrine that the qualities of experience are determined by the receptors that respond to different kinds of stimulation. According to the doctrine, we feel pain because a particular receptor responds to pain; we see red because a certain receptor, and not another, responds to "red wavelengths."

For most of the century and a third since Müller put forth this doctrine, the weight of scientific opinion has been on his side. The doctrine helped to inspire a great proportion of the work done in physiology and psychology during that period. On the other hand, it has had its worthy opponents, particularly in the field of the skin senses, and lively controversies have raged over the validity of the idea. Opponents have looked for, and argued for, some sort of signaling system in sensory pathways that would convey information about the nature of stimuli, say by the timing or patterning of impulses.

It can now be said with confidence, thanks largely to single-unit recording, that Müller's principle is essentially correct. There may still be a little room for doubt in certain quite special cases, but in every sense there is now good evidence that different receptors respond uniquely or in some unique combination to different kinds of stimulation and that this "coding" of information is conveyed all the way to the cerebral cortex.

The term *somesthesis*, as used here, refers to the various senses of the skin and the sense of movement or, more briefly, to the skin and kinesthetic senses. The term *somatic senses* is also used to apply to these senses and will be used interchangeably with somesthesis.

CUTANEOUS EXPERIENCE

The first and most basic question to ask about the somatic senses is, How many are there? What are the fundamental qualities of experience arising from the body? A second, closely related question is, What receptors are responsible for the qualities of sensation? What are the receptor mechanisms for conveying qualitative information to the central nervous system? It is impossible to separate these questions clearly, for evidence concerning one also throws light on the other. They should therefore be kept in mind as the discussion proceeds.

Let us begin by considering everyday experiences. What kinds of experiences do people commonly report when they are touched, scratched, pricked, or otherwise stimulated through their skins or within their bodies? If they are all counted, there are quite a number of such experiences, or at least different names for them. There are warmth and cold, tickle and itch, quick pricking pains and duller, longer-lasting pains. There are sensations of pressure or touch and of vibration. There are many other words in our vocabulary for somatic experiences, but most people would agree that this list pretty well covers them. Now let us see how these experiences are related to each other. For the moment, we shall refer only to the skin senses and later bring muscle or movement experiences into the picture.

PUNCTATE SENSITIVITY

The first step, in modern times, toward the classification of basic cutaneous qualities was the discovery of the punctate sensitivity of the skin. This discovery was made in 1883–1884 (see Boring, 1942). It was observed that the skin was not uniformly sensitive to all sorts of stimuli but had spots that were very sensitive, surrounded by areas of relatively poor sensitivity. If, for example, a warm rod is touched to various points on the back of the hand, there are some points where it can be felt as warmth and others where it is just something being touched to the hand. This phenomenon is called punctate sensitivity of the skin.

The phenomenon has many implications that have fostered research. One of them is the possibility of finding which are the fundamental qualities of cutaneous sensation. The idea is simple. By making maps of punctate sensitivity for different kinds of stimuli, one can see which ones are alike and which are unalike. For example, one can take a stylus that is slightly cooler than the normal skin temperature and make a map of any convenient area of the skin, finding the points where the observer can feel "cold." Then, with a stylus slightly warmer than the skin temperature, the area can be remapped to find the points at which the observer can feel "warmth." If these two maps are not the same—if the points for "cold" are different from those for "warmth"—then it seems quite clear that the "cold" sense and the "warmth" sense are really different senses.

SENSORY QUALITIES

That, in fact, is exactly the result and the conclusion of making maps for cold and warm stimuli (see Woodworth and Schlosberg, 1954). Many research workers have proved it over and over again. It is therefore quite certain that warmth and cold are different. There is a similar story for "pain" and for "touch." If one takes a needle and with light pricks maps the points in an area of the skin at which there is a report of pain and then makes a similar map for reports of "touch" when a stylus is placed lightly on the skin, the two maps are different enough to show that the two senses are different. Comparison of the maps for pain or for touch with those for cold or warmth shows that they also are different. Thus it is apparent that there are at least four different basic qualities of cutaneous sensation: touch, pain, cold, and warmth.

The next question is whether there are any more than these four fundamental qualities. There have been a good many experiments, and at times some controversies, about that question. However, the answer to it is beginning to be fairly certain. It looks as though such experiences as vibration, itch, and tickle are derivations or variations of the four fundamental qualities.

Let us consider first the experience of vibration. There were some investigators who thought that there must be a separate sense and separate receptors for appreciating vibration. There may still be some who think so, but the evidence is now marshaled against it (Geldard, 1953). There are several kinds of evidence, but one is the clearest and easiest to understand (Geldard, 1940). With the appropriate sort of mechanical vibrator in hand, one can find the threshold of vibration—the amount of movement of the vibrator that can be detected as vibration—for different spots in some region of the skin. As in other similar cases, there are peaks and valleys of sensitivity. This map can be compared with one obtained for touch alone—the points where a small stylus of a given weight is felt. The two maps match with each other within the limits of experimental error. Thus it seems clear that the same receptors are involved in vibratory sensitivity as in simple pressure or touch sensitivity.

There is a similar story for prick pain and itch. With either a needle or an electrical stimulus, one can find the "spots" that produce the experience of pain—a sharp pricking sensation. Then, by adjusting the needle or the electrical stimulus to give a few repeated stimuli, one can produce an "itching" sensation. The "spots" that will give "itch" are the same as those which will give "prick pain." Thus it is now rather well accepted that "itch" is a variant of the pain experience and employs the same sensory mechanisms.

The experience of "tickle" is the last member of the list. Tickle is something experienced when adjacent points on the skin are touched lightly in rapid succession. The common view of tickle is that it is a special variety of touch sensation, but it may possibly involve pain. However, whether "tickle" is an "itch," a "touch," or a combination of the two (Bishop, 1946), no one believes that it is a primary sensation. It may therefore be called a derived experience.

PATTERNS OF EXPERIENCE

So far the picture seems simple. There are four basic varieties of cutaneous experience—and by implication four receptor mechanisms—and all other types of experience are made up of these four components. Such a statement, although perhaps true from a physiological point of view, is a bit misleading. We must continually bear in mind that sensory phenomena are not simple additions and subtractions of a few basic elements. In everyday life, we seldom feel pain without touch, nor warmth or cold without touch, for the same stimulus that produces "warmth" or "cold" or pain also can be felt as "touch." Moreover, although itch may be tied up with the pain mechanisms, in a very real sense it is unique; it makes one scratch. The uniqueness is in the temporal pattern of events and in the reaction to it. Tickle is similarly unique because of the pattern of receptors involved and their order of stimulation. Thus, although sensation may be broken down into four components—and there is more to follow on this point below—we must not miss the point that cutaneous experience is always the result of some particular pattern of sensory events.

Concerning kinesthetic experience, most of us would agree that the experiences that come from within the body are not basically different from those generated in the skin. When we move our limbs, we feel pressure as a sensation essentially like that of contact on the skin. When a muscle is injured or tired, we feel pain, just as injury to the skin is painful. Perhaps kinesthetic pain or internal pain is duller or has a less definite locus than cutaneous pain, but it is pain just the same. Thus, kinesthesis included, it can be said that there are four basic qualities.

SOMATIC RECEPTORS

If there are four different qualities of experience, it may seem logical to expect that there might be four different kinds of receptors, each responsible for one of the qualities. Actually, this is probably not logical, but it has seemed so, and thinking this, investigators launched a search for specific receptors to match up with the qualities of experience. In Figures 9.1 and 9.2, one can see the principal structures they found.

STRUCTURE

There are many variations on the structures shown in the illustrations. Indeed, some of them are probably variations of each other. For our purposes, the structures shown may be classified into three general categories: (*1*) free nerve endings not associated with any specialized organ that, after much or little branching, end on epithelial cells or on the linings of the tissues of the body; (*2*) hair follicles in which the base of the follicle is served by a nerve ending; and (*3*) encapsulated end organs of various types in which the nerve fiber terminates within some sort of shell having a lining and perhaps other complex structures.

Because encapsulated end organs vary so much in size and structure, in-

FIGURE 9.1—Diagrams of the principal receptors of the skin. (Adapted from J. F. Fulton. *Physiology of the nervous system.* 2d ed. Fair Lawn, N.J.: Oxford University Press, 1943. P. 3. By permission of the publishers.)

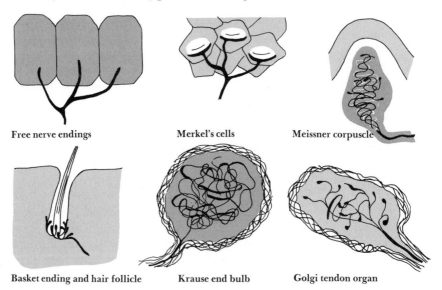

Free nerve endings	Merkel's cells	Meissner corpuscle
Basket ending and hair follicle	Krause end bulb	Golgi tendon organ

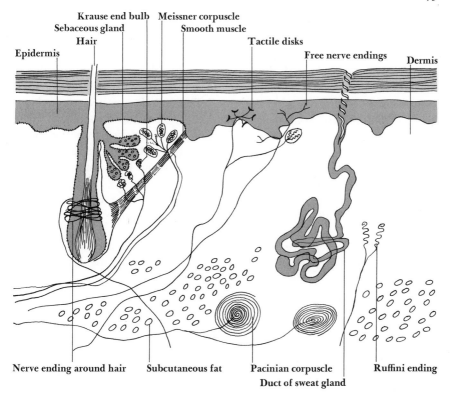

FIGURE 9.2—Schematic drawing of a cross section of the human skin (Adapted from H. H. Woollard, G. Weddell, and J. A. Harpman. Observations on the neurohistological basis of cutaneous pain. *J. Anat.*, 1940, 74, 413–440, and E. Gardner. *Fundamentals of neurology.* Philadelphia: Saunders, 1947. P. 111.)

vestigators have been tempted to classify them. One type of corpuscle (see Figure 9.1) is called the Meissner corpuscle, another the Krause end bulb (Figure 9.1), and another the Ruffini cylinder (Figure 9.2). All these are found in the skin relatively near the surface. Deeper in the body are the Pacinian corpuscle (Figure 9.2), the Golgi tendon organ (Figure 9.1), and the muscle spindle organ (see page 257). Such a classification, particularly of the last three, has its uses, but there is some doubt that there is really any clear line to be drawn among the first three and other variations not mentioned (see page 246).

DISTRIBUTION

Eighty years ago, investigators were more naïve. They were inclined to think of a few simple types of end organs. One of them, von Frey, attempted to correlate each of the cutaneous qualities with one type of end organ (see

Dallenbach, 1939). To find clues, he compared the distribution of different corpuscles in different regions of the body with differences in cutaneous sensitivity in these regions. It seemed to him that the Meissner corpuscle was more frequent in regions of the body where sensitivity to touch stimuli is greatest. The Krause end bulb appeared most plentiful where cold sensitivity was greatest. And another corpuscle, the Ruffini cylinder, seemed to correlate in its distribution with warmth sensitivity. Finally, free nerve endings—without any capsules—were correlated with pain sensitivity. Von Frey therefore proposed that the Meissner corpuscle is the organ of touch, the Krause end bulb the organ for cold, the Ruffini cylinder the organ for warmth, and the free nerve ending the pain receptor organ.

In another, more modern experiment the male prepuce was the region studied (Bazett et al., 1932). Here there are about fifteen cold spots per square centimeter and about one warm spot per square centimeter. The count for numbers of Krause end bulbs and Ruffini cylinders is just about the same as the number of spots. This correlation made some people believe that von Frey was right in naming these encapsulated end organs as thermal receptors.

HISTOLOGICAL STUDIES

But it takes more than a very rough correlation between regions of sensitivity and regions of greatest numbers of end organs (which are difficult to identify correctly anyway) to show that a given structure is *the* receptor for a particular sensory quality. A much better experiment is to find what receptor in the skin underlies a sensitive spot. The straightforward way of doing this experiment—but somewhat disturbing to the subject—is to make maps of the skin for "cold," "warmth," and "touch" spots and then do *biopsies,* that is, cut out that portion of the skin, stain it, slice it, and look at it under a microscope to see what is there. The results of this kind of experiment ought to be decisive.

The experiment has been made many times. The verdict goes against any fixed relation between encapsulated end organs and the quality of sensation subserved (Gilmer, 1942). Very frequently, there is no encapsulated end organ under, or even very near, a sensitive spot. This is true for all four qualities of sensation. The only thing one can be sure of finding is a nerve ending of some kind, either with an encapsulated organ or as a free nerve ending. Hence it must be concluded that free nerve endings may mediate any quality and that one cannot tell the kind of receptor by its structure. There are certain exceptions to this which will be mentioned below.

Confirming this conclusion is a recent experiment that is a model of controlled research in this area (Lele and Weddell, 1956). It was done on the cornea, which contains only free nerve endings and Krause end bulbs. Using a fine nylon hair, the investigators pressed it lightly against the cornea. To this stimulus, subjects uniformly reported "touch" without any pain whatsoever. With a larger, more brittle nylon hair, however, the subjects consistently blinked and reported sharp pain. To study temperature sensitivity, jets of air and cylinders appropriately heated or cooled were used. To employ a warm stimulus with contact, an infrared beam was used. With all these methods, subjects most of the time reported sensations of "cold" and "warmth." Consequently, it was well established that the cornea is sensitive in all modalities even though it has only free nerve endings and one type of encapsulated end organ.

Strengthening this conclusion further is a histological study of end organs in the human cornea (see Weddell, 1961). Methylene blue was injected to stain the organ, then it was photographed, and this was done in the same region at intervals over several weeks. A surprising result was obtained. The encapsulated end organs were in a constant state of degeneration and regeneration. An organ that was plainly present at one time of observation may have totally disappeared a few weeks later. Conversely, what was on one occasion a free nerve ending later was seen to have an encapsulated end organ around it. From this it would appear that the presence of the end organ was rather incidental to the function of the receptor.

CONCLUSIONS

Despite results of this sort, there are a few positive statements that can be made. The sensation reported when a hair is deflected, thus stimulating the fiber serving a hair follicle, is invariably one of "touch" or "pressure." The Pacinian corpuscle is also an organ of "pressure" but, in this case, deep pressure. Pacinian corpuscles are generally much larger than cutaneous encapsulated organs. They consist of a capsule made up of several layers of fibrous tissue in which nerve endings ramify (see Figure 9.2). They are distributed widely in the body: in the sheaths of tendons and muscles, in the linings of various organs of the body, and in the subcutaneous adipose tissue. They are organs of deep-pressure sensitivity and are excited by deformation of the tissue in which they are housed. They are served by large myelinated fibers, whose significance will be pointed out later. Finally, there can be no doubt either that the *muscle* spindle found in the equatorial region of muscle and the Golgi tendon organs are also organs of "pressure." However, as we shall see, signals from muscle spindles probably are never appreciated as sensation; rather they are significant only in reflex functions.

It is clear, then, that certain encapsulated end organs are unequivocally concerned in "pressure" reception. On the other hand, pain is clearly subserved by free nerve endings. There have been virtually no reports of organs other than free nerve endings being involved in pain. This does not mean that free nerve endings are *the* organs for pain, for, as indicated above, such endings may also serve all four qualities of sensation. In addition, encapsulated end organs are sometimes involved in "cold" and "warmth."

THERMAL SENSITIVITY

In this and the following sections, we shall consider in turn the peripheral mechanisms of temperature, tactile, pain, and kinesthetic sensitivity. After that, the somatic sensory pathways in the nervous system will be described, and finally we shall discuss the central mechanisms of the somatic senses.

DEPTH OF RECEPTORS

It was long ago established that the reaction time for warmth is longer than that for cold (see Woodworth and Schlosberg, 1954). If it is assumed that conduction rates for impulses in the two modalities are about the same, this fact suggested that the receptors for warmth and cold might lie at different depths in the skin. This is indeed the case.

To measure the depth of warmth and cold receptors, the prepuce of the human penis was chosen as a convenient tissue (Bazett et al., 1932). A thermocouple was placed on one side of the prepuce and a thermostimulator on the other side. With this arrangement the rate at which temperature changes were transmitted through the tissue could be measured. This was about 1 millimeter per second (confirmed by Hensel & Zotterman, 1951). It was also possible to correlate this rate with the time and temperatures at which subjects reported thermal experience. And from these data the depth of receptors could be estimated. The average depth of warmth receptors, it was found, was about 0.30 millimeter, and that for cold receptors was about 0.17 millimeter.

FIBER SIZES

As was pointed out in Chapter 3, it is possible to classify fibers according to their size. Usually in the compound action potential from a nerve containing fibers for all the somatic senses, several distinct humps can be distinguished (Figure 9.3). There has been some confusion about the labeling of these humps, but we shall use the terminology longest in use (Erlanger and Gasser, 1937). This divides somesthetic fibers into two general groups called, respectively, A and C fibers. The A fibers are myelinated and the C unmyelinated. The A fibers can in turn be subdivided into three or four subgroups, but for our purposes a division into "fast A fibers" and "slow A fibers" is sufficient because that is as far as the correlation with specific function can be carried.

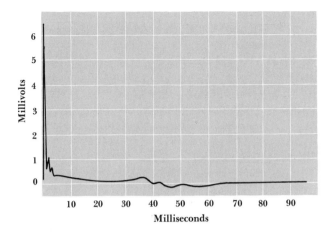

FIGURE 9.3—Compound action potential of cutaneous sensory fibers showing fast A (first peak), slow A (second pair of peaks), and very slow C (peaks at 35 to 50 milliseconds) fibers. (Adapted from W. K. Livingston. What is pain? *Scient. American*, 1953, 188, 59–66. Reprinted by permission. Copyright © 1953 by Scientific American, Inc. All rights reserved.)

The unmyelinated C fibers are, of course, slower than the "slow A fibers" (see Rose and Mountcastle, 1959).

As we shall see, tactile impulses and pain impulses can be carried by both A and C fibers. However, it seems fairly clear that cold and warmth impulses are carried by the slow A fibers. Whether these slow A fibers are the exclusive property of cold and warmth receptors is not known, but perhaps they are. Direct measurement of isolated cold fibers of the cat gives diameters of 1.5 to 3 microns; these are the slow thinly myelinated A fibers. Warmth fibers have somewhat larger spikes than cold fibers and may be presumed therefore to be somewhat larger.

NERVE AS TEMPERATURE RECEPTOR

It has been known for a long time that potentials can be obtained in nerve fibers—not just warmth or cold fibers—when they are cooled or warmed (see Granit and Skoglund, 1945). A systematic study of this phenomenon has been made (Bernhard and Granit, 1946). In this study, a thermode—a sort of cuff whose temperature can be controlled precisely—was placed around a bundle of nerve fibers. Then electrical measurements were made with different conditions of warming or cooling the nerve.

The results are summarized in Figure 9.4. They illustrate two electrical changes that follow cooling or warming. One is a local *generator potential*; the other, a *compound action potential*. The local potential is called a gen-

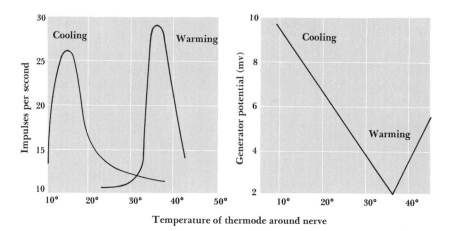

FIGURE 9.4—Some results of experiments on nerve as a model of a temperature end organ. (Adapted from C. G. Bernhard and R. Granit. Nerve as a model temperature end organ. *J. gen. Physiol.*, 1946, 29, 257–265. By permission of The Rockefeller Institute Press.)

erator potential because it would appear to be responsible for initiating the action potential. The existence, incidentally, of a separate generator potential has been demonstrated in kinesthetic receptors (Lowenstein et al., 1963). The action potential consists of a number of spike potentials summed, and in this case it was possible to count them. The frequency of impulses increased and decreased according to the change in temperature produced in the region of the nerve stimulated. Note that cold (lowered temperature) is somewhat more effective in evoking both generator potential and spike impulses than is warmth (increased temperature), but both are effective.

From these facts one might expect that any nerve fiber, whether concerned with temperature or not, might respond to differences in temperature. This, indeed, is sometimes the case. In one experiment, receptors known to be mechanical receptors were definitely excited by cooling (Hensel and Zotterman, 1951). However, the amount of change and the rate of change required to produce this nonspecific effect are greater than that required for true thermal receptors and their fibers.

THERMAL FIBERS

Since these earlier experiments on the general temperature sensitivity of nerve, it has been possible to isolate and to study individual thermal fibers. When found, such fibers invariably are either cold fibers, i.e., responsive to cold, or warmth fibers, i.e., responsive to warmth. That they are quite specific in their function is established by the fact that they respond to a thermal stimulus applied to their respective receptive fields but do not respond to mechanical stimuli, including pin pricks. Figure 9.5 gives the measurements made of the number of impulses per second for two such individual fibers, one a cold fiber and the other a warmth fiber (Zotterman, 1953).

THERMAL EXPERIENCE

From the simple data given in Figure 9.5 it is possible to make a number of predictions about the phenomena of thermal experience, all of which have proved to be correct. It happens that the phenomena were known long before the curves were explained, and so the curves actually explain the phenomena rather than predict them (see Zotterman, 1959).

PARADOXICAL SENSATION—First of all, the long-known phenomena of paradoxical cold and paradoxical warmth can now be understood. In mapping the punctiform sensitivity of the skin, investigators have frequently found paradoxical cold spots when they applied temperatures of between 45 and 50°C. In this region a cold fiber is set into excitation by a hot stimulus. Moreover, at these temperatures, warmth fibers have quit responding. Similarly, investigators have also mapped paradoxical warm spots, spots where warmth is experienced even though a cool stimulus—one cooler than body temperature—is applied. These spots are not so numerous or so stable as paradoxical cold spots. In Figure 9.5, warmth fibers continue to respond to cool stimuli though not so vigorously as to warm stimuli. Ordinarily, however, if a cold spot is stimulated at the same time, which would usually be the case, the paradoxical warmth would be masked by cold fibers, since their response is so much more vigorous.

FIGURE 9.5—Impulse frequency of the steady discharge of a single cold fiber (open circles) and of a single warm fiber (filled circles) as a function of the temperature of the receptors within the range of 10 to 50°C. (Adapted from Y. Zotterman. Special senses: Thermal receptors. *Ann. Rev. Physiol.*, 1953, 15, 357.)

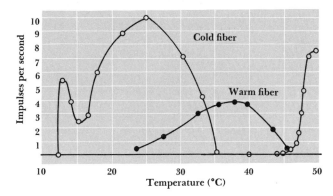

PERSISTENCE OF "COLD"—Secondly, a phenomenon that has long puzzled students of the skin senses is so-called "persistence of cold." This refers to the fact that, if a rather cold stimulus is applied to the skin and then removed, the experience of cold persists for a time (after a silent interval) when the warming of the skin during this period would seemingly predict an experience of warmth. It can be seen from Figure 9.5 that cold receptors respond better at 25° than they do at 15°. Hence, while the skin is warming toward skin temperature, the number of impulses in cold fibers actually increases.

THRESHOLDS—Thirdly, one might expect the threshold for cold to be less than that for warmth, because cold receptors respond more vigorously to a slight downward shift in temperature than the warmth receptors do to an upward shift in temperature. This difference in thresholds is a long-established fact, although the exact values vary with different conditions and regions of the body.

OTHER PHENOMENA—Two other observations not directly connected with the curves in Figure 9.5 can be made. In making maps of punctiform sensitivity, it is observed that warm spots are less stable, that is, less repeatable, than cold spots. This is probably due in part to the deeper location of warmth receptors and to the fact that warmth receptors respond less vigorously than cold ones do. Related to this is the observation that adaptation to a warm stimulus is typically greater and faster than adaptation to cold. Corresponding to this phenomenon is the fact that warmth fibers in the cat typically adapt faster than cold fibers.

The fact that mechanoreceptors sometimes respond to temperature, particularly cold, explains another phenomenon known as "Weber's deception." This is a sensation of pressure or contact caused by cooling of the skin even when there is no object in contact with the skin.

One other observation can be gleaned from Figure 9.5. It is that the warmth and cold receptors are in action even at skin temperature (about 35°). This is a kind of spontaneous activity of a fiber. It takes place without any energy being transferred to the receptor and illustrates the fact that nerve fibers can fire without being stimulated.

PRESSURE AND PAIN

Pressure and pain are clearly separate qualities of experience. In experiments, however, it is hard to separate them. When a man is stuck with a needle, he is also touched, and he feels both pressure and pain. Only by some rather ingenious methods is it possible to separate the sensory mechanisms of the two experiences in animals and in man. Thus we find it easier to start out discussing them together, and later in the section we can make the appropriate distinctions between them.

END ORGANS

Histologists have reported on the receptors for pain and pressure. They have sliced up sections of skin from various parts of the body, stained the slices, and described carefully what they saw. Their descriptions include several points of interest for understanding what happens when the experiences of pain and pressure are aroused (Woollard, et al., 1940; Tower, 1943).

For one thing, they report a good deal of ramification and interlocking of nerve terminals. Small groups of fibers leave the main nerve trunk in the subcutaneous adipose layer. In the dermis these small fiber groups split up into individual nerve fibers. Then in the upper dermis and epidermis, each fiber divides into a number of branches. These branches, however, come back together and split off again from one another, making a plexus, or anastomosis. Out of the plexus arise the numerous small terminals serving the skin receptors.

There are two important points to keep in mind about the small nerve plexus serving the skin (see Tower, 1943). One point is that the branches of two different fibers (of different neurons) do not join together. Each neuron preserves its identity in the terminals. The interlocking in the plexus is only of the branches of one fiber. The second point concerns the area served by one fiber; this can be much larger than one might expect. Sometimes, as in the viscera of the frog, one fiber or neuron unit may serve as much as 6 square centimeters. There are some regions of the skin of the frog and of man where the area is more than 1 square centimeter. In more sensitive regions, however, the area is smaller. On the back of a man's hand, for example, the net or plexus of one fiber serves about ⅛ square centimeter, and on the monkey's thumb the area is about 1 millimeter.

Another point of interest in the histologists' studies is the overlapping of innervation. Although the branches of different fibers do not join with each other, they serve overlapping areas of the skin. Thus a needle or a hair touched to any part of the skin is likely to stimulate the branches of more than one fiber. The degree of overlapping of terminals varies greatly from one region of the body to another.

PERIPHERAL UNIT FOR PAIN

It is not necessary to trust entirely to the histologists' reports for this conception of the receptors. A very neat method has been devised for mapping the sensory units for pain in man (Bishop, 1944). The main trick of the method is to use a short electric spark for the stimulus. A voltage of the right amount applied to an electrode near the skin, but not touching it, will cause a spark discharge to the skin. Either a pressure or a prick-pain experience will result —sometimes both. Points that give only the prick-pain experience can be selected and marked, and with appropriate adjustments in the voltage, the thresholds of the points can be found.

This method gives the conventional map of "pain spots" that can be obtained with needles or direct electrical stimuli. But it also does more than that. By using spark discharges of the right strength, it is possible to stimulate directly through the skin the nerve fiber whose branches serve the areas that have been mapped. Once several fibers have been located in this fashion, it is possible to anesthetize the fibers, singly or in combination, by squirting a little cocaine into the skin along the route of the nerve fiber. With various fibers anesthetized, one can remap the points sensitive to prick pain and see just what areas of the skin are served by various neuron units.

The results of one such experiment are pictured in Figure 9.6. There one can see the areas of overlap of eight different sensory units. These areas were found by anesthetizing the fibers serving them at the points indicated with large black dots. For example, by anesthetizing at points 2 and 3 and at points 7 and 8 and remapping the skin, the areas serving unit 4 could be mapped, and so on with the other units. In this way the peripheral units for pain on the forearm can be directly plotted. The units are relatively large— of the order of several centimeters—and the degree of overlapping is great.

LOCALIZATION

What does this overlapping of sensory units mean? They do not represent separate receptors. Instead, they are simply the points of greatest sensitivity in a much larger net of an individual fiber. This is a fact proved in the experiments with the electric-spark stimulus for prick pain. It was in the center of the area of a sensory unit that there was the greatest sensitivity. In the margins of the area that overlap with other areas, thresholds were the poorest.

A second point is to be noted from these experiments on the overlapping of sensory units. A stimulus, unless it is very small and placed in the center of one sensory unit's distribution, ordinarily excites more than one unit. It is the difference in stimulation of units serving a region that gives the local sign, i.e., makes possible localization of the place of stimulation. Thus the mechanism of discriminating space on the skin is like that for visual acuity. In vision, also, there is considerable overlapping of the connections of neurons (see page 148), but nevertheless fine visual detail can be appreciated from the pattern of visual fibers that are excited. It has been found that the somesthetic receptor mechanisms are organized in essentially the same way.

FIBER TYPES AND EXPERIENCES

Investigators more than sixty years ago described two different kinds of pain experience. One, called prick pain, is a bright, relatively short pain; the other, called dull pain, is longer-lasting and less well localized. Observers seem

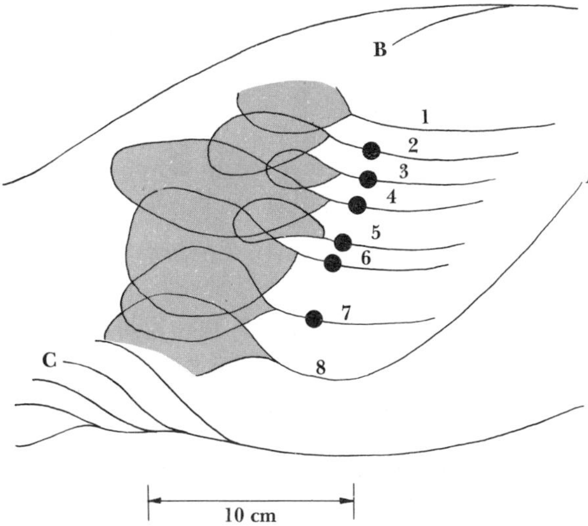

FIGURE 9.6—Sketch of pain units mapped by electrical stimulation and selective anesthetization of fibers. Dark areas are endings of nerve fibers 1, 2, etc., which are branches of the A group of fibers. B and C are the other groups. Dark dots are the spots anesthetized. (Adapted from G. H. Bishop. The peripheral unit for pain. *J. Neurophysiol.*, 1944, 7, 71–80.)

fairly well agreed that the subjective experiences of pain can be so categorized. Whether this subjective difference has any physiological basis is another question; some think yes, others no (see Sweet, 1959).

As previously indicated, both A and C fibers serve areas in which pain arises. Moreover, it seems clear from a variety of evidence that pain fibers are of both the A (slow) and C variety. It has been suggested that the A pain fibers signal prick (or bright) pain and that C fibers subserve dull pain. If this is so, and investigators disagree about it, there is no firm evidence for it. All that is reasonably certain is that both A and C fibers are involved in pain.

PAIN FROM EXCESSIVE STIMULATION?

One of the controversies concerning the Müller doctrine has centered on the question whether pain is always a unique, specific experience or whether it may result from the intense stimulation of any or all of the other somatic senses. The physiological evidence is in favor of the Müller doctrine and against the idea of pain arising from the excessive stimulation of other modalities. The argument goes something like this.

Individual pain fibers have been isolated that respond to pin prick but not to mechanical stimulation. Similarly, tactile fibers have been isolated that respond to mechanical stimulation but not to pin prick. Accordingly, there are clearly fibers responding uniquely to different kinds of stimulation. In addition, in those fibers that respond to pin prick (pain fibers), the number of impulses is proportional to the intensity of stimulation. With weak stimulation, the impulse rate may be made to vary in this way between 5 and 100 per second. On the other hand, in tactile fibers, which can respond usually at faster rates, frequency of fibers is similarly proportional to intensity of stimulation. Here, by intense stimulation, a fiber can be driven at, say, 300 or 400 per second, yet the animal used in the experiment gives no evidence of experiencing pain (Adrian, 1928).

It is true, of course, that strong mechanical stimulation, e.g., strong pressure, may be painful and may excite the pain receptors, but in this case the stimulus is an injurious one that can be expected to arouse pain.

STIMULUS FOR PAIN

This brings us to the question of what kinds of stimuli elicit pain. We can feel pain not only when we are stuck or cut but when a stimulus is too hot or too cold. That would suggest that any kind of intense stimulus, whether pressure or temperature, may excite pain receptors. Loosely speaking, that is true. It would appear, however, that there is another criterion for excitation. That is whether the stimulus actually damages tissue or is very close in intensity to the point where tissue damage would result. The case of cutting or pin prick is obvious. In the case of thermal stimulation, it appears that pain is experienced very close to the point where destructive changes normally take place in the tissues in which pain receptors are embedded (see Edwards, 1950).

The question has been raised whether in the excitation of receptors there is an intervening step in which some chemical is liberated and whether such a chemical is the immediate excitant for the pain receptor. No definite answer to this can be given. It can be stated, however, that in some cases a chemical (e.g., histamine) is liberated in connection with the excitation of pain receptors (Lewis, 1942). It can also be stated that such chemicals can cause pain (see Sweet, 1959). Both histamine and acetylcholine when injected in very small amounts (10^{-5} and 10^{-8} gram mole per milliliter, respectively) cause pain. So also does serotonin, a substance liberated in the destruction of blood platelets. But these substances are frequently quite potent in exciting neurons and muscle fibers at their synaptic junctures, and so perhaps this is a general effect not specific to pain fibers.

TACTILE FIBERS

Just to round out the picture of the peripheral mechanisms of pain and pressure, we may note that individual tactile fibers have been isolated and studied (see Rose and Mountcastle, 1959). For the technical reason that large fibers give larger potentials and thus are easier to study, most fibers isolated have been of the fast A type even though it is known that there are slower, smaller fibers involved in tactile experience. The tactile fibers studied regularly are responsive to mechanical stimuli, such as stroking or touching with hairs, and not to other kinds of stimuli, with the special exception of cold noted above. Hence, there is little doubt that the four modalities of experience discussed early in the chapter have their individual receptors.

KINESTHETIC SENSE

We shall come shortly to the central centers and pathways concerned in somesthesis. Before we do, however, there is still one somatic sense that we must take up briefly. This is kinesthesis. The receptors for this sense are to be found in the muscles, tendons, and joints. Although we are seldom aware of them, they are important. Unlike the skin receptors, which are stimulated now and then by energy from outside the body, the kinesthetic receptors are always being stimulated from within the body. Indeed, they are involved in every movement.

KINESTHETIC RECEPTORS

Besides free nerve endings in blood vessels, there are two general classes of kinesthetic end organs: muscle spindles and joint receptors.

The *muscle spindle* is a somewhat complicated structure found in the equatorial region of muscles. As can be seen in Figure 9.7, it consists of muscle fibers innervated by sensory nerve endings, all enclosed in a tissue fluid and a capsule of connective tissue. Within the muscle spindle are nerve endings of two types, each named more or less according to its appearance:

FIGURE 9.7—The sensory and motor innervation of muscle. (Adapted from D. Denny-Brown. In J. F. Fulton, *Physiology of the nervous system.* 2d ed. Fair Lawn, N.J.: Oxford University Press, 1943. P. 7. By permission of the publishers.)

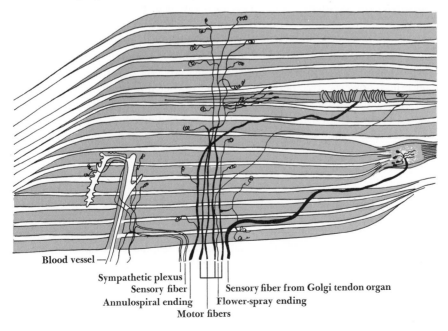

Blood vessel —
Sympathetic plexus
Sensory fiber
Annulospiral ending
Sensory fiber from Golgi tendon organ
Flower-spray ending
Motor fibers

(1) the annulospiral endings and (2) the flower-spray endings. The annulo-spiral endings are the terminals of large fibers arranged spirally around the muscle fibers. The flower-spray endings are terminals of smaller, less myeli-nated fibers, which end in spraylike arborizations upon the muscle fibers. Both these receptors are so arranged that they are stimulated when the muscle stretches. For that reason they are called *stretch afferents*.

Considerable evidence has piled up in recent years that stretch afferents are not concerned in experiences of events in muscles but rather serve in reflex inhibition of certain muscles (Rose and Mountcastle, 1959; Lloyd and McIntyre, 1950). For that reason they will not be referred to again here but will be discussed later in Chapter 10.

Actually, it is not the muscles but the joints that supply kinesthetic in-formation about the movement and position of the limbs. At least, all the evidence points in that direction. Instead of the muscle sense, as so many textbooks term it, one should more properly refer to the joint sense, for that is where the sense is.

Joints contain two types of end organs. The type that occurs most fre-quently is a "spray type" somewhat like the Ruffini organ mentioned earlier. These receptors are arranged at different positions in the joint along the range of movement, so that certain ones function with the limb in any position. The receptors fire when the limb moves, but they also have a steady firing rate when a limb is in a fixed position. A second type of receptor organ is the Golgi end organ. Organs of this type are found on the ligaments of the joints. Both types of joint receptors adapt very slowly to continued stimulation.

A third receptor, the Pacinian corpuscle, participates in the sensing of movement and position. This end organ is found in the deeper tissues and is frequently stimulated by "squeezing" whenever there is a change in the posi-tion of the body or a limb. It is served by large myelinated A fibers.

Free nerve endings are also kinesthetic receptors. They tell of certain events deep within the tissues and muscles of the body. As far as the muscles are concerned, however, free nerve endings are restricted to the blood vessels that serve the muscles; they do not end directly on muscle fibers. Unfortunately, not very much is known about the free nerve endings, how many there are, and just where they end. From what is known of pain arising from within the body, however, it may be assumed that the tendons and joints are espe-cially well supplied with free nerve endings.

KINESTHETIC FIBER TYPES

There is a nice relation between types of kinesthetic nerve fibers and the receptor organs that they serve. That has been learned from experiments in which nervous impulses have been recorded in nerves while the receptors are stimulated in various ways. Kinesthetic nerve fibers can be divided into four main groups (Matthews, 1933). They have been called A_1, A_2, B, and C.

These letters, however, have been assigned for convenience; they do not correspond to A and C fibers of the cutaneous nerves. The A, B, and C kinesthetic fibers, in fact, do not include any pain fibers comparable to the cutaneous C fibers. Altogether, they are much thicker and more myelinated and conduct impulses faster than the average fibers from the skin receptors. The B fibers have a higher threshold than the A_2 or A_1 fibers, they conduct more slowly, and they have smaller diameters. They are believed, upon good evidence, to serve the joint receptors. Their rate of response—nervous impulses—is increased by either active contraction or passive stretch of the muscles. Thus the B fibers can be called *tension recorders*. The C fibers are associated with Pacinian corpuscles, for responses in them disappear when the muscle sheaths containing Pacinian corpuscles are dissected away. These fibers are somewhat smaller and slower than the A or B fibers.

SOMATIC SENSORY PATHWAYS

We shall return to the question of specificity of function in the somatic senses, but in order to have a background for further discussion, it is necessary first to consider the anatomy of the somatic sensory pathways so that references may later be made to them.

DERMATOMES

One of the chief features of vertebrate animals is that their bodies, and particularly their bony structures, are divided into segments. One can see this most easily in fishes. In the higher vertebrates, such as the rat and man, it is a bit harder to see the segments, but they are there and are especially prominent in the very early stages of the embryo. Even in the adult, the vertebrae and spinal nerves are spaced in fairly regular steps. Each spinal nerve represents a segment or *metamere* in the embryo, and although the body itself has lost a segmental appearance, each spinal nerve serves a limited area of the body. This area is called a *dermatome*. In the human adult each dermatome is somewhat irregular in shape and size, but the position and shape of the various dermatomes look roughly as they are in Figure 9.8.

The boundaries of the dermatomes are not really as clear as they are shown in the illustration. There is considerable overlapping. In fact, in mapping dermatomes in experiments with animals, it is necessary to cut three nerves below and three nerves above the one to be studied in order to determine the area served by a nerve. This method is called the method of "remaining sensibility" (Sherrington, 1893).

Figure 9.8 shows only the map for the skin. Under the skin there is a similar grouping. In fact, fibers of the same nerves that serve the skin also go

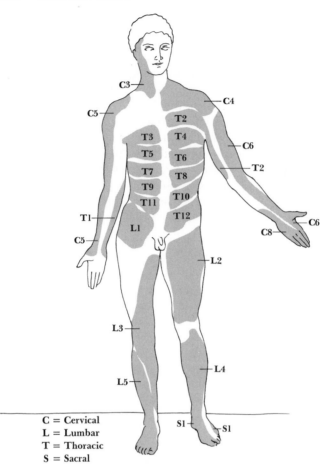

FIGURE 9.8—The dermatomes of the human body. (Adapted from
T. Lewis. *Pain*. New York: Macmillan, 1942. P. 20. By permission
of the publishers.)

to the muscles, tendons, joints, and deep tissues. The entire distribution, regardless of type of receptor, is divided in terms of spinal segments.

SPINAL ROOTS

As we follow the somesthetic nerves inward toward the spinal cord—we shall
consider the face and head later—we find that, just before the cord is
reached, all the nerves from a body segment join together in one nerve. Thus
the fibers for pain, temperature, and pressure and from the skin, muscles, and
deep parts of the body get together in one bundle to enter the cord. In fact,
for a short distance outside the cord both the motor and the sensory fibers are

joined in one nerve. On approaching the cord, however, they divide into sensory and motor roots. The somesthetic fibers make up the dorsal root and the motor fibers the ventral root. And as we noted in Chapter 1, all the cell bodies of the *sensory* fibers lie outside the cord in the dorsal ganglion, whereas the cell bodies of the *motor* fibers are inside the cord in the ventral horn.

Between the dorsal ganglion and the cord itself, the sensory roots divide into two bundles, one medial and the other lateral. The medial bundle goes to the dorsal column of white matter (fibers) and the lateral bundle goes to the dorsal horn of gray matter (chiefly somas). This division has functional significance. The medial bundle has mostly large myelinated fibers and represents pressure receptors, both kinesthetic and cutaneous. The lateral bundle, on the other hand, is made up of the smaller fibers, unmyelinated and lightly myelinated. It has in it the fibers from the pain and temperature receptors, both deep and cutaneous. Thus, at this point, the fibers divide, not according to skin, muscle, or tissue from which they came, but according to the kinds of receptors they serve. All the fibers, after they enter the cord, divide and send branches both upward and downward in the cord.

SPINAL CORD

The relations of various tracts and nuclei of the somesthetic system are fairly well known. The matter, however, is rather complex, and in the space we have to give to it here we cannot be completely accurate. Moreover, to make the pathways clear, we need two illustrations, one for the skin senses and the other for kinesthesis. Otherwise the diagrams would be too cluttered to read. In what follows, therefore, refer to either Figure 9.9 or 9.10, whichever is appropriate.

Many of the fibers from both medial and lateral bundles do not go very far, once they enter the cord. These are concerned in one way or another with various spinal reflexes. A few fibers may go directly to the ventral horn cells, where they make synapse directly with motor cells to effect the simplest reflexes. Others end on interneurons in the gray matter of the cord, and these interneurons make reflex connections with the motor cells. These connections can, of course, involve more than one level of the cord. Since they are concerned with reflexes, which we shall come to in the next chapter, rather than with sensory experience, we shall pay no more attention to them here. Instead, let us turn to the ascending tracts and consider them according to the bundle from which they arise.

MEDIAL BUNDLE—This bundle, it was pointed out, represents pressure receptors, both kinesthetic and cutaneous. Fibers enter the dorsal (posterior) columns, run upward for some distance, and then cross over to the opposite side of the cord. On each side of the cord there are two dorsal columns, called *gracilis* and *cuneatus*, respectively. Many kinesthetic fibers remain in the

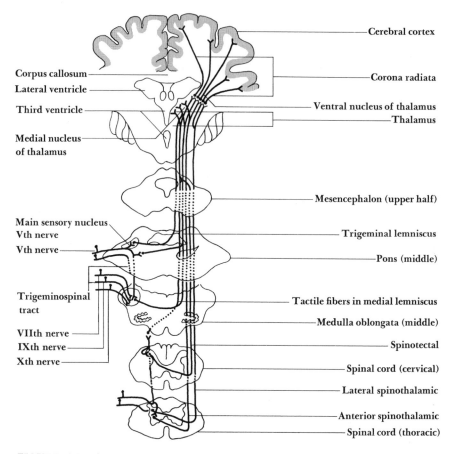

FIGURE 9.9—Diagram illustrating the chief centers and pathways of the cutaneous sensory system. (Adapted from A. Kuntz. *A textbook of neuroanatomy.* 4th ed. Philadelphia: Lea & Febiger, 1945. P. 214. By permission of the publishers.)

columns and ascend upward without making any synapses until they reach the *gracile nucleus* and *cuneate nucleus* of the medulla. Some kinesthetic fibers from the dorsal columns, however, end in the gray matter before they go very far. There they make synapses with cells that send fibers upward in another tract, the ventral spinal cerebellar tract. The purpose of these fibers is to connect with the centers in the cerebellum that aid in the coordination of movements (see Chapter 10).

Many of the fibers that represent pressure receptors of the skin do not remain in the dorsal columns but leave them at some point to run over to the ventral part of the cord. There they course upward in a tract known as the *central spinothalamic tract.*

LATERAL BUNDLE—This bundle, we noted before, contains fibers representing pain and temperature. Most of these fibers cross the cord as soon as they enter and end in the gray matter of the dorsal horn. With them connect second-order neurons that assemble nearby and ascend in the *lateral spinothalamic tract*.

This tract appears to have two divisions, although they are not distinctly separated. One, located more to the side, represents temperature receptors. The other lies more ventrally and conveys impulses from pain receptors. The thermal division, for the most part, continues all the way to the thalamus without making any synapses. The division for pain, however, has many endings in the gray matter on the way upward. The higher-order cells located there send upward fibers that may also end in gray matter of the cord. Thus the tract for pain is really a chain of neurons rather than a continuous

FIGURE 9.10—Diagram of the centers and pathways of the kinesthetic system. (Adapted from A. Kuntz. *A textbook of neuroanatomy.* 4th ed. Philadelphia: Lea & Febiger, 1945. P. 212. By permission of the publishers.)

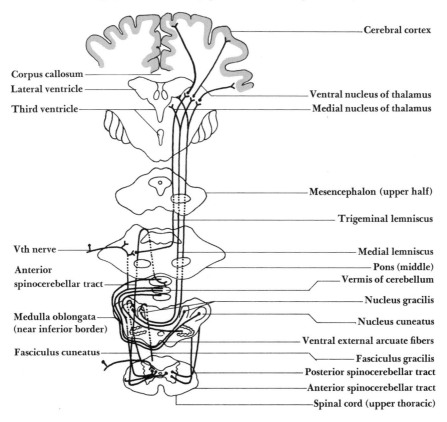

Cerebral cortex

Corpus callosum
Lateral ventricle
Third ventricle

Ventral nucleus of thalamus
Medial nucleus of thalamus

Mesencephalon (upper half)

Trigeminal lemniscus

Vth nerve
Anterior spinocerebellar tract

Medulla oblongata (near inferior border)

Fasciculus cuneatus

Medial lemniscus
Pons (middle)
Vermis of cerebellum
Nucleus gracilis
Nucleus cuneatus
Ventral external arcuate fibers
Fasciculus gracilis
Posterior spinocerebellar tract
Anterior spinocerebellar tract
Spinal cord (upper thoracic)

tract. However, the ultimate ending of both the pain and thermal divisions of the lateral spinothalamic tract is, as the name implies, in the thalamus.

HINDBRAIN

Now let us move on to the centers of the brain. The spinothalamic tracts of the spinal cord continue upward until they reach the thalamus. But in the hindbrain (medulla and pons) there are additions to the system, consisting of pathways for the head and face. The sensory tracts of the spinal cord serve only the trunk and limbs. Somesthetic impulses from the head enter the brain directly over cranial nerves. Several nerves take part in this pathway, among them the trigeminal, the facial, the glossopharyngeal, and the vagus. The pathway is called the bulbothalamic tract.

TRIGEMINAL NERVE—The most important contribution to the bulbothalamic tract is made by the trigeminal nerve. Upon approaching the hindbrain, it divides into three main roots which go to their respective nuclei of the hindbrain.

One of these nuclei is the *spinal nucleus,* so called because it extends downward in the medulla to the upper part of the spinal cord. This nucleus receives the smaller fibers concerned mainly with temperature and pain. It corresponds to the lateral spinothalamic tract of the spinal cord. Axons from this nucleus ascend to the thalamus.

A second nucleus of the trigeminal is the main *sensory nucleus.* It receives the larger myelinated fibers serving the pressure receptors of the skin. It corresponds to the ventral or anterior spinothalamic tract of the the spinal cord. Its axons, like those of the other nucleus, course upward to the thalamus.

Finally, there is the *mesencephalic nucleus* of the trigeminal nerve. It has this name because it extends through the pons into the lower part of the midbrain (mesencephalon). It has another distinctive feature, too. Most spinal and cranial sensory nerves, it will be recalled, have their cell bodies in the dorsal or cranial ganglia outside the central nervous system. The mesencephalic nucleus, however, is an exception. Although it lies within the hindbrain and midbrain, it contains the cell bodies of first-order sensory fibers. The final point to remember about the mesencephalic division and nucleus of the trigeminal is that it is kinesthetic in function. It serves the muscles and joints of the head and cranium. It is comparable, therefore, to the gracile and cuneate pathways of the spinal cord. Its axons, like those of the other somesthetic pathways, go on up to the thalamus.

GRACILE AND CUNEATE NUCLEI—The hindbrain, aside from these inputs from the cranial nerves, is also a way station for the kinesthetic pathways of the spinal cord: the gracile and cuneate tracts. In the medulla are two nuclei, the gracile and cuneate nuclei, and the long kinesthetic fibers of the dorsal columns end in these nuclei. In these nuclei also are the cell bodies of second-order neurons that send axons up to the thalamus.

These axons projecting to the thalamus, together with those arising from the main sensory nucleus, form a pathway to the thalamus called the medial lemniscus. At the level of the midbrain, then, there are two somatic pathways headed upward: the *spinothalamic tract* and the *medial lemniscus*.

RETICULAR FORMATION—There is no doubt but that one or the other of these two pathways gives off collaterals to the reticular formation throughout much of its length. Stimulation of cutaneous nerves is followed in the reticular formation by evoked potentials. There is no anatomical information to indicate which pathway or whether both pathways account for this activity. It is believed, however, that the collaterals are provided by the spinothalamic pathway and not the medial lemniscus (Rose and Mountcastle, 1959). This would fit with the fact that pain and temperature stimulation is activating; the spinothalamic tract is, of course, the pathway for these modalities.

FOREBRAIN FUNCTIONS

The tracts and nuclei of both the spinal cord and hindbrain, we have said, are so segregated that different kinds of impulses are, for the most part, kept in different tracts. The kinesthetic impulses travel in the gracile, cuneate, and medial lemniscus. The touch impulses from the skin run in the ventral spinothalamic tract and in the chief sensory pathway of the trigeminal. Pain and temperature impulses run in the lateral spinothalamic and spinal division of the trigeminal.

THALAMUS

When all these pathways reach the thalamus, there is no longer any segregation according to function. In fact, impulses from the taste pathways also join the procession and end in the same nucleus of the thalamus. That nucleus is the *posteroventral nucleus*. It shows no separate parts for pain, temperature, or pressure, although those for taste are partially segregated (Chapter 5). Instead, it is arranged—so far as is known now—largely on a topographical basis (Mountcastle and Henneman, 1949). One part of it represents all somesthetic senses of the legs, another the same senses of the arms, and still a third part the face. This last part, because it is relatively larger and more important, has its own special name, the *arcuate nucleus*, although it is part of the posteroventral nucleus.

In the first sections of this chapter, we considered at length the question of specificity of function of receptors and their sensory fibers. With the aid of single-fiber studies, it was shown that different sensory fibers respond to the respective stimuli for touch, warmth, cold, and pain. We should like to know whether this specificity of modality is preserved throughout the somesthetic pathways to the thalamus and cortex.

Unfortunately, at the present writing, there is no clear-cut experimental answer to this question, for studies of individual units in which the stimulating conditions or the sensory fibers stimulated are known. However, one pair of investigators (Gaze and Gordon, 1955) has recorded single-unit activity in the thalamus while at the same time recording the compound action potential of a cutaneous nerve and varying the stimulating conditions. They found units corresponding to different kinds of stimulation and to different groups of fibers in the sensory nerve. It appears from this that fibers in the thalamus, and hence presumably also in the cortex, retain their specificity of modality. It appears further that fibers for the different modalities are intermixed with each other in the thalamus and cortex just as they are in the skin and the sensory nerves. How messages in the cortex are sorted out so as to produce the respective sensations of touch, warmth, cold, and pain is still a mystery. All that is fairly certain is that the information for subjective quality is coded throughout the somesthetic pathways by the specificity of fibers.

CORTICAL PROJECTION

The posteroventral nucleus of the thalamus projects upward to the postcentral gyrus of the cortex (see page 43). In animals below primates, such as the rat or rabbit or cat, where there is no true central sulcus and consequently no true postcentral gyrus, the projection is nevertheless to an area corresponding to the postcentral gyrus. In primates, this area in the Brodmann number system is often referred to as area 3-1-2 (see page 49).

PRIMARY PROJECTION—The area is laid out topographically. At the top near the longitudinal fissure is the leg area. Then below it and more to the side is the arm area. Between is a small strip for the trunk. Then, far to the side, toward the temporal lobe, is the face area. This receives projections from the arcuate portion of the posteroventral nucleus. The relative space given to these different areas does not correspond with the size of the parts of the body but rather to the relative importance of these areas in somatic functions. Thus in higher animals such as the primates, the face is given much more space on the cortex than the arm or leg.

SECONDARY PROJECTION—By the method of tracing anatomical projections, one can distinguish a second relay from the thalamus and a second area of the cortex. The relay occurs through the *lateral nucleus* of the thalamus, which sends its dendrites to the posteroventral nucleus and its axons to the cortex. This relay was mentioned in Chapter 2. The receiving area of the cortex for this relay is back of the postcentral gyrus. Its limits are not well defined, but for practical purposes it may be considered to be the *posterior parietal lobule,* the major part of the parietal lobe other than the postcentral area.

SOMATIC SENSORY AREAS

For reasons that are not clear as yet, a different picture of the somatic cortex results if it is mapped with evoked potentials rather than with anatomical methods. In employing the method of evoked potentials, electrodes are placed at different positions on the cortex (or other areas) while different sense organs or sensory nerves are being stimulated. This method provides a number of facts about the somatic cortex that are probably more meaningful functionally than are the anatomical facts (see Woolsey, 1952).

SOMATIC AREA I—The electrical method reveals two main somatic areas in the cortex (see Figure 9.11). To avoid confusion with other systems of naming, these areas have been called somatic areas I and II (see Figure 2.11). Area I corresponds fairly well with the postcentral gyrus which we have just been discussing. It gives potentials whenever the skin or the muscles or their afferents send impulses into the nervous system. It is divided into three main parts, one for the legs, another for the arms, and another for the face. There is a small area for the trunk between the arm area and the face area.

The general arrangement of somatic area I is as one would expect from anatomical data. There are, however, some new features that are revealed by the electrical method (see Zubek, 1951; Rose and Mountcastle, 1959). In the first place, it shows in more detail how parts of the body are represented in each of the subordinate areas. The leg area, for example, is arranged in the same way as the segments of the spinal cord serving the skin. The serial order of the dermatomes is kept in the cortex. The same is true for the arm area, with the important exception that the entire serial order is reversed *en bloc.* This reversal of the arm area means that the top part of the cervical region of the spinal cord serving the arm and trunk is represented in the cortex next to the arm area and that the bottom part of the cervical region is also reversed so that its cortical counterpart lies next to the face area.

The main projection in somatic area I is contralateral; one side of the body is projected to the opposite cortex. In addition, however, the electrical method shows that there is also an ipsilateral representation of the face—and the face only—lying just in front of the main face area. This has been given the name *ipsilateral face area* as an additional subdivision of area I.

If, in the process of stimulation, kinesthetic receptors or nerve fibers are added to those of the skin, potentials appear not only in the postcentral cortex but also in the *precentral cortex.* This, we have already seen, is a motor cortex. It is the area from which motor impulses go down to the spinal cord

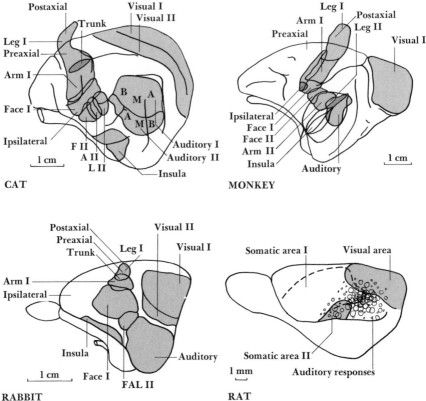

FIGURE 9.11—Somatic cortical areas of the cat, monkey, rabbit, and rat in relation to the visual and auditory areas. (Adapted from C. N. Woolsey. Patterns of localization in sensory and motor areas of the cerebral cortex. In Milbank Memorial Fund. Twenty-seventh Annual Conference. *The biology of mental health and disease.* New York: Hoeber, 1952. P. 195.)

and out to skeletal muscles. Therefore, in regard to kinesthesis, area I also includes the motor or precentral cortex, whereas for the skin senses it consists only of postcentral cortex. One can imagine that the projections are arranged in this fashion so that kinesthetic impulses can help directly in motor coordination.

SOMATIC AREA II—A second somatic, as revealed by electrical methods, does not correspond to the posterior parietal lobule. Instead, it lies on the lateral surface of the cortex between somatic area I and the temporal auditory area. This area II (see Figure 9.11) also has its face, arm, and leg sectors. They are laid out, however, in a slightly different way than in area I. The face area of II is near the face area of I, but the arm and leg areas of II lie to the rear toward the auditory area. The positions are somewhat different for different animals. The important point, however, is that in all animals there are two distinct somatic areas, I and II. One of them corresponds to the postcentral area, but the other has a unique position near the auditory area.

There are some interesting features of somatic area II. In the first place, unlike area I, it receives impulses from *both sides* of all parts of the body. Despite this bilateral representation, the impulses from the opposite side of the body are better represented than those from the same side; at least, they give cortical potentials about twice as large. Somatic area II also seems to be not only a sensory area but a motor area as well. At least, it lies in a position that has long been known to be a part of the extrapyramidal motor system (see Chapter 10). Electrical *stimulation* of this area can produce small movements of face, arm, or leg, depending on the site of stimulation (see Zubek, 1951).

SOMESTHETIC SENSITIVITY

Now we shall summarize what is known of the sensory functions of the somesthetic cortex. Here, as in the other senses, we must distinguish between sensory capacity and learned discriminations. The latter are considered in Chapter 17. Not much research has been done on cortical somesthetic function, and what there is is not very clear. It will be convenient to consider it according to the species of animal used as subjects.

RAT AND CAT—A few studies have been made with rats, in which they learned a roughness discrimination followed by lesions of the cerebral cortex and then by postoperative testing. In an early study of such a discrimination (Smith, 1939), lesions in the general vicinity of what is now known to be the somesthetic areas caused animals to lose their memory of the preoperatively learned discrimination, but they could always relearn the habit. The same general result has been obtained in more recent studies (Zubek, 1951, 1952). In these, however, different combinations of lesions were made in somatic areas I and II. Removal of SII, by itself, had relatively little effect on the discrimination. Removal of SI alone had considerably more effect, and removal of the two together had an even greater one. It is not entirely clear how much of the impairments observed was a matter of learning or memory and how much was a decrease in sensory capacity, but some of the latter seems to occur. Research on the cat confirms the results with the rat, except that ablation of SI and SII together permanently abolished the capacity of the cat to make a roughness discrimination (Zubek, 1952). In this case, sensory capacity surely was impaired.

MONKEY—In studies with the monkey before the existence of SI and SII was known, the subjects were taught to make kinesthetic discriminations of weights (Ruch, 1935). Lesions in the postcentral area, more or less equivalent to SI, did no harm to this discrimination. What did cause impairment, however, was combined lesions of SI and the posterior parietal lobule. Postoperative training enabled the animals to recover some of the loss that followed the operation, but they never recovered to their preoperative level of performance. They remained unable to discriminate differences in weights that they could distinguish preoperatively. Apparently, the lesions caused some real loss of sensory capacity. No lesions were made in SII for it was unknown at the time.

In a later study, a number of different somesthetic discriminations were employed (Orbach and Chow, 1959). Most of them were tactual. Area SII was included in the study. However, it proved to have relatively little importance, for when it was removed by itself there was no effect on the tests. The more important area was SI. Lesions in it resulted in losses of retention for somesthetic discriminations and considerable difficulty in relearning them. Another study of the posterior parietal area revealed a detectable difference in performance in the discrimination of sandpapers, but still the animals discriminated rather well (Wilson et al., 1960).

CHIMPANZEE—In contrast to the monkey and lower animals, the posterior parietal lobule appears to assume greater importance than SI in the chimpanzee (Ruch et al., 1938). Experiments were made with different combinations of lesions in SI and the posterior parietal area. The functions tested were weight discrimination, roughness, and tactual form.

In the case of roughness discrimination, removal of the postcentral area made no difference. It had an appreciable effect on weight discrimination, but this was effaced by further training and probably did not represent a loss of sensory capacity. In each case, however, removal of the parietal lobe, including both the postcentral and posterior parietal areas, caused a profound impairment in discrimination from which the subject could not recover entirely by lengthy postoperative training. Although the design of the study leaves something to be desired by present standards, it seemed to show that the posterior parietal area was more important than the postcentral area in the functions tested.

This conclusion is strengthened by the results of tests of form discrimination. The subject was trained to choose a cone from between a cone and a pyramid, solely on the basis of touch; another problem was to discriminate a pyramid from a wedge. This kind of discrimination was seriously impaired by removal of the posterior parietal area. Some, but not all, of the capacity for discriminating pyramids and wedges was recovered with time and training, but one animal never was able to discriminate again a cone and a pyramid. From this limited work, it is concluded that the parietal area is concerned in the capacity for making tactual form discriminations.

MAN—Data of two types are available for man. One consists of studies of the sensory capacities of individuals suffering from gunshot wounds. The other consists of records of human experience during electrical stimulation of the cortex carried out in the course of neurosurgery.

In the case of gunshot wounds, one is handicapped by not knowing very precisely the location and size of the cortical lesions. Some fairly careful studies of the behavioral capacities of such individuals, however, have been made (Ruch et al., 1938; Semmes et al., 1960). They typically require the individual to make some sort of discrimination with his hands, e.g., weight discrimination, roughness discrimination, or form discrimination. It might be expected, therefore, that the "hand areas" of the brain might be those most involved. This fits roughly with the facts, for the area most concerned in somesthetic impairments is one that includes the hand area of the post-central cortex and the part of the parietal lobe behind it. Individuals with substantial lesions in this area show deficits in all sorts of somesthetic tests. As in the chimpanzee, the most dramatic effects appear in form discrimination.

Studies of electrical stimulation are interesting, though they yield the kinds of results one might expect (Penfield and Boldrey, 1937; Penfield, 1958). If an electrical stylus is applied systematically to different points on the cortex of a conscious patient under local anesthesia, he reports some sort of sensation in much of the precentral and postcentral areas. Some points outside these areas also elicit experiences, but the stimulus required is usually greater. The postcentral cortex, particularly along the lip of the central sulcus, is most productive of reported experiences at low levels of stimulation.

The reports show, as might be expected, the topographic arrangement of the cortex. A stimulus, for example, in the dorsal leg area of the postcentral cortex is reported by the patient to be in his leg. Also, as expected, there is no segregation of experiences in different areas. Various experiences are reported from stimulation in the same areas. With the kinds of electrical stimulation used, sensations of pain, warmth, or cold are rarely recorded. Most common are sensations of numbness, tingling, or movement. Thus such studies do not show how different types of somatic experiences are set apart from each other in the functioning of the cerebral cortex.

10 MOTOR FUNCTIONS

Beginning with the classical work of Sherrington (1906), much of modern neurophysiology has centered around motor and reflex functions. Spinal reflexes are convenient responses to study. These, along with electrophysiological methods of stimulating and recording, have received a great deal of attention. Although this work is of interest in its own right, it is not of detailed interest to the physiological psychologist, for it is not directly concerned with the mechanisms of perception, learning, and motivation. Accordingly, our treatment of reflexes and of motor functions will be cursory; it will present only a bird's-eye view. The interested reader may refer to textbooks (Ruch and Fulton, 1960) or handbooks (Field et al., 1960) for more extended treatments. Our discussion in this chapter will begin with the anatomy and physiology of the motor system. It will then move on to spinal and higher-level reflexes and will end with the topic of motor coordination.

THE MOTOR SYSTEM

The motor system for reflexes, posture, and coordination includes the striated muscles, the nerves innervating them, and various structures of the spinal cord and brain. The best way of describing the system, or systems, is to begin with neuromuscular relations and then work up from the spinal cord to the cerebral cortex.

NEUROMUSCULAR RELATIONS

A striated muscle is a group of muscle fibers gathered together in a bundle. This bundle is covered by sheaths of connective tissue, and it is also joined to bones by tendons of connective tissue. In some instances, muscles are attached to each other.

MOTOR UNITS—Muscle fibers are served by both sensory and motor neurons. The cell bodies of the *motor* neurons are in the ventral horns of the spinal cord or, in the case of muscles of the head, in the motor nuclei of the brain stem. From these places in the central nervous system, axons go out to the various muscles of the body. Just before reaching them, the axons divide into a number of axon fibrils. Each axon fibril ends upon a muscle fiber, and each muscle fiber usually gets only one axon fibril. Thus one motor neuron has complete control of a number of muscle fibers. A functional *motor unit*, therefore, is made up of one neuron and a number of muscle fibers. The several fibers of a motor unit may not be all together—they may be separated by muscle fibers or another motor unit—but they are nevertheless a unit because they are all served by one neuron.

The size of a motor unit varies from place to place in the body. How big it is is indicated by the *innervation ratio*. This is the ratio of muscle fibers to nerve axons. In some parts of the body the ratio is as high as 150:1; in others it may be as low as 3:1. These ratios are significant, for an impulse in an axon fiber with a high ratio causes a relatively large contraction compared with that in an axon fiber with a small number of muscle fibers. Thus, in the large muscles of the body that are used in walking and in large, crude movements, the ratio is quite high. In the small muscles, like those of the eye or the fingers, which make very fine adjustments, the innervation ratio is rather small. The innervation ratio, therefore, is related to the precision and fineness of movements.

MUSCLE INNERVATION—The kind of innervation just described is only one of two kinds of motor innervation of muscle. It is called *alpha* innervation. Fibers supplying this innervation are relatively large, ranging from 9 to 13 microns in diameter. They constitute about 70 percent of the motor fibers innervating muscle. Impulses in these fibers cause contractions of muscle fibers throughout their length and hence are responsible for the contractions that make up the various patterns of motor behavior.

Also, innervating muscles are other groups of fibers called *gamma efferents*. These are somewhat smaller, ranging in size from about 3 to 6 microns. They constitute about 30 percent of motor fibers. These efferents, only recently discovered, have a special function. They go to one of the two types of receptor structures found in muscle, namely, to the muscle spindles (see page 257). There, when delivering impulses, they cause minute contractions of fibers within the receptor, thereby affecting the sensitivity of the receptor. Their function, which will be described in more detail below, is therefore not to cause large contractions but merely to affect sensory information returning from the muscle. In this way, they provide a feedback loop regulating the input of kinesthetic information.

Besides motor innervation, muscles have sensory innervation (page 258). In addition to pain receptors in the regions of blood vessels and the giant Pacinian corpuscles found in tissues near muscles, the principal sense organs connected with muscle are (1) the Golgi tendon organs and (2) the muscle spindles. These have already been described, but additional points will be made here about their function.

The Golgi tendon organs are embedded in tendons near their connection with muscle. Whenever tension is put on the tendon, they are stimulated; hence they are *tension* recorders. Because they are in "series" with the muscle-tendon system, they cannot distinguish between active *contraction* and the *stretch* of a muscle that occurs when an antagonistic muscle contracts (see Figure 10.1). In either case, the muscle-tendon system is put under tension, and the Golgi tendon organ records the resulting tension.

The muscle spindle, on the other hand, is arranged in "parallel" with the muscle (see Figures 10.1 and 10.2). It envelops a few muscle fibers, called *intrafusal*, detached from the larger group of *extrafusal* fibers. Because of this arrangement, a contraction of the regular extrafusal fibers reduces tension on the intrafusal fibers, thus decreasing pressure on the receptors of the spindle. Conversely, when the muscle relaxes or, more typically, when it is stretched by the action of an antagonistic muscle, the intrafusal fibers are stretched, thereby exerting pressure on the receptors of the muscle spindle. The consequence is that the muscle spindle is a *stretch receptor*, responding to stretch but, ordinarily, not to contraction of the muscle.

The last statement was qualified with the word "ordinarily" because there is one case in which the stretch receptors may be active during contraction. This is when the *gamma efferents*, which end on intrafusal fibers just be-

MUSCLE STRETCHED   MUSCLE CONTRACTED

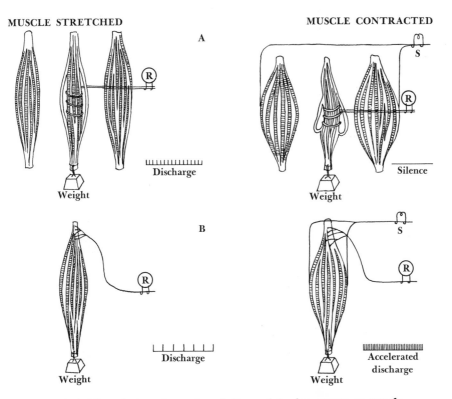

FIGURE 10.1—The relation of muscle spindles and tendon organs to muscle fibers. A, muscle spindles; B, Golgi tendon organs. (Adapted from T. C. Ruch and J. F. Fulton. *Medical physiology and biophysics.* 18th ed. Philadelphia: Saunders, 1960. P. 178.)

yond the poles of the muscle spindle (see Figure 10.2), deliver impulses to the intrafusal fibers, causing them to contract at the same time as extrafusal fibers also contract enough to take up the slack that would otherwise occur by the extrafusal contraction. In this case, the muscle spindles may be stimulated and their afferents may fire even though the muscle is contracted rather than stretched. This exception can be important in cases of prolonged tension in muscles.

Within the muscle spindle, as previously noted (page 257), are two kinds of receptors: the *primary, annulospiral* ending, which wraps around the intrafusal fibers near the center of the spindle, and the *secondary flower-spray* endings that ramify inside the spindle near its ends. These two kinds of receptors have quite different functions in reflex behavior (see below).

MUSCLE GROUPS—The striated muscles of the body form a system of balances in which the contraction of one muscle may cause another muscle to stretch,

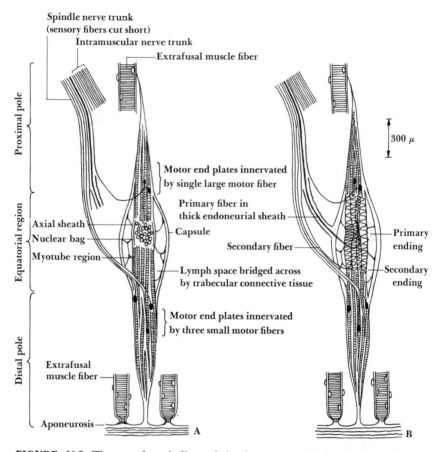

FIGURE 10.2—The muscle spindle and its innervation. (Adapted from D. Barker. *Quart. J. micr. Sci.*, 1948, 89, 143–186.)

and vice versa. Muscles having this relationship are called *antagonistic* muscles (see Figure 10.3). The most clear-cut cases of such antagonism are found in the limbs where one set of muscles, called *flexors,* make the limb bend, while another set, called *extensors,* make it extend or straighten. Extensor muscles normally are used to support the body, whereas the flexors are used in defensive reactions to noxious stimuli. The two working alternately or in complex patterns provide for locomotion and the manipulation of objects.

Usually more than one muscle is involved in any particular activity, say flexion or extension. Those that work together in that activity are called *synergistic* muscles. For example, all concerned in the extension of the hind limb are synergistic. In discussing reflex pathways *within* a synergistic group, a distinction is sometimes made between homonymous and heteronymous reflex arcs. A *homonymous* reflex arc is one that begins with stimulation in a muscle and ends with contraction of the *same* muscle. A *heteronymous* arc is one in which sensory impulses begin in one muscle and cause another muscle, but one in the same synergistic group, to contract. These distinctions will prove useful in the next section.

SYNAPTIC RELATIONS

By means of many intricate and often ingenious experiments, physiologists have established the particular receptors involved in various reflexes, the synapses traversed in them, and various other effects in reflex action. In this section, we shall summarize what has been learned in this work without going into the experimental details.

MOTONEURONS—A spinal motor neuron, commonly called a *motoneuron*, has its cell body in the ventral horn of the spinal cord (page 38). Its cell body and dendrites are served by many other neurons, some located at the same level of the spinal cord, others at other levels, and still others at points as far away as the cerebral cortex. The fact that a motoneuron has many inputs is evident in its microscopic anatomy, for about 40 percent of the somadendritic surface of the motoneuron is covered by the end knobs of axons terminating on it. These axons, as we shall see, have different sources of origin and different effects on the motoneuron.

FIGURE 10.3—The reciprocal relations of monosynaptic and multisynaptic reflex arcs. (Adapted from T. C. Ruch and J. F. Fulton. *Medical physiology and biophysics.* 18th ed. Philadelphia: Saunders, 1960. P. 153.)

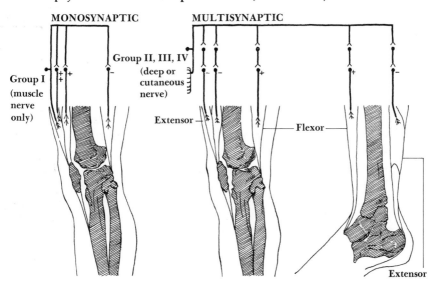

If a motoneuron serves an extensor muscle, it is an extensor motoneuron, and, of course, if it serves a flexor muscle, it is a flexor neuron. There are some differences in the connections of the two kinds of neurons, for extensor muscles are generally concerned in maintaining posture and upright support whereas flexor muscles act in locomotion, manipulation, and briefly executed reflexes. For our purposes, it is best to take the extensor neuron as a model, and, unless it is stated otherwise, the discussion that follows will refer to *extensor motoneurons*.

Three effects of axon activity on the motoneuron may be distinguished: *discharge, facilitation,* and *inhibition* (see Figure 10.4). Some axons can discharge the motor neuron. These axons have a relatively large number of terminations on the motoneuron, enough to build up a postsynaptic response above the threshold of discharge of the motoneuron. Among the axons capable of discharging motoneurons without any help from other axons are those of sensory neurons originating in annulospiral endings of the muscle spindle of the *homonymous* muscle of the same side. These sensory neurons, in other words, come from the same muscle served by the motoneuron.

There are other axons ending on an extensor motoneuron that are not individually capable of discharging the motoneuron. They are only able to *facilitate* its discharge when several axons deliver impulses to it at about the same time. This effect is one of spatial summation; the postsynaptic effects of several discharging axons summate to a level sufficient to fire the motoneuron. The axons that behave in this way come from *heteronymous* synergistic muscles. Like those capable of discharging motoneurons, they arise in the primary annulospiral endings of the muscle spindle.

With appropriate techniques, it may also be shown that impulses in some axons that end on the motoneuron have inhibitory effects. Either they prevent the motoneuron from discharging in response to the axons described above, or they raise the threshold for such discharge. They do this by hyperpolarizing the motoneuron and hence by creating IPSPs in the postsynaptic membrane of the motoneuron (page 74).

The inhibition of extensor motoneurons has several sources (see Figure 10.4). One is contralateral activity in the corresponding muscle. In other words, when a muscle stretches on one side so that the primary annulospiral endings are excited, the afferent stimulation excites extensor motoneurons on the same side and inhibits them on the opposite side. Another source is afferent activity in the same receptor of an antagonistic muscle. Other cases are shown in Figure 10.4. The general principle is that inhibition and facilitation mesh together so that antagonistic muscles do not work against each other, nor do the two sides of the body work against each other. In one case, a flexor should relax while an extensor contracts, and vice versa; in the other, the limb of one side should extend (in order to provide support) while the limb on the other side is flexed.

Let us now turn our attention briefly to the kinds of synaptic connections involved in excitation and inhibition of reflex pathways.

Monosynaptic arcs

Reflex	Receptor	Fiber type
Stretch reflex-tone and posture	Annulospiral (spindle)	IA homonymous
	Annulospiral (spindle)	IA heteronymous synergistic
	Annulospiral (spindle)	IA heteronymous antagonistic

Multisynaptic arcs

Reflex	Receptor	Fiber type
Flexion-stepping	Flower-spray (spindle)	II (muscle nerve)
	Touch-pressure	II (skin nerve)
Flexion-nociofensor	Free nerve endings	III, IV
Clasp-knife or inverse myotatic-overload protection	Golgi tendon organ	IB homonymous
	Golgi tendon organ	IB heteronymous synergistic
	Golgi tendon organ	IB heteronymous antagonistic

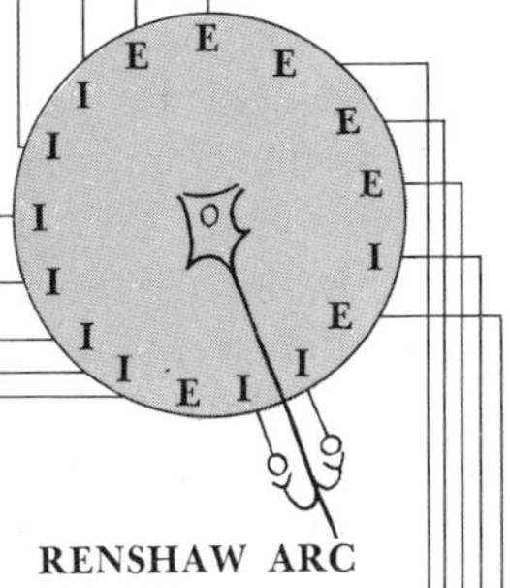

CONTRALATERAL INPUTS

RENSHAW ARC

Reflex	Receptor	Fiber type
Crossed extension-stepping	Flower-spray (spindle)	II (muscle nerve)
	Touch-pressure	II (skin nerve)
Crossed extension	Free nerve endings	III, IV
Phillipson's reflex	Annulospiral (spindle)	IA
	Golgi tendon organ	IB

FIGURE 10.4—Diagram of excitatory and inhibitory inputs to an extensor motoneuron. (Adapted from T. C. Ruch and J. F. Fulton. *Medical physiology and biophysics.* 18th ed. Philadelphia: Saunders, 1960. P. 188.)

MONOSYNAPTIC ARCS—The simplest conceivable synaptic relationship between two or more neurons is a *monosynaptic arc*. In this, a sensory fiber whose cell body lies in the dorsal ganglion (page 38) sends its axon through the spinal cord to the motoneuron. Such a monosynaptic arc exists. Its afferent component consists of fibers from the primary muscle-spindle receptors of the homonymous muscle of the same side. This is the same afferent source that causes discharge in the motoneuron. It is also the mechanism of the stretch or *myotatic reflex,* which has already been mentioned and will be described further below.

DISYNAPTIC ARCS—Physiologists usually distinguish only two classes of arcs: monosynaptic and disynaptic (see Figures 10.3 and 10.4). However, among the multisynaptic arcs, one can identify arcs possessing only two synapses, the disynaptic arcs and those having more than two synapses. A disynaptic arc is one in which there is one intervening neuron, between the sensory neuron and the motoneuron (see Figure 10.4). Such an arc differs from a mono-synaptic arc in three respects: First, it originates in a different receptor, namely, the Golgi tendon organ. The monosynaptic arc, by contrast, arises in the primary, annulospiral ending of the muscle spindle. Secondly, its reflex consequences are exactly the opposite of those at the monosynaptic arc. Where the monosynaptic arc is excitatory, the disynaptic arc is inhibitory, and vice versa. Thirdly, its threshold is higher than that for the monosynaptic arc. The higher threshold appears to be due to the extra neuron in the arc rather than to the receptors involved.

These three differences account for what happens when a muscle is stretched. If it is stretched slightly, only the monosynaptic arc comes into play. This causes contraction of the same muscle and hence resistance to stretching. However, if the stretch is applied with more force, the disynaptic arc is activated. This being inhibitory for the same muscle, it overcomes the monosynaptic stretch reflex and collapses the resistance of the muscle to stretch.

MULTISYNAPTIC ARCS—Besides the monosynaptic and disynaptic arcs, there are multisynaptic arcs that have their origin in the secondary, flower-spray endings of the muscle spindle, in touch and pressure receptors, and in pain receptors (see Figure 10.4). In general, their effects are like those of di-synaptic arcs and are opposite to those of monosynaptic arcs. A pin prick on the hand, for example, activates a multisynaptic arc for a flexion reflex. In this reflex, the limb is quickly bent while at the same time the stretch reflex is inhibited.

RECIPROCAL INNERVATION—This last statement, like similar statements made previously, is a specific instance of a more general principle known as *reciprocal innervation.* The formal statement of the principle is: "When the motoneurons supplying a given muscle are reflexly excited by an afferent volley, the motoneurons supplying antagonistic muscles are inhibited by that afferent volley" (Patton, 1960, p. 152). In other words, the same sensory input causes excitation in one set of muscles and inhibition in their antag-onists. This is a general principle of nervous function. It applies to remote influences on behavior exercised by higher centers of the brain as well as to spinal reflex arcs. Seldom is there in nervous function an isolated inhibition of response. On the contrary, it is typical to see the inhibition of some activities, at the same time that other, antagonistic responses occur. This is *reciprocal inhibition.*

SPINAL MECHANISMS

We have already discussed the segmental structure of the spinal cord (page 28). This makes a good basis for distinguishing two varieties of reflex mechanisms in the spinal cord. Some mechanisms are segmental and others are intersegmental.

SEGMENTAL ARCS—We have been referring to the neuron pathways that make up the reflex mechanisms as *arcs.* Except for monosynaptic arcs, these arcs are made up of three parts: *sensory neurons, interneurons,* and *motoneurons.* The cell bodies of the interneurons lie in the central gray matter of the spinal cord. When all three parts of the arc connect at one segmental level of the spinal cord, the arc is a segmental arc. Later on, we shall see examples of reflexes that depend on such segmental arcs. Some such arcs are uncrossed; i.e., all three parts are on one side of the spinal cord. There are, however, crossed arcs in which the interneuron crosses from one side of the spinal cord to the other and the motoneuron is on the opposite side of the cord from the sensory neuron.

INTERSEGMENTAL ARCS—Intersegmental arcs are formed when either the axons of incoming sensory neurons or the fibers of interneurons travel up or down the segments of the spinal cord before making connection with a motoneuron. There is, in fact, a special tract called the *fasciculi proprii* which lies near the gray columns of the spinal cord and connects various segments. This tract is made up of interneurons. These intersegmental connections may be unilateral; i.e., they may remain on the same side, or they may cross over the midline of the spinal cord to make a crossed intersegmental arc.

We shall come later to the description of various reflexes, but it may help to make clear here the anatomical basis of an intersegmental arc if we take a specific example, the *scratch reflex* of the dog. This is a reflex that we have all observed, and it is one that has been studied carefully by anatomical methods. The arc for this reflex is as follows: (1) If, for example, the stimulus is a tickling of the shoulder, a sensory neuron goes in from the skin of the shoulder to the corresponding segment of the spinal cord and ends in the gray matter of the segment. (2) Then a long interneuron descends from that segment to the spinal segments for the hind limb. (3) This interneuron connects finally with a motoneuron that goes out to the flexor muscle of the leg. There are other intersegmental reflexes, and we shall describe them later in this chapter.

FINAL COMMON PATH—Many reflexes can be observed in the spinal animal in the absence of connections with the brain. Some of these reflexes are essentially the same as those seen in the intact animal. In the latter case, however, motor tracts descending from the brain have an important influence on reflexes. We shall describe these pathways below.

In the meantime, it should be realized that the motoneurons are parts, not only of segmental and intersegmental arcs, but also of much more complicated arcs that include ascending and descending pathways to and from the brain. Consequently, motoneurons do not belong exclusively to any one arc but serve as the final channel for many arcs. The motoneurons are "funnels" upon which many different impulses converge. For this reason, they have been referred to as the "final common path." What happens in motoneurons determines behavior, but activity in motoneurons is in turn determined by various excitatory and inhibitory influences playing on them from all levels of the nervous system.

BRAIN MECHANISMS

Within the brain, as distinguished from the spinal cord, are three systems concerned in reflexes, posture, and movement: (1) the pyramidal system, (2) the extrapyramidal system, and (3) a system centering about the cerebellum but involving connections with several other structures. The three systems will be discussed in this section. In addition, the electrical stimulability and motor areas of the cerebral cortex will be considered.

PYRAMIDAL SYSTEM—The pyramidal system consists of motor neurons originating in the cerebral cortex and running downward to the brain stem and spinal cord. They are uninterrupted by synapses. Axons of cell bodies located in the cortex travel downward to end on the motoneurons of the brain and spinal cord that connect directly with peripheral muscles.

The pyramidal system gets its name from the fact that the pyramidal tracts cross in the medulla, forming a structure that is pyramidal in shape. Some of the cells of origin in the cortex happen to be pyramidal in shape, but that is a coincidence; many of them are not. Indeed, there is no consistent characteristic of either the place or the cells of origin of the tract that would distinguish it from other motor systems. It is defined solely by the fact that its fibers cross in the medullary pyramids. The fact that it is almost entirely a crossed system means that activity originating in one side of the cortex is accompanied by movements on the opposite side of the body.

The area of the cortex making the single, largest contribution to the pyramidal system is the so-called *motor area* of the cortex. In primates, this lies immediately in front of the central sulcus and is also called the *precentral gyrus* or, in the Brodmann system, area 4. For a long time, this was thought to be *the* origin of the pyramidal tract. Various kinds of studies, however, now make it clear that this is only one area of origin. Pyramidal fibers also originate in the premotor area in front and in the postcentral somatosensory area to the rear. Even these, taken together, account for only about 60 percent of the pyramidal tract (see Figure 10.5). Fibers also originate in other areas of the cerebral cortex, particularly in the prefrontal and parietal lobes.

EXTRAPYRAMIDAL SYSTEM—By contrast with the simplicity of the pyramidal system, the extrapyramidal system is quite complex. The latter system, by definition, consists of all those descending pathways that originate in the cortex but are not contained in the pyramidal system. The system is characterized by relays in many structures of the brain. For our purposes here, we need note only that two of the more important subcortical structures of this system are the basal ganglia, which include the corpus striatum (see page 52), and the reticular formation. Each of these receives downward projections from the cortex and, in turn, sends projections back to the cortex. Each of them also gives rise to descending pathways running downward in the brain stem and spinal cord to terminate on motoneurons.

The origin of the extrapyramidal system in the cerebral cortex is diffuse. Contributions are made to it by each of the four lobes of the brain. However, fibers to the reticular formation that make up the corticoreticular tract originate mainly in the sensorimotor region of the cortex. Taken together, the cortical areas of origin for the extrapyramidal tract overlap those of the pyramidal system. The pyramidal tract, however, has its densest projection

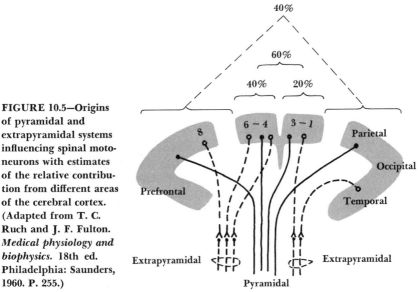

FIGURE 10.5—Origins of pyramidal and extrapyramidal systems influencing spinal motoneurons with estimates of the relative contribution from different areas of the cerebral cortex. (Adapted from T. C. Ruch and J. F. Fulton. *Medical physiology and biophysics.* 18th ed. Philadelphia: Saunders, 1960. P. 255.)

around the central sulcus, whereas the areas contributing most to the extrapyramidal system lie somewhat forward of the motor area.

ELECTRICAL STIMULABILITY—The electrical stimulability of the cerebral cortex was established in 1870 by Fritsch and Hitzig. In general, the best patterns of movement with the lowest thresholds are found on stimulation of the precentral cortex. However, some sort of movement can be obtained by stimulating many parts of the cortex, particularly the parietal and frontal lobes. By sectioning the pyramidal tract at the medullary pyramids and comparing the movements obtained through cortical stimulation with those observed in the intact animal, it has been possible to distinguish the effects of pyramidal and extrapyramidal stimulation. After section of the pyramids, stimulation of the precentral gyrus still produces some movement. However, the movements obtained are reduced in variety, accuracy, and skill. Thus it can be said that much of skilled or volitional movement is controlled by the pyramidal system. On the other hand, with only extrapyramidal pathways intact, some movements such as clutching and climbing can be observed on cortical stimulation. Therefore both pyramidal and extrapyramidal pathways appear to participate in the movements of normal animals.

Stimulation of the extrapyramidal pathways, on the other hand, often produces an inhibition of movement. Indeed, it is clear that this system can both facilitate and inhibit movement. Some of its function is undoubtedly to restrain movement and to inhibit such structures as the reticular formation that, because of other inputs, would otherwise deliver an excess of stimulation to lower motor points (see below). Figure 10.6 gives a diagram of some of the inhibitory and facilitatory components of the extrapyramidal system.

SOMATOTOPIC ORGANIZATION—A most outstanding feature of the stimulable cortex is that it is laid out in a very orderly fashion to represent different parts of the body (see Figure 10.7). This arrangement is much like that of the somesthetic areas that lie just behind the pyramidal cortex in the postcentral

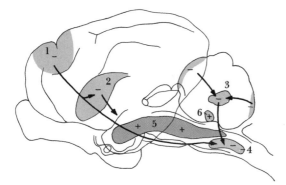

FIGURE   10.6—Facilitating (+) and inhibiting (−) portions of the extrapyramidal system. (Adapted from T. C. Ruch and J. F. Fulton. *Medical physiology and biophysics.* 18th ed. Philadelphia: Saunders, 1960. P. 208; see also D. B. Lindsley, L. H. Schreiner, and H. W. Magoun. An electromyographic study of spasticity. *J. Neurophysiol.*, 1949, 12, 197–205.)

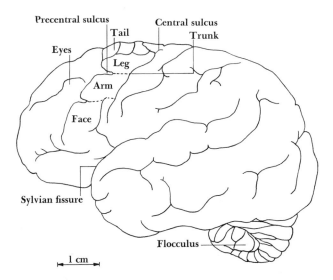

FIGURE 10.7—Side view of the right hemisphere of the spider monkey showing the tail, leg, arm, and face representation of the motor area. (Adapted from J. F. Fulton and J. G. Dusser de Barenne. The representation of the tail in the motor cortex of primates, with special reference to spider monkeys. *J. cell. comp. Physiol.*, 1933, 2, 408.)

gyrus. In animals that have a tail (Figure 10.7 has been taken from the spider monkey just to illustrate this point) the extreme dorsal portion of the stimulable motor cortex represents the tail. Electrical stimulation of this part will make the tail move. Then, if the electrical stimulus is moved to the more lateral parts of the pyramidal cortex, there is found, in order, a leg area, a small trunk area, an arm area, and finally, in the extreme lateral and ventral sector, a face area. Stimulation of these sectors causes movements of corresponding parts of the body. Even the muscles for speech are included in this arrangement, for a stimulus applied to a certain part of the face area will produce vocalizations of one sort or another.

It is interesting to see how much space on the motor cortex is assigned to movements in different parts of the body. In Figure 10.7 one can see that each part of the body does not get its fair share according to its size. Instead, space is assigned according to the skill and precision of movements controlled by the respective sectors. The *homunculus* of Figure 10.8 illustrates this fact very well. The trunk, whose movements are large and crude, has relatively little space. The legs have comparatively more, but the hands, which are used in refined skilled movements, have more than either the trunk or the legs. Then, in the head, the eyes, jaws, lips, tongue, and vocal cords have proportionately more space. This goes along with the fact that the eyes make extremely precise movements in fixating and pursuing visual objects and the lips, tongue, and vocal cords are involved in the very precise movements of speech.

SUPPLEMENTARY MOTOR AREAS—The homunculus just described refers to the precentral motor cortex and some of the cortex immediately in front of it. This has been called the primary motor area. In the anesthetized animal, this is the area that is most easily mapped. Under certain conditions, however, movements can be obtained from many parts of the cortex. Not all of these have a somatotopic organization. Two of them, however, do have such an organization. One is called *the supplementary motor area*, although some writers speak of *areas*. This lies along the longitudinal tissue and for the most part is embedded within it. This supplementary area has an organization but in a different orientation from the primary area (see Figure 10.8). There is another supplementary area that has a somatotopic organization and appears to be approximately coextensive with the second somatic area (SII, page 268). No one seems quite sure at present just how stimulation of the supplementary and the second somatic area causes movement.

FIGURE 10.8—Somatotopic organization of the primary (lower) and supplementary (upper) areas. (Adapted from T. C. Ruch and J. F. Fulton. *Medical physiology and biophysics.* 18th ed. Philadelphia: Saunders, 1960. P. 267; see also C. N. Woolsey. Patterns of localization in sensory and motor areas of the cerebral cortex. In Milbank Memorial Fund. Twenty-seventh Annual Conference. *The biology of mental health and disease.* New York: Hoeber, 1952.)

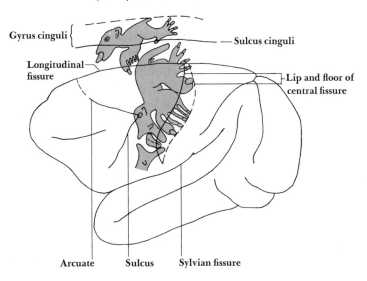

THE CEREBELLUM—Last to be mentioned as part of the motor mechanisms of the brain is the cerebellum. This is an extremely complex structure with many internal and external connections. Its general function is to regulate the other cortical and subcortical structures already described. It receives afferent inputs from all the senses and has reciprocal connections with the structures of both pyramidal and extrapyramidal systems.

The principal inputs to the cerebellum are from the somatic and vestibular senses. The cerebellum, in fact, is the terminus of information arriving from the vestibular receptors. These receptors located in the vestibular portion of the internal ear give rise to fibers of the vestibular portion of the VIIIth nerve. Such fibers join with auditory fibers in the nerve and then, just outside the medulla, separate into a *vestibular nuclei* of the medulla, but some continue on into the cerebellum. On the other hand, the vestibular nuclei themselves send fibers to the cerebellum so that, directly or indirectly, vestibular inputs terminate in the cerebellum.

The cerebellum also is the end station of a major ascending tract of the spinal cord, the *spinocerebellar tract*. This conveys information from the proprioceptors, particularly from the muscles. In addition, all the other senses, by one route or another, send fibers to the cerebellum. This fact has been established by the recording of potentials evoked by sensory stimulation. There is even a somatotopic organization of the cerebellar cortex, somewhat like that of the somatosensory cerebral cortex, but it is not as refined.

There are also inputs to the cerebellum from many areas of the cerebral cortex, but the cerebellum also sends back fibers to these areas. The relation, then, between cerebellum and cerebral cortex is reciprocal. One part of the cerebellum is reciprocally connected with somatosensory area I, another with SII, and another with the motor area of the cerebral cortex. In each case there is a fair degree of somatotopic organization. To be noted finally is the fact that the cerebellum sends fibers to most of the structures of the extrapyramidal system, including the reticular formation. It also sends fibers via the vestibulospinal tract to the spinal cord.

This is a very brief summary of a complex set of relationships, but it will serve for our purpose. We see from it that the cerebellum is not itself a motor system, but its role is to coordinate incoming sensory information and to interconnect with the motor systems of the brain. Thus it functions as a regulator or modifier of motor activities without itself directly controlling such activities.

SPINAL REFLEXES

Usually when we think of reflexes, we have in mind some specific movement. We think of the leg jerking when the knee is tapped or the eyelid winking when a light is flashed. Such brief, specific movements are indeed reflexes, but they constitute only one class of reflexes, the *phasic reflexes*. A second class, which is just as important but not so obvious, is the *postural reflexes*. These are always at work in the intact organism and consist of longer-lasting, sustained reactions. They keep the head up and the trunk erect as well as help support us in a standing position.

Another way of classifying reflexes hinges on the level of the nervous system involved. Those that take place over pathways of one spinal segment are *segmental reflexes;* those involving more than one spinal segment are *intersegmental reflexes*. These two kinds of reflexes taken together make up spinal reflexes. In addition, those reflexes that involve the participation of the brain are called *suprasegmental reflexes*.

SEGMENTAL REFLEXES

Now we may take up briefly some of the more important segmental reflexes. First of all, we should note that there are two varieties of such reflexes, the *flexion* and *extension* reflexes.

FLEXION REFLEXES—A flexion reflex is any response of a leg or arm in which part or all of the limb bends toward the body and away from the ground. In the main, a flexion reflex is a phasic response, although in certain special cases it may be a sustained postural response. The reflex is one of the most primitive of the phasic reactions because it occurs in response to any painful stimulus and is the means by which an animal avoids or escapes such a stimulus.

There are many variations in the pattern of the flexion reflex, and there are many factors that affect it. The flexion may take place at the ankle, the hip, or the knee, or it may involve all these points in varying degrees. How much flexion occurs depends in part on the kind of sensory stimulus that produces it and in part on its intensity. Painful stimuli bring forth the greatest flexion reflexes—those that involve the ankle, knee, and hip—as do also very intense stimuli. Pressure stimuli sometimes call forth flexion reflexes, but usually somewhat smaller ones, for pressure is also the stimulus for some antagonistic extension reflexes.

Also affecting the vigor and pattern of the flexion reflex are the impulses that come down from the brain to the segmental levels. When these are eliminated, by cutting the descending motor pathways, larger and more complete flexion reflexes are obtained than when part or all of the brain is allowed to send its impulses to the reflex center. Apparently the motor impulses from the brain tend to "inhibit" the flexion response, partly perhaps by direct inhibition and partly by helping extension reflexes that inhibit the flexion reflex through reciprocal inhibition (see above).

MYOTATIC REFLEXES—There are several types of extension reflexes. One is called the *stretch reflex* or, sometimes, the *myotatic reflex*, which has already been mentioned. This is an increased tension or contraction in extensor muscles. Such muscles support the animal's body against the pull of gravity and for this reason are sometimes called the antigravity muscles. It will be recalled that the muscles are stretched whenever their antagonists, the flexor muscles, contract, but the stretching stimulus calls forth the myotatic reflex, which makes the extensor muscles contract. Thus the myotatic reflex is really a circular reflex. Stretching the muscle sets up impulses that go into the spinal cord and out again to contract the muscle.

The myotatic, or stretch, reflex constitutes a fine balancing mechanism. As such, it can work as both a phasic and a postural mechanism. The phasic reflex occurs when an extensor muscle is suddenly stretched, and the result is a quick increase of tension in the muscle. The myotatic reflex is also a postural reflex, however, because it maintains a constant *tonus*, or a slight tension, in an extensor muscle even when the limb is not being flexed. Put another way, any tendency of the muscle to stretch sends some impulses back over the reflex pathway to keep it slightly contracted.

The myotatic reflex, whether phasic or postural, is usually limited to the muscle in which stretching (the stimulus) occurred. Sometimes, however, it may include other extensor muscles of the same limb that are related in function to the muscle stretched, i.e., synergistic muscles. This reflex, as we shall see below, is a basic reaction in many aspects of behavior.

EXTENSOR THRUST—There is another type of extension reflex, the *extensor thrust*, which is worth mentioning briefly. This is a reaction of a limb in which the limb straightens out to support the body against gravity or to thrust the body into the air. The stimulus that produces an extensor thrust is any pressure on the pads of the foot or, in animals like the dog or cat, a quick separation of the toe and foot pads. The extensor thrust is one of the reflexes that enable us to walk or run, for it comes into play to support the body whenever the foot touches the ground.

CROSSED EXTENSION REACTIONS—Closely related to the extensor thrust is another type of extension reflex, the *crossed extension reaction*, which also helps in walking and running. This reaction is an extension of the leg opposite to the leg that is stimulated to flex. It comes into play more slowly than does the extensor thrust, and it is slower both in reaching its peak and in relaxing. The timing of this reaction is quite important, for it counteracts the flexion reflex in the limb that is raised from the ground, and it prepares this limb for extension at the same time that the other limb is on the ground and supporting the body.

INTERSEGMENTAL REFLEXES

There are two general classes of intersegmental reflexes, the *somatic* and the *autonomic,* which correspond to two general divisions of the nervous system. We have already indicated the general pathway for autonomic reflexes in

Chapter 1, and we shall deal with such reflexes again in connection with emotion (Chapter 11). Here, therefore, we shall deal only with the somatic intersegmental reactions.

In general, use of the term intersegmental reflex does not imply any essentially new type of response. Instead, it refers to a composite or pattern of segmental reactions that occurs because several stimuli are present at the same time or in quick succession at different segmental levels of the spinal cord. Thus the term intersegmental reflex does not, in general, indicate responses fundamentally different from segmental reflexes, but it refers rather to a different level of neural organization.

COOPERATIVE REFLEXES—Intersegmental patterns sometimes involve the cooperation and sometimes the competition of the more elementary reflexes that comprise them. Thus we can think of two types of intersegmental patterns, the cooperative and competitive reflexes. In cooperative reflexes, two or more reflexes mutually aid each other or follow each other in a smooth pattern. In competitive reflexes, the pattern comes about because two or more incompatible reflexes are instigated by different stimuli acting at the same time.

A good example of a cooperative reflex is the *scratch reflex*. This is a repetitive rhythmic movement of a limb, and, analyzed into its parts, it is the alternation of two reflexes, a flexor and an extensor reflex. It has a rhythmic pattern because, by reciprocal inhibition, a flexor reflex first suppresses an extension response and then the resulting stretching of extensor muscles sets up an extension reflex in which the flexion is suppressed. Thus it goes on in alternation.

It is the peculiar quality of the stimulus that makes the two components cooperate in the scratch reflex. The stimulus for the reflex is "bright" pressure on two nearby points of the skin, either at the same time or one right after the other. Put another way, it is an "itching" or "tickling" stimulus that calls forth the scratch reflex. In an earlier chapter on the skin senses, we saw that this kind of stimulus arouses both the pain and pressure pathways. Pain impulses tend to call forth flexion responses, and pressure impulses call forth the extension reflexes. When these two stimuli are combined, the result is not a conflict of reflexes but rather a rhythmic cooperation of the two that serves a very good purpose, especially if there happen to be any fleas around.

COMPETITIVE REFLEXES—Competitive reflexes involve two or more sensory stimuli competing for a final common path. When there is such competition, one of several things may happen: (1) One stimulus may take over the final common path to evoke one of the two possible reflexes and to inhibit the other one; (2) exactly the reverse may happen; or (3) the final common path may be taken over first by one stimulus and then by the other so that the two stimuli take turns at calling forth their respective reflexes.

Which of these three possibilities occurs depends on certain factors affecting the priority of reflexes. One is a priority built into the nervous system. Flexion reflexes, apparently because they protect the organism from harm, tend to win out over scratch or extension reflexes. Another is stimulus intensity; other things being equal, the stronger stimulus calls out its reflex and suppresses the reaction to the weaker, competing stimulus. For example, a scratch reflex can win over a flexion reflex if the "itch" is relatively strong and the painful stimulus rather weak. Another factor is timing. If a reflex has been in operation for some time, it is likely to lose out to a competing reflex initiated at a later time. Again, to take the flexion and scratch reflexes as examples, a flexion reflex tends to win over the scratch reflex if the latter has been going on for some time.

SUCCESSIVE INDUCTION—There is one particular phenomenon of competition that deserves attention because it shows how we manage to walk and move around. The phenomenon is *successive induction*. It is the outcome of competition among reflexes, in which antagonistic reflexes follow each other in a definite pattern. If, for example, a pressure stimulus is applied to the bottom of the foot, it tends to call forth the antagonistic reactions of flexion and extension. Suppose, however, that for some reason the flexion reflex temporarily dominates and the leg lifts. Then an extension reaction tends to follow. One reason for this sequence is the factor mentioned above: Once the flexion reflex has had its turn, it tends to give way to the antagonistic extension reflex. Another factor, of course, is that the flexion stretches the extensor muscle and initiates a myotatic-reflex reaction of the extensors. The net result is the successive induction of two reflexes in a pattern of flexion and extension.

THE REFLEX FIGURE—The principle of successive induction also works to produce more complex patterns of reflexes. One such pattern is the reflex figure, which is basic to walking and running. The pattern involves interaction of reflexes in all four limbs (Figure 10.9). A flexion reflex in one hind limb causes a crossed extension reaction in the opposite hind limb. The flexion reflex of a hind limb is also accompanied by an extension of the forelimb on the same side. The result is a precise alternation of steps in the limbs used—by animals and human beings alike—in walking.

SUPRASEGMENTAL REFLEXES

Now we shall move on to study the reflexes that depend upon the centers and pathways of the brain: the suprasegmental reflexes. None of the reflexes of this type can be carried on by the brain alone, for they all require the pathways of the spinal cord and the muscles of the limbs and trunk for their expression. The suprasegmental reflexes, in fact, are made up of segmental and

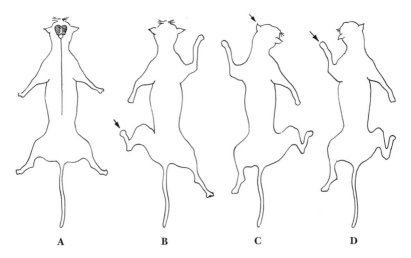

FIGURE 10.9—The reflex figure. A, resting position; B, C, and D, positions taken following stimulation of part of body indicated by arrow. (Adapted from C. S. Sherrington. In C. H. Best and N. B. Taylor, *The physiological basis of medical practice.* Baltimore: Williams & Wilkins, 1939. P. 1317. By permission of the publishers.)

intersegmental reactions, but they are more complex patterns that are put together in the brain and controlled by the brain.

We have previously distinguished between the quick phasic reflexes and the sustained postural reflexes. This is also a good general distinction between the suprasegmental and the spinal reflexes. Not all the spinal reflexes are phasic, but in general they are more phasic than those controlled at the higher levels. Even the extension reactions that are basic components of postural reactions tend to be phasic when controlled only at the spinal level. It is when the extensor reactions are controlled and organized into patterns by the action of the higher centers that they make up true postural mechanisms. As a general principle, then, the suprasegmental centers organize reflexes into postural patterns.

DECEREBRATE RIGIDITY

This principle has a striking illustration in a phenomenon that has come to be called decerebrate rigidity. Such rigidity is pictured in Figure 10.10. It is a complex postural pattern, but its main feature is the contraction of all the extensor, or antigravity, muscles of the arms and legs as well as other muscles of the body that normally contract with them. Indeed, it is basically an exaggeration of the extensor stretch reflexes. Sometimes, therefore, decerebrate rigidity is also called extensor rigidity.

LEVEL OF DECEREBRATION—In principle, a decerebrate preparation is one in which the cerebral hemispheres have been cut away from the rest of the nervous system. In practice, transections are often done at lower levels. The resulting preparation is named according to the level of the transection. The one with the thalamus intact but not the cerebral hemispheres is a *high decerebrate*; one with the midbrain as the highest structure left intact is called a *midbrain decerebrate*; and so on.

The general rule concerning decerebrate rigidity is that, down to a bulbar preparation, the lower the transection, the greater is the resulting decerebrate rigidity. Since the pyramidal system makes no synapses between the cerebral cortex and motoneurons, cutting of this system at any level should have the same effect. Since, on the contrary, the effect depends on the level of decerebration, this system is eliminated as a major factor in decerebrate rigidity. Another fact supporting this conclusion is that, if midbrain decerebration is carried out on only *one side*, extensor rigidity develops on the *same* side. Since the pyramidal system crosses below the level of the midbrain, its interruption could not cause the defect.

VESTIBULOSPINAL SYSTEM—Aside from the pyramidal system, there are two other candidates for involvement in decerebrate rigidity. One is the extrapyramidal system; the other is the vestibulospinal system. Without going into the details of experiments proving the point, let us simply assert that both of

FIGURE 10.10—Extensor rigidity in the decerebrate cat. A, intact labyrinths; B, labrinthectomized. (Adapted from L. J. Pollack and L. E. Davis. In C. H. Best and N. B. Taylor, *The physiological basis of medical practice.* Baltimore: Williams & Wilkins, 1939. P. 338. By permission of the publishers.)

A   B

these systems are known to be involved. The vestibulospinal system normally exerts a facilitatory effect on stretch reflexes. This system is always intact with all levels of decerebration that result in decerebrate rigidity. And it is facilitation from this source that causes such rigidity in the decerebrate preparation.

A simple deduction can be made from these facts. It is that decerebrate rigidity must be the consequence of the release from inhibition of systems functioning in the intact animal. Otherwise, why would extensor rigidity develop from decerebration while the vestibulospinal system is intact? The answer to this question involves the extrapyramidal system and the relation of both facilitatory and inhibitory structures within that system.

RETICULAR SYSTEM—At this point the reader should refer to Figure 10.6 (page 284) which shows various facilitatory and inhibitory systems concerned in decerebrate rigidity. It will be seen there that much of the reticular system is facilitatory, a fact established by observing the effects of electrical stimulation of the reticular formation. Some of it is also inhibitory. In addition, both regions of the reticular formation are under the control of inhibitory influences from the cerebral cortex and the caudate nucleus. In decerebration, the reticular formation is released from the inhibitory influences of the higher structures of the extrapyramidal system. At the same time, the excitatory part of the reticular system continues to receive afferents from the senses of the body, including the muscles. Thus a facilitation of extensor reflexes that is normally restrained by higher extrapyramidal structures is released from such restaint by decerebration. The conclusion, then, is that extensor rigidity is due to facilitation both by the reticular descending system and the vestibulospinal system. This occurs because of the removal of inhibitory influences from above.

ALPHA AND GAMMA EFFERENTS—The experimental analysis of decerebrate rigidity has been carried to the point of stating how the vestibulospinal and reticular systems, respectively, cause extensor tonus. The action of the vestibulospinal system is primarily through the *alpha* motoneurons, which constitute the regular innervation of extrafusal fibers. The reticular influence is exerted primarily through *gamma* motoneurons to intrafusal fibers of the muscle spindles of extensor muscles. It will be recalled that these efferents cause small contractions in the spindle which are sensed by the primary spindle receptors. Through this loop, stretch reflexes are exaggerated.

PLASTICITY OF BEHAVIOR

Closely related to extensor rigidity are some other reactions seen in the decerebrate preparations, the *lengthening* and *shortening* reactions. Taken together, these reactions make up the so-called *plastic* reactions because they allow the positions of limbs to be molded much as one might mold some plastic or clay.

The lengthening and shortening reactions are illustrated in Figure 10.11. The base line of the figure represents a limb that is partly flexed to make an angle of about 60° at the knee. The lines moving away from the base line indicate greater and greater flexion up to an angle of about 110°. The shortening reaction can be seen when the limb is being flexed and the lengthening reaction when it is extended. In either case, the terms "shortening" and "lengthening" refer to what is happening in the extensor muscles of the limb.

SHORTENING REACTION—A shortening reaction is a tendency for an extensor muscle to shorten either actively or passively. There are two ways to demonstrate the tendency in decerebrate animals. (1) When one passively *flexes* a limb, he encounters some resistance. The leg does not "want" to flex. This is due to a reflex contraction of the extensor muscles that counteracts flexion. (2) If, on the other hand, an experimenter passively *extends* a limb, there is no special resistance, and the leg easily assumes the new position to which it has been extended. In this case, the extensor muscles shorten with the passive extension. A series of shortening reactions is pictured in Figure 10.11. Such shortening reactions are manifestations of *stretch reflexes*. They come about because passive flexion of the leg slightly stretches the extensor muscles, and this stretching sends back impulses from the primary spindle receptors that reflexly cause the extensor muscles to shorten.

LENGTHENING REACTION—Superficially, the lengthening reaction appears to be just the reverse of the shortening reaction, but it involves a different mechanism. If, in the same situation as above, an attempt is made to flex a leg forcibly, first resistance is encountered because the shortening reaction is keeping the extensor muscles partly contracted. But, if the flexion is con-

FIGURE 10.11—Shortening and lengthening reactions. Numbers refer to angle of leg. (Adapted from C. S. Sherrington. On plastic tonus and proprioceptive reflexes. *Quart. J. exp. Physiol.*, 1909, 2, 118. By permission of the publishers.)

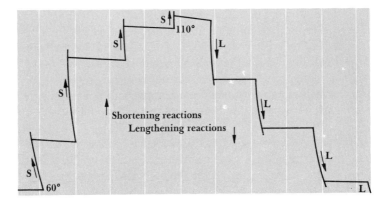

tinued rapidly, the resistance suddenly "melts" away and the leg can very easily be set in a new fixed position. The "melting away" of resistance in the face of forced flexion is called the lengthening reaction. It is also called the clasp-knife reaction, for it is like the resistance encountered in closing a jackknife.

The lengthening reaction is also referred to as *autogenic inhibition,* meaning self-induced inhibition. This inhibition is obviously due to some sensory mechanisms having a *higher threshold* than the myotatic shortening reaction and having exactly the opposite effect on the extensor muscle. It is now fairly certain, as we indicated earlier in the chapter, that this sensory mechanism consists of the Golgi tendon organs (see Figure 10.1). These organs have a higher threshold of activation; they provide an inhibition that overrides the excitation set up by spindle stimulation.

POSTURAL REFLEXES

The extensor reactions just described constitute one general aspect of posture. Also involved in the maintenance of posture are a number of reflexes known as the *postural reflexes.* Some of these reflexes are little more than changes in tonus in certain parts of the body, but others are rather complex movements. Indeed, one can grade postural reflexes on a scale ranging from the most general tonic reactions, such as extensor rigidity, to more specific and complex adjustments. In general, the higher the status on such a scale, the more are higher brain centers involved. Extensor tonus, the more basic and general postural mechanism, is organized, as we have just seen, at the level of the medulla and reticular formation. Some of the more specific postural reflexes, however, are tied together at the higher levels of the brain. Let us now examine some of these reflexes.

SUPPORTING REACTIONS—First are some postural reactions for maintaining support of the body in an upright position. They can be seen best in a dog or cat from which the cerebellum has been removed. One of these reactions is the *positive supporting reaction.* It is the contraction of both the flexor and extensor limb muscles at the same time so that the limb becomes a stiff pillar able to give the maximum of support to the animal's body. This reaction can be obtained in a decerebellate or bulbar animal by applying a tactual or kinesthetic stimulus to the pads or toes of the foot. Just the opposite sort of reaction, called the *negative supporting reaction,* is the relaxation of all the muscles of the limb. Without these negative and positive supporting reactions working in alternation, neither man nor animals could walk.

SHIFTING REACTIONS—Quite akin to the supporting reactions is the so-called shifting reaction. If an experimenter passively flexes the left hind limb of a dog and at the same time causes the animal's body to veer toward the left, a strong extensor tonus develops in the flexed limb. This is the shifting reaction. Its "purpose" is to support the body under the new conditions of shifted weight. This sort of response can be seen almost any day in an animal if one pushes the animal's body from one side to the other or forward or backward. The response is due to kinesthetic impulses from the limb muscles *stretched* or extended when the body veers. The reaction is primarily organized in the medulla, for it can be seen in bulbar animals. The reaction, however, is somewhat more dependable and precise in the midbrain preparation.

TONIC OR ATTITUDINAL REFLEXES—There is another group of reflexes that involve the muscles of the body more or less as a whole. They have been called tonic because they involve an increase in muscle tonus, but they are also called attitudinal reflexes because they are seen in an animal when it is putting itself in readiness to make some complex response, as when a cat is about to pounce on a mouse.

Many different patterns of attitudinal responses have been distinguished. They include various positions of the head and the body. The sources of stimulation for these reflexes have also been identified by experiments in which different sensory pathways have been eliminated. There are two general sources of stimulation. One is *kinesthetic* influences from the neck that cause the posture of the body to adjust to the position of the head. The other is *vestibular* stimulation which also results in postural adjustments to the head position. These two sensory sources normally work together in postural adjustments.

RIGHTING REACTIONS—There is a family of reflexes called the righting reactions that help an animal or human being to regain its balance when, for some reason, it has been thrown off balance. Different sensory stimuli can set off these reactions, and different parts of the body are involved. Three sources of stimulation may elicit the reactions: vestibular, kinesthetic, and optic. It is possible to identify righting reactions based on any of these three kinds of sensory input. The optic righting reflexes clearly depend on the striate cortex being intact. The other reflexes depend on subcortical structures located primarily at the brain-stem level.

THE GRASP REFLEX—Still another postural reflex is the grasp reflex. This is easily demonstrated in human babies and infant monkeys before the cerebral cortex is mature and in primate animals with certain parts of their cerebral cortex destroyed. It consists of an "involuntary grasping" of objects placed in the palm of the hand. Sometimes the reflex is so powerful it can support the entire weight of the body for a considerable length of time. It is present in most human infants at birth, but it grows less pronounced with age and tends to disappear after five or six months. Its appearance after this age is taken by neurologists to signal some disorder of the motor system. In monkeys, it is observed when the motor and premotor areas of the cortex are destroyed. Although technically a flexion reflex, it appears under the same circumstances as decerebrate rigidity when extensor tonus is generally increased. It therefore appears to be part of the postural mechanisms for supporting the body.

PLACING AND HOPPING REACTIONS—The last two types of postural reactions to be discussed are closely linked. They are the placing and hopping reactions. Both depend for their existence upon the integrity of certain areas of the cerebral cortex. Both are adjustments of the limbs in such a way as to bring about better support for the body.

Placing reactions may arise from either visual or somesthetic stimuli. In the visual reaction, an animal that is being held in the air with its legs hanging free will attempt to place its legs on any solid object nearby in the field of vision, so long as the eyes are not blindfolded and the visual cortex is intact. There are, on the other hand, several kinds of somesthetic placing reactions. In one, when an animal is held with the edge of a table in contact with the back of its feet, the legs will be put on the table. In other reactions, the animal similarly places its legs on a table in response to various kinds of stimuli.

Hopping reactions are complex. They consist first of a flexion of the leg, then a lateral movement, and finally an extension, all in quick succession, much as a person behaves when he has been shoved off balance. The reaction is easy to obtain in an animal (e.g., a monkey) that has been made to stand on one leg and then, by a push, is made to veer forward, backward, or sideways. The animal then makes a series of hops that serve the purpose of placing the limb squarely beneath him again for support. Such hopping reactions have been studied in the rat, cat, and monkey.

Both hopping and placing reactions depend upon particular areas of the cortex. In the rat, the reactions are abolished when a rather large but definite dorsal area of the cortex is taken out on both sides. In the cat, the reactions are "localized" somewhat more precisely in areas analogous to the motor areas of higher animals. And in monkeys, the functions of hopping and placing are confined to the precentral and postcentral cortical areas.

MOTOR COORDINATION

A distinction, though not a very fine one, can be made between reflexive, involuntary movements on the one hand and coordinated, voluntary movements on the other. The preceding sections have dealt with the first kind of movement; in this section we shall consider the second kind. First to be dealt with are the mechanisms for executing coordinated movements. Finally, problems of recovery of function after injury to the nervous system will be discussed.

EXECUTION OF MOVEMENT

A number of structures in the brain are concerned in one way or another with motor coordination. As one might expect, some of these are the same ones also involved in reflexes and posture, but some play relatively unique roles in coordinated acts, such as controlling the timing or accuracy of movement. First, however, let us consider the question of how coordinated movements are executed. What structures are concerned, and in what way, in carrying out coordinated acts?

PHYLOGENETIC DEVELOPMENT—The answer to this question depends in part on what species of animal one is discussing. A corticalization of motor functions takes place in the upper levels of the phylogenetic series similar to the corticalization of other functions. More specifically, motor functions are transferred from subcortical to cortical levels in the evolution of mammals, say, from rat to man. This transfer of motor functions in general includes manipulative motor ability. It is important in understanding how movements are executed by the brain.

In rats, cats, and dogs, the motor areas of the cortex are not very highly developed. Neither is manipulative ability. When the so-called motor areas in these animals are removed—indeed, when a very large portion of the cerebral cortex is removed—there is no great lasting effect on motor function. The animals can stand, walk, and get about much as normal animals do. When, however, rather small but circumscribed areas of motor function in the cortex of monkeys, apes, and man are removed, there is a marked paralysis that lasts for a long time. In general, the paralysis is greater in man than in monkeys. Because of the important difference between the primates and lower animals, we should keep in mind that the rest of this discussion refers to the primates.

CORTICAL AREAS—In the primates, then, the cerebral cortex is needed for coordinated movements, other than basic postural reflexes, to be carried out. Of all the cortical areas, moreover, area 4, the so-called motor area or precentral gyrus, is the most important. Removal of this area causes relatively severe paralysis. If the lesion is confined to area 4, the consequence is a flaccid paralysis; i.e., the muscles involved are relaxed but cannot be moved. People or monkeys suffering injuries to this area carry their arms or legs limply and find it difficult or impossible to move them voluntarily.

The motor area, however, is not the only area involved in the execution of acts. Greater and more lasting paralyses occur when larger areas of the cortex are involved, including the premotor area (Brodmann 6) and the supplementary motor areas. When the premotor area is greatly involved, either by itself or in addition to the motor area, the paralysis tends to be spastic. Voluntary movements are hampered, but instead of the affected part of the body being limp, it is taut, and it may look somewhat like it does in extensor rigidity.

SUBAREAL ORGANIZATION—The motor areas, it will be recalled, are arranged somatotopically. There is an "arm area," a "leg area," a "trunk area," and a "face area." Removal of the arm area of the motor cortex causes some paralysis of the arm. Similarly, some paralysis of the leg follows removal of the leg area. It is interesting, however, that these areas are not entirely independent. Removal of the leg area in addition to the arm area causes a greater paralysis of any particular part of the body than removal of only the subarea representing that part. Thus there is a real collaboration and overlapping of executive functions, even though they are to a large degree segregated into areas (cf. Figure 10.7).

BILATERAL ORGANIZATION—A similar principle holds for the two sides of the brain. The pyramidal system is almost entirely crossed; e.g., taking out the arm area from the left cortex causes paralysis of the right arm. There is, however, some bilateral overlap, so that removal of the arm area on both sides causes a more profound paralysis of the right arm than removal of only the left-arm area of the cortex. Similarly, there is more rapid recovery from a lesion on one side if the corresponding area on the other side of the cortex is intact than if it has been removed. Thus, although the executive functions are largely segregated according to the side of the body represented, they are not entirely so.

MOTOR SYSTEMS—Because lesions of the precentral motor areas cause the greatest paralysis, compared with lesions of other areas, and because this is the point of origin of many fibers of the pyramidal tract, it was once thought that damage to the pyramidal system was the key factor in flaccid paralysis following cortical injury. It is now known, however, that pyramidal fibers originate in many areas of the cortex and also that extrapyramidal fibers also emerge from the motor cortex. In addition, the pyramidal tracts have been experimentally sectioned at the level of the pyramids, thus separating their contributions from those of the extrapyramidal system.

These various anatomical and behavioral studies permit the following conclusions about the relative contributions of the pyramidal and extrapyramidal motor systems. Some, but not all, of the paralysis caused by cortical lesions is due to the interruption of the pyramidal pathways. Pyramidal section alone does not cause as great a loss as corresponding cortical lesions. The paralysis assignable to the pyramidal system is *flaccid* paralysis. Damage to the extrapyramidal system also causes some paralysis and when added to pyramidal damage increases the severity of the paralysis. Extrapyramidal lesions cause *spastic* paralysis and an exaggeration of the deep (muscle) reflexes.

COMPOSITION OF MOVEMENT

It is possible to distinguish different aspects of motor coordination and to point out various centers and pathways responsible for them. One important aspect of motor coordination is the composition of movement, i.e., the sequence and pattern of movements making up an act. There are two areas of primary importance in the composition of movements: the premotor area and the neocerebellum.

PREMOTOR AREA—As we have already seen, the premotor area (area 6) lying in front of the precentral gyrus is an important source of the extrapyramidal system. This system, as we have also seen, is concerned in the postural reflexes, but since posture and movement are inseparable, it is concerned, in addition, in the integration of movements into coordinated acts.

That the premotor area contributes a good deal to the composition of skilled movements can easily be seen by removing it. Without the premotor areas, either the monkey or chimpanzee shows a good many deficits in skilled movements. For one thing, the animal requires a good deal of practice to reacquire proficiency in the manipulatory movements that it acquired preoperatively, say in solving a problem box. Some abilities are never completely regained. In such a pattern of behavior as, for example, grooming, there is marked impairment. The animal is very awkward in attempting to remove fleas from the body, and it has difficulty particularly in coordinating the thumb and index finger as this should be done in grooming. In man, too, injury to the premotor areas causes awkwardness of movement and a very prominent difficulty in approximating thumb and index finger and in making the adjustments in buttoning a shirt or fingering a musical instrument.

NEOCEREBELLUM—The entire cerebellum is concerned in one way or another with the motor aspects of behavior. Some of it is mostly concerned with postural reactions that we have considered before. The most important part of the cerebellum for motor coordination, however, is the dorsal lobe or neocerebellum. This is the newest part from an evolutionary point of view, and it is highly developed in the primates.

The neocerebellum contributes in several ways to motor coordination, but one of the ways is like that of the premotor cortex. It contributes to the composition of movement. Its functions show up most clearly when it is removed either experimentally in monkeys or chimpanzees or by injury in man.

Disturbances in the pattern or composition of movement are particularly apparent in neocerebellar lesions. If a patient with such a lesion is asked to bring his finger from a position above his head to the tip of his nose, he may move his shoulder and upper arm before he begins to flex his elbow, which is an awkward thing to do. If asked to put one heel on the opposite knee, he may bend his hip completely before he bends his knee. Thus he raises his heel much too high and lowers it to his knee. On attempting to feed himself, a patient may first fix his elbow firmly to the side and move the spoon to his mouth, bending his elbow only. Frequently such a patient holds his arm or leg too rigidly in attempting to reach out and touch an object.

These are just a few examples that have been reported in the clinical and experimental literature. With lesions either of the premotor cortex or of the neocerebellum it is hard to say just what it is that is wrong. In either case, however, the various component movements that make up a coordinated act are not put together in the correct way.

RESTRAINT OF MOVEMENT

Probably the most important of all factors in coordinated movement is restraint or inhibition. There are several different factors at work in motor coordination that fit in this category.

KINESTHESIS—We have already seen how kinesthetic afferents are involved in reflex behavior (see page 278). Through their inhibitory influences, they keep reflexes from starting or stopping too abruptly, and they generally smooth out the reflex to make it better serve its purpose. Kinesthesis plays a similar role in voluntary behavior.

In man or primates, injury to the kinesthetic pathways, thus cutting off kinesthetic influences to the brain, causes severe disturbances of motor coordination called *voluntary ataxia*. Individuals suffering from such a disorder have trouble, for example, in feeding or in making other rather specific coordinations. Their limbs usually shoot rather wide of the mark and look as though "they do not know where they are going." That is because the kinesthetic impulses are necessary to guide a coordinated movement.

The disturbances seen when kinesthesis is lacking affect different limbs and parts of the body in different amounts. The effects are what one might predict from the homunculus (see page 286), which represents the amount of motor cortex assigned to various movements. In general, the parts of the body, such as the mouth, face, and fingers, that are most involved in precise coordination are affected most by loss of kinesthetic impulses. Impairment is slight in the hip, more marked in the distal joints, and so great in the digits that these are virtually useless. It is easy to show, however, that there is nothing wrong in the executive pathways from the cortex, for electrical stimulation of these pathways will elicit the movements that normally can be obtained. What the motor cortex lacks, apparently, is adequate information concerning the events taking place in the muscles.

The neurology underlying the role of kinesthesis in motor coordination is not simple. Fibers of the kinesthetic system project directly to the motor cortex (area 4). The postcentral gyrus, which is the main cortical area receiving kinesthetic impulses, is also involved in motor functions. Thus there is direct kinesthetic information being supplied to the cerebral cortex at all times. In addition, however, some of the kinesthetic influences in motor coordination undoubtedly are carried by way of the cerebellum. This organ was once called the "great proprioceptive ganglion." Although such a description overstates the case, kinesthetic impulses make their way in large numbers to the cerebellum, and the cerebellum in turn exerts its influence on the motor cortex.

NEOCEREBELLUM—The neocerebellum is also concerned in the restraint of movements. In fact, unrestrained movements that are excessive in range are about the most easily recognized sign that there is a disorder of the neocerebellum. For example, when a patient with a neocerebellar lesion attempts to touch his finger to his nose, he is likely to strike his cheek violently. Or a monkey, when walking, may lift its foot entirely too high from the ground or put it down too forcefully. These are just two examples. The general point is that the neocerebellum when functioning normally contributes impulses that restrain excessive movements and make them more precisely timed and coordinated.

TREMOR—When people try to thread needles or make any extremely fine movement, their fingers or hands usually tremble a little. When people get excited or emotionally upset, they may tremble excessively. Ordinarily, however, they do not tremble much—if they are normal—but in certain kinds of injuries to the nervous system there is a great deal of tremor in coordinated movements.

Two different kinds of tremor appear in diseases of the nervous system. One is *tremor at rest*. Neurologists frequently see it in Parkinson's disease, which involves many subcortical lesions in the brain. The tremor at rest develops when the patient holds his hands or head still, but it disappears whenever a voluntary skilled movement is made. The other kind of tremor is *intention tremor*. It is a very conspicuous tremor that appears only when a skilled movement is made, and it disappears when the hands or head are at rest. This tremor, as we shall see, is the result of injury to the cerebellum.

A number of different circuits are implicated in smoothing out coordinated movements and hence in preventing tremor. One group of circuits involves the extrapyramidal system and a pathway leading down to the brain stem and back to the cerebral cortex. Some interference with these circuits appears to be at fault in the tremor at rest seen in Parkinsonism. Another circuit passes from the cerebral cortex, particularly the precentral and frontal cortex, to the cerebellum and back again to the cerebral cortex. Injury to this circuit causes *intention tremor*. In fact, the clinical neurologist uses the presence of intention tremor as one of his signs that something is wrong with the cerebrocerebellar circuit. The lesion is very frequently in the cerebellum.

RECOVERY OF MOTOR FUNCTIONS

Complete bilateral extirpation of all the areas concerned with voluntary movement, including 4, 6, and 3-1-2, results in compelte motor paralysis of all voluntary movements in man, chimpanzee, and monkey. From such profound paralysis there is no recovery. If, however, the experimental injuries are made only to a part of the crucial areas, there is some improvement in function and effacing of the paralysis over a period of months following the operation. This recovery of motor functions has been known for a long time, but only recently has research been throwing some light on how and why it occurs.

COMPENSATION—So long as injuries do not include all the cortical areas participating in motor coordination, the areas remaining are, in time, capable of providing some compensation. Ordinarily, for example, when the motor cortex is removed simultaneously on both sides, a rather severe paralysis results. If, however, a lesion is made only on one side and a period of three or four months is allowed to elapse before taking out the other side, the result is not the usual paralytic signs of bilateral injury. Obviously there has been compensation taking place between the removal of one cortex and the second operation. Moreover, this compensation must involve some areas other than those of the motor cortex (area 4). It has been found that the postcentral gyrus (3-1-2) is responsible for this compensation, for, if it is also removed along with the extirpation of the corresponding precentral cortex, paralysis occurs after the second operation just as it would have if both sides had been removed simultaneously in one operation.

INJURY IN INFANCY—Compensation is also seen in the effects of cortical removal in infant monkeys. It is interesting that when cortical areas 4 and 6, the motor and premotor areas, are removed from infant monkeys, there is very little immediate effect on motor performance; i.e., there is no paralysis. As time goes on and the monkeys grow older, some signs of paralysis make their appearance, but these are much more moderate than if the injury were made in adult monkeys. From this fact it is possible to draw several conclusions. Some kind of reorganization of brain functions goes on after the removal of the motor areas; this reorganization is greater in the young monkey than in the mature animal, occurring to the greatest extent in the first six months of life. Apparently the parts of the cortical motor system that remain are responsible for the compensation.

To test this hypothesis, several experiments have been carried out (see Morgan and Stellar, 1950, p. 338). They make use of different methods for determining what reorganization has taken place. One method is to use a pharmacological stimulant during the period of recovery following the operation. A second is the use of a sedative after the operation.

STIMULANTS—The stimulant used was strychnine. This is a well-known nervous stimulant and probably acts by interfering with cholinesterase activity at the site of transmission of nervous impulses. Also used were two other chemicals that are known to have a stimulating action on the nervous system: thiamin (vitamin B_1) and doryl. By using these drugs postoperatively, singly or in combination, it was observed that all animals suffering removal of the cerebral cortex on one side were aided considerably in both the rate and degree of recovery of their motor functions. This increased rate of recovery appeared to be due to the fact that the stimulus accelerated the rate of functional reorganization in the parts of the motor system remaining after operation.

SEDATIVES—The opposite result was observed with the use of sedatives. Several monkeys were deprived of their motor and premotor cortices (areas 4 and 6) on one side and were treated with sedatives such as phenobarbital and dilantin during the postoperative period. The phenobarbital, in doses so small that they had no observable effect on the cage behavior of the monkeys, produced a very marked slowing in the rate of recovery of motor functions. In fact, the animals never reached a level of recovery typical of monkeys subjected to this lesion without the use of sedatives. The experimenters concluded that the sedatives interfered with the reorganization of the remaining tissues of the cortical motor system.

11 EMOTION

$\mathbf{T}$HIS CHAPTER FORMS a bridge between the chapters preceding it and those that follow. The reason is that, on the one hand, emotion has its sensory and motor aspects, and, on the other, it has its motivational aspects. Relatively little is known about its sensory or experience aspect because this has been difficult to study and to quantify. More is known about its motor and motivational aspects. For that reason, this chapter will be largely devoted to them.

EMOTIONAL MECHANISMS

Let us first consider some of the general problems and methods of studying emotion. In this way, we shall dispose of some points that need making, but only briefly, and thus put the topic in a perspective from which we can launch into more detail. In this section, we shall consider (1) kinds of emotion, (2) aspects of emotion, (3) theories of emotion, and (4) methods of studying it.

KINDS OF EMOTION   (1)

If we consider emotions as we observe them in people in everyday life, it is obvious that emotions have many shades and intensities. There are hundreds of words in the English language employed to denote these varieties of emotion. Perhaps some day the physiological basis of some of these varieties of emotion will be discovered. At the present time, however, we are limited to a relatively few categories of emotion. For our purposes, the following methods of classification will be quite adequate.

An age-old way of classifying emotions is into three categories: pleasure, fear, and anger. The latter two are disquieting emotions. They involve tension and disturbance of the organism's responses, both internal and external. Anger is a "fight" reaction; fear, one of "flight" or "fright." Pleasure is not so easily pigeonholed. In part, it is relief from fear and anger and hence a calming of the organism. In part, it may involve excitement. But it is usually distinguishable, at least if the situation giving rise to it is known, from anger and fear (Klineberg, 1954).

It helps in understanding the relation of emotions to each other to consider the way in which emotion develops in children (Bridges, 1932). This has been depicted as a tree (see Figure 11.1) in which the first expression of emotion is one of general excitement. Later in development, excitement differentiates into distress and delight (or pleasure). Still later, distress further

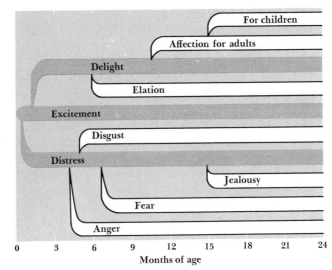

FIGURE 11.1—The development of emotion in human infants. (Adapted from K. M. B. Bridges. Emotional development in early infancy. *Child Develpm.* 1932, 3, 324–334.)

For children

Affection for adults

Delight

Elation

Excitement

Disgust

Distress

Jealousy

Fear

Anger

0   3   6   9   12   15   18   21   24

Months of age

shades into fear and anger. There are other steps in between, but the point is that, out of a common core of excitement or arousal, anger, fear, and pleasure are differentiated.

Still another method of classification has proved useful in judging human facial expression (Schlosberg, 1954). This method represents emotion as some mixture of three polar components: tension-sleep; pleasantness-unpleasantness; and attention-rejection. The advantage of this system, as well as the developmental system, is that it emphasizes the component of tension or arousal. Certainly in intense fear and anger, the organism is aroused; and without arousal, there is little or no emotion. This fact, as we shall see, has physiological significance.

In physiological experiments, which are for the most part done with animals, it is most often possible to observe and study arousal, fear, and anger. Other aspects of emotion, no matter how important, have not yet yielded to physiological methods of study.

ASPECTS OF EMOTION

At the outset of this chapter, we said that emotion has three aspects: sensory, motor, and motivational. Put another way, emotion can be an experience, a kind of behavior, or a motive. Let us review each of these briefly.

EMOTIONAL BEHAVIOR—There are a great many kinds of behavior included under the term *emotion*. Some involve primarily the musculature of the body. In man, for example, some of the somatic emotional reactions are smiling, laughing, crying, screaming, running in flight, startle responses to sudden loud sounds, and various facial expressions of emotion. Animals show some of these same reactions but also such patterns as snarling, purring, yelping, tail wagging, baring of fangs, hissing, and certain other patterns of facial and bodily reaction that go along with them. In physiological experiments with animals, the latter will be mentioned most often.

In both man and animals, a variety of autonomic responses are also part of emotion. There is the pallor of fear, in which blood tends to leave the head. There is fainting, which is a more extreme case of circulatory change accompanied by loss of consciousness and changes in bodily posture. Increase or decrease in the heart rate or in blood pressure occurs in emotion. Secretions of various glands may be increased or lowered, with resulting changes in the metabolism of the body. These, briefly, are a few of the autonomic emotional reactions. They will be described in more detail later.

EMOTIONAL EXPERIENCE—People and animals not only act emotional; they "feel" emotional. People can give verbal reports of such emotional experiences, while they can only be inferred from the behavior of animals. There are, moreover, many shades of emotional experience. People may feel "afraid," "mad," "happy," "excited," "depressed," "quiet"—such words could be multiplied almost indefinitely. Because of all the patterns and shades of emotional *experience,* it has been very difficult to work with it scientifically or, more specifically, to understand its physiological basis. Consequently, we shall discuss this problem briefly, referring particularly to pain and somesthetic mechanisms.

The relationship of pain to "unpleasantness" is obvious. Pleasure and pain are often used in hedonistic terminology as synonyms for pleasantness and unpleasantness, respectively. In what ways painful stimuli are directly appreciated in experience is not known (see Chapter 9). One point, however, is clear: The effect of pain on experience is amplified through the behavior that it evokes; this in turn excites other pain receptors in the interior of the body. Pain causes specific muscular tension and also reflexes that may feel unpleasant. It also causes changes in the activity of glands, in smooth muscles, in respiration, in blood pressure, and in the size of blood vessels. From these effects, impulses are evoked in the various interoceptors, particularly in pain receptors serving the organs involved. Thus the behavior elicited by the original painful stimulus also adds some more painful stimulation.

Although the sensory mechanisms of pain play a prominent role in feeling, these are not the only peripheral senses concerned. Touch or pressure, warmth, cold, and tickle have affective consequences. Warmth and tickle possess a pleasant character; pressure and cold are frequently "unpleasant." Sexual sensations are also a case in point. In these, excitation appears to arise from tactual receptors in the erotic regions, and the effect is usually judged to be "pleasant."

AUTONOMIC RESPONSES—Many experimenters with emotional states have wondered whether the difference between "pleasantness" and "unpleasantness" might not lie in sensory excitations arising respectively from the two general types of autonomic activity, parasympathetic and sympathetic responses (see Allport, 1924; Arnold, 1945). There are arguments in favor of such a distinction. One is that warmth stimulation, when it is not so intense as to produce pain, is generally "pleasant." Such stimulation, like parasympathetic discharge, produces dilation of blood vessels. Various functions connected with eating are parasympathetically governed, and these are usually pleasurable. The secretion of saliva in the anticipation of food and the secretion of gastric juices in hunger, for example, are parasympathetic activities. In sexual behavior, vasodilation and certain muscular responses leading up to orgasm are of parasympathetic origin.

There are, on the other hand, glaring exceptions to any rule that parasympathetic activity underlies pleasantness (Gellhorn, 1961). Crying is parasympathetic. Bad odors, as well as good food, elicit parasympathetic salivation and gastric contractions so severe as to cause vomiting. The motor activity of the bladder and rectum, which may be greatly augmented in fear, are also parasympathetic. Thus it is obvious that there is no simple relation between the activity of the autonomic divisions and emotional experience (or behavior). There may, nevertheless, be the possibility of distinguishing biochemically between sympathetic activities in fear and anger (see Autonomic Functions below).

K

THEORIES OF EMOTION (*3*)

Emotion has been the subject of considerable theorizing, perhaps because it has been so difficult to understand (Ruckmick, 1936; Young, 1961). The theories that have been put forth have concerned various aspects of emotion, but usually not all of them are encompassed in one theory. Some have focused on evolutionary development and how it serves the survival of the organism. Some have speculated about the role of the brain and nervous system. Others have dealt with the stimuli for, and the causes of, emotions. Four of the most prominent theories dealing with physiological mechanisms will be reviewed.

l. JAMES-LANGE THEORY—The theory that held the stage for many years and is still often quoted was put forth separately by Lange and James (see Gellhorn, 1961). What the theory attempted to explain, in general terms, was how emotional behavior and emotional experience are interrelated physiologically. At the time of its popularity, little was known about specific brain mechanisms. The important point that it made was that emotional response comes first and emotional experience is the result of that response. As James saw it, an emotional stimulus sets off autonomic responses in the blood vessels, glands, and so on, as well as in skeletal effectors. These responses act as stimuli for internal receptors, which send impulses back into the nervous system. These impulses give rise to emotional experience. Thus, said James, "We are afraid because we run; we do not run because we are afraid."

2. CANNON-BARD THEORY—In his classic work on reflexes, Sherrington (1906) objected to the James-Lange theory on the grounds that he had observed emotion in animals deprived of a large part of the sensory feedback from the structures of the body (see Gellhorn, 1961). Later Cannon (1927) and Bard (1928) prepared cats in which the sympathetic system was sectioned along the whole length of the spinal cord, thus depriving the animals of the usual autonomic responses in emotion. Bard also demonstrated the role of the hypothalamus in the expression of emotion.

Knowing these facts and also that the afferent pathways had way stations in the thalamus, Cannon and Bard postulated the so-called thalamic theory of emotion. In this, the experience of emotion was regarded as arising cortically from thalamic processes at the same time that emotional behavior at the hypothalamic level was released. Thus the two arose from the same source, not one from the other. However, there is virtually no evidence that emotional experience, other than the perception of pain or of primary sensory experience, arises from the thalamus (Lashley, 1938). In fact, exactly how emotional experience arises is still a mystery. Today, about all that is left of the Cannon-Bard theory is the emphasis on the hypothalamic *expression* of emotion. As we shall see below, however, parts of the thalamus *are* concerned in emotion.

LINDSLEY'S ACTIVATION THEORY—Shortly after the importance of the reticular *3.* system in arousal was demonstrated, Lindsley (1951) put forth an "activation theory" of emotion. He, of course, accepted the hypothalamus as a primary locus for organizing the expression of emotion, but he also stressed the recently demonstrated fact that the reticular system must be active to have any significant expressive behavior. As we shall see, animals with very much of the reticular system damaged are somnolent, apathetic, and distinctly unemotional. He regarded the reticular system as the source of general excitement or tension within which particular forms of emotion might be expressed through the hypothalamus.

Lindsley was certainly correct in emphasizing the activation aspects of emotion, as the facts known then and now clearly show. On the other hand, perhaps the role of the reticular system was overemphasized. More recently, it has become evident that the hypothalamus, aside from the fact that reticular substance is part of it, has its own activating functions, both by its connections with the cerebral cortex and also through autonomic activities that in turn activate the reticular system (see Gellhorn, 1961). Thus the activation ⋋ theory mainly integrates the reticular system, and the behavioral arousal and activation accompanying its activity, into the picture of brain mechanisms of emotion.

PAPEZ-MACLEAN THEORY—In 1937, the neurologist Papez published a specu- *4.* lative paper that bordered on the incredulous. He proposed a theory of emotion that involved many structures of the brain either considered to be primarily olfactory in function or not known definitely to have any function at all. These included the hippocampus, fornix, mammillary bodies of the hypothalamus, and cingular gyrus—in short, the structures now included in the limbic system (see page 52). He connected these together according to the neuroanatomy known at the time. This, subsequently supplemented by more studies (see Brady, 1958), showed that they belonged together in one system. Later on, as experimental studies began to indicate that there was some truth in Papez' theory, MacLean (1949, 1958) developed it further.

There are some differences in the details of the theories put forth by Papez and MacLean. These differences, however, are relatively inconsequential and mostly concern the as-yet-unknown basis of emotional experience. Both ascribe to the limbic system as a whole the mediation of emotional experience and expression. Both, of course, point out the significant connections of the system with the hypothalamus and its role in the expression of emotion. Both stress the strategic location of the limbic system for the correlation of feelings, particularly those arising from the internal organs of the body. Although precise knowledge of how these structures affect experience is still lacking, it is now known, as will be seen below, that they are involved in it. The Papez-MacLean theory is now much more than a theory. It is a general description of what experiment has established, namely, that the limbic system is the central system in emotion.

METHODS OF STUDY (4)

Before we get into the details of research on emotion, let us consider briefly the methods used in such research. These are like those used in several other areas of physiological psychology. They consist primarily of (1) ablations and lesions of the nervous system; (2) stimulation and recording, usually electrical, in the various parts of the brain; and, of course, (3) behavioral methods.

1. LESIONS—The method that has been most often used is that of making ablations and lesions in the nervous system. In the earlier work of the 1930s, complete transections of the brain at levels varying from the spinal cord to the thalamus were used to get an idea of the gross contribution of different parts of the brain. Later, more selective ablations were made, some limited to a single structure and others to a combination of structures. Most recently, with the perfection of stereotaxic techniques, lesions have often been made in restricted sites of one or two structures.

2. STIMULATION AND RECORDING—Methods other than those of ablation have had more limited use. The method of stimulation, however, has been increasingly employed, particularly since the technique of chronic implantation of electrodes has been perfected and mastered by a number of experimenters. Methods of recording events such as respiration, pulse, galvanic skin response, and other autonomic responses have been available for some time, but only recently and to a very limited extent has there been any recording of central electrical events in emotion.

3. BEHAVIORAL METHODS—Most research on the brain and emotion has been done in the dog and cat, some on rats and the monkey. Let us consider the kinds of emotional behavior that can be observed in these animals.

Patterns of emotion in animals are relatively easy to identify. The rage reaction in the dog, for example, consists of lashing of the tail, arching of the trunk, thrusting and jerking of the limbs, protrusion of the claws and clawing movements, snarling, movements of the head from side to side, attempts to bite, and very rapid, panting respiration. A somewhat similar and definite description can be given for rage in the rat, cat, and monkey. The fear reaction in the cat is displayed by dashing off in a furtive or precipitate manner, mewing plaintively, trembling, and taking cover behind any available object.

In general, fear in animals can be identified as freezing behavior or dashing away from the fearsome object into a corner or under cover. The *pleasure* reaction in dogs and cats is familiar to the layman. Its most evident sign in dogs is tail wagging, and in cats it is purring. Other reactions such as those to petting and stroking are also signs of pleasure. These various patterns of emotional reaction make it practicable to study emotion in animals.

Early studies of emotion simply attempted to determine whether familiar patterns, or parts of them, were present or absent. In these, it was also frequently possible to obtain a crude *threshold* of emotional response. How hard the tail must be pinched to elicit a rage reaction, how much of a threatening gesture must be made to provoke fear or rage, how readily an animal comes to the experimenter for stroking and petting, and other similar signs have been taken to indicate changes in the threshold of emotional response.

More precise measures of emotionality have occasionally been used. One of these is a *rating scale* for expressing numerically the degree of emotionality (Stone, 1932; Tryon et al., 1941). Six or seven different components of emotionality may be selected and each rated on a scale of four points (Brady and Nauta, 1953) or even of seven points (King, 1958). The components selected generally include resistance to capture and/or handling, vocalization during testing, startle and flight reactions to tapping the animal on the body, startle and attack reaction to a pencil presented visually to the animal, and urination and defecation during handling. The reliability of rating these components is usually quite high and provides a satisfactory measure of emotionality.

Another method involves the conditioning of an emotional response and is called the conditioned emotional response (CER) (see Brady and Hunt, 1951). This method is described in Chapter 16 and will not be covered in this chapter.

THALAMUS AND LOWER CENTERS

In the rest of this chapter, our treatment of emotion will be largely organized around the neural structures involved. First, we shall consider the thalamus and lower centers and then the cerebral cortex and limbic system. At the end of the chapter is a section on brain stimulation in which the subject, usually an animal, controls whether or not he will receive such stimulation.

SPINAL CORD AND MEDULLA

Most autonomic components of emotional behavior can be seen in spinal animals deprived, by transection between the medulla and spinal cord, of influences of the brain. On the other hand, the bulbar animal, i.e., one with the medulla and spinal cord intact, gives a more coherent picture of autonomic response than the spinal animal. Because the "vital" centers for respiration, heart rate, and control of circulation are found in the medulla, in the bulbar animal respiratory and circulatory changes are more nearly like those in the normal animal. To obtain relatively complete autonomic responses in mammals, an intact medulla is therefore needed.

BRAIN STEM

Besides autonomic responses, there are also somatic emotional patterns to consider. In fact, these are of the greatest interest to the psychophysiologist. Studies of such responses have been made with transections at various levels of the brain stem (Kelly et al., 1946; Macht and Bard, 1942).

a. SUBTOTAL RESPONSES—The principal conclusion to be drawn about animals with transections of the brain stem is that only "subtotal responses" appear in such animals. They may growl, hiss or spit, lash their tails, thrash with their forelegs, protrude their paws, increase their breathing, and urinate, showing nearly all the signs of rage in normal animals. These responses, however, are not always combined; typically they appear as isolated bits of behavior. Moreover, brain-stem animals never show the integrated "attack reaction" that one can see in normal animals, which attack with claws and teeth, directing their attack forward and downward and adopting the posture of preparing to attack. Thus midbrain and bulbar animals, although they show some of the fragments of emotional response, do not show integrated rage behavior. That, as we shall see, is put together at a higher level of the brain.

b. LEVELS OF INTEGRATION—A second feature of emotional behavior in midbrain and bulbar animals is that emotional reactions become more fragmentary, the lower the brain-stem section is made. Cats with an intact midbrain can right, stand, and walk, and they can express the items of emotional response listed above. With a section through the lower part of the midbrain or through the pons, animals no longer can right, stand, or walk. These animals do not show as many of the fragments of rage response as do those with somewhat higher section. Hence, it may be concluded that various items of rage behavior have their "seats" in the lower brain stem; that the lower the section in the brain stem, the more likely that some of them will be missed; but that the organization of total emotional responses is carried out at a level above the midbrain.

c. EFFECTIVENESS OF STIMULI—A third feature of emotional behavior in brainstem animals is that some stimuli lack their normal effectiveness in evoking emotional responses. In particular, auditory and visual stimuli are ineffective. This is not unexpected, since the main auditory and visual centers in mammals are above the medulla and midbrain. The effective stimuli for the midbrain animal are somesthetic and nociceptive stimuli: pinching, electrical shock, squeezing, and rubbing the animal. In some animals, only painful stimuli are capable of provoking emotional responses; in others, merely stroking or rubbing the animal brings forth growls or emotional acts (see Bard and Mountcastle, 1947).

LEVEL OF AROUSAL—These conclusions apply to the animal with brain-stem transection. Naturally, other results are obtained when lesions are made selectively in the brain stem. Some lesions in the so-called "vital centers" cause such profound autonomic disturbances of respiration or circulation that they kill the animal. Of more interest to the psychophysiologist are lesions made in the reticular activating system (RAS). These lesions cause profoundly somnolent animals (see Chapter 12). Such animals sleep or are sleepy most of the time, although they may be aroused temporarily by sufficient sensory stimulation (Lindsley, 1960). As one might expect, they are difficult or impossible to arouse emotionally. This fact, given an important place in the "activation theory of emotion," means that emotional reactivity, like other forms of reactivity, depends on a general level of arousal or excitement provided by the reticular formation. Hence, reticular activation is a necessary, if not sufficient, condition for emotional behavior.

HYPOTHALAMUS

If there is a "seat of emotion," it is the hypothalamus. Such a term can be misleading, but it points to the fact that the hypothalamus is the principal center in which the various components of emotional reaction are organized into definite patterns. The components in fragments are governed at lower points in the brain stem. Moreover, the hypothalamus is subject to powerful influences, both excitatory and inhibitory, from other structures in the limbic system, and there are, as we shall see, important cortical influences on the hypothalamus. Nevertheless, the hypothalamus is the focal, organizing structure in emotional behavior. This conclusion comes out of a number of experiments, some of which will now be summarized.

THE PREPARATION—The classic experiments that point up the importance of the hypothalamus were made with dogs and cats (Bard, 1928). The procedure was straightforward (see Figure 11.2). In some animals, the cerebral cortex was removed, while the thalamus and all lower structures were left intact. In other animals, the thalamus as well as the cortex was sectioned, but the hypothalamus and midbrain structures were untouched. Finally, in other animals, the section of the brain stem was made below the hypothalamus or below the midbrain.

The emotional responses of the animals were studied before and after these various operations. There were several striking results. For one thing, the threshold for rage response was lowered after the removal of the cerebral cortex. In other words, it was easier to get a rage response from an animal

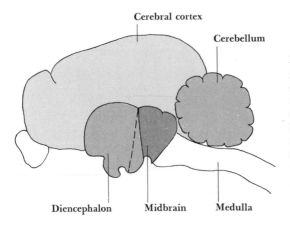

Cerebral cortex

Cerebellum

Diencephalon   Midbrain   Medulla

FIGURE 11.2—Schematic longitudinal section of the cat's brain, showing the different parts removed or left intact in studies of the neural basis of emotion. (Adapted from W. B. Cannon. The mechanism of emotional disturbance of bodily function. *New England J. Med.*, 1928, 198, 879. By permission of the publishers.)

after decortication than before (more on this below). Hence, removal of the cortex apparently released some inhibiting or restraining influences of the cortex that keep subcortical rage mechanisms in check.

Another result was that the complete rage response could be elicited only so long as the hypothalamus was intact. With sections below the hypothalamus, as we have just seen, emotional responses became fragmentary, subtotal responses. The rage response seen in hypothalamic animals, however, seemed just as complete as in normal animals. The conclusion, therefore, was that there is some mechanism in the hypothalamus for organizing the somatic patterns of emotional response. It is also known, of course, that the main centers for integrating patterns of autonomic effects (page 46) is in the hypothalamus.

The statement that the hypothalamus can mediate complete patterns of rage must be qualified. Actually, hypothalamic preparations exhibit certain behavioral deficiencies in emotion. They have, for example, some rigidity of the extensor muscles such as is seen in decerebrate preparations (page 292). In general, too, hypothalamic animals lack some of the postural reactions that accompany full-fledged emotional response. On the whole, however, a relatively well-organized and integrated pattern of rage response can be obtained with the hypothalamus intact, and only so long as it is, in decerebrate preparations.

STIMULATION—If the hypothalamus is the focal point for emotional expression, it would be expected that emotional reactions could be elicited by hypothalamic stimulation. A number of studies have demonstrated that this is the case (de Molina et al., 1959; Yasukochi, 1960; see also Hess, 1954, and Brady, 1960). It is possible to implant electrodes in the hypothalamus and to stimulate it with electrical currents while an animal is unanesthetized or only lightly anesthetized. When this is done, various kinds of emotional expression may be observed: fear, anxious behavior, irritation, rage, full-fledged attack reactions, and something resembling yearning or curiosity.

The arrangement of centers and pathways in the hypothalamus is undoubtedly complicated and has no clear topographical pattern (see Brady, 1960). Reports of the kinds of behavior elicited by stimulation at different points are not always consistent. It does seem well established, however, that stimulation of the lateral hypothalamus produces well-organized attack behavior (Nakao and Maki, 1958). Cats that otherwise do not attack rats—some do and some do not—can be made to attack savagely a rat placed in the home cage when hypothalamic stimulation is applied. The attack stops when the stimulation is turned off. In another recent study (Yasukochi, 1960), fearful behavior was seen in stimulation of the anterior hypothalamus, aggressive behavior in the middle portion, and curiosity and alertness in the posterior part.

LESIONS—A somewhat clearer picture, but still not entirely satisfactory, emerges from studies in which restricted lesions of the hypothalamus are made (see Brady, 1960). Posterior lesions generally produce stolid, somewhat somnolent animals that are difficult to arouse emotionally (Ranson, 1939). In fact, lesions in this area virtually abolish emotional behavior. The area contains structures associated with the reticular activating system and also some concerned in sympathetic activity. Hence, it is possible that the effect is one of generally lowered arousal. On the other hand, lesions of the more medial and ventromedial aspects of the hypothalamus may cause generally ferocious animals easily aroused to rage (Wheatley, 1944). Relatively small lesions produced here may cause "extremely, chronically and incurably savage" behavior in cats.

It is interesting that the rage reactions seen in such lesions are well integrated and directed reactions. The reactions are not "blind or senseless." Rather they are complete, savage reactions directed at some object. The lesions therefore appear to release from inhibition patterns of behavior otherwise organized by the hypothalamus and other structures. In the next sections, we shall see what some of these structures are.

THALAMUS

The nineteenth-century neurologist Henry Head was led, on the basis of both experiment and clinical cases of thalamic injury, to believe that the thalamus contained structures concerned in affective or hedonic reactions (1920). Some years later, Lashley (1938) examined the evidence then available and concluded that Head was wrong. According to Lashley, "There is no evidence whatever that the thalamus contributes facilitative impulses which might form a basis for the motivational aspects of emotion. Thus, the only part of the thalamic theory of emotion which has factual support is the localization of motor centers for emotional expression within the hypothalamus." (Also see Gellhorn, 1961, p. 404.)

Subsequent work, however, appears to side with Head rather than Lashley.

Although interpretation of the experiments is sometimes difficult, it appears that, directly or indirectly, the thalamus is concerned with emotional reactions and probably emotional experience as well. There are three different areas of the thalamus implicated: the anterior nuclei, the dorsomedial nucleus, and the posteroventral (somatosensory) nucleus. The anterior nucleus will be discussed later, along with the limbic system of which it is a part.

POSTEROVENTRAL NUCLEUS—There are several reports of electrical stimulation of the *posteroventral nucleus* (Brady, 1960; Roberts, 1962). This elicits behavior variously described as "anxiety, defensive and offensive movements, vocalizations, and autonomic manifestations" (Delgado, 1955) or a "pain-like" response (Roberts, 1962). This particular fact fits in with Lashley's point of view (1938), for it is to be expected that this nucleus, being a somesthetic relay center, would arouse pain when stimulated. And pain, whether evoked peripherally or with shock or centrally with electrical stimulation, naturally gives rise to emotional responses of fear and anger.

DORSOMEDIAL NUCLEUS—Siding with Head rather than Lashley, however, are observations of other areas of the thalamus. Stimulation of the dorsomedial nucleus of the thalamus evokes a fearlike crouching response. This nucleus, which projects to the frontal lobes, has in other ways been associated with anxiety and fear (see Chapter 19). Although it is risky to say what an emotion is just by looking at a "fear-crouching response," stimulation of the dorsomedial thalamic nucleus is clearly "unpleasant" and aversive, for cats learn a conditioned response to avoid such stimulation just as readily as they learn to avoid peripheral shock or stimulation of the posteroventral nucleus (Roberts, 1962).

Complementing this work with electrical stimulation are studies employing lesions restricted fairly well to the dorsomedial nucleus. One study reports increased irritability and rage (Schreiner et al., 1953), but other studies agree in observing that cats (see Roberts, 1962) and monkeys (Brierley and Beck, 1958) show less fearfulness after dorsomedial lesions. It would appear, then, that the dorsomedial nucleus is somehow concerned with fear or "unpleasant" experience.

CEREBRAL CORTEX AND LIMBIC SYSTEM

It is convenient to consider together the functions of the cerebral cortex and limbic system in emotion, first because some of the limbic system, namely, the cingular gyrus and the ventral cortical areas, is part of the cerebral cortex and, secondly, because some of the studies were so designed that they separate or involve the interaction of the two.

DECORTICATION

In early work on cortical functions in emotion and before the limbic system was known to be important, experiments were done with relatively complete ablations of the cerebral cortex (see Bard and Mountcastle, 1947). Actually, for surgical and other reasons, it is seldom practical to remove every bit of cerebral cortex, but these experiments came close enough to be described as "total decortication." The animal subjected to such decortication is a different one in several aspects of its emotional behavior. The principal differences are in the (1) threshold, (2) direction, and (3) timing of behavior.

THRESHOLD—One characteristic of emotional behavior in a decorticate dog or cat is its lower threshold. The animal is overreactive to slight pinches and pressures on different parts of the body. It usually displays a rage response at the slightest provocation. Oftentimes any handling or stroking of the animal, even gently, brings out a full-fledged rage response. The picture, then, is one of increased sensitivity or a lowered threshold for emotional stimuli. From this fact, it would appear that the cerebral cortex normally suppresses or restrains the activities of lower centers.

DIRECTION—Another characteristic of emotional reactions in decorticate animals is that they lack "direction." Although rage behavior is full-blown and well coordinated in decorticates, the animal seems to lack any appreciation of what it is that disturbs him. When, for example, the experimenter produces rage by pinching the decorticate dog's tail, the experimenter can feel quite safe from attack, because the dog's snapping and biting will be directed to the front rather than to the rear where the painful stimulus is being applied. The reason for this lack of direction is fairly clear; the principal sensory mechanisms concerned with spatial orientation and perception of space are at the cortical level. Removal of the cortex deprives the animal of his basic perceptual equipment for making directed emotional attacks. A similar phenomenon in the sexual behavior of decorticate male animals also occurs (see Chapter 14).

TIMING—Another characteristic of decorticate emotional responses is their different timing. When a normal animal is once excited by an emotional stimulus, it continues in an emotional state for some time. This is not so in the decorticate. Such an animal recovers from its madness very quickly. In other words, normal animals show an afterdischarge in emotional reactions, but this afterdischarge is considerably reduced in the decorticate animal. For example, an experimenter may pinch the tail of the decorticate dog and elicit rage behavior, but immediately afterward he may place his finger in the dog's mouth with little danger of being bitten; this is not nearly so safe in the case of the normal angry dog. The cerebral cortex, then, seems to have some braking or smoothing action on emotion; it makes emotional responses a bit more difficult to elicit but, once they are aroused, contributes to their continuation for a time.

LIMBIC SYSTEM

After it was suspected that the limbic system played a role in emotional behavior, experiments were made in which much of the cerebral cortex was removed but structures of the limbic system (see page 52 for anatomical diagram), particularly the cingulate gyrus and the ventral cortical areas, were left intact (Bard and Mountcastle, 1947).

Animals selectively decorticated so as to spare the limbic system are completely different from "totally" decorticate animals. They are *placid*. Indeed, they are so peaceful and stolid that their rage responses are almost entirely suppressed, and it is virtually impossible to elicit a rage response from them. Such a result means that the cortical portions of the limbic system must exercise an inhibiting influence on subcortical structures. Indeed, it might appear that the changed threshold of decorticate animals described above is due to the loss of these inhibiting or restraining structures.

To test this possibility, limbic lesions were made in animals previously made placid by decortications sparing the limbic cortex (Bard and Mountcastle, 1947). It was shown that a lesion in *either* the cingulate gyrus *or* the ventral complex (including the amygdala, pyriform lobe, and hippocampus) turns placid animals into ferocious ones. Now they are much like the "totally" decorticate animals in being very easily aroused to rage. It would, therefore, appear that both the cingulate and the ventral limbic regions exercise a restraining influence on subcortical structures. Just why the removal of either of these areas in addition to the removal of the neocortex causes a release from restraint is not clear. Quite probably other subcortical structures which, as we shall see, also have a restraining influence were also involved in these operations.

It was logical that this result should be followed up with an experiment in which the cingulate and ventral limbic regions were ablated in otherwise intact animals. This was done. Changes following removal of the cingulate were not marked although they were in the direction of a raised threshold and less emotionality for a period of time after the operation. Such a result is not easy to understand, and it implies that the influence of the cingulate gyrus is delicately balanced with other cortical and subcortical influences.

AMYGDALA AND TEMPORAL LOBE

Another logical follow-up of the work by Bard and Mountcastle (1947) on the limbic system was to study in detail the contributions of the ventral limbic complex. They did this, taking out the pyriform lobe, amygdala, and hippocampus, but with results that are hard to understand. Their cats with such lesions were made more ferocious, although the effect did not appear until several weeks after the operation.

Other repetitions of the experiment, removing substantially the same areas, have not confirmed the result (Schreiner and Kling, 1956, cat; Smith, 1950, monkey). Instead, the consequence of the operation most consistently seems to be greatly increased placidity and docility. Probably the difference lies in structures other than the amygdala and hippocampus, for lesions restricted to these structures regularly produce docility (see Brady, 1960). This result has been obtained so frequently with lesions differing in size and position, but always including the amygdala, that it may be concluded with little hesitation that the amygdala normally exercises an exciting influence on the expression of emotion, particularly the emotion of anger.

STIMULATION—If this conclusion be correct, stimulation of the amygdala would be expected to evoke an emotional response. Such an experiment has been made, with the predicted result (Ursin, 1960). Rage behavior is elicited when one part of the amygdala is stimulated; fearlike behavior, when another part is stimulated. From this fact, as well as from anatomical study of the amygdala, it appears that this structure may well have two or more subdivisions concerned with fear and anger. In the experiment just mentioned, stimulation of the temporal cortex also produced a fearlike response. Part of the temporal lobe appears closely associated with the hippocampus and amygdala, and in other experiments in which it has been destroyed along with the underlying limbic structures, the result has typically been one of "taming" or docility (Thompson and Walker, 1951).

It is generally thought that the amygdala plays its role in emotion through the hypothalamus, although it undoubtedly has other connections. This is the belief because the amygdala connects with the hypothalamus, because the hypothalamus is the important center in the integration of emotional behavior, and finally because the hypothalamus also connects with other structures known to exercise a restraining influence on it (see below).

All this seems to be true. Yet results are sometimes obtained that do not fit in with this picture. One is the effects of combined stimulation of the hypothalamus and the amygdala (Egger and Flynn, 1962). In this experiment, electrodes were embedded in the hypothalamus of cats in a position known to elicit attack reactions in rats. Electrodes were also embedded in the amygdala, and stimulation was applied at the same time the hypothalamus was stimulated. The effect was to suppress the attack reactions otherwise elicited hypothalamically. From this it would appear that the amygdala has a suppressing influence, while from the experiments with lesions of the amygdala, the opposite would be expected. The discrepancy is so far unexplained, but perhaps it is related to the suggestion made earlier that the amygdala has two or more subdivisions with different functions.

LESIONS—Another experiment that is somewhat difficult to interpret is one in which both the amygdala and the hypothalamus were ablated in succession (Kling et al., 1960). In this experiment, cats were first subjected to removal of the amygdala and the pyriform cortex. The expected docility and placidity followed. After that, they were operated again, this time with lesions in the part of the hypothalamus that normally produces savageness when ablated. And savageness resulted, just as if the animals had not previously been given amygdala lesions. About all one can say from this outcome is that, whatever the restraining influences on the hypothalamus in the absence of the amygdala, they are destroyed with this particular hypothalamic lesion. Apparently the relations of the limbic system and of structures within the hypothalamus are complicated.

That the effects of amygdalectomy are not simple and predictable is also brought out by another experiment that studied the effects of amygdalectomy on social behavior (Rosvold et al., 1954). In this experiment, eight male monkeys were studied preoperatively in a colony situation. As is usually the case, a dominance hierarchy was established in which monkey 1 (Dave) was "king," dominating all others; monkey 2 (Zeke) dominated all but Dave, and so on down the line (Figure 11.3). After amygdalectomy, however, Dave, the formerly dominant male, dropped to the bottom of the hierarchy. Once dominant and aggressive, he was now submissive and fearful. Next Zeke was operated; and he, too, dropped down to the bottom. He, however, was submissive to all other monkeys except Dave with whom he was intermittently aggressive. The conclusion seems to be that amygdalectomy can make an animal submissive in isolated cage situations or with particular monkeys that are also submissive. There are also some data on cats that fit in with this general picture (Clemente et al., 1957; also see Pribram, 1962).

SEPTAL AREA

In previously describing the limbic system, we included the septal region lying in the midline below the anterior part of the corpus callosum. This contains several nuclear groups and is difficult to define. Moreover, fibers run from this region to the hypothalamus in the median forebrain bundle, and lesions in this fiber tract seem to have about the same effect as lesions in the septum. This fact implicates the connection between the septum and the hypothalamus as being important in septal function. Hence the term septal area or region is used for the region itself and for pathways leading from it to the hypothalamus.

So far, the consequences of making lesions in the septal area have been quite consistent (Brady and Nauta, 1953; King, 1958). There is always a considerable increase in emotionality, which can be noticed with the naked eye or scaled more precisely by the rating-scale technique described earlier in this chapter. The animals become savage and dangerous to handle, they are jumpy and easily startled, they resist capture and handling, and they readily attack a pencil or other object thrust in their direction. This savageness does not last, however (Reynolds, 1963). It is greatest immediately after the opera-

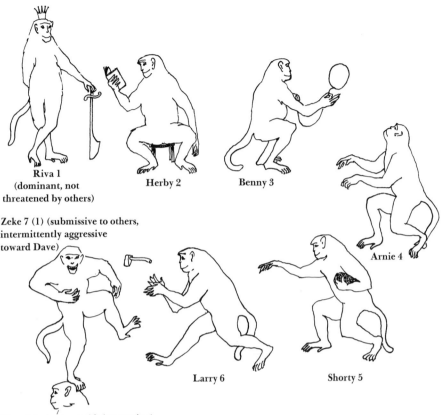

Riva 1
(dominant, not
threatened by others)

Herby 2

Benny 3

Arnie 4

Zeke 7 (1) (submissive to others,
intermittently aggressive
toward Dave)

Larry 6

Shorty 5

Dave 8 (cringer, avoids interaction)

FIGURE 11.3—The social hierarchy in a group of monkeys after Dave and Zeke had received bilateral amygdalectomies. (Adapted from K. H. Pribram. In S. Koch (Ed.), *Psychology: A study of a science*, vol. 4. New York: McGraw-Hill, 1962. P. 147. By permission of the publishers.)

tion and declines gradually over a period of several days, although some differences between septal and normal animals may be detectable for a long time afterward.

From the established fact that septal lesions cause ferocity and savageness, it has been concluded that the septum normally exercises a restraining influence on the hypothalamus. Since lesions of the amygdala usually cause placidity and docility, it is assumed that the two structures are opposed to each other, the amygdala being excitatory and the septum inhibitory.

On this reasoning, it is logical to determine the effects of the removal of the septal area and amygdala in combination. That has been done, and in two orders, the septum first and the amygdala first (King and Meyer, 1958). In the septal-amygdaloid order, the animals were first given a septal operation, rated for three days, and then given amygdalectomy. In this case, the amygdalectomy completely wiped out the hyperemotionality caused by the septal lesion. When the order was reversed, little happened with the amygdalectomy, perhaps because the subjects (white rats) were already very tame animals and because the lesions were not total lesions of the amygdala. Then, three days later, the septal lesions caused some increase in emotionality, an increase that was progressive for a few days, but this hyperemotionality was considerably less than that caused in a septal animal without amygdalectomy.

The time course of emotionality following operations is not understood, but lesions to the nervous system are seldom complete enough to destroy all tissue concerned with a function, and some recovery is the rule rather than the exception. It should therefore not be surprising. Neither is it clear why amygdalectomy following septal lesion completely wipes out the septal effect when it does so only partially in the reverse order. What does seem clear, however, is that the two structures work in opposition to each other and the removal of one tends to cancel out the removal of the other.

ANTERIOR NUCLEUS

Last to be considered in the limbic system is the anterior nucleus of the thalamus. This part of the system is connected with several structures but particularly with the cingulate gyrus and the mammillary bodies of the hypothalamus. Actually, not too much is known about its behavior functions. Such information as is available indicates that lesions in the anterior nuclei cause marked reductions in emotionality (see Brady, 1960). On the other hand, direct stimulation of the nucleus may cause fearlike crouching (Hunter and Jasper, 1949) or at least an aroused or alerting response. This area is also one in which electrical stimulation has a rewarding effect (see below).

BRAIN STIMULATION AS MOTIVATION

We covered in the sections above the use of brain stimulation to evoke patterns of emotional behavior. In recent years, brain stimulation has also been used as punishment (Delgado et al., 1954) and as reward (Olds and Milner, 1954) to motivate animals in learning situations. The characteristics of the learning with such stimulation, with certain exceptions which seem related to the motivational properties of the stimuli used, are very much like learning with other incentives such as shock and food. Thus the learning per se is not particularly interesting. Rather, it is the motivating effect of the stimulation that is unique and interesting from the physiological point of view. Exactly what the stimulation motivates is not clear, but it seems more closely related to emotion than to anything else. That is why the topic is treated at this point in the book rather than later in the chapters on motivation and learning.

First, we shall consider brain stimulation as an aversive or punishing stimulus motivating an animal to escape or avoid the stimulus. Next, we shall summarize the effects of such stimulation when it serves as a reward motivating the animal to continue or repeat behavior that produces it. Finally, we shall see what anatomical positions and other conditions of stimulation cause a stimulus to be either aversive or rewarding. All that is necessary to know for the present is that electrical stimulation in certain positions and at certain intensities and frequencies is rewarding; in other positions and with other parameters of stimulation, it acts as aversive stimulation.

AVERSIVE EFFECTS

The fact that brain stimulation can be aversive and can serve as punishment in a learning situation was first established by Delgado et al. (1954). These investigators, in various combinations and with other collaborators, have since conducted a number of experiments with aversive stimulation. For our purposes, some illustrative experiments bring out the kinds of results obtained (Miller, 1958).

In one experiment, cats were the subjects. Each cat was placed in an apparatus having a grill for a floor and a wheel in the side wall. Shock could be administered through the grill, and the cat could switch it off by turning the wheel. Cats in which brain electrodes had previously been implanted were trained to do this. Thus they learned to escape shock by turning a wheel. After they had learned the wheel-turning response, central stimulation was substituted for shock given through the grill, and the central stimulation was continued until the cat turned the wheel. On the first few trials of this procedure, the cat seemed somewhat "surprised" and disorganized, but it quickly transferred the habit of wheel turning from peripheral to central stimulation. Evidently, the central stimulation was painful or unpleasant.

In another experiment, rats were the subjects. They were prepared with implanted electrodes and after that placed in a maze. As the rat wandered through the maze, the experimenter turned on a central shock whenever the rat entered an incorrect alley and kept it on until the rat left the alley and got into a correct one, at which time it was turned off. The rats learned the maze in much the same way that they would if electric shock had been administered peripherally at the wrong turn, Again, central stimulation appeared to be punishing or aversive.

In general, animals learn just as fast with central aversive stimulation to make an escape or an avoidance response as they do with peripheral shock as punishment. It is tempting to conclude from this fact that central stimuli merely tap into pain pathways and that that is the simple explanation of these experiments. In some cases, this is undoubtedly the correct interpretation, though it is still a superficial one. In other cases, as we shall see, the electrode placements that are effective are not in the recognized pathways. Moreover, we should remember that peripheral shock, repeatedly administered, has the effect of eliciting fear in an animal, and this conditioned fear is clearly an important motivating element in the learning (see Chapter 16). More specifically, some electrode placements that serve as aversive stimuli also can be observed to elicit fear responses in animals (Roberts, 1962). It has therefore been concluded that the aversive motivation produced by central stimulation is one of fear. Hence fear, rather than pain—although pain may sometimes be involved—is the common property of learning motivated by central brain stimulation.

REWARDING EFFECTS

The fact that brain stimulation may sometimes be rewarding is one of the most interesting and important discoveries of recent years (Olds and Milner, 1954). It has led to a deluge of research, and it probably will continue to receive a great deal of attention in the years to come. For that reason, we shall explain, in the words of one of its discoverers (Olds, 1955, pp. 83ff.) just how it happened:

> In the Fall of 1953, we were looking for more information about the reticular activating system. We used electrodes permanently implanted in the brain of a healthy, behaving rat. . . . Quite by accident, an electrode was implanted in the region of the anterior commissure (a structure near the septum).
>
> The result was quite amazing. When the animal was stimulated at a specific place in an open field, he sometimes moved away but he returned and sniffed around that area. More stimulations at that place caused him to spend more of his time there.
>
> Later we found that this same animal could be "pulled" to any spot in the maze by giving a small electrical stimulus after each response in the right direction. This was akin to playing the "hot" and "cold" game with a child. Each correct response brought electrical pulses which seemed to indicate to the animal that it was on the right track.
>
> Still later, the same animal was placed on an elevated T maze. As there was an initial right-turn preference, he was forced to the left and stimulated at the end of the left arm. After three such trials, he proceeded to make 10 consecutive runs to the left for electrical stimulation alone, with decreasing running times. Then the stimulus was stopped on the left, and 6 runs were forced to the right with electrical stimulation in the right arm. After this, the animal made 10 runs to electrical stimulation in the right arm. Up to this point, no food had been in the maze at all.

Following these experiments and other exploratory tests, the experimenters (Olds and Milner, 1954) decided to study the phenomenon more systematically. They continued their studies by placing rats in a Skinner box so arranged that the rat need merely press a bar to obtain intracranial reinforcement. The Skinner box also provides for automatic recording of responses, permits a high rate of response, and is quite sensitive to changes in performance. Ever since these initial experiments, virtually all research on intracranial reinforcement has been done with the Skinner box. The following is a summary of the principal results obtained.

DRIVE STRENGTH—Intracranial reward can serve as an exceedingly powerful drive (Olds, 1958). With an optimal placement of the electrode, rats respond rapidly and for long periods of time. Rats usually make a response every two to ten seconds. They continue this, working for about three-quarters of the time, for hours on end. It is not uncommon for an animal to respond steadily at a rate of 2,000 responses per hour and to continue this for fifteen or twenty hours until completely exhausted. After a period of sleep, it resumes responding at the old rate for another period of several hours (see Figure 11.4).

There are other indications that the reward value of self-stimulation is very great. Hungry rats endure more painful shock from a grid in order to obtain central stimulation than they do to obtain a food reward (Olds and Sinclair, 1957). Central stimulation also appears to be a more powerful reward than is water or sexual activity (Olds, 1956). Opposed to these results, however, are instances in which animals respond no faster or not as fast for self-stimulation as for other kinds of reward (Bursten and Delgado, 1958; Kling and Matsumiya, 1962). But since electrode placement and other conditions of stimulation can lower self-stimulation rates, negative instances are not so persuasive as positive ones. In any case, there can be no question about self-stimulation under optimal conditions being a very powerful and sustained reward that has virtually no satiation point.

OTHER DRIVES—Experimenters have combined the deprivation of a drive, or increases in the strength of a drive, with tests of self-stimulation. For example, animals have been deprived of food or water at the same time that they are placed in the self-stimulation situation (Brady et al., 1957; Olds, 1958). In another instance, sexual drive was increased in castrated male rats by the injection of sex hormones (Olds, 1958). Under these circumstances, rats push the lever for self-stimulation more than they do under satiated conditions for other drives. There are also negative instances for this effect (Hodos and Valenstein, 1960), but again the conditions of self-stimulation may not have been optimal.

There may also be another explanation for differences in whether a drive such as hunger or sex augments the rate of responding for self-stimulation. This may depend on whether the electrode is located in a position in the

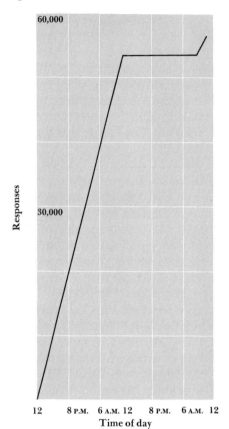

FIGURE 11.4—A record of bar pressing in a Skinner box, with the reinforcement being mild electric shock within the brain. Beginning at noon one day, the rat made about 2,000 responses an hour for twenty-six hours, then slept for nineteen hours, and then resumed self-stimulation at the same rate. (Adapted from J. Olds. Self-stimulation of the brain. *Science*, February 14, 1958, 127, 319. Adapted from *Science* by permission.)

brain relevant to the particular drive involved. If, for example, an electrode is placed in the lateral hypothalamic feeding area (see Chapter 13), this is a good location for obtaining high rates of self-stimulation (Hoebel and Teitelbaum, 1962). Moreover, the rate of self-stimulation is cut down either by excessively feeding the animal or by simultaneously stimulating the ventromedial nucleus of the hypothalamus. The latter is called a satiation center because its stimulation stops feeding and its ablation causes excessive overeating. It is quite possible that the sites for reward by self-stimulation are those connected with other drive systems (see below) and that a connection between other drives and self-stimulation may be expected only when the other drive is appropriate to the electrode placement. (For a full discussion of structures involved in hunger and thirst, see Chapter 13; for sex, Chapter 14).

LEARNING AND EXTINCTION—One of the interesting things about self-stimulation is the rapid pace of both the learning and the extinction of responses rewarded with self-stimulation. In a bar-pressing situation, rate of learning to press the bar for any reward, given appropriate motivation and other learning conditions, is so rapid that it is hard to make any comparison and to say which is faster. On extinction, however, the difference is clear-cut. It is quite slow for habits based on food or water reward but quite rapid for bar pressing based on self-stimulation. If the experimenter turns off the voltage to the rat's electrode, responses cease very abruptly (Olds, 1955). The animal proceeds to do something else like grooming, scratching, or sleeping. If now the experimenter gives the animal one or two stimulations, thereby showing that the current is on, the animal immediately starts responding again.

The fact that animals rapidly extinguish when stimulation is turned off and then resume quickly when it is turned on has led to experiments on the characteristics of extinction to self-stimulation. One approach is to study schedules of reinforcement in which animals receive a stimulation every so often with intervening responses going unrewarded. Such a schedule of partial reinforcement is a means of mixing reinforcement and extinction in one schedule. Up to a certain point, rats on self-stimulation behave in about the same way as animals rewarded, say, with food or water (Sidman et al., 1955). Cats respond at ratios of 7:1 (one reinforcement for every seven responses) or at intervals up to about fifteen seconds. However, beyond that point, a difference appears. Higher ratios can be reached only by very slow and gradual training of the animals (Brodie et al., 1960). This is to be compared with ratios of 100 or more that are not uncommon in reinforcement schedules involving food. From these facts, it appears that the drive for self-stimulation decays very rapidly between times of stimulation.

This conclusion has led to the idea that there may be no such thing as extinction of responses for self-stimulation (Deutsch, 1961). Rather, the only factor controlling response may be the motivation to obtain self-stimulation, and this may subside quickly after a stimulation. To test such a notion, one experiment compared the rate of "extinction" in animals that were not permitted to respond during an interval after the last stimulation with animals permitted to extinguish in the normal way (Howarth and Deutsch, 1962). If extinction is taking place during the interval, it should make a difference whether the animals are lever pressing and receiving no reward during the interval. In fact, it does not. A period of rest or no responding is followed later by the same rate of responding that occurs in rats allowed to respond during the interval. Hence, it appears that the important factor is simply a decay of the drive elicited by the stimulation.

NATURE OF REWARD—We have hinted above that self-stimulation may be rewarding when it activates some structure itself concerned in the satisfaction of a drive such as hunger, thirst, sex, or fear reduction. That is a possibility as yet unproved. Lending support to the idea, however, is an experiment in which fear evokes the bar-pressing habit for self-stimulation (Deutsch and Howarth, 1962). Rats were trained to press a bar for self-stimulation and then "extinguished" on this habit. After that, they were exposed to a frightening stimulus. This consisted either of a loud buzzer or, in some instances, of a loud buzzer that had been previously paired three or four times with shock. In many rats, this apparently frightening stimulus caused them to go to the lever and press it repeatedly or continuously even though they never again received any self-stimulation. This effect was fairly consistent in animals possessing electrodes in the tegmentum (see Figure 11.5) but rarely happened with hypothalamic electrodes, even though both locations were rewarding. Thus electrode placement is a factor in this effect. Nevertheless, it is of interest that animals resumed bar pressing merely because of the presence of a fearful stimulus. It is as though they expected to have their fears relieved by self-stimulation.

Other hints about the nature of the reward provided by self-stimulation come from studies of human beings in which electrodes have been implanted. In two cases, these studies are not very convincing because the subjects were severe psychotics not capable of communicating very satisfactorily (Heath, 1954; Bishop et al., 1963). In another study, patients suffering from Parkinson's disease were used (Sem-Jacobsen and Torkildsen, 1960). In exploring the brain, the investigators found several locations that seemed rewarding. Upon stimulation, the patients smiled or grinned and asked for more. Given an opportunity to press a button for stimulation, they did that too. When asked what it felt like, they said it "tickled" or "felt good." Apparently, the experience was not particularly clear-cut but was more like what some of us feel when we "feel real good today." This fits in with the idea derived from animal experiments that self-stimulation creates a temporary, satisfying feeling, but it is not like other drives in building up a deficit during deprivation.

ANATOMICAL LOCUS

Several studies have explored in varying degrees of thoroughness the placements in the brain that give either aversive or rewarding effects. Two relatively thorough investigations have been made on the rat (Olds et al., 1960) and the monkey (Lilly, 1958). The simplest way of determining whether a placement is aversive or rewarding is simply to see whether in a bar-pressing situation stimulation is "go" or "stop" (Lilly, 1958). That is to say, an animal that has been taught to press a bar for self-stimulation continues to press it if stimulation at a site is rewarding, but he immediately stops if it is aversive.

STIMULUS CONDITIONS—It is to be expected that the mapping of aversive and rewarding placements will depend on the characteristics of the electrical stimulus employed, and this is so. The frequency and the wave form of the stimulus make a difference, but within fairly wide limits it produces the same effect, either rewarding or aversive. Apparently, in the rat a frequency of 100 to 200 cycles per second is best for rewarding placements (Gengerelli

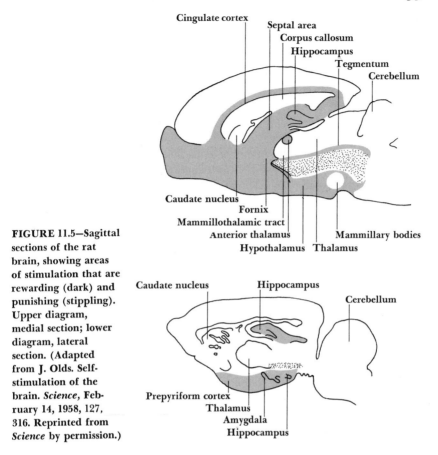

Cingulate cortex
Septal area
Corpus callosum
Hippocampus
Tegmentum
Cerebellum

Caudate nucleus
Fornix
Mammillothalamic tract
Anterior thalamus
Hypothalamus Thalamus
Mammillary bodies

Caudate nucleus
Hippocampus
Cerebellum

Prepyriform cortex
Thalamus
Amygdala
Hippocampus

FIGURE 11.5—Sagittal sections of the rat brain, showing areas of stimulation that are rewarding (dark) and punishing (stippling). Upper diagram, medial section; lower diagram, lateral section. (Adapted from J. Olds. Self-stimulation of the brain. *Science*, February 14, 1958, 127, 316. Reprinted from *Science* by permission.)

et al., 1960; Keesey, 1962), although many experimenters, for convenience, use the readily available 60-cycle current. Intensity, rather than frequency, is the more important variable, for in some sites the stronger the intensity, up to a certain point, the greater the responding, and in others, beyond a certain intensity, the rate of responding goes down (Olds, 1958). In some cases, high intensities become aversive, presumably by the spreading of current to aversive structures; again, in others, there is merely a reduction of responding, which may not mean any reduction in the reward value of stimulation (Reynolds, 1958).

The latter point is brought out in experiments in which animals may, in effect, choose the intensity by which they would like to be stimulated. This was accomplished in one experiment by providing two levers, one of which, when pushed, increased the current by a small step while the other reduced it by a small step (Stein and Ray, 1959). By alternating appropriately, the animals could keep the intensity at a relatively constant level. And they frequently did this. At some electrode placements, they did it rather poorly; at others, quite expertly. Another approach is to provide two levers but to have one intensity delivered by one lever, and another by the other lever (Hodos and Valenstein, 1962). In this case, it is interesting that animals frequently prefer an intensity at which their rate of responding is lower. This means that response rate, by itself, is not indicative of rewarding effect. Rather, the rat probably optimizes some overall physiological effect which may be a combination of intensity and frequency of reward.

AVERSIVE PLACEMENTS—The brains of both the rat (Olds et al., 1960) and the monkey (Lilly, 1958) have been systematically explored to find sites that are rewarding or aversive. In addition, aversive points in the cat's brain have been extensively plotted (Miller, 1958). The result of the study of the rat is illustrated in Figure 11.5 although some placements are not shown there. The rewarding placements shown will be discussed below. Some of the aversive placements are clearly in or near the sensory pathways and may represent activation of pain pathways. Others, however, are clearly out of the sensory system. In every instance, it is not understood from present knowledge of anatomy why the placement should be aversive. In others, however, emotional reactions seem to be involved; the animal appears to "experience" something like fear.

REWARDING PLACEMENTS—As is the case with the aversive placements, those having rewarding effects are spread liberally throughout the brain. There is no simple rule to explain all the sites that have been found to be rewarding. There are, however, a couple of general rules that will cover the majority of the placements. First, sensory and motor structures of the brain are not rewarding. Secondly, most rewarding sites are either in the limbic system or in structures closely associated with that system.

There seem to be two fairly distinct reward systems, one situated dorsally, the other ventrally (Olds et al., 1960). The dorsal system has its head in the region of the caudate nucleus and septum and then extends caudally through the dorsal part of the thalamus. The ventral system meets with the dorsal system at the anterior commissure extending downward to include the median forebrain bundle, the hypothalamus, the amygdala, the hippocampus, and the hypothalamus.

Throughout the two reward systems and even within the areas of the systems, there are differences in both the threshold for self-stimulation and the rate of responding. The two do not necessarily go together, for once the threshold is reached, the rate of responding may or may not be high. In general, very high rates are found in the septal area, amygdaloid complex, and anterior hypothalamus. Lower rates are found in the cingulate cortex, the hippocampus, anterior thalamus, and posterior hypothalamus.

REWARDING AND PUNISHING PLACEMENTS—As if life were not complicated enough, we must end this discussion by pointing out that in some locations brain stimulation may have both rewarding and punishing effects. This has been demonstrated in two cases in which identical electrodes delivering identical stimuli served either as reward or punishment.

In one experiment with cats (Brown and Cohen, 1959), the animals were taught two habits, one of approach and the other of avoidance. In an approach situation, the cats merely traversed a runway to receive brain stimulation at the end of the runway. This they learned to do. In the avoidance situation, they shuttled across a barrier in the middle of the box when they heard a buzzer, and if they did this in time, they were able to avoid brain stimulation. This they also learned to do. The electrodes in this experiment were in the lateral hypothalamus.

In a second study, the electrodes were located in the posterior hypothalamus of cats (Roberts, 1958), and two different experimental situations were employed. In one, the cats pushed a bar to turn on brain stimulation and performed a simple motor task to turn it off. They learned to do both: first to turn it on, then to turn it off. In the second experiment, a three-arm maze was employed. By oscillating back and forth between the arms, they could turn the stimulation on by going into one arm and turn it off by going into another one. This they learned to do. As the intensity of the stimulus was increased, they were more inclined to turn it off than to turn it on. On the other hand, the important point is that identical stimulation proved both rewarding and punishing. Why that should be so is not entirely clear unless in brain stimulation, as in other things in life, there can be "too much of a good thing."

BODILY CHANGES IN EMOTION

It has long been recognized that the autonomic system takes part in emotional reactions. In fact, autonomic effects, and the bodily changes brought about by them, were among the first physiological aspects of emotion to be carefully studied (Cannon, 1929). We shall consider these briefly. In recent years, attempts have been made to use certain autonomic effects as measures of emotional disturbance, conditioning, and personality. Also, attention has turned to the psychosomatic effects of continued emotional stress. We shall also review these topics briefly.

AUTONOMIC CHANGES

As the reader no doubt knows by now (page 29), the autonomic system has two principal divisions: the sympathetic and the parasympathetic. The sympathetic system is, in general, more diffuse in its effects than the parasympathetic; certain parasympathetic reflexes may occur without the involvement of other parts of the parasympathetic system, whereas the sympathetic system tends to discharge as a whole. The two systems are also usually antagonistic; the effect on an organ of one system is the opposite of the effect of the other. But this is an oversimplification, for in many instances the two work together in sequence or in a complementary fashion. Also, the balance of activities can swing in one direction or the other, the sympathetic being dominant or the parasympathetic being dominant. But, again, this statement tends to oversimplify the picture, for the activity of the two systems tends to be raised and lowered together. Hence, when one sees strong sympathetic activity, he may at the same time or within a short time interval see signs of strong parasympathetic activity.

INTENSE EMOTION—Most observations of autonomic effects have been made with intense emotions, usually of rage or fear. In intense emotion, the sympathetic system tends to dominate, so that most of the changes noted are sympathetic changes. Such changes may be summarized as follows:

Prominent changes take place in the gastrointestinal and urinary tracts. Salivation is restrained or stopped; hence dryness of the mouth is experienced in stage fright. Movement of the stomach, secretion of gastric juices, and peristaltic movements of the intestines are all inhibited. These effects together slow down digestion. The colon and bladder do not empty as easily as normally, and constipation may result. In some situations, however, when sympathetic effects have a rapid onset, there may be a brief compensatory outflow of parasympathetic impulses, giving rise to defecation and urination. The latter serve in tests with animals as measures of emotionality (see Lindzey, 1964).

Changes in the circulatory system also take place in strong emotion. Sympathetic impulses to the heart make it beat faster. They also cause constriction of the blood vessels of the gut and control blood flow in such a way as to direct more blood to brain and muscle. Speeding up the heart rate and constricting blood vessels at the same time make the blood pressure rise. On the other hand, a rapid rise in blood pressure can stimulate receptors for pressure in the carotid sinus, thereby bringing parasympathetic reflexes into play. Consequently, instead of increased pulse rate and blood pressure, both may suddenly fall and the heart may slow, sometimes to a standstill.

Other sympathetic effects that may be seen in strong emotion are as follows: The sweat glands may go into play; the "sweat" thus secreted helps dissipate heat generated by strenuous muscular activity and by increased metabolism. The muscles at the bases of the hair follicles contract, causing erection of hairs and "goose pimples." Profound changes in respiration may also take place, but these do not follow a set pattern. Gasps, catching of the breath, panting, and labored breathing are among the respiratory changes that may occur. Sympathetic impulses also dilate the bronchioles of the lungs, thus stepping up the exchange of oxygen and carbon dioxide. The pupils of the eyes dilate. And finally changes take place in the electrical resistance of the skin. The latter are closely associated with, but not identical with, sweat-gland activity.

Glandular changes also take place in strong emotion. In one way or another, several glands may be affected, but the most important changes take place in the adrenal gland. The medulla of this gland is directly innervated by the sympathetic system, and it discharges its secretions into the blood. These secretions, it will be recalled (page 94), are of two types: epinephrine and norepinephrine. Epinephrine has very general effects on various organs of the body, such as those directly affected by the sympathetic system. Thus, it is sympatheticomimetic. Norepinephrine has more restricted effects, the principal one being the contraction of small blood vessels that increases resistance to blood flow.

With prolonged emotional stress, the adrenal cortex and its hormones are also stimulated. In this case, however, there is no sympathetic innervation and the agent for its stimulation is itself glandular. Specifically, it is the adrenocorticotrophic hormone (ACTH) of the pituitary gland. And the pituitary is stimulated directly or indirectly by the activity of the hypothalamus. It is secretion of the adrenal cortex, brought about in this way, that is responsible for some of the psychosomatic effects discussed below.

AUTONOMIC MEASURES—Many of the autonomic changes just enumerated can be measured in the intact human or animal organism if appropriate apparatus is used. Even hormonal changes can be detected by appropriate assays of blood or urine or by using drugs known to counteract the effects of hormones. Measurements of autonomic changes have been employed for several purposes.

One is in an attempt to differentiate different emotions. If it were possible to tell what emotion an organism is experiencing, this would be interesting information about the physiology of emotion and also have practical applications. Earlier in this chapter we indicated that, in general, the pleasant emotions represent parasympathetic dominance and the unpleasant ones sympathetic dominance, but there are so many exceptions to the rule as to make it of little value. Since the so-called unpleasant emotions of fear and anger are marked by the various changes described above, there has usually been no way of distinguishing between them. There may, however, be one way of distinguishing physiologically between fear and anger. This is by means of the type of epinephrine secreted by the adrenal gland (Ax, 1953). Both epinephrine and norepinephrine raise blood pressure, but epinephrine does so by increasing the heart's pumping, whereas norepinephrine constricts blood vessels. By contriving situations in which subjects can be made either angry or fearful, it was shown that in anger a subject's reactions are like those induced by norepinephrine and in fear they are like those caused by epinephrine. Moreover, increases in blood pressure produced by the two hormones are affected differently by the drug mecholyl, a parasympathetic stimulant

(Funkenstein, 1955). When the pressure is increased by norepinephrine, mecholyl causes only a transient drop in pressure, but when it is increased by epinephrine the mecholyl drops the pressure markedly and keeps it down for several minutes. The implication of this work is that in anger the adrenal gland secretes mostly norepinephrine, whereas in fear it secretes mostly epinephrine.

Other uses for autonomic measures of emotion include any instances in which one wishes an indication of the presence of emotion. In lie detection, where the purpose is to measure a "guilty" emotional reaction, a battery of autonomic measures, which usually include respiration, blood pressure, and the galvanic skin response, is employed. The psychogalvanic response has been used in all sorts of psychological research as a measure of emotional conditioning or of emotional reactions to stimuli. Even a measure of pupil dilation has proved to be useful as an indicator of the "interest" value of various stimuli (Hess and Polt, 1960).

To be mentioned finally are autonomic measurements as and personality characteristics. In this role, such measurements have been found to correlate with many personality characteristics, including "frustration tolerance," recovery rate in psychotherapy, and the adequacy of various sensory and motor performances (see Lacey, 1956). The correlations are usually fairly low, however, because autonomic responses are relatively unstable and often relatively unreliable (Kaebling et al., 1960).

PSYCHOSOMATIC REACTIONS

For some years it has been recognized that emotional states, especially when they persist over long periods of time, can profoundly affect various organs of the body, sometimes directly damaging them and in others predisposing them to infection or to failure from precipitating causes (Dunbar, 1954). Since this book is not concerned with clinical and medical practice, we shall not go into such psychosomatic effects of emotions in any detail. We shall, however, mention briefly two topics on which there has been some considerable research. One is the general-adaptation syndrome of organisms in response to stress; the other is experimental work on psychogenic ulcers.

GENERAL-ADAPTATION SYNDROME—Some of the bodily changes that take place in emotion also occur in other kinds of stress: overwork, prolonged exposure to cold or heat, severe burns or pain, or the ravages of disease. The autonomic responses to all these, including emotion, are much the same. From a physiological point of view, they may all be considered reactions to stress. In fact, it has become customary to call a stress any condition that makes the body mobilize its resources and burn more energy than it normally does.

Three stages in the body's reaction to stress have been distinguished (Selye, 1950). Taken together, they are called the general-adaptation syndrome (see

Figure 11.6). The first stage, called the *alarm reaction,* consists of the typical bodily changes in emotion that we have reviewed above. If the stress continues for some time, however, an organism moves into a second stage called *resistance to stress.* In this stage, the organism recovers from its first burst of emergency reactions and endures the stress as best it can. Eventually, if the stress is severe and lasts long enough, a third stage of *exhaustion* is reached. In this stage, the organism may weaken and die.

The general-adaptation syndrome represents the organism's defense against stress. In making this defense, many complicated events take place that we shall not go into here (see Constantinides and Carey, 1949; or Selye, 1950). Chief among the events, however, is secretion of the adrenal gland. In this case, it is the cortex of the adrenal gland that is greatly involved. During the resistance stage, this part of the gland secretes much more than normal amounts of cortical hormones. This comes about through the pituitary hormone ACTH (see above and page 93). Animals kept under continued stress have greatly enlarged adrenal glands. Excessive cortical secretion may cause or aggravate such diseases as hypertension and heart disorder. In the later stages of the syndrome, when resources are exhausted, cortical secretions fall below normal, thus causing or aggravating such diseases as rheumatism and arthritis. These statements about disease come from medical experience, but the physiological reactions to stress have been established in the laboratory with such subjects as rats.

PSYCHOGENIC ULCERS—Among the disorders linked to emotional stress is the production of gastric and duodenal ulcers (Dunbar, 1954; Selye, 1950). It is a disorder that can be produced in experimental animals in a variety of ways, including drug and hormone administration and both lesions and stimulation

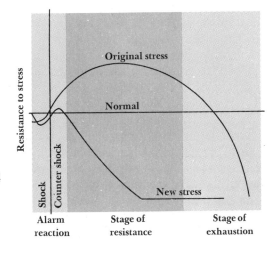

FIGURE 11.6—The general-adaptation syndrome. (Adapted from H. Selye. *The physiology and pathology of exposure to stress.* Montreal: Acta, Inc., 1950.)

of the hypothalamus. Of great interest to us here is the production of ulcers through psychological stress involving autonomic reactions.

Gastrointestinal ulcers are erosions of the mucosa of the stomach and intestine. They are produced by some combination of acid, pepsin (digestive enzyme), and the abrasive action of substances in the stomach. Other things being equal, the greater the production of acid in the stomach, the greater the chances of ulcerative lesions.

Several attempts to produce ulcers by psychological means involving conflict, emotion, and stress have failed; we shall not go into them. In 1956, however, there was the first report of the experimental production of gastric ulcers in rats by such means (Sawrey and Weiss, 1956; Sawrey et al., 1956). To accomplish this, rats were maintained for thirty days in a conflict box. The box was so designed that an electrically charged grill had to be crossed at one end to obtain water and a similar grill had to be crossed at the other end to obtain food. In the center was an uncharged grill. The animals were deprived of food and water for forty-seven hours and then allowed access to them under conflict conditions for one hour. Control animals were maintained in a similar box except that there was no shock, and food and water were available at all times. Under the severest of conditions, 76 percent of the animals developed gastric ulcers, whereas none of the controls had ulcers.

Experimental psychogenic ulcers have also been reported in the monkey (Porter et al., 1958). The experimental monkeys, restrained in a chair, were required to push a bar every twenty seconds in order not to be shocked; they had to do this for a period of six hours. After six hours rest, they were again required to perform in the avoidance conditioning situation for six hours, and so on. Control monkeys were subjected to all the same conditions including being shocked whenever the experimental monkey failed to push his button, but they did not have the button "to worry about." Two experimental monkeys developed ulcers while their controls did not.

Subsequently the procedure was changed to require the experimental monkeys to perform in the shock-avoidance situation for eighteen hours straight, rather than six "on" and six "off" (Brady et al., 1958). These monkeys, surprisingly, never developed ulcers. The investigators then concluded that in order for ulcers to develop the stress schedule needed to be intermittent. In this conclusion they were bolstered by measurements made of stomach acidity during the six-on six-off schedule and found that most of the acid production occurred during the "off" period as a kind of rebound effect from the stress during the "on" period. Another possible interpretation is that the experimental monkeys in the first study got their ulcers from causes unbeknown to the investigators, and it was simply luck that they developed in animals on the avoidance procedure.

In any case, even if results cannot always be duplicated, it seems clear that psychogenic ulcers can be experimentally produced in animals as a result of some kind of emotional stress.

12 SLEEP, AROUSAL, AND ACTIVITY

As THE TITLE OF THIS CHAPTER indicates, it is concerned with sleep and waking, alerting and attention, and general bodily activity. At first glance, these may seem to be unrelated topics, and for many years they were indeed thought to be so. Recent research, however, has tied them together to the extent that certain physiological mechanisms, particularly the reticular system, underlie all of them. Hence, they are treated together here. We shall begin with sleep, proceed to alerting and attention, and end with general bodily activity.

CHARACTERISTICS OF SLEEP

Organisms that are asleep differ from those that are awake in several ways (see Kleitman, 1963). Among them are the following: (*1*) Somatic activity is greatly reduced;

(2) thresholds of many reflexes are increased and responsiveness to most sorts of stimulation is lessened; (3) in man, consciousness is lost so that the organism is unaware of stimulation and unable to remember events occurring during sleep; and (4) the sleeping organism, as distinguished from one in a pathological state due to drugs, coma, or head injuries, can be aroused by strong sensory stimulation.

SOMATIC ACTIVITY

There are two conspicuous changes in behavior that are signs of an organism going to sleep: (1) The muscles supporting the body relax and the organism usually lies down; (2) there is a marked tendency for the eyes to close. Both of these somatic changes are commonly taken as signs of sleep or sleepiness. Both represent the elimination of major sources of afferent impulses that otherwise tend to keep the organism awake.

Once asleep, the organism remains relatively quiet, but somatic activity is not entirely absent. In fact, during sleep there are frequent bursts of activity interspersed among the periods of quiet. The average period of uninterrupted rest is only a few minutes. In relatively "restless" sleepers, some change in body position takes place every five to ten minutes; in others, the changes may occur only every twenty to twenty-five minutes.

AUTONOMIC ACTIVITY

In contrast to somatic activity, autonomic activity goes on whether one is sleeping or not, but there are some definite changes in autonomic activity accompanying sleep: (1) Heart rate is significantly reduced, in some cases by as much as 20 or 30 beats a minute. This shift, however, is about the same as occurs under conditions of muscular relaxation, as are the other autonomic changes in sleep. (2) Blood pressure also tends to go down in sleep by 20 or 30 millimeters. Usually blood pressure reaches a minimum in about the fourth hour of sleep, rising somewhat afterward and jumping up abruptly upon waking. (3) Respiration is somewhat slower, and its depth is greater in sleep than in waking, but the chief change is in its greater regularity. (4) Body temperature is lower during sleep than during waking. This lowering is part of a twenty-four-hour cycle in which the peak reached in the states of greatest arousal may be a degree or more higher than the minimum hit during deep sleep. (5) Gastric contractions and alimentary activity go on as usual, if not with somewhat greater vigor.

These various autonomic changes appear not to be caused by sleep per se. Rather, they are the same changes that can be observed while an organism is resting for a prolonged period of time without going to sleep. They represent a lowering of energy requirements during rest and inactivity.

REFLEX EXCITABILITY

In general, it is harder to elicit reflexes during sleep than in the waking state. This characteristic of sleep, however, does not apply equally well to all reflexes. While the threshold for eliciting proprioceptive reflexes is heightened, the cutaneous reflexes are nearly normal. The knee jerk, for example, disappears as one goes to sleep; this is a kinesthetic reflex elicited by sudden stimulation of the Golgi tendon organs (Chapter 9). Cutaneous stimulation, on the other hand, seems to bring out a rather normal response. Brushing the face produces a grimace, for example, or tickling stimuli may elicit scratching movements.

ELECTRICAL ACTIVITY

No aspect of sleep has been studied more thoroughly than the changes that take place in the electroencephalogram (EEG). Different stages in both waking and sleep are reflected in the EEG, and this fact permits the use of the EEG as an objective indicator of a person's state. He may feign sleep or protest that he is not sleepy, but his EEG can tell the investigator what the truth is.

EEG records taken from the human skull during various states from an excited waking state to deep sleep may differ in three respects: the amplitude (voltage) of the recorded waves; their frequency; and the regularity (synchronization) or irregularity in frequency (see Figure 12.1). For the present, we shall be concerned only with the changes taking place between relaxed wakefulness and deep sleep. The stages involved have been labeled somewhat differently by different investigators (see Lindsley, 1960), but there is good general agreement on what happens (see Figures 12.1 and 12.2).

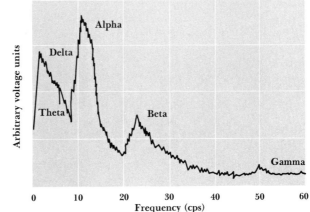

FIGURE 12.1—The frequency spectrum of electroencephalograms (EEGs).

In relaxed wakefulness, the record is likely to consist mainly of synchronized *alpha* waves of moderate voltage; in man, these are about 10 per second. The appearance of regular alpha waves in the record is a good sign the person is awake. As the person becomes drowsy, the amplitude of the alpha waves is reduced, and occasional low-amplitude slow waves, known as *delta* waves, are seen. This is sometimes referred to as the *low-voltage irregular* pattern. In light sleep, the alpha waves disappear, the slow waves (delta waves of 1 to 4 per second) become larger; in addition, *spindle* bursts of about 14 per second appear. The appearance of spindles is usually a good sign that the person is in light sleep. During the course of the first hour or so after going to sleep, the sleep becomes deeper. In deep sleep, the spindle bursts disappear, and the record is characterized by trains of large and very slow (delta) waves.

In recent years, another neurophysiologically unique phase of sleep has been discovered (Aserinsky and Kleitman, 1953). This occurs during a normal night of sleep about every 1½ to 2 hours after going to sleep. From only the EEG record, this phase might be mistaken for that of drowsiness, for the record looks very much like the one seen as a person is going to sleep.

There are, however, important differences between this state and drowsiness. For this reason, it is sometimes referred to as "paradoxical sleep." One difference is the appearance of rapid eye movements since these may be ob-

FIGURE 12.2—EEG records for different stages of sleep and wakefulness. (Adapted from H. H. Jasper. In W. Penfield and T. C. Erickson (Eds.), *Epilepsy and cerebral localization.* Springfield, Ill.: Charles C Thomas, 1941. Courtesy Charles C Thomas.)

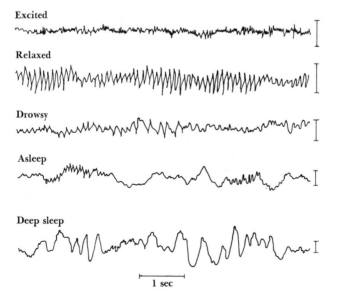

Excited

Relaxed

Drowsy

Asleep

Deep sleep

1 sec

jectively recorded; this stage of sleep has also been termed the REM (for rapid eye movements) stage. In addition, during this stage, if the person is awakened he is very likely to report dreaming activity (Dement and Kleitman, 1957). In fact, dreaming is highly correlated with the REM stage. At the same time, the person is more difficult to arouse in this stage than he is in the slow-wave phase of deeper sleep. Hence, this is not merely the awakening of the sleeper. The general conclusion is that the REM stage differs from the other stages in that the cerebral cortex is more active than in deep sleep, but at the same time thresholds for sensory stimuli are as high as they are in deep sleep (Williams et al., 1962).

DEPTH OF SLEEP

One of the advantages of using the EEG to study sleep is that it does not disturb the sleeper. To a certain extent, as we have seen, it can indicate the stage of sleep of the person (also see Lester, 1958). It does not, however, tell the whole story. Another method, used extensively before the EEG came into general use, was to determine the depth of sleep by finding the intensity of a stimulus required to awake a person, or at least to arouse him (Kleitman, 1963). An auditory stimulus was most commonly used for this purpose.

When auditory thresholds of arousal are used to measure the depth of sleep, it is found that the depth of sleep is not uniform throughout a night of sleep or even for very long periods (see Figure 12.3). Instead, a person passes cyclically through stages of deep and light sleep. These cycles are likely to be around ten to thirty minutes in length, but they vary greatly from one individual to another and even from one night to another for the same individual. No statistical generalizations are particularly meaningful. The point, however, is that the depth of sleep continually varies.

FIGURE 12.3—Diagram of the way in which the depth of sleep varies throughout a night of sleep, as measured by the intensity of sound required to wake the individual. (Adapted from N. Kleitman. *Sleep and wakefulness.* Chicago: University of Chicago Press, 1939. P. 146. By permission of the publishers.)

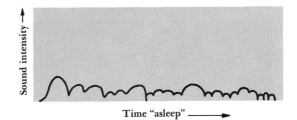

SLEEP RHYTHMS

Most adult human beings take their sleep in one long daily period. They did not, however, start life this way. As we all know, babies begin life taking their sleep in five to seven periods a day, each consisting of three or four hours of sleep. Otherwise said, the human adult is *monophasic* and the infant is *polyphasic*. During the first few months of life, human infants gradually change from a polyphasic to a monophasic pattern, although the transition is not complete until the afternoon nap is finally dropped at nursery school age (see Figure 12.4).

Some animals are monophasic and others polyphasic. Rats, rabbits, and most rodents are polyphasic. Canaries, snakes, and man are monophasic. The difference lies largely in the degree to which activity is controlled by the light-darkness cycle. Organisms that are very active in the light and live in such a way that they are well exposed to light tend to be monophasic; those that live in burrows or readily hide from the light tend to be polyphasic. This generalization, however, has many exceptions. Other factors, such as the availability of food and the temperature of the environment, also play a part.

KINDS OF WAKEFULNESS

Some years ago, Kleitman (1939) assembling the facts then available on sleep, including those summarized in the two preceding sections, proposed what he called an evolutionary theory of sleep. He called it "evolutionary" because he regarded patterns of sleeping and waking as depending on the evolutionary development of the cerebral cortex, particularly in mammals. He distinguished between a *wakefulness of necessity*, depending in all animals on afferent stimulation, and a *wakefulness of choice*, depending on the cerebral cortex. It turns out that Kleitman's distinctions fit well with more recent neurophysiological data to be described below (see Kleitman, 1963).

Wakefulness of necessity is characterized by the polyphasic alternation of sleep and wakefulness seen in the decorticate dog (see below), the newborn human, and many types of primitive animals. Whenever such an organism is relatively free from the barrage of afferent impulses arising from stimuli in the external world or from its own muscular activity, the activity of sub-cortical structures concerned in wakefulness is reduced. But when stimuli arise from the distension of the bladder, gastric contractions, or disturbances in the external world, these structures are excited and the organism is aroused from sleep. When it relaxes and escapes the external stimuli, the flow of afferent impulses is reduced. And so it goes in alternating cycles of sleep and wakefulness.

In the animal with a more highly developed cortex, the alternation of sleep and wakefulness becomes a joint function of subcortical and cortical structures. Wakefulness of necessity is maintained subcortically, but super-

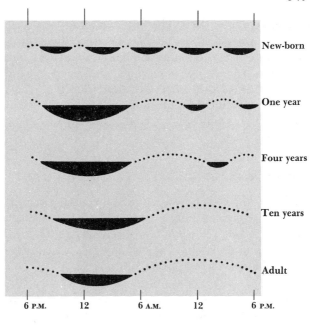

FIGURE 12.4—
Diagram illustrating
the cycles of sleep
and the change from
polyphasic to mono-
phasic sleep from
birth to adulthood.
(Adapted from
N. Kleitman. *Sleep
and wakefulness.*
Chicago: University
of Chicago Press,
1939. P. 515. By
permission of the
publishers.)

imposed on it is a wakefulness of choice maintained by the direct or indirect effects of cortical activity on subcortical waking mechanisms. Such cortical activity, Kleitman suggested, is largely determined by the learned and unlearned adjustments of the animal to the light-dark cycle of the world. In this way, sleep may be postponed and a monophasic rhythm of sleep and wakefulness may be developed in which the animal sleeps during the night and remains awake during the daytime.

Once the monophasic cycle is set up, it becomes a bona fide rhythm of the brain. It goes on whether or not the individual sleeps. In extensive studies of prolonged wakefulness (Kleitman, 1963), it was found that every aspect of the rhythm keeps up for considerable periods of time. Body temperature and activity, for example, drop at night and go up in the daytime. A subject is more awake on the third afternoon of prolonged wakefulness than he is on the second night. Thus, the sleep mechanism possesses periodicity even when wakefulness is forcibly extended far over the normal period.

NEURAL MECHANISMS OF SLEEP AND WAKING

Until twenty years ago, there were many different theories of sleep, none of which very satisfactorily encompassed all the facts. Some theorists were inclined toward a chemical theory of sleep in which some substance (hypnotoxin) was assumed to cause sleep by accumulating during waking hours and dissipating during sleep. The finger was first pointed clearly at brain rhythms and away from chemical mechanisms when it was demonstrated that siamese twins possessing two brains, as well as animals in which crossed circulation had been established, may sleep quite independently (Kleitman, 1939). Later research has made it reasonably clear what the brain mechanisms are. The principal structure concerned in waking is the reticular activating system (RAS). This point will be brought out by describing the roles of various brain structures.

CEREBRAL CORTEX

Studies of the cerebral cortex in both dogs and human beings make it clear that the cerebral cortex is responsible for monophasic sleep cycles or, in Kleitman's terms, the wakefulness of choice (see Kleitman and Camille, 1932; Kleitman, 1952). The evidence comes from the sleep and waking behavior of decorticate organisms.

Although adult normal dogs do some napping, their sleep patterns are generally like those of human beings; they are primarily monophasic. As puppies, they are like human infants; they are polyphasic. When deprived of their cerebral cortex, they revert to the sleep patterns of puppyhood, waking up occasionally to be fed or to take care of other bodily needs, then quickly going back to sleep (see Figure 12.4). Occasionally a decorticate human infant is born and survives for a year or two. Such infants follow the typical polyphasic cycle throughout their lives, never developing a monophasic cycle. Hence, it is concluded that the cerebral cortex in mammals such as the dog and man is necessary for the development of monophasic wakefulness of choice.

HYPOTHALAMUS

The facts just described were known in the 1930s. They pointed to some subcortical structure as being responsible for the wakefulness of necessity as distinguished from the wakefulness of choice. Clinical evidence at the time appeared to point toward the hypothalamus as the probable subcortical structure concerned in polyphasic sleep and waking. Tumors and inflammations in the region of the hypothalamus were commonly associated with abnormal tendencies to sleep (somnolence). In many of these cases, however, damage to the nervous system was extensive and usually involved parts of the brain other than the hypothalamus. More precise experimental work in animals seemed to be the next logical step.

Lesions were made in a number of regions of the thalamus and hypothalamus of monkeys (Ranson, 1939). The thalamus appeared not to be concerned, for even rather extensive bilateral destruction of the thalamus caused no disturbance of normal sleep and wakefulness. On the other hand, if the lesions were restricted to the posterior part of the hypothalamus, profound somnolence resulted. Monkeys with such a lesion slept almost continuously for four to eight days after operation and showed marked drowsiness for several months. At all times, they could be aroused by strong sensory stimulation, but immediately afterward they fell asleep again. Lesions in the more anterior portions of the hypothalamus failed to produce somnolence. Because wakefulness seemed to depend so crucially on the integrity of the posterior hypothalamus, this area was designated as a *waking center*.

Essentially the same findings were later duplicated in the rat except that, in addition, a *sleep center* lying more anteriorly in the hypothalamus was also discovered (Nauta, 1946). Control lesions in subcortical nuclei other than those of the hypothalamus had no effect on sleep. As in the earlier study of the monkey, bilateral lesions in the immediate vicinity of the mammillary bodies, however, produced profound sleep from which animals could be aroused only by intense stimuli.

In other animals suffering from bilateral lesions of the anterior hypothalamus, animals stayed awake continuously. Upon recovering from the operation, they were normally active, ate and drank voluntarily, and maintained normal body temperature. But they were never observed to sleep. After twenty-four hours, these rats began to show signs of fatigue. Their gait became unsteady and they would no longer eat or drink. In about three days they fell into a state of coma, from which they could not be aroused, and died shortly thereafter.

On the basis of these results, it was concluded that there is both a waking center in the posterior hypothalamus and a sleep center in the anterior hypothalamus. The finding of an anterior sleep center has not, however, been duplicated in other animals.

There have been experiments in which the hypothalamus has been stimulated, but the results have been conflicting. On the one hand, stimulation in the posterior hypothalamus was observed to induce sleep (Hess, 1929), whereas stimulation in the same regions not only has failed to produce sleep but has caused activity and excitement (1954). On the basis of what is now known (see below), the latter result is the more plausible, but the results obtained with stimulation depend on many characteristics of the stimulating current, and it is not uncommon for different results to be obtained in different experiments.

The one fact indicated by research on the hypothalamus is that there is a region in the posterior hypothalamus whose destruction causes sleep or somnolence. This is quite probably only part of a larger system controlling waking.

RETICULAR ACTIVATING SYSTEM

At the time of the experiments on decortication and the hypothalamus, the significance of the reticular formation of the brain stem was not known. Earlier (Bremer, 1935), it had been observed that decerebration at the midbrain level caused profound somnolence accompanied by a conversion of the normal cortical EEG pattern to one of sleep. At the time, the effect of transecting the brain stem was thought to be due to deafferentation, that is, to cutting the pathways of the specific sensory systems. Later it was shown (Lindsley et al., 1950) that cutting this system, leaving other midbrain pathways intact, had no such effect. Animals deprived of specific classical sensory pathways sleep and wake just as normal animals do. Rather, the somnolence produced by midbrain transection is related to the ascending portion of the reticular activating system (RAS).

The discovery of the importance of this system took place in two related steps, one electrocortical and the other behavioral. First, it was shown that electrical stimulation of the reticular formation caused "activation" of the cortical EEG (Moruzzi and Magoun, 1949). With such stimulation in the waking cat, the resting synchronized waves characteristic of relaxed wakefulness gave way to fast low-voltage activity or flattened EEG. This change in the EEG is variously called *activation, desynchronization,* or *arousal.* It also occurred when a new stimulus was presented to the animal or when it was aroused from a state of relaxed wakefulness. This result implied that the RAS was responsible for wakefulness.

This implication was confirmed by behavioral studies during stimulation or following lesions made in the reticular formation (Lindsley et al., 1950). The same stimulation that caused the activation pattern in the EEG also aroused a sleeping cat. Similar studies in the monkey (Segundo et al., 1955) also demonstrated that sleeping animals are readily awakened by reticular stimulation. On the other hand, lesions in the reticular formation that interrupt the RAS caused both the electrocortical and behavioral signs of somnolence. There have now been dozens of studies in various animals replicating these findings, and there can be little doubt that the reticular formation is the principal *waking center* of the brain.

At this point, one may ask whether there are two sets of waking centers, one in the hypothalamus and the other in the brain stem. There are slightly different views on this matter, one attributing more importance to the hypothalamus (Gellhorn, 1957) and the other stressing the reticular formation (Lindsley, 1960). However, the important anatomical fact is that the posterior hypothalamic area is so closely linked with the reticular formation that a part of it actually is considered to constitute one extension of the reticular formation. There undoubtedly are some differences in function between the hypothalamic and brain-stem portions of the RAS. In any event, the plausible view is that the two together form one waking center (Lindsley, 1960).

THALAMUS

Closely related to the brain-stem RAS is a group of nuclei in the thalamus which project diffusely to the cerebral cortex (see page 42). Sometimes this is referred to as the thalamic extension of the reticular formation, but since it has some properties that are different from those of the brain-stem RAS, it is frequently referred to separately as the diffuse thalamic projection system (DTPS). The essential facts about the DTPS are as follows:

Electrical stimulation of the DTPS at frequencies of 6 to 12 per second gives rise to a so-called *recruiting response* in several areas of the cortex (Morison and Dempsey, 1942). Each stimulating shock causes a response in the cortex, but as the shocks are repeated, the size of the response increases over the three or four stimulations. It is the increasing size of the cortical response that has been given the name recruiting.

In regard to activation and arousal, stimulation of the DTPS can cause both, just as RAS stimulation does (see Lindsley, 1960). However, the effect is more transient or less persisting than the RAS stimulation. Moreover, the effect seems to depend on the frequency of stimulation. High-frequency stimulation gives rise to cortical arousal responses, but if the frequency of electrical stimulation is much lower it may have just the opposite effect, namely, induce sleep (Akert et al., 1952).

The activating effect of the RAS appears stronger than, and takes precedence over, that of the DTPS. When the latter is destroyed or cut off from the cortex, stimulation of the RAS still causes a cortical arousal reaction.

The RAS and DTPS are differently affected by hormones and anesthetics. The barbiturate anesthetics, for example, greatly affect the RAS while not blocking the DTPS. In fact, the sleep induced by barbiturates is largely, if not exclusively, caused by their action on the RAS. On the other hand, the upper midbrain portion of the RAS is sensitive to the hormone epinephrine, whereas the DTPS is not. Indeed, the general arousal or activating effect of epinephrine is due as much to this specific stimulation of the RAS as it is to the peripheral effects of the hormone (Courville et al., 1962).

Aside from these differences, the exact relation of the DTPS to the RAS is not entirely clear. The best summary seems to be that the RAS provides a basic, general mechanism of arousal, determining persisting states of sleep and waking, whereas the DTPS is an accessory mechanism that participates in more transient increases in arousal and attention. In the words we have used to describe parallel differences in motor activities (page 287), the brain-stem RAS has longer-lasting *tonic* functions, whereas the DTPS has more *phasic* functions.

CORTICAL FEEDBACK

This story of the neural mechanisms of sleep and waking comes to an end just where it started, namely, with the cerebral cortex. At the beginning, we pointed out that the cerebral cortex provides a monophasic wakefulness of choice. Now we have seen that the polyphasic wakefulness of necessity, the basic waking mechanism, is seated in the brain stem and thalamic reticular system.

As pointed out elsewhere, the RAS constitutes an indirect sensory pathway to the cortex. It is activated by sensory stimuli, and the resulting wakefulness is a wakefulness of necessity. It is also activated by downward cortical projections. In other words, there is cortical feedback to the RAS (see Samuels, 1959). Hence a circuit exists in which the RAS activates the cortex and the cortex may activate the RAS. This mechanism is a suitable one for imposing a wakefulness of choice on one of necessity. For example, when we cannot sleep nights because something is on "our mind," cortical activity is feeding back to the RAS.

ALERTING AND ATTENTION

The picture that has emerged from research on the RAS is that this system not only provides a persistent waking mechanism but also functions during the waking state as a means of temporarily increasing the activation of the cortex. It would appear that there are two routes to the cortex, the direct and indirect, and that the indirect pathway alerts or prepares the way for messages arriving over the direct pathway. In this section, some experiments testing this point of view will be described. There are also scattered observations of the facilitation or inhibition of units at various points in the nervous system caused by alerting or attention-getting situations. These also will be described.

ALERTING AND REACTION TIME

One experiment with monkeys correlates reaction time with activation of the EEG. As has been described elsewhere (Chapters 3 and 16), the onset of almost any stimulus causes alpha blocking. This is another name for an EEG activation pattern in which the alpha rhythm that is characteristic of relaxed wakefulness is desynchronized into a fast low-voltage pattern. If activation of the cortex is a prerequisite to the prompt processing of information at the cortical level, the activation pattern should correlate with other behavioral measures of arousal. One that has been studied is reaction time (Lansing et al., 1959).

Monkeys were trained to make a response as rapidly as possible after the onset of a visual stimulus. Their reaction time in this case averaged about 280 milliseconds. Then an auditory stimulus was introduced as a ready or forewarning signal, and the interval between it and the onset of the visual stimulus was varied. At the same time, EEG records were taken. As was to be expected, the auditory stimulus caused alpha blocking, but this too had a reaction time (see Figure 12.5). As the interval between the auditory ready signal and the visual stimulus was lengthened, up to a point, the reaction time of both alpha blocking and of the overt response decreased. After about 300 milliseconds, however, lengthening the interval made little additional difference in either. The important point was that the curves of alpha block-

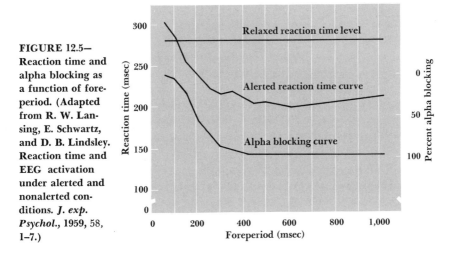

FIGURE 12.5—Reaction time and alpha blocking as a function of foreperiod. (Adapted from R. W. Lansing, E. Schwartz, and D. B. Lindsley. Reaction time and EEG activation under alerted and nonalerted conditions. *J. exp. Psychol.*, 1959, 58, 1–7.)

ing and of reaction time as a function of the ready interval looked very much alike. By inference, the activation seen in alpha blocking was responsible for the decreased reaction time.

In a related experiment, monkeys were trained to make a visual discrimination with tachistoscopic illumination of the objects (Fuster, 1958). After a brief flash in which the animals could see two stimuli, they were required to make a discrimination between them as rapidly as possible. As might be expected, the longer the flash, the better the performance of the monkey. In this case, however, the monkey carried indwelling electrodes in its reticular formation. Through these, the reticular formation was stimulated while the monkey was performing the visual discrimination. As seen in Figure 12.6, the monkey performed consistently better during reticular stimulation than it did otherwise. Again, the effect appeared to be due to the alerting or activating influence of the RAS.

There are other experiments correlating changes in the EEG with some aspect of perception. Among them is one on time perception and alpha voltage (Anliker, 1963). In this study, subjects were asked to push a key every three seconds, and the time between responses was used as a measure of time perception. When subjects were alert, as indicated by a high percentage of alpha waves in their EEG, their interresponse time was relatively constant. On the other hand, as the subjects became drowsy, their interresponse intervals lengthened and, at the same time, the percentage of alpha waves in the EEG decreased.

ATTENTION AND THE EEG

There are other experiments in which changes in attention have been correlated with changes in the EEG. Some of these involve conditioning procedures and will be described in the chapter on conditioning (Chapter 16).

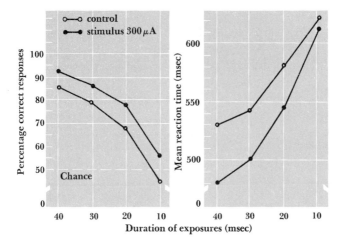

FIGURE 12.6—Percentage of correct responses and mean reaction times for exposures of different duration during electrical stimulation of the reticular formation as compared with control conditions. (Adapted from J. M. Fuster. Effects of stimulation of brain stem on tachistoscopic perception. *Science*, January 17, 1958, 127, 150. Adapted from *Science* by permission.)

The interpretation of these experiments is not very clear, but they would appear to reflect differences in alerting, orientation, or attention that occur in different phases of conditioning. Here two additional experiments will be described.

In one, EEG records were taken from the occipital cortex of the human adult (Jouvet, 1957). At the same time, the subject was exposed to repeated flashes of light. In this situation, each flash evokes a fairly complicated cortical EEG response. From this response, a trained observer can infer what is going on in the optic radiations leading up to the cortex and in the occipital cortex itself. In one part of the experiment, the EEG responses occurring during a state of relaxed wakefulness were compared with those obtained when the subject was instructed to attend to the flashes and to count them. There was a marked increase in the size of the responses in the optic radiation when the subject was attending. On the other hand, when distracting stimuli were presented to the subject, the responses in the optic radiation were drastically reduced. In short, attention to the visual stimulus enhanced signals coming to the visual cortex while attention to stimuli in other modalities reduced their strength.

There is a counterpart to this study in an experiment on the reticular formation and the lateral geniculate nucleus (Ogawa, 1963). With the aid of microelectrodes, records were taken from signal neurons in the lateral geniculate nucleus (LGN) during stimulation with a flickering light and during no stimulation at all. Then, the effect of electrical stimulation of the RAS was studied. The effect was clear. If a neuron was spontaneously firing, RAS activation caused an increase in the spontaneous firing rate. If the neuron was responding to a flickering light, the RAS stimulation considerably enhanced the number of impulses elicited by the flashes. Thus, RAS activation clearly augmented activity in LGN neurons that give rise to the optic radiations leading to the visual cortex.

SENSORY PATHWAYS

Comparable data have been obtained by electrodes implanted in structures "down the line" in sensory pathways. One of the first demonstrations of the role of attention in neural response was made with indwelling electrodes in the cochlear nucleus (Hernandez-Peón et al., 1956). When a cat prepared in this way is first exposed to repeated auditory clicks, there are good evoked potentials to these clicks. Presumably the animal is "paying attention." However, when a mouse is introduced in the cage—a fine attention-getting stimulus for the cat—the response to the clicks is greatly suppressed. So are they when other distracting stimuli such as odors or painful stimuli are presented. Hence the response in the auditory system, even at this low level, depends on the "attention" of the animal.

The opposite observation has been made from electrodes in the olfactory bulb of the cat (Lavín et al., 1959). In this case, almost any sensory stimulus, not necessarily olfactory, caused bursts of rhythmic activity in the olfactory-bulb record. These bursts were greater when the cat was more alert than relaxed. However, this result may be an artifact, for one of the things cats do when alerted is breathe more vigorously. It may be that activity in the olfactory bulb simply reflects respiratory responses under conditions of alerting (Gault and Leaton, 1963).

CORTICAL "ATTENTION" UNITS

One further example of the dependence of cortical activity on attention will be described (Hubel et al., 1959). Several investigators, using microelectrodes, have found neural units in the sensory areas of the cortex that are unresponsive to appropriate sensory stimuli. One can wonder why they are there. In one case, when such units of the auditory cortex had been isolated, many of the units responded only when the animal appeared to be "paying attention." What is "paying attention" is hard to define, but these units responded only when the experimenter, say, spoke sharply, made squeaks with a rubber mouse, scratched his fingernail on a nearby table, hissed, or tapped the table. The units did not respond to the regular presentation of a click normally used to study individual neurons in the auditory system.

From these various experiments, it may be concluded that activity at various points in sensory systems depends, not merely on the characteristics of the stimuli used, but also on the level of alerting and on the state of attention of the subject. It remains to be determined just what pathways are involved and what attention is in neurophysiological terms.

ACTIVITY

We turn now in this final section to the general bodily activity of the organism (see Roeder, 1955). During its waking hours, an organism may engage in a great variety of activities, such as exploring, sniffing, scratching, looking, and chasing things. For purposes of measurement, however, most of this activity may be categorized either as *locomotor activity* or as *restlessness*.

In locomotor activity, the animal goes somewhere, moving from one position in space to another. This kind of activity is the one most often measured, and it is usually measured with some kind of running wheel in which progression of the animal makes the wheel move and a counter attached to the wheel records the amount of such movement (see Young and Spector, 1957).

Restlessness is activity in which movements are made, but the animal does not walk any appreciable distance. Such activity is measured by a stabilimeter or "jiggle cage." This is a platform that will jiggle with any small movement of the animal, and by pneumatic or electronic means the jiggling is recorded.

The two kinds of measurements overlap, but the running wheel does not record much of the restless activity, and a jiggle cage distinguishes poorly or not at all the locomotor from restless activity. In general, the two kinds of activity are correlated; an animal that is highly active in a locomotor sense is also restless. There are, however, instances, for example, certain cases of poor nutrition, in which the animal may be quite restless but is at the same time low in locomotor activity. In most of the discussion that follows, locomotor activity is being measured unless statements to the contrary are made.

ACTIVITY RHYTHMS

One of the characteristics of activity recorded in revolving wheels is the regular variation in the amount of activity an animal displays over a period of time. In other words, activity characteristically occurs in rhythms. And there is not just one rhythm; rather, there are several rhythms superimposed on each other. Each of these rhythms has a different cause, either in internal physiological conditions or in stimulating factors of the environment. In the case of the rat, four different factors have been identified: hunger, light, temperature, and gonadal secretions.

HUNGER—Bodily activity and hunger are closely related. Rats, if allowed to eat freely, display rather regular rhythms of activity and feeding, which occur, on an average, about every four hours (Richter, 1927). The activity almost always begins first, and only after it has continued for some minutes does eating take place. Thereafter, activity soon ceases. This rhythm is the polyphasic rhythm of sleep and wakefulness described above. Wakefulness in such a rhythm is the "wakefulness of necessity," and the necessity has to do with hunger, feeding, and taking care of other biological urges.

LIGHT—Under conditions of natural lighting, many animals show regular daily fluctuations in activity as the environment changes from light to dark. This is true even though the basic sleep-wakefulness rhythm may remain polyphasic. Such cyclical variations are clearly seen in the rat, which is a nocturnal animal and displays about 70 percent of its activity in the dark. Rats distribute their activity in the same way under artificial-lighting schedules, even if these deviate widely from natural conditions (Browman, 1942). Birds and other diurnal organisms sleep during dark periods and are most active during daylight hours. In any case, the activity of most birds and mammals is closely correlated with light-dark cycles.

TEMPERATURE—Although light is the most important factor in maintaining daily activity rhythms, environmental temperature may also play a role. By arranging a regular schedule of alternating warm and cool periods, one can induce rhythms of activity in blinded rats (Browman, 1944). In general, animals are most active during cool periods and less active during warm ones. This generalization, however, depends on the temperatures, and it varies with the animal. If the temperature becomes too cold, nearly all animals try to find a place where they can get warm and then will remain quiet in it.

SEXUAL DRIVE—Gross bodily activity is also related in some cases to sexual drive. The female rat, for example, has a sexual cycle in which ovulation and sexual receptivity occur rather regularly at four- to five-day intervals. Correlated with this cycle is a prominent rhythm of somatic activity, which shows up well in measurements of the number of turns run in a rotating cage (see Figure 12.7). At the peak of the cycle, a female rat may run as much as 10 miles a day, whereas on other days only a fraction of a mile will be run. The period of greatest activity corresponds to the time of sexual receptivity. If at this time the female becomes pregnant, no further periods of heat will be seen throughout the length of pregnancy (about twenty-one days); during this period, activity remains at a very low level.

This relation between sexual drive and activity holds only for the female. Males do not have the underlying hormonal rhythms of the female. Moreover, there is little if any relation between general activity and the strength

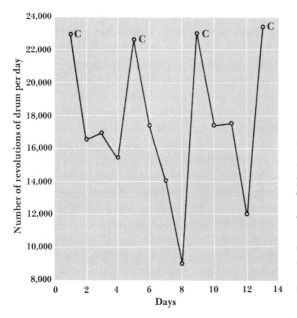

FIGURE 12.7—Rhythms of gross bodily activity corresponding to estrous periods in the female rat. C refers to presence of vaginal cornified cells, a sign of estrus. (Adapted from G. H. Wang. The relation between "spontaneous" activity and estrous cycle in the white rat. *Comp. Psychol. Monogr.*, 1923, 2, No. 6, p. 12. By permission of Williams & Wilkins, Baltimore, publishers.)

of male sexual drive, as measured by the readiness with which it will avail itself of a receptive female (Stone and Barker, 1934).

STIMULATION AND DRIVE

We have just seen that activity has causes both within and outside the organism. Below we shall consider still other physiological factors related to activity. The question has often been raised whether general activity is caused by stimulation, external and internal, or whether there is an internal activity drive. This is a difficult question to study because it is virtually impossible to free an animal from all stimulation. There are, however, experiments on which to base a conclusion, and these give the answer "both."

Activity, on the one hand, is certainly greatly affected by stimulation (Campbell and Sheffield, 1953). Lights, sounds, and other stimuli make organisms more active as well as keep them awake. And stimulation and drive deprivation interact (Hall, 1956). Food deprivation increases activity level, and external stimulation added to food deprivation increases it even more.

On the other hand, activity itself behaves like a drive. If one keeps animals in small cages that do not permit activity and then permits them to run in an activity wheel, the longer the animal is penned up, the greater the activity in the running wheel (Hill, 1956). Thus, a drive for activity can be deprived in much the same way that the hunger drive can be. In addition, the opportunity for activity can serve as a reward for learning a habit (Kagan and

Berkun, 1954; also see Hundt and Premack, 1963). Thus it seems fairly clear that activity is a drive quite apart from being a reaction to stimulation.

NUTRITIONAL FACTORS

We shall now consider physiological factors affecting activity level. Among these is the nutritional status of the animal. A great many experiments have been made to relate dietary treatment of animals with their activity level. The results are rather complicated, but we shall not go into them in any detail. A general rule, which holds for many but not all kinds of nutritional deprivation, is that, in the early stages of deprivation, activity increases but then when the deprivation weakens the animal, activity decreases. Such a relation has adaptive significance, for it means that the increased activity that at first accompanies deprivation augments the chances of the animal finding the food (or water) necessary to remedy the deficiency. Here are a few details.

When animals are deprived of all food or water, activity tends to increase in proportion to the severity of the deprivation (Wald and Jackson, 1944). When deprived of food alone, they become more active as the deprivation progresses. After five days of complete deprivation, their activity is about five times the normal level. After a similar number of days of water deprivation, roughly the same increase occurs. However, only two days of combined food and water deprivation are necessary to yield the fivefold increase in activity. The effects of the two kinds of deprivation appear to be roughly additive.

The composition of the diet affects activity. The diet may be altered to consist entirely of one kind of food stuff, say protein, fat, or carbohydrate. In this case, after an initial increase in activity, there is a decrease, but an all-protein diet causes the greatest depression, and an all-carbohydrate diet the least (Richter and Rice, 1942). Vitamin-deficient diets may be fed to animals. In this case, there is no general rule except that, when the deficiency is severe enough to impair the health of the animal, activity declines (Wald and Jackson, 1944). In the case of some deficiencies, however, there may be an initial increase in activity (B complex). In other cases, activity falls off continuously while the animals are on the deficient diet (A and D).

ENDOCRINE FACTORS

Since most of the endocrine glands are concerned in one way or another with energy metabolism, it is to be expected that they would be related to activity, and they are (see Reed, 1947). The relative size of the gonads and adrenal glands in rats is correlated with running activity. The larger the glands, the greater the general activity level (Riss et al., 1959). On the other hand, removal of any of the endocrine glands causes a reduction in general activity. Removal of the ovaries in the rat reduces activity to about one-fifth the normal level and completely eliminates the four- to five-day rhythm. Even in the male rat, castration is followed by a reduction of running activity. Complete removal of any of the adrenal glands, the thyroid glands, pancreas, *or* pituitary causes a substantial reduction in activity. In the case of the adrenal glands, the important factor seems to be the adrenal cortex, for after adrenalectomy, treatment with cortical extracts restores activity to normal.

Most of the work on endocrine factors has been done with the domestic rat. The effects of removing glands probably depends in some degree on the particular animal used. Apparently certain glands are more important to activity in some animals than in others. For example, the domestic and wild rat have been compared in the effects of adrenalectomy and gonadectomy (Richter and Uhlenhuth, 1954). The adrenal glands of the wild rat are normally larger than those of the domestic rat, and they are more important physiologically, for though the domestic rat can survive after adrenalectomy if it is given extra salt in its diet, the wild rat cannot survive with any amount of salt. On the other hand, while gonadectomy reduces the activity of the domestic rat, as indicated above, this operation has no significant effect on the wild rat. From these and other related facts, the conclusion has been drawn that in the wild rat activity is primarily controlled by the adrenal glands, whereas in the domestic rat activity is mostly controlled by the gonads.

NEURAL MECHANISMS

It is now clear, as might have been expected, that many factors, both internal and external, affect general activity. In the final analysis, however, all activity is mediated by the nervous system because muscular activity is under the control of the nervous system. It is therefore of interest to see how the nervous system is involved.

SUBCORTICAL STRUCTURES—There are reports of changes in activity following lesions to the hypothalamus, brain stem, and the caudate nucleus of the corpus striatum. In the case of the hypothalamus, damage to the ventromedial nucleus of the rat is sometimes accompanied by a reduction in activity (Hetherington and Ranson, 1942). This is the same nucleus that is implicated both in emotional behavior and in the control of hunger (see Chapters 11 and 13), and it is not entirely clear what the results mean. In an experiment on cats, lesions in the brain stem (interpeduncular nucleus) produced a change in the character of the activity (Bailey and Davis, 1942). The animals developed what was called the syndrome of "obstinate progression." They kept walking forward until they bumped into an object, knocked it over, or fell down and took a new direction. In some cases this behavior continued to the point of exhaustion.

Most of the work on subcortical structures has centered on the caudate nucleus of the corpus striatum. Apparently the results obtained here depend on the animal used. In the rat, lesions of the striatum produces no consistent effect (Beach, 1941). On the other hand, such lesions in the cat (Mettler, 1942) and the monkey (Richter and Hines, 1938) cause marked increases in activity. In the case of the cat, the increase is of the forward-going obstinate progression noted above for brain-stem lesions. Thus it would appear that in some animals some sort of inhibitory mechanism is to be found in the corpus striatum.

FRONTAL CORTEX—There are several studies of the effects of cortical lesions on general activity. They do not agree in every particular, but they permit some fairly clear-cut conclusions (see French, 1959; Isaac and de Vito, 1958).

One is that the frontal cortex is the only region of the cerebral cortex that, when damaged, causes changes in activity. No consistent changes in activity follow lesions in other areas (but see Stern, 1957). Frontal lesions, however, are accompanied by an increase in activity (see Zubek and de Lorenzo, 1952). In general, the larger the frontal lesion—and it should be bilateral—the greater is the effect on activity. Thus there is some equipotentiality of frontal function (see Chapter 18). But within the areas contributing to this effect, there is one area more important than others. In the rat, this is the frontal pole and particularly the orbital (lower) surface. In the monkey, the more important area lies in an orbital position but not so far forward.

Studies of the monkey suggest that lesions of the more important orbital area do not merely increase the activity of the animal. They change its character (Ruch and Shenkin, 1943). Random and spontaneous activities are not increased by the lesions. Rather, the complex and variable cage behavior of the unoperated monkey gives way to incessant methodical pacing or running from end to end of the cage. This stereotyped behavior has been recorded for periods of two or three hours with only momentary pauses. It has been described as "driven" (Kennard et al., 1941). Thus, although total activity is quantitatively increased, qualitatively some kinds of activity are reduced and replaced by locomotor activity (Stern, 1957).

13 HUNGER AND THIRST

HUNGER AND THIRST are closely related in two ways. In the first place, they are both needs for the ingestion of substances into the alimentary tract. The only difference between them in this respect is that thirst concerns water, whereas hunger concerns other solid and fluid substances. That makes thirst really only a special kind of hunger. In the second place, the uses of water and food within the body are interrelated. Water is required for the metabolism of most food stuffs. Hence it is to be expected that water intake will depend to a considerable extent on food intake. This is indeed the case, as has been demonstrated in a number of experiments.

One of the most thorough experiments on this point is illustrated in Figure 13.1 (Cizek, 1959). There it will be seen that, when the composition of the diet is held constant, there is a linear relationship between the amount of food consumed and the amount of water ingested. This experiment was made by varying the amount of food available in a day and allowing dogs to drink water at will. The graph shows that, as more food is provided, the water drunk is increased proportionately. In fact, most of the water consumed when food supplies are adequate is ingested in order to take care of water needs created by the eating of food. On the other hand, there is a basic water need that is independent of eating, for during periods in which no food at all is eaten, there is still some water drunk.

The degree to which water intake and food intake are related depends, of course, on the kind of food eaten. If, for example, the food contains a large amount of salt or mineral, more water will be drunk than normally, as anyone knows who has eaten a sizable amount of salty ham. There are similar differences with other kinds of food stuffs. The important point, however, is that there is a basic level of thirst, and hence water ingestion, that exists independently of food. But, beyond that, thirst depends on food intake.

Because of the close relationship between food ingestion and thirst, it is to be expected that hunger and thirst are closely related physiologically. That is true, as we shall see. We shall encounter instances in which one mechanism overlaps or involves the other. For clarity of exposition, however, we must treat hunger and thirst separately, taking up first hunger, then thirst.

REGULATION OF FOOD INTAKE

Hunger is both general and specific. It is general in that food stuffs are interchangeable up to a certain point in supplying the body's energy requirements. Hence the organism may be hungry for almost any kind of food. Hunger may also be specific in that the body needs certain kinds of substances and not others. This need, as we shall see, is reflected in the choice, if possible, of these particular substances. Our plan of treatment for the subject of hunger

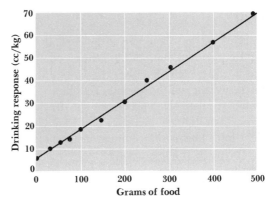

FIGURE 13.1—Drinking of one dog, illustrating the linear relationship between food intake and water intake. (Adapted from L. J. Cizek. Long-term observations on relationship between food and water ingestion in the dog. Amer. J. Physiol., 1959, 197, 344.)

will first consider the way in which the body regulates its overall intake of food stuffs and then secondly to cover the phenomena of specific hungers. After that we shall go into the various factors in the mouth, stomach, blood, and nervous system that make up the mechanism of hunger and of the control of food intake.

The simple and obvious relationship between hunger and eating is that after we have eaten a meal we are no longer hungry but after a period without food we become hungry again and eat. In other words, there is a circular relationship between hunger as a need and food ingestion. Through this relationship, food intake is regulated so as to maintain a relatively constant weight and to consume enough food to meet energy requirements.

A key word in this statement is "regulated." The question is, What is being regulated? What determines whether more or less is eaten in a given meal, in a day, or over a long period of time? The body has some norm or standard that is met by food ingestion. What is it? Actually, there is more than one standard. At least, it can be shown that there are several respects in which food intake is regulated to provide for a relatively constant state of nutrition.

MEAL SIZE AND FREQUENCY

Almost all organisms, particularly the mammals about which there is the most knowledge, have a rhythm of eating. They do not nibble constantly; they eat meals separated by some period of time without eating. A meal represents some kind of short-term regulation. After eating so much food, they stop. They have had "enough." There must be some mechanism for this stopping. And it cannot be the utilization of food eaten, for that does not occur until hours later. Rather, it is some immediate consequence of eating, either something connected with the act of eating itself or with the presence of food in the stomach. As we shall see, both are factors. The important point to be made here is that there is some regulator of the size of a meal.

WEIGHT

The total intake of an organism depends on the size of meals eaten and their frequency. Other things being equal, the more an organism eats, the more it will weigh. If either the size of its meals or their frequency is increased, weight will be gained. Yet adult organisms under normal conditions maintain a relatively constant weight. If, through food deprivation, they lose weight, their hunger increases and they eat more until they gain back the weight lost. This is the common method of motivating animals in laboratory experiments. Is the organism eating to maintain a constant weight? It would appear so.

There are several arguments for making this statement, but the most straightforward experimental demonstration is artificially, but temporarily, to increase an organism's weight and then see what happens to its food ingestion. Insulin can be used for this purpose. Later we shall consider why, but here let us simply note that a rat injected twice daily with protamine zinc insulin greatly increases its food intake; over a period of days, while the injections are continued, it gains weight until it becomes quite fat (see Teitelbaum, 1961). At this point, the insulin injections are stopped. As can be seen in Figure 13.2, it immediately cuts down on its food intake and consequently starts losing weight. In time, the weight returns to just what it had been at the beginning of the experiment. As the weight returns to the normal level, food consumption increases somewhat to a point that will sustain the normal weight. Pretty obviously, food intake is highly correlated with weight. There is some aspect of weight that somehow regulates food intake.

CALORIC INTAKE

To maintain a constant weight, other things being equal, an animal must consume a constant number of calories. This assumes that there is no change in the work done or the energy spent by the organism. There is considerable evidence that the organism normally regulates its caloric intake and that this is a link in the mechanism of maintaining a constant weight. Two experiments, among others, provide support for this conclusion.

FIGURE 13.2—A normal rat made obese by protamine zinc insulin injections brings its weight back to normal by eating less when the insulin injections are discontinued. (Adapted from P. Teitelbaum. In *Nebraska symposium on motivation*. Lincoln, Nebr.: University of Nebraska Press, 1961. P. 50.)

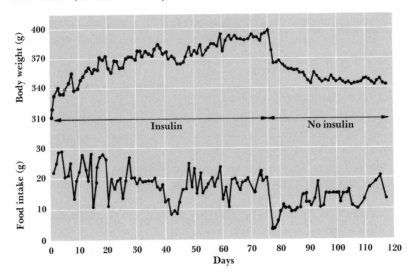

In one experiment, the caloric value of the diet eaten was manipulated by adulterating the food with nonnutritive material (Adolph, 1947). Various sorts of roughage materials, for example, cellulose, can be used for this purpose. When rats are fed foods containing various percentages of nonnutritive roughage, they make up for the roughage by eating more. In fact, within fairly wide limits, they compensate for the adulteration by eating enough more to maintain their caloric intake. In other words, caloric intake remains constant despite differences in the nutritional value of the food.

Another approach to this is to supply the rat with alcohol, in the form of either a "mixed drink," wine, or beer, along with its usual chow (Richter, 1953). It happens that rats, like many people, prefer a certain amount of alcohol. When offered "mixed drinks" consisting of 8, 16, and 24 percent alcohol, they always drink some alcohol, but they drink more of the lower concentrations than of the higher ones. Moreover, while alcohol is available, they reduce their food intake in proportion to the calories supplied by the alcohol. In other words, their caloric intake remains constant. If offered beer versus wine, they drink more than twice as much beer as wine, thus making up for the difference in alcohol and hence caloric content.

ENERGY REQUIREMENTS

The above experiments were carried out with constant energy requirements. Rats, living their normal lives, kept their caloric intake constant even though calories were offered in different forms. A corollary to the principle of constant caloric intake is that caloric intake should change with differing energy requirements of the body. For example, one can require an organism to do more work and thus to consume more calories to maintain a constant weight and at the same time put out the additional work.

This kind of experiment has been made with rats (Griffiths and Gallagher, 1953). Throughout the experiment, the rats were offered sugar (dextrose) and nonnutritive saccharine in addition to water and their stock diet. Their selection of these materials was compared for an eight-day rest period living in their cages and for a fourteen-day swimming period in which they were forced to swim in a tank for about two hours a day or until symptoms of exhaustion were evident. This kind of swimming expends a great deal of energy. It is interesting (1) that the rats increased their consumption of sugar by a factor of more than ten times and (2) they did not consume any more saccharine solution. Hence, they discriminated between foods giving energy, and they increased their intake of energy-rich food when their work required it.

Another way of increasing an organism's energy requirements is to lower its environmental temperature. A number of experiments have been made varying environmental temperature and measuring food intake (see Brobeck,

1960). They show that animals eat more in cold environments than in warm ones and that the increase is proportional to the additional heat production required in cold environments.

SPECIFIC HUNGERS

The principal point made so far is that organisms regulate the *amount* of their food intake according to the calories required for constant weight and according to varying energy requirements. Organisms also regulate the *kinds* of foods they eat, and they do this according to the requirements of the body for carbohydrates, proteins, fats, minerals, and vitamins. In this section, we shall see how they do this. Most of the research cited was done in the 1930s and 1940s. By 1950, the phenomena of specific hungers and dietary self-selection had been well established, and investigators turned their attention, as we shall see later, to biochemical and neural factors in hunger.

SELF-SELECTION OF DIETS

As a general rule, if an animal needs a particular dietary component because of a metabolic disorder or because that food has been excluded from its diet, it will develop a *specific hunger* for the food. There are some exceptions to this rule, but in cases where specific hungers show up clearly, three things can be demonstrated: (1) The organism prefers the food it needs to other foods that are available; (2) it usually ingests large enough amounts to meet its specific physiological requirements; and (3) it eats the needed food even when its stomach is full.

One of the best signs that there are specific hungers apart from general hungers is the ability of organisms to select a balanced diet from an assortment of all the necessary components of a good diet. Human adults would probably have difficulty doing this, for acquired habits, as we shall see, can and do override beneficial self-selections. Young children, however, have been reported to make good selections over a period of time (Davis, 1928). More convincing are experiments with rats (Richter, 1942a). If they are presented with several dishes of food, in each of which is one element, e.g., salt, sugar, or fat, necessary for the normal functioning of the body, they eat from each dish an amount that is just about correct for their needs.

FACTORS IN SELF-SELECTION

The self-selection feeding method works so well under some conditions that rats that obtain all their food in this way may actually grow more rapidly than animals maintained on standard laboratory food mixtures (Richter, 1942b).

However, not all animals make beneficial selections equally well. There are wide individual differences and perhaps even strain and species differences. In two different studies of rats, for example, about one-third of them failed to grow normally when allowed to select their own diets (Pilgrim and Patton, 1947; Scott, 1946).

A number of different factors are important in determining whether or not rats make beneficial food selections. Age may make a difference (Pilgrim and Patton, 1947). Rats that fail to grow adequately on self-selection diets at the age of 1½ months may grow normally when tested three months later in the same situation. Also, rats that do poorly on self-selection invariably fail to take adequate amounts of protein (casein). On the other hand, animals that do not grow normally on the protein casein may readily take some other form of protein such as fibrin or lactalbumen and grow normally. Rats that grow most slowly on self-selection diets also do most poorly on stock diets made from the same components used in the selection tests.

These individual differences in food preferences and the inability of some animals to make beneficial selections raise questions about the nature and operation of specific hungers. Perhaps in cases of failure the animals were not offered the right kinds of foods for their particular metabolic needs. Perhaps some learn strong preferences and aversions on the basis of taste, smell, or the consistency of foods, with the result that their natural preferences are obscured. A third possibility is that animals may sometimes be unable to taste particular kinds of foods and therefore are unable to select among them. Or conversely, certain purified foods, offered in self-selection diets, may not have a distinctive enough taste, smell, or consistency to be detected by animals.

All these factors operate in the regulation of food preferences and selections. Some idea of their relative importance can be obtained by considering experiments concerned with (1) the nature of food preferences; (2) the importance of body needs, including endocrine factors and vitamin deficiencies, in the development of specific hungers; and (3) the role of stimulus characteristics of food in the detection and selection of foods.

FOOD PREFERENCES

Two general methods of studying food preferences have been used.

One is the single-stimulus method (Stellar and Hill, 1952). In this, the animal is presented with only one food at a time, usually in solution, and its *rate* of ingestion is measured. This rate of ingestion for one food or substance on one occasion is compared with the rate for another food or sometimes for a different concentration of the substance in liquid form. A difference in rate is then taken to represent a difference in preference. This method has most often been used in experiments on taste and postingestion factors to be discussed later in the chapter.

A second method, most often used in the earlier studies of food preference, is the *two-stimulus method*. In this case, an animal is presented with two containers of food and allowed to eat it (Young, 1944). If this procedure is repeated a number of times, the animal selects or prefers one food more than the other. In this kind of situation, rats prefer sugar to casein (a protein). If they are deprived of casein and allowed ample supplies of sugar before being tested, they prefer casein, as they should in order to make a beneficial selection. As long as two foods are distinguishable, it can be accepted as a general rule than an animal will show a preference for the food of which it has been deprived.

The situation, however, is not always as simple as this. Rats that have consistently selected sugar under the influence of a sugar need may continue to prefer sugar at a later time when their need is for casein (Young and Chaplin, 1945). Only after a long series of trials do they shift their preferences to the casein. This apparent violation of the general principle just stated is explained in terms of habit. An animal prefers the foods it needs, but preference behavior becomes a habit, which may persist when the animal is tested in the same situation but with a *different need*. If, when the shift in body need is made, the animal is tested in an entirely different situation, for example, a T maze with the two substances presented on the respective arms, it shows a preference for the food it needs and not the one it learned to select in the old situation. In fact, if the animal is tested in both the old and the new situations on alternate trials, it shows a preference for sugar in the old and a preference for casein in the new situation. Hence, it is clear that animals can develop habits that obscure their "true" bodily needs (see Young, 1957).

INTERNAL ENVIRONMENT

One of the striking ways in which specific hungers are exhibited is in the organism's adjustment to changes in its internal environment. Such changes occur naturally in pregnancy and nursing, and they may be effected experimentally by the removal of endocrine glands or by feeding vitamin-deficient diets.

During pregnancy, because of the demands of the growing fetuses, the mother's need for many minerals, particularly sodium, phosphorus, and calcium, greatly increases. For the same reason, she needs more fats and proteins. Sugar, on the other hand, is of no greater importance and may, in fact, be less if the mother expends less muscular energy and maintains a somewhat lower metabolic rate. All these changes in physiological requirements during pregnancy are reflected in shifts in food intake (Richter, 1942). Specific hungers for minerals are much stronger; those for fat and protein are also raised; but sugar intake is lower. Much the same statement applies throughout nursing and lactation, but after young rats are weaned and physiological demands return to normal, so also do hungers for specific dietary materials.

The importance of the internal environment in arousing specific hungers can also be seen in the extirpation of endocrine glands. After removal of the pancreas, for example, rats develop diabetic symptoms while eating a standard stock diet because they have no way to alter their dietary balance. When allowed to select their own diets, however, they take very little sugar and compensate for the caloric loss by increasing fat intake (Richter and Schmidt, 1941). Similarly, after parathyroidectomy, which lowers calcium and increases phosphorus levels in the blood, rats show a great avidity for calcium, increasing their calcium intake by three or four times and showing a marked aversion for phosphorus (Richter, 1939). As a third example, after adrenalectomy, the excretion of salt is greatly increased and the animal becomes salt-deficient. Rats in this condition, if given the opportunity, ingest several times the normal amount of salt (Richter and Eckert, 1938; also see Lewis, 1960).

Specific hungers that develop in animals deprived of vitamins are particularly interesting. Such animals show specific hungers only when deprived of certain vitamins but not others. When deprived of vitamin A or D, for example, they show no changed preference for foods containing them (Wilder, 1937). The same is true of pantothenic acid deficiency, although specific hungers for the rest of the B complex are readily demonstrable (Scott and Quint, 1946). On the other hand, animals suffering vitamin deficiency show changes in specific hungers for other foods, depending on how they are related to the metabolic action of the missing vitamin (Richter and Hawkes, 1941). Thiamin-deficient rats, for example, decrease their sugar intake and increase their fat intake, as they should do to compensate for changes in their ability to metabolize these components.

STIMULUS CHARACTERISTICS OF FOOD

One reason, if not the principal reason, why animals sometimes do not show specific hungers for vitamins in which they are deficient is that they cannot taste them. Naturally, in order to select something, an organism must discriminate it, and this is not always within its capabilities. Rats, for example, which show no preference for pantothenic acid, select it accurately when it is flavored with anise, which they can taste (Scott and Verney, 1947).

PHYSIOLOGICAL BASIS

To summarize these various facts about specific hungers, we may say that learned habits sometimes interfere with beneficial self-selection and in some instances such selection fails because the animal is unable to discriminate the appropriate components. On the whole, however, beneficial selection has been demonstrated under a wide variety of conditions for many components of the diet. We may go on to ask what is the physiological basis of this ability to select the components needed by the internal condition of the animal.

At one time, it appeared that the answer might lie in changed taste thresholds. The hypothesis was that a preference for a component might be exaggerated by an animal becoming much more sensitive to the material. Fitting in with this hypothesis was the fact that adrenalectomized rats show a preference for salt solutions of much weaker concentrations than normal rats do (Bare, 1949). Conversely, rats fed on high-salt diets showed less than the normal preference for salt; in fact, at all detectable concentrations, they exhibit an aversion to salt (see Figure 13.3).

These shifts in preference do not represent changes in taste sensitivity. This has been established by measuring thresholds of sensitivity by means of neural discharges in the taste nerves and by behavioral means. In Figure 13.3 is a graph showing the neural response to different concentrations of salt in the normal and adrenalectomized animals (Pfaffmann and Bare, 1950). The curve for the neural response does not change with adrenalectomy. When animals are trained by a discrimination method and their thresholds measured, normal and adrenalectomized rats similarly do not differ (Carr, 1952). It must be concluded that, in the case of salt, the mechanism of the specific

FIGURE 13.3—A comparison of neural response (open circle) from a taste nerve with preference curves (filled circle) for different concentrations of NaCl. (Adapted from C. Pfaffmann. *Amer. J. clin. Nutrit.*, 1957, 5, 142.)

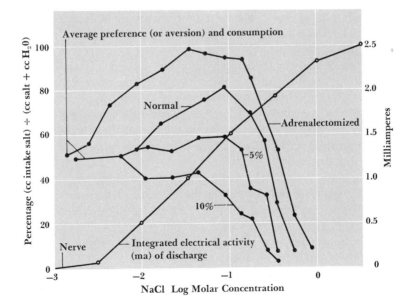

hunger does not lie in peripheral sensory changes. Rather, the internal environment must somehow affect the brain so that the ingestive response is greater for some substances than for others. Experiments to be described in the next sections throw some additional light on this problem.

PHYSIOLOGICAL MECHANISMS OF HUNGER

The preceding sections offer some hints about physiological mechanisms of hunger, but their principal purpose was to describe the phenomena of hunger. In other words, they present the problems for which physiological explanations are sought. Summing up what has been learned, we may say that food ingestion is regulated both in overall bulk and in specific kinds by physiological factors within the organism. It is now our purpose to take a closer look at these physiological factors.

GASTRIC CONTRACTIONS

Many years ago, Cannon and Washburn (1912) studied gastric contractions in human subjects by having their subjects swallow a balloon and by recording gastric pressure on the balloon. They observed that, when an individual reported hunger, gastric contractions were usually taking place. They concluded that the conscious experience of hunger comes from the sensory stimulation set up by these contractions.

It may be true that some individuals experience gastric contractions when they are hungry, but subsequent experiments make it clear that there is no essential relation between hunger and gastric contractions. In the first place, modern electrical methods of recording stomach contractions reveal that contractions of the empty stomach are relatively rare (Davis et al., 1959). It would appear that the balloon technique causes contractions that normally do not occur. Secondly, there are cases of individuals without stomachs who give all the normal signs of hunger. In one such case, the stomach was completely removed and the esophagus connected directly with the intestine (Wangensteen and Carlson, 1931). The patient ate normally and reported a normal desire for food.

There are also several experiments in man and animals that make it clear that hunger does not depend on the presence of the stomach or of sensory impulses arising from the stomach. Rats whose stomachs have been removed regulate their food intake about like normal animals (Tsang, 1938). Because they cannot store food as well as normals, they must eat more often and cannot withstand twenty-four-hour deprivations so well. But that is the principal difference. Similarly, rats (Bash, 1939) and dogs (Grossman et al., 1948) in which the vagus nerve, which carries sensory impulses from the stomach, has been cut display essentially normal hunger. The conclusion, then, is that gastric contractions are not essential to, nor important in, hunger. This conclusion, however, does not rule out other gastric factors, which, as we shall see, play a role in satiety.

ORAL FACTORS

The existence of specific hungers is proof that taste is one of the factors regulating food intake. Some substances taste "better than," that is, are preferred over, others when the body is in greater need of these substances. In order for the organism to select these substances, there must be some way in which a consummatory response to substances is altered according to the kind of specific hunger existing at the time.

There are several ways of studying oral factors in food intake. One is to look at patterns of ingestion of different substances. This has been done in the rat (Stellar et al., 1954; Davis and Keehn, 1959). When offered solutions of different substances, such as salt, sugar, or saccharin, all of them in acceptable concentrations, the rat, quite interestingly, licks these at about the same rate, regardless of its preference for them. What distinguishes the intake of substances is not rate of ingestion over the short term but rather the pauses between licking and the length of time the licks go on. In other words, the animal continues to ingest preferred substances longer and pauses more briefly for rest than it does for less preferred substances.

Under normal circumstances, of course, anything consumed passes first through the mouth and then into the stomach. This natural connection between intake and the stomach makes it difficult to separate oral factors from postingestion gastric factors. There are, however, artificial ways of separating the two, and these give additional information about the role of oral factors.

One is to use a fistulated preparation. For technical reasons, most experiments with fistulas employ only one fistula to the stomach. However, in some cases, the esophagus is sectioned, and its two ends are brought to the surface of the body in such a way that food may be introduced directly into the stomach and the food eaten by the animal passes out the fistula without ever entering the stomach. Feeding of this type is called sham feeding. It probably comes as no surprise that experiments with sham feeding show that it occurs and continues over periods of days (Hull et al., 1951). When hungry, fistulated animals sham feed and seem adequately motivated in other ways. For example, dogs can learn stable habits when their only reward for the learning is food that promptly passes out the fistula and is never available for the satisfaction of hunger.

In another experiment, food intake was compared under two conditions of prefeeding (Berkun et al., 1952). In one, milk was injected into the stomach; in the other, the rat drank a comparable amount of milk in the normal way. Following this, tests were run to measure the amount of additional milk drunk. It was found that milk drunk by mouth caused a greater subsequent reduction in milk intake than milk placed directly in the stomach. In other words, although milk in the stomach was "satisfying," milk taken through the mouth was even more "satisfying." This points to an oral factor in the inhibition or cessation of feeding.

GASTRIC FACTORS

This last experiment leads to an important distinction between the "start" and "stop" factors in food ingestion. A state of hunger leads an animal to eat and may determine the particular substances it prefers to eat, but then, as a result of eating, something happens that causes him to stop eating. The experiment above shows that the latter inhibition of eating may be influenced by mouth factors—some combination of taste and ingestion—but that it may occur through the presence of food in the stomach.

There are more experiments on this point. In general, they lead to the conclusion that the "start" or facilitating factor in eating is oral but that the "stop" or inhibiting factor is partly gastric. They also indicate that the oral factor is discriminating, that is, exhibits preferences, but the gastric factor is nondiscriminating. It does not "know" the difference between one kind of food and another. Let us consider three experiments illustrating these points.

In one experiment, the two sugars, glucose and sucrose, were presented to rats to determine equivalence of preference (Shuford, 1955; but see Young, 1957). Three concentrations of glucose were arbitrarily selected, namely, 5, 15, and 35 percent. Each of these was presented along with varying concentrations of sucrose until a concentration of sucrose was found that was equally preferable to the rat. These turned out to be 2.0, 9.6, and 27.6 percent, respectively. Then the rate of drinking was compared for each pair of equally preferred concentrations of the two sugars. The results are shown in Figure 13.4. At the beginning of a period of drinking, the rate was the same for each pair. In other words, if two sugars were equally preferred (presumably equally sweet), rats drank them at the same rate. After a few minutes, however, the curves of drinking rate began to diverge. This was particularly striking for the higher concentrations. The "stop," postingestion factor was beginning to operate, and it was different for the two sugars.

Now it happens that the concentrations of glucose and sucrose that are equally sweet have quite different osmotic pressures. That, indeed, was the reason for selecting the two sugars for comparison. The osmotic pressure of the sucrose solutions was 1.4, 8.0, and 30.0, respectively, while that of the glucose solutions was 7, 23, and 74, respectively. By pitting these numbers against the curves in Figure 13.4, it can be seen that the slowing down of intake was proportional to osmotic pressure, especially for the two higher concentrations. The rats drank less of the sugar with the higher osmotic pressure even though it was equally preferred at the outset.

Sucrose and glucose differ in ways other than sweetness and osmotic pres-

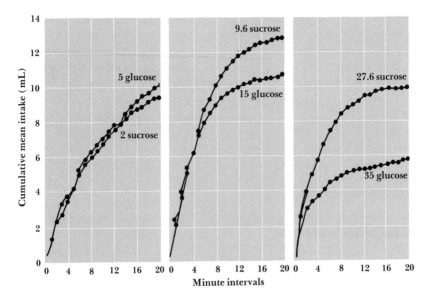

FIGURE 13.4—Intake curves of isohedonic solutions of glucose and sucrose. (Adapted from P. T. Young. In *Symposium on nutrition and behavior.* New York: National Vitamin Foundation, 1957. P. 53.)

sure. There is separate evidence, however, that osmotic pressure is an important variable, if not the principal variable, in the gastric inhibition of eating. This comes from an experiment in which rats were preloaded with three substances that are quite different both chemically and in acceptability to the rat, namely, urea, sodium chloride, and glucose (McCleary, 1953). The effect of these stomach loads on the drinking of a glucose or fructose solution was then measured. The result was that these substances had an equally depressing effect on sugar intake when they were equal in osmotic pressure. The kind of substance in the stomach made no difference; only its osmotic pressure.

Whether this result is a general rule for all kinds of substances and for all sorts of food intake cannot be said without more evidence. The experiment has been confirmed for food, as distinguished from sugar solutions, with the same results (Schwartzbaum and Ward, 1958). Thus osmotic pressure of substances in the stomach is at least an important factor in inhibiting food intake, and taste preference is important at the beginning of food ingestion.

SPECIFIC DYNAMIC ACTION

The experiments we have just discussed imply that there must be some means of communication between the stomach and the brain. It is probably not nervous, because severing the nervous connections in vagotomy has no appreciable effect on food intake (Grossman et al., 1947). At the same time, it is a relatively rapid form of communication, taking place within a few minutes after the beginning of eating. This is too soon for food to be digested or to meet the physiological need for food. Therefore the effect must take place through some temporary or intermediate link. At the present time, there is no good idea of the method of communication. Possibly it is related to the metabolic phenomenon of *specific dynamic action*. This is a release of energy in the body after a meal has been eaten but before food is digested. There is some evidence tying together food regulation with specific dynamic action (Strominger and Brobeck, 1953), but since the mechanism of a specific dynamic action itself is not known, that brings no nearer, at present, an answer to the mystery.

INTRAGASTRIC REGULATION

Whatever, the mechanism of communication may be, it is an effective one, not only for the inhibition of eating at the end of a meal but also for total food regulation. Recently rats have been prepared in such a way that they can feed themselves intragastrically (Epstein and Teitelbaum, 1962). A gastric tube is inserted directly into the stomach and hooked up to a pipetting machine (see Figure 13.5). The apparatus is so arranged that a press on the bar in the rat's box delivers a squirt of liquid food directly into the stomach. The animal soon learns to press the bar for intragastric squirts of food. After

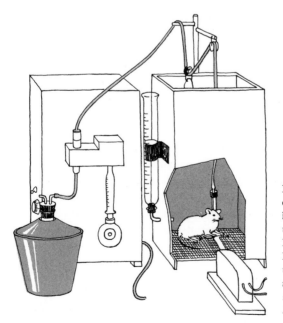

FIGURE 13.5—Schematic drawing of the apparatus for intragastric self-injection by the rat. (Adapted from A. N. Epstein and P. Teitelbaum. Regulation of food intake in the absence of taste, smell, and other oro-pharyngeal sensations. *J. comp. physiol. Psychol.*, 1962, 55, 155.)

that, it is left in the situation night and day, receiving all its food intra-gastrically. The remarkable thing is that animals are able, after some initial fluctuation, to regulate their intake with a precision about like that of normal animals.

There were other variations in this experiment. Quinine was put in the intragastric diet in a concentration that, taken orally, was so aversive that normal animals reduce their food intake. It made no difference to the intra-gastric rats. The diet was diluted with tap water. The size of individual "squirts" was halved. The number of bar presses per squirt was increased. The animals adjusted to all these conditions as normal animals would, chang-ing their intake so as to provide for relatively constant real-food intake. Evi-dently, without any oral factors at all, food regulation can be quite precise solely on the basis of intragastric factors.

BLOOD SUGAR

Hunger as a drive is obviously some state of the brain, but it must be aroused and sated by chemical factors in the blood representing conditions in the tissues of the body. Naturally, investigators have been trying to identify any chemical factors that might serve this function. Blood sugar has always been a fine candidate. It is the body's best short-term source of energy. Its supply in the blood is regulated by the release of glycogen in the liver, and the sup-plies of liver glycogen are known to be relatively small, being depleted in a matter of hours after a meal.

A simple hypothesis, put forth years ago (Carlson, 1916), is that hunger might be correlated with the rise and fall of blood sugar. In favor of the hypothesis is the well-established fact that insulin injections, which lower blood sugar, increase hunger (Teitelbaum, 1961). On the other hand, this action of insulin may not involve blood sugar, for certain drugs, such as amphetamine and atropine, counteract the insulin effect on hunger without affecting its hypoglycemic action (Soulairac et al., 1961). Moreover, there seems to be little or no correlation between normal fluctuations in blood-sugar level and the hunger drive (Scott et al., 1938).

It is now generally conceded that blood sugar per se is not related to hunger. There are some, however, who believe that the degree of utilization of glucose by tissues may be related to hunger (Mayer, 1955). In favor of the idea is the fact, as we shall see, that certain centers in the hypothalamus are sensitive to sugar. There also seems to be some relation between cycles of hunger and the rise and fall of glycogen levels in the liver (Anliker and Mayer, 1957). This theory of the role of blood glucose, called the *glucostatic theory*, therefore may have some merit.

It stands to reason, however, that there must be more than one biochemical factor regulating hunger and food intake. This is because animals regulate not only their total intake but also the relative amounts of food stuffs, minerals, and vitamins. The animal must have some way of "knowing" that it needs, say, proteins as well as food in general. It is not known what the messengers are, but when they are identified, there undoubtedly will be several of them.

NEURAL FACTORS

In recent years, with the development of more precise methods of stimulating and destroying neural tissue, much of the physiological research done on hunger has been on its neural mechanisms. Most of the work employs lesions, but some involves electrical stimulation.

When the brain is systematically explored with stimulating electrodes, one discovers that there are a number of areas concerned in one way or another with eating. In one experiment of this kind, carried out with monkeys, the procedure was to have food and water available at all times and to determine whether stimulation in a particular region caused the subjects to eat (Robinson and Mishkin, 1962). There are several places in the brain where this happens. The principal ones are portions of the frontal lobe, cingulate gyrus, thalamus, and hypothalamus. As will be seen later, some of these are also concerned in thirst. There are other points that, when stimulated, cause the animal to eject whatever he has in his mouth. Some cause vomiting. It remains to be seen just what these data mean and how the centers involved participate in the mechanism of hunger.

When lesions are made in some parts of the brain, there may be an effect on hunger. In some cases, hunger is decreased, but when that happens it is hard to tell whether the effect is specific or the result of some other effect on the animal's health. However, there is one area in the lateral hypothalamus destruction of which causes a drastic reduction in both hunger and thirst. So much is now known about this phenomenon that it is discussed separately in a section below.

There are three areas of the brain whose destruction is followed by sizable increases in hunger. Such augmented hunger is called *hyperphagia*. The areas are the frontal lobe, the amygdala, and the ventromedial portion of the hypothalamus. In many of the studies on the frontal lobe and general activity, discussed in the preceding chapter, hyperphagia was also reported (Richter and Hawkes, 1939; Langworthy and Richter, 1939). Not all studies reporting hyperactivity after frontal operation also report hyperphagia, but some do. Ablation of the frontal cortex, furthermore, sometimes leads to hyperactivity of the gastrointestinal tract and spasms of the stomach, which may last for several days. Thus the frontal lobe is clearly concerned somehow in the control of alimentary functions.

In several studies of temporal-lobe lesions, hyperphagia has also been reported (Klüver and Bucy, 1939). Most of these cases appeared to involve the amygdala, and it has now been established that lesions of the amygdala cause hyperphagia (Morgane and Kosman, 1957). As might be expected, along with the increase in hunger and food intake, there is a gain in weight.

Both the frontal lobes and the amygdala are connected with the hypothalamus. Beyond that, it is not known just why these two structures share an inhibitory control of eating. But it is known that the most important structures in the control of hunger and food intake are to be found in the hypothalamus. This part of the brain has been studied so thoroughly that we shall devote two separate sections to it, one on *hypothalamic hyperphagia* and the other on the so-called "lateral hypothalamic syndrome."

HYPOTHALAMIC HYPERPHAGIA

It has been known for thirty years that tumors or lesions of the hypothalamus of man and animals frequently cause them to become very obese (see Teitelbaum, 1961). Later, it was discovered that the reason for this obesity was that the affected individuals or animals overate and that the fundamental defect was one in the regulation of food intake (Brobeck et al., 1943). For this reason the syndrome was called *hypothalamic hyperphagia*.

It was also observed at this time that there are two distinct postoperative phases (see Figure 13.6): In the first, *dynamic phase,* animals eat two or three times as much as normal and rapidly gain weight. In the second, called the *static phase,* which occurs after the animals have become very obese, food intake drops back to about the preoperative level while weight is maintained at a constant level. Further research has attempted to determine why hyperphagics overeat and what the function is of the structures involved.

METABOLISM

The first step was to see whether there was anything wrong with the metabolism of hypothalamic hyperphagics. Conceivably, the lesions may derange the animal's metabolism and in this way cause the overeating. The answer, obtained in a whole series of experiments (see Teitelbaum, 1961), was clearly negative. The metabolism of the hyperphagic is normal. When restricted to a normal intake of food, the animal does not become obese. When starved, it loses weight at the same rate as normal animals. Intestinal absorption is normal. So is the respiratory quotient. Hence the only thing wrong with the hyperphagic is that it overeats.

MOTIVATION

The next question is why does the animal overeat? The answer to this is not simple. In the first place, the hyperphagic is not as hungry as normal animals, if by "hungry" is meant the amount of work the animal will do to obtain food.

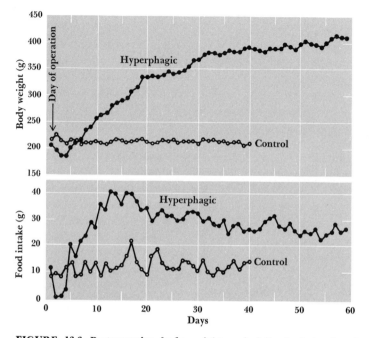

FIGURE 13.6—Postoperative body weight and daily food intake of a hyperphagic rat compared with that of a normal unoperated control. (Adapted from P. Teitelbaum. In *Nebraska symposium on motivation.* Lincoln, Nebr.: University of Nebraska Press, 1961. P. 41.)

If the animals are required to press a bar to obtain their food, they will not press it as much as normal animals (Miller et al., 1950; Teitelbaum, 1957). The difference is exaggerated if they are required to make several presses for each pellet. In a situation in which shock must be endured to obtain food, hyperphagics take less shock and thus appear less motivated than normal animals. There are other respects in which the two differ but, in every case, the hyperphagics are less highly motivated to obtain food than normal animals are.

PALATABILITY

Hyperphagics are also more finicky about their food than normal animals. As was indicated earlier, normal animals readily compensate for adulteration of their food. If nonnutritive cellulose is added to food, they eat more so as to maintain caloric intake and body weight at a constant level. This is not so with hyperphagics. A little adulteration of the food causes them to decrease their intake (Teitelbaum, 1955). If kaolin, rather than cellulose, is used as an adulterant, the effect is similar (Kennedy, 1950). It appears that hyper-phagics are less willing than normals to eat food they do not like. This shows up in studies with quinine, a bitter-tasting substance. Normal animals will stand substantial amounts of quinine in their food and still maintain their food intake, but only a very small amount of it in the food causes the hyper-phagic rat to eat practically nothing. Conversely, if food is sweetened with sugar, the normal rat does not eat more; rather he regulates his caloric intake. The hyperphagic, on the other hand, eats much more (Teitelbaum, 1955). Putting all these findings together, it appears that the hyperphagic rat is more sensitive to the palatability of his food than the normal rat.

WEIGHT REGULATION

If the hyperphagic rat is less hungry than the normal rat, and more sensitive to palatability, why does it eat more? There are two clues to the answer. One is in the size of the meals it eats (Teitelbaum and Campbell, 1958). If fed on a liquid diet, which is not bulky and not adulterated, the hyperphagic rat eats no more often than the normal rat. It does, however, eat longer and thus eats larger meals. The "stop" mechanism is altered so that it operates only after increased food intake. The other clue is to be found in the static phase of the syndrome. In this, after animals have become obese, they level off in weight, and they do this by reducing their food intake. Thus their food intake is regulated by their weight just as is the normal animal's. The difference is that the weight level at which the regulation takes place is markedly higher than in the normal animal.

This hypothesis was tested by inducing overeating and overweight in animals *before* operating them and making them hyperphagic (Hoebel and Teitelbaum, see Teitelbaum, 1961). This was done by injecting them with insulin as described earlier in this chapter. Unfortunately, this procedure does not result in rat weights that are typical of the static hypothalamic hyper-phagic, but it does result in weights close to them. Such preoperatively obese animals, after operation, do not eat very much, and they gain only a little more weight—just enough to take them to the weight they would arrive at postoperatively if they had not been obese to begin with. Otherwise said, hypothalamic hyperphagics level off at the same weight whether or not they were obese to begin with. It is the level of weight control that appears to be the factor altered by the hypothalamic operation.

PARABIOTIC RATS

This conclusion leads to a little speculation. The cells of the hypothalamus destroyed in the hyperphagic rat may be sensitive to some biochemical sub-stance related to the state of the animal's fat deposits. This substance may normally sensitize the "stop" mechanism in eating. As a consequence of the operation, the animal's brain may react less to this substance because some of the sensitive cells have been destroyed.

This inference is bolstered by experiments with parabiotic rats. These are pairs of rats with a common circulatory system so that substances in the blood of one animal can affect the blood of the other. In this particular case, one animal of the pair was made hyperphagic by a hypothalamic lesion (Hervey, 1959). After a period of time, as one might expect, the hypothalamic animal became quite obese. Interestingly, the normal partner of the pair became very thin and had hardly any fat. This is what would be expected if the hormone or other substance connected with fat exists at a high level in the obese animal. The cells in the hypothalamus of the normal rat that inhibit food intake would be stimulated by this substance more than is normally the case. Consequently, the normal rat's feeding would be curbed (see Teitelbaum, 1961).

SATIETY CENTER

The area of the hypothalamus whose destruction consistently causes hyperphagia is the *ventromedial nucleus* close to the midline. Because its destruction causes overeating, its normal function must be that of a "stop" or inhibiting mechanism in eating. For this reason, it has come to be called the *satiety center* (but see Reynolds, 1963). As we shall see below, there is a center in the lateral hypothalamus having the opposite function and called the *feeding center*. In recent years, investigators have been trying to analyze the roles of these centers by using various forms of direct stimulation and by recording electrical activity in them under different conditions of deprivation and satiation. Let us look briefly at some of the experiments that have been made along this line.

ELECTRICAL STIMULATION—When the ventromedial satiety center is electrically stimulated, the expected events occur. If the animal is in the course of eating, eating is inhibited (Wyrwicka and Dobrzecka, 1960). After the stimulation is turned off, there is a rebound effect (Morgane, 1961). An animal that was not eating before stimulation now begins to eat briefly, or one that was eating increases its rate of intake. Presumably this represents an aftereffect of stimulation in which the center is temporarily depressed—a common sequel to electrical stimulation. If animals have learned to cross a grid to obtain food or have learned some other response to obtain food, the responses are inhibited during the course of ventromedial stimulation. These various effects appear to be due to a reduction in hunger drive during ventromedial stimulation.

It is possible, on the other hand, that the inhibition of eating is not a primary effect on hunger (Krasne, 1962). Currents of the same intensity as those that inhibit have more general aversive effects. They also stop the animal's drinking, if drinking is in progress. They also serve as motivation for avoidance responses. Rats readily learn to press a bar to terminate the stimulation. Thus the conclusion to be drawn from experiments with electrical stimulation is not clear. However, those on chemical stimulation, about to be described, are more convincing.

CHEMICAL STIMULATION—By means of implanted cannulas, chemical substances either in crystalline form or in solution may be directly applied to the hypothalamus. Hypertonic saline solutions are usually stimulants to nerve tissue, and, as one might expect, they cause an inhibition of eating when applied to the ventromedial nucleus, much as electrical stimulation does (Epstein, 1960). On the other hand, procaine serves as a local anesthetic and transiently mimics the effects of destroyed tissue. As one might expect, procaine applied directly to the ventromedial nucleus causes an increase in eating. These results of chemical stimulation confirm those of electrical stimulation.

ELECTRICAL ACTIVITY—The *glucostatic* theory of hunger, mentioned earlier, holds that the degree of sugar utilization is at least one of the factors in hunger and more specifically that such utilization acts as a stimulus to the satiety center. More briefly, it holds that there are glucoreceptors in the satiety center. One way of testing this theory is to record electrical activity in the satiety center while manipulating blood glucose with glucose injections or with injections of glucagon which raises blood sugar. This has been done, with the expected result (Anand et al., 1962). Electrical signs of activity in the satiety center show no response to glucagon per se. They increase significantly, however, as blood sugar rises, and they fall with a reduction in blood sugar (Sharma et al., 1961).

Although experiments of this kind fit in with a glucostatic theory, they do not prove it. They merely indicate that the satiety center is somehow sensitive to glucose. The center may also be sensitive to a wide variety of biochemical conditions. Until these are explored, it will not be known whether the satiety center is sugar-specific or is more generally sensitive to metabolic conditions associated with satiation.

APHAGIA

Some years after the phenomenon of hypothalamic hyperphagia became known, it was discovered that there is another area of the hypothalamus whose destruction causes *aphagia* (Anand and Brobeck, 1951). This area lies lateral to the satiety area. Its destruction causes an animal to refuse to eat, and if special measures are not taken, the animal starves to death without ever again eating. If, on the other hand, the animals are tube-fed for a number of days and at the same time offered very palatable foods, most of them eventually recover to the point of maintaining an adequate food intake.

LATERAL HYPOTHALAMIC SYNDROME

There are four definite stages in the course of recovery from lateral hypothalamic lesions. These always occur in the same order (Teitelbaum and Epstein, 1962). They are illustrated in Figure 13.7 and will be described briefly. They constitute the so-called "lateral hypothalamic syndrome."

APHAGIA AND ADIPSIA—After a bilateral lesion of the lateral hypothalamic area, an animal refuses both to eat and to drink. It is therefore both aphagic and adipsic. They not only do not eat or drink; they do not swallow food or water placed in their mouths. If they get food on their paws, they shake it off. And in general they act as though mouth contact with food and water were highly aversive. The only way animals in this stage can be kept alive is to tube-feed them on a liquid diet that contains a proper combination of food stuffs and water for maintaining normal weight.

ANOREXIA AND ADIPSIA—When animals are kept alive by tube feeding, after several days they begin to eat again if the proper foods are offered to them. The food must be a highly palatable diet; for the rat, a liquid diet, milk chocolate, or cookies. They refuse to eat the dry pellets that preoperatively constituted their entire diet, and they do not drink water. Even on the

FIGURE 13.7—Stages in the recovery seen in the lateral hypothalamic syndrome. (Adapted from P. Teitelbaum and A. N. Epstein. The lateral hypothalamic syndrome. *Psychol. Rev.,* 1962, 69, 83.)

	STAGE ONE ADIPSIA, APHAGIA	STAGE TWO ADIPSIA, ANOREXIA	STAGE THREE ADIPSIA, DEHYDRATION-APHAGIA	STAGE FOUR RECOVERY
Eats wet, palatable foods	No	Yes	Yes	Yes
Regulates food intake and body weight on wet, palatable foods	No	No	Yes	Yes
Eats dry foods (if hydrated)	No	No	Yes	Yes
Drinks water; survives on dry food and water	No	No	No	Yes

palatable diet, however, they do not eat enough to maintain their normal weight, and they eventually starve to death if they are not also tube-fed. Thus animals in this stage are anorexic and do not show normal regulation of food intake.

ADIPSIA WITH A SECONDARY DEHYDRATION APHAGIA—In the third stage of recovery, lateral hypothalamic animals increase their intake of a liquid diet to the point of normally regulating their food intake and weight (Williams and Teitelbaum, 1959). They still do not drink, however. If their water balance is artificially maintained, palatability is no longer essential to their eating. They eat chow and other foods just as normal animals do. But if they become dehydrated, their food intake declines, and, as a consequence, they die just as they would in earlier stages. In this stage, however, the animals do not eat simply because they do not drink. The basic problem is an adipsia. Incidentally, by appropriately weaning them from liquid food to sugar solution and then to a saccharin solution, they can be induced to maintain adequate water intake. They still refuse plain water, but they "eat" the nonnutritive sweet saccharin solution and thus get their water as a by-product.

RECOVERY—Adipsia may be permanent in some animals. If so, they may live out their lives in the stage just described. Usually, however, thirst eventually returns, and the animals appear to be fully recovered. They get along on stock diets and water just as normal laboratory rats do. It can be shown, however, that they are still somewhat finicky. A very slight amount of quinine in their food may make them refuse to eat it. Similarly, they refuse water with an amount of quinine in it that a normal, thirsty rat readily accepts.

There are two general points to be made about the four stages of the lateral hypothalamic syndrome. One is that recovery presumably occurs because not all the cells concerned in the function have been destroyed in the operation. This seems to be the case whenever recovery occurs after brain injury, as we have pointed out in other chapters (Chapters 10 and 18). This interpretation is bolstered by the fact that those animals that have the largest lateral hypothalamic lesions are the ones that recover most slowly or the least completely (Morgane, 1961). Furthermore, additional lesions made near the site of the first lesions in animals that have recovered reinstate the syndrome (Teitelbaum and Epstein, 1962).

The other general point to make is that the lateral hypothalamic area is obviously concerned in both eating and drinking. Indeed, it is either more concerned in drinking than eating or the drinking structures are so arranged in relation to the feeding structures that lesions always affect the drinking more than the feeding system. At any rate, the adipsia is always more severe and lasts longer than the aphagia, and the two are not separable by hypothalamic lesions. As we shall see below, however, there are ways of separating them by means of chemical stimulation.

FEEDING SYSTEM

For the present, let us restrict ourselves to eating and feeding, leaving a discussion of thirst until later. The area of the lateral hypothalamus concerned has been called the *feeding system* or center because its normal function appears to be that of a "start" or facilitating system in eating. This interpretation is confirmed by the results of experiments in which the area is stimulated chemically or electrically.

Animals with food available and with stimulation applied to the lateral hypothalamic area are made to eat when such stimulation is turned on. The stimulation may be electrical (Wyrwicka et al., 1959), hypertonic salt solutions (Epstein, 1960), or certain adrenergic drugs such as epinephrine (Grossman, 1960). Moreover, if an animal (in this case a goat) has been taught to place its paw on a table to receive a food reward, electrical stimulation of the lateral area evokes the conditioned reaction (Wyrwicka et al., 1959).

It is interesting that the feeding center is also the same center in the lateral hypothalamus that is a good placement for electrical self-stimulation (Margules and Olds, 1962). When electrodes are implanted at different positions in the lateral hypothalamus, the sites that, upon stimulation, cause feeding responses are the same sites at which animals will press a bar for central stimulation. There were a few sites that were effective for self-stimulation and not for eating, but any site that produced feeding responses was also good for self-stimulation. In this region of the brain the feeding system and the self-reward system appear to be identical.

There are other facts that point to this same conclusion (see Figure 13.8). If the ventromedial satiety center is destroyed or anesthetized, thus releasing the lateral center from inhibition and causing a hyperphagic syndrome, both eating and the rate of self-stimulation are accelerated (Hoebel and Teitelbaum, 1962). Also, rats that are hungry self-stimulate themselves more than when they are satiated. Conversely, when an animal has been fully fed or when an electrical stimulus is applied to the ventromedial area self-stimulation of the lateral area either stops or is severely depressed. Hence it is clear that, in this case, the rewarding effect of self-stimulation depends on the lateral hypothalamic area and on the degree to which this area is inhibited by the ventral satiety center.

THIRST

The mechanisms of thirst, although not entirely understood, appear to be simpler than those of hunger. Perhaps this is because water is a single substance, not a mixture of many different ones playing different roles in metabolism. As in the case of hunger, our general plan of presentation is to start

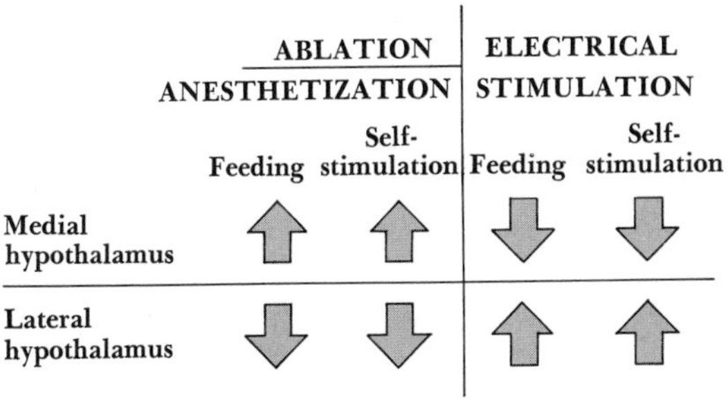

	ABLATION ANESTHETIZATION		ELECTRICAL STIMULATION	
	Feeding	Self-stimulation	Feeding	Self-stimulation
Medial hypothalamus	⬆	⬆	⬇	⬇
Lateral hypothalamus	⬇	⬇	⬆	⬆

FIGURE 13.8—Hypothalamic control of feeding and self-stimulation. (Adapted from B. G. Hoebel and P. Teitelbaum. Hypothalamic control of feeding and self-stimulation. *Science*, February 2, 1962, 135, 375. Adapted from *Science* by permission.)

with oral and gastric factors, then proceed to the blood and humoral factors, and end with the brain mechanisms involved.

WATER BALANCE

First, let us review briefly the salient features of water utilization in the body.

Water is involved in the metabolism of various food stuffs, and, as we have seen, both the need for water and the intake of water interact with food intake. In the end, however, it is water balance that counts in determining water intake. This is established by the relative rates of water loss and intake. There are three ways in which water is lost from the body: (1) by perspiration through the skin, (2) by evaporation of moisture in the respiratory passages, and (3) through urine and feces. There is only one way that water is taken into the body and that is by drinking it or by the ingestion of foods containing water.

Ingested water, of course, passes to the stomach. Virtually none of it is absorbed there. However, it normally passes on rapidly into the intestine, and most absorption of water occurs rapidly in the upper fifth or so of the small intestine. How rapidly it is absorbed, however, depends on the concentration of ions in it. Pure water in an empty gut passes through the intestinal wall in minutes. And, in general, all hypotonic solutions are rapidly absorbed but not so rapidly as pure water (O'Kelly et al., 1958). Hypertonic solutions, on the other hand, are not absorbed rapidly. Instead they draw water from the blood plasma into the intestine (Börnstein et al., 1959). Then, only after the intestinal contents have been made isotonic in this way does absorption begin to proceed. Hence, the absorption of hypertonic solutions may be quite slow. These facts, as we shall see, are related to the mechanisms of thirst.

Upon absorption, water is transported by the blood to the tissues, including the excretory organs. The amount of water in the blood tends to remain relatively constant, but this constancy is maintained at the expense of the tissues. These include the brain and the salivary glands. When the body is deprived of water, cells in these organs will be depleted. They may also lose water if the blood becomes more saline than normal. Just as in the case of intestinal absorption, salt in hypertonic concentrations tends to "pull" water in its direction until isotonic conditions are restored.

To summarize this, there is a chain of events from water ingestion to the tissues. Plain water and hypotonic solutions are absorbed into the blood, and water is then made available to the tissues. Conversely, hypertonic solutions in the gut pull water from the blood, and this, or any other condition, including water loss from the body, that increases the tonicity of the blood, is reflected in water loss from the tissues. So far as the mechanisms of thirst are concerned, the two most important tissues are the salivary glands and the brain.

ORAL FACTORS

Many years ago, the physiologist Cannon (1932) proposed a *local theory* of thirst. Simply stated, the theory asserted that thirst was an experience arising from dryness of the mouth. This dryness, in turn, reflected the state of water in the tissues of the body.

Many of the older experiments on thirst were attempts to test the local theory. In one experiment, the salivary glands were tied off, thus producing chronically dry-mouthed dogs. The intake of these dogs was no more than that of normal animals (Gregersen, 1932). In a similar study, salivary secretion was reduced by extirpating most of the salivary glands (Montgomery, 1931). Dogs prepared in this way drank water somewhat more often than normal dogs, but their overall intake remained the same. A human case with congenital absence of the salivary glands was like the "dry-mouthed" dogs (Steggerda, 1941). He drank more frequently than normal people, but he never ingested excessive amounts in any one day.

The conclusion to be drawn from these various studies is that dryness of the mouth is a minor factor in thirst. It may cause organisms to drink and thus may constitute a "start" factor in drinking. Dryness of the mouth is, however, not the only "start" factor nor a regulating factor in overall intake, for good water regulation takes place in chronically dry-mouthed individuals. Search for the principal "start" and "stop" mechanisms regulating drinking must be made elsewhere.

REGULATION OF DRINKING

Water intake, like food intake, is carefully regulated. It is very sensitive to minor losses of water from the body, and it occurs at intervals and in amounts necessary to maintain the water balance of the body within rather narrow limits (Robinson and Adolph, 1943). Dogs begin to drink, for example, when they have lost only 0.5 percent of their body weight in water. When no food is allowed during these tests, they take water at frequent intervals, in amounts proportional to the water they have lost. They do not, however, drink quite enough to make up their water losses completely unless they have access to food. If they can eat as well as drink, they take amounts of water that are proportional to both amount of solid food ingested and to their previous water losses. With food and water ad libitum, therefore, perfect water balance is maintained over long periods of time.

The same sort of accurate regulation of water intake is seen even more dramatically when dogs are deprived of water (Adolph, 1941; Bellows, 1939). In these experiments, the water deficits were estimated by measuring the difference in body weight under conditions of free water intake and after deprivation. If the dogs were allowed to drink after various amounts of water deprivation, they showed an ability to "estimate" very accurately their water deficits. The amount of water they ingested in a five-minute period, in fact, was directly proportional to the amount of water deficit they had accumulated during the deprivation.

GASTRIC FACTORS

In order to analyze the respective roles of oral and gastric factors in the regulation of water intake, investigators have studied dogs prepared with esophageal fistulas (Adolph, 1941). In these animals, the esophagus was cut; then the upper and lower ends of it were brought out to the surface so that the water the animals drank could not get to the stomach. Their drinking was sham drinking. In such sham drinking, just as in the normal drinking described above, the dogs drank water in proportion to their deficit (see Figure 13.9).

WATER LOADING—Carrying the experiment one step further, the investigator placed water directly into the stomach through the opening in the lower part of the esophagus. After a period of deprivation, he put into the stomach an amount of water equal to the animal's water deficit. Then, after varying periods of time, the dogs were allowed to drink. When they drank immediately after water had been placed in the stomach, they took enough to make up their water deficit just as if they had not been "prewatered." If drinking was delayed ten minutes, they took some water but not enough to make up the deficit. After a wait of fifteen minutes, the dogs did not drink at all. Similar results were also obtained in a normal animal given water through a stomach tube.

SALT-SOLUTION LOADING—This experiment shows that water in the gastrointestinal tract, after a brief delay, is capable of inhibiting drinking. This effect, however, depends on what else may be in the water or in the tract that may change the osmotic pressure of the fluid. This has been demonstrated in an experiment in which animals (rats) were preloaded with varying concentrations of salt solution from pure water to 3 percent salt (O'Kelly and

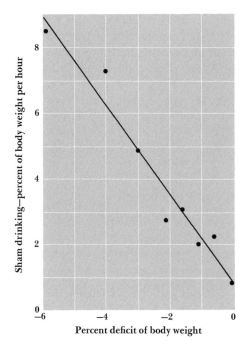

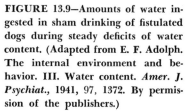

FIGURE 13.9—Amounts of water ingested in sham drinking of fistulated dogs during steady deficits of water content. (Adapted from E. F. Adolph. The internal environment and behavior. III. Water content. *Amer. J. Psychiat.*, 1941, 97, 1372. By permission of the publishers.)

Falk, 1958). After a fifteen-minute delay, they were tested for their rate of bar pressing to obtain water. All hypotonic loads, as one might expect, depressed water intake. Isotonic loads made no difference at all. It was as though no fluid had been placed in the stomach. But hypertonic loads increased water intake. As we indicated earlier, hypertonic fluids in the intestine cause water to be pulled from the blood into the intestine. This condition increases thirst.

From these experiments, the conclusion may be drawn that there are two "stop" factors regulating drinking. The first one appears to be the sheer act of drinking, for in the dog drinking stops within five minutes of the time it starts. This is too soon for the water to be absorbed and to affect the internal environment. A certain water deficit leads to a certain amount of drinking behavior, whether or not a bodily need is satisfied. Ultimately, of course, the bodily need must be relieved by water; otherwise drinking begins again. The second "stop" factor is gastric. Water placed in the stomach inhibits drinking in fifteen to thirty minutes. Here it may be presumed that some of the water has been absorbed, perhaps enough to change temporarily the osmotic pressure of blood.

STOMACH DISTENSION—It is possible that there is still a third "stop" mechanism, mechanical distension of the stomach. At any rate, distending the stomach by putting a balloon in it and filling the balloon with water inhibits drinking in dogs (Barker et al., 1954). Whether this is simply a reaction to discomfort or a normal factor in the regulation of drinking is not clear (Cheng, 1958).

INTRAGASTRIC REGULATION—It is clear, however, that normal regulation of water intake can take place when all the water ingested bypasses the mouth and enters the stomach directly (Epstein, 1960). The method for studying this is exactly the same as that described above for intragastric feeding. Tubes are permanently inserted in the stomach, and the rat learns to obtain all its water by pressing a bar that delivers a squirt of water for every bar press or for a certain number of presses. Normal rats studied over a long period of time regulate their intake of water by this means about as accurately as normal animals. Moreover, in experimental *diabetes insipidus* (see below), which considerably increases the normal requirements for water, a rat increases its water intake in proportion to the increased demand. There are special circumstances in which a rat's intragastric regulation may be thrown off, but under "normal" conditions it is quite good. From this fact, it may be concluded that oral factors, though operative in the normal animal, are not necessary for good water regulation. This may be accomplished by intragastric intake alone.

HORMONAL FACTORS

It has long been known that the posterior portion of the pituitary gland secretes a hormone that is important in the normal water balance of the body (see Patton, 1960). The hormone is called the *antidiuretic hormone* (ADH). More recently, it has become clear that the secretion of this hormone is not limited to the posterior hypophysis. Rather, the neurons having their cell bodies in the supraoptic nucleus of the hypothalamus and sending their fibers down the infundibular stalk to the pituitary are also secretory in function. Consequently, damage either to the supraoptic nucleus (Ralph, 1960), the infundibulum, or the posterior hypophysis (Barker et al., 1954) interferes with the production of ADH.

When the secretion of ADH is reduced, man and animals develop the symptoms of *diabetes insipidus*, i.e., abnormally severe thirst (polydipsia) and excessive urination (polyuria). ADH normally inhibits the output of water into the urine by promoting the reabsorption of water into the blood in the renal tubules. Without the normal level of ADH, excessive quantities of water are lost in the urine, thus causing a negative water load. The water deficit then causes excessive thirst. In other words, the increased thirst that follows reduction of ADH by damage to the hypothalamus or hypophysis is a consequence rather than a cause of the excessive urination (Richter, 1935).

It is not known whether the antidiuretic hormone normally plays any part in the mechanism of thirst. It may do so. When the body is dehydrated and needs to conserve water, the secretion of ADH is increased (see Pickford, 1945). Water deficit thus seems to affect the hormone, which in turn affects excretory activity of the kidney. It would appear that changes in osmotic pressure of the blood as a consequence of dehydration stimulate the neuro-secretory cells of the hypothalamic hypophyseal system. In other words, the neurosecretory cells secreting ADH may also function as osmoreceptors. That, at any rate, makes a plausible hypothesis.

CELLULAR HYDRATION

It seems quite clear that the crucial factor in thirst is dehydration of the cells of the body. Many signs point in this direction, but an experiment will illustrate it (Gilman, 1937). One group of dogs was injected with a 20 percent solution of sodium chloride, and another group was injected with 40 percent urea. These concentrations were selected because they are isomolar and produce the same rise in the osmotic pressure of the blood. On the other hand, they penetrate cells at different rates. The saline diffuses slowly into cells and as a result tends to draw water out of them soon after injection. Urea, on the other hand, is much more freely diffusible and permits equilibrium to be reached at the cell membranes without any loss of water. The difference in drinking after these two injections is unmistakable. When water is offered fifteen minutes after the saline injection, dogs drink large quantities. After urea injection, however, they do not drink until after an hour or more. It is only then that they begin to lose water through the kidney in the process of excreting the excess urea.

It can also be demonstrated that the same conditions that produce cellular hydration also inhibit drinking even when an overall deficit of water has built up. To produce this condition, injections of glucose may be used (Darrow and Yannet, 1935). A 5 percent solution of glucose injected intraperitoneally causes water to enter the cells of the body and thus temporarily alleviates cellular dehydration. When such a solution is injected into very thirsty dogs, they do not drink. Hence, the state of hydration of the cells of the body seems to be the important condition in thirst.

There are two implications of this conclusion. One is that dehydration of cells causes the relative concentration of minerals to increase, thus increasing osmotic pressure. It is undoubtedly this change in osmotic pressure, rather than the amount of water per se, that is significant in water metabolism and probably also in thirst. Secondly, the cells of the brain should be affected as much or more than others by changes in cellular hydration. Since it is known that different groups of cells in the brain are differentially sensitive to certain chemical stimuli, it is a good hypothesis that certain cells connected with the thirst mechanism that are especially sensitive to changes in osmotic pressure will be found.

NEURAL MECHANISMS

In covering the hypothalamic mechanisms of hunger, we learned that the lateral hypothalamus contains "start" areas for both feeding and drinking. Lesions in this area cause aphagia and adipsia. The areas for feeding and drinking are probably not identical, but they overlap so much that the lateral hypothalamic syndrome always includes deficits in both. In discussing hormonal factors in thirst, we also learned that the supraoptic area of the hypothalamus functions in a "stop" or inhibitory mechanism of thirst. This appears to differ from the corresponding area of the hypothalamus, the ventromedial nucleus, concerned in the inhibition of feeding, for it has its effects through the output of the antidiuretic hormone from the posterior hypophysis. Whether it has any other neurally mediated effects is not at present known.

The other information about neural mechanisms of thirst has to do with the so-called "start" mechanisms. These include both the lateral hypothalamic area already mentioned and portions of the limbic system. Studies have been made of the responses of these neural systems to various kinds of chemical stimulation.

SALT SOLUTIONS—Modern techniques of implanting cannulas in the brain make it possible to stimulate a given point in the brain with minute amounts of chemical substances either in solution or in crystalline form. The earliest use of the technique in behavior studies was with the hypothalamic drinking areas of the goat (see Andersson, 1953). Saline solutions of different concentration, both hypotonic and hypertonic, were injected into the lateral hypothalamus while goats were in a drinking situation and subjected to varying degrees of water deprivation. The results were rather simple and straightforward. Goats that had had all the water they wanted started drinking again when the area was injected with hypertonic salt solutions. These are solutions whose osmotic pressure is greater than normal. On the other hand, goats deprived of water and engaged in the act of drinking stopped drinking when the area was injected with hypotonic saline solution. Such a solution has an osmotic pressure less than normal.

Whether the crucial factor in these experiments was osmotic pressure in general or salt concentration in particular is not clear. From other work cited above, one might guess that it was osmotic pressure. However, since salt is a principal factor in determining the osmotic pressure of blood plasma, in the normal operation of the thirst mechanism, the difference may be academic.

ADRENERGIC VERSUS CHOLINERGIC STIMULATION—Although the feeding and drinking areas of the lateral hypothalamus are affected by the chemical composition of the blood, they are undoubtedly regulated by neural inputs from other parts of the brain. And although the feeding and drinking areas are difficult to distinguish anatomically, they can be differentiated chemically.

This has been shown in an experiment in which the areas have been chemically stimulated with cholinergic and adrenergic drugs (Grossman, 1960).

In this experiment, food and water were available to rats at all times. At intervals of three days or more, a drug was injected in crystalline form into the lateral hypothalamus and measures of drinking and eating following the injection were recorded. Two adrenergic drugs were used: norepinephrine and epinephrine (see page 94). Likewise, two cholinergic drugs were used: acetylcholine and carbachol. As controls, comparable amounts of solid NaCl and strychnine were deposited.

The results can be seen in Figure 13.10. They are quite dramatic. The adrenergic drugs greatly increased food consumption but, as compared with the cholinergic drugs, caused little water consumption. Indeed, the drinking that occurred with adrenergic drugs appeared to be secondary to eating, for it occurred largely after considerable food had been consumed. On the other hand, the cholinergic drugs caused a highly significant increase in drinking, while at the same time depressing food intake to a level well below that for control injections. From this experiment, it would appear that the effective inputs to the lateral hypothalamic drinking and feeding area are different for the two activities. That for drinking is cholinergic, whereas that for eating is adrenergic.

LIMBIC SYSTEM—There is other evidence that the neural mechanism for drinking is cholinergic (Fisher and Coury, 1962). This evidence also implicates several areas of the brain in the drinking mechanisms. Through permanently implanted cannulas that sampled many different brain areas, crystalline carbachol, a cholinergic drug, was deposited in varying amounts. The mean water intake just prior to this injection was compared with the intake during the hour after deposition. For many cannula positions, there was no difference, but for several others there was. In these, the mean intake after injection was 9 or more milliliters as compared with a control intake of 1.4 milliliters. Virtually all the areas involved in a significant increase in drinking were in the limbic system. Such areas included the hippocampus, septal region, lateral hypothalamus, anterior nucleus of the thalamus, and the cingulate gyrus. This result implicates the limbic system in thirst, which otherwise is known for its importance in emotion and self-stimulation (see Chapter 11). However, not all of any one of the limbic structures was implicated. Only one part of the hippocampus, for example, affected the increased drinking, while other parts did not. Hence, it is to be concluded that *some* of the circuits in the limbic system are concerned in thirst. These may or may not be those involved in emotion and self-stimulation.

ANTICHOLINERGIC DRUGS—The fact that the thirst system is cholinergic has been confirmed by other experiments in which anticholinergic drugs have

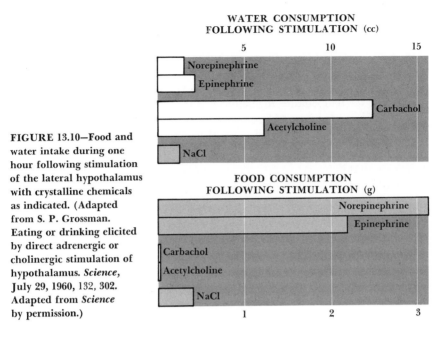

WATER CONSUMPTION
FOLLOWING STIMULATION (cc)

FIGURE 13.10—Food and
water intake during one
hour following stimulation
of the lateral hypothalamus
with crystalline chemicals
as indicated. (Adapted
from S. P. Grossman.
Eating or drinking elicited
by direct adrenergic or
cholinergic stimulation of
hypothalamus. *Science,*
July 29, 1960, 132, 302.
Adapted from *Science*
by permission.)

been used systematically. In this case, anticholinergic drugs were injected into the circulatory system via intraperitoneal injection (Stein, 1963). Two anticholinergic drugs known to have central effects (scopolamine and atropine) greatly depressed water intake whereas their (methylated) analogs, known to have relatively little central effect, did not.

TEMPERATURE DRIVE

We shall mention in passing another bodily need, the temperature drive. This is a drive to maintain environmental temperature within certain limits. In warm-blooded animals, this is tied to the maintenance of a relatively constant body temperature. But, as we shall see in Chapter 15, cold-blooded animals such as fish have temperature preferences, and a fish can be taught to press a bar to lower water temperature when it gets too high and in this way maintain the environmental temperature between 33.5 and 36.5°C most of the time (Rozin and Mayer, 1961).

The bar-pressing technique has also been used to study temperature drives in rats. When placed in a cold environment, say of 2°C, rats regularly push a bar to obtain brief bursts of heat (Carlton and Marks, 1958). The amount of such bar pressing varies with the animal's degree of acclimatization to cold (Laties and Weiss, 1960). It increases when anything is done that decreases metabolic rate, such as thyroidectomy (Laties and Weiss, 1959) or undernourishment or pantothenic acid deficiency (Weiss, 1957).

A center for temperature regulation is known to be located in the anterior part of the hypothalamus (Hardy et al., 1962). Changes in the temperature of this area cause circulatory changes throughout the body (Adams, 1963). Thus, although considerably more research needs to be done on the subject, it appears that there are hypothalamic mechanisms for the temperature drive just as there are for hunger and thirst.

14 SEXUAL BEHAVIOR

SINCE SEXUAL BEHAVIOR frequently leads to the birth of young, it is closely related to maternal and nesting behavior. Relatively more, however, is known about the physiological basis of sexual behavior than of these other behaviors. Hence it has been singled out for treatment in this chapter. Nesting and maternal behavior are considered in the next chapter along with other varieties of instinctive behavior.

In approaching the material to be presented here, it should be kept in mind that there are many species differences in sexual behavior (Beach, 1947). Some of these are species-specific; that is, differences in patterns of sexual behavior may be seen in closely related species at about the same level of the phyletic scale. Other differences are related, at least roughly, to position in the scale. With a few minor exceptions, our coverage here will be limited to birds and mammals, and particularly to mammals. Even with this restriction, we must at times note differences among species or phyletic groups of animals.

Since we are concerned with the physiological aspects of sexual behavior, little will be said here about the effects of learning or experience. It is possible, however, to observe such effects in virtually all animals from fishes to man. In general, organisms lower in the scale are more rigidly governed by physiological mechanisms. In higher mammals, particularly the primates, experience plays a relatively more important role in sexual behavior.

CHARACTER OF SEXUAL BEHAVIOR

As a background for discussing physiological factors in sexual behavior, we shall first describe briefly the patterns that may be seen in the warm-blooded animals (birds and mammals) most commonly employed in research (see Beach, 1949; Scott, 1961). The basic pattern of heterosexual behavior seen in most mammals and birds, as well as in many lower vertebrates, has three main parts: (1) orientation of the two partners, which may involve elaborate courtship behavior; (2) postural adjustments in which the female elevates and exposes her genitals while the male mounts her; and (3) the occurrence of genital reflexes until ejaculation occurs in the male. Let us look at these components of sexual behavior more closely.

BIRDS

Sexual behavior in birds may be divided into two types: primary, copulatory behavior and secondary, courtship behavior. It consists of several rather distinct activities, among them billing and cooing. In billing behavior, the bills of the male and female are interlocked in such a way that the lower beak of the female is usually below that of the male, the upper half being in the mouth cavity of the male. With their bills interlocked, the birds move their heads up and down with a vigor and quickness that suggest excitement. Interspersed with this billing may be vocalization, charging, and strutting—all characteristic of sexual behavior. Charging and strutting have much in common, but charging is more characteristic of some animals, e.g., pigeons, and strutting of others, e.g., turkey and peacock. Such secondary behavior prefaces copulatory behavior and in some instances clearly serves as a stimulus to it.

Courtship merges into copulatory behavior when the female assumes submissive and receptive posture. This consists of a slight spreading of the wings, extension of the tail, and flexing of the legs and is the posture that is conducive to copulation. The behavior of the male becomes dominant. He mounts the female and makes a balanced adjustment with his feet and wings, in some cases by grasping the feathers of the female's neck with his beak. Then copulation occurs and is followed by a period of inactivity, after which the sequence of mating activities may be reenacted. There are, of course, several variations in patterns of sexual behavior in the same animals and in different animals, but the highly organized character of the mating patterns is remarkable.

MAMMALS

The mammalian animals whose mating activities have been most extensively studied are the cat, rabbit, guinea pig, and rat (see Beach, 1949). The male sexual behavior of all these animals is quite similar. It consists in mounting, clasping the neck of the female in the mouth, and making pelvic thrusts (the basic copulatory movements). Patterns of mating behavior of the females of these animals are also highly organized in relatively stereotyped sequences, but they differ markedly in different species, as is indicated by the following descriptions.

Receptive behavior of the female rat consists simply of tense crouching for brief periods, interrupted by quick darts about the cage and a great amount of running activity. When mounted, the female rat assumes the posture that allows the male to achieve intromission and copulate successfully. It consists of an elevation of the rump, together with a tense receptive posture. In the rabbit, it includes also an adjustment of the tail. The guinea pig, along with this reflex pattern, frequently emits a characteristic vocalization. Whereas the mating pattern of the female rodent is rather simple, receptive behavior of the cat is much more highly organized and conspicuous. It begins with courtship, which leads to copulation, which in turn is followed by an afterreaction (Bard, 1940, p. 554).

> The courtship behavior includes playful rolling, excessive rubbing, a curious slow vocalization (the estrual call) and crouching and treading. The estrual crouch is a most specific posture. Resting on chest and forearms with pelvis raised somewhat and with tail elevated and turned to one side, the animal tends to execute treading movements of the hind legs. It is in this posture that the male is accepted. Many estrual cats crouch and tread quite spontaneously in the absence of any specific external stimulus. Others do not show this behavior unless they are in the presence of a male or receive some stimulation of the external genital region. . . . In most animals [the afterreaction] consists of more or less frantic rubbing, squirming, licking and rolling.

Infrahuman primates exhibit fundamentally the same pattern of behavior in mating as the lower animals. In monkeys and chimpanzees, the female bends forward at the hips, presenting the genitalia, and the male grips her hind legs with his feet and clasps her hips. Occasionally chimpanzees copulate in a face-to-face position. In this case the male keeps his feet flat on the ground and holds the female with his arms while she embraces him with her hind legs.

HOMOSEXUAL BEHAVIOR

The masculine and feminine patterns of sexual behavior just described are not confined to heterosexual situations (see Beach, 1949). Both male and female animals are capable of both masculine and feminine patterns and often show them. For example, male rats frequently display feminine receptive behavior when aggressive males attempt to mount them. Similarly, females, especially when highly receptive, often show mounting behavior that is characteristic of males. The occurrence of such homosexual behavior is seen in virtually all species of animals. It is not necessarily the result of sexual deprivation, for it may be seen when members of the opposite sex are available or have recently been copulated. Rather, it seems to go along with sexual excitement and is part of the normal spectrum of sexual behavior.

These observations are relevant to the explanation of homosexual behavior in man. They imply that homosexual behavior is not to be explained entirely by the constitutional or hormonal makeup of the person. Although, as we shall see later, homosexual tendencies can be altered by changing hormonal conditions at the appropriate stage in development, a certain amount of homosexual behavior is part of the normal array of sexual patterns. As Kinsey put it in his surveys of sexual behavior in man (1941, p. 428):

> Any explanation of the homosexual must recognize that a large portion of the younger adolescents demonstrates the capacity to react to both homosexual and heterosexual stimuli; that there is a fair number of adults who show this same capacity; and that there is only a gradual development of the exclusively homosexual or exclusively heterosexual patterns which predominate among older adults.

AUTOGENITAL STIMULATION

Somewhat similar statements can be made about autogenital activities (Beach, 1949). Some form of stimulation of the organism's own genitals is frequently seen in animals. It may consist of licking behavior, of making pelvic thrusts on inanimate objects such as sticks, or, in the higher mammals, of manual manipulation of the genitals. Such autostimulation frequently occurs in conjunction with heterosexual activities, taking place just before or after coitus. It may also occur at other times when the animal is isolated from or not in the company of members of the other sex. It is most prominent in the male, but it also occurs in females. It is most common in those primates that possess well-developed manipulative ability, and it may, in the case of the male, take the form of full-fledged masturbation in which ejaculation occurs. Hence, autogenital stimulation must be regarded as a "common element in the basic sexual pattern of mammals and is not to be characterized as a substitute or 'perverted' form of behavior" (Beach, 1949, p. 63).

GONADAL CYCLES AND SEXUAL BEHAVIOR

Sexual behavior runs in cycles; i.e., it has its ebbs and flows. In general, three main types of cycles may be distinguished: life cycles, seasonal cycles, and estrous cycles. All these cycles depend in one way or another on hormones. In this section, we shall describe the cycles that have been studied and the factors known to affect them. In the section that follows, we shall consider in detail the hormonal control of sexual behavior.

LIFE CYCLE

In the typical mammal, there is a major period in life during which sexual behavior may be seen. It begins with puberty and ends or declines during the last third of the animal's life. This life cycle of sexual activity is under the control of the pituitary gland and specifically of the gonadotrophic hormones of the adrenohypophysis (page 93). Through normal maturational processes, and in many animals as a result of external lighting and temperature conditions, the pituitary develops to the point of secreting large quantities of gonadotrophic hormones. This is the time of puberty in the typical mammal.

In the male, the gonadotrophic hormones stimulate sperm making and the secretion of androgens, the male gonadal hormones (page 98). In the female, the gonadotrophic hormones develop the ovaries and cause the secretion of estrogens, the female gonadal hormones. Once sufficient quantities of the gonadal hormones are produced under the influence of the pituitary hormones, they foster the development of secondary sex characteristics, such as the mature form of the reproductive organs, the distribution of body hair, and skeletal structure. At the same time, sexual behavior makes its appearance, although certain elements of it may be seen earlier.

After puberty, the period of sexual activity is continued intermittently throughout adulthood until some point at which the secretion of pituitary hormones begins to decline. Consequently, the gonads begin to regress, causing a reduction in gonadal hormones and also loss of the ability to produce eggs and sperm. In lower mammals, sexual behavior also tends to decline, although there are differences between females and males. In the primate and man, apparently because previous experience plays a more important role than it does in lower animals, sexual behavior may continue after gonadal regression has set in.

Certain of the fishes do not have prolonged periods of sexual activity. Rather, they have only one, relatively short period of spawning. Sometimes, as in the case of salmon, they die shortly after spawning is over (see Chapter 15).

SEASONAL CYCLES

In many animals, seasonal cycles of mating activities are superimposed on life cycles. The seasonal rise and wane of such activity goes along with the growth and decline of the gonads, which frequently can be measured directly by weighing them or by measuring their size (see Baggerman, 1957). The number and length of seasonal cycles vary in different animals. In the female dog, for example, there are two seasons of heat, one in the spring and another in the fall. Each lasts about two weeks. In mammals, seasonal cycles appear for the most part only in females, but in some species (marten and deer) they appear in the male as well. In birds, both male and female seasonal cycles are particularly prominent, and the male's gonadal development may be ahead of that of the female.

Various kinds of studies make it clear that the secretions of the pituitary gland are responsible for seasonal cycles (see Lehrman, 1959). In animals that can breed at any time of year, the pituitary keeps up its activity all the year round; but in seasonal breeders, it becomes active only just before and during the breeding season. One of the factors that is usually important in bringing the pituitary into action is the amount of light in the environment (Farner et al., 1953; Kirkpatrick and Leopold, 1953). Other factors, as we shall see below, also play a part. The important point is that seasonal fluctuations occur because of fluctuations in gonadotrophic activity of the pituitary gland.

ESTROUS CYCLES

Some animals are sexually active throughout the year. In mammalian males, for example, mating can occur at any time, for after puberty they do not have cyclic variations in gonadotrophic and hence of gonadal hormones. In many female mammals, however, there are short-run cycles in which sexual receptivity waxes and wanes with the ups and downs of ovarian activity. In infraprimate mammals, these short cycles are called *estrous cycles,* and the high points of gonadal and sexual activity are called *estrus* or *heat.* From a physiological and behavioral point of view, estrous cycles correspond closely to the *menstrual cycles* of primates. Both estrous cycles and menstrual cycles begin and end in a low point of sexual activity and ovarian development. At the midpoint of each cycle, about the time ovulation occurs, receptivity reaches a peak.

The physiological events underlying estrous and menstrual cycles have been worked out in considerable detail. The events are somewhat different, depending on whether pregnancy does or does not occur. Let us first take the case of the repeating estrous cycle that is not interrupted by pregnancy. In this case, three hormones are involved. One is estrogen; the other two are gonadotrophins: follicle-stimulating hormone (FSH) and luteinizing hormone (LH).

FOLLICLE-STIMULATING AND LUTEINIZING HORMONES—At the beginning of the cycle, the anterior hypophysis is secreting FSH (see Figure 14.1). This causes the primary, immature follicle to begin developing. It also causes the follicle to secrete *estrogen*. That is the first step. But estrogen has two effects on the anterior pituitary gland: It causes the gland to secrete LH and at the same time to inhibit, or to slow down, the production of FSH. At this stage, the large amount of FSH and small amount of LH present act synergistically to bring the follicle to a fully ripened state ready to discharge an ovum. At the same time, the estrogen from the follicle is shifting the balance of FSH and LH production so that the secretion of FSH falls off and that of LH rises. Although the two act synergistically in causing ovulation, the LH is the

FIGURE 14.1—Scheme of events taking place in the ovary and uterus during the estrous cycle.

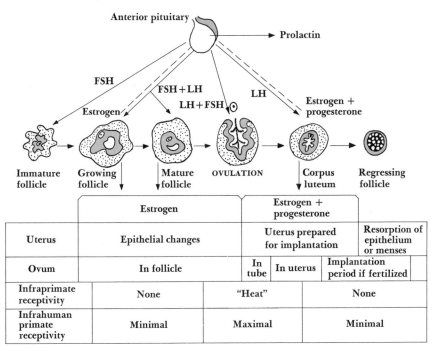

	Estrogen		Estrogen + progesterone	
Uterus	Epithelial changes		Uterus prepared for implantation	Resorption of epithelium or menses
Ovum	In follicle	In tube	In uterus	Implantation period if fertilized
Infraprimate receptivity	None	"Heat"	None	
Infrahuman primate receptivity	Minimal	Maximal	Minimal	

precipitating factor. In some cases and probably in most mammals, the concentration of LH is sufficient to cause spontaneous ovulation.

In some species such as the cat and the rabbit, ovulation does not occur unless copulation takes place. Then, the stimuli involved in copulation appear to cause a reflex discharge of LH from the anterior pituitary so that ovulation occurs within a few hours after copulation. At least, in such instances, the effects of copulation can be duplicated by electrical stimulation of the hypothalamus (see below).

After ovulation, the follicle begins a new stage of development and, under the influence of LH, becomes the *corpus luteum*. As the corpus luteum takes form, it continues to secrete estrogen, and, in addition, it elaborates a new hormone, *progesterone,* often called the *hormone of pregnancy* because it prepares the lining of the uterus for implantation by a fertilized egg. If pregnancy ensues, it maintains the conditions for supporting pregnancy. In that case, however, as we shall see, the progesterone comes largely from a different source.

PROLACTIN—When pregnancy follows copulation, a third gonadotrophin enters the picture. This is *prolactin*. It is actually present beforehand, along with the other two gonadotrophins, and helps LH in the formation of the corpus luteum. But after pregnancy takes place, and in some species merely after copulation, it becomes temporarily the dominant hormone. It preserves the corpus luteum, which otherwise would degenerate, for longer than the usual period. In man and in animals with a relatively long gestational period, this may be for as much as a month or more. During this period, it maintains the corpus luteum and causes it to secrete large amounts of estrogen and progesterone.

Several factors appear to be involved in maintaining prolactin secretion. In birds, this may be the presence of eggs in the oviducts (see Lehrman, 1961). The mechanical stimulation afforded by the egg after it has left the ruptured follicle apparently can both inhibit the pituitary production of LH, thus inhibiting the further maturation of follicles and egg production, and also stimulate the secretion of prolactin. In some species of mammals, the act of copulation appears to have somewhat the same effect. In these, pseudopregnancies occur that last for a number of days though not for as long as a true pregnancy. This may happen in rats and mice. Pseudopregnancies may also be induced by the injection of gonadotrophins, though not by FSH and LH in the absence of prolactin. Prolactin is necessary for the continuance of the corpus luteum with its production of estrogen and progesterone. Otherwise the luteum regresses, and a new estrous cycle begins.

PLACENTAL HORMONES—If pregnancy occurs, still another mechanism comes into play. This is the placenta, the body joining the young to the wall of the uterus (in mammals). First the fertilized egg implants in the uterine wall; then a placenta forms from the uterine epithelium and the developing, immature embryo. When the placenta has formed, it secretes gonadotrophins similar to those of the pituitary gland. These are called anterior-pituitary-like (APL) hormones. The APL hormones help to maintain the corpus luteum for a longer period than usual. By the time it regresses, the placenta takes over the major endocrine functions, secreting the large amounts of progesterone and estrogen that are characteristic of pregnancy.

If pregnancy does not occur after copulation, the corpus luteum regresses and the production of estrogen and progesterone drops. As a result, the uterine epithelium developed by these hormones is resorbed or, in animals that menstruate, is sloughed off and eliminated. In addition, the withdrawal of progesterone and estrogen permits the pituitary to secrete sufficient quantities of FSH to promote the development of a new follicle or follicles, thus starting a new cycle.

SEXUAL BEHAVIOR AND ESTRUS

Closely correlated with the physiological changes of the estrous cycle just described are variations in sexual receptivity of female animals (see Figure 14.1). The female rat, for example, has a four- to five-day estrous cycle and is receptive only during about six hours of this period. Usually heat occurs at night and can be identified by the appearance of cornified epithelial cells in the vaginal mucosa. When heat begins, there is an increase in general activity of the animal. The rat also hops and darts about its cage fitfully, and it responds to pressure stimulation of the lower back with an arching of the back called *lordosis*. During the rest of the cycle the female rat is relatively inactive and shows no signs of sexual receptivity. In fact, the anestrous female will fight off any attempts on the part of the male to mount. Here is a clear-cut case of the peak of sexual activity in an animal corresponding to the peak of estrogen production by the ripened ovary.

Essentially the same behavioral changes are seen in the menstrual cycle of infrahuman primates. Monkeys and chimpanzees show heightened sexual activity at about the time of ovulation. During this period the genitalia are characterized by reddening and swelling. The female in heat goes toward, and in general is sociable with, the male, whereas during anestrus the usual behavior is avoidance. In fact, the female in heat may actively try to attract the attention of the male and assume the specific receptive posture, thus "presenting" herself. In the case of the chimpanzee at least, the female in heat becomes socially dominant even in nonsexual matters such as food taking, whereas in anestrus she is subservient to the male.

Despite this correspondence of sexual behavior with the high points of estrogen production during heat, female monkeys and chimpanzees may show some signs of sexual activity during anestrus. In humans, departure from physiological cycles is even more marked. Sexual activity occurs at any time in the menstrual cycle but nonendocrine factors play an important role in human sexual behavior.

PREGNANCY AND ESTRUS

In most infrahuman animals, sexual drive is notably lacking in the female during pregnancy. In rats, for example, there are no further estrual periods of heat once pregnancy is started. Throughout the period of gestation, the female is not receptive to the male. But a few hours after birth of the young a period of estrus ensues, and impregnation may take place at this time (postparturitional heat). Immediately following this period, however, the mother goes into anestrus and does not display heat again until the end of the nursing period, about twenty-one days later. In spite of the lack of sexual drive and estrous cycles throughout these periods, there is a suggestion that ovarian cycles continue in pregnancy. In nearly all animals it is the common rule that the term of pregnancy is some multiple of the estrous cycle. Parturition seems to be associated, in fact, with the culmination of a cycle, for ovulation and postparturitional heat follow it closely. The hormonal causes of parturition, however, are still obscure.

ENVIRONMENTAL STIMULATION

The development of estrus and of sexual excitability is not purely endogenous; that is to say, it does not depend solely on factors within the organism. There are a number of environmental factors, aside from learning or experience, that play a part. No generalizations can be made that hold for all species, but one of the most potent environmental factors is light. In many fish, birds, and mammals, as has already been mentioned, the increasing length of the day during the winter and spring is normally an important, if not crucial, factor in seasonal cycles of sexual excitability (see Baggerman, 1957).

Light also affects estrous cycles. In the rat, estrus normally comes early in the dark part of a twenty-four-hour period and is accompanied by a characteristic burst of running. If the light-dark cycle is reversed, estrus and the burst of activity come during the new dark period. By keeping animals in constant light, moreover, the period of sexual receptivity can be prolonged although the running activity cannot (Browman, 1937; Hemmingsen and Krarup, 1937). On the other hand, rats kept in constant darkness reduce their activity and show prolonged periods of anestrus, coming into heat far less frequently than normally treated rats (Browman, 1937). From such facts as these, it has been learned that typically a cumulative effect of light on the organism helps to induce estrus and to prolong it once it is started.

In fish (Baggerman, 1957) and birds (Lehrman, 1961), other environmental factors play a part. Both temperature and light, working together but at somewhat different stages, are important in the gonadal development of many species and in both male and female members of it. Also, the availability of nesting materials and/or the presence of a male may be necessary for the culmination of sexual development (Lehrman et al., 1961). More will be said about this in the next chapter in connection with maternal behavior. Also, olfactory stimulation can play a part. In the male dog, there is little doubt that it is important both in tracking the estral female and in sexual excitability (Beach and Gilmore, 1949). On the other hand, olfactory stimulation from a strange male has been demonstrated to block the implantation of fertilized ova in mice recently inseminated (Bruce and Parrott, 1960). Other strange or disturbing environmental stimuli can do the same thing (Eleftheriou and Bronson, 1962).

These are just examples. Many more instances of environmental effects on gonadal and sexual activity could be cited. The important inference to be made from them is that there are hormonal responses to environmental stimuli (see Lehrman, 1959). It seems clear that in most, if not all, instances the effect is mediated through the anterior pituitary and its gonadotrophins. This is definitely true in the case of the effects of photic stimulation. Moreover, it is clear that the hypothalamus is involved. Since the anterior hypothalamus is not directly innervated by the hypothalamus, it appears that neurosecretory activities affect the anterior pituitary by way of the blood (see Chapter 15).

CASTRATION AND HORMONE ADMINISTRATION

All that we have said so far points to the hormones as the mainsprings of sexual behavior. That is partly true, especially in females and lower animals, and not quite so true in males and in higher mammals. Let us look into the matter in some detail, however, and consider exactly what happens to sexual behavior when the glands that make the hormones are removed or, conversely, hormone levels of the blood are increased (see Beach, 1948).

OVARIECTOMY

It is well established that monkeys and lower mammals become sexually unreceptive after complete removal of the ovaries. The effect on sexual activity is the same whether animals are castrated before or after puberty. But if castration is done during estrus, sexual behavior may persist for a short time, owing to the presence of large amounts of estrogens. Very shortly thereafter, however, sexual receptivity disappears permanently. If activity records are used as an index of sexual drive, they show that the gonadectomy has permanently abolished sex drive, for the usual cycles of activity (four to five days in the rat) are completely lacking.

In female primates and human beings, the effects of ovariectomy are not so definite (see Beach, 1947). Typically, there is a diminution of sexual desire, but in women this is highly variable. Some go on with about the same level of sexual activity as preoperatively. Others may sharply curtail such activity.

Undoubtedly, individual differences are important as well as attitudes toward sexual behavior. Certainly female sexual behavior in the higher primates and man is less crucially dependent on gonadal secretions than it is in lower animals.

MALE CASTRATION

The effects of gonadectomy on male animals differ considerably from the effects of ovariectomy on females (Beach, 1948). It is generally true that a male castrated before puberty never develops normal mating behavior. If castration is performed after puberty, however, copulation occurs normally for a short period and then diminishes slowly. In rats, for example, one month after castration, 33 percent of one group of castrates had ceased to copulate; after two months, 45 percent would no longer copulate; and in the subsequent fourth months, more and more animals lost their sexual drive (Stone, 1927). First to be lost was the capacity to ejaculate, and only later was the copulatory pattern dropped. Opportunity to practice copulation had no apparent effect on the length of time that sexual behavior would survive castration, for animals allowed to copulate behaved the same as those that were segregated.

Studies of higher animals show that some important changes have taken place in the course of evolution in the role of the sex hormones in the mating behavior of the male. While some dogs, castrated after sexual experience, show impairment of mating, others will copulate for as long as two years after operation. Supporting this finding is the fact that castration may have only slight effects on the sexual behavior of the male chimpanzee. In fact, it has been reported that a prepuberally castrated male chimpanzee was capable of vigorous sexual activity in adulthood (Clark, 1945).

Experience is one factor, though not the only one, affecting sexual activity following castration. Male cats that have sexual experience prior to castration show sexual performance after castration that is markedly superior to that of cats with little or no precastration experience, even though in both cases there is a decline of activity following castration (Rosenblatt and Aronson, 1958). Finally, although the data on man are not always in agreement, it seems to be the rule that sexual behavior will survive castration in adulthood and may even appear after castration before puberty. In the sexual behavior of males, then, the sex hormones have become less and less important in the course of evolution.

HYPOPHYSECTOMY

As one might expect, extirpation of the pituitary gland has an adverse effect on sexual behavior. The surprising fact about hypophysectomy, however, is that it has just as much effect on males as on females. In both cases, sexual behavior ceases rather promptly, and this effect seems to be permanent. It is not necessary, of course, to assume that the pituitary secretes a hormone that is crucial for male sexual behavior, for it is known that it governs the activity of several other glands, including especially thyroid and adrenocortical activity. In females, hypophysectomy and ovariectomy have just about the same effects. Following hypophysectomy, sexual receptivity promptly disappears and the ovaries and secondary sex apparatus rapidly regress.

REACTIVATION OF CASTRATES

As one can see, experiments with castration shed some light on the problem of hormones and sexual behavior. A natural partner of the method of castration is the method of replacement therapy, in which hormones in one form or another are used to treat animals (or people) suffering from various sorts of glandular deficiencies. As one might expect, it is possible to inject a gonadal hormone and offset the effects of removing the gonads. This will work in either male or female animals.

ANDROGEN—In castrated male guinea pigs, for example, sexual behavior returns after treatment with testosterone (Seward, 1940). The effects occur in the rat and in all infrahuman primates, even those that have been castrated before puberty. In the male rat, it is interesting that treatment with gonadal hormones first restores the copulatory pattern and sometime later the ability to ejaculate—just the reverse of the order of loss after castration (Beach and Holz-Tucker, 1949).

There are, of course, individual differences in the reactivation of castrates. These are due to both hormonal and nonhormonal factors. Also, such treatment produces an increase in sexual behavior in proportion to the effective dosage of hormones (Beach and Fowler, 1959). On the other hand, as in the effects of castration, previous experience makes a difference. The effects of androgen in reactivating castrated male cats depend to some extent on whether the animal has had prior copulatory experiences with females (Rosenblatt and Aronson, 1958). Therefore, the level of sexual activity seen in reactivated castrates is related both to hormone level and to sexual experience—and probably to other factors as well.

Unfortunately, statements about man cannot be so definite (see Beach, 1948). In some cases, injecting hormones in castrates seems to restore sexual potency and in others it does not. This is not surprising if we remember that castration in the first place sometimes seems to destroy sexual potency and sometimes not. Thus it appears that psychological and other factors are important enough in man to obscure the effects of castration and replacement therapy.

ESTROGEN—The effects of replacement therapy with ovariectomized females are much the same as those seen in the male. In castrated female rats, the injection of estrogen brings about estrus and sexual receptivity. The estrous cycle, however, is not entirely normal, for sexual receptivity does not wax and wane periodically nor does bodily activity come back to its usual peak in estrus. On the other hand, castrated female monkeys given estrogen show definite signs of sexual periodicity. There is, furthermore, a definite relation between the amount of hormone injected and the degree of sexual responsiveness induced.

The results with ovariectomized women are no clearer than those obtained with castrated men (see Beach, 1948). Many positive effects of hormone treatment are reported, but there have also been many failures. Unfortunately, one cannot tell from the literature whether suggestion and other "psychic" factors have been eliminated.

COMBINATION OF HORMONES—Although the androgens and estrogens are the primary sex hormones, their effectiveness sometimes depends on the presence of other hormones. In the guinea pig, for example, estrogen and progesterone given in sequence restore sexual behavior, as well as physiological signs of estrus, more effectively than estrogen alone (Boling et al., 1938). Species of animals differ, however, in their response to the combination. Most rodents react like the guinea pig. But receptivity in rabbits as well as in monkeys is actually inhibited by giving them progesterone; in castrated female monkeys it partly counteracts the effects of estrogen in restoring sexual behavior. Clinical reports say that progesterone also lowers the sexual desire of women (see Beach, 1948). All this, of course, fits in with the absence of sexual activity during pregnancy, when production of progesterone is high.

Reactivation of animals whose sexual drive has been lost as a result of hypophysectomy is also possible. Injection of gonadotrophic hormones will cause the gonads to mature again and will restore mating behavior. Gonadal hormones will do the same thing, and so it is known that the pituitary and its secretions are not crucial for mating behavior as long as there are adequate amounts of sex hormones.

INDUCED MATING IN NORMAL ANIMALS

Since there are many times in the life of normal animals when they are not sexually active, it would be interesting to know whether sex hormones can restore sexual activity at these times. Three kinds of studies bear directly on this question: (*1*) induction of mating behavior in immature animals, (*2*) stimulation of animals to breed out of season, and (*3*) reactivation of animals that have lost sexual powers in senility. All these studies are approaches to the question of whether animals that are inactive, presumably because of lack of gonadal hormones, are otherwise equipped to carry out mating behavior (see Beach, 1948).

PREMATURE DEVELOPMENT—Giving either gonadotrophins or gonadal hormones to immature animals, either male or female, makes them sexually active at an early age. Female rats given anterior pituitary extracts show signs of estrus at twenty-two days of age, although they normally do not show them until about fifty days. Just about the same thing happens when they are given estrogen. Similarly, male rats given androgen on the fourteenth day show sexual mounting as early as the sixteenth day. Similar reports have been made for mice and dogs. Taken together, they indicate that the neural mechanisms of sexual behavior are matured at an early age and that they simply wait to show themselves on the development of the gonads and their hormones.

ACTIVITY OUT OF SEASON—In many species that breed seasonally, sexual behavior can be induced off season in several ways. One way, as we saw previously, is by changing the light in the environment. Another is by injecting gonadotrophic or gonadal hormones. Similarly, in polyestrual animals like the rat, these same methods can be used to bring on or prolong periods of heat. Thus, again, it can be seen that hormones can arouse the neural mechanisms of sexual responsiveness quite apart from naturally occurring cycles.

DELINE WITH AGE—Sexual potency, of course, declines in man and animals as they get into old age. In lower animals, hormones sometimes succeed in bringing back sexual potency. In one study, for example, rats that were twenty-eight months old and had virtually ceased to copulate were reactivated by injections of testosterone (Minnick et al., 1946). Other studies of lower animals have come to similar conclusions. In man, however, the effects of hormones are not clear, and they frequently fail to restore sexual potency. That should not be very surprising in view of the fact that human beings can lose sexual potency even when they have adequate hormones. Also, psychological factors are more important in human sexual behavior than in lower animals.

SPECIFICITY OF SEX HORMONES

So far we have dealt only with the effects of male hormones on male animals and of female hormones on female animals. There are, of course, other possibilities. In fact, they raise the interesting question of what different kinds of hormones have to do with different patterns of behavior in the two sexes. Fortunately, there are a great many experiments on this question, and typical results are summarized in Table 14.1. The following are the main points:

1. In both male and female castrates androgen brings out masculine sexual behavior and estrogen feminine behavior. The sex of the animal, however, is of some importance, for it takes less male hormone to elicit masculine behavior in males than in females, and vice versa.

2. Androgen can bring out feminine behavior and estrogen masculine behavior in animals of both sexes. In such cases, however, it takes extremely high doses of hormones to produce rather slight effects in sexual behavior.

3. Under some circumstances, when an animal receives hormones of the

TABLE 14.1—The effect of androgen and estrogen on the masculine and feminine mating behavior of male and female animals

	EFFECT ON MALE	EFFECT ON FEMALE
Androgen	Normal masculine response	Sluggish or incomplete masculine response
	Very weak and incomplete feminine response	Sluggish or incomplete feminine response
	Inhibits masculine behavior of castrates if given early in life in large doses	May inhibit feminine responses slightly in intact females
Estrogen	Sluggish or incomplete feminine response	Normal feminine response
	Sluggish or incomplete masculine response	Very weak and incomplete masculine response
	May inhibit masculine responses slightly in intact males	Inhibits feminine behavior of castrates if given early in life in large doses

SOURCE: After F. A. Beach. *Hormones and behavior*. New York: Paul B. Hoeber, Inc., 1948. P. 220. By permission of the publishers.

opposite sex, its sexual behavior may be inhibited. When androgen is given to normal females, for example, it often inhibits feminine responses and facilitates masculine responses. The converse happens with estrogen given to males. Results such as these may simply mean that one set of responses is dominant over the other and not necesarily that there is any true inhibition by the hormone.

4. Male hormones given to males and female hormones given to females may inhibit the development of normal mating behavior if they are administered in large doses to animals castrated relatively early in life. When animals treated in this way become adults, they do not become sexually active even when treated with massive doses of the appropriate hormones.

EARLY ADMINISTRATION

This last point needs some elaboration because more than the activation of sexual behavior is involved. During development, the differentiation and maturation of various tissues both in the nervous system and in the sexual apparatus are subject to hormonal influences. Hence it may be asked how hormones affect the maturation of neural patterns and of the sex organs. In doing this, one should distinguish between homotypical and heterotypical hormones (Whalen and Nadler, 1963). Homotypical hormones are hormones of a given sex administered to the same sex; heterotypical hormones are those of one sex administered to organisms of the opposite sex.

PREGNANCY—During pregnancy, fetuses of both sexes are normally under the influence of high levels of estrogen circulating in maternal blood. This estrogen is homotypical for the female, heterotypical for the male. What happens if this normal relationship is reversed by administering testosterone to the mother, thus bringing female fetuses under the influence of the heterotypical hormone (Phoenix et al., 1959)? There are two consequences of such a treatment.

One is that females, if maternal testosterone injections are of very high dosage, are born as hermaphrodites. Their external genitalia are those of males and are, in fact, indistinguishable from those of normal males. To establish that they were genetic females, it was necessary to open the abdomen and note the presence of internal female tissues. From this fact, one can conclude that an unusual amount of male hormone during the fetal period markedly distorts organ development, partially reversing the normal, genetically determined differentiation of the sexual apparatus.

Secondly, the sexual behavior of the hermaphroditic females is altered when the animals are later tested as adults. When treated with estrogen and progesterone, the homotypical hormones, the animals (guinea pigs) show some elements of female sexual behavior, e.g., lordosis, but their capacity for this behavior is greatly reduced as compared with normal, control female animals. These animals, on the other hand, display more than a normal amount of male mounting behavior. Also, when treated with the heterotypical hormone, testosterone, they display an amount of male mounting behavior about like that seen in reactivated castrate males, while at the same time the female pattern of lordosis is suppressed.

From these results, it appears clear that the heterotypical hormone, administered during fetal development, not only reverses the sex of the external genitalia but also reverses markedly the differentiation of neural tissues mediating patterns of sexual behavior. On the other hand, there are no effects of the administration of maternal testosterone on either the sexual apparatus or the adult sexual behavior of the male fetuses.

INFANCY—Hormonal influences on the organism normally change abruptly at birth. The animal is no longer subjected to the high level of estrogens circulating in the blood of the mother. At the same time, its own gonads are immature. Only after the maturation of the gonads at puberty, brought about by the gonadotrophic hormones of the pituitary, is the animal once again under the influence of relatively large amounts of gonadal hormones. What happens if this normal course of development is interrupted by administering hormones during infancy?

The effects of heterotypical hormones are straightforward and dramatic.

The animals (guinea pigs), when they become adults, fail to mate even when given a "boost" by homotypical hormones. Females treated in infancy do not mate as spontaneously as adults (Barraclough and Gorski, 1962). They still fail to mate when given doses of estrogen and progesterone that normally bring the adult female into heat. The same effects are obtained with males treated in infancy with estrogen (Harris and Levine, 1962). They fail to copulate as adults either under normal circumstances or with doses of testosterone that are normally adequate. It may be concluded, then, that heterotypical hormones administered early in infancy suppress the development of normal sexual behavior. At this stage in development, however, it appears to be too late to reverse sexuality and to bring out behavior patterns of the opposite sex.

These results are probably what should be expected. Not so expected, however, are the effects of homotypical hormones administered during infancy. In this case, only data with the female rat are available (Whalen and Nadler, 1963). High doses of estrogen (estradiol) were administered in a single injection in infancy. The animals were then allowed to grow to adulthood and given the usual tests for sexual receptivity. Before testing, the animals were primed with estradiol and progesterone injections in a sequence and in amounts that regularly induce receptivity in spayed females. Receptivity, however, did not occur in the animals treated in infancy. Although some presented the mating posture (lordosis), virtually all of them kicked and rejected the male. As a consequence, the amount of mounting, intromission, and ejaculation on the part of the male was reduced to a small fraction of that occurring in control animals. Thus the homotypical hormone, estradiol, given in infancy, practically abolished female sexual behavior in adulthood. Just why this result should be obtained is at present obscure.

NEURAL MECHANISMS OF SEXUAL BEHAVIOR

We have seen, up to this point, that sexual behavior is under the control of sex hormones on the one hand and of experience and learning on the other. In the final analysis, the effects of both hormones and experience must be mediated by the nervous system. We shall now consider just how this mediation takes place. We begin with sensory factors in mating behavior because these are closely related to the role played by the cerebral cortex, which will be the second topic to consider. After that, we shall take up other parts of the nervous system (see Figure 14.2).

SENSORY FACTORS

If the kinds of sensory cues that male and female animals provide for each other are analyzed, it becomes obvious that every one of the senses may contribute in one way or another to arousing sexual behavior. There are odors

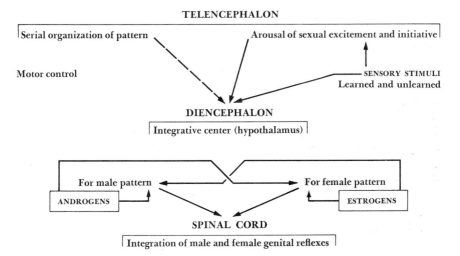

FIGURE 14.2—Schematic diagram of the hormonal and neural factors in the regulation of sexual behavior.

from the secretions of the genital tract of the female rat or dog in heat, the sounds of the "sex calls" of the cat, and the visual cues provided by the reddening of the sexual skin of monkeys or by the courtship behavior of birds. In addition, tactual and kinesthetic cues come into play when the male mounts and grasps the female and when actual contact of the genital organs occurs.

SENSORY DEPRIVATION—Much of the knowledge of the importance of these different kinds of stimulation comes from experiments in which mating behavior was studied after different avenues of sensory stimulation were eliminated. In many of the lower vertebrates, sexual behavior often depends upon one sense modality. Eliminating vision in the frog, for instance, reduces or eliminates mating (see Beach, 1942). Among mammals, however, the case is different. Indeed, no one kind of stimulation is crucial to the arousal of sexual behavior. Male rats mate normally after they have been deprived of vision, olfaction, or hearing. They also mate when surgically deprived of the sense of touch about the snout or ventral body wall and scrotum. In fact, experienced males will continue to mate until they are made blind, anosmic, and insensitive to touch around the snout. Inexperienced males, interestingly enough, fail to mate when they have been deprived of any two of these modalities. Results of the same type have been found in the case of the female cat. Removal of the olfactory bulbs and eyes and destruction of the cochlea do not abolish mating behavior.

GENITAL STIMULATION—Even if sight, sound, and smell are unnecessary for mating behavior, the sensory factors in the genital organs might be expected to be important. Even that is not the case, however (see Beach, 1942). Female rats show normal mating behavior after removal of the uterus and vagina (Ball, 1934). Similarly, in female cats both the sensory fibers innervating the sexual apparatus and the sympathetic motor fibers that play a prominent role in its function can be interrupted completely, and the cats still enter into mating behavior that is normal in every respect (Bard, 1935). Similarly, in the male cat the genitalia can be desensitized by sectioning a part of the lower spinal cord, without impairing sexual aggressiveness in any way (Root and Bard, 1937). Abdominal sympathectomy in addition to spinal injury abolishes ejaculation but in no way impairs the male cat's sexual activity. In the male hamster, moreover, removal of the seminal vesicles and prostate have no effect on normal mating behavior or on its rate of elimination after castration (Pauker, 1948).

Taken together, all these findings indicate that it is the total amount of relevant sensory stimulation rather than any particular kind of stimulation that arouses sexual behavior (Beach, 1942). It also appears that hormones do not have to sensitize any particular sensory structures for mating to occur.

In some instances, on the other hand, hormones may produce changes in genital or other organs that facilitate stimulation and thus aid in sexual arousal. An example of this is to be found in the glans penis of the rat (Beach and Levinson, 1950). In the normal rat, the periphery of this organ presents an irregular appearance somewhat like a cogwheel. This is caused by numerous epithelial folds or papillae. Directly beneath the base of these papillae are many touch receptors. After castration, these papillae degenerate and disappear, but after the administration of androgen they reappear. The time course of their reappearance and subsequent disappearance corresponds nicely with the rise and fall of copulatory behavior. There would appear to be a connection. The inference is that the papillae aid in the stimulation of the underlying touch receptors and thus assist in the copulatory act.

CEREBRAL CORTEX

Turning now to the central nervous system, we shall see below that the hypothalamus is the single most important structure of the nervous system in sexual behavior. On the other hand, the cerebral cortex is of some significance, particularly to the extent that sensory stimulation and perception are involved in such behavior. We shall therefore consider it first. There are marked differences between female and male animals in the role played by the cortex, and so it is necessary to consider them separately.

FEMALE ANIMALS—The female rat, rabbit, cat, and dog readily copulate despite complete decortication. In most gross respects the behavior pattern is quite normal, but the organization of the pattern is impaired in some of its finer aspects (see Beach, 1944). First, some of the component parts of copulatory behavior such as ear wiggling, hopping, and lordosis are absent or appear at atypical times in the sequence of responses. Second, any tendency the female has to take the initiative in instigating copulation is eliminated. Decorticate female rats fail, furthermore, to show any of the masculine responses, such as mounting, which occasionally appear in the intact female. The cortex in infraprimate females, then, is not essential for the arousal and satisfactory execution of the mating pattern. It does, however, play some role in the refinement of the pattern and in the extent to which the female takes an active part in initiating sexual activity.

MALE ANIMALS—In male animals the picture is somewhat different. Although complete decortication does not abolish mating behavior in the rabbit, destroying the olfactory bulbs in addition to the cortex does eliminate it. Apparently copulatory behavior in the male rabbit requires olfactory cues, whereas in the female it does not. If a sizable amount of the neocortex is left intact, however, one may destroy the olfactory bulbs without disturbing mating behavior in the male. Thus olfactory cues per se are not essential so long as other cues remain available to the animal.

There is available a rather extensive study of the effects of cortical lesions upon sexual behavior in the rat (Beach, 1940). Removal of small portions of the cortex up to about 20 percent does not abolish copulatory behavior, no matter where the lesion is. With more extensive destruction of the cortex, copulatory behavior may or may not be affected, but the larger the lesions, the greater are the number of animals affected. In this connection it is interesting that much larger lesions are required to eliminate sexual behavior in rats that are sexually vigorous before operation than in those that are less vigorous animals. Conversely, sexual behavior is possible in cases where it has been eliminated by relatively small cortical lesions if sufficient amounts of gonadal hormones are administered. Cortical lesions involving more than about 60 to 75 percent of the cortex, however, entirely eliminate sexual behavior, and even large doses of sex hormones cannot restore it. From these results, it is clear that the cortex is important in the male rat in the arousal of sexual behavior rather than in its execution.

EVOLUTIONARY STATUS—Cortical lesions have more pronounced effects upon male animals higher than the rat on the phylogenetic scale. In these cases, both the arousal and execution of sexual behavior are affected, but to different degrees. While mating behavior in the male cat is possible after unilateral hemidecortication or bilateral removal of any one of the major lobes of the cortex, it is not well integrated. Animals prepared in this way often approach the female from the side and begin copulatory movements before getting into the proper position. The more of the cortex involved in these operations, the more poorly organized are attempts at copulation. But interest in the female animals persists until relatively complete decortication is performed.

From the studies available, the following conclusions about the cortex and mating behavior in different species of animals may be drawn: (*1*) The cortex is not essential for copulation in any female animals studied. There is reason to believe, however, that the cortex normally plays a role in the intact female in the ordering of the responses that make up the pattern. Insofar as the female initiates mating responses, the cortex may also be important. (*2*) Sexual behavior survives fairly extensive cortical destruction in male animals, but the arousal of the behavior becomes difficult after lesions involving more than two-thirds of the cortex. (*3*) The execution of sexual behavior is not impaired in rats that have had the maximal destruction of cortex that still permits sexual arousal. In cats, however, large cortical lesions disturb motor capacities that are essential in the execution of mating behavior.

Apparently there has been a marked change in the course of evolution in the importance of the cortex in sexual behavior (Beach, 1947). This change is reflected not only in the more serious consequences of cortical damage in higher animals but also in that higher animals can be aroused by a greater variety of stimuli and can exhibit more variable patterns of sexual behavior than lower animals. Furthermore, animals that stand high on the phylogenetic scale depend far less upon the gonadal hormones for the arousal of sexual behavior than do lower animals. These developments reach their high point in man, who depends far less on gonadal hormones than any other animal and who is aroused by a wider variety of stimuli and shows a much more variable pattern of sexual behavior.

SPINAL CORD

We shall switch now from the "top" to the "bottom" of the nervous system, proceeding upward in our discussion from the spinal cord to the hypothalamus. In this way, the central role of the hypothalamus in sexual behavior, as in other kinds of motivated behavior, will become clear.

The spinal cord mediates certain elementary aspects of sexual behavior (see Beach, 1947). In spinal male animals, reflex erection of genital tissue and even ejaculatory responses may be obtained upon mechanical stimulation of the genital regions. Such findings have been obtained in the cat and dog, and the same sorts of reactions can be elicited in spinal human patients even though they are not aware of sensations arising from the genitals. In decapitate female cats, stimulating the genital region elicits lateral movement of the tail and treading of the hind feet like that seen in normal animals in heat. Such responses do not depend on estrus, however, for they occur in castrated animals and estrogen does not change them (Bromiley and Bard, 1940). One can see similar sexual reflexes in the spinal guinea pig, and they do not depend on sex hormones. What these studies show, then, is that certain of the responses typical of masculine and feminine sexual behavior are mediated by the spinal cord. Although sex hormones may influence these reflexes, hormones are not essential, at least, not in the female.

A number of studies indicate that the important "center" for the integration of sexual behavior lies somewhere in the hypothalamus or upper midbrain. Beyond that statement, however, matters are somewhat confused. The exact location of the center, as found in experiments, depends on the method of operation, the species of animal used, and the investigator doing the work.

One method, and the first method employed, for determining the structures that are essential for mating behavior is to make decerebrate sections at different levels of the brain. Such a section severs connections between points in front of and behind the section but otherwise leaves the brain intact. In one study with guinea pigs (Dempsey and Rioch, 1939), sections were made at different levels of the forebrain and brain stem. So long as the section passed in front of the mammillary bodies, estrual behavior followed hormone injection, but if the section passed behind the mammillary bodies, it did not. Similar studies in female cats gave the same results.

These results were confirmed and extended in the cat (Bromiley and Bard, 1940). Decerebration between the points of exit of the third nerve and the trapezoid body eliminated estrual responses. Animals decerebrated in this way, however, gave certain responses resembling estrual behavior that spinal animals do not show. When their genitals were stimulated, these cats lost extensor rigidity in the forelimbs and assumed a posture similar to the estrual crouch of the intact animal. Decerebrated male cats and decerebrated female dogs did not show such responses—they do not normally crouch during sexual activity—but the decerebrate female cat, both in and out of heat, did show them. Taken together, these data seem to point definitely to the hypothalamus and midbrain as the place where estrual mechanisms of sexual behavior are located.

HYPOTHALAMIC LESIONS

A rather different picture emerges from studies in which localized hypothalamic lesions are made. One series of studies points to the *anterior* hypothalamus as the structure of greatest importance in sexual behavior, whereas another series implicates the *central*, and sometimes the posterior, hypothalamus.

In one study of the first kind, male and female rats were used (Clark, 1942). Lesions in the medial part of the anterior hypothalamus impaired sexual activity more than lesions placed elsewhere in the hypothalamus. Similar and more clear-cut results were obtained in the guinea pig. In both male and female animals, lesions of the ventral portion of the anterior hypothalamus between the optic chiasm and the stalk of the pituitary consistently abolished normal mating behavior (Dey et al., 1940, 1942; Brookhart et al., 1940). Control experiments made it clear that the effect was due to a lesion in the hypothalamus and not to possible pituitary injury.

As indicated above, other studies implicate portions of the hypothalamus farther back than the anterior hypothalamus, although the results obtained depend somewhat on the size of lesions made. With relatively large electrolytic lesions made in the male guinea pig, an area in the more posterior part of the hypothalamus was found. Lesions here caused an immediate, almost complete and sustained loss of sexual behavior (Phoenix, 1961). The behavior could not be restored by the administration of androgens.

In an extensive study of 200 female rats, lesions both large and small were made in all parts of the hypothalamus (Law and Meagher, 1958). In this case, animals with large posterior lesions did some mating but not as much as normal controls. Animals with small lesions presented a different set of results in one respect. Although, as before, central lesions virtually abolished sexual behavior, *exaggerated* or hypersexual mating behavior was seen in animals having either anterior or posterior lesions. The hypersexuality was not as great in the anterior group as in the posterior group. It is possible that the hypersexuality that follows anterior lesions is due to the pituitary being released from inhibition. At least, that was the interpretation made in one study in which such lesions were found to accelerate the age at which puberty occurred (Donovan and van der Werff ten Bosch, 1959).

About the only conclusion to be drawn from these studies is that the hypothalamus is crucial for sexual behavior in both female and male animals. In all the studies, lesions somewhere in the hypothalamus abolished mating behavior. On the other hand, more work is needed before any detailed conclusions about the specific structures involved can be drawn.

HYPOTHALAMIC STIMULATION

Methods of implanting electrodes or cannulas so that the hypothalamus may be electrically or chemically stimulated have recently been put to work on the problem of sexual behavior, just as they have been in hunger and thirst (Chapter 13). The results show clearly that sexual behavior can be elicited by such stimulation and, moreover, that the normal mechanism of maintaining sex drive probably consists of direct excitation of the hypothalamus by hormones.

When electrodes are permanently implanted in the hypothalamus (in this case, the anterior dorsolateral region) and electrical stimulation is delivered through them, some of the electrode positions are capable of eliciting exaggerated sexual behavior in the male rat (Vaughan and Fisher, 1962). Within a few seconds after the current is turned on, animals begin mounting estrual females, and they continue sexual activity at a high rate until the current is turned off, whereupon the behavior immediately stops. Penile erection is virtually constant during stimulation. In the most dramatic cases, rats may have 15 or 20 ejaculations an hour under stimulation, while having none during similar periods without stimulation. There consequently is no doubt that direct electrical stimulation of the hypothalamus greatly increases sex drive.

Similar results have been obtained in female cats by implanting small amounts of solid estrogen in the hypothalamus (Michael, 1962). In this case, of course, the stimulation cannot be turned on and off; rather it is long-lasting. "Heat" or sexual receptivity induced in this way may last for as long as fifty or sixty days because the solid estrogen is absorbed very slowly. Incidentally, similarly implanting solid estrogen at other points in the brain has no effect; only a position in the hypothalamus has so far been effective.

Follow-up anatomical studies of the cats made receptive in this way reveal two important points: First, the vagina and uterus are in anestrual condition. In other words, while the cat is in heat behaviorally, it is not physiologically. This means that the effect of stimulation is directly on the hypothalamus and does not involve any intervening effect on gonadotrophins and gonadal hormones. Secondly, when the region of stimulation in the hypothalamus is examined microscopically, there are certain neurons, and not others, that show a selective affinity for the implanted estrogen. This was established by using C^{14}-labeled estrogen and making autoradiographs of sectioned tissue. Therefore it appears to be justifiable to conclude that certain neurons in the hypothalamus are especially sensitive to stimulation by gonadal hormones and that sex drive and receptivity are induced by direct hormonal stimulation of the hypothalamus.

AMYGDALA

To be mentioned, finally, is the role of the amygdala and hippocampus in sexuality. These nuclei are complex, and some parts of them have different functions than other parts. There is no doubt, however, that they are concerned in sexual drive and that they normally exert some kind of inhibitory function in sexual activity.

The evidence for this is that lesions in the amygdala frequently cause hypersexuality (Schreiner and Kling, 1953, 1954). Female cats show increased receptivity to manual stimulation and to the male. The males show even more aberrant sexual behavior, including "tandem copulation." They more frequently try to copulate with other animals and show increased homosexual behavior. Such hypersexuality appears to depend on certain parts of the amygdala, particularly the lateral portion (Wood, 1958). It also depends on gonadal hormones, for it disappears with castration and reappears when replacement therapy with gonadal hormones is given (Schreiner and Kling, 1954).

The effect of amygdalectomy on sexuality seems to hold only for adult animals, not for immature ones. The same results are not found if the lesions are made, say, in kittens (Kling, 1962). Such animals when they grow to adulthood are quite normal in every respect. For some reason, therefore, a certain level of neuroendocrine maturation must be attained before amygdaloid lesions have their effects on sexual behavior.

It appears that the hippocampus, a structure of the limbic system related to the amygdala, is also involved in sexual behavior. Lesions made in it are reported to increase frequency of mounting (Kim, 1960). The significance of this is not at present very clear.

15 INSTINCTIVE BEHAVIOR

I NSTINCTIVE BEHAVIOR is not easily defined. In the past, unfortunately, many have applied the term *instinct* rather loosely to any complex behavior that was not understood very well. Eventually the category of instincts became so broad that it was meaningless. At one point in history, it was almost completely abandoned.

In more recent years, the concept of instinctive behavior has been revived (Lashley, 1938; Lorenz, 1937). The concept has been particularly prominent in the work of European ethologists (see Tinbergen, 1957; Ewer, 1957). As used by them, the term instinctive behavior refers to behavior patterns that (1) are innate or develop through maturation, (2) are species-specific in that they are generally found in all members of a species and hence characterize the species, and (3) are released by certain patterns of stimulation. There are difficulties with this rather clearly defined concept (see Lehrman, 1953), but it has been used with enough caution to prove useful. Throughout this chapter, we shall have in mind the concept of instinctive behavior as used by the ethologists.

Even so, there is no clear line to be drawn between instinctive behavior and other kinds of behavior. Sexual behavior, for example, is sometimes regarded as instinctive behavior, sometimes not; and in some species, it seems to fit the definition of instinctive behavior better than in others. For convenience in organizing the chapters of this book, we have chosen to include the following topics in the area of instinctive behavior: parental behavior, including nest building and care of young; migration; hibernation; and hoarding. This is by no means an exhaustive list, but it covers those topics, other than those discussed in previous chapter, for which there is some knowledge of the physiological factors involved. The principal emphasis of this chapter is on parental behavior, for much is known about its physiological basis.

PHYSIOLOGICAL BASIS OF MOTIVATION

Before we take up specific kinds of instinctive behavior, we shall first consider in general outline the physiological factors at work in motivated behavior. This is a convenient point to consider such a general problem because of what is behind us and what lies ahead. Behind us are the chapters on hunger, thirst, and sexual motivation, which provide concrete illustrations of some of the factors in motivation. Ahead of us is a more complicated story in which many different factors are at work, often in intricate sequences. It will help us to summarize what has been covered and to preview what will be taken up later in the chapter (see Figure 15.1).

SENSORY CUES

In some kinds of motivated behavior, stimuli are important. They may not be the only factors of importance; indeed they usually are not. But given the right set of conditions, they may contribute to the arousal of a drive or pattern of motivated behavior. The female rat in heat, for example, arouses the male to sexual activity. This may be done with a variety of cues, including olfactory, visual, and tactual cues. In this case, sensory cues may be *alternatives* to each other, for any one cue may be eliminated without abolishing the reaction, but some cues are necessary to its arousal.

In other instances, sensory stimuli must be present in *combination* to elicit instinctive or motivated patterns. Gulls, for example, retrieve eggs or any other oval objects of similar texture but only if they can bring them to nests with which they are familiar (see Lashley, 1938). In some birds, nesting behavior is initiated only when accompanied by the stimulus of a courting male and in the presence of suitable nesting materials (see Lehrman, 1961). These are only two examples; we shall encounter more later.

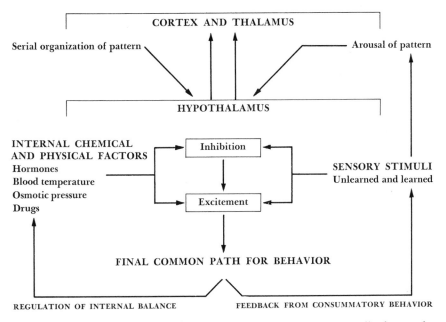

FIGURE 15.1—General scheme of the physiological factors contributing to the control of motivated behavior. (Adapted from E. Stellar. The physiology of motivation. *Psychol. Rev.*, 1954, 61, 6.)

SENSORY DEFICIT

In some kinds of instinctive behavior, no specific stimuli that are essential for the behavior pattern have been discovered. In fact, the "stimulus" seems to be the lack of a particular stimulus; it is a sensory deficit (Lashley, 1938). The spider, for example, can spin an intricate web of a specific design over and over again, and the only condition it seems to need to start this behavior is to have no web. The same is sometimes true of nesting by birds. Certain birds build nests that are characteristic of their species whenever the appropriate building materials are available. Once the nest is made, further activity stops. But if the nest is removed, the bird goes back to work again building a nest. In this type of motivated behavior, there seems to be a sensory deficit that impels the animal to work until the deficit is corrected.

HUMORAL ACTIVATION

In addition to sensory cues or sensory deficits, most instances of motivated behavior require priming or activation by a humoral factor in the blood of the organism. This has been given the name humoral motive factor (HMF) to emphasize its motivating character (see Morgan, 1960). Such a factor may be biochemical, for example, osmotic-pressure effects in hunger and thirst. It may be a hormone, as in the case of estrogen and female estrual behavior. And in each case, it appears that there are certain structures, or even specific neurons, in the brain that are selectively sensitive to the factor. Only when the chemical or hormonal factor activates these structures is the animal ready to react to stimulus situations with the appropriate motivated behavior.

PERIPHERAL CHANGES

We may summarize up to this point by saying humoral factors prime the nervous system so that certain behavior patterns are elicited by stimulus situations. But hormones interact with each other in complicated ways, one hormone often causing either the secretion or the inhibition of another hormone. Moreover, hormones affect other tissues of the body that in turn affect sensory stimulation. We saw one example in the changes effected in the glans penis by androgens (Chapter 14). We shall encounter other examples, such as crop engorgement in birds being caused by a hormone (prolactin) and the stimulation arising from this engorgement causing the bird to regurgitate food for the feeding of the young. Indeed, it seems fairly common in instinctive behavior for a hormone to affect some organ so that it provides stimulation for eliciting a pattern of behavior.

HORMONAL RESPONSES

Hormones not only affect responsiveness to stimuli, by sensitization of the nervous system and by acting on peripheral organs; they may be secreted in response to stimuli (see Lehrman, 1959). In most cases, the endocrine gland affected by such stimulation is the pituitary, which in turn sets off changes in the secretory activities of other glands. In some female birds, for example, the presence of a courting male causes an increased secretion of gonadotrophic hormones in the female, thus synchronizing readiness of the pair for copulation and parental activities. As another example, the stimulation afforded by eggs in a nest causes the secretion of prolactin. In this case, a loop is set up between the stimulation and the sensitizing effects of the prolactin, for the presence of prolactin helps to maintain the incubation behavior of sitting on eggs once this has been started by other hormones. In certain mammals, already referred to in the previous chapter, stimuli arising from copulation cause the pituitary gland to secrete luteinizing hormone which in turn causes ovulation.

These are examples of relatively specific stimuli causing a rather immediate increase in secretion. There are also long-term cumulative effects of environmental stimulation. As we have already seen, seasonal increases in illumination, affecting the pituitary gland, cause development of the gonads and readiness for copulatory behavior. The general point is that hormones are secreted not only in response to normal physiological changes in the body but also to environmental stimulation. Such changes often crucially determine whether patterns of motivated behavior will be aroused by external stimulation.

AVIAN PARENTAL BEHAVIOR

Throughout this section and the next one, the term parental behavior will be used. This will refer to all behavior prior to or following the birth of young that pertains to the care of young. Most such behavior is seen in the mother and hence is maternal behavior. In some cases, however, particularly in birds, some of this care may be paternal behavior, for it is carried out by the male. The term parental behavior covers both maternal and paternal activities.

Birds and mammals differ in the time at which a nest must be built. Since birds lay eggs in the nest at the time of ovulation, the nest must be ready for use at that time. Mammals, on the other hand, have a period of pregnancy before the young are delivered, and the nest is not needed until this later date. Birds and mammals also differ in the kind of care given young. Hence it is convenient to consider avian and mammalian parental behavior in separate sections.

Parental behavior by birds takes place in three stages: (1) nest building, largely before ovulation; (2) incubation of eggs before they hatch; and (3) parental care of the young. These aspects of parental behavior are related to egg laying and copulation and to the hormonal factors that underlie them. Consequently these two activities will also be considered. The following account leans heavily on a review of the hormonal regulation of parental behavior published by Lehrman (1961, but also see Eisner, 1960).

NEST BUILDING

There are wide variations in the nest-building behavior of birds. Some birds build neat and intricate nests; some, hardly any at all. Some build the nest in trees; others in burrows; others on mounds of earth; still others on semifloating structures. Among some birds, all the nest building is done by the female. Among others, the male and female may share about equally in nest building. Among still others, the male begins the nest and the female finishes it. The case of the female building all or part of the nest is the most common one and the one most thoroughly studied. That will be the one we have in mind here unless something to the contrary is said.

COPULATION—In general, there is a correlation between nest building and copulation. The female comes into a period of sexual receptivity through seasonal gonadal cycles described in the preceding chapter. At roughly the same time, but varying somewhat with the species, she begins nest building. In some instances, nest building begins and then copulation takes place, with the peak of copulation occurring later than the peak of nest-building activity. In general, the period of copulation is limited to the period of nest building or to a period immediately after the nest is completed. This correlation suggests that there may be a common physiological basis for the two activities.

EGG LAYING—Nest building is also related to egg laying. With most species of birds, the period of nest building leads up to and is terminated by egg laying. Where nest building continues beyond this time, it usually consists of finishing off the nest with materials that are particularly suitable for the incubation of eggs. Moreover, anatomical studies show that in the few days before egg laying there is an increased rate of maturation of the ovarian follicles containing the eggs. This period is associated, it will be recalled, with an increased production of estrogens and progesterone under the influence of the pituitary gland.

HORMONES—These associations suggest that one or both of these hormones may induce nest building. The experiments show, in general, that nest building is induced by the injection of estrogens. There is not perfect agreement on this, but in cases where it is difficult or impossible to induce nest building with estrogens there are probably also accessory stimulus factors involved. It seems reasonably certain that the secretion of estrogens is the principal factor causing the female to build nests. Even in those species where nest building requires the presence and courtship of a male, it appears that the stimulus of the male causes gonadotrophic responses which in turn stimulate estrogen secretion. On the other hand, the injection of progesterone does not induce nest building. Thus the crucial hormonal agent is estrogen, not progesterone.

Other factors in combination with estrogenic hormones may be involved in nest building. In the case of tropical birds, the occurrence of a rainy season may also be required. We have already mentioned the importance of suitable nest-building materials. Hence, although estrogen may sensitize nest-building behavior, other stimuli in the environment may be necessary to evoke it.

It was stated above that egg laying and nest building are correlated. Typically, this is because the ripening of the follicle must precede egg laying and also produce the estrogenic hormone that induces nest building. In some species, however, the connection between the two is closer than that. The presence of nesting materials is necessary for the bird to ovulate, that is, to release the egg into the oviduct. In this instance, a sequence is involved in which the ripening follicle secretes estrogen, which induces nest building; this in turn causes the release of luteinizing hormone from the pituitary, which subsequently causes ovulation. As we shall see, this sequence of cause and effect is extended still further into the incubation behavior that occurs after eggs are laid.

INCUBATION

When an egg or eggs have been laid, incubation behavior begins to appear. This consists of sitting on the egg(s) in such a way as to provide the proper warming temperature for the embryonic development of the fertilized egg(s). To accomplish this relationship, the bird erects certain feathers so that the egg comes in contact with the skin and is thus warmed more than it could be through the feathers. In many birds, there is an incubation patch (or patches) at this point in the skin. Such a patch has a characteristic vascular and swollen appearance due to changes in skin, muscles, and blood vessels. To get the eggs properly positioned under these incubation patches, the mother makes settling movements until the eggs contact the patch. After this, the erected feathers are relaxed around the sides of the eggs. In addition to settling movements, some birds poke at the eggs to help move them into place.

Incubation behavior develops at a different pace in different species, depending on the size of the clutch. In those laying a single egg, it may begin suddenly right after the egg is laid. With larger clutches, the behavior may be seen first after one or two eggs are laid, but it is not fully developed until the number of eggs characteristic of the species has been laid.

EGGS AS STIMULI—There are several questions that can be asked about this sequence of events. The basic one is, What causes incubation behavior? But before coming to that, let us first consider the relation between egg laying and eggs being present in the nest. There is a relationship because each species characteristically lays a certain number of eggs, and many follicles exist in various states of maturation in the ovary. Moreover, in experiments in which eggs are removed from the nest as they are laid, the hen goes on laying more than the usual number of eggs. There must, then, be some feedback from the presence of eggs in the nest to the laying of more eggs. The facts in this case are not clearly established. Circumstantial evidence, however, indicates that the eggs are a stimulus that inhibits gonadotrophic activity of the pituitary. At least the eggs, through some hormonal mechanism, inhibit ovulation and the laying of more eggs.

We may turn now to the question of what causes incubation behavior. One factor in many, if not all, cases is the presence of the egg itself. This is demonstrated by the fact that, if eggs do not hatch because they are sterile, birds characteristically go on sitting on the eggs long beyond the normal time of hatching. Also, when eggs are removed from a nest, birds usually stop incubating. Indeed, they return to the courtship stage and begin the cycle of copulation and egg laying all over again.

PRESENCE OF A MATE—Eggs, then, are important stimuli in incubation behavior, but they alone are not enough. If both the male and the female participate in incubation, as is the case with ring doves, the presence of the mate may be necessary for incubation (Lehrman et al., 1961). When kept singly, these birds do not incubate even though a nest with eggs in it is in the cage. The presence of a male may also be necessary. If eggs are present without a nest, a period of nesting behavior takes place before birds sit on the nest.

HORMONES—Hormones are also essential for incubation behavior. There are three possible candidates for hormonal induction of incubation behavior. These are estrogen, progesterone, and prolactin. All three are present as a consequence of gonadal conditions existing at the beginning of incubation, although estrogen levels subside during incubation (see Chapter 14). As might be guessed, estrogen alone does not induce incubation behavior by either laying or nonlaying birds. Indeed, in some instances it causes them to stop incubating. Progesterone and prolactin, however, do play a role.

The exact relationship of progesterone and prolactin to each other and to incubation is not entirely clear, but the available facts point to the following: Progesterone, which is normally at a high level at the time of egg laying, probably induces incubation. It does this when injected experimentally, provided a nest and eggs are present. On the other hand, the injection of prolactin may do the same thing. But normally prolactin levels rise during the course of incubation, and its injection induces incubation only if the birds are already laying eggs. It will cause the characteristic changes in incubation only after pretreatment with estrogen. It seems unlikely, then, that prolactin initiates incubation. Rather, the stimulation provided by sitting on the eggs is probably the cause of the pituitary secretion of prolactin. There therefore seems to be a chain in which progesterone initiates inclubation behavior; then incubation behavior provides the stimulus for the secretion of prolactin that may maintain such behavior once it is initiated. As we shall see presently, prolactin has a more important function in the final stage of parental behavior, namely, care of the young.

CARE OF YOUNG

Avian species, as well as mammalian species, vary widely in the degree of their development at birth. At one extreme are precocial types that are nearly able to take care of themselves at hatching and manage to do so within a brief time after hatching. At the other extreme are altricial young that are hatched without feathers and with eyes unopened; these are generally unable to move about to obtain their own food. In between are species with intermediate degrees of development. Naturally it is the young that are altricial in development that require the most parental care.

Parental care consists of brooding, which is the behavior that provides heat to the young, of feeding the young, of leading them to food, and of guarding them. Since brooding is the first thing required of the parent, and, if it occurs, it is usually followed by the other necessary elements of parental care, attention has focused on brooding and its physiological basis (see Lehrman, 1961). In the case of some species, the young are fed by regurgitation of crop milk, a food formed in the crop under the influence of prolactin in, for example, ring doves. This is a definable behavior characteristic that has been studied with some care (Lehrman, 1955).

PROLACTIN—The hormone on which attention has focused is prolactin. This hormone has repeatedly been demonstrated to induce broodiness and parental feeding when injected into birds. In the case of female birds, the effect is relatively fast. Animals caged with young birds and making no attempt to feed them begin parental feeding within hours after injection with prolactin. There is even a similar effect in males but it appears to be slower.

This fact would seem to ascribe broodiness and parental feeding to the relatively high prolactin levels that prevail late in incubation and at the time of hatching. But the situation, on further analysis, is more complicated than that. Prolactin, it has been shown, is not necessary for brooding behavior. Normally, the prolactin content of the pituitary drops sharply after the hatching of the young; yet broodiness is maintained during and after this drop. It will be recalled that prolactin rises during incubation and is maintained by the stimulus of eggs in the nest. At the same time, castrated and immature hens can be made broody by being kept with young without an increase in the prolactin content of the pituitary gland. Prolactin therefore seems not to be necessary even though it can facilitate broodiness.

PRESENCE OF YOUNG—This facilitating, but unessential, role appears to be accounted for by two other factors: One is the stimulus provided by the young; the other is the antigonadal action of prolactin. The first is probably the more important. As we just indicated, birds without mature gonads can be made broody just by being kept with young. Moreover, birds can be kept brooding for long after the normal duration of parental care merely by periodically replacing chicks so that there are young chicks in the nest. Apparently, the mere stimulus of the young is sufficient to invoke and maintain broodiness.

ANTIGONADAL ACTION—In both of the cases just cited, however, it should be noted that the birds have poorly developed or regressed gonads having a relatively low gonadal-hormone output. In the normal reproductive cycle, estrogen secretion goes down after ovulation in part under the influence of prolactin. In the case of castrated or immature birds, estrogen output is similarly low. This would implicate gonadal hormones and imply that they inhibit brooding behavior. Put otherwise, it might be inferred that broodiness is a response to the young only when gonadal hormones are at a low level. This inference has been amply confirmed by experiment. The injection of either androgens or estrogens into brooding hens promptly inhibits brooding.

From these facts, it has been concluded that the role of prolactin in broodiness is through its antigonadal effect. Being high during incubation and hatching, it inhibits the secretion of gonadal hormones. If gonadal-hormone level remains low, as it normally does, then the stimulation provided by the young is sufficient to induce broodiness and parental behavior.

MAMMALIAN PARENTAL BEHAVIOR

There are two important differences between birds and mammals in the bearing and rearing of young. First, birds lay fertilized eggs into a nest that must be ready shortly after copulation. In mammals, on the other hand, a period of pregnancy intervenes between copulation and delivery of the young. Secondly, mammals nurse their young with milk suckled from the mammary glands, whereas birds bring food to their young or supply them with regurgitated food. These differences are accompanied by differences in both the sequence and the character of parental behavior.

Three stages in the parental behavior of mammals may be distinguished: (1) nest building occurring prior to and sometimes after the birth of the young, (2) retrieving of the young, and (3) nursing and suckling behavior.

NEST BUILDING

Mammals, like birds, vary considerably in the kind of nests they build, in the quality of the nest built, and in the places they build nests. Some of this variation is related to the degree of development of the young at birth, for some mammalian young are almost ready to care for themselves at birth, while others must remain in the nest and under nursing care for a long time. Since we are interested in physiological mechanisms, rather than in patterns of behavior per se, we shall not concern ourselves with the details of nest-building behavior.

As one might expect, the physiological condition of an animal is clearly related to its nest-building activity. Most animals, including males and non-pregnant females under some circumstances, do some nest building. However, in the female rat, for example, nest building is related both to estrual cycles and to pregnancy. It is inversely related to estrus, being at a low during estrus when sexual receptivity is high, and it is at its height midway between estrual periods when the animal is not receptive. Then, during pregnancy, there is a great increase in nest-building behavior about five days before parturition. This continues, if necessary, until well after the pups are born. Thus, although nest building is sometimes seen in nonpregnant animals, it is greatest around the time of parturition. One might suspect from these facts that nest building is not regulated by any single or simple physiological mechanism.

Rather, it must be controlled by several factors, some of them operating in nonpregnant and nonparturitive animals. This is true.

TEMPERATURE—One of the factors, clearly, is the environmental temperature. This was demonstrated in one of the earliest experiments on nest building by rats (Kinder, 1927) and has since been repeated with mice (Koller, 1956). If room temperature is systematically varied, nest building varies inversely with the temperature. At high temperatures, say 85 to 90°F, very little nest-building material is consumed and either no nests at all or small, loose nests are constructed. At low temperatures, say 50 to 60°F, relatively large amounts of nesting material are used, and substantial, well-built nests are constructed. Such a relation to temperature would suggest that nest building is, in part, a thermoregulatory behavior pattern that conserves energy and helps to keep the animal warm.

THYROIDECTOMY—This conclusion is confirmed by the effects of thyroidectomy and of the injection of thyroid hormone. Thyroid hormone, as previously explained (page 96), regulates general metabolic rate. Animals with low thyroid output are deficient in energy expenditure and are particularly in need of ways of conserving energy. Thus it is not surprising that thyroidectomy causes a substantial increase in nest building (Richter, 1941). Conversely, the injection of thyroid extract reduces nest-building behavior in the rat (Richter, 1942–1943). Thus nest building is definitely related to the level of thyroid functioning. This relationship fits in with the work on environmental temperature in pointing to nest building as thermoregulatory behavior.

HYPOPHYSECTOMY—The thyroid gland is normally controlled to a considerable extent by the thyrotrophic hormone of the anterior pituitary gland. Removal of the pituitary should, among other things, reduce thyroid functioning and hence should increase nest building. That is exactly what happens (Richter, 1937; Stone and King, 1954); hypophysectomy and thyroidectomy have about the same effect on nest building. The pituitary and the thyroid are, in fact, the only two glands whose removal makes any substantial difference in nest building. Changes in nest building after adrenalectomy and gonadectomy are inconsequential.

In hypophysectomy and thyroidectomy, the effects of removal of the gland accumulate slowly so that nest building gradually increases after the operation until it is approximately double the normal amount about three weeks afterward. This slow buildup in both cases fits with the idea that metabolic rate is gradually lowered and that the cause of the effect is metabolic. This suggestion was put forth many years ago, and it has not been disproved. Possibly nest building is under the control of the thyroid, and any other effects, including hypophysectomy, are secondary ones exercised through the thyroid. If so, the chain of events leading up to this is complicated, for other hormones also are involved in nest building.

ESTROGEN AND PROGESTERONE—In the pregnant animal, nest building is in one way or another under the control of gonadal hormones. In nonpregnant mice, the injection of progesterone causes a striking increase in nest building (Koller, 1956). This increase takes place in either intact or gonadectomized mice. When estrogen, on the other hand, is injected, there is no immediate increase in nest building; indeed, there may be a slight depression. However, after the injections of estrogen are terminated, a marked increase (of the order of 2.5 times) follows. Since it is well known that progesterone secretion is normally linked to estrogen production (page 401), this result appears to be due to progesterone secretion stimulated by estrogen injection. The effect takes place only in the female; it does not occur in the intact or castrated male (Koller, 1956). Other hormones have been tried in the female, but the only hormone having the capacity to induce substantial nest-building behavior in the male appears to be progesterone. It should be noted that it is not known how it works, whether directly on the nervous system or by way of the pituitary and thyroid glands (see Lehrman, 1961).

EFFECT OF YOUNG—Hormones and environmental temperature are not the only agents inducing nest-building behavior. The mere presence of young in the nest is also effective. When young mice are introduced into the nest of a nonpregnant female, nest building increases sharply (Koller, 1952, 1956). There have been reports that the same thing happens with adult male animals, but the results are inconsistent. On the other hand, nest-building behavior is usually maintained at a high level throughout the period of rearing of the young, that is, so long as the young are in the nest. Yet progesterone secretion, which is at a high point at parturition, drops off abruptly immediately afterward. It has returned to normal, nonpregnant levels at a time when nest-building behavior is still continuing. Quite clearly, the presence of young in the nest maintains nest building at this point.

It may be concluded that in the nest-building behavior of parental mammals, as in the similar behavior of birds, nest building is controlled by two factors: (1) progesterone and (2) the stimulus of young in the nest. The two factors are complementary. Progesterone induces, or at least helps to induce, high levels of nest building around the time of parturition, but the young in the nest maintain nest building after the level of progesterone has decreased. It may be that the pituitary and thyroid are involved in this behavior, for they are factors in the nest building of nonpregnant animals. If so, it remains to be proved.

RETRIEVING BEHAVIOR

Retrieving behavior is the act of picking up and returning to the nest young that may have strayed from the nest or, in some instances, may have been born outside the nest. Different mammals retrieve in different ways, but retrieving is an integral part of parental behavior. Otherwise many young would soon die.

HORMONES—Retrieving and nest building are in many respects parallel. They appear at about the same time in the cycle of pregnancy and lactation, and they continue for about the same length of time, although retrieving may outlast nest building. They are affected in the same way by many hormonal factors, being increased by hypophysectomy and thyroidectomy and being inhibited by the estrogenic hormone. They can be seen in male and non-pregnant animals, but they are much more prominent in females before and after parturition. There are so many parallels between the two kinds of behavior that they would appear to be controlled by identical physiological and stimulus factors.

There are, however, differences between them that prevent the conclusion that they have exactly identical mechanisms. One difference is in the effects of prolactin injection. This has no effect on nest-building behavior, but it does induce retrieving behavior. Both progesterone and prolactin are capable of inducing retrieving behavior. Moreover, the effect of prolactin is essentially the same in hypophysectomized and gonadectomized animals. The effect is therefore not mediated through the pituitary gland nor by the antigonadal properties of prolactin. Hence it appears that hypophysectomy, progesterone, and prolactin all induce retrieving behavior by different mechanisms, the nature of which is not yet clear.

In the postparturitive female, prolactin secretion, unlike progesterone, holds up well during the period of lactation. In fact, as we shall see in the next section, it must do this for lactation to be maintained. One might be tempted to think, consequently, that prolactin maintains retrieving behavior throughout nursing. It may well assist in doing this, but it is not the only means of maintaining retrieving behavior. The behavior is also induced and maintained by the presence of young in the vicinity of the nest.

EFFECT OF YOUNG—Retrieving behavior, like nest building, may also be induced in nonpregnant animals by caging them with young, a procedure called concaveation and employed in the classical study of maternal behavior in rats (Wiesner and Sheard, 1933). Concaveation for a few days causes animals that have not previously been retrieving to begin retrieving young. The method works with virgin female mice, male mice, and with hypophysectomized mice, none of whom were retrieving when first placed with young (see Leblond, 1940). Concaveation does not always have the same effect on retrieving and on nest building. Certain individuals may begin retrieving while they show no signs of nest building. Hence, although the mechanisms of retrieving and nest building may be similar, they are, to emphasize the point made above, not identical (see Lehrman, 1961).

Analysis of the stimulus aspects of the young that induce retrieving has been carried somewhat further than it has in the case of nest building. In some species of animals, relatively specific stimuli, such as the bleating of the lamb or the cry of the kitten, may cause the mother to retrieve the young. In the case of the rat, several different kinds of stimuli may be involved (Beach and Jaynes, 1956). Dummy pups, anesthetized pups, or dead pups may all be retrieved, but normal live pups are retrieved better and more often. Olfactory cues are important, but so also are visual and auditory cues. In cases of sensory deprivation of retrieving mothers, the more senses that are available to the animal, the better the retrieving behavior (Beach and Jaynes, 1956).

The age of pups is also a significant factor. When this is carefully studied, retrieving behavior and other associated behavior, such as licking, decreases as the pups grow older (Rowell, 1960). This is not due to physiological changes in the mother, as can be demonstrated by substituting pups of different ages. Rather, it has to do with hair coat, size of pup, and other changing features of the pup as it grows.

We see, then, that retrieving and nest building have similar, but not identical, physiological mechanisms. They tend to appear roughly at the same time, but retrieving behavior may be artificially induced without nest-building behavior. One hormone, prolactin, effectively induces retrieving but not nest building, while progesterone induces both. Also, in both instances the behavior, although originally induced by the physiological condition of the mother, may also be induced, and probably is normally maintained, by stimuli provided by the young.

NURSING

In the mammal, nursing behavior is maintained until the time of weaning when the young are capable of finding and consuming their own food. Nursing behavior is any behavior on the part of the mother that fosters the young gaining access to the nipples. This may involve the mother moving so that the infant is better able to grasp the nipple or the mother repositioning the infant. The sucking of the nipple by the young is called suckling. It is, as we shall see, a positive stimulus for lactation and nursing behavior.

MAMMARY SECRETION—In order to make clear some of the hormonal relationships encountered in nursing, it is necessary to summarize briefly the physiology of mammary secretion. This secretion of milk is definitely under the control of the hormone prolactin, one of the hormones of the anterior pituitary, although other hormones may in complex ways be concerned in the preparation of mammary tissue for milk secretion. If the pituitary is removed, mammary tissue regresses and the glands dry up. Using replacement therapy with prolactin, it can be shown that the crucial factor in maintaining secretory activity in the gland is prolactin. This, as we have seen, is normally produced as a result of gonadal influences on the pituitary body (page 402).

Although milk has been secreted in the mammary gland, it is not all available to the suckling young. When suckling begins a small amount of milk is obtained, but for a full meal to be secured, the milk must be "let down" or ejected from the gland into the region of the nipple. This effect is called the milk-ejection reflex. It is a reflex because it is definitely elicited by the mechanical stimulus provided by the suckling infant. It is not, however, a motor reflex, for no secretory motor fibers in the mammary gland are known. Rather, it is a hormonal reflex requiring some seconds or a minute or two. Specifically, it is due to the secretion of oxytocin by the *posterior* pituitary gland. A suckling stimulus causes the hypothalamus via the pituitary stalk to discharge oxytocin. This, circulating in the blood, causes the mammary gland reflexly to let down milk. Here is a clear case of a *hormonal reflex* induced by suckling and executed by means of a circulating hormone. We shall not go into the evidence for these statements, but they are rather well established (see Lehrman, 1961).

NURSING BEHAVIOR—The factors that cause a mother to nurse her young are not yet clear. In many instances, there seems to be a correlation between mammary distension and amount of nursing (see Lehrman, 1961). Yet this cannot be the only factor, for estrogens injected into nursing rats cause them to stop nursing before the mammary glands regress. On the other hand, rats hypophysectomized during pregnancy may attempt to nurse even though no milk is secreted, owing to the lack of pituitary prolactin. Thus there is no one-to-one relation between either prolactin secretion or mammary distension and nursing care. The question of what induces nursing behavior is still open.

One thing that is clear is that the suckling stimulus maintains lactation even though it does not induce lactation. Rather, this happens because the prolactin secretion rises before and after parturition, thus preparing the mammary glands for nursing. But if the young are not nursed, the glands regress and provide no milk. Normally, however, as the young continue to suckle, the prolactin secretion is maintained, and thus the capacity of the mammary glands to supply the needed milk is also maintained.

One further point is reasonably clear. The maintenance of prolactin secretion takes place through essentially the same mechanism as the milk-ejection reflex. In this case, however, the oxytocin secreted by the posterior pituitary body in response to the suckling stimulus acts as a neurohumor to stimulate the anterior pituitary body to put forth prolactin. Thus prolactin prepares mammary tissue for suckling; then the suckling stimulus evokes the secretion of oxytocin which causes both the milk-ejection reflex and the further secretion of prolactin for the maintenance of lactation. In this way, suckling behavior maintains lactation. Here there is a two-step hormonal response to a peripheral stimulus.

OTHER INSTINCTIVE BEHAVIOR

Although many kinds of instinctive behavior have been studied in detail, relatively little of this work is concerned with physiological mechanisms. Parental behavior is by far the most thoroughly investigated. Relatively little can be said about other forms of instinctive behavior. What there is to say will be put briefly in the following sections.

MIGRATION OF FISHES

Most fishes have special areas to which they go for spawning. In typical instances, this is a certain area of a lake or river not far from the places they normally inhabit. In several species of fish, however, lengthy migrations of hundreds or thousands of miles take place. In the case of salmon, several species of which have been studied, breeding normally takes place in the small streams that constitute the headwaters of major rivers. The young salmon after a time move down the river and out into sea. Some years later, they migrate back to the river and up to its headwaters for breeding, thus closing the cycle. In the case of American eels, the cycle is just the reverse. These breed far out in the Atlantic Ocean in the Sargasso Sea; the young migrate to the brackish streams of the Atlantic coast, and then at the appropriate time they migrate back to the Sargasso Sea for breeding.

STICKLEBACKS—In a moment, we shall return to salmon, but first it is better to consider another species, the three-spined stickleback. This has been carefully studied (Baggerman, 1957). This fish breeds in the spring in fresh water. After the breeding season ends, it and its young migrate either to the sea or to brackish water to spend the winter. In the spring, it migrates back again to the breeding grounds. The timing of this migration coincides with the maturing of the gonads.

Some of the causal factors in this cycle of events are clear. Light is a controlling factor. The increasing length of the day during the winter causes the gonads to start developing. Presumably this relationship is mediated by the hypothalamus and pituitary gonadotrophins, as is the parallel relationship in birds. In the later stages of gonadal development, temperature becomes a critical factor. It, combined with increasing light, is necessary for full gonadal maturation.

Although gonadal development is necessary for breeding to take place, it is not the important factor in migration. This is thyroid activity, rather than gonadal activity, although gonadal secretions may have some slight modifying influence on migration. It would appear that the same external influences, principally light, that affect gonadal development also cause a secretion of thyrotrophin which increases thyroid activity.

This change in thyroid activity has been definitely correlated with preferences for fresh water. Whether this alone is responsible for migration tendencies is doubtful, but it is nevertheless a factor determining the fish's preference for fresh-water streams rather than for the saline sea. Within two months or so after breeding occurs, thyroid activity diminishes. At the same time, a change in preference from fresh water to salt water occurs. Then, the animals head again for the sea.

SALMON—Whereas the stickleback makes several round trips to and from the breeding area, the salmon of the Pacific Northwest makes only one. The young are hatched in various tributaries. In the second year, they migrate downstream to the ocean and there spend two or three years. After that, they reenter the river and proceed to its headwaters to spawn. After spawning, the parents die.

One interesting aspect of this round trip is that salmon quite uniformly return to the same stream in which they were hatched (Hasler, 1960). The precision of this homing is remarkable. Although there may be some straying, the overwhelming proportion of those completing the migration reach the exact spot in which they were hatched. This represents some kind of memory, quite probably imprinting (see Hess, 1959), and not any instinctive selection of streams. The proof is that, if eggs are transferred to another stream before hatching, the adults later return to the stream in which they hatched rather that to that of their parents (Donaldson and Allen, 1957). Thus it is clear that the fish remember quite precisely where they were born.

We may note in passing that the cue utilized in finding the home stream has been extensively investigated. All possibilities have just about been eliminated except for chemical cues, probably olfactory (Hasler, 1960). Most fish, including salmon, are exceedingly sensitive to differences in the chemical composition of water. It is believed that each stream has some distinctive chemical properties that can be remembered and utilized as a cue in returning to the home stream.

Most other aspects of salmon migration are still a mystery, although some facts are known (Fields, 1957). Young salmon migrating downstream are negatively phototropic. They avoid light, doing most of their traveling at night. They also prefer water of low velocity to rapidly moving water. Whether either or both of these factors account for downstream migration is not known with certainty.

It was formerly thought that salmon, once they reached the sea, lingered in the area of the river from which they came (Roule, 1933). Now it is clear from tagging studies that certain species migrate many thousands of miles to points near Alaska (Hasler, 1960). Two or three years later, when their gonads are maturing, they make the return trek to the home river.

The factors involved in either direction of migration are not known. Changing preferences for warmer or colder water might be one. However, on the return trip, the journey southward in the ocean is accompanied by increasingly warmer water, but the journey upstream is from warmer to colder water. Thus an unreasonable reversal of preference in the course of the trip would be required. Mature salmon swimming upstream are known to have a strong rheotropism, a tendency to swim against the current. This, plus a preference for fresh water and for waters of distinctive chemical composition, might take over as guide once the fish are in the home river. None of these factors, however, can adequately explain the accuracy of the direction of the migration at sea to the vicinity of the home river. The most plausible suggestion here is that the fish use the sun as a compass for navigation. At least some fish are clearly capable of such light-compass reactions (Hasler, 1960).

MIGRATION IN NEWTS

Newts are varieties of salamanders. Certain species have typical migration patterns (Twitty, 1959). These animals grow up high on the slopes of mountains. When, after four or five years, they reach sexual maturity in the spring, they migrate down the mountain side to a stream, do their breeding, and then return to the mountains. Through marking studies, it has been established that they return quite precisely to the point in the stream where they last bred or where they were born.

Two factors are known to play a part in this migration. One is chemical sensitivity. Animals deprived of any of the senses, except smell, retain the ability to migrate to their particular section of the stream. The other factor is some combination of pituitary hormones (Chadwick, 1941). Immature salamanders can be made to migrate to water if pituitary tissue is transplanted into their abdominal cavities or if they are injected with prolactin, a pituitary hormone. This fact, however, does not rule out the role of other glands such as the thyroid or gonads which may be influenced by pituitary hormones.

MIGRATION IN BIRDS

Many species of North American birds have migratory patterns in which they fly north in the spring and south in the fall. They have definite "homes" on each end of the line. In the typical case, the northward migration occurs in preparation for breeding that takes place in the northerly breeding grounds.

Much the same factors appear to be involved in bird migration as in the migration of other animals. In most species, light is an important external factor. In a now classical study, two groups of snowbirds were kept in cages under identical conditions of temperature and feeding (Rowan, 1931). For one group, the illumination each day was gradually shortened just as the day shortens in the fall. The other group had artificial days that gradually lengthened over a period of time, simulating the changes that occur in the spring. When released, birds in the first group did not move away from the vicinity in which they had been caged. Many birds of the second group flew away to the north as snowbirds typically do in the spring migration.

Associated with the effects of light on migration are changes in pituitary secretion (see Farner, 1961). This is a connection we have seen several times before. Pituitary activity is reflected in heightened hormonal output of several glands, among them the gonads (Wolfson, 1959). These are typically well developed at the time of spring migration and are regressed at fall migration. For this reason, many investigators have concluded that migratory tendencies are under the control of gonadal hormones. Despite this general agreement, instances have been reported in which migration occurs whether or not there are changes in light and even when the birds are castrated (see Beach, 1948). To explain such instances, it has been argued that the pituitary has an inherent rhythm, possibly influenced by seasonal changes in temperature as well as light. Also, as in the case of the migration of the stickleback, the significant hormonal changes induced by pituitary activity may be thyroidal rather than gonadal. Lending credence to the idea of the thyroid gland playing a significant role in migration is the fact that deposition of fat is pronounced in migrating birds (Wolfson, 1959). This fat appears to be the source of the great additional energy required in migration.

Unfortunately, less is known about how birds find their way in migration than about what makes them start migrating in the first place (see Griffin, 1953). To the extent that it has been possible to trace migration flights, it is known that birds can follow a migration route very well, even without the benefit of previous experience. In one study, for example, a group of newly hatched crows were held in cages in Alberta, Canada, for a month after all the adults had gone south toward Oklahoma (Rowan, 1945). After the young birds were released, over 50 percent of them were recaptured in a direct line southeast of their birthplace along the route to Oklahoma followed by their parents. Exactly how this sort of navigation is done remains a mystery (but see Griffin, 1953).

HIBERNATION

Hibernation is a state of inactivity resembling sleep but accompanied by a marked decrease in body temperature (see Kayser, 1961). True hibernation occurs only in warm-blooded mammals and birds that otherwise maintain a body temperature in the neighborhood of 100°F. The hibernating animal usually finds a warm, secluded place that provides protection from environmental cold and from predators. In most cases, hibernation is a seasonal affair, taking place during the long winter months in cold climates, but it also occurs diurnally in some animals, such as the Scandinavian birchmouse, when exposed to wide swings of temperature during the day-night cycle. The optimum body temperature for hibernation is usually about 40°F, a few degrees above freezing.

No one yet knows why animals enter hibernation, or why some animals do and some do not (Lyman, 1963). During the hibernating season, various endocrine glands typically regress, so that a reduction in pituitary activity and particularly of thyroid activity under pituitary control accompanies hibernation. On the other hand, no single endocrine gland controls hibernation, and removal of any endocrine gland does not consistently bring on hibernation. Typical of most hibernators is a pronounced fattening during the fall when food is plentiful and before the onset of hibernation. This fat is clearly a major source of heat in some hibernating animals (Smalley and Dryer, 1963). Yet the accumulation of fat is not a necessity, for thin animals also hibernate, though somewhat later than fat ones. Some animals, like the golden hamster, do not lay on fat but instead store food, which they periodically emerge from hibernation to eat. Thus far, no one has been able to discover the physiological causes of hibernation.

HOARDING

Many animals, particularly the rodents, hoard food and other objects by carrying it either to the home area or to other protected places. Hoarding can be observed in the common laboratory rat by providing a source of food at some distance from the cage and a connecting alley to the home cage. Some investigators regard hoarding as instinctive behavior (Morgan, 1947). Others feel that it is largely a learned behavior (Marx, 1950). And others place it somewhere in between, suggesting that it is the "canalization of an exteroceptive drive to manipulate" (Bevan and Grodsky, 1958).

Many factors affect hoarding behavior, including previous experience with the objects hoarded (Stellar and Morgan, 1943). Food deprivation is one factor. Hungry rats generally hoard much more than well-fed rats. Merely making rats hungry, however, is not enough; in fact, rats that are very hungry when they are given access to food pellets eat them rather than hoard them. However, the cumulative effect of keeping animals on a restricted diet for a week or more is pronounced (Morgan et al., 1943). Once these effects of deprivation have been built up, rats continue to hoard for some time after they have been satiated with all the food they can eat. Hunger as such, then, is not the basis of hoarding, but some physiological state associated with it may be.

Temperature is clearly a factor of importance (McCleary and Morgan, 1946). At normal room temperatures, rats that have always had ample food carry back very few pellets from the bins. As the temperature gets lower and lower, however, they increase their hoarding activity more and more until they are carrying back more than ten times as many pellets as they can eat in a day. Of course, rats eat more and are more active when they are cold, expending more energy than normally. Perhaps hoarding has something to do with rate of metabolic activity. In this case, one might expect hoarding to correlate with thyroid function.

Neither of these possibilities, however, has been confirmed by experiments. Neither thyroid function reduced by thyroidectomy or thiouracil treatment or increased by thyroxine injection has any sizable effect on hoarding (Stellar, 1950). Neither does changing the balance of sugar reserves in the body by injecting rats with glucose, insulin, or adrenalin several hours before a hoarding test (Stellar, 1943). Neither, finally, does rearing young rats on diets deficient in carbohydrate, fat, or protein (Bindra, 1947). Therefore, what biochemical conditions in the body, if any, affect hoarding are still unknown.

With respect to neural factors in hoarding, there are some data, although their meaning is not clear. Lesions made in the cortex seem to increase hoarding slightly, provided they are not too large and do not encroach appreciably on the midline (Zubek, 1951). On the other hand, rather large lesions placed anywhere in the cortex reduce hoarding activity (Stamm, 1953), and rather small lesions also reduce hoarding if they are made along the midline (Stamm, 1954). In the latter case, the degree of reduction in hoarding correlates quite highly with the length of the lesion along the midline. There is, at present, no clear interpretation to be made of such results, but it may be noted that the cingular gyrus of the limbic system, which we have seen to be implicated in motivation and emotion, lies along the midline.

16 CONDITIONING

L EARNING AND its physiological mechanisms are the subject of study in this and the next two chapters. This chapter considers classical and avoidance conditioning, Chapter 17 discriminative learning, and Chapter 18 instrumental and trial-and-error learning. Virtually all the work considered in these chapters is based on animal subjects, for there is very little research on the physiological aspects of learning in man. The reason is the usual one, namely, that in an experiment it is not possible to interfere physiologically with man's organs. There are, however, data on memory and intellectual abilities following human brain damage, and these will be treated in a later chapter (Chapter 19).

TYPES OF LEARNING

As an introduction to the three chapters on learning, we should first explain and understand the basic varieties of learning. No system of classification is entirely satisfactory (see Hebb, 1956), for in the final analysis there is no clear line between one kind of learning and another. Nevertheless, a rough, threefold classification is helpful in understanding many of the phenomena we shall encounter.

The threefold classification consists of (*1*) classical conditioning, (*2*) instrumental learning, and (*3*) discriminative learning. There are also several hybrids of these varieties; one—avoidance conditioning—will be described in this chapter along with classical conditioning. Other hybrids will be left to later chapters.

CLASSICAL CONDITIONING

In 1906, Pavlov described (in English) his now famous discovery of the conditioned reflex, elucidating various factors governing its acquisition and extinction. As Pavlov used the term *conditioning*, it applied to a situation in which two kinds of stimuli are presented to an animal (Figure 16.1). One stimulus, called the *unconditioned stimulus* (US), is any stimulus that evokes some definite response. This response, prior to learning, is called the *unconditioned response* (UR). (In many cases, the so-called UR may

FIGURE 16.1—Pavlov's method of conditioning the salivary reflex. (Adapted from R. M. Yerkes and S. Morgulis. The method of Pavlov in animal psychology. *Psychol. Bull.*, 1909, 6, 264.)

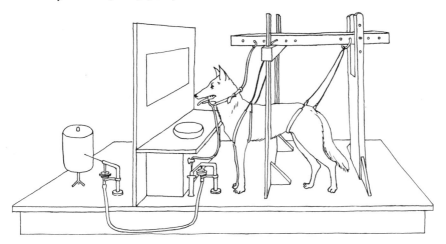

actually have been learned, but it is such an ingrained and stable habit that it can be treated as though it were unlearned.) In Pavlov's case, the US was food and the UR was salivation. Another stimulus, the *conditioning stimulus*, or, after learning has occurred, the *conditioned stimulus* (CS), is one that before learning evokes no significant response. In many of Pavlov's experiments, this was a bell. By pairing the CS and the US, the CS coming just before the US, and doing this for a number of trials, Pavlov observed that the CS (the bell) came to evoke the UR (salivation) which he now called the *conditioned response* (CR).

In the United States in recent years, the Pavlovian method of studying learning has been called *classical conditioning* (see Galambos and Morgan, 1960). In Russia, however, where Pavlov worked during his long life, it is more commonly called conditioning of the "first type," or type I conditioning.

The original procedures of classical conditioning were subsequently modified by substituting a noxious stimulus, usually a shock applied somewhere to the skin of an animal, in place of food as the US. If this is the only change made and if the presentation of a CS is always followed by the US, no matter what the subject does, the conditioning that occurs is still classical or type I conditioning. If, however, the response of the animal can affect whether or not the shock is applied or how long it lasts, then the procedure becomes one of *avoidance* or *escape* conditioning. In escape conditioning, the organism can terminate the shock after it is applied; in avoidance conditioning, it can avoid it altogether if it makes the proper response.

AVOIDANCE CONDITIONING

To be more specific, in avoidance conditioning an animal is presented with a CS (light or bell, for example) followed by a shock, but only if the animal fails to make some specified response, such as lifting its leg (CR). Thus the animal can avoid the shock (US) by leg lifting in response to the CS and before the shock is felt. In the United States, this is usually called *avoidance conditioning*; in Russia it is *defensive conditioning*, conditioning of the "second type," or type II conditioning. Since what the subject does is instrumental in avoiding shock, it falls into the more general category of instrumental conditioning, a term introduced to distinguish it from classical conditioning (Hilgard and Marquis, 1940).

There is evidence, to be presented later, that avoidance conditioning is really a hybrid consisting of two stages. One is classical conditioning of fear or at least of autonomic reactions; the other is instrumental conditioning. Moreover, in the learning of an instrumental avoidance response, the animal must first learn to escape from shock before it learns to anticipate, and hence to avoid, shock. Such escape learning may be studied separately from instrumental learning, and it appears to have somewhat different physiological mechanisms (see below).

INSTRUMENTAL LEARNING

Many years after the Russian development of type I and type II procedures, Konorski (see Konorski, 1950) in Poland and Skinner (see Skinner, 1938) in the United States applied the term conditioning to a still different learning procedure. They put hungry rats in a box and delivered a pellet to them each time they pushed a lever. In this case, food was the US and pushing the lever became the CR. This situation differs from both classical and avoidance conditioning in that (1) it contains no specifiable CS and (2) the CR (pushing the lever) is not originally a UR to the food (US). For this reason, Skinner called it *operant conditioning,* in contrast to the first two kinds of conditioning, which he called *respondent conditioning.* Nevertheless, since the animal's response is instrumental in obtaining food (US), this learning procedure must also be classified as a form of instrumental or type II conditioning. Many investigators prefer to call it instrumental learning, rather than conditioning, and that practice is followed in this book.

Skinner's instrumental-learning procedures, it should be noted, do not differ in principle from other learning methods that have been called "trial and error." Cats in a puzzle box, described by Thorndike about the same time (1898) that Pavlov came forth with conditioning, must do about the same thing as Skinner's rat, namely, push a pedal to get out of a box to reach food. Similarly, animals required to run through a maze to receive a food reward must learn to make a number of turns correctly to reach the goal of food. Although in the latter case the animal must make a series of responses, rather than just one, these responses are still instrumental responses which, as in the case of the rat in the Skinner box, are not themselves URs and are not evoked by any identifiable CSs. Hence, it is only a matter of convention, not one of fundamental difference, to call maze learning and learning in puzzle boxes trial-and-error learning while at the same time calling Skinner-box learning a kind of conditioning.

DISCRIMINATIVE LEARNING

In addition to the learning studied in classical-conditioning and instrumental-learning procedures, organisms also can learn something about the relation of stimuli and of objects in their environment. The general name for such learning is *discriminative learning,* or some prefer *perceptual learning,* because it involves a change in the perception of the environment. Although discriminative learning can be shown to take place independently of the acquisition of conditioned or instrumental responses (see Dodwell, 1964), still in most cases, especially those to be studied here, the perceptual change is built upon one or another of the kinds of learning just described. Conditioning procedures may, for example, be designed to require that the organism discriminate differences among stimuli. So may instrumental-learning procedures. Exactly how such discriminations are acquired, as well as the physiological mechanisms underlying them, will be described in Chapter 17.

We are now ready to come to grips with the main task of this chapter, which is to describe physiological research on conditioning. Although we have distinguished among different types of conditioning and shall make use of the distinctions, our outline will correspond, in its main headings, to the principal physiological methods used in research on conditioning. These are (1) brain lesions, (2) brain stimulation, (3) electrical correlates, and (4) physiological feedback. What is meant by this last topic will be clear when we discuss it.

BRAIN LESIONS

Ablating or destroying some region of the brain is the oldest method of studying the function of the brain. Until the 1930s it was, with few exceptions, about the only method available for studying the neural aspects of conditioning and learning. Although it has since been supplemented by other methods that we shall discuss later, it is still one of the favorite methods of experimenters in this field. When, in earlier days, the method was limited to gross surgical destructions or removals, most of the work was on the cerebral cortex. With the advent of stereotaxic methods of making lesions deep within the brain, more information has been forthcoming from subcortical regions. We shall start with the cerebral cortex and then discuss in turn the thalamus, the limbic system, the midbrain, and the spinal cord.

BEHAVIORAL METHODS

First we should describe the conditioning procedures that have been employed with brain lesions. Although there are a great many different experiments, there are a few basic procedures that, with minor variations, have been followed in all the work. They may be classified under the headings of (1) classical conditioning, (2) conditioned emotional response, and (3) avoidance conditioning.

CLASSICAL CONDITIONING—Relatively few experiments have been done with classical conditioning, although in some instances it is possible to observe a classical conditioned response in conjunction with more complex procedures. In one instance (Marquis, 1934) a conditioned eye blink was used. Conditioning was performed by pairing a flash of light with a puff of air to the eye (of a dog). After many such pairings, the dog learned to wink his eye in response to the light signal.

More typically, classical conditioning is carried out with a signal and an electric shock. A signal is presented and is then followed by an electric shock to some region of the body, usually the paws (of a dog or cat). For the procedure to be called classical conditioning, the shock must always follow the signal, at least during conditioning, and be administered so that there is nothing the animal can do to escape it.

Two kinds of responses may be observed in this situation. One is a specific anticipatory movement such as a flexion of the leg or the contraction of a muscle in the leg. Usually, when conditioned, the subject lifts, or at least twitches, the leg to which shock is regularly applied, and it does this to the signal in advance of the application of shock. The other kind of response is some sort of generalized fear response. It may be a crouching or change of posture, a squeal or a bark, or something the experimenter learns to identify with "fear." This kind of response is often observed in avoidance conditioning described below.

CONDITIONED EMOTIONAL RESPONSE—Conditioned fear, or more accurately a conditioned emotional response, may also be observed more objectively and precisely by studying its effect on some other quantitatively measured behavior (Hunt and Brady, 1951). The kind of behavior used for this purpose is lever pressing in a Skinner box (page 327). The animal (usually a rat) is first given a few classical conditioning trials in which a clicker is presented along with a shock. On each trial a clicker is run for, say, three minutes. At the end of this time, one or two substantial shocks are administered. It takes only three to six trials of this sort to build up a well-established, long-remembered emotional response to the clicker. The animal thereafter, upon hearing a clicker, "freezes" or otherwise plainly shows a "fear response." If this is the extent of the conditioning, it may be designated as CER(a).

The parenthetical a in this abbreviation is meant to distinguish it from another kind of CER. Subsequent to this conditioning (or prior to it) animals may be trained in a Skinner box to press a bar to obtain food or water. Ordinarily a partial-reinforcement procedure is employed in which the animal is rewarded at variable intervals rather than on every trial. This procedure keeps the animal pressing the bar at a high and relatively steady rate except when a clicker is turned on. When this happens, the animal immediately shows a CER(a) and at the same time either stops pressing the bar or considerably slows down its pressing. The effect on lever pressing is easily seen in a record of its performance, and this effect is also known as a CER but may be designated more specifically as a CER(b). Such an effect is really one of classical conditioning; the lever pressing is used merely as a quantitative, and very sensitive, measure of the strength of the conditioned emotional response.

AVOIDANCE CONDITIONING—Three different techniques of avoidance conditioning are commonly employed: (1) paw flexure, (2) a jumping response, and (3) a shuttle response.

Paw flexure as a conditioned response was introduced with dogs as subjects by Pavlovian investigators studying type II, or defensive, conditioning. A signal, which may be a light, sound, or a cutaneous stimulus, is first presented and then followed some seconds later by a shock to a paw if that paw is not raised in response to the signal. In other words, the animal may escape (at first) shock or avoid it (later) by raising its paw. Either the forepaws or hind-paws may be used. Sometimes, for a particular reason, both forepaws or hind-paws may be shocked and hence must be raised to avoid shock.

Paw-flexure conditioning may be used to establish *differential conditioning*. Actually, any method of avoidance conditioning can be employed for this purpose, but typically it has been paw flexure. To establish differential conditioning, two different stimuli are used. One is positive in that it, as in simple conditioning, is punished by shock if the leg is not lifted. The other is negative in the sense that it is not reinforced. Eventually, with this procedure, a normal dog learns to lift its leg to the positive stimulus and to leave its leg down when the negative stimulus is presented. Sometimes the two responses are called the *positive conditioned reflex* and the *negative conditioned reflex*. Since, after positive conditioning, the negative conditioned reflex represents an inhibition of the paw flexure, the negative reflex is sometimes referred to as an *inhibitory reflex*.

A jumping avoidance response has in recent years served as a convenient response to conditioning in the rat. If a rat receives a shock from a grill in the floor, one of its natural responses is to jump up in the air away from the source of stimulus. Hence this response is readily conditioned. All that is necessary is to provide a ledge within the jumping altitude of the rat so that the rat can jump up and cling to it for some arbitrary interval. As in paw-flexure conditioning, a signal is presented a few seconds before the shock. The rat first acquires a simple emotional response to the signal, then learns to escape the shock by jumping, and finally to avoid the shock by jumping in response to the signal.

A third variety of avoidance-conditioning procedure, the one employed more frequently than any other, is a *shuttle response*. In this case, the animal (rat, cat, dog, or monkey) is placed in a box with two compartments. The compartments may be separated by a hurdle, a swinging door, or even an imaginary line marking off the box into two sources of shock. In order to avoid shock, the animal must learn to respond to a signal by shuttling over from the compartment he is in to the other compartment. Aside from the shuttle response, other details of the procedure are similar to those in paw flexure or jumping.

With these procedures in mind, we may now describe the kinds of results obtained when lesions are made in different parts of the brain.

CEREBRAL CORTEX

We shall first consider the effects of lesions of the cerebral cortex. In doing this, we shall omit the cingular gyrus and the ventral regions of the cortex that are closely related to the limbic system, for these will be treated separately.

Research with cortical lesions can be classified into the following groups: complete decortication, hemidecortication, sensory areas, and frontal cortex.

COMPLETE DECORTICATION—In 1911, Zeliony, a Russian colleague of Pavlov, first attempted to study conditioning in the totally decorticate dog (a dog deprived of all neocortex). Zeliony failed. His failure caused Pavlov and many others to believe that conditioning was solely a property of the cerebral cortex. Many years later, in 1930, Poltyrew and Zeliony repeated the early attempts. This time they succeeded in obtaining conditioned responses in decorticates (dogs). In fact, two of their animals developed a rather sophisticated form of differential conditioning; they learned to lift one forepaw to avoid shock to the sound of a whistle and the other forepaw to the sound of a knock on wood.

These positive results with decorticates reopened the whole question. The Russian workers had not reported any postmortem checks of their animals, and it was possible that their animals were not really decorticate. Later checks by several American investigators (Girden et al., 1936; Bromiley, 1948), leave no doubt that decorticate animals can be conditioned. In all cases, avoidance conditioning was the kind of conditioning studied. Auditory, thermal, and tactile stimuli have all been successfully employed.

In the later work, however, a new question arose. It was, Are the conditioned responses of the decorticate qualitatively different from those of the normal animal? To Girden and his collaborators (see above), decorticate conditioned responses appeared to be more diffuse and less specific than normal responses. In acquiring a conditioned response, the normal animal first learns a diffuse conditioned reaction; it squirms, squeals, and makes a host of uncoordinated movements to the conditioned stimulus. With more and more trials, it drops out the "excess motion" and calmly executes a specific paw flexure to avoid shock. For Girden and his colleagues, this second stage did not develop in the decorticate animal.

Further research has since cleared up this point (Bromiley, 1948). Decorticate animals can learn to make specific avoidance responses, but they may or may not do this, depending on how they are handled. Decorticate animals are emotional animals (see Chapter 11), and their emotional responses are easily conditioned. If the investigator does not shock the dog when it is disturbed, thus keeping it as unemotional as possible, specific flexure of the front paw can be conditioned to the sound of a bell. Moreover, a differential discrimination can be built up; by appropriate training, the animal can learn to raise its paw to a light stimulus and not to respond to a bell stimulus.

It may be concluded, then, that, while the decorticate animal is at a handicap, both classical and avoidance conditioning, including differential conditioned responses, can take place in the absence of the neocortex. At least, this is true of the dog.

HEMIDECORTICATION—Several studies have been made of the dog and the cat deprived of all neocortex *on one side* (Bromiley, 1948; Kellogg and Bashore, 1950; and Kellogg and Hovorka, 1951). To understand the results, it should be remembered that hemidecortication causes a partial paralysis of limbs on the side opposite the decortication because the operation destroys the motor cortical areas as well as others (see Chapter 10).

If, as was the case in one study (Bromiley, 1948), the animal (cat) is allowed to avoid shock by lifting a foot on either side of the body, the animal learns to lift the foot on the normal side. In other words, it "favors" its partially paralyzed side. On the other hand, if forced to lift its disabled paw, by reinforcing only the lifting of this paw, the animal (dog) can learn to do this about as rapidly as a normal animal (Kellogg and Bashore, 1950). The amplitude of the leg lift on the affected side is, however, smaller than that on the normal side. Not only is this true of animals trained after hemidecortication; it also applies to the retention of responses learned prior to operation. Hemidecortication does not affect retention of a conditioned response; only the vigor of the response on the "bad" side is decreased.

SENSORY AREAS—As we have just seen, a cat or a dog *can* learn an avoidance response after decortication. From this fact, it might be expected that lesser ablations restricted to specific areas of the cortex would also permit an animal to learn an avoidance response. This expectation is confirmed in a number of studies, as we shall see.

On the other hand, there are other possible consequences of lesions restricted to limited areas of the cortex. (1) One is impairment of acquisition. Although an animal may eventually acquire an avoidance response, it may require more than the normal number of responses. Hence acquisition is impaired. (2) A second possible effect is impairment of retention. After operation, the animal may not "remember," at least perfectly, the habit learned beforehand and may require more trials, sometimes even more than preoperatively, to reacquire the habit. (3) Simple avoidance responses may be retained following operation, but differential responses requiring a discrimination between positive and negative stimuli may be impaired or lost. All three effects are seen under certain circumstances.

In research on these effects, restricted lesions of the cortex have been made in each of the sensory areas and in the frontal cortex. The sensory areas involved have been the visual, auditory, and somatic areas.

Few studies employing classical conditioning and lesions of specific sensory areas are available. In the case of vision, conditioned eye-blink responses to visual stimuli are unaffected by removal of the visual cortex (Marquis, 1934). It is a good guess that, if the data were available, the same would be true of other senses because some kind of response to the conditioning stimulus is invariably present following removal of any sensory area.

There similarly is little or no effect of sensory lesions on the *acquisition* of an avoidance response or of an instrumental response. Animals lacking the striate cortex are quite capable of learning to lift their leg in response to a flash of light (Wing and Smith, 1942) or even to a change in intensity (Wing, 1946). By a slight change in procedure, such animals can learn to lift their leg on signal to obtain food reward (Wing, 1947). In a word, then, animals do not need their striate cortex to acquire a simple avoidance or instrumental response. Essentially, the same results have been obtained with auditory stimuli and the auditory cortex (Raab and Ades, 1946). After bilateral removal of this cortex, they learn avoidance responses as readily as normal animals.

When the *retention* of responses following operation is considered, the results are not so clear. Avoidance responses to visual stimuli, including responses to changes in intensity as well as to the onset of a flash, are retained following removal of the striate cortex (Wing, 1947). Similarly, removal of somatic areas 1 and 2 (Chapter 9) in the dog has little if any effect on the retention of cutaneous foreleg avoidance responses (Allen, 1945, 1946). Animals continue to make responses to the positive stimulus following operation. In the case of hearing, however, different results are obtained, depending on the technique used. In the dog, conditioned paw flexure to a positive auditory stimulus is not affected appreciably by removal of auditory areas I and II and even somewhat larger cortical areas.

The most consistent and significant effect of cortical lesions in sensory areas is obtained with *differential* conditioned reactions. In these, it will be recalled, the subject raises its paw in response to a positive conditioned stimulus but must not respond to another stimulus. A discrimination of stimuli is involved; so also is the capacity to inhibit a conditioned response. In both cutaneous (Allen, 1946) and auditory (Allen, 1945) conditioning, this ability is not retained after bilateral lesions of the appropriate sensory areas. The severity of difficulty depends on the size of the lesion. With lesions smaller than areas I and II, the differential response is partly or completely lost, but it may be relearned in some number of trials. With lesions encompassing both areas I and II, animals may not be able to reacquire the differential response after hundreds or even thousands of trials (see Chapter 17).

FRONTAL CORTEX—The role of the frontal cortex in avoidance conditioning has been studied in several experiments. They differ in the animals used, the amount and position of lesions, and in the particular conditioning techniques employed. In general, however, it can be said that the frontal cortex is important in the retention of avoidance responses. Rats with frontal lesions show no retention of a jumping avoidance response learned preoperatively and are indeed unable to relearn it (Thompson, 1959). A similar result is obtained with rats (Brady et al., 1954). In monkeys, the effects of limited frontal lesions are less severe (Waterhouse, 1957; Pribram and Weiskrantz, 1957). Retention of an avoidance response is impaired, but the animals relearn.

However, certain areas of the frontal cortex appear to be more important than others. The area most consistently implicated is the area of projection of the dorsomedial nucleus of the thalamus which, as we shall see, is a thalamic center of importance in avoidance learning.

The interpretation to be made of these studies of the frontal cortex is not entirely clear. On the one hand, the frontal cortex is somehow concerned with fear; frontal animals appear not to be as fearful or to be as easily aroused by the conditioned stimulus (auditory or visual) as normal animals (Waterhouse, 1957). On the other hand, frontal animals do not lose their emotional response to the conditioning stimulus (Thompson, 1959). They exhibit anticipatory responses, such as squealing, muscle movements, and changes in respiration, to the conditioned stimulus. Hence the fundamental difficulty appears to be one of executing a specific avoidance response.

LIMBIC SYSTEM

The structure of the limbic system has been previously described (page 52). For the most part, it is a subcortical system but it includes the cingulate gyrus of the cerebral cortex (so-called transitional cortex). The effects of lesions on this structure have been studied; so also have lesions in the septum, hippocampus, amygdala, and hypothalamus. The principal behavioral techniques used have been the conditioned emotional response (CER) and either the jumping or shuttle avoidance responses (CAR). The effects obtained with lesions of the limbic system depend on the type of conditioned response employed and on the structures destroyed, as well as on whether original acquisition or retention is being measured.

SEPTUM—Lesions of the septum, it will be recalled (page 322), increase emotionality, although this effect gradually wears off in time. Animals (rats) have been studied during the period of heightened emotionality and tested for their rate of acquiring two different responses: a conditioned emotional response, type CER(a), which is a classical conditioned fear response, and the shuttle-box avoidance response (CAR).

On the first test, there is no difference in acquisition. Septal animals acquire it just as fast, but no faster, than normal animals (Brady and Nauta, 1953). This, however, is an extremely simple kind of conditioning for it occurs in very few trials, and it is hard to see how it could occur much faster. An avoidance response, on the other hand, is acquired somewhat *more rapidly* by septal than by normal animals (King, 1958). This is one of very few instances in which lesions improve performance. However, it is in accordance with the fact that septal animals are more emotional than normal animals.

If this is the explanation of more rapid acquisition of shuttle-box avoidance, one would not predict from it the effect of septal lesions on the retention of a

CER(*a*) or a CAR. In two different experiments, one using the CER(*a*) (Brady and Nauta, 1953) and the other a CAR (Tracy and Harrison, 1956), retention was impaired when the septal lesions were made *after* acquisition of the conditioned response. The effect is not great, but it is significant.

AMYGDALA—Lesions of the amygdala in normal, relatively tame animals have little effect on emotionality. In wild animals, however, or in animals previously subjected to septal lesions, destruction of the amygdala usually causes the animal to become more placid—less emotional (King, 1958). It might be expected, therefore, that amygdala lesions would impair both acquisition and retention of CERs and CARs. In general, this is the case, although there are exceptions.

Acquisition of an active CAR has been studied after amygdala lesions made in the rat and the cat. In the case of the rat, there is no difference in rate of learning the CAR although operated animals are somewhat more sluggish and have longer latencies in responding to the conditioning signal (King, 1958). In the cat, on the other hand, acquisition of a CAR is impaired, at least under the conditions studied (Brady et al., 1954). Since there were some differences in procedures and the acquisition of normal cats took about three times as long as that of rats, it has been suggested (King, 1958) that the problem for cats was more difficult. If that be true, then one would conclude that amygdala lesions impair acquisition when the problem is difficult but not when it is easy. This is plausible, for the difficulty of the learning task often is a crucial variable in the effects of brain lesions.

With respect to *retention*, there is also some disagreement in the available results. In cats—in fact, in the very study that showed impairment of acquisition of an active CAR—there was little or no difference in retention between amygdalectomized animals and normals (Brady et al., 1954). On the other hand, with the simpler CER(*a*) in the monkey, there was a significant impairment in retention (Weiskrantz, 1956). Again, these results are difficult to explain.

CINGULATE CORTEX—Lesions of the cingulate cortex have been studied with the CER(*a*), the conventional CAR, and also a variation of the CAR that yielded interesting results (McCleary, 1961) and require a brief description. This variation is called *passive* avoidance in contrast to the conventional CAR which is distinguished by the term *active* avoidance. In passive avoidance, an animal is first trained to enter a compartment or to stick its head in a box to obtain food reward. It may be trained to do this either in response to a signal or merely upon being placed in the testing box. Then shock is introduced and presented whenever the animal approaches the food after being given a signal. The animal, in order to avoid shock, must learn to withhold his approach to food. Otherwise it gets shocked. This behavior of *not* approaching food is *passive* avoidance, whereas an animal that must move or make some other response is displaying active avoidance. This distinction should be kept in mind for what follows.

In an experiment with rats that had acquired a CER(a) before operation, there was perfect retention of the habit following substantial lesions to the cingulate cortex (Brady and Nauta, 1953). Apparently the role of this cortex is more subtle than can be discerned with the simple CER(a). This is brought out in research that distinguishes between the anterior and posterior parts of the cingulate cortex as well as the kind of habit acquired (McCleary, 1961).

The investigator made anterior lesions in some cats, confining his surgical destruction to tissue beneath the knee of the corpus callosum, and in other cats he made posterior lesions above the corpus callosum. Postoperatively he taught, or attempted to teach, all the cats two habits: an active avoidance (shuttle-box) response and passive avoidance (refraining from approaching food). The two groups of cats were markedly different. Those with anterior lesions readily learned the *active* CAR, but they had great difficulty learning the passive avoidance response. They seemed unable to restrain their approach to food and were rather impervious to the shocks they received. On the other hand, cats with posterior cingulate lesions had just the opposite pattern. They readily learned the passive avoidance habit but had difficulty learning the active CAR.

The latter result, namely, the one obtained with the more conventional active CAR, has also been obtained in the monkey (Pribram and Weiskrantz, 1957) though with a somewhat different procedure. Monkeys with cingulate lesions *following* acquisition of a CAR were successively extinguished, reconditioned, and reextinguished. Quick extinction in this case is a sign of poor retention. And the monkeys extinguished almost immediately. More significantly, they had great difficulty reacquiring the active CAR, taking about thirteen times the number of trials normally required. After this they reextinguished more rapidly than normally.

The cingulate gyrus, then, plays a role in the acquisition and retention of conditioned avoidance responses, but different parts of it seem to be involved in different kinds of avoidance.

HIPPOCAMPUS—The last structure in the limbic system to be discussed is the hippocampus (page 53). It has been left until last because the results obtained are related to those obtained with other structures, particularly the cingulate gyrus.

Animals with large hippocampal lesions have no difficulty acquiring an active CAR (Isaacson et al., 1961). They learn avoidance shuttling about as rapidly as normal animals. One experiment (Thomas and Otis, 1958) appears to contradict this statement, but in that experiment damage was probably also done to the cingulate cortex. Hence the effect on active CAR might be explained by cingulate effects. It may be, on the other hand, that hippocampal lesions impair the retention of a CAR, for in an experiment on the monkey (Pribram and Weiskrantz, 1957) operated animals showed more rapid extinction than normals. On the whole, however, hippocampal damage does not appear to harm active CARs.

Still, as in the case of anteroventral cingulate lesions, hippocampal animals have trouble acquiring a passive avoidance (Isaacson and Wickelgren, 1962). Although normal rats and, indeed, rats with extensive cortical lesions are disturbed by shocks given to them while eating—and refuse to enter the goal compartment for many trials after a single shock—rats with hippocampal ablation show only a slight and transient passive avoidance of the shock. Hence, they are impaired in passive avoidance as distinguished from active avoidance.

THALAMUS

So far as is known at present, there are three areas of the thalamus concerned in avoidance conditioning (Thompson, 1963). These are (1) the dorsomedial nucleus which projects to the frontal lobe and particularly to the parts of the frontal that seem most concerned in avoidance habits, (2) the diffuse thalamic nuclei that constitute the thalamic portion of the reticular formation (page 348), and (3) the posterior (pretectal) nuclei. The first two are unspecific in that it makes no difference whether the conditioning stimulus is auditory or visual. The last is specific in that it is concerned with visual stimuli. It is possible that there is also a specific auditory structure, but so far it has not been discovered.

POSTERIOR NUCLEI—Let us consider the specific posterior area first. Some animals (rats) were trained to make a jumping avoidance response to the onset of a light; others were trained to make the same response to the sound of a 1,000-cycle tone. Following lesions in the posterior nucleus, retention was tested. There was no effect on those responding to auditory stimuli. On the other hand, those that learned the visual response were severely affected. Many of them were unable to relearn the habit after receiving twice the number of postoperative trials they had had preoperatively. (One can never say with complete assurance that an animal can *never* relearn, even if thousands of trials are run, but in avoidance conditioning the conclusion is tentatively accepted when animals show no progress after two or three times the number of trials required for original learning.)

Anatomical connections between the visual cortex and posterior thalamic nucleus are known to exist (Krieg, 1947). Whether these are in any way related to the importance of these nuclei in visual avoidance habits is not known. This nucleus, however, appears to be important in visual learning, not only in avoidance but also in other kinds of visual learning, as we shall see in the next chapter.

DORSOMEDIAL NUCLEUS—One of the two nonspecific structures in the thalamus concerned in avoidance conditioning is the dorsomedial nucleus. This has long been implicated in frontal lobe function (see Chapter 18). Animals with lesions in this structure show no retention of an active CAR learned preoperatively and show considerable difficulty relearning it. In some instances, the habit is not relearned in twice the number of preoperative trials. Thus the dorsomedial nucleus plays a major role in the functions involved in "active" avoidance conditioning. It has anatomical connections with the limbic system (Gillery, 1959) and also with the diffuse thalamic system (Nauta and Whitlock, 1954), but the significance of either of these is not known.

DIFFUSE THALAMIC SYSTEM—This is the upper extension of the reticular formation. It projects to several regions of the cerebral cortex, and it also receives fibers from the cortex. Generally it is regarded as a facilitating system that "alerts" and "primes" cortical processes. It is also connected with the limbic system, as was noted above.

Whatever the significance of these anatomical connections, the fact is that lesions in this system greatly impair both the retention of active CARs and the ability to relearn them. It makes no difference whether the avoidance signal is auditory or visual. Postoperatively, animals frequently make spontaneous responses; they also appear to react just as emotionally to the conditioned stimulus as before. What seems to be impaired is their ability to execute the avoidance response on cue from a signal.

OTHER BRAIN-STEM STRUCTURES

In addition to the "higher" structures of the brain that we have discussed, there are several "lower" centers that might conceivably play some role in conditioning. These are the hypothalamus, because of its important part in emotional behavior; the reticular formation, because of its part in emotional behavior; the reticular formation, because of its part in arousal and alerting; and the superior and inferior colliculi, because of their respective connections with the visual and auditory system. There is some information bearing on these various structures, although in some cases it is rather scanty. Both classical and avoidance conditioning have been employed, using cats and rats as subjects.

Some center, or centers, in the region of the posterior hypothalamus is important in conditioning. A cat conditioned preoperatively with a tone and an unavoidable shock but suffering a lesion that includes the posterior hypothalamus and mammillary bodies never shows any conditioned responses whatsoever after more than five times the number of preoperative trials (Doty et al., 1959). As we shall see later (Chapter 17), this same general area is implicated in discriminative learning. A deficit in avoidance conditioning has also been demonstrated in the interpeduncular nucleus, a nucleus of the brain stem that makes efferent connections with the posterior hypothalamus, but this deficit apparently is transient, occurring only in a period immediately after operation (Thompson and Rich, 1961).

Except for the posterior hypothalamic area, no other structure of the midbrain or hindbrain appears to be crucial for conditioning employing shock. Animals with virtually complete destruction of either the superior or inferior colliculus display essentially complete retention of a jumping CAR, whether the conditioning stimulus is sound or a light (Thompson, 1963). The whole brain-stem portion of the reticular formation has been destroyed with no significant effect on classical conditioned responses to shock (Doty et al., 1959). Thus none of the "indirect" sensory pathways seem important in shock-reinforced conditioning.

We have had to qualify the above statement with "shock-reinforced," because it does not hold for salivary conditioning of the Pavlovian type. In this case, relatively minor lesions of the brain-stem reticular formation abolish conditioned salivary responses in the dog (Hernández-Peón et al., 1958). Why there should be a difference is not apparent.

SPINAL CORD

This survey of the effect of brain lesions on conditioning leaves one with the conclusion that few areas of the brain are crucial for conditioning. Conditioning can be obtained after practically any region is injured. This is particularly true of simple classical conditioning. Some investigators have asked whether the brain is really necessary for very simple learning. Perhaps conditioning can take place in the spinal cord. The results of studies on this question are complex and contradictory. We shall review them briefly.

TECHNIQUES—Two basic techniques have been used in the study of spinal conditioning. One, employed by Shurrager (see Shurrager and Culler, 1940) and his collaborators, involves stripping out surgically the semitendinosus muscle in the thigh of a dog (see Figure 16.2). This muscle is a flexor which gives a reflex response when shock is applied to the foot pad. The conditioning stimulus in the experiments was shock or pressure applied to the tail.

Another investigator, Kellogg et al. (1947), employed a technique differing from Shurrager's in the following respects: Instead of using the muscle twitch of a single muscle, Kellogg observed the flexor response of the whole leg. His unconditioned stimulus was the same as Shurrager's (an electric shock to the foot pad of the same leg) but his conditioning stimulus was different. It was a shock applied to the opposite limb of the animal rather than a stimulus administered to the tail.

RESULTS—With these two different procedures, two groups of investigators have obtained different results. Shurrager and his collaborators reported that

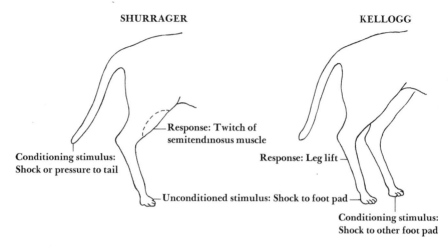

SHURRAGER   KELLOGG

Response: Twitch of
semitendinosus muscle

Conditioning stimulus: Response: Leg lift
Shock or pressure to tail

Unconditioned stimulus: Shock to foot pad

Conditioning stimulus:
Shock to other foot pad

FIGURE 16.2–Diagram of the techniques for spinal conditioning.

spinal conditioning takes place, whereas Kellogg's group was unable to obtain it.

Shurrager's positive results were obtained in 98 dogs. For some unexplained reason, he could not observe it in the remainder of 219 dogs studied. In those dogs that were conditioned, conditioning took place in 20 to 120 trials and the average rate of conditioning was 51 trials. This "spinal conditioning," like Pavlovian conditioning, could be extinguished by presenting the tail stimulus (conditioning stimulus) repeatedly without reinforcement from the foot-pad stimulus (US). On repeated reconditioning and extinction, it took progressively fewer trials on each occasion. There are a number of other results of these experiments, but these are the principal ones.

Shurrager's results have been subject to several criticisms: (1) It was probable that there was an *unconditioned* response to the tail stimulus; at least Shurrager himself reports the occasional occurrence of such a response. (2) There were no controls for pseudoconditioning, that is, for the possibility that the curves of learning and extinction would have taken place with repeated presentations of the shock alone.

There is the fact too that Kellogg's procedure obtained negative results. This is not compelling in itself, for there may have been reasons for them. Perhaps spinal conditioning occurs under such restricted conditions that it can be seen only in a muscle twitch and not in a gross response. Or perhaps the choice of the opposite leg for applying the CS was inappropriate. Such stimulation can cause an extension reflex of the opposite leg, the one in which an attempt was made to condition flexion (see page 289).

As matters stand at present, one can draw no final conclusion on the matter. Shurrager (Shurrager and Dykman, 1951) has reported that kittens whose spinal cords are transected early in life eventually learn something about walking. But this is a gross experiment and difficult to interpret. If there is conditioning or learning at the spinal level, it is certainly difficult to find, and it is not a conspicuous phenomenon. If it exists, it probably accounts for little or nothing of the learned behavior of adult mammalian organisms.

BRAIN STIMULATION

Studying the effects of brain lesions on conditioned responses is one way to investigate the neural mechanisms of conditioning. Stimulation of the brain with electrical currents is another. We say "by electrical currents" because virtually all the work using brain stimulation in conditioning has been with such currents. Conceivably chemical stimuli might also be used, as they have been in the area of motivation, but to date they have not been used.

Electrical stimulation of the brain has been employed in conditioning studies in two general ways. One is to use an electrical stimulus as a substitute for either a *conditioning stimulus* or an *unconditioned stimulus*. The other is to determine whether an electrical stimulus has some effect, say of *interference,* on a conditioned response acquired in the normal way. We shall consider each of these methods, giving particular attention to the first, since the most work has been done with it.

CONDITIONING STIMULUS

An electrical stimulus to the brain may be substituted for the usual auditory, visual, or somesthetic stimuli employed in conditioning. Such a substitution may be made in either classical conditioning or avoidance conditioning. For the present purposes, it makes no difference which, although this will not prove to be the case when we consider the unconditioned stimulus below. Most of the uses of an electrical stimulus (ES) as a conditioning stimulus (CS) have been on areas of the cerebral cortex.

As a preview of what is to come, we may say that electrical stimuli applied to the cortex usually serve well as conditioning stimuli. Also, one can usually obtain generalization between normal peripheral stimuli and cortical stimuli when one is used in conditioning and the other later used in a test of generalization. Finally, the route of the connections established with cortical CSs usually appears to be subcortical. Let us consider in more detail each of these points.

ELECTRICAL STIMULI AS CSs—In an early experiment on this subject, dogs were conditioned either to salivate in anticipation of food or to flex a paw to avoid shock. Electrical stimulation of the visual area of the cortex served as the CS (Loucks, 1938). Instead of the usual procedure of presenting a light prior to shock or food, an ES to the visual cortex served as the CS. Conditioning took place in a normal number of trials. This general result has since been confirmed in a number of experiments (see Doty, 1961).

In more recent experiments (also Doty, 1961), many different positions on the cerebral cortex have been tried. Although the auditory and visual cortical areas have been the favorite areas, because of the common use of visual and auditory stimuli in conditioning experiments, many other cortical areas, including some not considered to be sensory or even associative, have been tried. There is virtually no area of the cortex that will not yield conditioned flexion responses, after appropriate training, when electrical stimuli are applied as CSs to it, although there are a few exceptions.

Even stimulations of the motor cortex result in conditioning. In an early experiment on this point (Loucks, 1936), shock to the motor cortex was used to elicit a hind-limb movement, and this was later followed by a forelimb flexure to avoid shock. This procedure resulted in the conditioning of the forelimb to cortical elicitation of the hind-limb movement. Of course, the hind-limb movement might conceivably serve in this instance as the CS for the response. This possibility, however, was eliminated by narcotizing the hind limb during the conditioning series. Conditioning still occurred. Thus it was shown that it was the electrical stimulus to the motor cortex, not its indirect effects, that served as the CS. It is known that there is cutaneous representation in the motor cortex (Bucy, 1944) that might be activated with electrical stimulation. On the other hand, since other nonsensory areas can serve as loci for electrical CSs, that is not necessarily the explanation. At present, it is not at all certain why so many of the areas of the cortex may serve as CS spots. All that is known is that they generally do so.

STIMULUS GENERALIZATION—As psychologists have shown in many experiments, all learning involving stimuli has associated with it some stimulus generalization. That is to say, certain stimuli, not identical with those involved in learning, may evoke the learned response once the learning has been established. To study stimulus generalization, one normally trains an organism on one particular stimulus, or set of stimuli, and then tests at the end of training with other stimuli to determine the ones to which the response generalizes.

In an extensive study of generalization, two investigators (Doty and Rutledge, 1959) obtained results on several varieties of generalization. They trained all their animals (cats) to make foreleg flexions to avoid shock in response to a CS. For some animals the CS was tone, for others a light; for still other animals the CS was a shock to the auditory cortex, and for others a shock to the visual cortex. After training on the prescribed CS was complete, the animals were tested with other types of stimuli, including other placements of cortical electrodes. This was to test for generalization.

Generalization usually took place between auditory and visual stimuli.

(This, however, does not occur in all experiments and may depend on the technique employed.)

It also appears that generalization from peripheral to corresponding cortical stimuli was good, although the number of animals was small. For example, a cat trained on light responded well to an ES to the visual cortex, and a cat similarly trained to a tone generalized to an ES applied to the auditory cortex. The reverse, however, did not work so well; only about a quarter of the animals trained on cortical ESs generalized to the corresponding normal stimulus. Finally, there was good "homotopic" generalization to cortical CS. That is to say, an animal trained to an ES applied on one side generalized to an ES applied to the corresponding cortical area on the other side. (More will be said about this later.)

How to interpret these experiments is not entirely clear. From what is known of electrical stimulation of sensory areas in man (see page 271), one may surmise that the sensory experience evoked by cortical stimulation is rather bizarre—a buzz, noise, flickering light, or such—and something not usually duplicated in environmental stimuli. This might possibly explain why generalization from environmental to cortical stimuli was reasonably good, while generalization in the other direction was poor. The reason is not known. It is interesting, however, that there is any generalization at all.

ANATOMICAL PATHWAYS—Naturally, one of the central problems in the mind of investigators studying the neural mechanisms of learning is to determine, if possible, the routes employed in learning. That is to say, it would be desirable to know the pathways involved in learning and the place, if there be a place, in which the crucial changes in learning occur. Several experiments have been designed with this problem in mind.

One experiment concerns a kind of anatomical generalization as contrasted with stimulus generalization. Once a conditioned response employing an electrical CS at one point has been established, tests are made with the electrical CS applied at other points. If there is any generalization from one cortical area to another, it would imply a transcortical route or mechanism in conditioning.

The evidence on this point is negative. In the study described above (Doty and Rutledge, 1959) some heterotopic tests were made on 19 animals. Generalization occurred in six and was either equivocal or absent in the rest. The investigators concluded that heterotopic generalization may not occur, but their data were inconclusive. In another study (Grosser and Harrison, 1960), in which rats were trained to bar-press for food in response to an electrical ES to the posterior (visual) cortex, no generalization to electrode positions more than 1 millimeter away from the position employed in conditioning was found. This experiment would lead to the belief that very little transcortical generalization in conditioning occurs. This conclusion fits with other facts we shall present.

Another approach to the study of anatomical pathways in learning is to cut the corpus callosum. This is an intercortical pathway connecting homotopic (and other) points on the two sides of the cerebral cortex. In the study on cats (Doty and Rutledge, 1959) this was done. The effect on homotopic generalization was nil. In other words, the generalization that took place between corresponding points on the two hemispheres apparently did not involve the corpus callosum. Rather, some other (subcortical?) route was involved.

That subcortical pathways are more important than transcortical routes is shown by another pair of experiments (Doty, 1961). In one of these, the cortical area to which the electrical CS was applied was circumcised—cut off from surrounding cortex—upon the completion of conditioning. In the other, the white matter under the cortex, which communicates with subcortical centers, was undercut after conditioning. Both had an effect on postoperative tests, but circumcision had much the lesser effect. Circumcision traumatizes the cortex, and so it is not surprising that some retraining was required, but much less was necessary than was originally required. Hence there is considerable saving after this operation. On the other hand, undercutting the cortex caused the habit to be completely lost, and the animal had to be completely retrained, requiring somewhat more trials, on an average, than originally.

It is interesting that in this situation there is any relearning at all. The fact that relearning is possible means that, when circumstances make it "necessary," a transcortical route can be established. Such a route, however, appears not to be the cortical route in the intact animal.

The general conclusion from these studies is that a pathway downward from the cortex is normally the important anatomical route for the effects involved in using an electrical stimulus as the conditioned stimulus. In the next chapter on discriminative learning, we shall see that a similar conclusion holds in more complex kinds of learning.

UNCONDITIONED STIMULUS

A conditioning stimulus is normally a neutral stimulus. It is one that before conditioning has no meaning or motivating value for the organism. This may or may not be true of the unconditioned stimulus. Generally speaking, in classical conditioning, the US does not motivate; it merely evokes a response. This is the case in conditioning an eye blink or a knee jerk. On the other hand, in instrumental learning the unconditioned stimulus, say food or shock, is an incentive; it motivates the organism and can call out many kinds of behavior other than the one conditioned. The conditioned stimulus is that particular response that is rewarded, or punished if it is not made. This distinction must be taken into account when we consider the use of electrical stimuli as substitutes for the unconditioned stimulus in classical and instrumental learning.

CLASSICAL CONDITIONING—We have seen that an electrical stimulus may be substituted over much of the cerebral cortex for a conditioning stimulus. Is the same true of the unconditioned stimulus? In early experiments on this question, the answer was "yes" and "no," depending on the part of the brain stimulated. In general, movements may be evoked by electrical stimulation in many parts of the brain, if the stimulus is strong enough, but the most sensitive part is the motor area of the cerebral cortex. This area was the place of stimulation in one of the earliest systematic experiments on the question (Loucks, 1936).

The subjects were dogs. The procedure consisted of sounding a buzzer and then, in about a second, of shocking the motor cortex. The shock evoked a contraction of a hind limb. This pairing of stimuli was repeated in the usual way trial after trial. But no conditioning occurred. No matter how many trials the experimenter ran the dog, he was unable to obtain any responses to the buzzer alone. He did find, however, that he could obtain conditioning if he introduced a food reward for leg lifting, but this simply converted the problem into a conventional instrumental conditioning problem in which the electrical stimulation may have served as "guidance," helping the animal to make the correct response. It did not permit one to say that classical conditioning had occurred.

In a similar experiment a few years later, everything was done in much the same way except that the electrical stimulus was applied to the cerebellum rather than to the motor cortex (Brogden and Gantt, 1942). The cerebellar stimulation evoked a leg contraction much like that evoked from the motor cortex. Only in this instance conditioning occurred. And it took about the same number of trials, that is, the same number of pairings of a buzzer and cerebellar stimulation, as dogs normally require when the US is a shock to the foot.

For some years, it was a puzzle why a US to a remote point such as the cerebellum could produce conditioning when the same stimulus applied to the motor cortex, the beginning of the direct motor pathway, could not. Recently, the mystery seems to have been solved. Two investigators (Doty and Giurgea, 1961), checking on the findings made earlier by one of them (Giurgea in Rumania), were able to obtain good conditioning with electrical stimulation to the motor cortex in dogs, cats, and monkeys. The main difference between their positive experiment and the earlier negative one was in the timing of the trials. Apparently Loucks had been going too fast; the intervals between his trials were usually thirty to sixty seconds and always less than two minutes. If the interval is lengthened to three to five minutes, then positive results can be obtained. It is reasonably certain that this is the explanation, because, in the very animals in which conditioning has taken place, the conditioned response disappears when the intertrial interval is shortened from three minutes to less than two minutes. The fact that the intertrial interval is often critical in conditioning was earlier shown by Pavlov.

Thus it has now been established that movements directly elicited by stimulation of the motor cortex or the cerebellum may become conditioned responses when paired with the appropriate conditioning stimulus. This fact, coupled with the findings for the conditioned response, leads to the belief (see Sperry, 1955; Doty and Giurgea, 1961) that the important connection formed in conditioning is closely related to the motor side and may be subcortical.

It is always hazardous to say that something *cannot* happen. As we have just seen, the first attempts to obtain conditioning with the US to the motor cortex failed, but the trouble later proved to be a matter of procedure. Such may be the case in other unsuccessful attempts to obtain conditioning. There have been two such failures with stimulation in the hypothalamus. In one (Masserman, 1941), the ES elicited sham rage, a well-known phenomenon of stimulation at certain points in the hypothalamus (see Chapter 11). Electrical stimulation was paired with an auditory or visual conditioning stimulus. No animal was conditioned even though in some cases hundreds of trials were given. A similar result was obtained in an experiment on polydipsia (Andersson and Larssen, 1956). Electrical stimulation was applied to a point in a hypothalamic center where it causes an animal (goat) to drink. Such stimulation was paired with a tone. However, no conditioning took place; the goats did not drink in response to the tonal conditioning stimulus.

There is insufficient evidence of this kind to draw any general conclusions. Possibly there is something unique about the responses employed or about stimulation of the hypothalamus (but see below). At present, it is not known.

INSTRUMENTAL LEARNING—In instrumental conditioning, the unconditioned stimulus is typically a positive reward such as food or a negative incentive such as shock. Through trial and error, the animal learns some response, arbitrarily required by the experimenter, that is followed by reward, or it avoids a shock. The US does not directly elicit the response, as is the case in classical conditioning. The US is typically regarded as something that satisfies a motive.

As we have already seen (Chapter 11), central brain stimulation may serve as a reward in instrumental learning. Animals implanted with electrodes through which they receive shocks when they make an appropriate response will learn to press bars, run mazes, or to perform other acts to obtain central shock. In most respects, the learning with such central stimulation is like that seen with external rewards. Only it frequently is a more powerful incentive than external rewards. We have also seen that electrical stimulation in the brain may be aversive and that animals will learn habits to avoid such stimulation. Since we have fully discussed these phenomena elsewhere (Chapter 11), we shall not go into them here. Suffice it to say that the use of electrical stimulation as a US in these cases seems to be a matter of motivation, not learning.

INTERFERENCE EFFECTS

Besides being used as a CS or US, brain stimulation may be applied during or after normal learning to determine its effects on learning and retention. Such stimulation may conceivably facilitate learning, and certain instances of this have been reported (Gengerelli and Woskow, 1958). However, brain stimulation more often has an interference effect, if it has any effect at all. This can come about because electrical stimulation frequently causes an abnormal amount of neural activity at or near the site of stimulation. This activity can swamp or occlude normal activity. In theory, such an occlusion effect can be used to track down the structures important in a particular kind of learning. Brain stimulation can also cause prolonged discharges or seizure in certain structures. This can also be expected to be occluding. Finally, a period of prolonged depression sometimes follows electrical stimulation, thus rendering tissue or materially raising its threshold. Some examples of these effects on learning will be given. In order to avoid scattering the discussion of this subject, other kinds of learning besides conditioning will also be mentioned.

In one experiment (Rosvold and Delgado, 1956) monkeys were trained to perform a delayed alternation task in which they were supposed to look for food under one cup and then, after a delay, to look for it under another cup, and so on. The same monkeys were also trained to make a simple visual discrimination. After learning these tasks, brain stimulation was applied during the performance of the tasks. With electrodes in the caudate nucleus (page 283), the monkeys were adversely affected on the delayed alternation. While being stimulated, they were seldom able to alternate correctly. [A similar effect on avoidance responses has been reported (Nakao and Maki, 1958).] On the other hand, their ability to make a visual discrimination was unimpaired.

In another kind of experiment, cats were trained in the conventional instrumental task of bar pressing (Knott et al., 1960). Brain stimulation was applied during bar pressing. With the electrodes in some positions, namely, in the hippocampus, caudate nucleus, and thalamus, there was no effect on bar-pressing rate. However, with placements in the septum and the hypothalamus, bar pressing stopped during brain stimulation and was resumed only after the stimulation had ceased for some time. Since the septum and hypothalamus are concerned in emotion, it is quite possible that the reason for the effect was that brain stimulation aroused or affected emotional responses that in turn affected bar pressing.

Interference effects, however, have been reported in structures outside the limbic system, not only in the caudate nucleus discussed above but also in the brain-stem reticular formation (Glickman, 1958). The disturbance in the latter case may be one of "distraction of attention," but until all the consequences of such brain stimulation are better understood, its effect will be difficult to interpret.

One final experiment will illustrate the production of afterdischarges and their effect on learning (Flynn and Wasman, 1960). Electrodes were placed in the hippocampus of cats. A train of impulses was applied for ten seconds. Following this, afterdischarge activity could be measured in the hippocampus for ten to ninety seconds. Such an afterdischarge propagates throughout the hippocampus and also to other limbic structures. During this period of after-discharge, cats were given trials in an avoidance response. The task was to lift a leg to avoid shock in response to a sound.

The interesting thing about the experiment is that during training the cats seemed to learn little at all. They seldom avoided the shock, although occasionally they made avoidance responses. After the number of trials during which cats usually learn the avoidance response, the brain stimulation was discontinued. Then, surprisingly, the animals immediately began to make a large number of correct responses. In other words, learning was occurring in the trials conducted during afterdischarges even though no responses were made. Interference with the response evidently was a motor effect and not related to the learning mechanism.

ELECTRICAL CORRELATES

So far we have considered brain lesions and brain stimulation as methods of studying what goes on in the brain in conditioning. Another approach to the problem is to correlate recorded electrical events with the phenomena of conditioning (Morrell, 1961). For this purpose, electrical events may be put into two main classes: (1) electroencephalographic (EEG) changes, that is, changes in the rhythmic patterns of the brain, and (2) evoked potentials recorded either by gross electrodes or from microelectrodes on single units. We shall refer to both types of electrical events in what follows.

ALPHA BLOCK

Almost any novel stimulus, when first presented to an organism, calls forth an attentive response. In Russian circles, this behavioral reaction is called an *orienting response,* because an animal usually orients toward the stimulus, looking at it if it is a light, or listening to it if it is a sound. The animal's response seems to be the equivalent of saying "What is it?" This behavior is typically accompanied by the *activation* pattern in the EEG. Such activation (see page 348) is a disruption of the normal alpha rhythm and is frequently referred to also as *desynchronization* or *alpha block.* The term activation is most appropriate when one has the reticular formation in mind, for the reticular activating system is primarily, if not exclusively, responsible for the desynchronization.

Before blocking, the alpha rhythm is seen generally over the cerebral cortex, but it has certain foci in which it is most prominent. These include the primary visual, auditory, and somesthetic areas. Stimuli causing alpha block have both general and specific selective effects (Morrell, 1961). That is to say, a visual stimulus, while tending to block alpha all over the cortex, does it more clearly in the visual area; similarly, an auditory stimulus more effectively blocks alpha in the auditory region of the cortex than in other areas; a similar statement applies to somatic stimuli. We may also note that alpha activity is strongest in the visual area and that visual stimuli are consistently more effective than others in producing alpha block.

One of the first experiments to be made with electrical correlates of conditioning was a conditioning of the alpha block. That it can be conditioned was established in 1935 (Durup and Fessard, 1935), but the first detailed study of the phenomenon was made somewhat later (Jasper and Shagass, 1941). In this study, a sound signal was presented before a visual stimulus, in a sensory-sensory pairing, while the EEG was recorded. In some cases, the occipital alpha block to the sound signal first had to be habituated (see below), but once this was done, the pairing of CS and US was carried out in the usual way. At the beginning of conditioning, the light blocked the alpha, but the sound did not. After repeated pairings, the sound came to elicit the alpha block formerly produced only by the visual stimulus. In this study, it was possible to duplicate nearly all the phenomena of Pavlovian conditioning, including extinction, as well as differential, delayed, and trace conditioning.

EVOKED POTENTIALS

A novel stimulus (one the organism is not "accustomed to") not only desynchronizes the cortical alpha rhythms; it also produces evoked potentials that can be recorded. The two events are related, in that evoked potentials in the reticular formation traveling toward the cortex destroy cortical rhythms and institute vigorous unsynchronized activity. To a certain extent, the potentials evoked by a novel stimulus are signs of an orienting, attentive response just as is the alpha block. The facts concerning evoked potentials and conditioning are in some confusion (Morrell, 1961), but the following points seem fairly well established.

On first presentation of a stimulus, evoked potentials are fairly widespread in the brain. They may be recorded in the primary sensory pathways and the indirect reticular pathway, as expected, but they may also appear in many other places and in cortical areas not directly related to the sense being stimulated. On repeated presentation of the stimulus, there is a general tendency for evoked potentials to habituate, just as alpha blocks do. The habituation can be seen at most points of recording, but it occurs less in the primary sensory pathways than it does in other areas. (There will be more about habituation below.) It is usually necessary to habituate the response to a novel stimulus before proceeding with a conditioning experiment.

What happens to evoked potentials during conditioning depends on the kind of conditioning studied and, in general, on the procedures used. In classical conditioning, say of a click to a shock to the foot, evoked potentials become more prominent as conditioning proceeds. They become more widespread, reversing the effects of habituation, and they become greater in amplitude (Galambos, 1958). In particular, an evoked potential to an acoustic stimulus may appear in the motor cortex after repeated pairing of the CS with shock to the limb (Jouvet and Hernández-Peón, 1957). On the other hand, once conditioning has been well established so that the CS regularly evokes a conditioned leg response, the evoked potentials tend to wane in size (Hearst et al., 1960). Similarly, in avoidance conditioning, evoked potentials are prominent in the early stages of conditioning when the animal is being regularly shocked, but they subside when the animal successfully learns to avoid the shock (see Morrell, 1961).

One of the most comprehensive studies of the effects of a classical conditioning procedure on evoked potentials is illustrated in Figures 16.3 and 16.4 (Galambos and Sheatz, 1962). Indwelling electrodes were implanted in a variety of locations in the brains of cats and monkeys. In most instances, the conditioning stimulus was a click, but in a few it was a light flash. Before beginning the conditioning, the "naïve" animal was presented with a series of CSs (see Figure 16.3). These evoked potentials were of a given size. Then the animal was habituated by the presentation of a series of clicks or flashes. During this period, the evoked potentials became smaller in size (see Figure 16.3). When they no longer decreased in size, conditioning was begun by pairing a puff of air as the US with the CS. After a few such pairings, the evoked potential to the CS markedly increased in size, becoming larger than it was in the naïve animal. After conditioning, an extinction procedure was instituted, during which the size of the evoked potentials subsided to the habituated level. The evoked potential could be conditioned and extinguished in this way over and over again.

It is interesting that the conditioned enhancement of the evoked potential could be obtained in a great variety of brain locations (Figure 16.4). The effect could be found in extensive areas of the neocortex, paleocortex, thalamus, hypothalamus, medial midbrain, pons, and medulla. Thus it appears in brain areas far outside the classical sensory and motor systems.

HABITUATION AND INHIBITION

The points just made make one wonder whether evoked potentials are really a correlate of conditioning per se or of something else, such as "attention" or orientation. The same suspicion is aroused by the fact that both alpha blocks

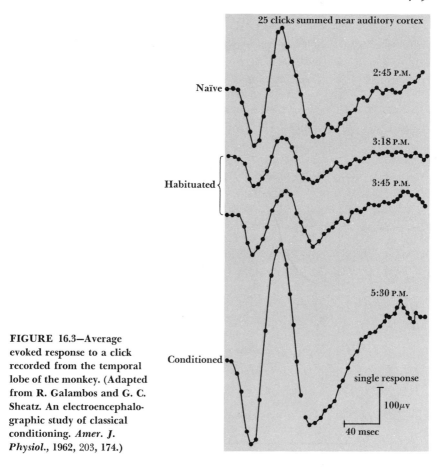

25 clicks summed near auditory cortex

Naïve

2:45 P.M.

3:18 P.M.

Habituated

3:45 P.M.

Conditioned

5:30 P.M.

single response

100μv

40 msec

FIGURE 16.3—Average evoked response to a click recorded from the temporal lobe of the monkey. (Adapted from R. Galambos and G. C. Sheatz. An electroencephalographic study of classical conditioning. *Amer. J. Physiol.*, 1962, 203, 174.)

and evoked potentials must typically be habituated to a novel stimulus before beginning a conditioning routine. Other data confirm this suspicion.

One piece of evidence comes from the inhibition of evoked potentials by "distracting" stimuli (Hernández-Peón et al., 1956). An unanesthetized cat was regularly giving evoked potentials to the sound of a click. The electrode was in the cochlear nucleus of the medulla, a point where evoked potentials become more prominent in conditioning (Galambos et al., 1956). The cat was then shown a mouse, which of course is a most powerful attention-getting stimulus for a cat. The evoked potentials to the click stopped abruptly and did not resume until the mouse was taken away or until the cat "tired" of looking at it. Somehow the presentation of the "interesting" visual stimulus inhibited or choked off evoked responses to the sound. It would appear from this that evoked potentials are more a sign of "attention" to a stimulus than of a conditioned response to it.

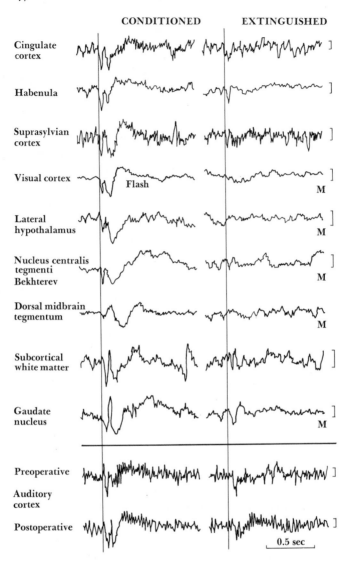

FIGURE 16.4—Evoked responses from several monkeys and cats in conditioned and extinguished states. (Adapted from R̥. Galambos and G. C. Sheatz. An electroencephalographic study of classical conditioning. *Amer. J. Physiol.,* 1962, 203, 175.)

This kind of inhibition also occurs in conditioning. Pavlov called it external inhibition. If a well-conditioned dog is presented with an unexpected, distracting, or attention-getting stimulus, its conditioned response is inhibited. Thus, to a degree, the electrical correlate and the behavioral effect correspond. In each case, however, the inhibition seems to be one of not letting the sensory information available at the receptor pass through the pathways of the brain.

The inhibition of evoked potentials by distracting stimuli is an interesting fact in its own right. Moreover, it is an example of one of the more exciting discoveries of recent years in neurophysiology. This is the discovery of efferent control over the sensory inputs to the nervous system (see Morrell, 1961). It is now well established that each of the sensory pathways contains efferent, as well as sensory, fibers and that these serve different points along the pathway, including the sense organs themselves. These efferent fibers control the level of sensory activity permitted to make its way upward in the sensory system. Thus there is in the brain a mechanism of "attention" that can selectively determine which sensory signals are allowed to make their way upward and which are not. Hence it looks as if it is the attention mechanism that is operative in studies of evoked potentials in conditioning rather than any direct correlate of conditioning per se. Further research, however, may alter this conclusion.

SLOW WAVES

Pavlov distinguished between two kinds of inhibition, the external inhibition just discussed and *internal inhibition*. While the first is caused by distraction of attention, the second is quite the opposite. It represents a relaxation of attention on the part of the organism. Pavlov noted internal inhibition in a variety of procedures all of which had in common the condition that the organism *not* respond.

DELAY INTERVALS—One condition is a long interval between the onset of a CS and the presentation of the US. This happens in delayed conditioning in which the CS comes on and stays on for, say, sixty seconds before the US is presented. It also occurs in trace conditioning; in this the CS comes on briefly and is followed by a long silent interval before the onset of the US. In both instances, the organism tends to relax during the CS-US interval. Pavlov's dogs sometimes relaxed so much they became drowsy and appeared to sleep briefly. Internal inhibition is also frequently seen in differential conditioning when a negative stimulus that requires no response is presented.

The electrical correlates of these procedures, and hence of internal inhibition, have been studied. In trace or delayed conditioning, where there is a long interval between CS and US, the typical sequence is as follows (Gastaut, 1957): When the CS comes on, the EEG shows the expected alpha block or activation pattern. Then, in the middle of the interval, relatively high-voltage, slow-frequency waves, sometimes called hypersynchronous slow waves, are seen (Iwami, 1950). These are in the neighborhood of three to five per second. Toward the end of the interval and prior to the onset of the US, the activation pattern appears again. Hence the onset of slow waves in the EEG signifies the relaxation, or even drowsiness, of internal inhibition.

DIFFERENTIAL CONDITIONING—Essentially similar results have been reported in a number of different experiments, some of which involved differential conditioning (Rowland, 1957). Sleep-deprived cats who might be more prone to drowsiness than rested animals were trained to make a response to an unavoidable shock when they heard a click. Another stimulus, a low steady tone, on the other hand, was not accompanied by shock. After conditioning had proceeded long enough for the animal to respond differentially, the CS regularly elicited an activation pattern, whereas the other stimulus was accompanied by a slow wave.

Slow waves also appear during the extinction of a conditioned response. In this case, they appear not only to a negative stimulus or during a long CS-US interval but also to the CS itself in the typical case of a brief interval between the CS and the US (Morrell and Ross, 1953).

Slow waves in the cortical EEG seem clearly to be a correlate of internal inhibition.

ATTENTION—Another kind of slow wave occurs in the hippocampus and in the part of the reticular formation served by the hippocampus (Green and Arduini, 1954). This wave is a little faster, being five to seven per second, although it is not always easily distinguished in rate from the cortical slow wave. It has been called the hippocampal "arousal" pattern. It is not, however, immediately aroused, as is the cortical activation pattern, by a novel stimulus. Such a stimulus causes desynchronization in the hippocampus as it does in the cortex. However, after a few presentations of the stimulus, that is, after some habituation, the hippocampal arousal pattern of slow waves appears in response to the stimulus. If, now, a conditioning procedure is instituted, the pattern persists as a response to the CS until conditioning is fairly far along (Grastyan et al., 1959). After the conditioned response is well formed and the orienting reflex subsides, the slow pattern also subsides and is replaced by the activation pattern that was present when the CS was presented for the first time. If the animal is subjected to an extinction procedure, the slow waves reappear.

What all this means is not clear, but it has been given an interpretation (Lissak and Grastyan, 1960). The initial activation is regarded as an initial orienting or alerting—a response of "What is it?" The slow waves are regarded as representing a more specific orienting response, one in which the animal has been conditioned to "attend" to the CS. They also appear to represent inhibition of the reticular formation by the hippocampus. It remains to be seen whether this is the correct interpretation.

RHYTHMIC STIMULATION

In studies of the EEG correlates of conditioning, one of the two stimuli, CS or US, has frequently been a flickering light. Such a light, it will be recalled (page 185), can induce "photic driving," if it is not too different in frequency from the normal alpha rhythm of 9 to 11 cycles per second (in man, but somewhat different in different animals). That is to say, the flickering light, unlike a flash of light, which induces desynchronization, causes a rhythmic oscillation in the EEG that is synchronized with the stimulus. It is interesting to correlate such a rhythm with events in conditioning (see Chow et al., 1957).

FLICKER AS US—Let us consider first the case in which a flickering light is used as a US, preceded by a steady tone as a CS. This is a sensory-sensory conditioning procedure. The general course of conditioning is as we described it for a tone and flash of light. However, midway in the conditioning, something else happens. Upon presentation of the tone, rhythmic waves appear in the EEG. At first they are not exactly the same as the rate of flicker, but they tend to approach this rate with repeated pairings. This is the case when the flicker rate is not too fast and is held in the range of 3 to 12 flashes per second. Thus, at this point in conditioning, the EEG is frequency-specific to the US. It is a rhythmic response to the CS of the same frequency as the US.

This frequency-specific response, however, is transient. It lasts only for a few trials, perhaps up to as many as 12. With further conditioning trials, it disappears and is replaced by the typical alpha block. This phenomenon has been confirmed by a number of workers. Moreover, rhythmic frequency-specific responses have also been seen in trace conditioning and even in animals simply placed in the experimental room where the conditioning procedure is carried out.

What the appearance of frequency-specific rhythm means is not at present clear. It would seem to represent some kind of memory, perhaps only an anticipation of the US. It probably does not, however, have any causative or mediational significance in conditioning. To test this possibility, cats were first trained in a shuttle avoidance habit; flickering light was the CS (Chow et al., 1957). The flickering light, of course, caused photic driving. Then the animals were put through a sensory-sensory conditioning regime in which a tone served as CS and the flickering light as US. At the point in conditioning when the frequency-specific responses appeared, the cats were put back in the shuttle box and presented with a tone. If the presence of the rhythmic pattern mediated responses, the cats should have performed the avoidance response to the tone. They did not.

LABELED RHYTHMS—When a flickering light of low frequency is used as a CS, rhythmic waves of the same rate as the flickering stimulus can be recorded not only in the visual cortex but at numerous places throughout the brain (John and Killam, 1959, 1960). Just as is the case in alpha block, this response may be habituated, at least in most places in the brain, although they remain in the visual pathway. At this point, a conditioning procedure can be instituted; the flicker is paired with a shock in an avoidance situation. As the training proceeds, the rhythmic responses reappear in a number of structures, viz., auditory cortex, reticular formation, superior colliculus, amygdala, and lateral geniculate body. These rhythmic responses in nonvisual pathways are seen before the animal acquires the conditioned response, that is, begins to make avoidance responses. About the time these responses to the CS appear, the rhythmic waves in most structures begin to disappear, remaining only in the classical visual pathway. In other words, at the beginning of conditioning, rhythmic waves are seen in the visual pathway; during conditioning, they spread to nonvisual structures; and when conditioning is complete they recede again to the visual structures. Obviously, whatever is happening here, it is not directly related to conditioning. Rather, it is some intermediate stage in the process.

PHYSIOLOGICAL FEEDBACK

From time to time in the history of psychology, psychological theorists have made use of a concept of internal feedback (see Solomon and Turner, 1962). The behaviorists assumed that proprioceptive feedback into the nervous system from skeletal-muscle responses was important in learning, particularly serial learning. The James-Lange theory of emotion (see page 310) assumed feedback from skeletal and autonomic muscles to play a part in emotional experience. There have been other specific hypotheses of feedback, some of which will be explained in this section.

Such hypotheses have led to experiments designed to assess the existence and importance of feedback from organs in the body. Some of the experiments have turned up with results that do not definitively answer the questions posed, but they still prove to be interesting in their own right. Others give a clear answer about the existence and probable importance of physiological feedback in learned behavior.

BLOCKING OF RESPONSES

A series of experiments extending over thirty years have been designed to block peripheral skeletal responses during conditioning and then, when the block is removed, to test whether or not conditioning has actually taken place. Such an experiment tests in principle whether it is necessary for a response to take place in order for learning to occur.

CRUSHED NERVE—In one set of experiments, the muscles involved in the conditioned response were paralyzed during training by crushing the motor nerves leading to them (Kellogg et al., 1940; Light and Gantt, 1936) or by surgically deefferenting the limb (Beck and Doty, 1957). A complete conditioning procedure was carried out while the animal (dog or cat) could not respond. Then time was allowed for the nerves to regenerate. When it was clear that the muscles could respond again, the animals were tested for conditioning. They showed by the appropriate paw flexure to the conditioning stimulus that learning had taken place while the muscles were paralyzed.

This type of experiment has been criticized, however, on the grounds that the paralysis of a limb does not prevent an animal, during the original conditioning, from giving generalized struggle responses centering about the limb. These generalized responses could conceivably be conditioned, and perhaps it was through them that the correct response was made after nerve regeneration.

ATROPINE—Another approach to the problem is to use a drug that specifically blocks a response while presumably having little effect on the ability of the nervous system to form conditioned responses. Several such drugs, as we shall see, have been used. One drug, atropine, blocks parasympathetic endings and is therefore suitable for blocking salivation in salivary conditioning.

In one experiment (Crisler, 1930), morphine was employed as the unconditioned stimulus for evoking salivation in a typical Pavlovian type of conditioning. The salivation, however, was blocked by giving the animal atropine during the conditioning trials. Testing later, without the atropine, produced conditioned responses of salivation to the conditioning stimulus. In a similar study (Finch, 1938), acid was used as the unconditioned stimulus for salivation, but salivation was again prevented with atropine. When conditioning tests were made later without atropine, the animal showed conditioned responses. These experiments in which the motor response is artificially blocked thus show clearly that a salivary response need not occur in order for learning to take place.

CURARE—The atropine experiments block an autonomic response. Thinking that there might be a difference between autonomic and skeletal responses and not being satisfied with the experiments with crushed or deefferented nerves, other investigators turned to the drug curare as an agent for blocking skeletal responses.

Curare is the poison used by Indians on arrowheads. It is a plant extract, not a pure drug, that varies considerably in both strength and purity. In the 1930s, however, it was the one drug available that might be expected to block skeletal response and at the same time have little effect on the nervous system. Its principal site of action is the neuromuscular juncture. It also has a considerable depressing effect on the brain, and this effect accounts for the interesting results obtained with it.

In the first experiments with curare (Harlow and Stagner, 1933), it was used on dogs and cats during conditioning. Both avoidance conditioning and classical pupillary conditioning were studied. In the case of avoidance conditioning, which involves a skeletal response, the animals made no responses at all during the conditioning procedure. When tested later in the normal state, the animals showed no evidence of conditioning. On the other hand, curare did not block the pupillary response. During training under curare, the animals gave dilation responses to a shock as the US, and in due course this response was conditioned to a bell. The investigators took this as evidence that curare did not depress cortical activity. Since the animals did not learn an avoidance response under curare, they concluded that "conditioned reflexes are only possible if a response is made, and do not result merely from stimuli presented simultaneously" (Harlow and Stagner, 1933, p. 293).

A few years later it was to become clear why this result has been obtained. Other investigators (Girden and Culler, 1937) devised a new technique for studying conditioning under curare. In this technique, the semitendinosus muscle, a muscle taking part in paw flexure of the rear leg, was dissected out while keeping the blood and nerve supply intact. Under curare, this muscle could be made to twitch with a shock applied to the leg even though gross movement of the limb did not occur. When the bell and a shock were repeatedly paired in a classical-conditioning procedure, conditioning was observed to take place. In a series of subsequent studies (Culler et al., 1939; Girden, 1940), the technique was used in both normal and curarized animals to observe the course of conditioning and of retention in the two states.

Without going into detail, we may state the general point—a most interesting point—to emerge from these experiments. The responses conditioned under curare vanished when the animal was returned to the normal state. The normal animal showed no sign of retention of the conditioning that had taken place under curare. Conversely, the conditioning that was established in the normal animal disappeared when the animal was put under curare. Thus there was a complete amnesia in one state for conditioning in another state.

Having discovered this, one could question the earlier finding that pupillary responses conditioned under curare carried over into the normal state. Is there a difference between autonomic and skeletal responses in this respect? On reexamining pupillary conditioning, it appeared that the earlier result was an artifact (Girden, 1942). The apparent conditioning seemed to be an unconditioned response to the bell. When light, instead of a bell, was used, there was no carry-over between normal and curarized states. Moreover, when other autonomic responses, such as blood-pressure change to shock, were used, the two stages clearly dissociated.

At this point, the investigators began to suspect that curare was doing more to the nervous system than simply blocking neuromuscular transmission. They made some threshold studies of cortical excitability in the two stages (Culler et al., 1939). They found that the excitability of the motor cortex, and perhaps the cortex as a whole, was considerably depressed. From this finding they theorized that normal conditioning involved the cerebral cortex but that conditioning under curare, because of cortical depression, might involve principally subcortical structures.

This thought led to another experiment (Girden, 1942). The auditory cortex was removed on both sides before the beginning of conditioning. Now, presumably, all conditioning would require subcortical activity, at least in the auditory pathway. One would not expect dissociation under these conditions. Indeed, when the comparisons were made between normal and curarized states, there was no dissociation. Conditioning in one state carried over to the other.

TUBOCURARINE AND BULBOCAPNINE—The research just reported, though interesting, had strayed a long way from its original intent. This had been to test whether peripheral responses were necessary for conditioning to occur. That problem still remained. Moreover, to solve it, a drug other than curare was required to block neuromuscular transmission without depressing the cerebral cortex. In the late 1940s, such a drug became available. This was D-tubocurarine, a synthetic drug with the neuromuscular-blocking properties of curare but without its central depressing effect. This fact was proved by giving it to a human subject (Smith et al., 1947). (Any organism given a paralyzing drug must be kept under artificial respiration because the skeletal respiratory muscles are paralyzed along with other muscles. Hence, the subject required artificial respiration.) Under the influence of D-tubocurarine, the subject was presented with a wide variety of stimuli, including some that were painful. After recovering from the drug, the subject could recount quite accurately the various effects. His senses and mental abilities were quite unimpaired. He had merely been paralyzed.

This fact established, the old experiments were repeated. Dogs taught an association between a signal and shock to the forelimb under the drug showed good transfer to a flexion response in the normal state (Lauer, 1951). Similar training for avoidance responses transferred from one state to another (Solomon and Turner, 1962). To check on the generality of the result for the autonomic system, pupillary and cardiac conditioning were also studied (Black et al., 1962). In the latter case, differential conditioning was also studied.

In every instance, there was transfer between normal and paralyzed states. Indeed, simple classical conditioning of a tone to shock carried out under the drug greatly facilitated the learning of an avoidance habit later in the normal state. These experiments then provide a definitive answer to the question of whether response is necessary for conditioning to take place. *It is not.* It may be mentioned in passing that similar results have been obtained with other immobilizing drugs that are now available: Flaxedil (Black et al., 1962) and bulbocapnine (Beck and Doty, 1957).

SENSORY INFORMATION—There is a corollary to the question of whether response is necessary for conditioning to occur. It is the question whether sensory information from the response being made by a limb is necessary. In other words, is the execution of a response centrally directed, or does it require somesthetic feedback from the limb? This has been studied by *de-afferenting* the limb used by a monkey after learning to make an avoidance response (Knapp et al., 1958). Such an operation renders the limb somewhat flaccid. While running, the animal holds it in a semiflexed position with the hand and fingers hanging loosely. He obviously prefers not to use it. When returned postoperatively to the conditioning situation, he at first does not make avoidance responses. He suffers some "lack of retention." On the other hand, with continued trials, he reconditions and again learns to use the limb in avoidance responses. Apparently the sensory information helped, but it was not crucially necessary.

AUTONOMIC FACTORS

Conditioning in a paralyzed state is necessarily classical conditioning. Since the organism cannot respond, it is incapable of instrumental or avoidance conditioning. All it can learn is an association between CS and US that may later facilitate acquisition of an avoidance response. Thus conclusions about response being necessary are limited to classical conditioning.

TWO-FACTOR THEORY—To understand better the mechanism of instrumental learning several theorists have proposed a two-process theory of instrumental conditioning (Skinner, 1935; Schlosberg, 1937; and Mowrer, 1947). In the case of avoidance conditioning, two-process theory goes something like this: The early part of avoidance conditioning consists of a classical conditioning of, say, sound and shock. What is conditioned is the emotional response to shock. This consists not only of skeletal responses but also of the autonomic responses involved in emotion. Put another way, this first learning consists of a conditioning of the fear response. Once this is acquired, the fear response aroused by the CS becomes the motivation for making an avoidance response. When the avoidance response is made, it reduces fear, and that is the reinforcement for learning. Thus, in this second stage, the avoidance response is a response to another response, the fear response.

AUTONOMIC FEEDBACK—If this theory is correct, it means that the fear response is a critical link in the learning of an avoidance response. Much of this feedback, though not all of it, is autonomic. The feeling of fear is partly a feeling originating in the organs of the body under autonomic control. From the theory, it could therefore be predicted that reducing or eliminating peripheral autonomic function should interfere with avoidance conditioning.

An experiment testing this prediction has been made (Wynne and Solomon, 1955). Dogs were subjected to surgical procedures in which much of the autonomic system, and particularly the sympathetic, was cut off from the central nervous system. They were trained in avoidance-conditioning procedures and compared with normal dogs. In several respects they were different from normal dogs: (*1*) They acquired the avoidance habit more slowly than normals; (2) they extinguished more rapidly than normal dogs—in fact, many extinguished spontaneously, when normal dogs may not extinguish after thousands of extinction trials; and (3) they were relatively indifferent to the shock, showing much less fear of it than normal animals. It is to be emphasized, however, that they did acquire the avoidance response. Hence it can be concluded that autonomic feedback makes a difference, and an important one, in the acquisition of avoidance behavior. It is not, however, crucial to avoidance learning.

AUTONOMIC CONDITIONING—Aside from the role of the autonomic system in avoidance conditioning, the conditioning of autonomic responses is of interest in its own right. They offer the best possibility of studying classical conditioning since, unlike skeletal responses, they are not instrumental in altering the external environment. (They may, however, alter the internal environment.) They also serve as signs of emotionality and of emotional conditioning.

A number of autonomic responses have been conditioned. The classic response, of course, is the salivary response studied by Pavlov. We have already mentioned the pupillary response as conditionable. In working with the pupillary response, however, one must always be wary of natural or previously conditioned responses to the conditioning stimuli one uses. Many stimuli cause a change in pupil size. It has even been shown recently that interest-arousing pictures viewed by the human subject cause increases in pupil size (Hess and Polt, 1960). Another autonomic response, commonly conditioned in all sorts of experiments, is the galvanic skin response (GSR). This is a change in the electrical resistance of the skin that accompanies almost any emotional response and is evoked and conditioned by using electric shock as the US (McCleary, 1950).

Two other autonomic responses that have been conditioned are nictitating-membrane response and hyperglycemia. Certain animals, such as the rabbit, possess a membrane, in addition to the eyelid, which is reflexly drawn across the eye when the eye is stimulated noxiously, as, for example, by a puff of air to the cornea. This response has been conditioned to a tone and exhibits the general phenomena of Pavlovian conditioning (Gormezano et al., 1962).

Hyperglycemia (a rise in blood sugar) is interesting because it is brought about indirectly, so far as nervous control is concerned, by the secretion of adrenalin. Hyperglycemia has been conditioned in rats simply by placing them in a cage and, after a waiting period of ten minutes, giving them an electric shock (Gutman and Jakoubek, 1960). After three trials of this sort, blood sugar starts to rise after the rat is placed in the cage. In this particular experiment, the investigators went on to make lesions in the brain. They found that the conditioned hyperglycemia was abolished by lesions made in the diffuse thalamic portion (page 349) of the reticular system. They theorized that this system exerts its influence via the hypothalamus and adrenal secretion.

The last two autonomic responses to be mentioned in this connection are respiration and heart rate. Although respiration is carried on by skeletal muscles, it is subject to autonomic as well as "voluntary" influences. Heart rate is completely under autonomic control, although it is affected mechanically by respiration (Westcott and Huttenlocher, 1961). In both cases, the effects observed in conditioning are complex. Either a slowing or an acceleration of respiration or heart rate may be a sign of emotional or autonomic involvement. And it is not always easy to tell what is being conditioned or consistently to condition the same effect, i.e., acceleration or deceleration.

Probably the most typical response in both respiration and heart rate is a slowing or inhibition. This has been reported in respiratory conditioning to a signal and shock (Friedman, 1951) and in heart-rate conditioning (Notterman et al., 1953). It is interesting that similar effects can also be obtained in the goldfish (Otis et al., 1957). However, in some cases, the heart rate accelerates when a warning stimulus is presented prior to shock. If there is any general rule, it is that general anxiety increases heart rate while anticipation of a specific pain such as shock decelerates it (Deane, 1961).

INTEROCEPTIVE CONDITIONING—Virtually all the work in conditioning done by American and Western investigators has employed exteroceptive stimuli: light, sound, or somesthetic stimuli. Russian research workers, on the other hand, have been paying increasing attention to conditioning in which either the CS, US, or both stimuli are applied to organs within the body. Conditioning, using such stimuli, is called interoceptive conditioning (Razran, 1961).

Russian students of interoceptive conditioning deliver their stimuli in a variety of ways. Air-filled or water-filled balloons may be introduced into the stomach, and the pressure in the balloon used as a stimulus. Fistulas with cannulas may be made in the stomach or trachea and stimuli—chemical, electrical, or mechanical—applied through the opening. Loops may be formed in the intestinal wall, and mechanical or electrical stimuli applied to them. Recording of the effects of such stimulation is done by putting devices through cannulas or embedding them in tissues that are sensitive to mechanical, thermal, or electrical changes.

Three kinds of interoceptive conditioning are distinguished. In one, the CS is interoceptive and so also is the US. In a second, the CS is interoceptive and the US exteroceptive. And in the third, the CS is exteroceptive and the US interoceptive. The following are examples of each type.

For *intero-interoceptive conditioning,* a dog is operated in such a way that toxic gases may be introduced through a trachea into the lungs, and the gas mixture breathed by the dog may be regulated. Carbon dioxide, introduced as a 10 percent mixture, behaves as a US, causing rapid breathing (hypercapnia). For a CS, intestinal loops are formed so that they may distend the intestine and thus serve as a pressure stimulus (CS) to the organ. After only a few trials of pairing the CS and US, the intestinal distension causes hypercapnic breathing. A stable conditioned response is built up in 5 to 16 trials.

As an example of *intero-exteroceptive* conditioning, a female dog is fistulated in the lower abdomen so that a jet of air can be blown on the wall of the uterus and employed as a CS. The US is an unavoidable shock to the right hind leg. Again, conditioned responses begin to appear in a few trials and are made consistently after 10 or 12 trials.

Finally, as an example of *extero-interoceptive conditioning,* the hypercapnic preparation in which gases may be introduced into the lungs may be used. Carbon dioxide serves as a US and hypercapnic breathing as an unconditioned response. A tone, employed as a CS, is presented before introducing the carbon dioxide to evoke the rapid breathing. A conditioned hypercapnic reaction builds up even more rapidly than when intestinal stimulation is used as the CS in intero-interoceptive conditioning.

There are many variations of these procedures, but these three examples illustrate Russian methods of studying interoceptive conditioning. There is a theoretical background for doing this work. It recognizes that interoceptive stimuli are organism-bound rather than arising in the environment as exteroceptive stimuli. Interoceptive stimuli are generated by the organism's own responses, and if they can serve as conditioning stimuli, as they can, then they can become conditioned to other responses occurring in the organism. Thus, many conditioned loops may be set up, some of them quite accidentally in the history of the organism. Such intervening interoceptive links may be important in psychosomatic activities and in "unconscious responses," both autonomic and skeletal.

17 DISCRIMINATIVE LEARNING

Thus chapter will deal with those kinds of learning in which the organism makes differential responses to two or more stimuli. Such learning is discriminative learning. Because conditioning methods are sometimes used in such learning, there will occasionally be some overlap with the preceding chapter. The bulk of research on discriminative learning, however, employs instrumental learning in which the organism chooses between two stimuli presented simultaneously and receives a reward for making a correct choice.

Most of the chapter is organized by sensory modality, that is, according to the sense involved in the discrimination. We begin with somesthetic learning, then consider auditory discrimination, and end with visual discriminations. As might be expected, visual discrimination has received by far the greatest amount of attention, and we shall break it down into several kinds of discrimination. The chapter will also consider the topics of generalization and transfer in discriminative learning. But, before getting into the details of work on discriminative learning, we should first consider some of the problems and methods involved in this work.

PROBLEMS AND METHODS

In trying to determine the neural mechanisms of discriminative learning, the main tools are training and extirpation. An animal is trained to master a particular discrimination. Then a test is made to see whether the animal is capable of remembering the discrimination or, if not, of learning it again after a particular part of the brain has been removed. Although there are some exceptions, this simple paradigm is typical of most of the work we shall discuss. In principle, it is simple. In practice, there are difficulties.

SENSORY CAPACITY

In the first place, we must distinguish between sensory capacity and learning capacity. It is theoretically possible for an animal's senses and sensory pathways to be normal and yet for it to be unable to learn a particular action. Conversely, in principle, an organism might be capable of learning a discrimination yet fail simply because the sense upon which the habit depends is impaired. But because tests of sensory capacity so often hinge on prior learning, it is not always possible to tell whether the failures observed are due to losses of learning ability or of sensory capacity. If, for example, an operated animal fails after long training to discriminate between a triangle and a circle, it is not certain whether the difficulty is that he cannot "see" the stimuli or that, seeing them, he cannot learn their meaning. Sometimes such a question can be settled by devising other methods of measuring sensory capacity, but this is not always feasible nor, if feasible, always done. Thus the problem is a persistent one.

LEARNING METHODS

It has sometimes been remarked that the answers one gets to questions put to organisms depend on the questions. This is particularly true in the present case. The questions put to animals are in the form of learning problems. They are, in effect, "Do you remember this one?" or "Can you learn this discrimination?" But the answer depends on the particular method used for training and testing.

In general, the methods employed in discriminative learning with animals are of two kinds: conditioning involving successive discrimination and two-choice methods involving simultaneous discrimination. In conditioning, stimuli are presented one at a time. If differential, or discriminative, conditioning is to be established, two different kinds of stimuli are used, positive and negative. The animal must, for example, learn to lift its leg (in paw-flexure conditioning) or shuttle to the other side of the box when one stimulus is presented and not to do this when the other one is presented. In two-choice methods, two stimuli are presented simultaneously, or at least in closely spaced pairs, and the animal chooses one or the other by pushing a lever, opening a door, pulling a string, pushing away a cup, etc. Very frequently the effects of a particular extirpation of the brain will be different, depending on which one of these methods is used.

Other details of method are also important. Are the stimuli to be discriminated quite similar and thus difficult, or are they very different so that the discrimination is an easy one? Is the discrimination merely one of distinguishing differences in a single dimension, such as intensity or frequency, or is it one of choosing between complex patterns or forms? Are the stimuli close together in space or time or are they separated? Factors like these that make a problem relatively easy or difficult have much to do with the results obtained.

POSTOPERATIVE EFFECTS

In general, three kinds of effects are encountered when an animal's postoperative performance on a discrimination learned preoperatively is measured. (1) One is no effect at all; the habit is performed as well by operated as by normal animals. However, in order for such a statement to be true, there must usually be controls, for many habits are partly forgotten with any lapse of time, whether or not surgery intervenes. And if operated animals perform as well as control animals, even though both have some loss, there is no postoperative effect on retention. (2) The habit may be partially or completely lost, as compared with controls, but the animal may be able to relearn the habit in some reasonable number of trials. This is a very common finding. It implies that the area destroyed was somehow important preoperatively in the normal animals, but in its absence other structures are capable of mediating the habit. (3) The animal may not only lose the habit but also be unable to relearn it after a large number of trials. In this case, great care must be taken to determine that the difficulty does not lie in a loss of sensory capacity. We shall regularly encounter postoperative effects of these three kinds.

One must also look for transient effects. Shortly after an operation, measurable effects of the operation may be seen, but after weeks or even months, the effects may either not be there or not be nearly so serious as they were at first. Why postoperative effects are so often transient is something of a mystery. It usually cannot be blamed on the shock or disability of the operation, but it nevertheless must be considered in interpreting the effects of operations.

ANATOMY

Another difficulty sometimes encountered in discriminative learning is that it is not always known where to look in the brain for structures of importance in learning. Cortical areas I and II, as mapped by evoked potentials in the various senses, are always good candidates. Beyond that, however, matters become hazier. Many connections in the brain are known, but many are not. Sometimes there seem to be too many possible connections to consider; sometimes not enough. In any event, frequently behavioral work is ahead of the anatomy. Making lesions in certain areas and measuring their postoperative effects on discriminative learning has uncovered important areas and structures that, on anatomical grounds, would not be very suspect. We shall see several examples of this, and it is not unlikely that future research will provide more.

To summarize, four factors determining the outcome of neural studies of discriminative learning must be kept in mind: (1) the separate effects of a lesion on sensory capacity and on learning capacity, (2) the particular learning methods used, (3) the possibly different effects of an injury on retention and relearning ability depending on time after the operation, (4) and the particular structures of the brain extirpated.

SOMESTHETIC DISCRIMINATION

Relatively little physiological research has been done on somesthetic discrimination. Some data exist, however, for four kinds of discrimination: thermal, kinesthetic, roughness, and form discrimination. Virtually all the work concerns the cerebral cortex. In particular, areas SI and SII have been studied in the rat, dog, and monkey. In addition, the posterior parietal cortex has been studied in the monkey and chimpanzee.

THERMAL DISCRIMINATION

The data on thermal discrimination are quite limited and are negative so far as the cerebral cortex is concerned (Downer and Zubek, 1954). Blinded rats taught to make a temperature discrimination retain the habit after lesions made anywhere in the cerebral cortex, whether in somatic areas I and II or in other areas of the cortex (see Figure 17.1). Evidently, neither the capacity for making the temperature discrimination nor habits making use of the capacity are mediated at the cortical level in the rat.

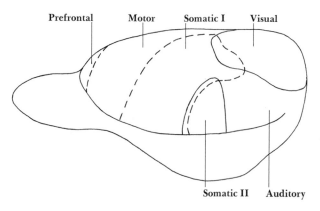

Prefrontal   Motor   Somatic I   Visual

Somatic II   Auditory

FIGURE 17.1—Lateral view of the motor and sensory areas of the rat's cerebral cortex. (Adapted from D. H. LeMessurier and C. N. Woolsey, personal communication.)

KINESTHETIC DISCRIMINATION

A relatively old set of experiments on kinesthetic discrimination has been reported for the monkey and chimpanzee (Ruch, 1935). They were made before the method of evoked potentials revealed the outlines of areas SI and SII. The results are roughly the same for the chimpanzee as for the monkey. Hence a description of the work on the monkey will suffice. The general procedure was to train monkeys preoperatively in making discriminations between lifted weights and then to measure the effect on retention of removing precentral, postcentral, and posterior parietal areas, taken separately or in combination (see Figure 17.2).

After the separate removal of any one of these areas, there was some loss of memory for the discrimination but, after retraining, the discriminations could be mastered again. The memory loss was much less after removal of the precentral and postcentral areas than after destruction of the posterior parietal areas. With combined lesions of the precentral and postcentral areas, there was still only a moderate loss of memory for the discrimination, and this was easily effaced with training. A combination of the postcentral and parietal areas, unfortunately, was not employed. From other data on tactual discrimination, to be described below, this combination could be expected to have the most serious effects.

ROUGHNESS DISCRIMINATION

Several experiments on the discrimination of roughness have been performed. One of the earliest (Smith, 1939) was done on the rat. Rats were run in a Y apparatus in which they found two different sandpapers, one rough and one smooth, at the fork of the Y. They were supposed to take the path of one of these sandpapers to reach food. This discrimination is comparable to a light-dark visual discrimination or an on-off auditory discrimination.

Various lesions, large and small, were made in different parts of the rat's cortex. Most of these ablations did little or nothing to the roughness discrimination. There were four rats, however, who showed complete amnesia for the habit and, in addition, three others whose performance was impaired. On reconstructing diagrams of the rats' brains, an area in common was found for the animals with postoperative amnesia. The area included some of the cortex now known to be somesthetic, but it also extended far forward and overlapped motor areas that probably have little to do directly with somesthetic discrimination. More recent work has focused on somatic areas I and II as defined by evoked potentials.

Results on the monkey and chimpanzee, in general, are parallel to those for the rat, except that cortical lesions generally have more serious effects (Ruch, 1935). Taking out the posterior parietal lobe in either the monkey or the chimpanzee causes some loss of memory for the roughness-discrimination habit. The loss is much greater in the chimpanzee than in the monkey. The postoperative amnesia, however, can be overcome by a moderate amount of training, more in the chimpanzee than in the monkey. Removing the entire parietal lobe, i.e., both the postcentral gyrus and the posterior parietal lobule, causes an even more serious disruption of the habit. This operation, as we have already learned (page 270), affects not only the habit but also the sensory capacity of primates to make somesthetic discriminations. It perhaps is no wonder, then, that it takes prolonged retraining for an animal to reestablish the roughness-discrimination habit.

There are some experiments on the dog that cannot be classified as experiments on roughness discrimination yet are of interest here (Allen, 1946, 1947). Dogs were conditioned to raise their forelegs when the stimulus was stroking in a particular direction on the back, with the "grain." They were also trained not to respond to a negative stimulus consisting, in some cases, of stroking in the opposite direction, against the "grain," or, in others, of stroking

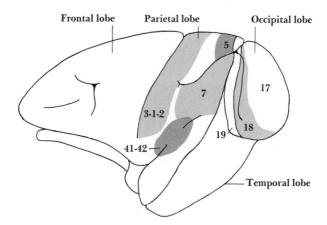

FIGURE 17.2—
Posterior cortex of
the monkey.

with the "grain" three times a second as contrasted with a positive stimulus of stroking once a second.

In some animals, lesions were placed in somesthetic area I. They had little effect. There was some loss of the habit but not much, and the dogs clearly had some retention. In other cases, both areas I and II were removed. In fact, the lesions were large enough to invade some surrounding territory. In these cases, they either retained or could quickly relearn the response to the positive stimulus. On the other hand, they lost the ability to discriminate between positive and negative stimuli and could not, after many trials, relearn the habit.

Even though the method was one of conditioning, the problem for the animal was a difficult one. A very subtle discrimination was required—one that is probably comparable in difficulty to making a difficult form discrimination. Perhaps, then, that is the reason the results were very much like those obtained in experiments on form discrimination, the next topic to be discussed.

FORM DISCRIMINATION

Tactual form discrimination has been studied in the rat, monkey, and chimpanzee, as well as in man. One experiment on the rat is negative; it shows no effects of operations anywhere in the cerebral cortex on the discrimination of a wedge-shaped from a cylindical lever (Zubek, 1952). The studies made on the monkey and man are the most thorough and systematic. The results coincide with other kinds of somesthetic discrimination except that form discrimination is clearly the most difficult and is the most sensitive to extirpations in the cortical somesthetic system.

If a lesion in a monkey is confined to somesthetic area I, there is little effect (Kruger and Porter, 1959). Animals retain almost perfectly discriminations learned preoperatively. If the lesions include both areas I and II, there is an effect on retention. The animals forget preoperatively acquired habits. However, they can relearn the discriminations, and the defect therefore is not permanent. However, if both the precentral gyrus, which includes some somesthetic projections, and postcentral areas I and II are removed on one side, animals have trouble with the more difficult discriminations. Neither of two animals tested could relearn to discriminate a three-dimensional figure L from its inversion.

Other experiments implicate the posterior parietal lobule as being important in tactual form discrimination (see Ruch and Fulton, 1935). Removal of the posterior parietal lobule alone, for example, is sufficient to cause complete amnesia for a form discrimination. In the case of complex form discriminations, no amount of retraining yields mastery of the discrimination, although with less difficult discriminations retraining is effective. If subjected to long retraining, a chimpanzee whose posterior parietal lobule has been removed may learn again to distinguish between a cone and a pyramid, but the capacity to discriminate a pyramid and a wedge, which are much more alike than a cone and pyramid, is never regained, no matter how many trials are given the subject.

These findings indicate (1) that tactual form-discrimination learning by the normal animal depends in part upon the posterior parietal area and (2) that after removal of the area some other structure takes over part, but not all, of the learning function. It is not known whether this structure is located cortically or subcortically.

One of relatively few systematic studies on the effects of cortical injury on learning by man has been done with somesthetic discrimination (see Teuber, 1960). Individuals suffering unilateral penetrating injury of the cerebral hemispheres were trained in making a tactual discrimination of different forms. Normal individuals using either hand and individuals with brain injury using the hand on the same side as the lesion were able to make progress in learning the discriminations. Individuals using the hand on the side opposite to their injuries were not, however, able to learn the discrimination. This failure to learn was not related to any sensory defect. Hence, it may be concluded that at least some kinds of learning depend on the hemisphere receiving the main sensory projections of the somesthetic system.

AUDITORY DISCRIMINATION

In the chapter on hearing, we reviewed what is known of the sensory pathways and projections of the auditory system. The cortical areas in which evoked potentials appear have been fairly well defined in the cat, dog, and monkey. Experiments on the learning of auditory discriminations, however, are limited largely to the rat, cat, and dog. Of these three, the most work, and most informative modern work, has been done on the cat.

In studies of auditory discrimination some of the difficulties mentioned earlier in this chapter are encountered. The factor of recovery from an operation has proved important in the effects of cortical ablations on such simple discriminations as absolute auditory thresholds (see Ades, 1959). The type and difficulty of the test also prove to be important variables. Finally, auditory areas other than those revealed by physiological methods participate in some learned auditory discriminations.

The kinds of discrimination that have been studied fall into four main categories: (1) intensity, (2) frequency, (3) tonal pattern, and (4) auditory localization in space. We shall consider each in turn.

INTENSITY

Early work on auditory discrimination employed the simplest of all habits, namely responding to the onset of a tone. Conditioning methods were used, for the most part. The animal was required to lift a leg or to run in a rotating cage when a tone was sounded. Once this habit was learned, the intensity of the tone was gradually reduced to threshold levels. Such a discrimination then served as a measure of sensory capacity.

It at first appeared that removal of auditory cortex—for the moment let us not worry about how much—caused a loss of auditory sensitivity (see Ades, 1959). However, it was found that a period of recovery is required postoperatively before testing the animal. If this is allowed and if the animal is retrained (see below), there is no loss of auditory sensitivity. This statement appears to be true regardless of how much auditory cortex is removed (page 234). Thus auditory sensitivity is subcortically determined. In some ways, this is a convenient result, for it shows that other difficulties displayed by animals postoperatively are not due to defects in basic auditory sensitivity (Kryter and Ades, 1943).

One of the difficulties that occurs repeatedly in experiments on extirpation of auditory cortex is loss of retention for the habit learned preoperatively. In the rat, removal of auditory areas always has serious effects on the habit, and the animals need training to reacquire it (Wiley, 1937; Pennington, 1941). The same is true of the dog and cat (Raab and Ades, 1946). Removal of the auditory areas, if complete enough, causes amnesia. This amnesia is quite complete even for a simple conditioned avoidance response to the onset of a tone. However, the animals were capable of relearning the response.

FREQUENCY

Most of the work just described was done before the auditory areas I and II were precisely delimited. Maps of these areas first became available between 1943 and 1947. About this same time, a third area yielding evoked potentials to auditory stimulation was discovered (Tunturi, 1945). It overlapped, as we have previously pointed out (page 216), somatic area II. Hence it is usually referred to as SII even though our interest in it here is that it has auditory functions (see Figure 8.6, page 217).

After work on intensity discrimination established that capacity for making such a discrimination is not cortically bound, attention turned to frequency discrimination and to other complex functions. By this time, AI, AII, SII and EP were known, but the importance of the more ventral, insular, and temporal areas shown on the map in Figure 8.6 was not. That fact came out of experiments about to be described.

Frequency discrimination has been studied by a number of investigators. In one set of experiments, lesions were made in some combination of areas AI, AII, EP, and AIII (or SII, Meyer and Woolsey, 1952). The effects depended on the combination removed. If any one of the areas was removed singly (but always bilaterally), there was no effect on the habit. The animals went on performing as they did preoperatively with little or no disturbance. If, on the other hand, AI and AII were removed in combination, the animals had an amnesia for the habit, and they were able to relearn it in a reasonable number of trials. On the other hand, if all the areas mentioned were removed, there was, as before, an amnesia but no relearning. The animals were incapable of relearning the frequency discrimination, in some cases after as many as 1,000 trials.

This experiment does not mean exactly what it appears to mean. It was subsequently repeated with somewhat different results (Butler et al., 1957). In the repetition, the main point of difference was in the ability of the animals to relearn the frequency discrimination. Animals with combined lesions of AI, AII, EP, and SII, though showing amnesia for the habit postoperatively, could relearn it with training. Why the discrepancy?

Possibly slight differences in method in the experiments account for the result, but probably not. Most probably the answer lies in the extent of the lesions. The repetition confined the lesion rather precisely to the areas chosen for the experiment. In the earlier experiments (also see Allen, 1945), the investigators in their attempts to make complete lesions overshot the mark, as frequently happens. They invaded the more ventral areas IN and TE, not then known to be significant. However, these areas contribute importantly to auditory function. This is especially true, as we shall see, when more complex discriminations such as tonal patterns are studied.

TONAL PATTERN

In hearing, a melody or tonal pattern is about the closest one can get to a form discrimination in vision or in somestheses. As we have seen and shall see, form discrimination depends most on cortical function and particularly on cortical areas other than the primary receiving areas. This is also true for hearing.

The simplest stimulus in which the discrimination of a total pattern may be required is one in which two tones are presented but in different orders (see page 224). One stimulus consists of tone A and tone B presented as ABA. The other stimulus is a pattern of BAB. In the experiment, a three-tone sequence of low-high-low was presented repetitively a number of times to animals in shuttle boxes. Then, abruptly, the pattern was changed to high-low-high. This was a signal for shock, which the trained animal could avoid by shuttling to the other compartment of the box.

Two different experiments with this discrimination have been made with the lesions differing in the two. In one, lesions were made in some combination of AI, AII, and EP (Diamond and Neff, 1957). Extirpation of AI alone had no effect; the habit was well retained. If extensive lesions were made in all three areas but some remnant of one or another of the areas was left, the animals lost the habit but it could be reestablished through retraining. With complete destruction of the three areas, however, the habit not only was lost; it could not be relearned even after prolonged retraining.

The second set of experiments concerned the cortex ventral to AII and EP, namely, areas SII, IN, and TE (Goldberg et al., 1957). These proved to be equivalent in function, so far as the tonal-pattern discrimination is concerned, to the dorsal areas. Cats trained in both frequency discrimination and in tonal-pattern discrimination have complete amnesia for both habits when these ventral areas are extirpated. However, they are able to relearn the frequency discrimination in about the same number of trials as was required originally. On the other hand, they are unable to relearn the tonal-pattern discrimination with prolonged retraining.

A significant feature of this second experiment is the clear separation of frequency discrimination and tonal-pattern discrimination. Since the animals can relearn the frequency discrimination, there is no sensory defect—no inability to "hear" the tones. But since they cannot relearn the tonal-pattern discrimination, the loss must be in a more complex capacity comparable to pattern vision in the rat. It is interesting that this capacity can be obliterated by destruction of areas other than AI and AII. It has, however, been demonstrated that these ventral areas receive projections from the medial geniculate nucleus even though the principal projection from the geniculate is to AI.

LOCALIZATION

Experiments have also been made on auditory localization in operated cats. Two or three boxes are placed in different parts of the room. A sound is made to emanate from one of the boxes, and the cat released in the room. The job for the cat is to go to the correct box. If he does, he is rewarded with food. The ability to make such a discrimination is quite sensitive to extirpations of auditory cortex. A lesion in AI alone causes severe impairment, and larger lesions make it impossible for the animal to reacquire the habit. Again, since lesions that abolish this habit leave intensity and frequency discrimination intact, some more complex capacity must be involved. But whether or not it is a perceptual or a learning capacity has not so far been established (see Neff, 1961).

VISUAL INTENSITY

In the preceding chapter we saw that, if an animal is conditioned, say, to lift its paw in response to a light, such conditioning is unaffected by cortical lesions (Marquis, 1934). Animals retain the habit after large lesions placed anywhere in the cortex. On the other hand, one of the best established facts in the area of discriminative learning is that animals trained to make a two-choice discrimination between a light stimulus and a dark one do not retain the habit after lesions to the striate cortex (VI). This has been demonstrated a good many times in various animals, including the rat (Lashley, 1929), cat (Smith, 1937), and monkey (Klüver, 1936). In all cases, too, it has been shown that, although retention is affected by striate lesions, the habit can be relearned.

POSTOPERATIVE LEARNING

In general, the postoperative learning of a brightness discrimination proceeds at the same pace as preoperative learning. The animals seem to start over again to learn the problem. There are, however, certain conditions under which this is not so. One is making the discrimination more difficult by requiring the animal to distinguish not merely between light and dark but between two lights not too different in intensity (Lashley, 1929; Mead, 1939). This discrimination is more difficult than a light-dark discrimination for all animals, normal and operated. However, striate animals are slower to learn postoperatively than normals. This could be due to a sensory loss for, as we saw in an earlier chapter, striate animals are never able, with any amount of retraining, to make as fine discriminations of intensity as normal animals.

Another factor affecting postoperative learning is the use of punishment (Krechevsky, 1936). Where animals are punished for incorrect responses and also rewarded for correct ones in learning a light-dark discrimination, postoperative learning proceeds at a normal rate. However, if punishment is omitted and learning takes place only on the basis of reward for correct responses, the learning of striate animals is retarded. They make more errors and require more trials to reach criteria than normal animals trained under the same conditions. Why this is true is not known.

A third factor affecting postoperative learning rate is the kind of task presented to the animal: successive versus simultaneous brightness discrimination. So far, we have talked about a simultaneous discrimination. A successive discrimination can be set up by having the animal go, say, to the left when he encounters a dark card and to the right when he is presented with a light one. This is more difficult than a simultaneous discrimination for normal animals, but it is enormously more difficult for striate animals. Such animals not only do not retain the preoperative habit; they are virtually incapable of relearning it (Thompson and Malin, 1961).

Finally, as was mentioned in the preceding chapter, the results with an avoidance-conditioning technique are different from those with light-dark discrimination. Following striate lesions, rats exhibit only a moderate loss of an avoidance habit, compared with a complete loss for light-dark discrimination (Thompson, 1960).

AMOUNT OF VISUAL CORTEX

So far we have been discussing complete extirpation of the striate cortex. In this case, as in those of somesthetic and auditory discriminations, we can ask what happens in cases of incomplete lesions leaving some remnants of striate cortex. Although there have been some conflicting results, the answer seems to be that, so long as a relatively small part of the striate cortex is left intact, there is little or no loss of retention (Lashley, 1935). The animals retain a light-dark habit postoperatively.

CAUSES OF MEMORY LOSS

We have now encountered many times the phenomenon of cortical lesions causing amnesia for a habit while sparing the ability of the subject to relearn the habit. We shall see it several more times. In no case, however, has the explanation been clear. The simplest conclusion to draw is that some structure of the brain takes over the capacity for relearning after a lesion destroys the structure normally involved. But this is hardly an explanation. Why the shift in structures involved?

One possible explanation is that the lesion so alters the perception of the organism that the learning situation is now a new one. It "looks" so different that there is no transfer between the two. Lending credence to this possibility is the fact that the striate animal's perception is definitely changed. The striate monkey is postoperatively unable to make a true discrimination of brightness, that is, to tell the difference between two stimuli of different size but equal in luminous flux (Klüver, 1937). The animal's vision becomes much like a photoelectric cell that knows only the total amount of light, not its distribution (Diamond and Chow, 1962).

This hypothesis was tested many years ago by destroying the lenses in rats' eyes, thus obliterating their detail vision, before giving them discriminative training (Lashley, 1937). In this way, it was hoped, animals would "see" the situation the same way before the operation as after it. After striate lesions, however, these animals showed the same loss of memory with ability to re-learn as did all the other experimental animals we have discussed. Apparently, the hypothesis was wrong.

On the other hand, it may not be entirely so. Postoperative amnesia in striate animals appears to be due to some lack of transfer between preoperative and postoperative situations. This has been demonstrated in the following way (Thompson, 1960). Normal animals were trained preoperatively as in the typical experiment but were operated in two stages. First, one side of the striate cortex was removed; then, after an interval of days or weeks, the other side was removed. This two-stage method of operating permits the animal to live and to have simultaneous visual experience with both the preoperative and postoperative worlds. Under these circumstances, the animals show no postoperative loss; there is good retention. Exactly why this happens is not yet known, but it points to transfer as a means of understanding the difference between preoperative and postoperative learning situations.

SUBCORTICAL MECHANISMS

Whatever the reason for the amnesia, the fact is that animals are able to re-learn postoperatively, and this ability does not depend on the cortex. It is necessary to look, then, for alternate structures subserving the ability at sub-cortical levels. It will be recalled that fibers of the visual system terminate in two subcortical stations: the superior colliculi of the midbrain and the pre-tectal nuclei of the thalamus, sometimes referred to as the posterior thalamic nuclei, in front of the colliculi. These two structures are candidates for investigation.

SUPERIOR COLLICULI—Several studies now have investigated the superior col-liculus (Ghiselli, 1938; Thompson and Rich, 1963). Bilateral removal of the superior colliculi by themselves does nothing to the memory of, or the ability to learn, a simultaneous intensity discrimination. Moreover, when destruction of the superior colliculus is performed in rats already lacking the striate cortex, there is still no disturbance in brightness discrimination. It is possible that the lesions in these studies were not as complete as they should be. It appears, however, that the superior colliculus has little to do with intensity discrimination. That leaves the pretectal posterior nucleus.

POSTERIOR NUCLEUS—A series of experiments involving lesions of the pos-terior nucleus clearly implicates this nucleus in intensity discrimination (Thompson and Rich, 1961, 1963). Indeed, it would appear to be the more important structure of the two terminal stations of the subcortical visual sys-tem. First of all, lesions in this nucleus disturb any visual habit set up pre-operatively: simultaneous brightness discrimination, successive brightness dis-crimination, light-avoidance conditioning, or form discrimination. In all these except light-avoidance conditioning, however, the disturbance is not great—there is some retention—and animals can relearn the habits. On the other hand, form discrimination is less affected than brightness discrimination. And, in contrast, avoidance conditioning to light is more affected than bright-ness discrimination. Indeed, rats with posterior lesions are virtually unable to relearn a light-avoidance response. To summarize these results and to interpret them in relation to the effects of removing the striate area, Thompson and Rich (1963, p. 65) have written as follows:

> On the basis of the present experiment, it would appear that the sub-cortical structure (nucleus posterior) which participates in mediating a brightness discrimination in normal animals is the very same structure which also subserves the habit in rats lacking the visual cortex. The prevalent notion that some subcortical region gains functional signifi-cance upon removal of the striate areas is unwarranted.

VISUAL FORM DISCRIMINATION

Visual form discrimination is the most extensively studied of the varieties of discriminative learning. There are dozens of experiments in which some part of the brain has been extirpated and its effect on some aspect of form-discrimination learning has been investigated. Many of the studies say essentially the same thing. Even where they may differ in detail, it would hardly be worthwhile in the present book to cover them all. Only the more general conclusions and representative studies supporting them will be presented and discussed.

METHODS OF STUDY

There seems to be no limit to the tasks involving form discrimination that can be concocted for use with animals. In general, the following types of tasks may be distinguished:

PATTERNED-STRING PROBLEMS—Patterned-string problems consist of two strings attached to cups that may be baited with food reward. The strings may be straight, crossed once, crossed twice, or placed in more complex arrangements. Such problems are mainly suitable only for primates who use their hands to manipulate things. Simple patterned-string problems are frequently included in a battery of tests to determine whether there is any visual defect. Animals with scotomas cannot see all the strings at once and usually have some difficulty with such a problem.

OBJECT DISCRIMINATION—In work with primates it is convenient to present three-dimensional objects, such as a block, a tobacco can, or almost anything one can pick up in the 5-and-10 store, as objects to be discriminated. In the Wisconsin General Test Apparatus or devices like it, such objects are placed over wells in a platform just outside the animal's cage. The well under the correct object is baited with food. The task for the animal is to learn to select the correct object and to brush it aside to pick up the food in the well.

A somewhat more difficult problem than simple object discrimination is the oddity problem. In this, three objects, two alike and one different, are presented. The animal, usually a monkey, is supposed to learn to select the odd object of the three as the correct one.

Another problem in object discrimination is matching from a sample. In this problem, a sample object is set apart from two other objects, one like it and the other different. The animal is first permitted to obtain food under the sample object. Then he is permitted access to the pair to be discriminated and is rewarded if he chooses the object that matches the sample.

PATTERN DISCRIMINATION—The task most often used with rats or cats, and sometimes with primates, is one in which patterns are painted or otherwise attached to cards. The patterns to be discriminated may be a triangle versus a circle, two circles that are different in size, or anything desired. Although the patterns presented in this way are usually simpler in design than objects used in object discrimination, the discrimination of patterns appears to be more difficult for animals than an object discrimination, perhaps because patterns are flat and lacking in depth. This same method may be used to present patterns of the same shape but of different sizes. In this case the discrimination is not one of pattern but rather one of size. Similarly, by painting cards with different shades of gray, a brightness-discrimination problem may be made in the same way.

CONDITIONAL REACTIONS—One of the more difficult problems to present to an animal is a conditional discrimination (Lashley, 1938). In this task, the animal must learn that, of two patterns repeatedly presented, the one that is correct depends, or is *conditional* upon, some other cue. Usually the conditional cue is a difference in background. For example, when a triangle and a circle are presented, the triangle may be correct if the background consists of horizontal stripes, but the circle is correct if the background is of vertical stripes.

LEARNING SETS—A learning-set problem is one consisting of many different problems, each presented for a limited number of trials (Harlow, 1951). One problem may be a triangle and a circle presented for six trials, another may be a tobacco can and a bottle also presented for six trials, and so on for problem after problem. The animal is supposed to learn the "rules of the game." If, each time he is presented with a new problem, he learns which one is correct on the first trial, then he should be able to perform perfectly on the second to the sixth trial. Actually, this kind of performance is seldom achieved. What does happen, however, is that as the animal works at many problems, sometimes hundreds of different ones, he does better and better on each succeeding problem. His improvement is evidence of learning to learn or of a learning set. The ability to learn such a set is phylogenetically correlated; monkeys do considerably better than rats or cats.

STRIATE CORTEX

It should be recalled from Chapter 7 that the striate cortex is essential for form vision in all adult animals. When it is completely removed, animals are unable to make any form discriminations at all. There is a slight exception to this statement in that striate cats can discriminate poorly an upright bar from a horizontal bar (Smith, 1938), but the statement is true of other varieties of form discrimination. It should also be recalled, however, that, if the striate cortex is removed shortly after birth (in kittens), no such deficit appears (page 194). When such animals mature, they behave in all respects like normal animals. In this case, then, the capacity for form discrimination must hinge on some other part of the brain.

A number of studies have been made on partial lesions of the striate cortex. In some, all but a small remnant was taken out (Lashley, 1939). In these cases, the rat could postoperatively make pattern discriminations. In other studies on the monkey (Settlage, 1939), the cortex was removed on only one side. This caused a temporary loss of retention but, with some retraining, the animals regained the habit. In general, it can be said that extensive lesions of the striate cortex cause some "loss of retention" that may be effaced by further training. The disturbance, however, is probably not one of retention. Rather, the animal with only a small part of the striate cortex remaining must learn new habits of fixation and looking at objects in order to make the discriminations it made preoperatively (Harlow, 1939).

In the case of the *rat*, there seems to be no area of the cortex other than the striate cortex that plays any part in pattern vision. Extensive lesions have been made all over the cortex before and after learning a form discrimination (Lashley, 1942) without finding any lesion that spared the striate cortex to have any effect on either the retention or the learning of a form discrimination.

It is quite possible that explorations such as these missed making exactly the right size and shape of lesion outside the striate cortex that might have produced a deficit. On the other hand, it probably represents the true state of affairs, for the rat has relatively little cortex not labeled as sensory or motor. There is certainly some evolution of "associative" pathways and cortical areas between the rat and primates. In any case, the situation for the monkey is rather different. There are nonstriate areas of significance in form-discrimination learning.

Altogether, three different areas have been implicated: (*1*) the preoccipital or prestriate areas near the striate area, (*2*) the frontal lobe, and (*3*) the temporal lobe. The evidence for the last is quite clear and will be detailed below, but that for the frontal and preoccipital areas is rather dubious.

PRESTRIATE AREAS

Relatively large lesions of the parieto-temporo-occipital cortex produce deficits in form discrimination (Blum et al., 1950). Monkeys with such lesions show amnesia on several tests of visual discrimination learning, including painted patterns, patterned-string problems, and conditional reactions. Not only is the amnesia usually complete, but ability to relearn the discriminations is impaired. It takes far more trials than preoperatively to reacquire the discriminations. They could, however, relearn them. The areas involved are not therefore crucial.

When more restricted lesions are made in the preoccipital or prestriate areas, the results are not so clear-cut. In fact, the experiments disagree with each other. In one set of experiments (Ades, 1946; Ades and Raab, 1949), monkeys learned three different discriminations, one of color, another of size, and a third of form. After they mastered the discriminations, the prestriate areas were extirpated (Figure 17.3). After an appropriate rest, the monkeys were retested. They had complete amnesia for all the habits. They could, however, be retrained to their preoperative levels of performance in about the same number of trials as was required originally.

In contrast to this, two other experiments obtained negative results (Lashley, 1948; Chow, 1952). Prestriate lesions had no effect on the retention or performance of visual form discriminations. Two possible explanations for the discrepancy have been offered, and perhaps both have some merit. One (Diamond and Chow, 1962) is that in the studies reporting deficits the lesions were better placed in the prestriate areas. In the negative studies, according to this view, enough of the prestriate areas was left to mediate retention. Certainly, the latter experiments invade more of the striate cortex than the positive ones, as indicated both by histology (Lashley, 1948) and by the fact that some of the monkeys showed a deficit on patterned-string problems but not on form discriminations.

A second possibility is that the amount of preoperative training makes a difference in retention (Riopelle and Ades, 1953; Riopelle et al., 1951). Animals that have been trained on many problems before operation and are relatively sophisticated seem to show little or no deficit in retention, whereas those given, say, only one form discrimination to learn show a loss. This factor of amount and kind of preoperative training frequently is as an important variable in determining whether there is or is not an amnesia following a lesion.

Figure 17.3—A sketch of the medial and lateral aspects of the monkey's brain, showing the prestriate areas. (Adapted from H. W. Ades. Effect of extirpation of parastriate cortex on learned discriminations in monkeys. *J. Neuropath. exp. Neurol.*, 1946, 56, 62. By permission of the publishers.)

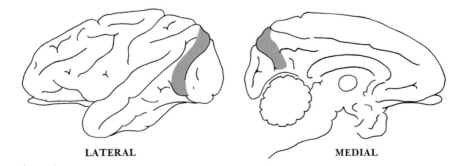

LATERAL   MEDIAL

FRONTAL AREAS

As we shall see later, interest in frontal-lobe functions has centered on the delayed response and on other measures of immediate memory. Frontal lesions have, however, frequently been made in animals trained on form-discrimination problems, often simply as an operative control for lesions in occipital and temporal areas where definitive effects were expected. In general, animals with frontal lesions are not seriously affected on discrimination problems. They show no large losses of retention. On the other hand, they often show loss and some inferiority to normal animals in performance on such problems (Harlow et al., 1952). The difference is not great, but sometimes it is definitely there. As testing continues postoperatively, however, the differences disappear (Warren and Harlow, 1952). Probably the difficulty is not in discrimination or in learning per se but rather in the fact that frontal animals tend to have strong, spontaneous object preferences and aversions. At least this is a phenomenon noted and offered in explanation (Brush et al., 1961).

TEMPORAL LOBE

For years it was assumed that a sensory "association" area for each of the senses is located adjacent to the primary projection area. It was thought that the prestriate area is the "association" area for vision. On that basis, one would expect it to be involved in visual discriminative learning, particularly of form or pattern. Then in 1938 Klüver and Bucy discovered that bilateral removal of the temporal lobe in the monkey is followed by a very striking visual agnosia (see Chapter 19). Monkeys with such lesions seem unable to recognize familiar objects and are generally deficient on visual tasks. That discovery, after some delay occasioned by World War II, initiated a program of research on the functions of the temporal lobe. Now, there are probably more papers on this topic than on any other part of the cerebral cortex, except possibly the frontal lobe (see Milner, 1954; Pribram, 1954; Diamond and Chow, 1962).

The general statement that can be made about the temporal lobes is that, following their removal, there is a deficit in visual habits—an amnesia for previously learned discriminations—but the habits can be relearned. Also, under some circumstances, temporal animals may be retarded in acquiring new visual habits. The degree of this memory loss or retardation in learning depends on the size and placement of the lesion, on the difficulty of the tasks employed, on the amount of preoperative training, and on other features of the tasks learned.

ANATOMICAL SITE—The inferotemporal or ventral temporal cortex appears to be the most important part of the temporal lobe in visual functions. At least, extirpation of this part results in deficits almost as severe as removal of the whole lobe. On the other hand, there is a difference, and one cannot say that the visual "associative" function is limited to the inferotemporal surface (Mishkin, 1954; Pribram, 1954).

Once it was established that the temporal lobe functions in visual discriminative learning, it became interesting to look into the anatomical basis of this function. Anatomical studies demonstrated that the temporal lobe receives projections from the pulvinar of the thalamus and sends fibers back to this region of the thalamus (Chow, 1950; Whitlock and Nauta, 1956). Consequently, attempts were made to assess the importance of these connections in visual function either by making lesions in the pulvinar (Chow, 1954) or by undercutting the cortex and thus severing the projections (Chow, 1961). Neither of these operations made any difference to the retention of visual habits. Apparently the connections involved are transcortical rather than thalamocortical. This was confirmed by cross-hatching the temporal cortex in such a way as to cut its transcortical connections. Monkeys operated in this way show the same memory loss for visual habits as those in which the temporal cortex is extirpated (Chow, 1961).

NATURE OF DEFICIT—On the behavioral side, several questions have been asked about the nature of the postoperative visual deficit. Is it a sensory defect or caused by a sensory defect? Or is it a true memory defect? It rather definitely is the latter. Temporal monkeys showing the amnesia have been tested for scotoma and found not to have any. They locate small pieces of food and thin threads as well as normal monkeys, when scotomatous monkeys cannot. Temporal monkeys that are deficient in acquiring form discriminations and learning sets have no difficulty with learning string-pattern problems, while monkeys with lateral occipital lesions have quite the reverse abilities (Wilson and Mishkin, 1959). Thus the postoperative deficit has not been traced to a sensory deficit.

Could it be an inability to "understand" or learn the testing procedure? Apparently not, because the deficit may appear with more difficult tasks, and not with easier ones, when both involve the same procedure. For example, monkeys were given learning-set training on two kinds of stimuli; one was with three-dimensional objects, and the other with painted patterns (Chow, 1954). As mentioned earlier, the first of these is easier for monkeys than the second. Postoperatively, the animals retained the learning-set performance for the three-dimensional objects, but they had a deficit for the painted patterns. Moreover, they were unable to relearn learning sets for the painted patterns. All the procedures were the same, and so the deficit had to do with the kind of learning involved rather than with the procedures.

NATURE OF TASK—Is the difficulty of the task important in the deficit? In general, the answer seems to be affirmative, although there are exceptions

(Chow, 1962). Animals may retain a very easy discrimination between circles of different sizes but show a deficit in a more difficult discrimination of circles of slightly different size. If stimuli are presented tachistoscopically, temporal monkeys have more difficulty compared with normal animals when the flashes are brief than when they are longer.

Is degree of mastery of the task important? It seems to be, and in two ways. If monkeys are overtrained before operation, that is, given many more trials than are required to learn to a criterion, they show no postoperative deficit; yet they show such a deficit on problems that they merely learn to a criterion before operation (Orbach and Fantz, 1958). Also when monkeys are given new visual discriminations to learn postoperatively and then are tested on tasks learned preoperatively they may show no memory loss, although they normally do so. Hence, postoperative retention or recovery may depend simply on the practicing of visual discriminations, not practice on the specific tasks (Chow, 1952).

All this work leaves the question of just what is the role of the temporal lobes in discriminative learning. Further research will undoubtedly produce a clearer idea. So far, the following are certain: The deficits of temporal animals are in the visual domain and not in other modalities; they are not sensory; they are not deficits in learning skills; but they are related to the nature of the tasks to be learned and remembered.

GENERALIZATION AND TRANSFER

The terms *generalization* and *transfer* are similar in meaning, but by custom they are applied to somewhat different situations. The term generalization is ordinarily used when an organism has learned to discriminate one set of stimuli and is now tested on another, different set of stimuli. If some feature of a test stimulus is similar to that of the training stimuli and is discriminated, *generalization* is said to occur. The term *transfer* is used where two different tasks are to be learned, and the question is whether the learning of the first task helps, or possibly hinders, the learning of the second. The two tasks are usually discriminations, and that is why we discuss transfer here in a chapter on discriminative learning, but transfer may also occur in motor or problem-solving tasks.

GENERALIZATION

Some years ago, the way in which rats learn pattern discriminations and then generalize them was studied in some detail (Lashley, 1938). A great variety of different patterns were made up on cards. After the animals had learned to discriminate any particular pair of cards, they were tested to see what aspects of the forms they were using. This was done by seeing which forms were chosen when many different pairs were presented to them. It was found that rats selected certain details from complex patterns and used these as the basis of discrimination. Any card having the particular detail used in learning the discrimination would be chosen.

In a follow-up study (Maier, 1939), it was found that rats, if they have the opportunity, tend to choose differences in intensity as a basis for discrimination. They can and do sometimes use size differences independently of intensity differences. And sometimes they choose some unique, or absolute, property of the stimulus card. In this study, a standard pair of cards was used for original learning; and a series of other cards was used as tests of generalization. From scores made on these tests, it could be determined what factors animals were using in their original learning. Also, the percentage of cards that were equivalent for a rat could be used as an index of visual generalization for the rat.

All this was preparatory to studying the effect of cortical lesions on visual generalization (Maier, 1941; Wapner, 1944). Lesions were made at various places and in varying sizes in the cortex prior to training. Then the animals postoperatively were trained on the standard discrimination and tested for generalization. The principal conclusion to be drawn from these studies was that generalization is greater in operated animals than in normals. In other words, operates are less discriminating and tend to choose more widely different stimuli in their generalization tests. Secondly, generalization in both normal and operated animals is based on some combination of intensity and size, but the intensity factor becomes relatively more important in the operated animals. There was no cortical localization of these effects; lesions anywhere in the cortex had these effects on generalization. There was a tendency for larger lesions to have greater effects on generalization, but this was not very marked.

TRANSPOSITION

The term *transposition* refers to a special case of generalization in which the important factor in the generalization is some relational aspect of the stimuli. Suppose, for example, the rat is taught to discriminate between two grays, choosing the lighter of a medium gray and dark gray. If he learns the relation "brighter," then, when he is tested with a light gray and a medium gray, he chooses the light gray rather than the medium gray which formerly was the lighter of two stimuli. Normal rats do this, and this kind of generalization is called transposition.

The effect of cortical lesions on such transposition has been studied in the rat (Hebb, 1938). The lesions, however, were restricted to the striate areas. Animals trained on an intensity discrimination were tested for transposition before and after the striate lesions were made. There was no difference. Striate lesions did not impair the transpositions made normally by the rat.

A similar experiment has been made in the monkey except that the structure considered was the amygdala (Schwartzbaum and Pribram, 1960). Operated animals were trained on a medium and dark gray and then tested on a light and medium gray. There was no significant difference between normals and operates in learning the original brightness discrimination. On transposition tests, however, there was a remarkable difference. Normal animals transposed almost perfectly, whereas operated animals performed at a chance level. They did not know which stimulus to choose.

In this study, the monkeys were subsequently trained on a sequential discrimination that was the opposite of a transposition. They were presented in random order with pairs of gray stimuli, sometimes a light and medium gray, and sometimes a medium and dark gray, but the medium gray (not the lighter of the two grays) was always positive. Despite the fact that normal animals readily transpose, they learned this sequential discrimination at a good rate, whereas the operated animals did not. Amygdalectomized animals eventually learned it, but they took five times as long as normal animals.

Most of what is known about the amygdala concerns its role in emotion (Chapter 11). Just what is its role here in transposition and sequential discrimination is not readily understood. There are theories about it (Pribram, 1962), but they are not very convincing, and so we shall not go into them here.

BILATERAL TRANSFER

We shall turn now to a most interesting set of experiments done on *bilateral transfer*. The general procedure in these experiments is to make use of one side of the body, say one eye or one hand, in original training and then to test for transfer using the corresponding member of the other side of the body. If, as is usually the case in normal individuals, there is excellent transfer, bilateral transfer is said to take place. If the transfer is from one hand to another, it is bimanual transfer. If it is from one eye to the other, it is interocular transfer. The majority of research done to date has been on interocular transfer.

The fact that bilateral transfer takes place in normal individuals is not surprising. In fact, it is pretty much taken for granted. However, in combination with surgical procedures that partly divide the brain into halves, some interesting results are obtained (Sperry, 1961). For example, with visual discriminations, the brain may be divided so as to split the visual system in two. Similar operations can be used to divide the somesthetic or motor system. Animals prepared in this way are known as *split-brain* animals.

VISUAL SYSTEM—The mammalian visual system, as we have seen (Chapter 6), is partly crossed. At the optic chiasm, fibers from each eye partly cross and partly stay on the same side (see Figure 17.4). To prepare a visual split brain, the optic chiasm is sectioned in such a way as to interrupt all crossed fibers, leaving only the homolateral fibers undisturbed. This by itself, however, is not sufficient to make a split brain. There are other commissural connections in the brain. One is the corpus callosum joining the two sides of the striate cortex. There is another commissure at the level of the superior colliculi. Altogether, then, there are three possible crossings of visual information in the mammalian brain: the chiasm, the corpus callosum, and the colliculi. However, the first two are quite important for at least some kinds of bilateral visual transfer.

But before going into these experiments, it should be pointed out that animals below the level of mammals more nearly approach split-brain preparations in their natural state without surgical intervention. Inframammalian animals have visual systems that are entirely crossed. With little or no cerebral cortex, the corpus callosum does not have to be reckoned with. That leaves the only bilateral visual connection at the level of the colliculus. In birds this commissure is only partial, connecting projections representing the relatively small binocular field of the animal. The monocular fields appear to have no bilateral connections.

INFRAMAMMALIAN ANIMALS—First we shall discuss the "natural" split-brain preparations found in the bird and fish and then the split-brain animals prepared surgically. The standard procedure in either case is to train the animal

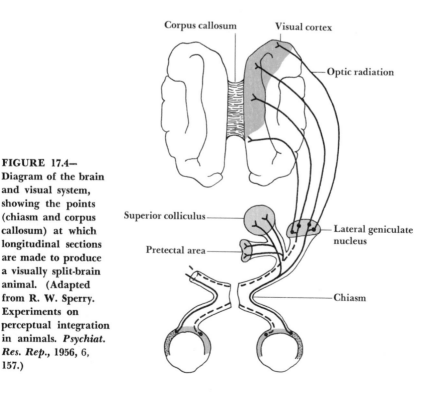

FIGURE 17.4—
Diagram of the brain and visual system, showing the points (chiasm and corpus callosum) at which longitudinal sections are made to produce a visually split-brain animal. (Adapted from R. W. Sperry. Experiments on perceptual integration in animals. *Psychiat. Res. Rep.*, 1956, 6, 157.)

Corpus callosum   Visual cortex

Optic radiation

Superior colliculus

Pretectal area

Lateral geniculate nucleus

Chiasm

on a visual discrimination with one eye covered or otherwise not used. (In the monkey, this can be done by arranging that the monkey must use only the eye on one side to peer through an aperture at the stimuli.) After the discrimination is learned through one eye, tests are made with the other eye.

Pigeons trained to discriminate patterns, color, or brightness show interocular transfer under some conditions and no such transfer under others (Levine, 1945a, 1945b). When the patterns are placed directly in front of them and they are trained while using only one eye, they do not show the slightest indication of memory when tested while the other eye is being used. Yet, when the stimuli used in discrimination are placed just beneath their heads, they exhibit perfect interocular transfer.

This interesting phenomenon, it seems, is explained by the part of the visual field used in its discrimination. Interocular transfer seems to occur when the small binocular field is used and to fail when the monocular field is used. This is in accord with the anatomy of the visual system in which only the binocular portions of the colliculi are connected together through a commissure. In some preliminary experiments (Levine, 1945), this commissure was cut. The pigeons so operated failed to show interocular transfer under the conditions in which transfer is seen in normal pigeons. These experiments ought to be confirmed. If they are, interocular transfer in the pigeon would be located within a little bundle of commissural fibers.

Similar experiments have been made in fish (McCleary, 1960) without any surgical interference. In this case, conditioning procedures were used. One procedure was of the classical type, pairing light with shock, and the response was a change in heart rate. For this conditioned response, there was good transfer between the two eyes. When the problem was changed, however, to one of conditioned avoidance, there was no interocular transfer. Fish trained to avoid shock, using one eye, showed no evidence of learning when tested with the other eye. In this situation, the learning apparently takes place at some point before the information from the two eyes is connected.

SPLIT-BRAIN ANIMALS—We shall turn now to the mammalian split-brain preparation and its performance in interocular transfer (Sperry, 1961). Most of the work has been done on cats and monkeys, a little on chimpanzees. The typical split-brain animal is prepared by longitudinally sectioning the optic chiasm to eliminate crossed visual fibers and, in the same animal, sectioning all or part of the corpus callosum to eliminate visual interhemispheral connections. The general effect of these operations is to abolish interocular transfer, though whether this happens or not depends on the kind of task used and on the degree of overtraining.

It was first established, as one might guess, that interocular transfer regularly takes place in chiasm-sectioned animals (Myers, 1955). Cats were trained on various pattern discriminations with a mask over one eye and were given different amounts of training. They were rewarded for correct choices by food and punished for incorrect choices by shock. When tested with the mask over the opposite eye, they showed immediate transfer. Their performance, however, was not quite so good on this test with the mask on the untrained side as with the mask on the trained side. Later work with several different problems showed that this difference depended on the difficulty of the problem (Myers, 1959). The more difficult the problem, the more inferior is the untrained side to the trained side.

The next step was to add callosal section to chiasm section, other features of the procedure remaining the same (Myers, 1956; Sperry et al., 1956). The operations were done before training. After training with one eye on several discriminations, the animals showed no transfer whatsoever when tested on the other eye. This result, however is limited to pattern discriminations or to brightness discriminations that are reasonably difficult (Meikle and Sechzer, 1960). If the learning task is a very simple discrimination, there may be good interocular transfer. Near-threshold brightness discriminations do not transfer (Meikle, 1960). It would appear that those functions that normally depend on the cortex, such as pattern vision, do not transfer in this split-brain preparation, whereas those that are carried out subcortically do transfer.

Once the independence of the two hemispheres in the split-brain animal was established, other studies attempted to analyze in more detail the anatomical factors in transfer, or lack of it. The corpus callosum was sectioned only partially to determine whether all of it or only certain fibers in it were important (Myers, 1956). Interocular transfer was found after section of the anterior portion of the callosum but not after posterior section. Since the visual interhemispheral fibers are in the posterior portion, this was to be expected.

Once the role of the callosum was established, the next problem was to find out just how it functions. In the chiasm-sectioned animal having the callosum intact, is the information from training stored in the trained hemisphere and later tapped? Or is it transmitted to the other hemisphere and stored there?

To answer this, chiasm-sectioned rats were trained monocularly on one easy discrimination (horizontal versus vertical stripes) and one difficult discrimination (circle versus ring) and given a good deal of overtraining (Myers and Sperry, 1958). Then lesions were made in the cortex of the trained side, some limited to the striate cortex and others encompassing a wider area. After that, the animals were tested for interocular transfer. On the easy task, all showed transfer regardless of size of lesion. On the more difficult task, there was less transfer for the striate lesion, and none at all for the larger lesions. From this result, it appears that, in simpler discriminations, the trained hemisphere lays down some information on the naïve side but that this is not so for the more difficult discriminations.

A number of other questions about the mechanism of interocular transfer have been investigated, but only one more point will be made here. In the split-brain preparation, the independence of the hemispheres seems to be complete (see Sperry, 1961). Two completely opposite habits can be learned by means of the two eyes. One can teach an animal either successively or alternately to select one of the two stimuli of a pair as positive when viewed with the left eye and the other member of the pair when viewed with the other eye. There is no apparent interference between the habits in the learning curves. Apparently, one side of the brain does not know what the other side is doing.

SOMESTHETIC TRANSFER—It may be mentioned in passing that somesthetic bilateral transfer has also been studied in cats (Stamm and Sperry, 1957) and in monkeys (Glickstein and Sperry, 1960). In the case of somesthesis, split-brain animals were prepared merely by sectioning the corpus callosum. They were tested by having them learn to make a roughness discrimination with one paw and then tested on the other paw. The results have been inconsistent. In fact, they are downright confusing. It would appear that there are some species differences and that the degree of transfer depends on the type and difficulty of the task and perhaps on other procedural factors not yet clearly identified. For that reason, no more will be said about them here (see Sperry, 1961).

Two other points may be made briefly. One is that temporary split-brain animals can be prepared by using Leão's (1944) spreading depression (Bureš and Burešová, 1960). By applying KCl to the cortex of one side, that side can be blocked long enough to conduct some training of the animal (rat). Testing may then be done while the other cortex is blocked. In this case, there is no bilateral transfer of a learned avoidance response. Secondly, bilateral transfer has been studied in the octopus (Muntz, 1961). Section of certain tracts and lobes in the brain of the octopus abolishes bilateral transfer for habits taught with one eye.

18 PROBLEM SOLVING

THIS IS THE LAST of three chapters on learning. The first covered classical and avoidance conditioning, the second discriminative learning, and this one covers other kinds of learning. The term "problem solving" applies loosely to these other kinds of learning and, for want of a better phrase, serves as the chapter title.

Three general classes of learning will be considered. (1) One is mazes, simple or complex. These may vary from a simple T maze to one involving many alleys and an elaborate pattern. (2) Another is the so-called problem box in which the animal must discover a bar to press or some act to perform in order to be rewarded. (3) The third is the delayed response. In this, the animal must remember over some period of delay what it has seen at the beginning of the delay period. Since performance on the delayed response is closely tied to the frontal lobes, the third section of the chapter dealing with the delayed response is mostly concerned with the frontal lobes.

The research covered in this chapter is, on the whole, older work than that discussed in the preceding chapters. That is because much of the early work on brain functions and learning focused on problem solving. In more recent years, emphasis has shifted to work on conditioning and discriminative learning. Research on the delayed response is an exception to this statement. Work on the delayed response has been fairly active in recent years. Even so, much of it does little more than confirm the results of earlier work.

MAZE LEARNING

The maze is one of the earliest instruments to be devised for studying animal learning. It is simple to construct, it can be made in a variety of forms, and its difficulty can be varied by changing its pattern or increasing the number of alleys in the maze. For these reasons, it also became one of the first instruments used in the study of brain functions in learning (Lashley and Franz, 1917). Since it is very handy for the size and capabilities of the rat and less convenient for use with larger animals, virtually all research with the maze has been on the rat.

CEREBRAL CORTEX

Much of the work on the role of the cerebral cortex in learning was done by Lashley (see Beach et al., 1960). His general procedure was to destroy areas of the cortex before and after learning had taken place, thus assessing the effects of lesions on learning and retention. He used mazes having three steps of difficulty. One maze, maze I, had only one blind alley; a second maze, maze II, had three blind alleys; and the most difficult maze, maze III, had eight blind alleys.

LEARNING—The results of Lashley's experiments are depicted in Figure 18.1. As one might guess, the effect of cortical lesions on ability to learn and to remember a maze habit was greater for maze II than for maze I. For the simplest (one-blind-alley) maze, small or moderate lesions of the cortex did not affect the rate of learning the maze. But quite large lesions destroying, say, 50 percent of the cortex had some deleterious effect on rate of learning. In any case, the place of the lesion in the cortex had nothing to do with whether the learning rate was impaired. Only the size of the lesion was important. The relationship between size of lesion and impairment of learning rate could be put in statistical terms as a correlation of .20. This was a small correlation, but it was significant.

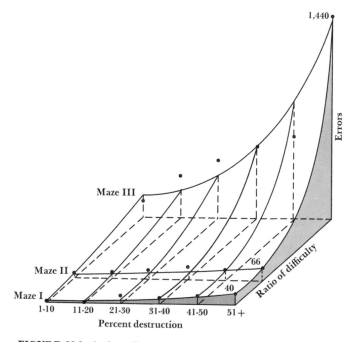

FIGURE 18.1—A three-dimensional representation of the results of a study in which difficulty of maze was varied, lesions of different sizes were made, and the degree of retardation (errors) in learning the maze was measured. (Adapted from K. S. Lashley. *Brain mechanisms and intelligence.* Chicago: University of Chicago Press, 1929. P. 74. By permission of the publishers.)

The correlation is considerably higher for mazes II and III, the more complex mazes. For maze II, the statistical correlation between size of lesion and rate of learning was .58. For maze III, it was .75. Thus the degree to which cortical lesions interfered with rate of learning was proportional to their size. Their location was not important.

The upshot of the series of experiments with the three mazes and with lesions before learning was this: (1) The rat's ability to learn any of the mazes does not depend upon any particular area of the cerebral cortex; (2) in general, learning ability after cortical lesions is proportional to the amount of cortex left intact; and (3) the relation between mass of cortex and maze-learning ability is more predictable—the correlation is higher—the more difficult the maze to be learned.

RETENTION—What we have said so far refers to initial learning of a maze. Lashley's experiments also included tests of retention after cortical lesions.

As one might expect, the same general conclusions apply to retention as to learning. Small lesions varying in size up to one-third of the cortex do not disturb retention of the simplest-maze habit. Larger injuries, however, cause some loss of retention in the one-blind-alley maze (maze I), even though they do not impair learning ability. The more difficult the maze, the more a lesion of a particular size impairs memory for the maze habit. Moreover, the larger the lesion, the greater the impairment of the habit. And in all cases of retention tests, just as in learning tests, there was no relation between the place of a lesion and the amount of impairment. Finally, as the last main point of these experiments, a lesion of a particular size does more harm to retention of a habit already formed than to ability to learn or relearn a maze habit.

Closely related to these conclusions about brain lesions and maze habits is an experiment with maze-bright and maze-dull rats (Ericksen, 1939). The experimenter picked some rats that were relatively bright in learning mazes and some that were rather poor. He made cortical lesions of about the same size, viz., 20 percent, in all of them. In comparing the preoperative learning with postoperative tests of retention, he found that the animals that had learned most rapidly before operation remembered the most after the operation and those that had learned most slowly retained the least, although both bright and dull animals had been trained to a high criterion of performance before the operations. The conclusion, then, from Ericksen's experiment is that, other things being equal, the effect of cortical lesions upon memory is less in bright rats than in dull ones. Or, put another way, intelligent rats seem better able to function without some of their cortex than dull rats.

MASS ACTION

The principal finding of Lashley's studies on maze learning is, as we saw above, that the effect of a cortical lesion on maze learning or retention is proportional to the mass of the lesion (see also Lashley and Wiley, 1933). Lashley interpreted this result to mean that the cortex is relatively nonspecific in its role in maze learning. Although admitting the specificity of the primary sensory and motor areas in perceptual and motor skills, respectively, he regarded them as also having, along with other "associative" areas of the cortex, a general function in learning. The name he gave to this concept was *mass action*.

EQUIPOTENTIALITY—Along with the concept of mass action, Lashley (1929) proposed a complementary concept, that of *equipotentiality*. By this, he meant that different parts of the cortex, and also of subcortical systems, are interchangeable in their roles in learning. Actually, Lashley had different parts of a given sensory system in mind in employing the term equipotentiality. For example, the fact seen in the preceding chapter that a brightness discrimination can be relearned after removal of the striate cortex would be an example of equipotentiality in the visual system. "Mass action," however, referred to the cortex as a whole and meant that different parts of the cortex were interchangeable in a learning task like maze learning. Thus the two concepts, mass action and equipotentiality, imply about the same thing but one refers to relationships *within* a system and the other to relationships *among* sensory, motor, and other systems.

SENSORY CONTROL OF MAZE LEARNING—Lashley's results were open to another interpretation which was not long in being offered (Hunter, 1930a, 1930b, 1931). Maze learning involves the use of several different sensory cues as well as motor activities. When increasingly large lesions are made in the cortex, the animal is deprived of more and more of his sensory-motor capacities for responding in the maze.

Additionally, it might be assumed that, in learning a maze, some animals use one sensory cue and that other animals mainly use some other type of cue. Yet the experimenter does not know which animal is which. Whether or not a lesion damages the particular area mediating the learned response in each case becomes, then, a matter of probability. The greater the size of the lesion, the greater is the likelihood of destroying the area through which learning takes place. On these assumptions, one might expect learning and memory for maze performance, as studied in the experiments described above, to look as though they do not depend upon a particular place in the cortex but rather upon mass of cortex.

These assumptions are bolstered by experiments. It is known, in the first place, that animals vary among themselves in the cues of which they make use in solving maze problems. One way of testing that is to remove different cues, after an animal has learned a maze, and see what effect this procedure has on his memory. In experiments in which rats were trained in the light and subsequently tested in the dark, for example, some animals were considerably disturbed and others were not (Dennis, 1929; Finley, 1941). Another test is to provide two different solutions of a problem, one employing visual cues and another positional ones (tactual-kinesthetic). In this case, some rats take one "hypothesis" and other animals the second "hypothesis" (see below).

A second assumption, stated above, is that cortical lesions of increasing size deprive the animal, in increasing amounts, of necessary sensory cues. This can be tested by studying the effects of the destruction of sense organs upon learning (Honzik, 1936). Here one finds results essentially comparable to those of mass action (see Figure 18.2). If animals are blind while learning a maze, the lack of vision has little or no effect upon their learning. The same is true if one destroys the olfactory bulbs. Combining anosmia and blindness, however, makes a great deal of difference; animals are appreciably retarded in their learning of maze problems. It is a little difficult to make more extensive combinations, but even this result points rather definitely to the conclusion

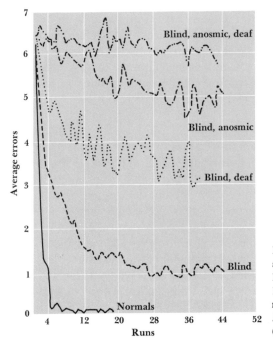

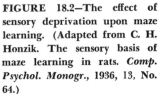

FIGURE 18.2—The effect of sensory deprivation upon maze learning. (Adapted from C. H. Honzik. The sensory basis of maze learning in rats. *Comp. Psychol. Monogr.*, 1936, 13, No. 64.)

that in sensory deprivation, as in cortical destruction, there is a "law" of mass action. In the former case, however, it is plain that no mass factors are concerned but, on the contrary, only specific sensory factors.

MASS VERSUS SPECIFIC FACTORS—These various experiments offer two possible interpretations of the statistical relationship between mass of lesion and the effects of a lesion on maze learning. They do not offer a clear decision. In an attempt to arrive at one, other experiments have been carried out. These fall into two general categories: One is to see whether some specific area of the cortex has a function in learning not ascribable to its sensory function; the other is to see whether some areas of the cortex may not be more important in maze learning than Lashley's results would lead one to believe.

Experiments of the first class have attempted to compare the effects of blinding an animal with removal of the striate cortex. Presumably, if the sensory hypothesis is correct, destruction of the striate cortex should have no more effect than blinding. If it has more, then a mass-action function can be ascribed to the striate cortex. Several experiments on this problem will be described.

In the first one (Tsang, 1934), it was found that removal of the striate cortex, in addition to the blinding of an animal, caused more retardation in maze learning than blinding alone. In another closely related experiment (Tsang, 1936), removal of the visual cortex alone caused more retardation in learning than simply blinding the animals. The results, it was concluded, were definite evidence for a mass-action factor of the visual cortex in maze learning.

These experiments, however, were not entirely satisfactory because, in an attempt to remove completely the striate cortex, other surrounding areas were sometimes invaded. Therefore it was quite possible that the additional effects of cortical lesions were due to removing more than the projection area of the visual system. For this reason the experiments were repeated (Finley, 1941), this time taking care to keep the lesions from exceeding the boundaries of the striate cortex. Since cortical operations in the rat are by no means precise, the result was that most of the operations did not remove all the striate area. Thus, although the striate cortex in the rat averages about 20 percent of neocortex, the lesions in this particular experiment averaged only about 10 percent. Perhaps it is not surprising that this experiment gave no evidence of mass action. Indeed, the rats with cortical lesions got along better in maze learning than did blinded rats. And in experiments in which visual cues were not necessary for learning the maze (in the dark), the animals with cortical lesions were just as good as the normal animals.

The experiment was repeated still a third time (Lashley, 1943). The attempt was to make the lesions cover more of the striate cortex but still not to exceed it. In this case, positive evidence for mass action was found. The rats with striate lesions did more poorly than blinded rats. But again the lesions were somewhat too large and, on an average, exceeded the area of the visual cortex. The problem seemed, and still seems, insoluble.

The experiment has been repeated recently in the monkey where it is possible to make more precise lesions of the visual cortex (Orbach, 1959). Monkeys learned a Lashley type III maze. After mastery of the habit, they were peripheral-blinded. This caused "complete loss of the habit, prolonged immobility in the maze . . . and retarded relearning of the maze" (Orbach, 1959, p. 54). Apparently the monkeys had relied on visual cues in the original learning. Once the blinded monkeys relearned the maze, however, the habit was relatively stable. Then bilateral removal of striate cortex was performed and the animals retested. This caused a mild retardation in relearning the maze. It appears that, in addition to the visual function of the striate cortex, it possesses some nonvisual function, which might be regarded as a "mass-action" function. The investigator's conclusion, however, was a little more specific than that. He concluded that the "occipital cortex in the monkey serves as a substrate for nonvisual orientation involving a locomotor sequence" (Orbach, 1959, p. 54).

It may be concluded that, although cortical areas in the rat may have nonspecific functions in maze learning, the concept of mass action has its limitations. Cortical areas have both specific and nonspecific functions. This is brought out in a recent experiment (Smith, 1959) in which animals with different rearing conditions were tested on another kind of maze, the Hebb-Williams closed-field maze (Hebb and Williams, 1946). Some animals were reared in a free environment and others in a cage. Each group was divided into two surgical subgroups, one receiving large anterior lesions and the other small posterior lesions outside the striate areas. They were then run on a number of problems in the Hebb-Williams maze. The cage-reared group gave results predicted from Lashley's concept of mass action. Those with large anterior lesions were the most retarded. Not so with the free-environment rats. In these, the smaller posterior but nonstriate lesions produced the greater deficit. In the case, then, of animals reared in a free environment and learning to solve spatial problems, the concept of mass action does not hold.

SUBCORTICAL MECHANISMS

Work on subcortical mechanisms involved in maze learning is relatively meager. It is not particularly exciting either. Some of the results are exactly what one would predict, knowing the effects of cortical lesions. Some, on the other hand, are not easy to interpret at present. The research we shall describe concerns decortication, the thalamus, and the limbic system.

DECORTICATION—There are basically two ways to study the role of subcortical mechanisms. One is to see what they can do while intact but without accompanying cortex. The other is to determine the difference it makes when subcortical structures are damaged, leaving the cortex intact. Let us first see what happens in decortication.

As already noted, in Lashley's early studies (1929) of maze learning, he used one relatively simple maze, and he had animals with varying sizes of lesions. His simple maze presented rats with a problem that amounts to the formation of a position habit. All they had to do was make one turn and make it consistently; this is what psychologists call a position habit. He found that with lesions up to 80 percent there was little or no retardation in the learning of such a habit.

More recently, this work has been extended (Thompson, 1959) in two ways. First, very large lesions were made, so large, in fact, that two animals suffered virtually complete decortication. The other was to train the animals on a simple T maze so that learning consists of the mastery of a position habit. The results confirmed what might be guessed from Lashley's work. There was no effect of decortication on the learning of the position habit. Decorticate animals learned it just as well as normals.

Even the extremely simple habit of learning a T maze can be made more difficult by delaying reward. If, after animals have made a correct response, an interval of thirty seconds is interposed before they are given food, a larger number of trials is required to learn the habit (Pubols, 1958). In the case of the decorticates and their controls, some animals were trained in this way—with a thirty-second delay of reward. Although the normals required about twice as long to learn under these conditions, the nearly complete operates did the same. There was thus no significant difference between them. This is interesting because such learning is generally considered to involve a "memory trace." If so, such a "memory trace" seems not to require any appreciable amount of cortex.

THALAMUS—Stereotaxic lesions made in the anterior portion of the thalamus have relatively little effect on maze learning in the rat (Ghiselli and Brown, 1938). Neither do lesions in the pretectal nuclei. The latter result is in contrast to the effects of such lesions on brightness discrimination (see page 201). Lesions in other thalamic structures impair somewhat the learning of a maze, but the most important thalamic structures are the sensory and association nuclei which project to the cortex. This is what might be expected. Although no statistical correlations were run, the mass of thalamic lesions correlates fairly well with the amount of impairment of learning ability. No structure or group of structures, however, is essential for maze learning.

LIMBIC SYSTEM—The septum and hippocampus have been studied. In both cases, deleterious effects on maze learning have been noted. In the case of septal lesions, the effect seems to depend on whether the lesion is sufficient to make animals irritable (Thomas et al., 1959). (It will be recalled that lesions in the septum cause rats to be savage and irritable, although the effects usually wear off in time.) The rats that showed no irritability after the septal operation did not differ from normals in the learning of a (Lashley type III) maze. On the other hand, those which were jumpy and irritable made significantly more errors, though only slightly more errors, to learn the maze. In this case, it appeared that the effect of the lesion on learning was due to the excessive exploratory behavior of the "jumpy" animals.

It also seems well established that lesions of the hippocampus impede learning. In two different studies of rats with hippocampal lesions (Kaada et al., 1961; Thomas and Otis, 1958), such lesions impaired the learning of a maze. The reasons for the impairment are not clear, for the role of the hippocampus in any kind of learning is not clear. From studies of electrical correlates of learning in the hippocampus (page 53) it appears that it does something, possibly in connection with attention or reinforcement, in the early stages of learning. It has been suggested (Thomas and Otis, 1958) that the effect on maze learning is through some interference with the mechanisms of secondary reinforcement.

PROBLEM–SOLVING BEHAVIOR

Investigators have devised a considerable number of apparatuses posing problems to be solved through trial-and-error learning. In the early days of animal-learning research, the maze was the most popular apparatus. Later, other kinds of "problem boxes," including the much-used Skinner bar-pressing situation, came into frequent use. In some cases, the maze was reduced to its simplest form, a runway or single T. In addition, special apparatuses were devised for special problems. In this section we shall consider the physiological aspects of learning and retention in situations other than the multiple-unit maze discussed above.

LATCHES AND BARS

In one of Lashley's early studies (Lashley, 1935; also see Beach et al., 1960), a series of latch boxes was used. Four different problems involved the learning of manipulative behavior on the part of the rat. One required a string to be pulled, another a strip of paper to be torn in a certain way, and so on. A fifth problem was simpler, at least in motor function, for it required the animal to step successively on two platforms in order to obtain food.

The effects of brain lesions were different for the two types of problems. In the double-platform, locomotor problem, the ability of animals to learn it was not affected by cortical lesions of considerable magnitude, in fact up to 58 percent. The rate of learning was not correlated with the magnitude of any lesions made. With other boxes, however, which required manipulative behavior, there was considerable retardation in learning with cortical lesions. The correlations between extent of lesion and amount of damage to the cortex ranged from .48 to .72, depending on the particular problem.

Lashley's observations of his operated animals and his analysis of results convinced him that the difficulty of operated animals in the manipulative problem boxes was basically a matter of variability of behavior. They had more trouble varying their behavior in such a way as to strike on the right kind of coordinated act to solve the problem. Most of Lashley's lesions involved the motor areas, which are relatively large in the rat. Hence some of the difficulty in learning manipulative skills was undoubtedly motor.

HANDEDNESS—Many years ago, Lashley (1924) also made a related observation, this time in the monkey. He had taught his animals a manipulative problem in which they could use only one hand at a time. After they had learned to use one hand consistently, he removed the (opposite) motor cortex responsible for that limb. Upon postoperative testing, the animal promptly used the other, unparalyzed limb to solve the problem. The paralysis following operation was, of course, to be expected. The interesting point was that, upon being paralyzed, the animals immediately transferred the habit learned with one hand to the other.

This observation has been repeated in rats and in a variety of ways (Peterson, 1938; Peterson and Barnett, 1961). The rat does the same thing as the monkey. Moreover, the result occurs when the animal originally learns with his preferred hand and a lesion is made in the contralateral cortex. It does not take much of a lesion to produce this result. Relatively small lesions that impose a hardly perceptible paralysis cause the transfer. And it is reversible if a larger lesion is made on the side opposite to the first lesion.

BAR PRESSING

Bar-pressing behavior of the sort required in a Skinner box is very close in difficulty to the simple locomotor behavior of Lashley's double-pedal box. This, we have seen, does not depend importantly on the cerebral cortex. Relatively large cortical lesions do not impair the learning of a simple pedal or bar-pressing habit.

The student of animal learning will know that in recent years bar pressing has most often been used to study the effects of schedules of reinforcement. There are several ways in which schedules may be arranged, but one of them is the fixed-interval schedule. In such a schedule, the animal is reinforced at fixed intervals regardless of how often he pushes in the meantime. All he must do is make at least one push during the interval. In fact, however, animals typically make a number of responses, and the frequency of their responses increases—their bar pressing speeds up—as the time approaches when they are to be rewarded. In an accumulative graph, this gives a scalloped effect (see Figure 18.3). The curve rises slowly at the beginning of an interval, increasing in slope up to payoff time, and then drops back to a low rate.

The effects of several different lesions on the shape of the bar-pressing function have been studied. In monkeys (Weiskrantz, 1953; see Pribram, 1962), lesions of the prefrontal cortex have been compared with control resections of the frontal lobe and with normal animals. Only the prefrontal lesions make a difference. Such a lesion does nothing significant to the general level of bar pressing. It does, however, change the shape of the slope. In prefrontal animals, the scallop is considerably flattened out (see Figure 18.3). What this means is that the animals lose their sense of timing. They respond almost at the same rate, though not entirely so, throughout the interval. The control and normal animals, on the other hand, anticipate the moment of reward by responding more rapidly as that time approaches. This effect of frontal lesions corresponds with other deficits of frontal-lobe animals to be discussed in a later section of this chapter.

The same sort of bar-pressing function has also been studied in amygdalectomized animals (Schwartzbaum, 1960a, 1960b). In this case, there is an effect, but it is not on the distribution of responses. Rather, it concerns the amount of food given at the end of the two-minute period between reinforcements. The normal animal is sensitive to the size of reward. If the amount of reward is increased, the scallop of responding—the crescendo—becomes steeper. This is not the case with amygdalectomized animals. These animals are relatively insensitive to changes in the amount of reward. This is in accord with the fact that such animals also are less affected by the amount of hunger deprivation.

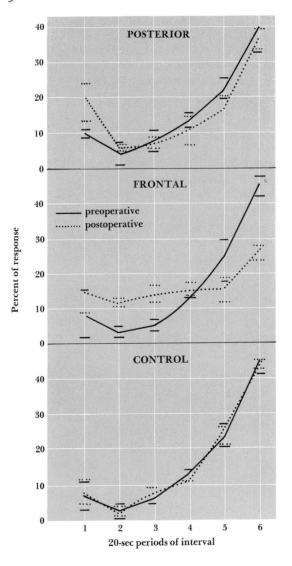

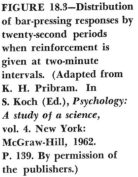

FIGURE 18.3—Distribution of bar-pressing responses by twenty-second periods when reinforcement is given at two-minute intervals. (Adapted from K. H. Pribram. In S. Koch (Ed.), *Psychology: A study of a science,* vol. 4. New York: McGraw-Hill, 1962. P. 139. By permission of the publishers.)

HYPOTHESIS BEHAVIOR

Mazes or discrimination apparatuses may be so constructed that there is more than one way to solve them. Alternate pathways to a goal may be provided. Or different cues, say a visual cue versus a right-left spatial cue, may be available for reaching the goal. Much of this work, now some years old, was done by Krechevsky, and he chose to use the term *hypothesis* to refer to behavior in which an animal rather consistently employed one cue, or one kind of response, over other alternatives. His terminology has therefore been followed here, even though it is doubtful that rats employ hypotheses in the sense human beings do.

SPATIAL VERSUS VISUAL HYPOTHESES—In Krechevsky's first experiment (1933), he demonstrated that rats tend to have different hypotheses in running a maze that offers alternative routes to the goal. Some react consistently to spatial cues, some to visual cues, and some use both. This was determined by analyzing the pattern of turns made by each animal on each trial in the maze.

The next question investigated was the effect of cortical lesions on such hypothesis behavior (Krechevsky, 1935). Lesions of various sizes were placed at different locations on the cortex so that the whole cerebral cortex was explored. The conclusion was that cortical lesions reduce the number of hypotheses employed by rats. Whereas normal animals tend to use both visual and spatial hypotheses and to vary from one to another, animals with cortical lesions are inclined to take one hypothesis and stick to it.

The reason for this became clear when the brains were studied anatomically. One cortical area, which corresponded fairly exactly with the striate area, was responsible for the visual hypothesis. When it was removed, animals shifted to the use of spatial hypotheses. On the other hand, an area a little in front of center on the cortex was crucial for spatial hypotheses. Animals with this area destroyed preferred to use visual hypotheses.

The same maze used in these investigations can be arranged to study a type of intensity discrimination simply by placing lights over correct alleys and eliminating spatial cues. Two investigators (Krechevsky, 1936; Ghiselli, 1938) have done that. One used small lesions of about 10 or 12 percent, in most cases overlapping the visual area. The other used considerably larger lesions, up to 55 percent, distributed over the entire cortex.

Both investigators found, strangely, that lesions anywhere in the cortex interfered with the learning of the brightness discrimination. The finding is strange because Lashley found (see page 200) that *no* cortical lesions retarded the original *learning* of a brightness discrimination. Even more interesting is the fact that there was a correlation of .80 between retardation in rate of learning and the size of the cortical lesion, its locus being of no importance (Ghiselli, 1938). This is mass action again. The reasons for the discrepancy between these results and those of Lashley are still not clear.

SINGLE ALTERNATION—One of the curious things about rat behavior, discovered years ago (Dennis and Sollenberger, 1934), is that a rat tends not to repeat its responses. If it has gone into one alley on one trial, it will tend to go into another one on another trial. In a simple T maze, where both sides are rewarded, this tendency is evidenced in simple alternation behavior. Normal animals tend to alternate their choice of right or left about 80 percent of the time.

This particular behavior has been studied in rats with cortical lesions (Morgan and Wood, 1943). In general, animals with such lesions reduce their variability and tend more often than normals to repeat the last response made, thereby adopting simple position habits. However, this effect is more pronounced in animals with frontal lesions; all animals with such lesions adopted stereotyped behavior. Some animals with parietal lesions did so too, but those with occipital lesions continued a high degree of alternation.

Besides the frontal lobes, the hippocampus somehow is involved in spontaneous alternation (Roberts et al., 1962). Rats in which hippocampal lesions are made have their alternation rate reduced to chance levels.

VARIABLE PATHS—The degree of stereotyping versus variability of behavior may also be studied in block mazes so arranged that any one of several paths may lead the animal to the goal. The effects of lesions in such an apparatus have been investigated (Krechevsky, 1937a, 1937b, 1937c). Without going into details, we may note that cortical lesions reduce variability of behavior and increase its stereotyping. Even relatively minor injuries to the cortex may cause increased stereotyping. In general, there is a mass-action effect; the degree of stereotyping correlates with the size of the lesion. The exact results obtained, however, depend on the particular way in which the block maze is designed.

REASONING

Several years ago one investigator (Maier, 1932) devised a problem for rats that he considered to involve reasoning ability. It has been questioned whether the problem actually involves reasoning in the sense used in human behavior. At any rate, normal rats can solve the problem a good percentage of the time, and the effect of cortical lesions on ability to solve it has been studied.

The problem was this: Rats were first allowed to explore thoroughly a three-table arrangement until they became familiar with all parts of it. Then they were allowed to feed on one of the three tables. Afterward, they were placed on one of the other tables. Screens prevented the animal from seeing where the food was or where he had just been. The rat was forced to put together its knowledge of the maze with its previous experience of feeding on one table in order to go immediately to the correct table.

Rats subjected to cortical lesions could not solve the problem nearly as well as normal rats. Very small lesions of less than 10 percent made little difference, but lesions greater than 18 percent—an area roughly equivalent to the size of the striate cortex—completely abolished the ability. The lesion did not have to be in any particular locus to have this effect. Thus, whatever the task involved, be it reasoning or not, it is extremely sensitive to a lesion anywhere in the cortex. And the lesion does not have to be very large.

PREFRONTAL–LOBE FUNCTION

In 1935, Jacobsen made the now classical discovery that the prefrontal areas of monkeys have a unique function. After lesions of these areas, monkeys were unable to perform a task in which a delay of several seconds occurs between the time the animal is shown the cue for making a response and the time he is permitted to make the response. Because delay is the important element in the problem, the task has been called the *delayed-response* problem. In the years since Jacobsen's discovery, many variations of the problem have been employed, as we shall see, and in most variations Jacobsen's finding has been upheld. Prefrontal animals are usually unable to solve the delayed-response problem (see Warren and Akert, 1964).

In recent years, a special variety of delayed response, namely, delayed alternation, has frequently been employed. In delayed alternation, an animal must make a response, say "right," after a period of delay, which is the opposite of the response, say "left," made before the delay. Prefrontal animals are usually unable to solve this problem when the delay is several seconds.

LOCALIZATION OF FUNCTION

After Jacobsen's discovery, attention immediately turned to the question of how well localized this particular function is. Very early it was established that lesions of the temporal lobe (Jacobsen and Elder, 1936) do not impair the delayed response, and this has subsequently been confirmed several times (see below). Similarly, it was established that the lesions of the motor and premotor areas have no effect on the delayed response, although they do, of course, cause other symptoms (Jacobsen and Haslerud, 1936). Later comparisons of the effects of posterior and of frontal lesions have been made (Harlow et al., 1952). In these experiments and in others, animals have frequently been trained in visual discriminations as well as in delayed response. Although posterior lesions may impair slightly and transiently performance on a delayed response, the effect is not nearly as devastating as a prefrontal lesion. Similarly, although prefrontal animals sometimes show slight and transient losses in discrimination, the effect of prefrontal lesions is not nearly so marked as those of posterior lesions (Harlow and Dagnon, 1943). Thus it is now definitely established that a significant disturbance of delayed-response performance is limited to prefrontal lesions.

Research in recent years has attempted to determine more precisely the parts of the prefrontal areas, as well as the subcortical structures with which they are related, most directly concerned in delayed-response tasks and some related tasks that will be described below. Many types of lesions, large and small and placed both unilaterally and bilaterally in different positions of the prefrontal areas, have been made. The following is a summary of the results of such research:

UNILATERAL LESIONS—Hemicerebrectomies have some effect on delayed response, for such animals are slower than normals in learning it (Kruper et al., 1961), but in general unilateral lesions, large or small, have little effect (Meyer et al., 1951). For lesions to impair markedly or to destroy ability to solve the delayed-response task, they must be bilateral. Hence all further statements will refer to bilateral lesions or operations.

MIDLATERAL AREAS—Large, radical lesions of the prefrontal areas are usually more damaging than smaller lesions, although this depends somewhat on the particular behavioral methods used (see Rosvold et al., 1961). It appears that all the prefrontal areas make some contribution to delayed-response performance. However, some areas are more important than others. Lateral lesions, as distinguished from either dorsal or ventral lesions, have the most effect, but within the lateral areas, the midlateral seems to be somewhat more important than the dorsolateral (Pribram et al., 1952; Mishkin, 1957). It is to be emphasized, however, that, although these areas are the ones most concerned, sizable lesions in other parts of the prefrontal areas, such as anterofrontal (Mishkin and Pribram, 1956) and the frontal eye fields (Pribram, 1955), also have measurable and usually long-lasting effects on delayed response and delayed alternation.

SUBCORTICAL STRUCTURES—Following the demonstration of the role of the prefrontal areas in delayed response and alternation, some interest (but not a great deal) has been shown in subcortical centers associated with the prefrontal areas. Two important structures are the caudate nucleus, which has extensive interconnections with the prefrontal areas, particularly to the ventrolateral portion of the lobe, and the dorsomedial nucleus of the thalamus which projects to the midlateral portion of the lobe (Blum, 1952; Pribram et al., 1952).

Lesions have been made in both of these subcortical structures. Curiously enough, lesions of the dorsomedial nucleus, which might be expected to be deleterious because of their projection to the midlateral frontal lesions, have no effect on delayed response or alternation (Peters et al., 1956; Chow, 1954). On the other hand, lesions of the caudate nucleus are not as harmful to delayed alternation as large frontal lesions, but they do abolish delayed response (Dean and Davis, 1959) and delayed alternation for delays of more than five seconds (Battig et al., 1960). With training, the monkeys are able to exceed mere chance to about 70 percent correct, but they never perform as well as normal or operative control animals. These results are somewhat paradoxical because the caudate nucleus projects to an area whose ablation makes less difference than the projection area of the dorsomedial. Relatively little research, however, has been done on this problem, and it may be that further research will modify and clarify these conclusions.

TRANSCORTICAL CONNECTIONS—If, as the above experiments seem to indicate, subcortical projections are not critically important, possibly transcortical connections are. This is a traditional problem that has been raised before in a number of settings. The usual approach to it has been to compare the effects of circumcision of the cortex—cutting it off from surrounding cortex—with either removal of cortex (lobectomy) or a cutting of the projection fibers to the cortex (lobotomy). This experiment has been done for the prefrontal areas (Wade, 1952).

Preoperatively, monkeys were trained on a variety of problems: multiple latch box, a rake problem, a conditional discrimination, and a delayed response. Three groups of animals were compared: prefrontal lobectomy, prefrontal lobotomy, and prefrontal circumcision. None of these operations affected performance on any problem except the delayed response. In the case of the delayed response, the lobotomized and lobectomized groups were unable to perform above chance level on delays of five seconds. That was to be expected. On the other hand, circumcision of the cortex had no appreciable effect on the delayed response. This result points to the importance of the connections between the prefrontal areas and subcortical structures.

There is, then, a not-too-clear picture of the antomical basis of prefrontal defects. What is clear is that the prefrontal areas are uniquely important in these defects and that, within this region, some areas, particularly the mid-lateral, are more critical than others. It also appears that the connections between the prefrontal areas and subcortical structures, rather than transcortical connections, are important but, beyond that, the picture is still muddied.

The remainder of this discussion of the prefrontal areas will be concerned with the nature of the psychological deficit. Why are prefrontal monkeys unable to solve delayed-response and alternation problems? What is the nature of the impairment caused by prefrontal lesions?

MEMORY FUNCTIONS

On the basis of the limited data Jacobsen had in his early studies, he concluded that the underlying loss in prefrontal deficit was of *immediate memory*. Because the animals failed to solve problems involving delay, while being quite competent in other tasks, particularly discriminations, it would appear that their difficulty was in remembering something over a brief period of time.

This hypothesis was soon put to a test (Finan, 1939). Prefrontal monkeys were run in several kinds of problems in which an immediate memory of recent events was required for the animals to make the correct choice. In one problem, modified from the conventional shuttle box, the monkeys had to shuttle from one grill to another after a delay of several seconds following a signal. In another, they learned a temporal maze in which one route took a longer time than the other. Both prefrontal and normal monkeys solved these problems. At the same time, prefrontal animals failed the delayed response. The conclusion therefore seemed justified that, whatever was wrong with prefrontal monkeys, it was not simply a matter of immediate memory. They had demonstrated in other situations that they had such memory. There must be some other basis of the difficulty with the delayed reaction.

ATTENTIVE FUNCTIONS

An alternative cause of prefrontal deficits might be a disturbance of attention. Perhaps the prefrontal animal has trouble paying "attention" to the predelay cue; that is to say, perhaps he does not note well where the food is placed to begin with and therefore has nothing to remember during the delay interval. Several experiments of somewhat different sorts lend some credence to this hypothesis, although, as we shall see, attentional difficulties do not seem to be the whole story.

PREDELAY REINFORCEMENT—In the traditional procedure of Jacobsen, the monkey was shown which of two cups was baited. After the delay, he had to choose the cup previously baited. One possible way to make the monkey pay better attention to the correct stimulus was to give him some food, that is, a predelay reinforcement, from the same cup that would also be correct after the delay. This was tried (Finan, 1942). And, as might be expected on the hypothesis of a disturbance of attentional functions, prefrontal monkeys were able to solve it. Thus, the first ammunition was gathered for the "attentional" hypothesis.

SEDATIVES—If one observes prefrontal monkeys, they appear to be more distractable and less attentive than normal monkeys. Perhaps they do not attend because they are too "jumpy and distractable." One way to lessen their distractability is to slow them down a little with a sedative. Accordingly, the effects on prefrontal monkeys of a sedative in less than anesthetic doses was studied (Wade, 1947). The hypothesis was confirmed. Prefrontal animals under light sedation could solve the delayed-response problem. This experiment has been repeated, and although some retraining is typically involved, sedatives have usually improved the delayed-response scores of prefrontal monkeys and baboons (Pribram, 1950; Mishkin et al., 1953). There is one negative report (Blum et al., 1951), but this may have been due to insufficient training under the sedative. The use of insulin and of environmental cooling for three hours before testing also improves the scores of prefrontal animals while "pep pills" of Benzedrine cause the animals to stop responding in the situation (Pribram, 1950).

INTERVENING DARKNESS—Another way to test the attentional hypothesis is to keep animals in the dark during the delay period. If they cannot remember because they cannot "keep their mind on the task," distractions would be considerably reduced by giving them nothing to look at during the delay period. This experiment was made, with results fitting the hypothesis (Malmo, 1942). With darkness during the delay, prefrontal monkeys could solve the delayed-response problem.

REACTION TIME—Also fitting in with the idea that prefrontal animals have attentional difficulties are the results of a rather simple reaction-time test (Harlow and Johnson, 1943). A piece of food was exposed to the monkey for a given number of seconds. If the animal did not take it in the time allowed, he lost it. For reasonable time limits, both normal and prefrontal animals can make the response. When, however, the time limit is reduced to one second, normal animals can still react in time, but prefrontal animals cannot.

SPATIAL FACTORS

There is justification for the conclusion that some sort of disturbance of attention is involved in prefrontal lobectomy. This, however, is not saying a great deal. Just what aspects of attention are disturbed? Exactly how is the prefrontal animal handicapped? Attempts to answer such questions have led to a variety of experiments. Such experiments indicate more specifically some of the deficits suffered by prefrontal animals.

One such deficit has to do with the spatial aspects of the delayed-response and alternation problems. In traditional research with these problems, the animal is required to remember *where* the correct goal lies. In delayed response, he is shown *where* the food is to be found following the delay. And in delayed alternation, he must know *where* it is because it will be in the opposite position, right or left, from the place he last found food. Perhaps prefrontals have some difficulty with remembering *where* things are.

GO–NO-GO—To test this hypothesis, a go–no-go delayed-response problem was devised and compared with the traditional left-right problem. In go–no-go, there is a single cup, not two, and the animal is shown before the delay whether or not there will be food in the cup after the delay. To show the monkey which it is, the experimenter either baits the cup in view of the monkey, then covers it over, or shows the monkey his empty hand before covering it. The problem for the animal, after the delay, is either to reach for food or not to reach, depending on what he saw before the delay.

A comparison of the two procedures on prefrontal monkeys gives a clear-cut result (Mishkin and Pribram, 1956). Prefrontal animals can perform in the go–no-go situation when they fail as expected on the traditional procedure.

The same result has been obtained when the problem is one of delayed alternation, the animal "going" on one trial and not on the next (Mishkin and Pribram, 1955). Results with go–no-go procedures in the prefrontal chimpanzee are similar to those obtained in the monkey (Rosvold et al., 1961).

Incidentally, the prefrontal animals are not perfect on the go–no-go, and most of their mistakes occur on the no-go trial. They reach for food when they should not. This indicates some difficulty with "not responding," which is in line with studies of conditioning and the prefrontal cortex (see page 451).

OBJECT VERSUS POSITION—Sparked by the finding that prefrontal animals can solve delayed-response problems when they must know *whether* rather than *where* to go, further efforts to vary spatial and nonspatial aspects of the test situation were made. Actually, many years ago it was shown that prefrontal monkeys could perform on delayed matching-from-sample tasks (Spaet and Harlow, 1943). If presented with a sample object, they could choose this object from a pair of different objects after a delay. However, in this study, predelay reinforcement was also used, and ability to solve the problem may have depended more on that than on the fact that objects were used. Therefore it still seemed wise to see whether prefrontal animals might do better with *objects* to remember during the delay than with spatial position.

To follow up this lead, monkeys were trained on object alternation. This is like a delayed alternation except that objects rather than right-left positions are the cues. Each time one of two different objects is correct, but the animal must alternate from trial to trial, with delays between trials, in picking the object. The results turned out to be disappointing, at least for the hypothesis that the prefrontal defect is spatial (Pribram and Mishkin, 1956). The problem is not an easy one, and all operates have trouble with it, but temporal animals can perform above the 80 percent point while anterofrontal animals do about as badly on this task as they do on delayed alternation. Hence one cannot conclude that the prefrontal deficit is confined to spatial discriminations. In a two-choice situation, it extends to objects as well as to spatial position.

The prefrontal animal, on the other hand, undoubtedly has more trouble with spatial factors than the normal animal. This has been demonstrated by comparing him with normals in a simple visual discrimination in which the separation of the stimulus objects is varied (French, 1962). Both normal and prefrontal animals have increasing difficulty as the objects are moved farther apart, but the prefrontal animals have more difficulty with increasing separations than normal animals do.

REVERSAL LEARNING

There are still other aspects of the deficit suffered by prefrontal animals. In some of the experiments with rats, it appeared that prefrontal rats in simple linear mazes made more errors of anticipation (Carpenter, 1952) and of perseveration (Maher, 1955) than normal rats. It was hard to interpret these results, but they suggested that the prefrontal deficit might include some rigidity of behavior or some resistance to doing things differently from the procedure learned in the past.

This hypothesis was put to test by using reversal-learning problems. In these, animals are taught a simple discrimination, or a simple pattern of responses in a maze, and then are required to learn exactly the opposite of the responses they first learned. A task of this sort has been used with prefrontal rats (Bourke, 1954) and with monkeys (Brush et al., 1961). In each case, the prefrontal animals had more difficulty with the reversal learning than normal animals even though they were comparable to normals on original learning.

REWARD

As research has proceeded, it is apparent that there are several aspects of prefrontal deficit. There is not space here to mention them all. The last general point to be covered here is the effects of the conditions under which reward is administered.

It has long been known (Hull, 1943) that the time of presenting a reward affects rate of learning. In general, if reward is delayed after the performance of a response, learning is slowed. And the greater the delay, the slower the learning. This is true of the normal animal, but it is even more true of the prefrontal preparation (Mishkin and Weiskrantz, 1958). Actually, prefrontal monkeys can master problems involving delay of reward, but the delay must be gradually lengthened from 0 to several seconds for them to perform well at the longer delays, say of eight seconds. If the shift is made abruptly, normal animals continue to perform, but the prefrontals do not. Hence there appears to be a deficit here, although it is only a mild one.

Last to be mentioned is the question whether it makes any difference in prefrontal animals whether the motivation for performing is a reward or a punishment. Prefrontal monkeys have been compared with normals on delayed response and delayed alternation when food reward or shock is the motivation (Miles and Rosvold, 1956). Prefrontal animals do not differ from normals in this respect. Thus the fact that food reward rather than shock has been used in most experiments on prefrontal function appears to be of no significance.

19 BRAIN DISORDERS

<hr>

UP TO THIS POINT in the book, virtually everything we have considered has dealt with animals as subjects. This, as we have repeatedly pointed out, is because people cannot be employed as subjects for surgical and most other physiological methods of experimentation. We have, however, occasionally referred to data collected from human subjects suffering from disorders of brain or glandular function. In this chapter we shall make such disorders, and specifically brain disorders, our main subject of study. We shall do this in order to bring into focus what is known about the psychological functions of the human brain and also because there are a number of facts that, for one reason or another, it was not convenient to consider in other chapters.

The chapter will not be long, because knowledge is limited. In fact, much of what we say will point up how little is known in this area and why there is difficulty in drawing firm conclusions in it. In addition to the new material introduced in the chapter, it will serve as a means of summarizing various points made throughout the book.

FACTORS IN IMPAIRMENT

The study of the psychological effects of brain disorders is a study of impairment, for injuries or lesions to the brain almost without exception cause impairment if they have any effect at all. There are a number of factors that enter into any such impairment. Some are sources of confusion; others are interesting in their own right. Among the sources of confusion are (1) inability, usually, to know exactly the nature and extent of the injury to the brain and (2) often a lack of knowledge of the patient's behavior before the lesion that would otherwise permit comparisons of before and after. These are rather obvious difficulties for which there usually is no remedy. Other important factors that determine whether impairment occurs or whether it can be assessed are described in the following sections.

VARIATIONS IN STRUCTURE

One factor is individual differences in the structure of brains. Just as people have different shapes of faces and bodies, so their brains vary in both gross and microscopic structure (Lashley, 1947). The positions of the primary fissures and sulci certainly vary from one person to another. So, too, do the shapes and sizes of some of the major gyri and convolutions. Such individual differences enter the clinical picture. In two different individuals, lesions that sometimes appear to involve exactly the same regions of the brain may actually involve somewhat different functional areas. If the lesions do not produce the same impairments, the difference may be due to individual differences in the size and shape of parts of the brain.

FUNCTIONAL DUPLICATES

Another problem is to distinguish between functional and organic states. Many of the symptoms seen in brain damage can also occur in individuals with normal brains. Stage fright may make a person just as speechless as he sometimes is after certain brain lesions. In hysteria and neurotic disorders, there are sometimes cases of inability to recall names of familiar persons or objects—the same kind of inability that occurs in some brain injuries. Moreover, even where there is brain disorder, it frequently has its functional consequences. People seldom suffer brain damage without it rather seriously affecting their lives—their personal relationships, finances, employment, and so on. These may cause psychological symptoms of impairment or change quite apart from the direct effects of brain damage. The functional and organic causes of change are thus difficult to separate.

INDIVIDUAL DIFFERENCES

Individual differences among people often are related to the effects of brain disorders. We have previously seen (page 512) that bright rats are less affected by a brain lesion of a given size than dull rats. This sort of relationship sometimes, but not always, may occur in human brain injuries (but see Weinstein and Teuber, 1957). Besides general intelligence, people differ somewhat in their specific abilities. Some are high on visual factors, others on motor factors, others on verbal factors, and so on. Such individual differences may affect the kind and degree of impairment caused by brain injury.

MOTIVATION AND TRAINING

Two related factors affecting impairment in brain disorders are motivation and training. Lack of motivation may sometimes make a person act as though he had a brain lesion. And people in hospitals are usually not very highly motivated—except possibly to get out—and behavior deficits due to lack of motivation may mistakenly be assigned to a brain lesion. Even where there is such a lesion, however, motivation may be a factor in the degree of impairment shown. Lashley (1938) tells the story of a patient, for example, who seemed to have lost a good deal of memory for language after a brain operation. The hospital staff, in fact, was trying to teach the patient the alphabet again. After 900 repetitions the patient was still failing. All he needed, however, was a little incentive, for when offered a bet of some cigarettes that he could not learn the alphabet, he promptly learned it perfectly in 10 trials and remembered it until he collected his bet.

As this story implies, people with brain injuries nearly always are capable of some retraining. As we shall see below, there seems to be some recovery of function without retraining but, in addition, an impairment usually can be effaced partially by practice or training following the injury. This means that when an attempt is made to assess the nature and degree of impairment the assessment will depend on the amount of the retraining that has taken place between the time of the injury and the time of the assessment. Since motivation, or at least some effort, is required for a person to relearn what he has lost through injury, the two factors of motivation and training are interlocked.

RECOVERY OF FUNCTION

After a brain lesion, there may be great losses of memory, but memory may gradually come back in the course of time. Sometimes even after severe lesions, recovery is so great that one would hardly know that the patient had

had a brain injury. The same thing may be true of motor coordination and skills. To understand the processes involved in such recovery of functions has long been a problem.

RETRAINING—In many cases, the recovery of function after an injury is quite slow and there is plainly an opportunity for the patient to relearn. On the other hand, memories previously obliterated by cerebral damage may suddenly reappear weeks or months after the injury occurred. What is the reason for this? Is the recovery spontaneous or the result of relearning experiences prior to the recovery?

It is difficult to keep an organism, particularly a human being, in a situation in which he cannot learn. Therefore it is virtually impossible to separate experimentally the effects of training from those of spontaneous recovery. In all probability, however, much of recovery from the effects of brain damage can be ascribed to retraining. Sometimes the individual does not practice the particular skill that recovers. Rather he practices something related to it, and the recovery is a transfer effect.

This last point can be illustrated by an old experiment with monkeys (Klüver, 1933). The monkeys were trained before operation to make various sensory discriminations. In these discriminations, they reacted by pulling a string attached to the "correct" box. After relatively small lesions in several different areas of the brain, the animals appeared to have a complete amnesia for all the habits. They pulled strings and boxes at random, no matter what discrimination was asked of them. The forgetting, however, seemed to be a general affair—one of "comparing" and "choosing" between two stimuli— rather than a loss of a specific habit. When the animals were retrained on just one of the discrimination habits, they were able without any further training to make the other discriminations that they seemed to have forgotten after the operation.

MECHANISMS OF RECOVERY—Let us assume then that recovery from the effects of a brain injury is chiefly a matter of practice or retraining, allowing for transfer to take place from the relearning of one skill to the recovery of another. We may now go on to ask, How is it possible for a memory or skill lost through injury to be recovered through training? Why is not impairment permanent? Two different, though related, proposals have been made about the answer to this question.

One relies on the concept of *vicarious function*. According to this notion, almost any part of the brain can, if necessary, take over a function lost because of injury in some other part. This assumes that functions are not very well localized in the brain, which is true. Another idea is that of *equipotentiality*, a concept introduced previously (page 512). This assumes that certain functions are localized in certain systems but that the parts of a system may take over the functions of that system if they remain after an injury to another part. This idea is probably closer to the truth than the first, for the possibilities of recovery are not unlimited, and if the major portion of a system is destroyed, insofar as a system can be identified, there is relatively little recovery.

MASS AND RECOVERY—Adding support to this conclusion are the facts concerning mass of a lesion and the degree of recovery. The two are inversely related; the larger the lesion, the less is the recovery of the functions impaired by the lesion. We have seen this to hold true in animal experiments, and it seems also to be true of injuries to the human cerebral cortex.

AGE

The age at which a brain injury is sustained is a factor in the degree and kind of impairment caused by the brain injury. This is seen in a comparison of individuals injured at birth or in early infancy with individuals receiving their injuries in adolescence or adulthood. The difference between these two groups, other things being equal, depends, however, on the kind of capacities measured.

As we have seen in discussing both the senses and motor functions, brain lesions occurring in infancy have less incapacitating effects than those made in adulthood. The sensory losses sustained by lesions in the primary sensory areas and the paralysis suffered by lesions in the motor areas are much less severe when the injury occurs in infancy than when it occurs later. This same general rule applies also to human beings.

However, in the case of the kinds of intellectual abilities measured by an intelligence test, it is a different story. In the first place, the effect of brain injury on overall intelligence is greater when the injury occurs early than when it occurs later in life (Bryan and Brown, 1957). In the second place, if tests of intelligence are broken down into verbal and nonverbal items, there is another difference. Those injured early show impairment on both verbal and nonverbal items, whereas those injured in adolescence show impairment only on nonverbal items, so long as the injury is not specifically in "speech areas" (Hebb, 1942).

The explanation of these findings appears to lie in the difference between learning ability and the retention of things already learned. Injuries occurring early in life impair learning ability, and this impairment affects the development of all skills. More specifically, learning of nonverbal skills underlies verbal learning, for words stand for other things, acts and experiences. Consequently, a general impairment of learning ability affects the development of language as well as nonlinguistic skills. On the other hand, once language is acquired, a brain injury may impair the skills necessary for its acquisition without impairing its present function.

LATERALITY OF FUNCTION

The brain is symmetrical. The left side is like the right. That raises the question of the equivalence of the two sides. Do we need both sides or will one serve? Do we normally use both sides or only one? If we use one and lose it, can the other take over the job? Clues to the answers to these questions come from both behavior and from neurological disorders.

For each of the things we do, most of us have a major side and minor side. We write, throw balls, and carry objects with our right hands. A few, of course, are left-handed. Some are "switch hitters"; they can use either hand, but these are relatively few. Most show some *laterality* of function. This is also true, it will be recalled (page 518), of animals. But in many individuals, the major side is not the same for all activities. Some write with the left hand and throw balls with the right hand, or vice versa. In fact, if several different tests of laterality are considered together, it is found that there is an imperfect correlation among them (Jasper and Raney, 1937; Zangwill, 1960).

These statements about laterality can be applied to the brain. Voluntary behavior, we have seen, is executed through the pyramidal system, and this is almost entirely crossed. If, therefore, the right arm is the major arm, the left motor cortex is the major side of the cortex, for it controls the right arm. Hence, for many skills, there is a simple "crossover" rule.

In speech and in many sensory functions, however, the problem is quite different. These activities are bilateral, not lateral. The vocal cords, the tongue, and the lips are bilateral organs, which are not used in halves but rather all at once. In listening to sounds or in looking at objects, we use both ears or both eyes, as the case may be. Here the "crossover" rule does not work. In these cases, the interesting question arises of whether both sides of the brain are used or only one.

The clinical evidence from brain disorders speaks rather clearly on this question. Psychological functions tend to depend more on one hemisphere than on the other, but there is not a unitary characteristic of cerebral dominance (Zangwill, 1960). That is to say, the side that is dominant for speech may or may not be the side that is dominant for handedness. There is, however, a general tendency for speech to be represented in the left hemisphere, as there is for handedness, even though the two may not be related.

This conclusion is based on the study of individuals with cerebral injuries (Kimura, 1961) and also on a relatively new technique for testing cerebral dominance in speech (Lansdell, 1962). Sodium amytal is injected into the carotid artery on one side, so that one side of the brain is more anesthetized than the other. If the injection causes difficulties in speech, the side of the injection is the dominant side so far as speech is concerned.

It can be seen, then, that one hemisphere or the other tends to be dominant in speech, although there are gradations in cerebral dominance. Usually, the dominant hemisphere is the left hemisphere. Similarly, one side tends to be dominant in nonverbal intellectual functions. This hemisphere is more often the right hemisphere than the left (Reitan and Tarshes, 1959; Piercy et al., 1960). For example, when patients with right-sided lesions are given tests like the Wechsler picture arrangement or block design, they do more poorly than the controls. This is in contrast to those with left-sided lesions who perform as well as the controls (Heilbrun, 1959). In general, it appears that intellectual functions of the two hemispheres are divided so that one side is dominant in verbal activities and the other in nonverbal functions.

This conclusion applies to normal people and to those who have recently sustained cortical injuries. However, if the dominant side, say, for speech is seriously injured, then the formerly nondominant side begins to function and is capable of mediating the acquisition of speech. This is particularly true of individuals in which the dominant side is damaged in childhood (Roberts, 1958). They are able to learn speech, and although their IQs, like those of birth-injured, tend to remain low, they show none of the disabilities of speech observed in individuals suffering recent injuries to the side dominant for speech.

Since the cortex of the two hemispheres is connected by the corpus callosum, it is pertinent to ask whether the corpus callosum plays any role in cerebral dominance. A system of fibers as massive as this ought to have some purpose. Earlier, we saw that in some split-brain preparations discriminations learned with one side do not transfer to the other side (page 506). Similar studies have been made in people whose corpus callosa have been sectioned completely or partially for the purpose of limiting epileptic activity in the brain. These patients were extensively studied with psychological tests before and after the operation. Although some minor differences were found, it is fair to say that no great change, even on the transfer of tasks between the two sides of the body, was found (Smith, 1951). Neither were there other significant effects on learning capacity or memory (Akelaitis, 1944). It was concluded that, in the absence of the corpus callosum, other pathways between the two hemispheres must exist and function to transfer information from one side of the brain to the other.

PSYCHOLOGICAL DEFICIT

In this section, we shall consider the kinds of psychological impairment seen in the brain-injured. For the moment, we shall not be concerned with the locus of lesions. This is often difficult to determine or not even known, and hence we shall deal with that problem in a separate section.

Psychological impairment may be seen in either or both of two ways: clinical symptoms and test performance. For many years, the only guides that neurologists had in their practice were the clinical signs shown by a patient. These consist of pathological changes in EEG or reflexes, of complaints of the patient, or of the more obvious defects in his behavior. In more recent years, with the aid of psychologists, a number of tests have been developed for the purpose of assessing impairments from brain injury.

CLINICAL SYMPTOMS

Leaving aside pathological signs, which are not in our domain, we may classify the clinical signs of impairment seen at one time or another in brain-injured patients into three general categories: sensory and motor disturbances, disturbances of memories and learned skills other than language, and language disorders.

SENSORY AND MOTOR DISORDERS—What there is to say about these has been said at earlier points in the book. When lesions encroach on the primary sensory areas, there is usually some fairly obvious sensory disturbance. The person has a scotomatous area in his visual field, he is unable to make appropriate discriminations in the field of touch, or he has difficulty hearing. The latter, incidentally, is one of the less frequent signs of brain injury. In each case, the symptom corresponds with what would be expected when a primary sensory area of the cortex is damaged. Similarly, lesions of the motor and premotor areas are accompanied by paralyses, flaccid or spastic (page 300), as the case may be.

RECOGNITION AND SKILLED ACTS—Above the level of sensory capacity and at the level of memory is recognition of the meaning of objects. If we see a banana, we know that it is for eating. Or we know that doors are for opening and walking through. Bolts are to fasten things together. Or more generally, we learn what to do, or what we can do, when any particular stimulus is presented to us. The simplest case of recognition of objects occurs in conditioning an animal to respond to a signal or choose one of two stimuli to get food. Even this kind of memory can, of course, become rather complicated in man.

When the ability to recognize certain familiar objects is lost in brain injury, it is called *agnosia*. There are all sorts of agnosias. The main classes are obvious: visual agnosia, auditory agnosia, and tactile agnosia. Theoretically, there may be olfactory and gustatory agnosias, but they seldom are reported as clinical symptoms. On the other hand, there may be rather specific agnosias within a modality, e.g., color agnosia, finger agnosia, form agnosia, and so on. There are names for many agnosias, some of which are given and defined in Table 19.1.

At the same level as recognition of objects but on the motor side is memory for acts and skills. These are matters of putting together particular movements

TABLE 19.1—A brief outline of memory disorders

SENSORY APHASIA

Auditory aphasia (word deafness): difficulty in understanding the meaning of words and language as heard.

Visual aphasia (word blindness, alexia): disturbances of the perception of the meaning of language as read.

MOTOR APHASIA

Manual aphasia (agraphia): difficulty in writing language.

Speech aphasia (word muteness): inability to express language vocally or to think in terms of it. Head distinguishes four types of speech aphasia:

> *Verbal*: "defective power of forming words, whether for external or internal use."
>
> *Syntactical*: "lack of that perfect balance and rhythm necessary to make the sounds uttered easily comprehensible." Articles and prepositions binding words together tend to be dropped or slurred.
>
> *Nominal*: inability to use words as names and failure to appreciate the nominal character of words.
>
> *Semantic*: disturbances of the connected sequence of verbal or written expression.

AGNOSIA: disturbances in the perception of the significance of sensory stimuli or defects of imagination.

Astereognosis: "difficulty in the recognition of objects or forms by touch."

Auditory agnosia: "psychic deafness for noises and music deafness" (sensory amusia).

Visual agnosia: disorders of visual recognition of

1. Objects or pictures.
2. Color—not color blindness or color defect but "difficulty in understanding colors as qualities of objects, a faulty color concept, and an inability to evoke color images."
3. Visual cues orienting the person in space.

APRAXIA: disturbances of the memory of movements.

Limbkinetic: the patient "appreciates the nature of the movement but cannot carry it out with ordinary skill." It is thought to be a loss of innervatory memories for complex forms of movement.

Ideokinetic: a disorder attributed to a break between the kinesthetic processes and others of the brain; consists of loss of memory of how to make movements.

Ideational: faulty conception of the movement as a whole. The patient, for example, is unable to strike a match.

Constructive: "In typical cases the patient experiences difficulty in laying out sticks to copy a given design, in building with blocks, in drawing," and so on.

into a pattern that accomplishes something. A rat or cat put into a latch box learns, for example, to go to one end of the box, pull a string, and push a door with its head. People with brain lesions can forget skills or acts of this sort without becoming paralyzed or showing major signs of motor disorder. When they do so, they are said to suffer from *apraxia,* which means "inability to do things." The apraxic person may, for example, not remember how to do what he has been doing all his life, such as buttoning his shirt, driving a car, opening the door, eating with knife and fork, and so on.

There are different descriptions and names for various apraxias; some are given in Table 19.1. One might note there the definition of *constructive apraxia* as "difficulty in laying out sticks to copy a given design, in building with blocks, in drawing." This kind of apraxia lends itself to systematic testing and is frequently studied in the brain-injured (McFie and Zangwill, 1960).

LANGUAGE DISORDERS—The last level of memory to consider in this connection is that of language. By the term "language," we mean all symbolic stimuli and responses that are learned and used by both people and animals—mainly people. Various sorts of signals and gestures fall within the scope of the term. So do arithmetic, algebra, and higher mathematics. Any item of behavior may be called linguistic behavior if it is a symbol for some other behavior. And any stimulus may be called linguistic if it stands for some other stimulus. It is the symbolism that makes language a higher-order memory function.

Language, of course, has its own levels of complexity. There are alphabets to learn, words to be spelled, names to be learned, words to be put together in sentences. The meaning of words and sentences may merely be recognized, or names of objects may be recalled and words and sentences constructed. Thus linguistic behavior has all the aspects of any other kind of behavior. It is simply a variety of behavior in which man has specialized and which makes up an amazingly large part of his memories as well as his repertoire of adjustments to the world.

Any disorder of language that results from brain injury or disease is called *aphasia.* There are several shades and varieties of aphasia seen in the brain-injured. They are divided into two general categories: the sensory aphasias and the motor aphasias. Sensory aphasias include auditory aphasia, in which there is disability in understanding the heard word, and visual aphasia, sometimes called alexia, which is impairment in reading. On the motor side, any difficulty in speaking is called dysphasia; verbal aphasia refers to some impairment in forming and saying words; and nominal aphasia refers to disability in naming people or objects. For other varieties of aphasia, see Table 19.1.

RELATION BETWEEN LEVELS—The distinctions we have just made between levels of psychological function and kinds of disorder are more easily made in principle than they are in practice. All sorts of patterns of impairment are encountered in patients, and it is not always clear which disabilities are primary and which are secondary. A patient, for example, may have a verbal aphasia; he may not be able to speak words or sentences. He may have his "mind" full of things to say, and he may know what he wants to say, but he may simply be unable to say it. He may prove that fact by writing everything perfectly well. If that is the case, the patient has a true motor aphasia. On the other hand, he may say nothing because he has nothing to say. He may have lost his ability to read, to understand what he hears, to recognize the meaning of objects—he may have a widespread agnosia and sensory aphasia—and thus it may be a sensory rather than a motor disorder that keeps him from talking. For this reason, it is often necessary to use some ingenuity to determine exactly what is wrong.

PSYCHOLOGICAL TESTS

Since World War II, psychologists have become increasingly involved in the diagnosis and care of neuropsychiatric patients, including those with brain damage. This has given them an opportunity to administer tests to thousands of such individuals. Sometimes they have been able to do this both before and after the damage, when the damage is caused by neurosurgery performed to remove cancers or for other therapeutic purposes. Consequently, there is now a veritable mountain of test data on the brain-injured.

These data bear on two kinds of questions. One is the question of what impairments are characteristically found in individuals suffering a brain disorder. A second question is whether psychological tests can be used in the diagnosis of such disorders. We shall discuss each in turn.

IMPAIRMENT—To the extent that different functions are localized in different parts of the brain, to that extent the impairment one finds on psychological tests depends on where the brain injury is. It is not surprising therefore that certain visual tests (page 192) show impairment when the injury is in the visual cortex; the same is true of tactual tests when the injury is in the primary somesthetic cortex. On the other hand, there are several psychological tests that tend to show impairment no matter where the damage is located. One of these is a flicker-fusion test; another is the hidden-figure (Bender-Gestalt) test previously described (page 193); another is a test of spiral aftereffects in which the patient is shown an expanding or contracting spiral and tested for an aftereffect; another is a memory-for-designs test. In fact, most tests that involve any combination of attention, spatial organization, and memory tend to show differences between normal individuals and the brain-damaged (Haynes and Sells, 1963).

DIAGNOSIS—It is one thing to say that the brain-injured typically show impairment on certain tests, and another matter to use tests to determine whether or not a person is brain-injured. In order to do the latter, the tests must be sensitive both qualitatively and quantitatively to the impairments found in the brain-injured. Unfortunately, there are wide individual differences in test performance among normal persons, and so it is difficult to tell whether an impairment is real or simply a matter of individual differences. Brain injury, for example, frequently impairs IQ as measured by a standard intelligence test (Wechsler), yet a low IQ does not necessarily indicate brain injury. Indeed, it usually does not.

This problem has plagued the use of psychological tests for diagnostic purposes. Indeed, performances, on single-variable tests, such as hidden figures or spiral aftereffects, although impaired by brain injury, usually give so many false positives and false negatives that they are of very little use (Haynes and Sells, 1963). Put another way, although these tests are better than chance for picking out individuals with brain injury, they also pick normals as brain-injured, and vice versa, in such numbers that one is never very sure in any individual case about the correctness of diagnosis. Batteries of tests, however, serve considerably better, for here impairment on a number of tests increases the accuracy of prediction. And the use of ratios within the batteries, that is, comparisons of performance among different tests and items, is even better (Bryan and Brown, 1957). Even so, psychological tests are at best only aids that must be interpreted along with other medical information in the diagnosis of brain injury.

BIOLOGICAL INTELLIGENCE—One of the more effective sets of psychological tests for diagnostic purposes is the Halstead Battery of Tests. Halstead (1960, p. 1674) describes his battery as follows:

> The components of the Halstead Battery of Tests consists of a category test (with instantaneous auditory reinforcement of correct and incorrect responses); a tactual form-board test (which is never experienced visually by the subject); a test for critical fusion frequency; a test for auditory flutter-fusion frequency (frequency of interruption at which bursts of white noise fuse subjectively into continuous noise); a speech perception test; a rate of tapping test; and a time-sense memory test (repeated setting of an electric clock with and without the aid of vision).

Out of his work with this test battery, Halstead has developed the concept of biological intelligence. This kind of intelligence is considered to be relatively independent of the usual intelligence tests, which are not especially helpful in diagnosing brain injury. Whereas such tests predict well a person's ability to do school work, the Halstead tests predict with some degree of accuracy the capacities that characterize the normal functioning of the forebrain. From scores made by a patient on the Halstead Battery of Tests, a measure may be computed known as the Halstead Impairment Index of biological intelligence. Halstead believes biological intelligence to involve the frontal lobe more than other parts of the forebrain.

LOCALIZATION OF FUNCTION

The question of the degree to which different psychological functions are localized in the brain has long been the subject of debate. On one side have been those who have believed in a strict localization of function (e.g., Kleist, 1962); they have sometimes been referred to as the "map makers." An example of the kind of map constructed by those taking this view is given in Figure 19.1. On the other side are those who believe there is very little localization of function outside the primary sensory and motor areas (Goldstein, 1939).

The truth appears to lie somewhere between these views. In the first place, some functions seem to have little or no localization, whereas others do. Impairment, for example, on the Bender-Gestalt hidden-figure test does not seem to be associated with lesions in any particular place. On the other hand, impairment in certain kinds of language skills or of tactual recognition has a certain degree of localization. In the second place, even when there is localization, except for primary motor and sensory functions, the localization is not very precise. Relatively large areas, as we shall see, are involved. Evidence on these points comes from the study of individuals with brain lesions and also from instances of direct stimulation of the brain.

FIGURE 19.1—Composite diagram of the supposed association areas of the cerebral cortex of man.

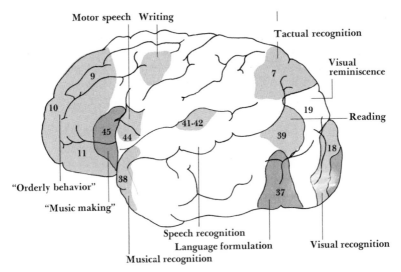

RECEPTIVE DISORDERS

A rough way of classifying disorders seen in the brain-injured is into those that are receptive and those that are expressive (Weisenburg and McBride, 1935). The receptive disorders include the agnosias and the sensory aphasias described earlier. Most studies of individuals with receptive disorders indicate that the lesions are primarily in the posterior part of the cerebral cortex (Conrad, 1954). In Figure 19.2, for example, is a plot of the skull positions of the wounds of a number of brain-injured who exhibited receptive disorders. Nearly all cases fall into the posterior cortex.

We can go even farther and say that there is some localization of different kinds of receptive disorders (Zangwill, 1960). Patients displaying difficulties in visuospatial aspects of language, e.g., reading, more often than not have lesions in the posterior parietal cortex. On the other hand, those that have difficulty with the understanding of words and with those aspects of speech that depend on auditory cues tend to have lesions in the temporoparietal cortex. Nevertheless, the localization is not very definite.

EXPRESSIVE DISORDERS

Expressive disorders consist of the apraxias and motor aphasias, that is, any difficulty in executing acts and speech. The general rule is that patients with such disorders have lesions in the frontal lobes (see Figure 19.2). There are exceptions, but even these do not wander very far from the anterior cortex. In making this statement, however, it is necessary to separate nominal aphasia, which is difficulty in the naming of things, from other varieties of motor aphasia. Lesions causing nominal aphasia are very frequently found in the parietal and temporal cortex. Perhaps this is because the act of naming is

FIGURE 19.2—Localization of lesions in sensory (left) and motor (right) aphasia. (Adapted from K. Conrad. In J. Field, H. W. Magoun, and V. E. Hall (Eds.), *Handbook of physiology*, vol. 3. Washington, D.C.: American Physiological Society, 1960, p. 1718. Reprinted by permission of the publishers.)

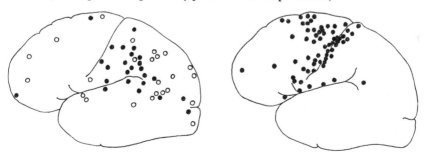

really a complex one that depends on sensory as well as motor capacities and even to a considerable extent on ability to abstract.

BRAIN STIMULATION

It is logical at this point to correlate data obtained by the method of brain stimulation with the above. We have already mentioned (page 271) the use of this method to study the sensory experiences evoked by cortical stimulation. Here there are two additional points to note. One has to do with speech and the other with memories.

Electrical stimulation of the human cerebral cortex, if it affects speech, may cause either an arrest of speech when speech is in progress or an involuntary vocalization (Figure 19.3). The vocalization, when it occurs, is a well-sustained vowel sound that cannot be inhibited voluntarily by the patient. Such vocalization occurs, as might be expected, upon stimulation of the mouth areas of the precentral and postcentral gyrus. This is a pure motor effect. It also sometimes occurs upon stimulation of the dorsal frontal lobe, as indicated in Figure 19.3.

There are also points in the frontal, parietal, and temporal lobes (see Figure 19.3) where speech is arrested, but here the reason does not seem to be an interference with motor activities. Rather, it causes a verbal amnesia, that is, a disturbance of the ability to find or recall words. It has therefore been called an aphasic arrest as distinguished from a speech arrest. The places at which this phenomenon occurs are localized, but the localization is not very precise. Moreover, there are three areas of localization, not just one.

In these studies of the effects of brain stimulation, another interesting result has occasionally been obtained, usually in epileptic patients (Penfield, 1959). This is the induction of memories. Typically, the site of stimulation is the temporal cortex. Upon stimulation, the patient has a flight of images in which he vividly recalls past experiences in his life. The effect is as if the electrode tapped the "neuron record of the past." Why this result is not obtained in all patients is not clear, but it ties in with work on animals reviewed in Chapter 17 and indicates some localization of functions in the temporal cortex.

PREFRONTAL LOBES

No part of the human brain has received more attention in the past thirty years than the prefrontal lobes. This is because surgeons have deliberately removed or undercut these lobes in an attempt to alleviate psychotic conditions, usually schizophrenia, and also in some instances to relieve intolerable pain. In the former case, the theory is that frontal lobes are involved with recent memory (cf. delayed response, Chapter 18) and also with planning functions that are often interlinked with anxiety. These presumably become

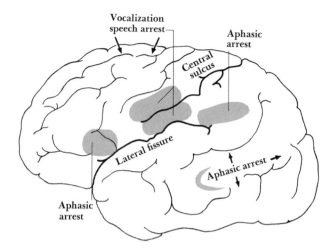

Vocalization
speech arrest

Aphasic
arrest

Central
sulcus

Lateral fissure

Aphasic arrest

Aphasic
arrest

FIGURE 19.3—Summary of areas in which stimulation may interfere with speech. (Adapted from W. Penfield and T. Rasmussen. *The cerebral cortex of man.* **New York: Macmillan, 1950. Reprinted by permission of the publishers.)**

deranged, or overworked, in certain forms of psychosis, particularly those where anxiety and depression are evident, and the situation can be improved by reducing the activity of the prefrontal areas.

The topic is a confusing and controversial one. Only a few facts stand out as being relatively well established. One is that some patients, suffering intolerable pain because of other neurological disorders, are relieved by prefrontal lobotomy or lobectomy (Towe and Ruch, 1960). Another is that the frontal lobes appear to have some special role in biological intelligence; at least, prefrontal damage, more than damage to any other part of the brain, is reflected in a change on the Halstead Impairment Index (Halstead, 1960). On the other hand, systematic administration of many tests before and after operation on the prefrontal lobes yields no consistent and permanent pattern of change (Mettler, 1949). There is, for example, no consistent impairment in capacity to do the delayed-response test, as there is in monkeys. There are, however, detectable intellectual changes if the "right" set of factor-analytic intelligence tests is given (DeMille, 1962). All in all, then, it is not possible to draw any very definite conclusions about the functions of the prefrontal lobes in man.

20 PSYCHOCHEMISTRY

T HE TITLE OF THIS CHAPTER was only recently coined (see Polidora and Bowman, 1963). The term, however, is an appropriate one to cover a wide range of facts and theories relating to biochemical factors in behavior. We have, of course, already seen at various points throughout the book instances in which biochemical and endocrine factors are concerned in behavior. This chapter will round out the study of such factors.

As the coinage of a new term implies, psychochemistry has taken a spurt in recent years. This is largely because of remarkable advances in the biochemical aspects of biology and in the development of psychotherapeutic drugs. These advances hold forth some fascinating possibilities for understanding complex behavior in terms of biochemical events in the nervous system. The field, however, still has a long way to go. Although it possesses some hard facts, it also has a profusion of theories and data that are difficult to sift and to organize into a coherent structure. All this chapter can do is present a picture of some of the more important ideas and facts in the field.

MEMORY TRACE

When an organism learns something, its nervous system must somehow be changed. This change, whatever it may be, has usually been called the memory trace. Sometimes it is spoken of as a connection, for learning appears in the simplest analysis to be the formation of connections. Those interested in brain function have long been trying to determine just what the change is that is represented by this connection or trace (see Morgan, 1943, p. 518). We shall review here some current ideas on this subject.

ELECTROCONVULSIVE SHOCK

First, we must review briefly experiments on the effects of electroshock on memory. These experiments do not bear directly on psychochemistry. They are, however, concerned with the memory trace, and they have some implications for theories of the neural mechanism of the memory trace. Hence they are best discussed at this point in the book.

Electroconvulsive shock (ECS) came into use in the late 1930s as a therapy for certain kinds of disturbed patients. Since that time, psychologists have been studying experimentally the effects of electroshock on learning and memory. There is now a very substantial literature on the subject, most of it on the rat. For our purposes, just a few points will be made.

LEARNING—Earlier experiments sought to establish an effect of electroshock convulsions on learning. The convulsions were induced either before a series of learning trials or interspersed during the course of learning. Many experiments of the first sort found no effect at all on learning. After trying a good many different learning tasks, it finally became apparent that significant effects are obtained on subsequent learning only when the tasks are relatively difficult for the rat (Russell, 1949).

RECENT MEMORY—In an effort to find a situation with a clearer effect of electroshock, experimental conditions were rearranged so that one convulsion was given every day during the course of learning (Duncan, 1949). The learning task in this case was one of simple avoidance and the animal was given only one trial a day. In addition, the time of giving the convulsion during the twenty-four-hour period between trials was varied. It was found that very significant effects were obtained when the convulsion was given within a few minutes after a learning trial, but convulsions given an hour or more after a trial had little effect. The importance of the convulsion being induced shortly after a learning trial has been confirmed in a number of subsequent experiments (e.g., Leukel, 1957).

Two interpretations of this relationship have been made. One is that electroshock impairs recent memory (Duncan, 1949). The other is that electroshock is a kind of punishment that, if it comes close enough to the completion of a learning trial, causes the rat to acquire a fear associated with the trial (Coons and Miller, 1960). Although the matter may not be conclusively settled, it seems as though this second interpretation is incorrect. The argument against it consists of experiments in which ECS (Madsen and McGaugh, 1961) or immediate anesthetization (Pearlman et al., 1961) causes an animal to forget a *punished* response just as it does an *avoidance* response.

CONSOLIDATION THEORY—If the first interpretation is correct, it implies what has come to be called the *consolidation theory* of memory (see Hebb, 1949). According to this theory, the connections or traces formed in learning are not laid down, at least completely, at the time of a learning experience. Rather, something goes on for minutes or even hours afterward, during which the trace is in some way consolidated. There are a number of facts of human and animal learning that fit in with such a theory, but the fact that electroconvulsive shock affects memory only when it comes shortly after a learning trial and not either before the trial or at some later time is the strongest argument for such a theory of the consolidation of memory traces.

It may be mentioned in passing that electroshock may differentially affect memories for different tasks. This was demonstrated dramatically with the conditioned emotional response (see page 447) when it was shown that memory for this response can be obliterated without the bar-pressing habit, on which it is ordinarily superimposed, being affected at all (Hunt and Brady, 1951). In this case, it makes no difference which was learned first (Geller et al., 1955), even though in some instances the convulsions seem to affect recent memory more than older, more established memories. Here the electroshock affects conditioned emotional responses without affecting instrumental bar pressing.

SYNAPTIC CONNECTIONS

Any physiological theory of the memory trace must, then, meet two requirements. The first is to provide an explanation for the simple phenomenon of learning itself. In learning, some sort of connection is formed so that a stimulus or situation not formerly connected with a response acquires the power to evoke that response. The second requirement is that the laying down of such a connection takes some time, at least for it to be complete and permanent. What sort of events in the nervous system could meet these two requirements? There are a good many possibilities (see Morgan, 1943), but two have merited the most attention in recent years.

NEUROBIOTAXIS—The term neurobiotaxis was introduced many years ago by the embryologist Kappers (1921). He was interested in explaining how nervous connections are formed in the embryological development of the organism. There was evidence that stimulation or activity in one part of the nervous system caused fibers to grow toward, and to form connections with, the source of the activity. This idea is applicable to learning as well as to maturation, and it has been employed as a possible explanation of the neural basis of learning (Hebb, 1949). The neurobiotactic theory of learning is that the connecting parts of a neuron grow closer together under the influence of the stimuli involved in learning. When the parts have grown closer together, a connection is made that enables a conditioning stimulus, for example, to evoke a response formerly called forth only by the unconditioned stimulus. Nothing is said about exactly why neurobiotactic growth takes place, but presumably it would take some time and be a response to chemical or metabolic traces left by the learning experience.

SENSITIZATION—Another proposal, based on current knowledge of transmitter action, which is quite different in detail from the neurobiotactic theory, has been called the sensitization theory (Milner, 1961). This assumes that changes take place in presynaptic knobs. These are the knobs containing the synaptic vesicles from which the neurotransmitter is secreted when an impulse terminates in their vicinity. It is assumed that some of these knobs cannot fire until other knobs ending on the same cell also fire. The theory further assumes that when such a knob has been repeatedly fired under these conditions it somehow is sensitized so that in the future it can fire without the companion knob firing. This scheme of things is quite parallel to the paradigm of the conditioning process. The forming of a connection in this way could very well involve local chemical changes and might require time for its consolidation. Moreover, since acetylcholine is the principal transmitter substance in the central nervous system, the theory implies that acetylcholine may somehow be involved in learning. We shall discuss below the role of acetylcholine in learning and memory.

PROTEIN HYPOTHESES

With advancing knowledge in protein chemistry, and particularly in the role played by enzymes in nervous function, attempts have been made in recent years to develop a protein theory of events taking place in learning. The first theory, like earlier ones, assumed that synaptic connections are somehow formed in learning (Katz and Halstead, 1950). It proposed, however, that the lattice structure of proteins in the membranes of neurons was so altered that better conduction or sensitivity resulted. This theory came along before recent breakthroughs in the chemistry of nucleic acids and thus was largely ignored. Today, a similar but more specific theory of memory seems more plausible (Hydén, 1962). In order to explain this theory, it is necessary briefly to summarize the present conception of the nucleic acids (Hurwitz and Furth, 1962).

DNA—The chromosomes, and the genes of which they are made, constitute a biological memory system. They contain all the information necessary for developing a new organism that is like the parent. This information is coded on giant protein molecules of desoxyribonucleic acid (DNA). Each of these consists of two helically wound strands which are comprised in turn of long sequences of complex units called nucleotides (Figure 20.1). A nucleotide consists of a sugar, a phosphate, and a base. Actually, the helical strands consist of a sugar and a phosphate in alternation. The bases connect the two strands like the rungs of a ladder. There are only four bases used as such rungs, but the sequence of the bases formed by the rungs varies. And it is this sequence that contains genetic information.

RNA—Outside the cell in the cytoplasm are some closely related giant molecules, called ribonucleic acid (RNA). Molecules of RNA are the factories that make many sorts of proteins, including the enzymes involved in the body's chemical reactions. Actually, there are two kinds of RNA. One is messenger RNA; the other, transfer RNA. Messenger RNA is formed in the nucleus as a copy of certain aspects of the structure of DNA which serves as a template for making it. This messenger RNA carries information out to the cytoplasm where transfer RNA is formed, again by template action, and this in turn forms proteins.

This is an extremely brief sketch of a mechanism that is now known in considerable detail (Hurwitz and Furth, 1962). For our purposes, two important points should be brought out. First, the activities of a cell, including its development and biochemical functions, are governed by RNA, which in turn receives its instructions from the genetic memory material, DNA. Secondly, the coding of information is contained in the sequences of the bases joining the sugar-phosphate strands. Differences in these sequences and differences in the relative proportions or ratios of the bases constitute different sets of information.

THEORY OF MEMORY TRACE—The idea has been advanced that learning causes certain changes in RNA (Hydén, 1962). According to theory, the novel excitation involved in a learning situation somehow excites bases, causing them to be replaced by other bases so that the "base ratios" change. The RNA, altered in this way, then manufactures different proteins that represent

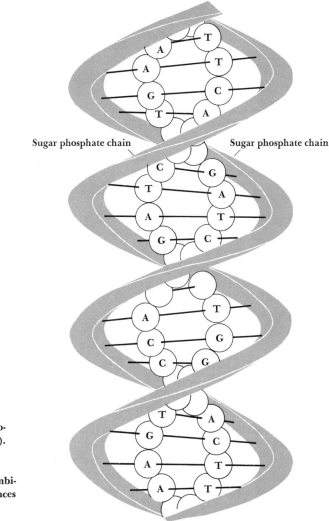

Sugar phosphate chain   Sugar phosphate chain

FIGURE 20.1—A
strand of deoxyribo-
nucleic acid (DNA).
A, C, G, and T are
four kinds of bases
whose different combi-
nations and sequences
encode genetic
information.

the results of a learning experience. These in turn cause neurotransmitters to be excited or activated so that they modify the output of neurons to other neurons and hence change the pattern of firing in a neuronal network. Although developed independently, this scheme fits in with the sensitization theory described above.

The RNA theory, based on firm knowledge of biochemical genetics and protein chemistry, is still relatively new. It is too early to say whether it will be accepted. There are, however, two sets of experiments that lend some credence to it.

EXPERIMENTAL EVIDENCE

One set demonstrates that changes in base ratios may take place in certain parts of the nervous system as a result of "experience" (Hydén, 1962). Whether the "experience" is learning or merely exercise is not clear. Rats were trained to climb a rope. The base ratios of proteins found in a certain vestibular nucleus were measured in rats having this experience and compared with those found in control rats. The ratios were significantly different. It is to be noted, however, that the structure studied was a sensory relay nucleus which has not otherwise been implicated in learning. The difference may prove to be caused by vestibular stimulation. Even so, the result is interesting because it indicates a change due to experience.

Another set of experiments is interesting in its own right. These were made with planaria, a flatworm (Thompson and McConnell, 1955). Planaria have the rare capacity of regenerating missing parts. In fact, if they are cut in two so that the head is separated from the tail, the head section regenerates a new tail, and the tail section regenerates a new head. Presumably this regeneration takes place only through the DNA-RNA template system.

In behavioral experiments designed to exploit this capacity, the worms were first trained in a classical conditioning procedure. The sequence was one of light and shock. After repeated pairings, they acquired a conditioned response of contraction to the presentation of the light. They were then cut in two, and the front and tail halves allowed time to regenerate their missing halves. After that, they were tested again in the conditioning situation. Each of the organisms showed substantial retention of the conditioned response.

This phenomenon, assuming that it is not due to some artifact of procedure, implies something about the memory trace. Although a connectionistic explanation is not impossible, some sort of transfer of information from the old half to the new half seems to be involved. On the assumption that this might be RNA, another follow-up experiment was made (Corning and John, 1961). After conditioning and sectioning, some animals were put in a solution containing ribonuclease during the period of regeneration, while a control group lived during this time in pond water, their natural habitat. Ribonuclease is an enzyme that destroys, or at least degrades, RNA. One might expect this to interfere with memory if RNA is involved in memory. In the case of the tail section, it did so. The organism regenerated from the tail did not show retention of the previously conditioned response. On the other hand, the treatment did not harm the head section. The worm regenerated from this retained the conditioning. Why there was a difference between the two is not explained. But the inhibiting effect on the tail section affords support for the hypothesis that RNA may be concerned in memory.

Neither this experiment nor any one experiment is likely to prove with any conclusiveness the RNA hypothesis. In fact, it will probably take a good many experiments to evaluate the hypothesis. This is because a hypothesis is not proved simply by establishing a correlation between RNA levels and learning or memory. In varying RNA, any number of other things may also be varied, including protein chemistry, metabolic by-products, and even other remotely related biochemical variables. However, such evidence as there is supports the RNA hypothesis. Three further examples of such experiments will be described.

In one, an RNA inhibitor was used (Dingman and Sporn, 1961). In this case, the inhibitor was 8-azaguanine-2C^{14}. This seems to be incorporated into rat brain RNA but, like some other inhibitors (see page 98), make RNA less able to perform its normal functions. When fed to rats that had learned a water maze and learned it well, it had no effect. In other words, it did not affect memory. On the other hand, when fed before learning a maze, it depressed the learning of a new maze.

A second experiment gave more dramatic results (Cook et al., 1963). Rats were injected intraperitoneally each day with a solution of powdered RNA for some days before and during the learning of an avoidance response. The avoidance response was to jump onto a pole when a buzzer sounded. The RNA-treated animals were markedly better than controls at learning this response. They were also much slower to extinguish when an extinction procedure was instituted. In fact, by every criterion, RNA-treated animals learned faster, reached a higher level of performance, and retained this performance longer than control animals.

Another experiment employed the antibiotic puromycin (Flexner et al., 1963). This substance markedly inhibits or suppresses protein synthesis in the cell. For this reason, it was studied to see whether it affects memory. It does, but the circumstances under which it does so are rather restricted. In the first place, it must be injected directly into the brain; subcutaneous injection has no effect. In the second place, it must be administered three to six days after learning has taken place. Given at that time, it blots out a habit (Y maze) previously learned and leaves intact habits learned before or after this particular period. Since there is no good reason for either condition, it remains to be seen whether the experiment has any bearing on the role of protein synthesis in memory traces.

Further work on the relation of proteins, and their constituent amino acids, to learning and intellectual ability is discussed in the next section. At this point, it may be concluded that the RNA hypothesis of learning and memory has much to recommend it, and the data so far available support it, although they do not by any means prove it.

NEUROTRANSMITTERS

Another possible hypothesis about the memory trace is that it involves changes in neurotransmitters. That is to say, as a result of learning, greater supplies of neurotransmitters might be developed and thus make synaptic transmission easier. Such a notion is not incompatible with either the protein hypotheses or the sensitization hypothesis described above. In one case, the RNA might transmit its message by affecting supplies of neurotransmitter. In the other, the sensitization might consist of an augmented secretion of neurotransmitters.

As we saw earlier (Chapter 4), neurotransmitters are of two general types: cholinergic and adrenergic. Of these, only the cholinergic transmitters have been proved to be transmitters within the brain. Although the adrenergic transmitters are established as transmitters in the autonomic system, it is still a question whether they play any transmitter role in the CNS. This statement also applies for the companion biogenic amine, serotonin. On the assumption that they may be central transmitters, or at least integrally concerned in brain metabolism, attempts have been made to correlate drug effects as well as stress effects with changing levels of the biogenic amines. These effects are best discussed in a later section. There is, however, considerable research on acetyl-choline and the hypothesis that it is somehow concerned in the establishment of the memory traces.

The research is by no means satisfactory, and there are contradictions in some of the results (see Polidora and Bowman, 1963). However, certain facts implicating acetylcholine seem reasonably well established (Rosenzweig et al., 1960, 1961). To understand this work, it should be recalled that cholines-terase (ChE) is an enzyme that promptly breaks down acetylcholine after it has been secreted, thus limiting cholinergic influences to the synapse at which it is secreted. It is easier to measure ChE than ACh, and it has been assumed that high ChE activity indicates high ACh activity, an assumption that may not always be true. The following are some of the facts based on this measure-ment and its related assumption:

Strains of rats formerly developed as either bright or dull in a particular maze (Tryon, 1940) were compared for ChE activity of the cortex (see Rozenzweig et al., 1961). The bright strain had the higher ChE activity. On the other hand, when new strains are developed based on the cortical level of ChE so that one strain has a high ChE and the other a low (relatively) ChE, the relationship is reversed. High-ChE strains make more errors on most tests, usually mazes, than low-ChE strains. In still another experiment, ani-mals that had had considerable training on especially difficult problems were compared with those in which there was little or no training. A significantly higher level of ChE activity was found in *subcortical* structures in the highly trained rats than in the naïve ones. This appears to be a demonstration of learning or memory being accompanied by increased levels of ChE and of, inferentially, acetylcholine activity.

Another approach to this general problem is to employ anticholinesterases, that is, substances that inhibit or destroy ChE and thus leave acetylcholine to accumulate in larger than normal amounts (Russell et al., 1961). A substance known as Systox is such a ChE inhibitor. It can be included in the normal diet. Animals were put through an avoidance training procedure and after that an extinction procedure. There was no difference in avoidance training between animals fed Systox and normal controls. However, in extinction, the Systox animals, that is, the low-ChE, high-ACh animals, were much slower in extinction than normal animals.

In summary, there are indications that the metabolism of acetylcholine may be involved with the memory trace, but considerably more research is necessary to clarify the nature of the relationship.

LEARNING AND INTELLIGENCE

No sharp line can be drawn between the material we have just covered and that which we shall consider in this section. The principal difference is that we have been concerned up to now with the theoretical question of what changes in the nervous system underlie learning and memory. At this point, we turn to more practical questions of how biochemical factors influence for good or ill, usually ill, learning and intelligent behavior. Learning and intelligence are grouped together because in human beings learning ability is usually measured with some kind of intelligence test whereas in animals it is customary to employ rate of learning a maze or a problem.

INBORN ERRORS

Two varieties of feeblemindedness are now traceable to genetic defects: mongolian idiocy and phenylpyruvic oligophrenia. These terms will be defined below. The presence of a genetic defect implies some structural or metabolic defect. Since in each case the nervous system appears normal in structure, one may suspect that the linkage is through some alteration of enzyme systems that in turn causes metabolism to be disturbed. In one case, phenylpyruvic oligophrenia, this is certainly true. In mongolian idiocy, it is probably true but it is not yet known exactly how.

MONGOLIAN IDIOCY—The mongolian type of feeblemindedness is called that because individuals who fit this category have certain mongoloid features. Among such features are the epicanthic fold of the eyes that distinguishes Orientals from Caucasians. Such individuals, born to Caucasian parents, usually suffer severe mental retardation.

It was thought for some years that this kind of feeblemindedness was caused by some abnormal conditions of pregnancy, such as a poor circulatory connection between the fetus and mother, with resulting anoxia. Recently, however, it has been shown that the defect is genetic (see Rowley, 1962). Mongols have an extra chromosome in the 21 position. Human chromosomes are numbered from 1 to 22 in order of decreasing length except that the sex chromosomes are designated X and Y (see Human Chromosomes Study Group, 1960). Although further research is necessary to understand the genetic rules underlying mongolism, there now seems little doubt about its being an inborn error (see Forssman et al., 1961).

The mechanism by which the extra chromosome causes mongolism is unknown, but some defect in metabolism is definitely indicated. Early studies showed that cerebral metabolism is not normal in mongols (Himwich and Fazekas, 1940). Careful measurements of the respiration of brain tissue in these defectives indicated that their brains are incapable of using normal amounts of oxygen and carbohydrate. There is probably also a defect in protein metabolism, for the levels of uric acid found in the serum of mongoloids is significantly higher than it is in nonmongoloid feebleminded on the same diet (Mertz et al., 1963). The details of the derangement of metabolism, however, remain to be determined.

PHENYLPYRUVIC OLIGOPHRENIA—This jaw-breaking term applies to those feebleminded (oligophrenia) who have a defect characterized by the excretion in their urine of an excessive amount of phenylpyruvic acid or its metabolites. The disorder is easily detected by a urine test and for this reason is sometimes called phenylketonuria or, briefly, PKU (see Lyman, 1962). Occasionally PKU is found in cases of nonretarded children, but it is nearly always accompanied by feeblemindedness (Allen and Gibson, 1961). Actually, this kind of retardation is quite rare, accounting for about 0.1 percent of the population of feeblemindedness. It nevertheless has evoked considerable interest because it is inherited and also because the general nature of the metabolic defect causing it can be traced.

The defect is an inability to metabolize properly the amino acid phenylalanine (see page 89). Not all the details of this metabolic derangement are known (see Tashian, 1959), but it is certain that an enzyme is lacking that is necessary for the normal metabolism of phenylalanine. This means, as a practical matter, that the condition can be alleviated by putting defective individuals on a diet free of phenylalanine. Conversely, for experimental purposes, it is possible to create animals suffering from this type of disorder by overfeeding with phenylalanine. When this is done, the body does not have sufficient enzymatic resources to cope with the excess phenylalanine, and the animal seems to resemble in every way the human case of PKU and its accompanying feeblemindedness (Yuwiler and Louttit, 1961; see also Waisman et al., 1959).

NUTRITIONAL FACTORS

For both theoretical and practical reasons, considerable research has been carried out on the relation of nutrition to learning and intelligence (see Brozek and Vaes, 1961; Brozek and Fabrykant, 1962). If a diet that is deficient in some respect adversely affects behavioral capacities, it should be known so that such deficiencies can be remedied. On the other hand, from the effects of dietary deficiencies we can get some clues about important links in metabolism. There is also the hope that some way of feeding people better might be found so that their intellectual capacities might be increased. The nutritional factors that have been investigated with these purposes in mind are deficiencies in total intake, protein deficiency, and vitamin deficiency.

SEMISTARVATION—Some of the early studies on nutritional factors and behavioral capacity concerned the effects of semistarvation. One dealt with the effects of a severe regime of food deprivation of rats for as long as 100 days after weaning (Anderson and Smith, 1926). Three groups of rats were used. One was a control group. A second was a group of animals kept at almost constant weight by limiting their food intake. A third group was stunted by feeding it a diet in which the only protein source was gliadin. No significant differences in maze-learning ability were found among these groups when the animals were tested, either right after the period of stunting or after a long period of refeeding. The same negative results came from a similar study in which rats were kept almost at birth weight until they were thirty days old (Biel, 1938). Apparently, then, severe food deprivation, even to the point of stunting growth, has no effect on either the rat's learning ability or its capacity to perform in the maze situation.

PROTEINS—It will be recalled that the body manufactures proteins from amino acids and that certain amino acids are essential for this process. The essential amino acids cannot be made by the body but must be present in the protein eaten. Other amino acids, though not essential, may also be important in that they spare some of the ones that are essential. Still other amino acids can be made within the body. It is the essential and the sparing amino acids that are of interest here. Not all of them have been studied, and so no general conclusion can be drawn. In certain instances, however, diets deficient in amino acids cause an impairment in learning ability. For example, rats deprived of lysine, an essential amino acid, and those deprived of cystine, a sparing amino acid, are inferior to their litter-mate controls in rate of learning a maze (Riess and Block, 1942). The deficient animals, however, seem to be on a par with their controls in tests of activity and motivation. Hence the effect appears to be on learning ability and not on sensory or motor performance.

One amino acid that has evoked considerable interest in recent years is glutamic acid. This interest arose because it was demonstrated that it is important, or at least the most important of the amino acids, in maintaining oxygen uptake in the brain. This fact raised the possibility that glutamic acid might be crucially related to brain function and even that excesses of glutamic acid in the diet might increase learning capacity and intelligence. There are now more than thirty published studies on the effects of feeding glutamic acid to animals and human beings (Astin and Ross, 1960). About half of the studies are positive in the sense that they report a beneficial effect of glutamic acid on some measure of learning ability or intelligence; about half are negative. But of the positive studies, the majority lack any reasonable controls. And of the studies with some sort of control, the great majority are negative. Even the few positive instances employed controls that are questionable. The upshot of the matter is that any effect of glutamic acid, beneficial or otherwise, is very doubtful.

VITAMINS—Because vitamins, by definition, are essential to the health and normal growth of organisms, they have come in for a great deal of attention. The general procedure has been to feed animals vitamin-deficient diets and, after a fairly severe deficiency has been created in this way, to compare their ability in learning and other tests with that of control animals.

In general, vitamins not concerned in energy metabolism of the brain have no substantial effect on learning ability. Such vitamins include A and D. Animals suffering severe deficiencies of these vitamins are essentially normal in learning ability even though they may be so debilitated that they have trouble getting through the maze (Bernhardt, 1936). On the other hand, vitamins that are known to serve as coenzymes in brain metabolism give significant results in deficiency experiments. Several of the B vitamins are in this category (see Young and Spector, 1957; Morgan and Stellar, 1950).

Without going into details of the many experiments on the B vitamins, the results will be briefly summarized. The age at which vitamin B deficiency is induced is important. If young animals are placed on a deficient diet or if their mother is fed a deficient diet during pregnancy, learning ability as well as retention of a maze habit is definitely impaired even after the animals have been put back on a complete diet. On the other hand, similar deficiencies induced in adult animals have little or no effect. Of the various B vitamins, thiamin appears to be the one of greatest importance. It functions as a coenzyme in carbohydrate metabolism. In studies of thiamin deficiency in human beings, there are some conflicting reports. Most of the studies and the best controlled ones, however, show no effects on measures of intelligence either of thiamin deficiency or of feeding extra thiamin to those who have been underfed or on inadequate diets. It is possible, however, that if vitamin deficiency occurs early enough in life, say, during pregnancy or infancy, there is permanent impairment of intelligence.

HORMONAL FACTORS

As in the case of vitamin deficiency, there are numerous studies of the effects of manipulating hormone levels on learning ability. The usual technique is to extirpate a gland and later run tests. In a few instances, hormone inhibitors have been used (page 98). The results are not always in agreement, but we shall summarize the general conclusions that can be drawn.

There is usually little or no effect of removing a gland in adulthood. No observable changes in maze-learning ability follow castration or hypophysectomy in adult animals. Learning ability has seldom been altered by thyroidectomy or the administration of thyroid hormone in adulthood. In one case, however, the thyroid inhibitor, allyl thiourea, was reported as producing much poorer maze learners than the control animals (Scow, 1946). It is possible that in this case the inhibitor causes a more complete state of thyroid deficiency than surgical extirpation of the gland. Also, it has been reported that moderate doses of adrenal cortical hormones *increase* the maze-learning ability of rats (Riess, 1947). It was thought that this resulted from the fact that the adrenal cortical hormones play a role in the metabolism of carbohydrate. Despite these exceptions, the general rule seems to be that hormonal factors are not particularly important in the adaptive behavior of adults.

The rule does not hold, however, in certain instances in infancy or during embryonic development. A notable instance, long known clinically, is thyroid insufficiency. Individuals who suffer from such insufficiency are known as cretins and are usually feebleminded. This result has been produced experimentally by thyroidectomizing rats at birth (Scow, 1946). Such animals are markedly impaired in later tests of maze-learning ability.

There has been some interest in the biogenic amines, namely, epinephrine, norepinephrine, and serotonin. Interest in serotonin has arisen in recent years because it is suspected of being involved in some of the mental disorders, which we shall discuss later in this chapter. It has been demonstrated that the epinephrines, and their metabolic derivatives, increase in blood plasma when animals are subjected to emotional disturbances (Mason et al., 1961). This is to be expected. On the other hand, no effect is obtained on avoidance-learning rates when the adrenal medullas of rats are removed (Moyer and Bunnell, 1959) or when they are injected with adrenalin (Moyer and Bunnell, 1958).

The results of experiments in which brain serotonin is manipulated are mixed. In one report, an excess of cerebral serotonin decreases maze-learning ability of adult mice; whereas a deficiency of serotonin and the catechol amines increases it slightly (Woolley and van der Hoeven, 1963). On the other hand, other investigators report that the injection of a substance that differentially depletes serotonin and norepinephrine disrupts the pecking behavior of pigeons on a schedule of intermittent reinforcement (Hingtgen and Aprison, 1963). In the latter case, performance rather than learning was the measure, but it is not easily understood why a reduction of serotonin should improve maze-learning ability while impairing the performance of an already-learned habit. Undoubtedly more research on the role of serotonin in learning will be forthcoming in the future.

DRUG EFFECTS

As might be expected, hundreds of experiments have been carried out over the years on the relation of various drugs to learning, retention, and intelligence (see Ross, 1960). Some of these are best discussed below in conjunction with behavior disorders. The others, although they often have some practical value in indicating dosages that may impair *performance*, produce little of significance with respect to learning and intelligence. In general, activating drugs like Benzedrine and caffeine may speed up performance for a time, but they do not produce any marked effects on intelligence-test scores or learning. Similarly, depressants like phenobarbital and alcohol in moderate doses may impair performance temporarily, but they do not have any particular long-range effects on intelligence.

PERSONALITY

The prevailing psychological view of personality disorders, such as the neuroses and "functional" psychoses, is that they develop through experience with the environment. According to this view, learned habits of reacting to stressful and conflictful situations underlie neurotic and psychotic behavior. On the other hand, for several decades now, many investigators have been searching for, and frequently have reported, some physiological basis for personality disorders. The two views are not necessarily contradictory, for physiological differences among people may account in part for the ways in which they react to stress (Meehl, 1962). That is the assumption made here, but because this is a book on physiological psychology our treatment will be restricted to physiological factors in personality disorders.

GENETIC PREDISPOSITIONS

If there is a physiological difference accounting in part for personality disorders, it should be reflected in a genetic linkage. Such differences might, of course, arise in embryological development or even through trauma or dietary effects in development. Still, with the widespread incidence of personality disorders, a most plausible hypothesis is that genetic differences determine many physiological differences underlying such disorders.

Genetic studies in human beings are difficult to carry out in such a way that they are clearly separated from environmental effects. Circumstantial evidence comes from the study of the incidence of personality disorders in families. Even more convincing evidence is found in the study of twins. Both kinds of evidence will be summarized. The evidence has been subjected to criticism, some of which is undoubtedly justified. And the results may appear more impressive than they should be, but there can be hardly any doubt that they prove the existence of a genetic component in personality disorders.

SCHIZOPHRENIA IN FAMILIES—All the more common functional psychoses have been studied from the genetic point of view. Data are available for manic-depressive psychoses, for involutional melancholia, and for schizophrenia (see Table 20.1). The data are more extensive, however, for the most prevalent of the three disorders, namely, schizophrenia, and it will serve as an illustration of the points to be made.

In one series of studies (Kallmann, 1946), over 1,000 schizophrenics and 9,000 of their relatives were studied. This work, plus other relevant information, leaves no doubt that schizophrenia occurs more often in the blood relatives of schizophrenics than in the general population. For example, although schizophrenia occurs in only 0.85 percent of the population, there is a rate of about 4 percent in the distant relatives of schizophrenics and one of 10 to 12 percent among the parents and siblings of schizophrenics. It is even more frequent in families where it is known that two individuals have the disorder. When only one parent is schizophrenic, for example, about 16 percent of the children are afflicted, but when both parents are schizophrenic, about 68 percent of the children are schizophrenic.

SCHIZOPHRENIA IN TWINS—The roles of genetic and environmental factors are even more clearly separated in the study of twins. When the fraternal twins

TABLE 20.1—*Incidence of schizophrenia*

	PREVIOUS MORBIDITY STUDIES OF KALLMANN	RANGE OF MORBIDITY RATES OF OTHER INVESTIGATORS
Incidence of schizophrenia in general population	0.85	0.3– 1.5
Incidence of schizophrenia in consanguineous groups related to:		
One ordinary index case		
Nephews and nieces	3.9	1.4– 3.9
First cousins	—	2.6
Grandchildren	4.3	
Half-siblings	7.6	
Parents	10.3	7.1– 9.3
Full siblings	11.5	4.5–11.7
Children	16.4	8.3– 9.7
Two ordinary index cases		
Siblings	20.5	20.0
Children	68.1	53.0
One twin index case		
Dizygotic co-twins	12.5	14.9
Monozygotic co-twins	81.7	68.3

of schizophrenics are investigated, it is found that they are no more prone to the disease than the siblings of schizophrenics. This would be expected if genetic factors were the important ones, since fraternal twins are no more alike in genetic background than siblings. On the other hand, among the identical twins of schizophrenics, the incidence of schizophrenia is 81.7 percent. The interesting thing, too, is that schizophrenia occurs in the fraternal and identical twins of schizophrenics almost as often when they are reared apart in dissimilar environments as it does when they grow up in the same household. On the basis of these studies, it may be concluded that a predisposition to schizophrenia is inherited and probably depends on rather specific genetic factors. However, everyone recognizes that establishing a genetic basis for schizophrenia does not answer the question of what causes individuals predisposed to schizophrenia to develop the disorder. Undoubtedly, there must be structural or metabolic differences in the nervous system, as well as environmentally precipitating causes.

BIOCHEMICAL CORRELATES

For many years, investigators have been attempting to isolate some substance or substances from the blood or urine of psychotics or to find some biochemical test to distinguish psychotics from normal individuals. There is now a vast literature on this subject. It has been accelerating in recent years. Despite all the effort expended in this direction, there is very little that can yet be said with any assurance about the biochemical correlates of psychosis. For that reason, this section will constitute a very brief summary of the field. Its purpose will be to indicate some of the pitfalls of the research and some of the principal ideas guiding it (see Kety, 1959). Because schizophrenia is the most prevalent psychosis, most of our remarks will concern schizophrenia.

SOURCES OF ERROR—Probably no field of investigation is fraught with more possibilities of error than this one. Some of the principal sources of error are as follows:

Schizophrenia is probably a heterogeneous, not a unitary, disorder. From the behavioral point of view, schizophrenia is a fairly well-defined syndrome that includes disorganization of thought, disorientation in time and space, withdrawal and autistic behavior, and depersonalization. At the same time there are wide variations in the pattern of these symptoms, which is recognized in part by the subclassifications in common use. It is quite possible that schizophrenia represents a number of different disorders or, at least, that different biochemical abnormalities may be involved. The fact that different investigators may have drawn rather different samples of schizophrenic subjects may account in part for their often failing to confirm each other's research findings.

Conditions of institutional living often have biochemical correlates that are unrelated to schizophrenia disorders per se. Certain infectious diseases of the digestive tract, liver, and other organs are more common in institutions than in normal individuals, and these have their biochemical correlates. Diets are also frequently different, and these may cause differences in metabolism showing up in tests of the blood and urine. One study, for example, disclosed higher quantities of urinary phenolic acids in schizophrenics than in normal individuals, but these compounds are metabolites of substances in coffee, and they are correlated with the ingestion of coffee rather than with schizophrenia per se (Mann and LaBrosse, see Kety, 1959).

Schizophrenics also frequently do not eat the same things as other subjects. Even with institutional cooking, the bizarre nature of schizophrenia often leads to imbalances in food intake. These in turn are reflected in biochemical tests that can appear to indicate fundamental biochemical aberrancies in schizophrenia. In some studies, for example, schizophrenics had abnormalities of thyroid function, but these were traceable to dietary deficiency in iodine easily correctable with iodized salt. In other studies, what appeared to be biochemical abnormalities of schizophrenia turned out to be due to deficiencies in vitamin intake.

Some of the biochemical differences seen in schizophrenics are by-products of their reactions to emotional stress. Such stress, even in normal persons, may cause changes in such things as adrenocortical or thyroid function, in excretion of the catechol amines, and in the excretion of a number of metabolites. Schizophrenics are often characterized by emotional disturbances much more severe and prolonged over much longer periods of time than those of so-called normal individuals in stressful situations. Although these biochemical by-products of stress are interesting in their own right and tell something about autonomic reactions to stress, they are not to be mistaken as having a primary or causative role in the disorder.

There are, finally, in the study of schizophrenia, as in all sorts of scientific research, the usual hazards of inadequate sampling and subjective bias. Investigators have sometimes appeared unaware of the fact that, if 100 biochemical comparisons are made, about 5 percent can be expected to deviate by chance at the 5 percent level of confidence. Investigators have sometimes been so anxious to establish a correlation that they select data to fit in with their hypotheses.

BIOCHEMICAL HYPOTHESES—From time to time, reports have been published that the injection of some substance extracted from blood or urine into normal human beings or into animal subjects produces schizophreniclike symptoms. In one of many possible examples, intraperitoneal injections of blood substances from schizophrenics caused monkeys to take much longer to complete a precise timing task in which they had previously been trained (Ferguson and Fisher, 1963). In this case, however, a control sample of blood taken from *stressed* normal individuals was used with essentially the same result. This illustrates a general conclusion that some fraction of schizophrenic blood is frequently capable of producing schizophrenic symptoms, but whether this is due to some by-product of stress reactions or to some causative agent in schizophrenic blood is still unproved. Theories of causative agents, however, continue to abound and can be divided into three general classes.

One class of theories concerns carbohydrate metabolism. It once appeared that schizophrenia brains were deficient in their rate of cerebral glucose consumption. It may well be that such a defect characterizes patients with long-standing disease. It has not been confirmed, however, in patients maintained under special laboratory conditions where diet and other factors of maintenance have been controlled (see Kety, 1959). There are variations of this carbohydrate theory in which schizophrenics are supposed to have abnormal tolerances for injected glucose, to have greater than normal anti-insulin or hyperglycemic activity, or to have defects in the oxidation of phosphates. However, investigators usually fail to confirm any defects implied by the theories when other conditions of maintenance and feeding are controlled.

Similar statements can be made of another class of theories about the amino acids and their metabolism. Several studies have reported amino acids and their metabolites to appear in abnormally high concentrations in the urine of schizophrenics. A number of different amino acids have been named in such studies, some of which, when used as drugs, seem to have psychotomimetic properties. Many of these, however, are a consequence of drug therapy or of vitamin deficiencies; some have been shown to be of dietary origin. Hence the hypothesis that a disorder of amino acid metabolism is of causative significance in schizophrenia remains to be proved.

Probably the most attractive hypothesis of all those that have been advanced is the so-called epinephrine hypothesis. This theory postulates that the symptoms of schizophrenia are caused by abnormal, hallucinogenic derivatives of epinephrine. The two derivatives often suggested are adrenochrome and adrenolutin. The fact that epinephrine is released in individuals under stress and that a genetic defect in an enzyme might alter its metabolism makes the hypothesis plausible. And there are many papers reporting abnormalities in epinephrine in schizophrenics. The most telling arguments against the theory, however, are that (1) epinephrine metabolites vary greatly with the level of ascorbic acid (vitamin C) in the blood and (2) epinephrine injected into schizophrenics does not aggravate their psychotic symptoms. In the first instance, ascorbic acid levels were uncontrolled in most of the positive studies. In the second, if schizophrenics are unable to handle epinephrine metabolism as well as normals, presumably its injection should make some significant difference. It does not.

PSYCHOTROPIC DRUGS

The concept of the psychotropic drug has been introduced earlier (Chapter 4). Such a drug is any drug whose effect is primarily psychological. Psychotropic drugs fall into three main classes: tranquilizers, activators (also called energizers), and psychotogens (also called psychotomimetic drugs). The first two classes of drugs are being used in therapy to reduce and control psychological symptoms and also as aids in psychotherapy. The psychotogens are being used primarily as research tools to promote a better understanding of the nature of personality disorders (see Himwich, 1958).

There seems to be no question but that the tranquilizers are frequently effective in ameliorating many symptoms of psychotic and neurotic disorders. In general, the tranquilizers are useful in treating depressive and hyperactive disorders arising from anxiety. This is true whether the patient is a neurotic or a schizophrenic. The tranquilizers are so effective in quieting highly disturbed patients that isolation rooms and other devices for the restraint of patients have virtually disappeared in institutions where such drugs are used.

There are many different tranquilizers, and new ones are making their appearance at a rapid rate. Some of the better established ones have been named and described earlier. There appear, however, to be no established rules for the choice of tranquilizers. Most tranquilizing drugs have some beneficial effect on disturbed patients, but their effectiveness varies widely. The only way a physician can determine the best one is to try them. If one drug does not work very well, he switches until he finds one that appears most effective. The fact that different drugs of different chemical constitutions may be differentially beneficial makes it appear that these are not unitary disorders or at least not disorders always having the same physiological basis.

Considerable research has been directed toward finding the physiological events that are affected by psychotropic drugs. Some of this parallels the work on biochemical correlates described above. In this case, however, the research has attempted to find those conditions in the brain that are altered by, or in some cases mimic, the action of drugs. In this way, it is hoped to uncover physiological factors related to, or causing, personality disorders.

Two general approaches to the anlysis of therapeutic effects are to study (1) chemical changes in the brain or blood brought about by psychotropic drugs and (2) sites of action in the brain where the drugs have their greatest effects. In regard to the first approach, research has generally implicated the biogenic amines: serotonin, epinephrine, and norepinephrine. Serotonin is an indole amine, the other two catechol amines, but epinephrine can be oxidized to form the indole amine adrenochrome, and this yields serotonin or can be a product of serotonin. Thus, biochemically, the biogenic amines are closely interrelated. There are, however, few firm conclusions to be drawn about these biogenic amines and the psychotropic drugs. Some tranquilizers definitely alter, say, serotonin levels in the brain, but some do not. Some psychotogens, for example, are similar to serotonin and enter into some of the same chemical reactions as serotonin, possibly functioning as inhibitors, but some do not. Hence more research must be awaited before one can say much that makes any scientific sense in this area.

It can be demonstrated that the tranquilizers have different sites of action on the brain. Chlorpromazine, for example, probably acts in part by depressing the reticular formation. Reserpine, on the other hand, activates the reticular system. Its value as a tranquilizer must have some other basis. Probably both chlorpromazine and reserpine exert some of their effects through the hypothalamus. In addition, both drugs affect the amygdala, in each case increasing its activity. Such activity is associated with a calming or tranquilizing effect on emotional responses. Other facts are known about the sites of action, and some of them have been indicated earlier (page 105). These examples illustrate the findings. Knowledge of both sites of action of drugs and of the specific roles played by the sites in the control of aberrant behavior is still, however, so incomplete that no specific conclusions can be drawn.

The research literature of recent years is inundated with studies of drug effects on behavior. Much of this literature has a practical purpose of determining how drugs might be used to improve human performance or of assaying the effects of drugs for pharmaceutical purposes. Some is directed at an understanding of drug action on behavior. One experiment that illustrates how animal techniques may be used in assaying the effects of a drug and also how two drugs may have quite different effects on behavior is the following (Brady, 1956):

First a conditioned emotional response (CER) previously described (page 452) is developed. This CER may then be used to suppress bar pressing in a Skinner box. A rat is placed in a Skinner box on a schedule of partial reinforcement and taught to press the bar to obtain food (or fluid). Then the animal is given a few conditioning trials in which a clicker is sounded for a period, followed at the end by an electric shock. In this way, anxiety (CER) is conditioned to the sound of the clicker. Thereafter, whenever the clicker goes on, the normal animal stops pushing the bar and does not resume pressing it again until the clicker stops. Hence, the CER can be measured as a cessation of bar pressing.

Figure 20.2 presents a graph showing the effects of two drugs on the CER. Amphetamine (Benzedrine) is an activator which, like caffeine, tends to pep up an organism; reserpine is a tranquilizer; and saline serves as a control. The downward step in the curves marks the onset of the clicker, and the upward step marks its cessation. When this step is flat, it means that the rat stops pressing the bar during the sounding of the clicker. If it is not flat but is still of less slope than the rest of the line, the rat has merely slowed its bar pressing.

The latter is the case for the normal saline control; the clicker-induced emotional response only slows bar pressing. With the stimulant amphetamine, however, the record during periods of clicking is substantially flat, indicating that the rat's emotionality is heightened. Note, too, that bar pressing between periods of clicking is more rapid than normal; the recording line is much steeper. Quite the reverse happens with the tranquilizer, reserpine. The general rate of responding is slower than normal—tranquilizers may have general

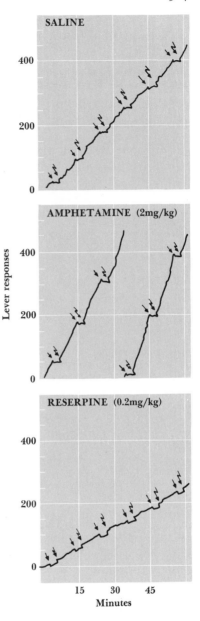

FIGURE 20.2—Effect of activator and tranquilizer on CER. (Adapted from J. V. Brady. Assessment of drug effects on emotional behavior. *Science*, June 8, 1956, 123, 1034. Adapted from *Science* by permission.)

sedation effects, especially in heavy doses—but it is just the same during both periods of time. In other words, the tranquilizer completely abolishes the conditioned emotional response to the clicker. Thus both the tranquilizing and activating effects of drugs can be demonstrated in the same experimental situation.

General References

DOCUMENTATION for specific experiments referred to in the text will be found in the combined Bibliography and Author Index that follows this section. Most of the citations are to the original journal literature. These citations were selected from the enormous amount of currently available literature and are by no means exhaustive.

Some students, after reading this text or parts of it, may want to find other more general sources for a more comprehensive or more detailed account than is given here. The references listed in this section, mostly books, are intended to serve this purpose.

Most of the general references cover more ground than any individual chapter. Some are as broad as physiological psychology itself or at least touch upon several different aspects of the subject. These are given immediately following this paragraph. Others are somewhat narrower and fall into the major groups of chapters described in the Introduction. These are given under the appropriate headings on the following pages.

BEACH, F. A., D. O. HEBB, C. T. MORGAN, and H. W. NISSEN (Eds.). *The neuropsychology of Lashley: selected papers of K. S. Lashley.* New York: McGraw-Hill, 1960.

BRAZIER, M. A. B. (Ed.). *The central nervous system and behavior.* (Transactions of five conferences.) New York: Josiah Macy, Jr., Foundation, 1959–1963.

DETHIER, V. G., and E. STELLAR. *Animal behavior: its evolutionary and neurological basis.* Englewood Cliffs, N.J.: Prentice-Hall, 1961.

ESTES, W. K., and E. STELLAR (Eds.). *J. comp. physiol. Psychol.* Washington, D.C.: American Psychological Association (bimonthly publication).

FARNSWORTH, P. R., O. MCNEMAR, and Q. MCNEMAR (Eds.). *Annu. Rev. Psychol.* Palo Alto, Calif.: Annual Reviews (annual publication, 1950–present).

FIELD, J., H. W. MAGOUN, and V. E. HALL (Eds.). *Handbook of physiology.* Section 1. *Neurophysiology.* 3 vols. Washington, D.C.: American Physiological Society, 1959–1960.

HARLOW, H. F., and C. N. WOOLSEY (Eds.). *Biological and biochemical bases of behavior.* Madison, Wis.: University of Wisconsin Press, 1958.

ISAACSON, R. I. (Ed.). *Basic readings in neuropsychology.* New York: Harper & Row, 1964.

MAGOUN, H. W. *The waking brain.* 2d ed. Springfield, Ill.: Charles C Thomas, 1963.

SOLOMON, H. C., S. COBB, and W. PENFIELD (Eds.). *The brain and human behavior.* Baltimore: Williams & Wilkins, 1958.

WOLSTENHOLME, G. E. W., and M. O'CONNOR (Eds.). *CIBA Foundation symposium on the neurological basis of behaviour: in commemoration of Sir Charles Sherrington.* Boston: Little, Brown, 1958.

ANATOMY AND PHYSIOLOGY OF THE NERVOUS SYSTEM

BRAZIER, M. A. B. *The electrical activity of the nervous system.* 2d ed. New York: Macmillan, 1960.

GALAMBOS, R. *Nerves and muscle.* Garden City, N.Y.: Doubleday, 1962.

GARDNER, E. *Fundamentals of neurology.* 4th ed. Philadelphia: Saunders, 1963.

GELLHORN, E. *Autonomic imbalance and the hypothalamus: implications for physiology, medicine, psychology, and neuropsychiatry.* Minneapolis: University of Minneosta Press, 1957.

GERARD, R. W. *Unresting cells.* New York: Harper & Row, 1940.

MCGUIGAN, F. J. *Biological basis of behavior: a problem.* Englewood Cliffs, N.J. Prentice-Hall, 1963. (A programed text.)

VON BONIN, G. *The evolution of the human brain.* Chicago: University of Chicago Press, 1963.

WALTER, W. G. *The living brain.* New York: Norton, 1963.

WOOLDRIDGE, D. E. *The machinery of the brain.* New York: McGraw-Hill, 1963.

THE SENSES

BARTLEY, S. H. *Vision.* Princeton, N.J.: Van Nostrand, 1941.

BARTLEY, S. H. *Principles of perception.* New York: Harper & Row, 1958.

BÉKÉSY, G. V. *Experiments in hearing.* (Translated and edited by E. G. Wever.) New York: McGraw-Hill, 1960.

BRAZIER, M. A. B. (Ed.). *Brain and behavior,* vol. 1. Washington, D.C.: American Institute of Biological Sciences, 1961.

DAVIS, H., and S. R. SILVERMAN. *Hearing and deafness.* Rev. ed. New York: Holt, 1960.

GELDARD, F. A. *The human senses.* New York: Wiley, 1953.

LE GRAND, Y. *Light, colour and vision.* New York: Wiley, 1957.

NOORDENBOS, W. *Pain: problems pertaining to the transmission of nerve impulses which give rise to pain.* Amsterdam: Elsevier, 1959.

POLYAK, S. (Edited by H. Klüver.) *The vertebrate visual system.* Chicago: University of Chicago Press, 1957.

SEMMES, J., S. WEINSTEIN, L. GHENT, and H. L. TEUBER. *Somatosensory changes after penetrating brain wounds in man.* Cambridge, Mass.: Harvard, 1960.

TEUBER, H. L., W. S. BATTERSBY, and M. B. BENDER. *Visual field defects after penetrating missile wounds of the brain.* Cambridge, Mass.: Harvard, 1960.

MOTIVATION AND EMOTION

ANAND, B. K. Nervous regulation of food intake. *Physiol. Rev.,* 1961, **41**, 677–708.

CANNON, W. B. *Bodily changes in pain, hunger, fear and rage: an account of researches into the function of emotional excitement.* 2d ed. New York: Harper & Row, 1963.

CLOUDSLEY-THOMPSON, J. L. *Rhythmic activity in animal physiology and behavior.* New York: Academic, 1962.

GELLHORN, E., and G. N. LOOFBOURROW. *Emotions and emotional disorders: a neurophysiological study.* New York: Harper & Row, 1963.

JASPER, H. H., L. D. PROCTOR, R. S. KNIGHTON, W. C. NOSHAY, and R. T. COSTELLO (Eds.). *Reticular formation of the brain.* Boston: Little, Brown, 1958.

JONES, M. R. (Ed.). *Nebraska symposium on motivation.* Lincoln, Nebr.: University of Nebraska Press (annual publication).

OSWALD, IAN. *Sleeping and waking: physiology and psychology.* Amsterdam: Elsevier, 1962.

RHEINGOLD, H. L. (Ed.). *Maternal behavior in mammals.* New York: Wiley, 1963.

ROSENZWEIG, M. R. The mechanisms of hunger and thirst. In L. Postman (Ed.), *Psychology in the making.* New York: Knopf, 1962.

SHEER, D. D. (Ed.). *Electrical stimulation of the brain.* Austin, Tex.: University of Texas Press, 1961.

SIMON, A., C. C. HERBERT, and R. STRAUS. *The physiology of emotion.* Springfield, Ill.: Charles C Thomas, 1961.

WOLF, H. A. *Thirst: physiology of the urge to drink and problems of water lack.* Springfield, Ill.: Charles C Thomas, 1958.

WOLSTENHOLME, G. E. W., and M. O'CONNOR (Eds.). *The nature of sleep* (CIBA Foundation Symposium). Boston: Little, Brown, 1961.

YOUNG, P. T. *Motivation and emotion: a survey of the determinants of human and animal activity.* New York: Wiley, 1961.

YOUNG, W. C. (Ed.). *Sex and internal secretions.* Baltimore: Williams & Wilkins, 1961.

LEARNING AND PROBLEM SOLVING

GERARD, R. W., A. FESSARD, and J. KONORSKI. *Brain mechanisms and learning.* Springfield, Ill.: Charles C Thomas, 1961.

KIMBLE, G. A. *Hilgard and Marquis' Conditioning and learning.* Rev. ed. New York: Appleton-Century-Crofts, 1961.

LASHLEY, K. S. *Brain mechanisms and intelligence: a quantitative study of injuries to the brain.* New York: Dover, 1963.

PAVLOV, I. P. *Lectures on conditioned reflexes,* vol. 1. (Translated and edited by W. H. Gantt.) New York: International Publishers, 1963.

WARREN, J. M., and K. AKERT. *Frontal granular cortex and behavior.* New York: McGraw-Hill, 1964.

BRAIN DISORDERS

HALSTEAD, W. C. *Brain and intelligence: a quantitative study of the frontal lobes.* Chicago: University of Chicago Press, 1947.

KLEIST, K. *Sensory aphasia and amusia: the myelarchitectonic basis.* (Translated from German.) New York: Pergamon Press, 1962.

MOUNTCASTLE, V. B. (Ed.). *Interhemispheric relations and cerebral dominance.* Baltimore: Johns Hopkins, 1962.

OSGOOD, C. E., and S. M. MURRAY (Eds.). *Approaches to the study of aphasia.* Urbana, Ill.: The University of Illinois Press, 1963.

PENFIELD, W., and L. ROBERTS. *Speech and brain mechanisms.* Princeton, N.J.: Princeton, 1959.

RUSSELL, W., W. RITCHIE, and M. L. E. ESPIR. *Traumatic aphasia: a study of aphasia in war wounds of the brain.* Fairlawn, N.J.: Oxford University Press, 1961.

WEPMAN, J. M. *A selected bibliography on brain impairment: aphasia and organic psychodiagnosis.* Chicago: Language Research Associates, 1961.

WINDLE, W. F. (Ed.). *Neurological and psychological deficits of asphyxia neonaturium with consideration of use of primates for experimental investigations.* Springfield, Ill.: Charles C Thomas, 1958.

ZANGWILL, O. L. *Cerebral dominance and its relation to psychological function.* Edinburgh and London: Oliver & Boyd, 1960.

PSYCHOCHEMISTRY AND PSYCHOPHARMACOLOGY

ABRAMSON, H. A. (Ed.). *Neuropharmacology.* (Transactions of five conferences.) New York: Josiah Macy, Jr., Foundation, 1955–1960.

BENSON, W. M., and C. S. BURTRUM. *Tranquilizing and antidepressive drugs.* Springfield, Ill.: Charles C Thomas, 1962.

COLE, J. W., and R. W. GERARD (Eds.). *Psychopharmacology: problems in evaluation.* Washington, D.C.: National Academy of Sciences–National Research Council. Publication 583, 1959.

GORDON, H. L. (Ed.). *The new chemotherapy in mental illness.* New York: Philosophical Library, 1958.

HIMWICH, H. E. (Ed.). *Tranquilizing drugs.* Washington, D.C.: American Association for the Advancement of Science, 1957.

NASH, H. *Alcohol and caffeine.* Springfield, Ill.: Charles C Thomas, 1962.

RINKEL, M. (Ed.). *Chemical concepts of psychosis*. New York: McDowell, Obolensky, 1958.

ROESSLER, R., and N. S. GREENFIELD. *Physiological correlates of psychological disorder*. Madison, Wis.: The University of Wisconsin Press, 1962.

UHR, L., and J. G. MILLER (Eds.). *Drugs and behavior*. New York: Wiley, 1960.

WIKLER, A. *The relation of psychiatry to pharmacology*. Baltimore: Williams & Wilkins, 1957.

WILLIAMS, R. J. *Biochemical individuality: the basis for the genetotrophic concept*. New York: Wiley, 1956.

Bibliography and Author Index

The following list of names and titles serves as a bibliography and author index. The bibliography is cross-indexed by listing all names in alphabetical order and giving the names of senior authors whenever a junior author's name appears in the order. Numbers in parentheses are the page numbers of the text in which the reader will find the name referred to. When a complete title appears in the legend of an illustration or in a general reference at the end of a chapter, the title is not repeated in the index, only the author's name and the page number on which it appears are given. There are a few cases of names mentioned for their historical reference for which no bibliographic reference is given.

ABRAMSON, H. A., reference given in text. (571)

ACHENBACH, K., see Kaelbling.

ADAMS, T. Hypothalamic temperature in the cat during feeding and sleep. *Science,* 1963, **139,** 609–610. (394)

ADES, H. W. Effect of extirpation of parastriate cortex on learned visual discrimination in monkeys. *J. Neuropath. exp. Neurol.,* 1946, **5,** 60–65. (499)

ADES, H. W. Central auditory mechanisms. In J. Field, H. W. Magoun, and V. E. Hall (Eds.), *Handbook of physiology,* Vol. 1. Washington, D. C.: American Physiological Society, 1959. (216, 217, 222–224, 234, 236, 489, 490)

ADES, H. W., see Culler, Kryter, Raab, Riopelle.

ADES, H. W., and RAAB, D. H. Effect of preoccipital and temporal decortication on learned visual discrimination in monkeys. *J. Neurophysiol.,* 1949, **12,** 101–108. (499)

ADEY, W. R. The sense of smell. In J. Field, H. W. Magoun, and V. E. Hall (Eds.), *Handbook of physiology,* Vol. 1. Washington, D. C.: American Physiological Society, 1959. (123)

ADOLPH, E. F. The internal environment and behavior: III. Water content. *Amer. J. Psychiat.,* 1941, **97,** 1365–1373. (387, 388)

ADOLPH, E. F. Urges to eat and drink in rats. *Amer. J. Physiol.,* 1947, **151,** 110–125. (364)

ADOLPH, E. F., see Barker, Robinson.

ADRIAN, E. D. The "all-or-none" principle in nerve. *J. Physiol.,* 1914, **47,** 450–474. (65)

ADRIAN, E. D. *The basis of sensation: The action of the sense organs.* London: Christophers, 1928. (232, 256)

ADRIAN, E. D., 1954, cited by Pfaffmann, 1959. (127)

AJURIAGUERRA, J., see Piercy.

AKELAITIS, A. J. A study of gnosis, praxis, and language following section of the corpus callosum and anterior commissure. *J. Neurosurg.,* 1944, **1,** 94–102. (536)

AKERT, K., reference given in text. (571)

AKERT, K., see Benjamin, Warren.

AKERT, K., KOELLA, W. P., and HESS, R., JR. Sleep produced by electrical stimulation of the thalamus. *Amer. J. Physiol.,* 1952, **168,** 260–267. (349)

ALCOCER-CUARÓN, C., see Hernández-Peón, Lavín.

ALLEN, G. H., see Donaldson.

ALLEN, R. J., and GIBSON, R. M. Phenylketonuria with normal intelligence. *Amer. J. Dis. Children,* 1961, **102,** 145–152. (556).

ALLEN, W. F. Effect of ablating the frontal lobes, hippocampi, and occipito-parietotemporal (excepting pyriform areas) on positive and negative olfactory conditioned reflexes. *Amer. J. Physiol.,* 1940, **128,** 754–771. (128)

ALLEN, W. F. Effect of ablating the pyriform-amygdaloid areas and hippocampi on positive and negative olfactory conditioned reflexes and on conditioned olfactory differentiation. *Amer. J. Physiol.,* 1941, **132,** 81–92. (128)

ALLEN, W. F. Effect of destroying three localized cerebral cortical areas for sound on correct conditioned differential responses of the dog's foreleg. *Amer. J. Physiol.*, 1945, **144**, 415–428. (451, 491)

ALLEN, W. F. Effect of bilateral destruction of three lateral cerebral cortical areas on correct conditioned differential responses from general cutaneous stimulation. *Amer. J. Physiol.*, 1946, **147**, 454–461. (451, 487)

ALLEN, W. F. Effect of partial and complete destruction of the tactile cerebral cortex on correct conditioned differential foreleg responses from cutaneous stimulation. *Amer. J. Physiol.*, 1947, **151**, 325–337. (487)

ALLISON, A. C. The morphology of the olfactory system in vertebrates. *Biol. Rev.*, 1953, **28**, 195–244. (126)

ALLPORT, F. H. Social psychology. Boston: Houghton Mifflin, 1924. (309)

AMASSIAN, V. E., see Patton.

ANAND, B. D., reference given in text. (570)

ANAND, B. D., see Sharma.

ANAND, B. D., and BROBECK, J. R. Hypothalamic control of food intake. *Yale J. biol. Med.*, 1951, **24**, 123–140. (381)

ANAND, B. D., CHHINA, G. S., *and* SINGH, B. Effect of glucose on the activity of hypothalamic "feeding centers." *Science*, 1962, **138**, 597–598. (381)

ANDERSON, J. E., and SMITH, A. H. The effect of quantitative and qualitative stunting upon maze learning in the white rat. *J. comp. Psychol.*, 1926, **6**, 337–359. (557)

ANDERSSON, B. The effect of injections of hypertonic NaCl-solutions into different parts of the hypothalamus of goats. *Acta Physiol. Scand.*, 1953, **28**, 188–201. (391)

ANDERSSON, B., LANDGREN, S., OLSSON, L., and ZOTTERMAN, Y., 1950, cited by Pfaffmann, 1959. (118)

ANDERSSON, B., and LARSSON, S., 1956, cited by Doty, 1961. (464)

ANLIKER, J. Variations in alpha voltage of the electro-encephalogram and time preception. *Science*, 1963, **140**, 1307–1309. (351)

ANLIKER, J., and MAYER, J. The regulation of food intake. Some experiments relating behavioral, metabolic and morphologic aspects. *In Symposium on nutrition and behavior.* New York: National Vitamin Foundation, Inc., 1957. (375)

APRISON, M. H., see Hingtgen.

ARANA, R., see Segundo.

ARDUINI, A., see Green.

AREY, L. B., reference given in text. (133)

ARIETI, S., see Minnick.

ARNOLD, M. B. Physiological differentiation of emotional states. *Psychol. Rev.*, 1945, **52**, 35–48. (309)

ARONSON, L. R., see Rosenblatt.

ASERINSKY, E., and KLEITMAN, N. Regularly occurring periods of eye motility, and concomitant phenomena, during sleep. *Science*, 1953, **118**, 273–274. (343)

ASHER, H. The electroretinogram of the blind spot. *J. Physiol.*, 1951, **112**, 40–41. (143)

ASTIN, A. W., and ROSS, S. Glutamic acid and human intelligence. *Psychol. Bull.*, 1960, **57**, 429–434. (558)

AX, A. F. The physiological differentiation between fear and anger in humans. *Psychosom. Med.*, 1953, **15**, 433–442. (335)

BAGGERMAN, B. An experimental study of the timing of breeding and migration in the three-spined stickleback (Gasterosteus aculeatus L). *Arch. Neerl. Zool.*, 1957, **7**, 105–318. (400, 404, 436)

BAGSHAW, M. H., and PRIBRAM, K. H. Cortical organization in gustation (Macaca Mulatta). *J. Neurophysiol.*, 1953, **16**, 499–508. (122)

BAILEY, C. J., see Miller.

BAILEY, P., and DAVIS, E. W. The syndrome of obstinate progression in the cat. *Proc. Soc. exp. Biol. Med.*, 1942, **51**, 307. (358)

BALL, JOSEPHINE. Sex behavior of the rat after removal of the uterus and vagina. *J. Comp. Psychol.*, 1934, **18**, 419–422. (414)

BARD, P. A diencephalic mechanism for the expression of rage with special reference to the sympathetic nervous system. *Amer. J. Physiol.*, 1928, **84**, 490–515. (310, 315)

BARD, P. The effects of denervation of the genitalia on the oestral behavior of cats. *Amer. J. Physiol.*, 1935, **113**, 5. (414)

BARD, P. The hypothalamus and sexual behavior. *Res. Publ. Ass. Res. Nerv. Ment. Dis.*, 1940, **20**, 551–579. (397)

BARD, P. *Medical physiology.* St. Louis: Mosby, 1956, 1176. (155)

BARD, P., see Bromiley, Macht, Root.

BARD, P., and MOUN·CASTLE, V. B. Some forebrain mechanisms involved in the expression of rage with special reference to suppression of angry behavior. *Res. Publ. Ass. Res. Nerv. Ment. Dis.*, 1947, **27**, 362–404. (315, 319, 320)

BARE, J. K. The specific hunger for sodium chloride in normal and adrenalectomized white rats. *J. comp. physiol. Psychol.*, 1949, **42**, 242–253. (369)

BARE, J. K., see Pfaffmann.

BARKER, A. N., see Hull.

BARKER, D., reference given in text. (276)

BARKER, J. P., ADOLPH, E. F., and KELLER, A. D. Thirst tests in dogs and modification of thirst with experimental lesions of the neurohypophysis. *Amer. J. Physiol.*, 1954, **173**, 233–245. (389)

BARKER, R. G., see Stone.

BARLOW, H. B., and HILL, R. M. Selective sensitivity to direction of movement in ganglion cells of the rabbit retina. *Science*, 1963, **139**, 412–414. (150)

BARNETT, P. E., see Peterson.

BARRACLOUGH, C. A., and GORSKI, R. A., 1962, cited by Whalen and Nadler, 1963. (412)

BARTLEY, S. H. Temporal and spatial summation of extrinsic impulses with intrinsic activity of the cortex. *J. Cell. comp. Physiol.*, 1936, **8**, 41–62. (184)

BARTLEY, S. H. Some factors in brightness discrimination. *Psychol. Rev.*, 1939, **46**, 337–357. (142, 187)

BARTLEY, S. H. *Vision, a study of its basis.* New York: Van Nostrand, 1941. (136)

BARTLEY, S. H. Central mechanisms of vision. In J. Field, H. W. Magoun, and V. E. Hall (Eds.), *Handbook of physiology*, Vol. 1. Washington, D. C.: American Physiological Society, 1959. (156, 157, 185, 186)

BARTLEY, S. H., reference given in text. (570)

BARTLEY, S. H., and NELSON, T. M. A further study of pulse-to-cycle fraction and critical flicker frequency. A decisive theoretical test. *J. Opt. Soc. Amer.*, 1961, **51**, 41–45 (187)

BARTLEY, S. H., and NELSON, T. M. Some relations between sensory end results and neural activity in the optic pathway. *J. Psychol.*, 1963, **55**, 121–143. (155, 159, 161, 184–186)

BASH, K. W. An investigation into a possible organic basis for the hunger drive. *J. comp. Psychol.*, 1939, **28**, 109–134. (370)

BASHORE, W. D., see Kellogg.

BATTERSBY, W. S., reference given in text. (570)

BATTERSBY, W. S., see Teuber.

BATTIG, K., ROSVOLD, H. E., and MISHKIN, M. Comparison of the effects of frontal and caudate lesions on delayed response performance and alternation in monkeys. *J. comp. physiol. Psychol.*, 1960, **53**, 400–404. (524)

BAUMEISTER, A. A., see Thompson, R.

BAY, E. Disturbances of visual perception and their examination. *Brain*, 1953, **76**, 515–550. (196)

BAZETT, H. C., MC GLONE, B., WILLIAMS, R. G., and LUFKIN, H. M. Studies in sensation. I. Depth, distribution and probable identification in the prepuce of sensory end-organs in sensations of temperature and touch; thermometric conductivity. *Arch. Neurol. Psychiat.*, 1932, **27**, 489–517. (246, 248)

BEACH, F. A. Effects of cortical lesions upon the copulatory behavior of male rats. *J. comp. Psychol.*, 1940, **29**, 193–245. (397)

BEACH, F. A. Effects of lesions to corpus striatum upon spontaneous activity in the male rat. *J. comp. Psychol.*, 1941, **31**, 145–178. (359, 415)

BEACH, F. A. Analysis of the stimuli adequate to elicit mating behavior in the sexually inexperienced male rat. *J. comp. Psychol.*, 1942, **33**, 163–207. (413)

BEACH, F. A. Analysis of factors involved in the arousal, maintenance and manifestation of sexual excitement in male animals. *Psychosom. Med.*, 1942, **4**, 173–198. (413, 414)

BEACH, F. A. Effects of injury to the cerebral cortex upon sexually-receptive behavior in the female rat. *Psychosom. Med.*, 1944, **6**, 40–55. (414)

BEACH, F. A. A review of physiological and psychological studies of sexual behavior in mammals. *Physiol. Rev.*, 1947, **27**, 240–307. (416)

BEACH, F. A. Evolutionary changes in the physiological control of mating behavior in mammals. *Psychol. Rev.*, 1947, **54**, 297–315. (395, 405)

BEACH, F. A. *Hormones and behavior.* New York: Hoeber, 1948. (405–408, 410)

BEACH, F. A. *A cross-species survey of mammalian sexual development in health and disease.* New York: Grune & Stratton, 1949. (396–399)

BEACH, F. A., reference given in text. (570)

BEACH, F. A., and FOWLER, H. Individual differences in the response of male rats to androgen. *J. comp. physiol. Psychol.*, 1959, **52**, 50–52. (407)

BEACH, F. A., and GILMORE, R. W. Response of male dogs to urine from females in heat. *J. Mammalogy*, 1949, **30**, 391–392. (405)

BEACH, F. A., HEBB, D. O., MORGAN, C. T., and NISSEN, H. W. (Eds.). *The neuropsychology of Lashley.* New York: McGraw-Hill, 1960. (510, 518)

BEACH, F. A., and HOLZ-TUCKER, A. M. Effects of different concentrations of androgen upon sexual behavior in castrated male rats. *J. comp. physiol. Psychol.*, 1949, **42**, 433–453. (407)

BEACH, F. A., and JAYNES, J. Studies of maternal retrieving in rats. III. Sensory cues involved in the lactating female's response to her young. *Behaviour*, 1956, **10**, 104–125. (434)

BEACH, F. A., and LEVINSON, G. Effects of androgen on the glans penis and mating behavior of castrated male rats. *J. exp. Zool.*, 1950, **114**, 159–168. (414)

BEATON, L. E., see Kelly.

BECK, E. C., see Brierley, Doty.

BECK, E. C., and DOTY, R. W. Conditioned flexion reflexes acquired during combined catalepsy and de-efferentation. *J. comp. physiol. Psychol.*, 1957, **50**, 211–216. (474, 477)

BEER, B., see Hearst.

BEIDLER, L. M. In *Chemistry of natural food flavor.* Chicago: Quartermaster Research and Engineering Center, 1957. Pp. 7–42. (118)

BEIDLER, L. M., see Kimura.

BÉKÉSY, G. V., reference given in text. (570)

BÉKÉSY, G. V., see also Von Békésy.

BELLOWS, R. T. Time factors in water drinking in dogs. *Amer. J. Physiol.,* 1939, **125,** 87–97. (387)

BENDER, M. B. *Disorders of perception.* Springfield: C. C. Thomas, 1952. (193)

BENDER, M. B., reference given in text. (570)

BENDER, M. B., see Teuber.

BENJAMIN, R. M. Cortical taste mechanisms studied by two different test procedures. *J. comp. physiol. Psychol.,* 1955a, **48,** 119–122. (122)

BENJAMIN, R. M. The effect of fluid deprivation on taste deficits following cortical lesions. *J. comp. physiol. Psychol.,* 1955b, **48,** 502–505. (122)

BENJAMIN, R. M., and AKERT, K. Cortical and thalamic areas involved in taste discrimination in the albino rat. *J. comp. Neurol.,* 1959, **111,** 231–260. (120)

BENJAMIN, R. M., and PFAFFMANN, C. Cortical localization of taste in albino rat. *J. Neurophysiol.,* 1955, **18,** 56–64. (122)

BENNETT, E. L., see Rosenzweig.

BENSON, R. W., see Davis.

BENSON, W. M., reference given in text. (571)

BERESFORD, W. A. Fibre degeneration following lesions of the visual cortex of the cat. In R. Jung and H. Kornhuber (Eds.), *Neurophysiologie und Psychophysik des visuellen Systems.* Berlin: Springer-Verlag, 1961. (157)

BERGER, F. M. Classification of psychoactive drugs according to their chemical structures and sites of action. In L. Uhr and J. G. Miller (Eds.), *Drugs and behavior.* New York: Wiley-Interscience, 1960. (105)

BERKUN, M., see Kagan.

BERKUN, M. M., KESSEN, M. L., and MILLER, N. E. Hunger-reducing effects of food by stomach fistula versus food by mouth measured by a consummatory response. *J. comp. physiol. Psychol.,* 1952, **45,** 550–554. (371)

BERMAN, A. J., see Knapp.

BERNHARD, C. G., and GRANIT, R. Nerve as a model temperature end organ. *J. gen. Physiol.,* 1946, **29,** 257–265. (249, 250)

BERNHARDT, K. S. Protein deficiency and learning in rats. *J. comp. Psychol.,* 1936, **22,** 269. (558)

BERRY, C. M., see Dey.

BERSH, P. J., see Notterman.

BERSON, S. A., see Roth.

BEST, C. H., and TAYLOR, N. B. *The physiological basis of medical practice.* Baltimore: Williams & Wilkins, 1940. (27, 292, 293)

BEVAN, W., and GRODSKY, M. A. Hoarding in hamsters with systematically controlled pre-test experience. *J. comp. physiol. Psychol.,* 1958, **51,** 342–345. (440)

BIEL, W. C. The effect of early inanition upon maze learning in the albino rat. *Comp. Psychol. Monogr.,* 1938, **15,** 1–33. (557)

BINDRA, D. Hoarding behavior of rats: Nutritional and psychological factors. Unpublished Ph.D. thesis, Harvard University, 1947. (441)

BISHOP, G. H. The peripheral unit for pain. *J. Neurophysiol.,* 1944, **7,** 71–80. (253, 255)

BISHOP, G. H. Neural mechanisms of cutaneous sense. *Physiol. Rev.,* 1946, **26,** 77–102. (243)

BISHOP, M. P., ELDER, S. T., and HEATH, R. G. Intracranial self-stimulation in man. *Science,* 1963, **140,** 394–396. (330)

BISHOP, P. O., BURKE, W., and DAVIS, R. Synapse discharge by single fibre in mammalian visual system. *Nature,* 1958, **182,** 728–730. (158)

BISHOP, P. O., BURKE, W., and DAVIS, R. Activation of single lateral geniculate cells by stimulation of either optic nerve. *Science,* 1959, **130,** 506–507. (158)

BLACK, A. H., CARLSON, N. J., and SOLOMON, R. L. Exploratory studies of the conditioning of autonomic responses in curarized dogs. *Psychol. Monogr.,* 1962, **76,** No. 29, 31 pp. (Whole No. 548). (477)

BLAKE, L. The effect of lesions of the superior colliculus on brightness and pattern discrimination in the cat. *J. comp. physiol. Psychol.,* 1959, **52,** 272–278. (196)

BLOCK, R. F., see Riess.

BLUM, J. S., CHOW, K. L., and BLUM, R. A. Delayed response performance of monkeys with frontal removals after excitant and sedative drugs. *J. Neurophysiol.,* 1951, **3,** 196–202. (526)

BLUM, J. S., CHOW, K. L., and PRIBRAM, K. H. A behavioral analysis of the organization of the parieto-temporo-pre-occipital cortex. *J. comp. Neurol.,* 1950, **93,** 53–100. (498)

BLUM, R. A. Effects of subtotal lesions of frontal granular cortex on delayed reaction in monkeys. *Arch. Neurol. Psychiat.,* 1952, **67,** 375–386. (524)

BLUM, R. A., see Blum, J. S.

BODANSKY, M. *Introduction to physiological chemistry.* New York: Wiley, 1938. (102)

BODIAN, D. The generalized vertebrate

neuron. *Science*, 1962, **137**, 323–326. (18)

BOLDREY, E., see Penfield.

BOLING, J. L., YOUNG, W. C., and DEMPSEY, E. W. Miscellaneous experiments on the estrogen-progesterone-induced heat in the spayed guinea pig. *Endocrinology*, 1938, **23**, 182–187. (408)

BOLL, F., reference given in text. (136)

BOREN, J. J., see Brady, Brodie, Sidman.

BORING, E. G. *Sensation and perception in the history of experimental psychology*. New York: Appleton-Century-Crofts, 1942. (241)

BORING, E. G. *A history of experimental psychology*. 2nd ed. New York: Appleton-Century-Crofts, 1950. (112)

BORING, E. G., LANGFELD, H. S., and WELD, H. P. *Foundations of psychology*. New York: Wiley-Interscience, 1948. (205)

BÖRNSTEIN, A. M., DENNIS, W. H., and REHM, W. S. Movement of water, sodium, chloride and hydrogen ions across the resting stomach. *Amer. J. Physiol.*, 1959, **197**, 332–336. (385)

BÖRNSTEIN, W. S. Cortical representation of taste in man and monkey. I. Functional and anatomical relations of taste, olfaction, and somatic sensibility. *Yale J. Biol. Med.*, 1940a, **12**, 719–736.

BÖRNSTEIN, W. S. Cortical representation of taste in man and the monkey. II. The localization of the cortical taste area in man and a method of measuring impairment of taste in man. *Yale J. Biol. Med.*, 1940b, **13**, 133–156. (120)

BOURKE, W. T. The effects of frontal lobe damage upon habit reversal in the white rat. *J. comp. physiol. Psychol.*, 1954, **47**, 277–282. (529)

BOWMAN, R. E., see Polidora.

BOYNTON, R. M., KANDEL, G., and ONLEY, J. W. Rapid chromatic adaptation of normal and dichromatic observers. *J. opt. Soc. Amer.*, 1959, **49**, 654–666. (175)

BOYNTON, R. M., and RIGGS, L. A. The effect of stimulus area and intensity upon the human retinal response. *J. exp. Psychol.*, 1951, **42**, 217–226. (143)

BRADY, J. V. Assessment of drug effects on emotional behavior. *Science*, 1956, **123**, 1033–1034. (566, 567)

BRADY, J. V. The paleocortex and behavioral motivation. In H. F. Harlow and C. N. Woolsey (Eds.), *Biological and biochemical bases of behavior*. Madison: University of Wisconsin Press, 1958.

BRADY, J. V. Emotional behavior. In J. Field, H. W. Magoun, and V. E. Hall (Eds.), *Handbook of physiology*, Vol. 3. Washington, D. C.: American Physiological Society, 1960. (316–318, 324)

BRADY, J. V., see Geller, Hunt, Mason, Porter, Sidman.

BRADY, J. V., BOREN, J. J., CONRAD, D., and SIDMAN, M. The effect of food and water deprivation upon intracranial self-stimulation. *J. comp. physiol. Psychol.*, 1957, **50**, 134–137. (327)

BRADY, J. V., and HUNT, H. F. A further demonstration of the effects of electroconvulsive shock on a conditioned emotional response. *J. comp. physiol. Psychol.*, 1951, **44**, 204–209. (313)

BRADY, J. V., and NAUTA, W. J. H. Subcortical mechanisms in emotional behavior: affective changes following septal forebrain lesions in the albino rat. *J. comp. physiol. Psychol.*, 1953, **46**, 399–346. (313, 322, 452–454)

BRADY, J. V., PORTER, R. W., CONRAD, D. G., and MASON, J. W. Avoidance behavior and the development of gastroduodenal ulcers. *J. exp. Anal. Behav.*, 1958, **1**, 69–73. (338)

BRADY, J. V., SCHREINER, L., GELLER, I., and KLING, A. Subcortical mechanisms in emotional behavior: The effect of rhinencephalic injury upon the acquisition and retention of a conditioned avoidance response in cats. *J. comp. physiol. Psychol.*, 1954, **47**, 179–186. (451, 453)

BRAZIER, M. A. B., reference given in text. (570)

BREMER, F. Cerveau "isole" et physiologie du sommeil. *Compt. rend. Soc. de Biol.*, 1935, **118**, 1235–1241. (347)

BRIDGES, K. M. B. Emotional development in early infancy. *Child Develpm.*, 1932, **3**, 324–341. (307)

BRIDGMAN, C. S., and SMITH, K. U. The absolute threshold of vision in cat and man with observations on its relation to the optic cortex. *Amer. J. Physiol.*, 1942, **136**, 463–466. (200)

BRIERLEY, J. B., and BECK, E. The effects upon behavior of lesions in the dorsomedial and anterior thalamic nuclei of cat and monkey. In G. E. W. Wolstenholme and C. M. O'Conner (Eds.), *Neurological basis of behavior*. Boston: Little, Brown, 1958. (318)

BROBECK, J. R. Food and temperature. *Recent progress in hormone research*, 1960, **16**, 439–446. (364, 377)

BROBECK, J. R., see Anand, Strominger.

BROBECK, J. R., TEPPERMAN, J., and LONG, C. N. H. Experimental hypothalamic hyperphagia in the albino rat. *Yale J. Biol. Med.*, 1943, **15**, 831–853. (377)

BRODIE, D. A., MALIS, J. L., MORENO, O. M., and BOREN, J. J. Nonreversability of the appetitive characteristics of intracranial stimulation. *Amer. J. Physiol.*, 1960, **199**, 707–709. (329)

BRODWICK, M., see Roberts.

BRODY, P. N., see Lehrman.

BROGDEN, W. J., and GANTT, W. H. Intraneural conditioning. *Arch. Neurol. Psychiat.*, 1942, **48**, 437–455. (463)

BROMILEY, R. B. Conditioned responses in a dog after removal of neocortex. *J. comp. physiol. Psychol.*, 1948, **41**, 102–110. (449, 450)

BROMILEY, R. B. The development of conditioned responses in cats after unilateral decortication. *J. comp. physiol. Psychol.*, 1948, **41**, 155–164. (450)

BROMILEY, R. B., see Galambos.

BROMILEY, R. B., and BARD, P. A study of the effect of estrin on the responses to genital stimulation shown by decapitate and decerebrate female cats. *Amer. J. Physiol.*, 1940, **129**, 318–319. (416, 417)

BRONSON, F. H., see Eleftheriou, Kaelbling.

BROOKHART, J. M., DEY, F. L., and RANSON, S. W. Failure of ovarian hormones to cause mating reactions in spayed guinea pigs with hypothalamic lesions. *Proc. Soc. exp. Biol. Med.*, 1940, **44**, 61–64. (418)

BROWMAN, L. G. Light in its relation to activity and oestrus rhythms in the albino rat. *J. exp. Zool.*, 1937, **75**, 375–388. (404)

BROWMAN, L. G. The effect of bilateral optic enucleation on the voluntary muscular activity of the albino rat. *J. exp. Zool.*, 1942, **91**, 331–344. (355)

BROWMAN, L. G. Modified spontaneous activity rhythms in rats. *Amer. J. Physiol.*, 1944, **142**, 633–637. (355)

BROWN, C. W., see Ghiselli.

BROWN, C. W., and GHISELLI, E. E. Subcortical mechanisms in learning. IV. Olfactory discrimination. *J. comp. Psychol.*, 1938, **26**, 109–120. (128)

BROWN, G. W., and COHEN, B. D. Avoidance and approach learning motivated by stimulation of identical hypothalamic loci. *Amer. J. Physiol.*, 1959, **197**, 153–157. (333)

BROWN, H. D., see Smith, S. M.

BROWN, M. A., see Bryan.

BROWN, P. K., see Wald.

BROZEK, J., and FABRYKANT, M. *Psychodietetics: fundamentals and applications.* Unpublished manuscript, 1962. (556)

BROZEK, J., and VAES, G. Experimental investigation on the effects of dietary deficiencies on animal and human behavior. *Vitam. Horm.*, 1961, **19**, 43–94. (556)

BRUCE, H. M., and PARROTT, D. M. V. Role of olfactory sense in pregnancy block by strange males. *Science*, 1960, **131**, 1526. (405)

BRUSH, E. S., MISHKIN, M., and ROSVOLD, H. E. Effects of object preferences and aversions on discrimination learning in monkeys with frontal lesions. *J. comp. physiol. Psychol.*, 1961, **54**, 319–325. (500)

BRUST-CARMON, H., see Hernández-Peón

BRYAN, E., and BROWN, M. A. A method for differential diagnosis of brain damage in adolescents. *J. nerv. ment. Dis.*, 1957, **125**, 69–72. (534, 541)

BUCHER, V. M., see Nauta.

BUCY, P. C. Effects of extirpation in man. In P. C. Bucy (Ed.), *The precentral motor cortex.* Urbana, Ill.: Univ. Illinois Press, 1944. (460)

BUCY, P. C., see Klüver.

BULLOCK, T. H. Neuron doctrine and electro-physiology. *Science*, 1959, **129**, 997–1002. (68)

BURES, J., and BUREŠOVÁ, OLGA. The use of Leão's spreading depression in the study of interhemispheric transfer of memory traces. *J. comp. physiol. Psychol.*, 1960, **53**, 558–563. (508)

BUREŠOVÁ, O., see Bures.

BURKE, W., see Bishop.

BURSTEN, B., and DELGADO, M. M. R. Positive reinforcement induced by intracerebral stimulation in the monkey. *J. comp. physiol. Psychol.*, 1958, **51**, 6–10. (327)

BURSTEN, S. D., see Riss.

BURTRUM, C. S., reference given in text. (571)

BUTLER, R. A., DIAMOND, I. T., and NEFF, W. D. Role of auditory cortex in discrimination of changes of frequency. *J. Neurophysiol.*, 1957, **20**, 108–120. (491)

CAMILLE, N., see Kleitman.

CAMPBELL, B. A., see Teitelbaum.

CAMPBELL, B. A., and SHEFFIELD, F. D. Relation of random activity to food deprivation. *J. comp. physiol. Psychol.*, 1953, **46**, 320–322. (356)

CANNON, W. B. The James-Lange theory of emotions: a critical examination and an alternative theory. *Amer. J. Psychol.*, 1927, **39**, 106–124. (310)

CANNON, W. B. *Bodily changes in pain, hunger, fear, and rage.* New York: Appleton-Century-Crofts, 1929. (31, 333)

CANNON, W. B. *The wisdom of the body.* New York: Norton, 1932. (386)

CANNON, W. B., reference given in text. (316, 570)

CANNON, W. B., and WASHBURN, A. L. An explanation of hunger. *Amer. J. Physiol.*, 1912, **29**, 441–454. (370)

CAREY, N., see Constantinides.

CARLSON, A. J. *The control of hunger in health and disease.* Chicago: Univer. Chicago Press, 1916.

CARLSON, A. J., see Wangensteen.

CARLSON, N. J., see Black.

CARLTON, P. L., and MARKS, R. A. Cold exposure and heat reinforced operant behavior. *Science*, 1958, **128**, 1344. (394)

CARMICHAEL, L., reference given in text. (130)

CARPENTER, J. A. Anticipatory behavior in the rat following frontal lesions. *J. comp. physiol. Psychol.*, 1952, **45**, 413–418. (529)

CARR, W. J. The effect of adrenalectomy upon the NaCl taste threshold in rat. *J. comp. physiol. Psychol.*, 1952, **45**, 377–380. (369)

CERF, J. A., see Otis.

CHADWICK, C. S. Further observations on the water drive in triturus viridescens. II. Induction of water drive with lactogenic hormone. *J. exp. Zool.*, 1941, **86**, 175–187. (438)

CHANG, H.-T. The evoked potentials. In J. Field, H. W. Magoun, and V. E. Hall (Eds.), *Handbook of physiology*, Vol. 1. Washington, D. C.: American Physiological Society, 1959. (77)

CHANG, J. J., see Tasaki.

CHAPLIN, J. P., see Young, P. T.

CHASE, A. M., see Hecht.

CHENG, F-Y. The effects of stomach distention on thirst: The value of using a variety of measures. *Acta Psychol. Taiwanica*, 1958, **1**, 144–152. (389)

CHHINA, G. S., see Anand.

CHOW, K. L. A retrograde cell degeneration study of the cortical projection field of the pulvinar in the monkey. *J. comp. Neurol.*, 1950, **93**, 313–340. (501)

CHOW, K. L. Further studies on selective ablation of associative cortex in relation to visually mediated behavior. *J. comp. physiol. Psychol.*, 1952, **45**, 109–118. (499, 502)

CHOW, K. L. Lack of behavioral effects following destruction of some thalamic association nuclei in monkeys. *Arch. Neurol. Psychiat.*, 1954, **71**, 762–771. (524)

CHOW, K. L. Effects of temporal neocortical ablation on visual discrimination learning sets in monkeys. *J. comp. physiol. Psychol.*, 1954, **47**, 194–198. (501)

CHOW, K. L. Effect of local electrographic after-discharge on visual learning and retention in monkey. *J. Neurophysiol.*, 1961, **24**, 391-400.

CHOW, K. L., see Blum, Diamond, Orbach.

CHOW, K. L., DEMENT, W. C., and JOHN, E. R. Conditioned electrocorticographic potentials and behavioral avoidance response in cat. *J. Neurophysiol.*, 1957, **20**, 482–493. (473)

CIZEK, L. J. Long-term observations on relationship between food and water ingestion in the dog. *Amer. J. Physiol.*, 1959, **197**, 342–346. (360, 361)

CLARK, G. Sexual behavior in rats with lesions in the anterior hypothalamus.

CLARK, G. Prepubertal castration in the male chimpanzee with some effects of replacement therapy. *Growth*, 1945, **9**, 327–339. (406)

CLARK, G., see Lashley.

CLARK, W. E. L., reference given in text. (45)

CLARK, W. G. Psychotomimetic (hallucinogenic) drugs. *Mind*, 1963, **1**, 293–317. (108)

CLAUSEN, J. *Visual sensations (phosphenes) produced by AC sine wave stimulation.* Copenhagen, Denmark: Ejnar Munksgaard, 1955. (188)

CLEMENTE, C. D., GREEN, J. D., and DEGROOT, J. Studies on behavior following rhinencephalic lesions in adult cats. *Anat. Rec. Amer. Ass. Anat.*, 1957, 127, 279. (322)

CLOUDSLEY-THOMPSON, J. L., reference given in text. (570)

COAKLEY, J. D., see Culler.

COBB, S. *Foundations of neuropsychiatry.* Baltimore: Williams & Wilkins, 1941. (49)

COBB, S., reference given in text. (570)

COHEN, B. D., see Brown.

COHEN, M. J., LANDGREN, S., STRÖM, L., and ZOTTERMAN, Y. Cortical reception of touch and taste in the cat. *Acta Physiol. Scandinav.*, 1957, **40**, Suppl. 135. (120)

COLE, J. O., see Ross.

COLE, J. W., reference given in text. (571)

COLE, K. S., and CURTIS, H. J. Electric impedance of the squid giant axon during activity. *J. gen. Physiol.*, 1939, **22**, 649–670. (63)

CONCON, J. M., see Mertz.

CONGER, J., see Sawrey.

CONRAD, D. G., see Brady, Mason, Porter, Sidman.

CONRAD, K., reference given in text. (543)

CONSTANTINIDES, P. C., and CAREY, N. The alarm reaction. *Scient. Amer.*, 1949, **180**, (Mar.), 20–23. (337)

COOK, L., DAVISON, A. B., DAVIS, D. J., GREEN, H., and FELLOWS, E. J. Ribonucleic acid: Effect on conditioned behavior in rats. *Science*, 1963, **141**, 268–269. (553)

COONS, E. E., and MILLER, N. E. Conflict versus consolidation of memory traces to explain "retrograde amnesia" produced by ECS. *J. comp. physiol. Psychol.*, 1960, **53**, 524–431. (548)

CORDEAU, J. P., see Courville.

CORNING, W. C., and JOHN, E. R. Effect of ribonuclease on retention of conditioned response in regenerated planarians. *Science*, 1961, **134**, 1363–1365. (552)

CORNSWEET, J. C., see Riggs.

CORNSWEET, T., see Riggs.

CORRELL, J. W. Adipose tissue: Ability to

respond to nerve stimulation in vitro. *Science*, 1963, **140**, 387–388. (88)

COSTELLO, R. T., reference given in text. (571)

COURVILLE, J., WALSH, J., and CORDEAU, J. P. Functional organization of the brain stem reticular formation and sensory input. *Science*, 1962, **138**, 973–975. (349)

COURY, J. N., see Fisher.

COVELL, W. P., see Davis.

CRISLER, G. Salivation is unnecessary for the establishment of the salivary conditioned reflex induced by morphine. *Amer. J. Physiol.*, 1930, **94**, 553–556. (475)

CROZIER, W. J. Regarding the existence of the "common chemical sense" in vertebrates. *J. comp. Neurol.*, 1916, **26**, 1–8. (110)

CROZIER, W. J. Chemoreception. In C. Murchison (Ed.), *Handbook of general experimental psychology*. Worcester, Mass.: Clark Univer. Press, 1934. Pp. 987–1036. (123)

CROZIER, W. J. The theory of the visual threshold. I. Time and intensity. *Proc. Nat. Acad. Sci., Wash.*, 1940, **26**, 54–60. (190)

CROZIER, W. J., and HOLWAY, A. H. Theory and measurement of visual mechanisms. III. ΔI as a function of area, intensity, and wavelength, for monocular and binocular stimulation. *J. gen. Physiol.*, 1939, **23**, 101–141. (182)

CROZIER, W. J., and WOLF, E. Theory and measurement of visual mechanisms. IV. Critical intensities for visual flicker, monocular, and binocular. *J. gen. Physiol.*, 1941, **24**, 505–534. (183)

CULLEN, J. W., see Gengerelli.

CULLER, E., see Girden, Shurrager.

CULLER, E. A., COAKLEY, J. D., SHURRAGER, P. S., and ADES, H. W. Differential effects of curare upon higher and lower levels of the central nervous system. *Amer. J. Psychol.*, 1939, **52**, 266–273. (476)

CUMMINS, G. M., see Grossman.

CURTIS, H. J., see Cole.

DAGNON, J., see Harlow.

DALLENBACH, K. M. Pain: history and present status. *Amer. J. Psychol.*, 1939, **52**, 331–347. (246)

DARROW, D. C., and YANNET, H. The changes in the distribution of body water accompanying increase and decrease in extracellular electrolyte. *J. clin. Invest.*, 1935, **14**, 266–275. (390)

DAVIS, C. M. Self selection of diet by newly weaned infants. *Amer. J. Dis. Child.*, 1928, **36**, 651–679. (365)

DAVIS, D. J., see Cook.

DAVIS, E. W., see Bailey.

DAVIS, G. D., see Dean.

DAVIS, H. (Ed.). *Hearing and deafness.* New York: Holt, 1947. (230)

DAVIS, H. Biophysics and physiology of the inner ear. Theory of origin of various potentials. *Physiol. Rev.*, 1957, **37**, 1–49. (227–229)

DAVIS, H. Excitation of auditory receptors. In J. Field, H. W. Magoun, and V. E. Hall (Eds.), *Handbook of physiology*, Vol. 1. Washington, D. C.: American Physiological Society, 1959. (211, 217, 226, 227, 232)

DAVIS, H., reference given in text. (570)

DAVIS, H., see Galambos, Stevens.

DAVIS, H., BENSON, R. W., COVELL, W. P., FERNÁNDEZ, C., GOLDSTEIN, R., KATSUKI, Y., LEGOUIX, J.-P., MC AULIFFE, D. R., and TASAKI, I. Acoustic trauma in the guinea pig. *J. Acoust. Soc. Amer.*, 1953, **25**, 1180–1189 (228)

DAVIS, H., MORGAN, C. T., HAWKINS, J. E., JR., GALAMBOS, R., and SMITH, F. W. Temporary deafness following exposure to loud tones and noise. *Acta Otolaryng.*, 1950, Suppl. 88, 1–57. (228)

DAVIS, J. D., and KEEHN, J. D. Magnitude of reinforcement and consummatory behavior. *Science*, 1959, **130**, 269–271. (371)

DAVIS, L. E., reference given in text. (293)

DAVIS, R., see Bishop

DAVIS, R. C., see Kellogg

DAVIS, R. C., GARAFOLO, L., KVEIM, K. Conditions associated with gastrointestinal activity. *J. comp. physiol. Psychol,.* 1959, **52**, 466–475. (370)

DAVIS, R. T., see Harlow.

DAVISON, A. B., see Cook.

DEAN, W. H., and DAVIS, G. D. Behavior changes following caudate lesions in rhesus monkey. *J. Neurophysiol.*, 1959, **22**, 525–537. (524)

DEANE, G. E. Human heart rate responses during experimentally induced anxiety. *J. exp. Psychol.*, 1961, **61**, 353–359. (480)

DEAUX, E., see Gormezano.

DEESE, J., see Kellogg.

DE GROOT, J., see Clemente.

DELGADO, M. M. R. Study of some cerebral structures related to transmission and elaboration of noxious stimulation. *J. Neurophysiol.*, 1955, **18**, 261–275. (318)

DELGADO, M. M. R., see Bursten, Rosvold.

DELGADO, M. M. R., ROBERTS, W. W., and MILLER, N. E. Learning motivated by electrical stimulation of the brain. *Amer. J. Physiol.*, 1954, **179**, 587–593. (324, 325)

DE LORENZO, A. J., see Zubek.

DEMBER, W. N., see Roberts.

DEMENT, W., and KLEITMAN, N. Cyclic variations in EEG during sleep and their relation to eye movements, body motility, and dreaming. *EEG clin. Neurophysiol.*, 1957, **9**, 673–690. (343)

DEMENT, W. C., see Chow.

DE MILLE, R. Intellect after lobotomy in

schizophrenia. *Psychol. Monogr.*, 1962, **76**, No. 16, 1–18. (545)

DE MOLINA, FERNANDEZ, A., and HUNS-PERGER, R. W. Central representation of affective reactions in forebrain and brain stem: Electrical stimulation of amygdala, stria terminalis, and adjacent structures. *J. Physiol.*, 1959, **145**, 251–265. (316)

DEMPSEY, E. W., see Boling, Morison.

DEMPSEY, E. W., and RIOCH, D. MC K. The localization in the brain stem of the oestrous responses of the female guinea pig. *J. Neurophysiol.*, 1939, **2**, 9–18. (417)

DENNIS, W. The sensory control of the white rat in the maze habit. *J. genet. Psychol.*, 1929, **36**, 59–89. (513)

DENNIS, W., and SOLLENBERGER, R. T. Negative adaptation in the maze exploration of albino rats. *J. comp. Psychol.*, 1934, **18**, 197–206. (521)

DENNIS, W. H., see Börnstein.

DENNY-BROWN, D., reference given in text. (257)

DE ROBERTIS, E., SALGANICOFF, L., ZIEHER, L. M., and RODRIGUEZ DE LORES ARNAIZ, G. Acetylcholine and cholinacetylase content of synaptic vesicles. *Science*, 1963, **140**, 300–301. (72, 91)

DETHIER, V. G., reference given in text. (570)

DETHIER, V. G., and STELLAR, E. *Animal behavior: Its evolutionary and neurological basis.* Englewood Cliffs, N. J.: Prentice-Hall, 1961. (54)

DEUTSCH, J. A. *The structural basis of behavior.* Chicago: Univer. of Chicago Press, 1961. (329)

DEUTSCH, J. A., see Howarth.

DEUTSCH, J. A., and HOWARTH, C. I. Evocation by fear of a habit learned for electrical stimulation of the brain. *Science*, 1962, **136**, 1057–1058. (329)

DE VALOIS, R. L. Color vision mechanisms in the monkey. *J. gen. Physiol.*, 1960, **43**, Part 2, 115–128. (159, 160)

DE VALOIS, R. L., JACOBS, G. H., and JONES, A. E. Effects of increments and decrements of light on neural discharge rate. *Science* 1962, **136**, 986–987. (158)

DE VITO, J. L., see Isaac.

DEY, F. L., see Brookhart.

DEY, F. L., FISHER, C., BERRY, C. M., and RANSON, S. W. Disturbances in reproductive functions caused by hypothalamic lesions in female guinea pigs. *Amer. J. Physiol.*, 1940, **129**, 39–46. (418)

DEY, F. L., LEININGER, C. R., and RANSON, S. W. The effect of hypophyseal lesions on mating behavior in female guinea pigs. *Endocrinology*, 1942, **30**, 323–326. (418)

DIAMOND, I. T., see Butler, Goldberg.

DIAMOND, I. T., and CHOW, K. L. Biological psychology. In S. Koch (Ed.), *Psychology: A study of a science*, Vol. 4. New York: McGraw-Hill, 1962. (494, 499, 500)

DIAMOND, I. T., and NEFF, W. D. Ablation of temporal cortex and discrimination of auditory patterns. *J. Neurophysiol.*, 1957, **20**, 300–315. (225, 491)

DIMMICK, F. L., and HUBBARD, M. R. The spectral location of psychologically unique yellow, green, and blue. *Amer. J. Psychol.*, 1939, **52**, 242–254. (171)

DIMMICK, F. L., and HUBBARD, M. R. The spectral components of psychologically unique red. *Amer. J. Psychol.*, 1939, **52**, 348–353. (171)

DINGMAN, W., and SPORN, M. B. The incorporation of 8-azaguanine into rat brain RNA and its effect on maze-learning by the rat: An inquiry into the biochemical basis. *J. Psychiat. Res.* (London), 1961, **1**, 1–11. (553)

DOBRZECKA, C., see Wyrwicka.

DODWELL, P. C. Further evidence on learning without performance in a water maze. *Psychon. Sci.*, 1964, **1**, 23–24. (445)

DONALDSON, L. R., and ALLEN, G. H., cited by Hasler, 1960. (437)

DONHOFFER, H., see Grastyán.

DONOVAN, B. T., and VAN DER WERFF TEN BOSCH, J. J. The hypothalamus and sexual maturation in the rat. *J. Physiol.*, 1959, **147**, 78–92. (418)

DOTY, R. W. Potentials evoked in cat cerebral cortex by diffuse and by punctiform photic stimuli. *J. Neurophysiol.*, 1958, **21**, 437–464. (161, 163)

DOTY, R. W. Functional significance of the topographical aspects of the retinocortical projection. In R. Jung and H. Kornhuber (Eds.), *The visual system: Neurophysiology and psychophysics.* Berlin: Springer-Verlag, 1961.

DOTY, R. W. Conditioned reflexes formed and evoked by brain stimulation. In D. E. Sheer (Ed.), *Electrical stimulation of the brain.* Austin, Tex.: Univer. Texas Press, 1961. (192, 194, 196, 460, 462)

DOTY, R. W., see Beck.

DOTY, R. W., BECK, E. C., and KOOI, K. A. Effect of brain-stem lesions on conditioned responses of cats. *Exp. Neurol.*, 1959, **1**, 360–385. (456, 457)

DOTY, R. W., and GIURGEA, C. Conditioned reflexes established by coupling electrical excitation of two cortical areas. In J. Delafresnaye (Ed.), *Brain mechanisms and learning.* London: Blackwell Scientific Publications, 1961. (463, 464)

DOTY, R. W., and GRIMM, F. R. Cortical responses to local electrical stimulation of retina. *Exp. Neurol.*, 1962, **5**, 319–334. (161)

DOTY, R. W., and RUTLEDGE, L. T. Generalization between cortically and peripherally applied stimuli eliciting conditioned reflexes. *J. Neurophysiol.*, 1959, **22**, 428–435. (460–462)

DOUGLAS, R. J., see Isaacson.

DOWNER, J., and ZUBEK, J. P. Role of the cerebral cortex in temperature discrimination in the rat. *J. comp. physiol. Psychol.*, 1954, **47**, 199–203. (485)

DRYER, R. L., see Smalley.

DUA, S., see Sharma.

DUNBAR, H. F. *Emotions and bodily changes.* 4th ed. New York: Columbia Univer. Press, 1954. (336, 337)

DUNCAN, C. P. The retroactive effect of electroshock on learning. *J. comp. physiol. Psychol.*, 1949, **42**, 32–44. (547, 548)

DURUP, G., and FESSARD, A. L'électroencéphalogramme de l'homme. *L'année Psychol.*, 1935, **36**, 1. (467)

DUSSER DE BARENNE, J. G., reference given in text. (285)

DYKMAN, R. A., see Shurrager.

ECCLES, J. C. Neuron physiology—Introduction. In J. Field, H. W. Magoun, and V. E. Hall (Eds.), *Handbook of physiology*, Vol. 1. Washington, D. C.: American Physiological Society, 1959. (62–64, 72–74)

ECKERT, J. F., see Richter.

ECKHAUS, E., see Hernández-Peón.

EDWARDS, W. Recent research on pain perception. *Psychol. Bull.*, 1950, **47**, 449–474. (256)

EGGER, M. D., and FLYNN, J. P. Amygdaloid suppression of hypothalamically elicited attack behavior. *Science*, 1962, **136**, 43–44. (321)

EISNER, E. The relationship of hormones to the reproductive behaviour of birds, referring especially to parental behaviour: A review. *Anim. Behav.*, 1960, **8**, 155–179. (425)

EKMAN, G. Dimensions of color vision. *J. Psychol.*, 1954, **38**, 467–474. (171, 172)

ELDER, J. H., see Jacobsen.

ELDER, S. T., see Bishop.

ELEFTHERIOU, B. E., and BRONSON, F. H. Interaction of olfactory and other environmental stimuli on implantation in the deer mouse. *Science*, 1962, **137**, 764. (405)

EPSTEIN, A. N. Water intake without the act of drinking. *Science*, 1960, **131**, 497–498. (389)

EPSTEIN, A. N. Reciprocal changes in feeding behavior produced by intrahypothalamic chemical injections. *Amer. J. Physiol.*, 1960, **199**, 969–974. (381, 384)

EPSTEIN, A. N., see Teitelbaum.

EPSTEIN, A. N., and TEITELBAUM, P. Regulation of food intake in the absence of taste, smell, and other oropharyngeal sensations. *J. comp. physiol. Psychol.*, 1962, **55**, 753–759. (374)

ERICKSON, T. C., see Penfield.

ERIKSEN, S. C. The relative effect of a cerebral lesion upon learning, retention and transfer. *J. comp. Psychol.*, 1939, **27**, 373–391. (512)

ERLANGER, J., and GASSER, H. S. *Electrical signs of nervous action.* Philadelphia: Univer. Penn. Press, 1937. (78, 248)

ERULKAR, S. D., and FILLENZ, MARIANNE. Single-unit activity in the lateral geniculate body of the cat. *J. Physiol.*, 1960, **154**, 206–218. (158)

ESPIR, M. L. E., reference given in text. (571)

ESTES, W. K., reference given in text. (570)

EVANS, C. L. *Starling's principle of human physiology*, 9th ed. Philadelphia: Lea & Febiger, 1945, P. 192. (20)

EWER, R. F. Ethological concepts. *Science*, 1957, **126**, 599–603. (421)

FABRYKANT, M., see Brozek.

FALK, J. L., see O'Kelly.

FANTZ, R. L., see Orbach.

FARNER, D. S. Comparative physiology: Photo periodicity. *Annu. Rev. Physiol.*, 1961, **23**, 71–96. (439)

FARNER, D. S., MEWALDT, L. R., and IRVING, S. D. The roles of darkness and light in the activation of avian gonads. *Science*, 1953, **118**, 351–352. (400)

FARNSWORTH, P. R., reference given in text. (570)

FATT, P. Skeletal neuromuscular transmission. In J. Field, H. W. Magoun, and V. E. Hall (Eds.), *Handbook of physiology*, Vol. 1. Washington, D. C.: American Physiological Society, 1959. (75, 80)

FAZEKAS, J. F., see Himwich.

FEINBERG, M., see Kellogg.

FELLOWS, E. J., see Cook.

FERGUSON, D. C., and FISHER, A. E. Behavior disruption in Cebus monkeys as a function of injected substances. *Science*, 1963, **139**, 1281–1282. (563)

FERNÁNDEZ, C., see Davis.

FESSARD, A., reference given in text. (571)

FESSARD, A., see Durup.

FIELD, J., MAGOUN, H. W., and HALL, V. E. (Eds.), *Handbook of physiology.* Washington, D. C.: American Physiological Society, 1959 (Vol. 1), 1960 (Vols. 2 & 3). (165, 272, 543, 570)

FIELDS, P. E. Guiding migrant salmon. *Scient. Monthly*, 1957, **85**, 10–22. (437)

FILLENZ, M., see Erulkar.

FINAN, J. L. Effects of frontal lobe lesions on temporally organized behavior in monkeys. *J. Neurophysiol.*, 1939, **2**, 208–226. (525)

FINAN, J. L. Delayed response with predelay reinforcement in monkeys after removal of the frontal lobes. *Amer. J. Psychol.*, 1942, **55**, 202–214. (526)

FINCH, G. Salivary conditioning in atropinized dogs. *Amer. J. Physiol.*, 1938, **124**, 136–141. (475)

FINCH, G., see Girden.

FINLEY, C. B. Equivalent losses in accuracy of response after central and after peripheral sense deprivation. *J. comp. Neurol.*, 1941, **74**, 203–237. (513, 515)

FISHER, A. E., see Ferguson, Vaughan.

FISHER, A. E., and COURY, J. N. Cholinergic tracing of a central neural circuit underlying the thirst drive. *Science*, 1962, 691–693. (392)

FISHER, C., see Dey.

FLEXNER, J. B., FLEXNER, L. B., and STELLAR, E. Memory in mice as affected by intracerebral puromycin. *Science*, 1963, **141**, 57–59. (553)

FLEXNER, L. B., see Flexner, J. B.

FLINT, D., see O'Kelly.

FLYNN, J. P., see Egger.

FLYNN, J. P., and WASMAN, M. Learning and cortically evoked movement during propagated hippocampal after discharges. *Science*, 1960, **131**, 1607–1608. (466)

FORSSMAN, H., LEHMANN, O., and THYSELL, T. Reproduction in mongolism. *Amer. J. Ment. Defic.*, 1961, **65**, 495–498. (556)

FOUNTAIN, G., JR., see Kennard.

FOWLER, H., see Beach.

FRANK, K. Identification and analysis of single unit activity in the central nervous system. In J. Field, H. W. Magoun, and V. E. Hall (Eds.), *Handbook of physiology*, Vol. 1. Washington, D. C.: American Physiological Society, 1959. (79)

FRANK, M., see Lashley.

FRANK, S., see Maturana.

FRANKENHAEUSER, M., see Russell.

FRANZ, S. I., see Lashley.

FREEDMAN, B. Conditioning of respiration and its psychosomatic implications. *J. nerv. ment. Dis.*, 1951, **113**, 1–19. (480)

FRENCH, G. M. Locomotor effects of regional ablations of frontal cortex in rhesus monkeys. *J. comp. physiol. Psychol.*, 1959, **52**, 18–24. (359)

FRENCH, G. M. Spatial discontiguity in monkeys with lesions of the frontal cortex. *Science*, 1962, **135**, 728–729. (528)

FRENCH, J. D. The reticular formation. *Scient. Amer.*, 1957, **196**, 54–60. (42)

FRENCH, J. D., see Segundo.

FRITSCH, G., and HITZIG, E., historical, no reference given. (284)

FUENTES, I., see Gormezano.

FULLER, R. W., see Mertz.

FULTON, J. F. *Physiology of the nervous system*. 1st ed. New York: Oxford, 1938. (32, 44, 131, 285)

FULTON, J. F. *Physiology of the nervous system*. 2nd ed. New York: Oxford, 1943. (244)

FULTON, J. F., see Ruch.

FUNKENSTEIN, D. H. The physiology of fear and anger. *Scient. Amer.*, 1955, **192** (May), 74 (336)

FURTH, J. J., see Hurwitz.

FUSTER, J. M. Effects of stimulation of brain stem on tachistoscopic perception. *Science*, 1958, **127**, 150. (351, 352)

GALAMBOS, R. Some recent experiments on the neurophysiology of hearing. *Ann. Otol. Rhin. Laryngol.*, 1956, **65**, 1053–1059. (214).

GALAMBOS, R. Suppression of auditory nerve activity by stimulation of efferent fibers to the cochlea. *J. Neurophysiol.*, 1956, **19**, 424-437. (218)

GALAMBOS, R. Electrical correlates of conditioned learning. In M. Brazier (Ed.), *The central nervous system and behavior*. New York: Josiah Macy, Jr. Foundation, 1958. (468)

GALAMBOS, R. A glia-neural theory of brain function. *Proc. Nat. Acad. Sci.*, 1961, **47**, 129–136. (21)

GALAMBOS, R., reference given in text. (570)

GALAMBOS, R., see Davis, Hearst, Hubel, Porter, Rose, Simmons.

GALAMBOS, R., and DAVIS, H. The response of single auditory-nerve fibers to acoustic stimulation. *J. Neurophysiol.*, 1943, **6**, 39–57. (220, 221, 232, 236, 237)

GALAMBOS, R., and DAVIS, H. Inhibition of activity in single auditory nerve fibers by acoustic stimulation. *J. Neurophysiol.*, 1944, **7**, 287–304. (222)

GALAMBOS, R., and DAVIS, H. Action potentials from single auditory-nerve fibers? *Science*, 1948, **108**, 513. (220)

GALAMBOS, R., and GRIFFIN, D. R. Obstacle avoidance by flying bats: the cries of bats. *J. exp. Zool.*, 1942, **89**, 475–490. (227)

GALAMBOS, R., and MORGAN, C. T. The neural basis of learning. In J. Field, H. W. Magoun, and V. E. Hall (Eds.), *Handbook of physiology*, Vol. 3. Washington, D. C.: American Physiological Society, 1960. (444)

GALAMBOS, R., MYERS, R. E., and SHEATZ, G. C. Extralemniscal activation of auditory cortex in cats. *Amer. J. Physiol.*, 1961, **200**, 23–28. (215, 224)

GALAMBOS, R., ROSE, J. E., BROMILEY, R. B., and HUGHES, J. R. Microelectrode studies on medial geniculate body of cat. II. Response to clicks. *J. Neurophysiol.*, 1952, **15**, 359–380. (233)

GALAMBOS, R., and RUPERT, A. Action of the middle ear muscles in normal cats. *J. Acoust. Soc. Amer.*, 1959, **31**, 349–355. (226, 227)

GALAMBOS, R., SCHWARTZKOPFF, J., and

RUPERT, A. Microelectrode study of superior olivary nuclei. *Amer. J. Physiol.*, 1959, **197**, 527–536. (237, 238)

GALAMBOS, R., and SHEATZ, G. C. An electroencephalographic study of classical conditioning. *Amer. J. Physiol.*, 1962, **203**, 173–184. (468–470)

GALAMBOS, R., SHEATZ, G., and VERNIER, V. G. Electrophysiological correlates of a conditioned response in cats. *Science*, 1956, **123**, 376–377. (469)

GALLAGHER, T. J., see Griffiths.

GANTT, W. H., see Brogden, Light.

GARAFOLO, L., see Davis.

GARDNER, E. *Fundamentals of neurology.* Philadelphia: Saunders, 1947. (29, 124, 570)

GARNER, W. R. Auditory signals. In *Human factors in undersea warfare.* Washington, D. C.: National Research Council, 1949. Pp. 201–217. (235)

GASSER, H. S., see Erlanger.

GASSER, H. S., and GRAHAM, H. T. Potentials produced in the spinal cord by stimulation of dorsal roots. *Amer. J. Physiol.*, 1933, **102**, 303–320. (65)

GASTAUT, H. Etat actuel des connaissances sur l'electroencephalographie du conditionnement. Colloque de Marseille. *EEG clin. Neurophysiol.*, 1957, Suppl. 6. (471)

GAULT, F. P., and LEATON, R. N. Electrical activity of the olfactory system. *EEG clin. Neurophysiol.*, 1963, **15**, 299–304. (353)

GAZE, R. M., and GORDON, G. Some observations on the central pathway of cutaneous impulses in the cat. *Quart. J. exp. Physiol.*, 1955, **40**, 187–194. (266)

GEBHARD, J. W. Threshold of the human eye for electric stimulation by different wave forms. *J. exp. Psychol.*, 1952, **44**, 132–140. (188)

GEBHARD, J. W. Motokawa's studies on electric excitation of the human eye. *Psychol. Bull.*, 1953, **50**, 73–111. (188)

GELDARD, F. A. The perception of mechanical vibration: IV. Is there a separate "vibratory sense"? *J. gen. Psychol.*, 1940, **22**, 291–320. (242)

GELDARD, F. A. *The human senses.* New York: Wiley-Interscience, 1953. (164, 240, 570)

GELLER, I., see Brady.

GELLER, I., SIDMAN, M., and BRADY, J. V. The effect of electroconvulsive shock on a conditioned emotional response: A control for acquisition recency. *J. comp. physiol. Psychol.*, 1955, **48**, 130–131. (548)

GELLHORN, E. Autonomic imbalance and the hypothalamus. Minneapolis: Univer. Minnesota Press, 1957. (348, 570)

GELLHORN, E. Prolegomena to a theory of emotions. In *Perspectives in biology and medicine*, Vol. 4, No. 4. Chicago: Univer. Chicago Press, 1961. Pp. 403–436. (309–311, 317)

GELLHORN, E., reference given in text. (571)

GENGERELLI, J. A., and CULLEN, J. W. J. Studies in the neurophysiology of learning: II. Effect of brain stimulation during black-white discrimination on learning behavior in the white rat. *J. comp. physiol. Psychol.*, 1955, **48**, 311–319. (465)

GENGERELLI, J. A., PROCTOR, D. M., and WOSKOW, M. H. Studies in the neurophysiology of learning: V. Differential effects of various rates of cerebral "driving" on behavioral modification. *Psychol. Rep.*, 1960, **7**, 123–141. (331)

GENGERELLI, J. A., and WOSKOW, M. H. Studies in the neurophysiology of learning: IV. Effect of brain stimulation on learning behavior of the white rat in the Skinner box. *Psychol. Rep.*, 1958, **4**, 109–208. (465)

GERALL, A. A., see Phoenix.

GERARD, R. W., reference given in text. (570, 571)

GERMAN, W. J., see Ruch.

GHENT, L., reference given in text. (570)

GHENT, L., see Semmes.

GHISELLI, E. E. The relationship between the superior colliculus and the striate area in brightness discrimination. *J. genet. Psychol.*, 1938, **52**, 151–157. (200)

GHISELLI, E. E. Mass action and equipotentiality of the cerebral cortex in brightness discrimination. *J. comp. Psychol.*, 1938, **25**, 273–290. (495, 521)

GHISELLI, E. E., see Brown.

GHISELLI, E. E., and BROWN, C. W. Subcortical mechanisms in learning: VII. The effect of cerebral injury upon the relative distribution of errors in a spatial maze. *J. comp. Psychol.*, 1938, **26**, 301–309. (517)

GIBSON, R. M., see Allen.

GILLERY, R. W. Afferent fibers to the dorsomedial thalamic nucleus in the cat. *J. Anat., London,* 1959, **93**, 403–419. (456)

GILMAN, A. The relation between blood osmotic pressure, fluid distribution, and voluntary water intake. *Amer. J. Physiol.*, 1937, **120**, 323–328. (390)

GILMER, B. V. H. The glomus body as a receptor of cutaneous pressure and vibration. *Psychol. Bull.*, 1942, **39**, 73–93. (246)

GILMORE, R. W., see Beach.

GIRDEN, E. Cerebral mechanisms in conditioning under curare. *Amer. J. Psychol.*, 1940, **53**, 397–406. (476)

GIRDEN, E. The dissociation of blood pressure conditioned responses under erythroidine and curare. *J. exp. Psychol.*, 1942, **31**, 219–231. (476)

GIRDEN, E. The acoustic mechanism of the cerebral cortex. *Amer. J. Psychol.*, 1942, **55**, 518–527. (234, 477)

GIRDEN, E., and CULLER, E. Conditioned responses in curarized striate muscle in dogs. *J. comp. Psychol.*, 1937, **23**, 261–274. (476)

GIRDEN, E., METTLER, F. A., FINCH, G., and CULLER, E. Conditioned responses in a decorticate dog to acoustic, thermal, and tactile stimulation. *J. comp. Psychol.*, 1936, **21**, 367–385. (449)

GIURGEA, C., see Doty.

GLICK, S. M., see Roth.

GLICKMAN, S. E. Deficits in avoidance learning produced by stimulation of the ascending reticular formation. *Canad. J. Psychol.*, 1958, **12**, 97–102. (465)

GLICKSTEIN, M., and SPERRY, R. W. Intermanual somesthetic transfer in split brain monkeys. *J. comp. physiol. Psychol.*, 1960, **53**, 322–327. (508)

GOLDBERG, J. J., DIAMOND, I. T., and NEFF, W. D. Auditory discrimination after ablation of temporal and insular cortex in cat. *Fed. Proc.*, 1957, **16**, 47–48. (492)

GOLDBERG, M. M., and NEFF, W. D. Frequency discrimination after bilateral section of the brachium of the inferior colliculus. *J. comp. Neurol.*, 1961, **113**, 265–282. (224, 225)

GOLDSTEIN, K. *The organism.* New York: American Book, 1939. (542)

GOLDSTEIN, R., see Davis, Landau.

GOODMAN, L. S., see Smith, S. M.

GORDON, G., see Gaze.

GORDON, H. L., reference given in text. (571)

GORMEZANO, I., SCHNEIDERMAN, N., DEAUX, E., and FUENTES, I. Nictitating membrane: Classical conditioning and extinction in the albino rabbit. *Science*, 1962, **138**, 33–34. (479)

GORSKI, R. A., see Barraclough.

GOULD, J., and MORGAN, C. T. Auditory sensitivity in the rat. *J. comp. Psychol.*, 1942, **34**, 321–329. (227)

GOY, R. W., see Phoenix.

GRAHAM, C. H., see Riggs.

GRAHAM, C. H., and HSIA, Y. Color defect and color theory. *Science*, 1958, **127**, 675–682. (177, 178)

GRAHAM, H. T., see Gasser.

GRANIT, R. Color receptors of the frog's retina. *Acta Physiol. Scand.*, 1941, **3**, 137–151. (146)

GRANIT, R. *Sensory mechanisms of the retina.* London: Oxford Univer. Press, 1947. (142)

GRANIT, R. Neural activity in the retina. In J. Field, H. W. Magoun, and V. E. Hall (Eds.), *Handbook of physiology,*

Vol. 1. Washington, D. C.: American Physiological Society, 1959. (142, 144, 148)

GRANIT, R., see Bernhard.

GRANIT, R., MUNSTERHJELM, A., and ZEWI, M. The relation between concentration of visual purple and retinal sensitivity to light during adaptation. *J. Physiol.*, 1939, **96**, 31–44. (180, 181)

GRANIT, R., and SKOGLUND, C. R. The effect of temperature on the artificial synapse formed by the cut end of the mammalian nerve. *J. Neurophysiol.*, 1945, **8**, 211–217. (249)

GRANIT, R., and THERMAN, P. P. Excitation and inhibition in the retina and in the optic nerve. *J. Physiol.*, 1935, **83**, 359–381. (184)

GRASTYÁN, E., see Lissák.

GRASTYÁN, E., LISSÁK, L., MADARÁSZ, I., and DONHOFFER, H. Hippocampal electrical activity during the development of conditioned reflexes. *EEG clin. Neurophysiol.*, 1959, 11, 409–430. (472)

GRAY, J. A. B. Initiation of impulses at receptors. In J. Field, H. W. Magoun, and V. E. Hall (Eds.), *Handbook of physiology,* Vol. 1. Washington, D. C.: American Physiological Society, 1959. (66, 67, 72)

GREEN, H., see Cook.

GREEN, J. D., see Clemente.

GREEN, J. D., and ARDUINI, A. Hippocampal electrical activity in arousal. *J. Neurophysiol.*, 1954, **17**, 533–557. (472)

GREGERSEN, M. I. Studies on the regulation of water intake. II. Conditions affecting the daily water intake of dogs as registered continuously by a potometer. *Amer. J. Physiol.*, 1932, **102**, 344–349. (386)

GRIFFIN, D. R. Sensory physiology and the orientation of animals. *Amer. Scient.*, 1953, **41**, 209–244. (439)

GRIFFIN, D. R., see Galambos.

GRIFFITHS, W. J., and GALLAGHER, T. J. Differential dietary choices of albino rats occasioned by swimming. *Science*, 1953, **118**, 780. (364)

GRIMM, R. F., see Doty.

GRODSKY, M. A., see Bevan.

GROSSER, G. S., and HARRISON, J. M. Behavioral interaction between stimulated cortical points. *J. comp. physiol. Psychol.*, 1960, **53**, 229–233. (461)

GROSSMAN, M. I., CUMMINS, G. M., and IVY, A. C. The effect of insulin on food intake after vagotomy and sympathectomy. *Amer. J. Physiol.*, 1947, **149**, 100–102. (370, 374)

GROSSMAN, S. P. Eating or drinking elicited by direct adrenergic or cholinergic stimulation of hypothalamus. *Science*, 1960, **132**, 301–332. (384, 392, 393)

GRUNDFEST, H. Synaptic and ephatic transmission. In J. Field, H. W. Magoun, and V. E. Hall (Eds.), *Handbook of physiology*, Vol. 1. Washington, D. C.: American Physiological Society, 1959. (66, 67)

GUTMANN, E., and JAKOUBEK, B. Nervous regulation of conditioned hyperglycemia to nociceptive stimulation. *Science*, 1959, **131**, 1096–1098. (479)

GUYER, M. F. *Animal biology*, 3rd ed. New York: Harper, 1941. (22)

HAIG, C., see Hecht.

HAHN, H. Die Adaptation des Geschmackssinnes. *Z. Sinnesphysiol.*, 1934, **65**, 105–145. (117)

HAHN, H. *Beitrage zur Reizphysiologie.* Heidelberg: Scherer, 1949. (117)

HALL, J. F. The relationship between external stimulation, food deprivation, and activity. *J. comp. physiol. Psychol.*, 1956, **49**, 339–341. (356)

HALL, V. E., reference given in text. (570)

HALL, V. E., see Field.

HALSTEAD, W. C. Thinking, imagery and memory. In J. Field, H. W. Magoun, and V. E. Hall (Eds.), *Handbook of physiology*, Vol. 3. Washington, D. C.: American Physiological Society, 1960. (541, 545)

HALSTEAD, W. C., reference given in text. (571)

HALSTEAD, W. C., see Katz.

HALSTEAD, W. C., KNOX, G. W., and WALKER, A. E. Modification of cortical activity by means of intermittent photic stimulation in the monkey. *J. Neurophysiol.*, 1942, 5, 349–355. (187)

HAMMEL, H. T., see Hardy.

HARDY, J. D., HAMMEL, H. T., and NAKAYAMA, T. Observations on the physiological thermostat in homoiotherms. *Science*, 1962, **136**, 326. (394)

HARLOW, H. F. Recovery of pattern discrimination in monkeys following unilateral occipital lobectomy. *J. comp. Psychol.*, 1939, 27, 467–489. (498)

HARLOW, H. F. Thinking. In H. Helson (Ed.), *Theoretical foundations of psychology*. New York: Van Nostrand, 1951. (497)

HARLOW, H. F., reference given in text. (570)

HARLOW, H. F., see Brady, Meyer, Riopelle, Spaet, Waisman, Warren.

HARLOW, H. F., and DAGNON, J. Problem solution by monkeys following bilateral removal of prefrontal areas. I. Discrimination and discrimination reversal problems. *J. exp. Psychol.*, 1943, **32**, 351–356. (523).

HARLOW, H. F., DAVIS, R. T., SETTLAGE, P. H., and MEYER, D. R. Analysis of frontal and posterior association syndromes in brain-damaged monkeys. *J. comp. physiol. Psychol.*, 1952, **45**, 419–429. (500, 523)

HARLOW, H. F., and JOHNSON, T. Problem

solution by monkeys following bilateral removal of the prefrontal areas: III. Test of initiation of behavior. *J. exp. Psychol.*, 1943, **32**, 495–500. (527)

HARLOW, H. F., and STAGNER, R. Effect of complete striate muscle paralysis upon the learning process. *J. exp. Psychol.*, 1933, **16**, 283–294. (475, 476)

HARPMAN, J. A., see Woolard.

HARRIS, G. W., and LEVINE, S. Sexual differentiation of the brain and its experimental control. *J. Physiol.*, 1962, **163**, 42–43. (412)

HARRISON, J. M., see Grosser, Tracy.

HARRISON, J. M., WARR, W. B., and IRVING, R. E. Second order neurons in the acoustic nerve. *Science*, 1962, **138**, 893–895. (214)

HARTLINE, H. K. The response of single optic nerve fibers of the vertebrate eye to illumination of the retina. *Amer. J. Physiol.*, 1938, **121**, 400–415. (147, 148)

HARVEY, J A., see Thomas.

HASLER, A. D. Guideposts of migrating fishes. *Science*, 1960, **132**, 785–792. (437, 438)

HASLERUD, G. M., see Jacobsen.

HAWKES, C. D., see Richter.

HAWKINS, J. E., JR., see Davis.

HAYNES, J. R., and SELLS, S. B. Assessment of organic brain damage by psychological tests. *Psychol. Bull.*, 1963, **60**, 316–325. (540, 541)

HEAD, H. *Studies in neurology*, Vols. 1 & 2. London: Frowde, Hodder & Stoughton, 1920. (317)

HEARST, E., BEER, B., SHEATZ, G., and GALAMBOS, R. Some electrophysiological correlates of conditioning in the monkey. *EEG clin. Neurophysiol.*, 1960, **12**, 137–152. (468)

HEATH, G. G. Luminosity curves of normal and dichromatic observers. *Science*, 1958, **128**, 775–776. (330)

HEATH, R. G. (Ed.), *Studies in schizophrenia*. Cambridge, Mass.: Harvard Univer. Press, 1954. (177)

HEATH, R. G., see Bishop.

HEBB, D. O. The innate organization of visual activity. III. Discrimination of brightness after removal of the striate cortex in the rat. *J. comp. Psychol.*, 1938, **25**, 427–437. (503)

HEBB, D. O. The effect of early and late brain injury upon test scores, and the nature of normal adult intelligence. *Proc. Amer. Philos. Soc.*, 1942, **85**, 275–292. (534)

HEBB, D. O. *The organization of behavior*. New York: Wiley-Interscience, 1949. (548, 549)

HEBB, D. O. The distinction between "classical" and "instrumental." *Canad. J. Psychol.*, 1956, **10**, 165–166. (443)

HEBB, D. O., reference given in text. (570)

HEBB, D. O., see Beach.

HEBB, D. O., and WILLIAMS, K. A method of rating animal intelligence. *J. gen. Psychol.*, 1946, **34**, 59–65. (515)

HECAEN, H., see Piercy.

HECHT, S., reference given in text. (191, 199)

HECHT, S., HAIG, C., and CHASE, A. M. The influence of light adaptation on subsequent dark adaptation of the eye. *J. gen. Physiol.*, 1937, **20**, 831–850. (178, 179)

HEILBRUN, A. B., JR. Lateralization of cerebral lesion and performance on spatial-temporal tasks. *AMA Arch. Neurol.*, 1959, **1**, 282–287. (536)

HEMMINGSEN, A. M., and KRARUP, N. B. Rhythmic diurnal variations in the oestrous phenomena of the rat and their susceptibility to light and dark. *K. danske vidensk. Selsk. Skr.*, 1937, **13**, No. 7. Pp. 61. (404)

HENNEMAN, E., see Mountcastle.

HENSEL, H., and ZOTTERMAN, Y. Action potentials of cold fibres and intracutaneous temperature gradient. *J. Neurophysiol.*, 1951, 14, 377–385.

HENSEL, H., and ZOTTERMAN, Y. The response of mechanoreceptors to thermal stimulation. *J. Physiol.*, 1951, 115, 16–24. (248, 250)

HENSEN, C. O., see Hubel.

HERBERT, C. C., reference in text. (571)

HERNÁNDEZ-PEÓN, R., see Jouvet, Lavín.

HERNÁNDEZ-PEÓN, R., SCHERRER, H., and JOUVET, M. Modification of electrical activity in cochlear nucleus during "attention" in unanesthetized cats. *Science*, 1956, **123**, 331–332. (353, 469)

HERNÁNDEZ-PEÓN, R., BRUST-CARMON, H., ECKHAUS, E., LOPEZ-MENDOZA, E., and ALCOCER-CUARON, C. Effects of cortical and subcortical lesions on salivary conditioned response. *Acta neur. latinoam.*, 1958, **4**, 111–120. (457)

HERVEY, G. R. The effects of lesions in the hypothalamus in parabiotic rats. *J. Physiol.*, 1959, **145**, 336–352. (380)

HESS, E. H. Imprinting. *Science*, 1959, **130**, 133–141. (437)

HESS, E. H., and POLT, J. M. Pupil size as related to interest value of visual stimuli. *Science*, 1960, **132**, 349–350. (336, 479)

HESS, W. R. Hirnreizversuche ueber den Mechanismus des Schlafes. *Arch. Psychiat.*, 1929, **86**, 287–292. (347)

HESS, W. R. *Diencephalon—Autonomic and extra-pyramidal functions.* New York: Grune & Stratton, 1954. (347)

HESS, W. R. *Das Zwischenhirn: Syndrome, Lokalisationen, Funktionen.* 2nd ed. Basel: Schwabe, 1954. (316)

HESS, W. R., JR., see Akert.

HETHERINGTON, A. W., and RANSON, S. W. The spontaneous activity and food in-

take of rats with hypothalamic lesions. *Amer. J. Physiol.*, 1942, **136**, 609–617. (358)

HILGARD, E. R., and MARQUIS, D. G. *Conditioning and learning.* New York: Appleton-Century, 1940. (444)

HILL, J. H., see Stellar.

HILL, R. M. Unit responses of the rabbit lateral geniculate nucleus to monochromatic light on the retina. *Science*, 1962, **135**, 98–99. (159, 160)

HILL, R. M., see Barlow.

HILL, W. F. Activity as an autonomous drive. *J. comp. physiol. Psychol.*, 1956, **49**, 15–19. (356)

HIMWICH, H. E. Psychopharmacologic drugs. *Science*, 1958, **127**, 59–72. (95, 565)

HIMWICH, H. E., reference given in text. (571)

HIMWICH, H. E., and FAZEKAS, J. F. Cerebral metabolism in mongolian idiocy and phenylpyruvic oligophrenia. *Arch. Neurol. Psychiat.*, Chicago, 1940, 44, 1213–1218. (556)

HIND, J. E. An electrophysiological determination of tonotopic organization in auditory cortex of cat. *J. Neurophysiol.*, 1953, **16**, 475–489. (223)

HINES, M., see Richter.

HINGTGEN, J. N., and APRISON, M. H. Behavioral response rates in pigeons: effect of -Methyl-m-tyrosine. *Science*, 1963, **141**, 169–171. (559)

HITZIG, E., see Fritsch.

HODOS, W., and VALENSTEIN, E. S. Motivational variables affecting the rate of behavior maintained by intracranial stimulation. *J. comp. physiol. Psychol.*, 1960, **53**, 502–508. (327, 332)

HOEBEL, B., reference given in text. (379)

HOEBEL, B. G., and TEITELBAUM, P. Hypothalamic control of feeding and self-stimulation. *Science*, 1962, **135**, 375–376. (328, 384, 385)

HOLWAY, A. H., see Crozier.

HOLZ-TUCKER, A. M., see Beach.

HONZIK, C. H. The sensory basis of maze learning in rats. *Comp. Psychol. Monogr.*, 1936, **13**, No. 64. (513, 514)

HOOKE, R., historical, no reference given. (12)

HOSKINS, R. G. *Tides of life.* New York: Norton, 1933. (92)

HOVORKA, E. J., see Kellogg.

HOWARTH, C. I., see Deutsch.

HOWARTH, C. I., and DEUTSCH, J. A. Drive decay: The cause of fast "extinction" of habits learned for brain stimulation. *Science*, 1962, **137**, 35–36. (329)

HSIA, Y., see Graham.

HUBEL, D. H. Single unit activity in lateral geniculate body and optic tract of unrestrained cats. *J. Physiol.*, 1960, **150**, 91–104. (158)

HUBEL, D. H. Integrative processes in ven-

physiological correlates of avoidance conditioning in the cat. *J. Pharmacol. exp. Therapeut.*, 1959, **125**, 252–274. (473)

JOHN, E. R., and KILLAM, K. F. Electrophysiological correlates of differential approach-avoidance conditioning in cats. *J. nerv. ment. Dis.*, 1960, **131**, 183–201. (473)

JOHNSON, E. P. The character of the B-wave in the human electroretinogram. *AMA Arch. Ophthalmol.*, 1958, 565–591. (143)

JOHNSON, O., see Morgan.

JOHNSON, R. W., see Riss.

JOHNSON, T., see Harlow.

JOLLIFFE, C. L., see Sperling.

JONES, A. E., see de Valois.

JONES, M. H. A study of the common chemical sense. *Amer. J. Psychol.*, 1954, **67**, 696–698. (110)

JONES, M. R., reference given in text. (571)

JOUVET, M., 1957, cited by Lindsley, 1960.

JOUVET, M., see Hernández-Peón.

JOUVET, M., and HERNÁNDEZ-PEÓN, R. Mecanismes neurophysiologiques concernant l'habituation, l'attention et le conditionnement. In H. Fischgold and H. Gastaut (Eds.), Conditionnement et reactivité en electroencephalographie. *EEG clin. Neurophysiol.*, 1957, **39**, Suppl. 6. (468)

KAADA, B. R., RASMUSSEN, E. W., and KVEIM, O. Effects of hippocampal lesions on maze learning and retention. *Exp. Neurol.*, 1961, **3**, 333–335. (517)

KABAT, H., see Ranson.

KAELBLING, R., KING, F. A., ACHENBACH, K., BRANSON, R., and PASAMANICK, B. Reliability of autonomic responses. *Psychol. Rep.*, 1960, **6**, 143–163, Monogr. Suppl. 4–16. (336)

KAGAN, J., and BERKUN, M. The reward value of running activity. *J. comp. physiol. Psychol.*, 1954, **47**, 108. (356)

KALLMANN, F. J. The genetic theory of schizophrenia; and analysis of 691 schizophrenic twin index families. *Amer. J. Psychiat.*, 1946, **103**, 309–322. (561)

KANDEL, G., see Boynton.

KAPLAN, S. J., see Pribram.

KAPPERS, C. U. A. On the structural laws in the nervous system. The principles of neuro-biotaxis. *Brain*, 1921, **44**, 125. (549)

KASDON, S. C., reference given in text. (45)

KATSUKI, Y., see Davis, Sumi.

KATZ, J. J., and HALSTEAD, W. C. Protein organization and mental function. *Comp. Psychol. Monogr.*, 1950, **20**, 1–39. (549)

KAYSER, C. *The physiology of natural hibernation.* New York: Pergamon, 1961. (439)

KEEHN, J. D., see Davis.

KEESEY, R. E. The relation between pulse frequency, intensity, and duration and the rate of responding for intracranial stimulation. *J. comp. physiol. Psychol.*, 1962, **55**, 671–678. (331)

KEESEY, U. T., see Riggs.

KELLER, A. D., see Barker.

KELLOGG, W. N., and BASHORE, W. D. The influence of hemidecortication upon bilateral avoidance conditioning in dogs. *J. comp. physiol. Psychol.*, 1950, **43**, 49–61. (450)

KELLOGG, W. N., DEESE, J., PRONKO, N. H., and FEINBERG, M. An attempt to condition the chronic spinal dog. *J. exp. Psychol.*, 1947, **37**, 99–117. (457)

KELLOGG, W. N., and HOVORKA, E. J. Are localized CRs lost or eradicated following unilateral cortical damage? *J. comp. physiol. Psychol.*, 1951, **44**, 37–49. (450)

KELLOGG, W. N., SCOTT, V. B., DAVIS, R. C., and WOLF, I. S. Is movement necessary for learning? *J. comp. Psychol.*, 1940, **29**, 43–74. (474)

KELLY, A. H., BEATON, L. E., and MAGOUN, H. W. A midbrain mechanism for faciovocal activity. *J. Neurophysiol.*, 1946, **9**, 181–190. (314)

KENNARD, M. A., SPENCER, S., and FOUNTAIN, G., JR. Hyperactivity in monkeys following lesions of the frontal lobes. *J. Neurophysiol.*, 1941, **4**, 512–524. (359)

KENNEDY, G. C. The hypothalamic control of food intake in rats. *Proc. Roy. Soc.*, Ser. B., 1950, **137**, 535–549. (379)

KENNEDY, J. L. The effects of complete and partial occipital lobectomy upon the thresholds of visual real movement in the cat. *J. genet. Psychol.*, 1939, **54**, 119–149. (197)

KESSEN, M. L., see Berkun.

KETY, S. S. Biochemical theories of schizophrenia. *Science*, 1959, **129**, 1528–1532. (562, 564)

KILLAM, J. F., see John.

KIM, C. Sexual activity of male rats following ablation of hippocampus. *J. comp. physiol. Psychol.*, 1960, **53**, 553–557. (420)

KIMBLE, G. A., reference given in text. (571)

KIMURA, D. Some effects of temporal-lobe damage on auditory perception. *Canad. J. Psychol.*, 1961, **15**, 156–165. (535)

KIMURA, K., and BEIDLER, L. M. Microelectrode study of taste bud of the rat. *Amer. J. Physiol.*, 1956, **187**, 610. (115)

KINDER, E. F. A study of nest-building activity of the albino rat. *J. exp. Zool.*, 1927, **47**, 117–161. (431)

KING, F. A. Effects of septal and amygdaloid lesions on emotional behavior and conditioned avoidance responses in the rat. *J. nerv. ment. Dis.*, 1958, **126,** 57–63. (313, 322, 452, 453)

KING, F. A., see Kaelbling, Stone.

KING, F. A., and MEYER, P. M. Effects of amygdaloid lesions upon septal hyper-emotionality in the rat. *Science*, 1958, **128,** 655–656. (323)

KINNEY, J. A. S. Sensitivity of the eye to spectral radiation at scotopic and mesopic intensity levels. *J. Opt. Soc. Amer.*, 1955, **45,** 507–514. (174)

KINSEY, A. C. Homosexuality: Criteria for a hormonal explanation of the homo-sexual. *J. clin. Endocrinol.*, 1941, **1,** 424–428. (398)

KIRKPATRICK, C. M., and LEOPOLD, A. C. Photoperiodicity in animals: The role of darkness. *Science*, 1953, **117,** 389–391. (400)

KISTIAKOWSKY, G. B. On the theory of odors. *Science*, 1950, 112, 154–155. (123)

KLEFFNER, F. R., see Landau.

KLEIST, K. *Sensory aphasia and amusia: The myeloarchitectonic basis.* (Trans. by F. J. Fish and J. B. Stanton) New York: Pergamon Press, 1962, (542, 571)

KLEITMAN, N. *Sleep and wakefulness.* Chicago: Univer. of Chicago Press, 1939. (342, 344, 346)

KLEITMAN, N. Sleep. *Scient. Amer.*, 1952, **187** (Nov.), 34–38. (346)

KLEITMAN, N. *Sleep and wakefulness* (Rev. ed.). Chicago: Univer. of Chicago Press, 1963. (339, 343, 344)

KLEITMAN, N., see Aserinsky, Dement.

KLEITMAN, N., and CAMILLE, N. Studies on the physiology of sleep. VI. Be-havior of decorticated dogs. *Amer. J. Physiol.*, 1932, **100,** 474–480. (346)

KLINEBERG, O. *Social psychology* (Rev. ed). New York: Holt, 1954. (307)

KLING, A. Amygdalectomy in the kitten. *Science*, 1962, **137,** 429–430. (420)

KLING, A., see Brady, Schreiner.

KLING, A., ORBACH, J., SCHWARTZ, N. B., and TOWNE, J. C. Injury to the limbic system and associated structures in cats. *Arch. gen. Psychiat.*, 1960, **3,** 391–420. (321)

KLING, J. W., and MATSUMIYA, Y. Relative reinforcement values of food and intra-cranial stimulation. *Science*, 1962, **135,** 668–670. (327)

KLÜVER, H. *Behavior mechanisms in mon-keys.* Chicago: Univer. of Chicago Press, 1933. (533)

KLÜVER, H. An analysis of the effects of the removal of the occipital lobes in monkeys. *J. Psychol.*, 1936, **2,** 49–61. (493)

KLÜVER, H. Certain effects of lesions of the occipital lobes in macques. *J. Psychol.*, 1937, **4,** 383–401. (194)

KLÜVER, H., and BUCY, P. C. Preliminary analysis of functions of the temporal lobes in monkeys. *Arch. Neurol. Psy-chiat.*, Chicago, 1939, **42,** 979–1000. (376, 500)

KNAPP, H. D., TAUB, E., and BERMAN, A. J. Effect of deafferentation on a condi-tioned avoidance response. *Science*, 1958, **128,** 842–843. (478)

KNIGHTON, R. S., reference given in text. (571)

KNOWLES, W. B., see Lindsley.

KNOX, G. W., see Halstead.

KOELLA, W. P., see Akert.

KOLLER, G. Der Nestbau der weissen Maus und seine hormonale Auslösung. *Verh. dtsch. zool. Ges.*, Freiburg, 1952, 160–168. (432)

KOLLER, G. Hormonale und psychische Steuerung beim Nestbau weiser Mäuse. *Zool. Anz.* (Suppl.), 1956, **19,** 123–132. (431, 432)

KONORSKI, J. In *Physiological mechanisms in animal behavior.* Society of Experi-mental Biology Symposium, No. 4. New York: Academic Press, 1950. (445)

KONORSKI, J., reference given in text. (571)

KOOI, K. A., see Doty.

KOSKOFF, Y. D., see Kruper.

KOSMAN, A. J., see Morgane.

KRARUP, N. B., see Hemmingsen.

KRASNE, F. B. General disruption resulting from electrical stimulus of ventromedial hypothalamus. *Science*, 1962, **138,** 822–823. (380)

KRECH, D., see Krechevsky, Rosenzweig.

KRECHEVSKY, I. Hereditary nature of "hypotheses." *J. comp. Psychol.*, 1933, **16,** 99–116. (521)

KRECHEVSKY, I. Brain mechanisms and "hypotheses." *J. comp. Psychol.*, 1935, **19,** 425–468. (521)

KRECHEVSKY, I. Brain mechanisms and brightness discrimination learning. *J. comp. Psychol.*, 1936, **21,** 405–445. (493, 521)

KRECHEVSKY, I. Brain mechanisms and variability: I. Variability within a means-end-readiness. *J. comp. Psychol.*, 1937a, **23,** 121–138. (522)

KRECHEVSKY, I. Brain mechanisms and variability: II. Variability where no learning is involved. *J. comp. Psychol.*, 1937b, **23,** 139–163. (522)

KRECHEVSKY, I. Brain mechanisms and variability: III. Limitations of the effect of cortical injury upon variability. *J. comp. Psychol.*, 1937c, **23,** 351–364. (522)

KRIEG, W. J. S. Connections of the cerebral cortex. I. The albino rat. C. Extrinsic connections. *J. comp. Neurol.*, 1947, **86,** 267–394. (455)

KRUGER, L., and PORTER, P. A behavioral study of the functions of the rolandic cortex in the monkey. *J. comp. Neurol.*, 1958, **109**, 439–467. (488)

KRUPER, D. C., KOSKOFF, Y. D., and PATTON, R. A. Delayed alternation in hemicerebrectomized monkeys. *Science*, 1961, **133**, 701–702. (524)

KRYTER, K. D., and ADES, H. W. Studies on the function of the higher acoustic nervous centers in the cat. *Amer. J. Psychol.*, 1943, **56**, 501–536. (234, 490)

KUFFLER, S. W. Discharge patterns and functional organization of mammalian retina. *J. Neurophysiol.*, 1953, **16**, 37–68. (148, 149)

KUNTZ, A. *A textbook of neuroanatomy.* 4th ed. Philadelphia: Lea & Febiger, 1945. (48, 262, 263)

KUZNETS, G., see Tryon, R. C.

KVEIM, K., see Davis.

KVEIM, O., see Daada.

LACEY, J. I. The evaluation of autonomic responses: toward a general solution. *Ann. N. Y. Acad. Sci.*, 1956, **67**, 123–164. (336)

LANDAU, W. M., GOLDSTEIN, R., and KLEFFNER, F. R. Congenital aphasia: A clinicopathologic study. *Neurology*, 1960, **10**, 915–921. (233)

LANDGREN, S., see Andersson, Cohen.

LANGELD, H. S., see Boring.

LANGWORTHY, O. R., and RICHTER, C. P. Increases in spontaneous activity produced by frontal lobe lesions in cats. *Amer. J. Physiol.*, 1939, **126**, 158–161. (376)

LANSDELL, H. Laterality of verbal intelligence in the brain. *Science*, 1962, **135**, 922–923. (535)

LANSING, R. W., SCHWARTZ, E., and LINDSLEY, D. B. Reaction time and EEG activation under alerted and nonalerted conditions. *J. exp. Psychol.*, 1959, **58**, 1–7. (350, 351)

LARSSON, S., see Andersson.

LASHLEY, K. S. Studies of cerebral function in learning. V. The retention of motor habits after destruction of the so-called motor areas in primates. *Arch. Neurol. Psychiat.*, Chicago, 1924, **12**, 249–276. (518)

LASHLEY, K. S. *Brain mechanisms and intelligence.* Chicago: Univer. of Chicago Press, 1929. (493, 511, 512, 516, 571)

LASHLEY, K. S. The mechanism of vision: XII. Nervous structures concerned in the acquistion and retention of habits based on reactions to light. *Comp. Psychol. Monogr.*, 1935, **11**, 43–79. (494)

LASHLEY, K. S. Studies of cerebral function in learning: XI. The behavior of the rat in latch-box situations. *Comp. Psychol. Monogr.*, 1935, **11**, 4–42. (518)

LASHLEY, K. S. The mechanism of vision:

XIII. Cerebral function in discrimination of brightness when detail vision is controlled. *J. comp. Neurol.*, 1937, **66**, 471–479. (494)

LASHLEY, K. S. Factors limiting recovery after central nervous lesions. *J. nerv. ment. Dis.*, 1938, **88**, 733–755. (532)

LASHLEY, K. S. The mechanism of vision. XV. Preliminary studies of the rat's capacity for detail vision. *J. gen. Psychol.*, 1938, **18**, 123–193. (497, 502)

LASHLEY, K. S. Experimental analysis of instinctive behavior. *Psychol. Rev.*, 1938, **45**, 445–471. (421–423)

LASHLEY, K. S. The thalamus and emotion. *Psychol. Rev.*, 1938, **45**, 42–61. (311, 317, 318)

LASHLEY, K. S. Conditional reactions in rat. *J. Psychol.*, 1938, **6**, 311–324. (502)

LASHLEY, K. S. The mechanism of vision: XVII. The functioning of small remnants of the visual cortex. *J. comp. Neurol.*, 1939, **70**, 45–67. (195, 498)

LASHLEY, K. S. Thalamo-cortical connections in the rat's brain. *J. comp. Neurol.*, 1941, **75**, 67–121. (157)

LASHLEY, K. S. The mechanism of vision. XVII. Autonomy of the visual cortex. *J. genet. Psychol.*, 1942, **60**, 197–221. (498)

LASHLEY, K. S. Studies of cerebral function in learning. XII. Loss of the maze habit after occipital lesions in blind rats. *J. comp. Neurol.*, 1943, **79**, 431–462. (515)

LASHLEY, K. S. Structural variation in the nervous system in relation to behavior. *Psychol. Rev.*, 1947, **54**, 325–334. (531)

LASHLEY, K. S. The mechanism of vision: XVIII. Effects of destroying the visual "associative areas" of the monkey. *Genet. Psychol. Monogr.*, 1948, **37**, 107–166. (499)

LASHLEY, K. S., and CLARK, G. The cytoarchitecture of the cerebral cortex of Ateles: a critical examination of architectonic studies. *J. comp. Neurol.*, 1946, **85**, 223–306. (161)

LASHLEY, K. S., and FRANK, M. The mechanism of vision. X. Postoperative disturbances of habits based on detail vision in the rat after lesions in the cerebral visual areas. *J. comp. Psychol.*, 1934, **17**, 355–391. (194)

LASHLEY, K. S., and FRANZ, S. I. The effects of cerebral destruction upon habit-formation and retention in the albino rat. *Psychobiol.*, 1917, **1**, 71–139. (510)

LASHLEY, K. S., and SPERRY, R. W. Olfactory discrimination after the destruction of the anterior thalamic nuclei. *Amer. J. Physiol.*, 1943, **139**, 446–450. (128)

LASHLEY, K. S., and WILEY, L. E. Studies of cerebral function in learning: OX. Mass action in relation to the number of elements in the problem to be learned. *J. comp. Neurol.*, 1933, **57**, 3–55. (512)

LATIES, V. G., and WEISS, B. Thyroid state and working for heat in the cold. *Amer. J. Physiol.*, 1959, **197**, 1028–1034. (394)

LATIES, V. G., and WEISS, B. Behavior in the cold after acclimatization. *Science*, 1960, **131**, 1891–1892. (394)

LAUER, D. W. The role of the motor response in learning. Unpublished doctoral dissertation, Univer. of Michigan, 1951. (477)

LAVÍN, A., ALCOCER-CUARÓN, C., and HERNÁNDEZ-PEÓN, R. Centrifugal arousal in the olfactory bulb. *Science*, 1959, **129**, 331–332. (353)

LAW, O. T., and MEAGHER, W. Hypothalamic lesions and sexual behavior in the female rat. *Science*, 1958, **128**, 1626–1627. (418)

LAWRENCE, M., see Lempert.

LAYMAN, J. D. The avian visual system. I. Cerebral functions of the domestic fowl in pattern vision. *Comp. Psychol. Monogr.*, 1936, **12**, No. 58. (194)

LEÃO, A. A. P. Spreading depression of activity in the cerebral cortex. *J. Neurophysiol.*, 1944, **7**, 359–390. (508)

LEATON, R. N., see Gault.

LEBLOND, C. P. Nervous and hormonal factors in the maternal behavior of the mouse. *J. genet. Psychol.*, 1940, **57**, 327–344. (433)

LEGOUIX, J.-P., see Davis.

LE GRAND, Y., reference given in text. (570)

LEHMANN, O., see Forssman.

LEHRMAN, D. S. A critique of Konrad Lorenz's theory of instinctive behavior. *Quart. Rev. Biol.*, 1953, **28**, 337–363. (422)

LEHRMAN, D. S. The physiological basis of parental feeding behavior in the ring dove (Streptopelia risoria). *Behaviour*, 1955, **7**, 241–286. (429)

LEHRMAN, D. S. On the origin of the reproductive behavior cycle in doves. *Trans. N. Y. Acad. Sci.*, 1959, Ser. II, **21**, 682–688. (400)

LEHRMAN, D. S. Hormonal responses to external stimuli in birds. *Ibis*, 1959, **101**, 478–496. (405–424)

LEHRMAN, D. S. Hormonal regulation of parental behavior in birds and infrahuman mammals, pp. 1268–1382. In W. C. Young (Ed.), *Sex and internal secretion* (3rd ed.), Baltimore; Williams and Wilkins, 1961. (402, 404, 422, 425, 429, 432, 433, 435)

LEHRMAN, D. S., BRODY, P. N., and WORTIS. R. P. The presence of the mate and of nesting material as stimuli for the development of incubation behavior and for gonadotropin secretion in the ring dove (Streptopelia risoria). *Endocrinology*, 1961, **68**, 507–516. (428)

LEININGER, C. R., see Dey.

LELE, P. P., and WEDDELL, G. The relationship between neurohistology and corneal sensibility. *Brain*, 1956, **79**, 119–154. (246)

LE MESSURIER, D. H., reference given in text. (486)

LEMPERT, J., WEVER, E. G., and LAWRENCE, M. The cochleogram and its clinical applications. *Arch. Octolaryng.*, 1947, **45**, 61–67. (228)

LEOPOLD, A. C., see Kirkpatrick.

LESTER, D. Continuous measurement of the depth of sleep. *Science*, 1958, **127**, 1340–1341. (343)

LETTVIN, J. Y., see Maturana.

LEUKEL, F. A comparison of the effects of ECS and anesthesia on acquisition of the maze habit. *J. comp. physiol. Psychol.*, 1957, 50, 300–306. (548)

LEVINE, J. Studies in the interrelations of central nervous structures in binocular vision. I. The lack of bilateral transfer of visual discriminative habits acquired monocularly by the pigeon. *J. genet. Psychol.*, 1945a, **67**, 105–129. (506)

LEVINE, J. Studies in the interrelations of central nervous structures in binocular vision. II. The conditions under which interocular transfer of discriminative habits takes place in the pigeon. *J. genet. Psychol.*, 1945b, **67**, 131–142. (506)

LEVINE, S., see Harris.

LEVINSON, G., see Beach.

LEVITT, K., see Pechtel.

LEWIS, M. Behavior resulting from sodium chloride deprivation in adrenalectomized rats. *J. comp. physiol. Psychol.*, 1960, **53**, 464–467. (368)

LEWIS, T. Pain. New York: Macmillan 1942. (256)

LICKLEY, J. D. *The nervous system.* New York: Longmans, 1919. (40, 210)

LIGHT, J. S., and GANTT, W. H. Essential part of reflex arc for establishment of conditioned reflex. Formation of conditioned reflex after exclusion of motor peripheral end. *J. comp. Psychol.*, 1936, **21**, 19–36. (474)

LILLY, J. C. Learning motivated by subcortical stimulation: The start and stop patterns of behavior. In H. H. Jasper (Ed.), *Reticular formation of the brain.* Boston: Little, Brown, 1958. (330, 332)

LINDSLEY, D. B. Emotion. In S. S. Stevens (Ed.), *Handbook of experimental psychology.* New York: Wiley-Interscience, 1951. (311)

LINDSLEY, D. B. Attention, consciousness, sleep and wakefulness. In J. Field. H. W. Magoun, and V. E. Hall (Eds.), *Handbook of physiology*, Vol. 3. Washington, D. C.: American Physiological Society, 1960. (315, 341, 348, 349)

LINDSLEY, D. B., see Lansing.

LINDSLEY, D. B., SCHREINER, L. H., KNOWLES, W. B., and MAGOUN, H. W. Behavioral and EEG changes following chronic brain stem lesions in the cat. EEG clin. Neurophysiol., 1950, 2, 483–498. (348)

LINDSLEY, D. B., SCHREINER, L. H., and MAGOUN, H. W. An electromyographic study of spasticity. J. Neurophysiol., 1949, 12, 197–205. (284)

LINDZEY, G., WINSTON, H. D., and WHITNEY, G. D. Defecation in stressful and non-stressful situations. Psychon. Sci., 1964, 1, 3–4. (334)

LISSÁK, L., see Grastyán.

LISSÁK, K., and GRASTYÁN, E. The changes of hippocampal electrical activity during conditioning. In H. H. Jasper and G. D. Smirnow (Eds.), The Moscow colloquium on electroencephalography of higher nervous activity. EEG clin. Neurophysiol., 1960, Suppl. 13. (472)

LIVINGSTON, J. R., see Hull.

LIVINGSTON, R. B. Central control of receptors and sensory transmission systems. In J. Field, H. W. Magoun, and V. E. Hall (Eds.), Handbook of physiology, Vol. 1. Washington, D. C.: American Physiological Society, 1959. (216)

LIVINGSTON, W. K. What is pain? Scient. Amer., 1953, 188, 59–66. (249)

LIVINGSTON, W. K. Cerebrospinal fluid. In T. C. Ruch and J. F. Fulton (Eds.), Medical physiology and biophysics, 18th ed. Philadelphia: Saunders, 1960. (54)

LLOYD, D. P. C., and MC INTYRE, A. K. Dorsal column conduction of group I muscle afferent impulses and their relay through Clarke's column. J. Neurophysiol., 1950, 13, 39–54. (258)

LONG, C. N. H., see Brobeck.

LOOFBOURROW, G. N., reference given in text. (571)

LOPEZ-MENDOZA, E., see Hernández-Peón.

LORENTE DE NO, R. Analysis of the activity of the chains of internuncial neurons. J. Neurophysiol., 1938, 1, 207–244. (81)

LORENTE DE NO, R. Continuous conduction of action potentials by peripheral myelinated nerve fibers. Science, 1963, 140, 383. (71)

LORENZ, K. Z. Ueber die Bildung des Instinktbegriffs. Die Naturwissenschaften, 1937, 25, 289–300, 307–318, 324–331. (421)

LOUCKS, R. B. The experimental delimitation of neural structures essential for learning: The attempt to condition striped muscle responses with faradization of the sigmoid gyri. J. Psychol., 1936, 1, 5–44. (460, 463)

LOUCKS, R. B. Studies of neural structures essential for learning. II. The conditioning of salivary and striped muscle responses to faradization of cortical sensory elements, and the action of sleep upon such mechanisms. J. comp. Psychol., 1938, 25, 315–332. (460)

LOUTTIT, R. T., see Yuwiler.

LOWENSTEIN, W. R., TERZUOLO, C. A., and WASHIZU, Y. Separation of transducer and impulse-generating processes in sensory receptors. Science, 1963, 142, 1180–1181. (250)

LUCKHARDT, A. B., see Scott.

LUFKIN, H. M., see Bazett.

LURIE, M. H., see Stevens.

LUTZ, A., see Riss.

LYMAN, C. P. Hibernation in mammals and birds. Amer. Scient., 1963, 51, 127–138. (440)

LYMAN, F. L. (Ed.). Phenylketonuria. Springfield: C. C. Thomas, 1962. (556)

MACHT, M. B., and BARD, P. Studies on decerebrate cats, in the chronic state. Fed. Proc., 1942, 1, 55–56. (314)

MACLEAN, P. D. Psychosomatic disease and the "visceral brain." Psychosomat. Med., 1949, 11, 338–353. (311)

MACLEAN, P. D. The limbic system with respect to self-preservation and the preservation of the species. J. nerv. ment. Dis., 1958, 127, 1–11. (52, 311)

MACNICHOL, E. F., JR., see Svaetichin, Wagner.

MACNICHOL, E. F., JR., and SVAETICHIN, G. Electric responses from the isolated retinas of fishes. Amer. J. Ophthal., 1958, 46, 26–40. (151)

MADARÁSZ, I., see Grastyán.

MADSEN, M. C., and MC GAUGH, J. L. The effect of ECS on one-trial avoidance learning. J. comp. physiol. Psychol., 1961, 54, 522–523. (548)

MAGOUN, H. W. The waking brain. 2nd ed. Springfield, Ill.: C. C. Thomas, 1963. (41, 570)

MAGOUN, H. W., see Brady, Field, Kelly, Lindsley, Moruzzi, Ranson.

MAHER, B. A. Anticipatory and perseverative errors following frontal lesions in the rat. J. comp. physiol. Psychol., 1955, 48, 102–105. (529)

MAIER, N. R. F. Cortical destruction in the posterior part of the brain and its effects on reasoning in rats. J. comp. Neurol., 1932, 56, 179–214. (522)

MAIER, N. R. F. Qualitative differences in the learning of rats in a discrimination situation. J. comp. Psychol., 1939, 27, 289–331. (503)

MAIER, N. R. F. The effect of cortical injury on equivalence reactions in rats. J. comp. Psychol., 1941, 32, 165–189. (503)

MAKI, T., see Nakao.

MALIN, C. F., see Thompson, R.

MALIS, J. L., see Brodie.

MALMO, R. B. Interference factors in delayed response in monkeys after removal of frontal lobes. *J. Neurophysiol.*, 1942, **5**, 295–308. (527)

MANCIA, M., MEULDERS, M., and SANTIBANEZ-H., G. Changes of photically evoked potentials in the visual pathway of the cerveau isole cat. *Arch. Ital. Biol.*, 1959, **97**, 376–398. (158)

MANGAN, J. G., see Mason.

MARGULES, D. L., and OLDS, J. Identical "feeding" and "rewarding" systems in the lateral hypothalamus of rats. *Science*, 1962, **135**, 374–375. (384)

MARQUIS, D. G. Effects of removal of the visual cortex in mammals with observations on the retention of light discrimination in dogs. *Res. Publ. Ass. Res. Nerv. Ment. Dis.*, 1934, **13**, 558–592. (446, 450, 492)

MARQUIS, D. G. Phylogenetic interpretation of the functions of the visual cortex. *Arch. Neurol. Psychiat.*, Chicago, 1935, **33**, 807–815. (194)

MARQUIS, D. G., see Hilgard.

MARX, M. H. A stimulus-response analysis of the hoarding habit in the rat. *Psychol. Rev.*, 1950, **57**, 80–93. (440)

MASON, J. W., see Brady, Porter.

MASON, J. W., MANGAN, J. G., BRADY, J. V., CONRAD, D., and RIOCH, D. MCK. Concurrent plasma epinephrine, norepinephrine and 17-hydroxycorticosteroid levels during conditioned emotional disturbances in monkeys. *Psychosom. Med.*, 1961, **23**, 344–353. (559)

MASSERMAN, J. H. Is the hypothalamus a center of emotion? *Psychosom. Med.*, 1941, **3**, 3–25. (464)

MASSERMAN, J., see Pechtel, Schreiner.

MATSUMIYA, Y., see Kling.

MATHEWS, B. H. C. Nerve endings in mammalian muscle. *J. Physiol.*, 1933, **78**, 1–53. (258)

MATURANA, H. R., and FRANK, S. Directional movement and horizontal edge detectors in the pigeon retina. *Science*, 1963, **142**, 977–979. (150)

MATURANA, H. R., LETTVIN, J. Y., MCCULLOCH, W. S., and PITTS, W. H. Evidence that cut optic nerve fibers in a frog regenerate to their proper places in the tectum. *Science*, 1959, **130**, 1709–1710. (163, 196)

MAYER, J. Regulation of energy intake and the body weight: The glucostatic theory and the lipostatic hypothesis. *Ann. N. Y. Acad. Sci.*, 1955, **63**, 15–43. (375)

MAYER, J., see Anliker, Rozin.

MCAULIFFE, D. R., see Davis.

MCBRIDE, K. E., see Weisenburg.

MCCLEARY, R. A. The nature of the galvanic skin response. *Psychol. Bull.*, 1950, **47**, 97–117. (479)

MCCLEARY, R. A. Taste and post-ingestion factors in specific-hunger behavior. *J.*

comp. physiol. Psychol., 1953, **46**, 411–421. (373)

MCCLEARY, R. A. Type of response as a factor in interocular transfer in the fish. *J. comp physiol. Psychol.*, 1960, **55**, 311–321. (506)

MCCLEARY, R. A. Response specificity in the behavioral effects of limbic system lesions in the cat. *J. comp. physiol. Psychol.*, 1961, **54**, 605–613. (453, 454)

MCCLEARY, R. A., and MORGAN, C. T. Food hoarding in rats as a function of environmental temperature. *J. comp. Psychol.*, 1946, **39**, 371–378. (440)

MCCONNELL, J. V., see Thompson, R.

MCCULLOCH, W. S., see Maturana.

MCELROY, W. D. The mechanism of inhibition of cellular activity by narcotics. *Quart. Rev. Biol.*, 1947, **22**, 25–58. (87)

MCFIE, J., and ZANGWILL, O. L. Visual-constructive disabilities associated with lesions of the left cerebral hemisphere. *Brain*, 1960, **83**, 243–259. (539)

MCGAUGH, J. L., see Madsen.

MCGLONE, B., see Bazett.

MCGUIGAN, F. J., reference given in text. (570)

MCINTYRE, A. K., see Lloyd.

MCNEMAR, Q., reference given in text. (570)

MEAD, L. C. The curve of visual intensity-discrimination in the cat before and after removal of the striate area of the cortex. Unpublished Ph.D. thesis, Univer. of Rochester, 1939. (200, 493)

MEAGHER, W., see Law.

MEEHL, P. E. Schizotaxia, schizotypy, schizophrenia. *Amer. Psychol.*, 1962, **17**, 827–838. (560)

MEIKLE, T. H., JR. Role of corpus callosum in transfer of visual discriminations in cats. *Science*, 1960, **132**, 1496. (507)

MEIKLE, T. H., JR., and SECHZER, J. A. Interocular transfer of brightness discrimination in "split brain" cats. *Science*, 1960, **132**, 734–735. (507)

MERTZ, E. T., FULLER, R. W., and CONCON, J. M. Serum uric acid in young mongoloids. *Science*, 1963, **141**, 535. (556)

METTLER, F. A. Relation between pyramidal and extrapyramidal function. *Res. Publ. Ass. Res. Nerv. Ment. Dis.*, 1942, **21**, 150–277. (359)

METTLER, F. A. (Ed.). *Selective partial ablation of the frontal cortex.* New York: Hoeber, 1949. (545)

METTLER, F. A., see Girden.

MEULDERS, M., see Mancia.

MEWALDT, L. R., see Farner.

MEYER, D. R., see Harlow.

MEYER, D. R., HARLOW, H. F., and SETTLAGE, P. H. A survey of delayed response performance by normal and brain-damaged monkeys. *J. comp.*

physiol. Psychol., 1951, **44**, 17–25. (524)

MEYER, D. R., and WOOLSEY, C. N. Effects of localized cortical destruction upon auditory descriminative conditioning in the cat. *J. Neurophysiol.*, 1952, **15**, 149–162. (490)

MEYER, P. M., see King.

MICHAEL, R. P. Estrogen-sensitive neurons and sexual behavior in female cats. *Science*, 1962, **136**, 322–323. (419)

MILES, J. E., and ROSVOLD, H. E. The effect of prefrontal lobotomy in rhesus monkeys on delayed response performance motivated by pain shock. *J. comp. physiol. Psychol.*, 1956, **49**, 286–292. (529)

MILLER, J. G., reference given in text. (572)

MILLER, N. E. Central stimulation and other new approaches to motivation and reward. *Amer. Psychol.*, 1958, **13**, 100–108. (325, 332)

MILLER, N. E., see Berkun, Coons, Delgado.

MILLER, N. E., BAILEY, C. J., and STEVENSON, J. A. F. Decreased "hunger" but increased food intake resulting from hypothalamic lesions. *Science*, 1950, **112**, 256–259. (378)

MILNER, B. Intellectual function of the temporal lobes. *Psychol. Bull.*, 1954, **51**, 42–62. (500)

MILNER, P. M. The application of physiology to learning theory. In R. A. Patton (Ed.), *Current trends in psychological theory*. Pittsburgh, Pa.: Univer. of Pittsburgh Press, 1961. (549)

MILNER, P. M., see Olds.

MINER, N., see Sperry.

MINNICK, R. S., MARDEN, C. J., and ARIETI, S. The effects of sex hormones on the copulatory behavior of senile white rats. *Science*, 1946, **103**, 749–750. (409)

MIRSKY, A. F., see Peters, Rosvold.

MISHKIN, M. Visual discrimination performance following partial ablations of the temporal lobe: II. Ventral surface vs. hippocampus. *J. comp. physiol. Psychol.*, 1954, **47**, 187–193. (501)

MISHKIN, M. Effects of small frontal lesions on delayed alternation in monkeys. *J. Neurophysiol.*, 1957, **20**, 615–622. (524)

MISHKIN, M., see Battig, Brush, Pribram, Robinson, Rosvold, Wilson.

MISHKIN, M., and PRIBRAM, K. H. Analysis of the effects of frontal lesions in monkeys: I. Variations of delayed alternations. *J. comp. physiol. Psychol.*, 1955, **48**, 492–495. (528)

MISHKIN, M., and PRIBRAM, K. H. Analysis of the effects of frontal lesions in the monkey: II. Variations of delayed response. *J. comp. physiol. Psychol.*, 1956, **49**, 36–40. (524, 527)

MISHKIN, M., ROSVOLD, H. E., and PRIBRAM, K. H. Effects of Nembutal in baboons with frontal lesions. *J. Neurophysiol.*, 1953, **16**, 155–159. (526)

MISHKIN, M., and WEISKRANTZ, L. Effects of delayed reward on visual-discrimination performance in monkeys with frontal lesions. *J. comp. physiol. Psychol.*, 1958, **51**, 276–281. (529)

MITCHELL, P. H. *General physiology*. 5th ed. New York: McGraw-Hill, 1956. (57, 111)

MONCRIEFF, R. W. *The chemical senses*. London: Leonard Hill, 1944; New York: Wiley, 1946. (110, 113, 123)

MONTGOMERY, M. F. The role of the salivary glands in the thirst mechanism. *Amer. J. Physiol.*, 1931, **96**, 221–227. (386)

MOORE, R. Y., see Isaacson, Thomas.

MORENO, O. M., see Brodie.

MORGAN, C. T. The nature of discrimination of movement in the cat with preliminary observations concerning its relation to the visual area of the cortex. Unpublished Master's thesis, Univer. of Rochester, 1937. (197)

MORGAN, C. T. *Physiological psychology*. New York: McGraw-Hill, 1943. (547, 549)

MORGAN, C. T. The hoarding instinct. *Psychol. Rev.*, 1947, **54**, 335–341. (440)

MORGAN, C. T. Physiological theory of drive. In S. Koch (Ed.), *Psychology: A study of a science*, Vol. 1. New York: McGraw-Hill, 1960. (423)

MORGAN, C. T., see Beach, Davis, Galambos, Gould, McCleary, Stellar.

MORGAN, C. T., and STELLAR, E. *Physiological psychology* 2nd ed. New York: McGraw-Hill, 1950. (304, 558)

MORGAN, C. T., STELLAR, E., and JOHNSON, O. Food deprivation and hoarding in rats. *J. comp. Psychol.*, 1943, **35**, 275–295. (440)

MORGAN, C. T., and WOOD, W. M. Cortical localization of symbolic processes in the rat: II. The effect of cortical lesions upon delayed alternation. *J. Neurophysiol.*, 1943, **6**, 173–180. (522)

MORGANE, P. J. Alterations in feeding and drinking behavior of rats with lesions in globi pallidi. *Amer. J. Physiol.*, 1961, **201**, 420–428. (380)

MORGANE, P. J. Electrophysiological studies of feeding and satiety centers in the rat. *Amer. J. Physiol.*, 1961, **201**, 383–844. (383)

MORGANE, P. J., and KOSMAN, A. J. A rhinencephalic feeding center in the cat. *Amer. J. Physiol.*, 1957, **197**, 158–162. (377)

MORGULIS, S., reference given in text. (443)

MORISON, R. S., and DEMPSEY, E. W. A

study of thalamo-cortical relations. *Amer. J. Physiol.*, 1942, **135**, 281–292. (349)

MORLOCK, H. C., see Williams.

MORRELL, F. Electrophysiological contribution to the neural basis of learning. *Physiol. Rev.*, 1961, **41**, 443–494. (466–468, 471)

MORRELL, F., and ROSS, M. Central inhibition in cortical conditioned reflexes. *AMA Arch. Neurol. Psychiat.*, 1953, **70**, 611–616. (472)

MORUZZI, G., and MAGOUN, H. W. Brain stem reticular formation and activation of the EEG. *EEG clin. Neurophysiol.*, 1949, **1**, 455–473. (348)

MOTOKAWA, K. Retinal processes and their role in color vision. *J. Neurophysiol.*, 1949, **12**, 291–303. (188)

MOUNTCASTLE, V. B., reference given in text. (571)

MOUNTCASTLE, V. B., see Bard, Rose.

MOUNTCASTLE, V. B., and HENNEMAN, E. Pattern of tactile representation in thalamus of cat. *J. Neurophysiol.*, 1949, **12**, 85–100. (265)

MOWRER, O. H. On the dual nature of learning—a reinterpretation of "conditioning" and "problem solving." *Harv. Educ. Rev.*, 1947, 102–148. (478)

MOYER, K. E., and BUNNELL, B. N. Effect of injected adrenalin on an avoidance response in the rat. *J. genet. Psychol.*, 1958, **92**, 247–251. (559)

MOYER, K. E., and BUNNELL, B. N. Effect of adrenal demedullation on an avoidance response in the rat. *J. comp. physiol. Psychol.*, 1959, **52**, 215–216. (559)

MÜLLER, J., historical, no reference given. (240)

MUNSTERHJELM, A., see Granit.

MUNTZ, W. R. A. The function of the vertical lobe system of octopus in interocular transfer. *J. comp. physiol. Psychol.*, 1961, **54**, 186–191. (508)

MURRAY, S. M., reference given in text. (571)

MYERS, R. E. Interocular transfer of pattern discrimination in cats, following section of crossed optic fibers. *J. comp. physiol. Psychol.*, 1955, **48**, 470–473. (506)

MYERS, R. E. Localization of function within the corpus callosum—visual gnostic transfer. *Anat. Rec.*, 1956, **124**, 339–340. (507)

MYERS, R. E. Function of corpus callosum in interocular transfer. *Brain*, 1956, **79**, 358–363. (507)

MYERS, R. E. Interhemispheric communication through corpus callosum: limitations under conditions of conflict. *J. comp. physiol. Psychol.*, 1959, **52**, 6–9. (507)

MYERS, R. E., see Galambos, Sperry.

MYERS, R. E., and SPERRY, R. W. Interhemispheric communication through the corpus callosum: mnemonic carryover between the hemispheres. *Arch. Neurol. Psychiat.*, 1958, **80**, 298–303. (507)

NADLER, R. D., see Whalen.

NAKAO, H., and MAKI, T. Effect of electrical stimulation of the nucleus caudatus upon conditioned avoidance behavior in the cat. *Folia psychiat. neurol. Jap.*, 1958, **12**, 258–264. (317, 465)

NAKAYAMA, T., see Hardy.

NASH, H., reference given in text. (571)

NAUTA, W. J. H. Hypothalamic regulation of sleep in rats; an experimental study. *J. Neurophysiol.*, 1946, **9**, 285–316. (347)

NAUTA, W. J. H., see Brady, Whitlock.

NAUTA, W. J. H., and BUCHER, V. M. Efferent connections of the striate cortex in the albino rat. *J. comp. Neurol.*, 1954, **100**, 257–286. (157)

NAUTA, W. J. H., and WHITLOCK, D. G. An anatomical analysis of the non-specific thalamic projection system. In J. F. Delafresnoye (Ed.), *Brain mechanisms and consciousness, a symposium.* Springfield, Ill.: C. C. Thomas, 1954, 81–104. (456)

NEFF, W. D. The effects of partial section of the auditory nerve. *J. comp. physiol. Psychol.*, 1947, **40**, 203–216. (227, 231)

NEFF, W. D. Sensory discrimination. In J. Field, H. W. Magoun, and V. E. Hall (Eds.), *Handbook of physiology*, Vol. 3. Washington, D. C.: American Physiological Society, 1960. (200)

NEFF, W. D. Discriminatory capacity of different divisions of the auditory system. In M. A. B. Brazier (Ed.), *Brain and behavior.* Vol. 1. Washington, D. C.: Amer. Inst. Biol. Sci., 1961. Pp. 205–216. (206, 224, 234, 239, 492)

NEFF, W. D., see Butler, Diamond, Goldberg, Schuknecht, Wever.

NELSON, T. M., see Bartley.

NISSEN, H. W., reference given in text. (570)

NISSEN, H. W., see Beach.

NOORDENBOS, W., reference given in text. (570)

NOSHAY, W. C., reference given in text. (571)

NOTTERMAN, J. M., SCHOENFELD, W. N., and BERSH, P. J. Conditioned heart rate response in human beings during experimental anxiety. *J. comp. physiol. Psychol.*, 1953, **45**, 1–8. (480)

OAKLEY, B., and PFAFFMANN, C. Electrophysiologically monitored lesions in the gustatory thalamic relay of the albino rat. *J. comp. physiol. Psychol.*, 1962, **55**, 155–160. (122)

O'CONNOR, M., reference given in text. (570, 571)

OGAWA, T. Midbrain reticular influences

upon single neurons in lateral geniculate nucleus. *Science,* 1963, **139,** 343–344. (158, 352)

o'KELLY, L. I., and FALK, J. L. Water regulation in the rat: II. The effects of preloads of water and sodium chloride on the bar-pressing performance of thirsty rats. *J. comp. physiol. Psychol.,* 1958, **51,** 22–25. (388)

o'KELLY, L. I., FALK, J. L., and FLINT, D. Water regulation in the rat: I. Gastrointestinal exchange rates of water and sodium chloride in thirsty animals. *J. comp. physiol. Psychol.,* 1958, **51,** 16–21. (385)

OLDS, J. Physiological mechanisms of reward. In M. Jones (Ed.), *Nebraska symposium on motivation,* Vol. 3. Lincoln, Neb.: Univer. Nebraska Press, 1955. (326, 329)

OLDS, J. A preliminary mapping of electrical reinforcing effects in the rat brain. *J. comp. physiol. Psychol.,* 1956, **49,** 281–285. (327)

OLDS, J. Self-stimulation of the brain. *Science,* 1958, **127,** 315–323. (327, 328, 331)

OLDS, J., see Margules, Olds, M. E.

OLDS, J., and MILNER, P. Positive reinforcement produced by electrical stimulation of septal area and other regions of rat brain. *J. comp. physiol. Psychol.,* 1954, **47,** 419–427. (324, 326, 327)

OLDS, J., and SINCLAIR, J. Self-stimulation in the obstruction Dox. *Amer. Psychol.,* 1957, **12,** 464. (Abstract) (327)

OLDS, J., TRAVIS, R. P., and SCHWING, R. C. Topographic organization of hypothalamic self-stimulation. *J. comp. physiol. Psychol.,* 1960, **53,** 23–28. (330, 332)

OLMSTED, J. M. D. Effects of cutting the lingual nerve of the dog. *J. comp. Neurol.,* 1921, **33,** 149–154. (111)

OLSSON, L., see Andersson.

ONLEY, J. W., see Boynton.

ORBACH, J. Disturbances of the maze habit following occipital cortex removals in blind monkeys. *AMA Arch. Neurol. Psychiat.,* 1959, **81,** 49–54. (515)

ORBACH, J., see Kling.

ORBACH, J., and CHOW, K. L. Differential effects of resections of somatic areas I and II in monkeys. *J. Neurophysiol.,* 1959, **22,** 195–203. (270)

ORBACH, J., and FANTZ, R. L. Differential effects of temporal neo-cortical resections on overtrained and non-overtrained visual habits in monkeys. *J. comp. physiol. Psychol.,* 1958, **51,** 126–129. (502)

OSGOOD, C. E., reference given in text. (571)

OSWALD, I., reference given in text. (571)

OTIS, L. S., see Thomas.

OTIS, L. S., CERF, J. A., and THOMAS, G. J. Conditioned inhibition of respiration and heart rate in the goldfish. *Science,* 1957, **126,** 264–265. (480)

PAPEZ, J. W. A proposed mechanism of emotion. *Arch. Neurol. Psychiat.,* Chicago, 1937, **38,** 725–743. (311)

PARKER, G. H. *The elementary nervous system.* Philadelphia: Lippincott, 1919. (16)

PARROTT, D. M. V., see Bruce.

PASAMANICK, B., see Kaelbling.

PATT, M., reference given in text. (199)

PATTON, H. D., see Ruch.

PATTON, H. D. Spinal reflexes and synaptic transmission. In T. C. Ruch and J. F. Fulton (Eds.), *Medical physiology and biophysics,* 18th ed. Philadelphia: Saunders, 1960. (280)

PATTON, H. D. Higher control of autonomic outflows: The hypothalamus. In T. C. Ruch and J. F. Fulton (Eds.), *Medical physiology and biophysics.* Philadelphia: Saunders, 1960. (389)

PATTON, H. D., and AMASSIAN, V. E. Cortical projection zone of chorda tympani nerve in cat. *J. Neurophysiol.,* 1952, **15,** 245–250. (120)

PATTON, H. D., and RUCH, T. C. Preference thresholds for quinine hydrochloride in chimpanzee, monkey and rat. *J. comp. Psychol.,* 1944, **37,** 35–49. (121)

PATTON, H. D., and RUCH, T. C. The relation of the foot of the pre- and postcentral gyrus to taste in the monkey and chimpanzee. *Fed. Proc.,* 1946, **5,** 79. (Abstract) (122)

PATTON, H. D., RUCH, T. C., and WALKER, A. E. Experimental hypogeusia from Horsley-Clarke lesions of the thalamus in Macaca mulatta. *J. Neurophysiol.,* 1944, **7,** 171–184. (120, 121)

PATTON, R. A., see Kruper, Pilgram.

PAUKER, R. S. The effects of removing seminal vesicles, prostate and testes on the mating behavior of the golden hamster, Cricetus auratus. *J. comp. physiol. Psychol.,* 1948, **41,** 252–257. (414)

PAVLOV, I. P., reference given in text. (443, 571)

PEARLMAN, C. A., JR., SHARPLESS, S. K., and JARVIK, M. E. Retrograde amnesia produced by anesthetic and convulsant agents. *J. comp. physiol. Psychol.,* 1961, **54,** 109–112. (548)

PECHTEL, C., see Schreiner.

PENFIELD, W. Functional localization in temporal and deep Sylvian area. *Res. Publ. Ass. Res. Nerv. Ment. Dis.,* 1958, **36,** 210–226 (271)

PENFIELD, W. The interpretive cortex. *Science,* 1959, **129,** 1719–1725. (544)

PENFIELD, W., and BOLDREY, E. Somatic motor and sensory representation in the cerebral cortex of man as studied by electrical stimulation. *Brain,* 1937, **60,** 389–443. (271)

PENFIELD, W., reference given in text. (545, 570, 571)

PENFIELD, W., and ERICKSON, T. C. (Eds.) *Epilepsy and cerebral localization.*

Springfield, Ill.: C. C. Thomas, 1941, (342)

PENNINGTON, L. A. The effects of cortical destruction upon responses to tones. *J. comp. Neurol.*, 1941, **74**, 169–191. (490)

PESKIN, J. C., reference given in text. (199)

PETERS, R. H., ROSVOLD, H. E., and MIRSKY, A. F. The effect of thalamic lesions upon delayed response type tests in the rhesus monkey. *J. comp. physiol. Psychol.*, 1956, **49**, 111–116. (524)

PETERSON, G. M. The influence of cerebral destruction upon the handedness of the rat in the latch box. *J. comp. Psychol.*, 1938, **26**, 445–459. (518)

PETERSON, G. M., and BARNETT, PATRICIA E. The cortical destruction necessary to produce a transfer of a forced-practice function. *J. comp. physiol. Psychol.*, 1961, **54**, 382–385. (518)

PFAFFMANN, C. Taste and smell. In S. S. Stevens (Ed.), *Handbook of experimental psychology*. New York: Wiley, 1951. (110)

PFAFFMANN, C. Gustatory nerve impulses in rat, cat, and rabbit. *J. Neurophysiol.*, 1955, **18**, 429–440. (115, 116)

PFAFFMANN, C. Taste mechanisms in preference behavior. *Amer. J. clin. Nutrit.*, 1957, **5**, 142–147. (369)

PFAFFMANN, C. The sense of taste. In J. Field, H. W. Magoun, and V. E. Hall (Eds.), *Handbook of physiology*, Vol. 1. Washington, D. C.: American Physiological Society, 1959. (111, 113, 114, 116)

PFAFFMANN, C., see Benjamin, Oakley.

PFAFFMANN, C., and BARE, J. K. Gustatory nerve discharges in normal and adrenalectomized rats. *J. comp. physiol. Psychol.*, 1950, **43**, 320–324. (369)

PHOENIX, C. H. Hypothalamic regulation of sexual behavior in male guinea pigs. *J. comp. physiol. Psychol.*, 1961, **54**, 72–77. (418)

PHOENIX, C. H., GOY, R. W., GERALL, A. A., and YOUNG, W. C. Organizing action of prenatally administered testosterone propionate on the tissues mediating mating behavior in the female guinea pig. *Endocrinology*, 1959, **65**, 369–382. (411)

PICKFORD, MARY. Control of the secretion of anti-diuretic hormone from the pars nerosa of the pituitary gland. *Physiol. Rev.*, 1945, **25**, 573–595. (390)

PIERCY, M., HECAEN, H., and DE AJURIAGUERRA, J. Constructional apraxia associated with unilateral cerebral lesions: Left and right sided cases compared. *Brain*, 1960, **83**, 225–242. (536)

PIERON, H. *The sensations.* New Haven: Yale Univer. Press, 1952. (235)

PILGRAM, F. J., and PATTON, R. A. Patterns of self-selection of purified dietary components by the rat. *J. comp. physiol. Psychol.*, 1947, **40**, 343–348. (366)

PITTS, W. H., see Maturana.

POLIDORA, V. J., and BOWMAN, R. E. Psycho-chemistry. In J. E. Sidowski (Ed.), *Methodology and instrumentation in psychology*. New York: McGraw-Hill, 1966. (546, 554)

POLLACK, L. J., reference given in text. (293)

POLT, J. M., see Hess.

POLTYREW, S. S., and ZELIONY, G. P. Grosshirnrinde und Assoziationsfunktion. *Z. Biol.*, 1930, **90**, 157–160. (449)

POLYAK, S. L. *The retina.* Chicago: Univer. of Chicago Press, 1941. (132)

POLYAK, S., reference given in text. (570)

PORTER, P., see Kruger.

PORTER, R. W., see Brady.

PORTER, R. W., BRADY, J. V., CONRAD, D., MASON, J. W., GALAMBOS, R., and RIOCH, D. Some experimental observations on gastro-intestinal lesions in behaviorally conditioned monkeys. *Psychosom. Med.*, 1958, **20**, 379–394. (338)

PREMACK, D., see Hundt.

PRIBRAM, K. H. Some physical and pharmacological factors affecting delayed response performance of baboons following frontal lobotomy. *J. Neurophysiol.*, 1950, **13**, 373–382. (526)

PRIBRAM, K. H. Toward a science of neuropsychology: Method and data. In *Current trends in psychology and the behavioral sciences*. Pittsburgh: Univer. Pittsburgh Press, 1954. (500, 501)

PRIBRAM, K. H. Lesions of "frontal eye fields" and delayed response of baboons. *J. Neurophysiol.*, 1955, **18**, 105–112. (524)

PRIBRAM, K. H. Interrelations of psychology and the neurological disciplines. In S. Koch (Ed.), *Psychology: A study of a science*, Vol. 4. New York: McGraw-Hill, 1962. Pp. 119–157. (322, 323, 504, 519, 520)

PRIBRAM, K. H., see Bagshaw, Blum, Mishkin, Rosvold, Schwartzbaum, Wilson.

PRIBRAM, K. H., and MISHKIN, M. Analysis of the effects of frontal lesions in monkey: III. Object alternation. *J. comp. physiol. Psychol.*, 1956, **49**, 41–45. (528)

PRIBRAM, K. H., MISHKIN, M., ROSVOLD, H. E., and KAPLAN, S. J. Effects on delayed-response performance of lesions of dorsolateral and ventromedial frontal cortex of baboons. *J. comp. physiol. Psychol.*, 1952, **45**, 565–575. (524)

PRIBRAM, K. H., and WEISKRANTZ, L. A comparison of the effects of medial and lateral cerebral resections on conditioned avoidance behavior of monkeys. *J. comp. physiol. Psychol.*, 1957, **50**, 74–80. (451, 454, 455)

PROCTOR, D. M., see Gengerelli.

PROCTOR, L. D., reference given in text. (571)

PRONKO, N. H., see Kellogg.

PUBOLS, H. H., JR. Delay of reinforcement, response perseveration, and discrimination reversal. *J. exp. Psychol.*, 1958, **56**, 32–40. (516)

QUINT, E., see Scott.

RAAB, D. H., see Ades.

RAAB, D. H., and ADES, H. W. Cortical and midbrain mediation of a conditioned discrimination of acoustic intensities. *Amer. J. Psychol.*, 1946, **59**, 59–83. (451, 490)

RALPH, C. L. Polydipsia in the hen following lesions in the supraoptic hypothalamus. *Amer. J. Physiol.*, 1960, **198**, 528–530. (389)

RANEY, E. T., see Jasper.

RANSON, S. W. Somnolence caused by hypothalamic lesions in the monkey. *Arch. Neurol. Psychiat.*, Chicago, 1939, **41**, 1–23. (317, 346)

RANSON, S. W., see Brookhart, Dey, Hetherington.

RANSON, S. W., KABAT, H., and MAGOUN, H. W. Autonomic response to electrical stimulation of hypothalamus, preoptic region and septum. *AMA Arch. Neurol. Psychiat.*, 1934, **33**, 467–474. (347)

RASMUSSEN, E. W., see Kaada.

RASMUSSEN, T., reference given in text. (545)

RATLIFF, F., see Riggs.

RAY, O. S., see Stein.

RAZRAN, G. The observable unconscious and the inferable conscious in current Soviet psychophysiology: Interoceptive conditioning, semantic conditioning, and the orienting reflex. *Psychol. Rev.*, 1961, **68**, 81–147. (480)

REED, J. D. Spontaneous activity of animals. A review of the literature since 1929. *Psychol. Bull.*, 1947, **44**, 393–412. (357)

REHM, W. S., see Börnstein.

REITAN, R. M., and TARSHES, E. L. Differential effects of lateralized brain lesions on the Trail Making Test. *J. nerv. ment. Dis.*, 1959, **129**, 257–262. (536)

REYNOLDS, R. W. The relationship between stimulation voltage and rate of hypothalamic self-stimulation in the rat. *J. comp. physiol. Psychol.*, 1958, **51**, 193–198. (331)

REYNOLDS, R. W. Ventromedial hypothalamic lesions without hyperphagia. *Amer. J. Physiol.*, 1963, **204**, 60–62. (380)

RHEINGOLD, H. L., reference given in text. (571)

RICE, K. K., see Richter.

RICH, I., see Thompson, R.

RICHTER, C. P. Animal behavior and internal drives. *Quart. Rev. Biol.*, 1927, **2**, 307–343. (355)

RICHTER, C. P. The primacy of polyuria in diabetes insipidus. *Amer. J. Physiol.*, 1935, **112**, 481–487. (389)

RICHTER, C. P. Hypophyseal control of behavior. *Cold Spr. Harb. Sympos. quant. Biol.*, 1937, **5**, 258–268. (431)

RICHTER, C. P. Mineral appetite of parathyroidectomized rats. *Amer. J. med. Sci.*, 1939, **198**, 9–16. (368)

RICHTER, C. P. The internal environment and behavior. Part V. Internal secretions. *Amer. J. Psychiat.*, 1941, **97**, 878–893. (431)

RICHTER, C. P. Total self regulatory functions in animals and human beings. *Harvey Lect.*, 1942a, **38**, 63–103. (363, 367, 431)

RICHTER, C. P. Physiological psychology. *Annu. Rev. Physiol.*, 1942b, **4**, 561–574. (365)

RICHTER, C. P. Alcohol, beer and wines as foods. *Quart. J. Stud. Alcohol*, 1953, **14**, 525–539. (364)

RICHTER, C. P., see Langworthy.

RICHTER, C. P., and ECKERT, J. F. Mineral metabolism of adrenalectomized rats studied by the appetite method. *Endocrinology*, 1938, **22**, 214–224. (368)

RICHTER, C. P., and HAWKES, C. D. The dependence of the carbohydrate, fat, and protein appetite of rats on the various components of the vitamin B complex. *Amer. J. Physiol.*, 1941, **131**, 639–649.

RICHTER, C. P., and HAWKES, C. D. Increased spontaneous activity and food-intake produced in rats by removal of the frontal poles of the brain. *J. Neurol. Psychiat.*, Chicago, 1939, 231–242. (368, 376)

RICHTER, C. P., and HINES, MARION. Increased spontaneous activity produced in monkeys by brain lesions. *Brain*, 1938, **61**, 1–16. (359)

RICHTER, C. P., and RICE, K. K. The effect of thiamine hydrochloride on the energy value of dextrose studies in rats by the single food choice method. *Amer. J. Physiol.*, 1942, **137**, 573–581. (357)

RICHTER, C. P., and SCHMIDT, E. C. H. Increased fat and decreased carbohydrate appetite of pancreatomized rats. *Endocrinology*, 1941, **28**, 179–192. (368)

RICHTER, C. P., and UHLENHUTH, E. H. Comparison of the effects of gonadectomy on spontaneous activity of wild and domesticated Norway rats. *Endocrinology*, 1954, **54**, 311–322. (358)

RIESS, B. F. Some effects of adrenal cortical steroid hormones on the maze behavior of the rat. *J. comp. physiol. Psychol.*, 1947, **40**, 9–11. (559)

RIESS, B. F., and BLOCK, R. J. The effect of amino acid deficiency on the behavior of the white rat: I. Lysine and cystine deficiency. *J. Psychol.*, 1942, **14**, 101–113. (557)

RIGGS, L. A. The human electroretinogram. *AMA Arch. Ophthalmol.*, 1958, **60**, 739–754. (143)

RIGGS, L. A., see Boynton.

RIGGS, L. A., and GRAHAM, C. H. Effects due to variations in light intensity on the excitability cycle of the single visual sense cell. *J. cell. comp. Physiol.*, 1945, **26**, 1–13. (198, 200)

RIGGS, L. A., RATLIFF, F., CORNSWEET, J. C., and CORNSWEET, T. The disappearance of steadily fixated visual test objects. *J. Opt. Soc. Amer.*, 1953, **43**, 495–501. (191)

RIGGS, L. A., RATLIFF, F., and KEESEY, U. T. Appearance of Mach bands with a motionless retinal image. *J. Opt. Soc. Amer.*, 1961, **51**, 702–703. (192)

RINKEL, M., reference given in text. (572)

RIOCH, D. MC K., see Dempsey, Mason, Porter, Schreiner.

RIOPELLE, A. J., and ADES, H. W. Visual discrimination performance in rhesus monkeys following extirpation of prestriate and temporal cortex. *J. genet. Psychol.*, 1953, **83**, 63–77. (499)

RIOPELLE, A. J., HARLOW, H. F., SETTLAGE, P. H., and ADES, H. W. Performance of normal and operated monkeys on visual learning tests. *J. comp. physiol. Psychol.*, 1951, **44**, 283–289. (499)

RISS, W., BURSTEIN, S. D., JOHNSON, R. W., and LUTZ, A. Morphologic correlates of endocrine and running activity. *J. comp. physiol. Psychol.*, 1959, **52**, 618–620. (357)

RITCHIE, W., reference given in text. (571)

ROBERTS, L. Functional plasticity in cortical speech areas and the integration of speech. *Res. Publ. Ass. Res. Nerv. Ment. Dis.*, 1958, **36**, 449–466. (536)

ROBERTS, L., reference given in text. (571)

ROBERTS, W. W. Both rewarding and punishing effects from stimulation of posterior hypothalamus of cat with same electrode at same intensity. *J. comp. physiol. Psychol.*, 1958, **51**, 400–407.

ROBERTS, W. W. Fear-like behavior elicited from dorsomedial thalamus of cat. *J. comp. physiol. Psychol.*, 1962, **55**, 191–197. (318)

ROBERTS, W. W., see Delgado.

ROBERTS, W. W., DEMBER, W. N., and BRODWICK, M. Alternation and exploration in rats with hippocampal lesions. *J. comp. physiol. Psychol.*, 1962, **55**, 695–700. (522)

ROBINSON, B. W., and MISHKIN, M. Alimentary responses evoked from forebrain structures in Macaca mulatta. *Science*, 1962, **136**, 260–261. (376)

ROBINSON, E. A., and ADOLPH, E. F. Pattern of normal water drinking in dogs.

Amer. J. Physiol., 1943, **139**, 39–44. (386)

RODRIGUEZ DE LORES ARNAIZ, G., see de Robertis.

ROEDER, K. D. Spontaneous activity and behavior. *Sci. Mon.*, 1955, **80**, 362–370. (354)

ROESSLER, R., reference given in text. (572)

ROOT, W. S., and BARD, P. Erection in the cat following removal of lumbo-sacral segments. *Amer. J. Physiol.*, 1937, **119**, 392–393. (414)

ROSE, J. E., see Galambos.

ROSE, J. E., GALAMBOS, R., and HUGHES, J. R. Microelectrode studies of the cochlear nuclei of the cat. *Bull. Johns Hopkins Hosp.*, 1959, **104**, 211–251. (223)

ROSE, J. E., and MOUNTCASTLE, V. B. Touch and kinesthesis. In J. Field, H. W. Magoun, and V. E. Hall (Eds.), *Handbook of physiology*, Vol. 1. Washington, D. C.: American Physiological Society, 1959. (249, 256, 258, 265, 267)

ROSE, J. E., and WOOLSEY, C. N. Organization of the mammalian thalamus and its relationship to the cerebral cortex. *EEG clin. Neurophysiol.*, 1949, **1**, 391–404. (215)

ROSENBLATT, J. S., and ARONSON, L. R. The decline of sexual behavior in male cats after castration with special reference to the role of prior sexual experience. *Behaviour*, 1958a, **12**, 285–338. (406, 407)

ROSENBLATT, J. S., and ARONSON, L. R. The influence of experience on the behavioral effects of androgen in prepuberally castrated male cats. *Anim. Behav.*, 1958b, **6**, 171–172. (406, 407)

ROSENZWEIG, M. R. Cortical correlates of auditory localization and of related perceptual phenomena. *J. comp. physiol. Psychol.*, 1954, **47**, 269–276. (238)

ROSENZWEIG, M. R., reference given in text. (571)

ROSENZWEIG, M. R., KRECH, D., and BENNETT, E. L. A search for relations between brain chemistry and behavior. *Psychol. Bull.*, 1960, **57**, 476–492. (554)

ROSENZWEIG, M. R., KRECH, D., and BENNETT, E. L. Heredity, environment, brain biochemistry, and learning. In R. A. Patton (Ed.), *Current trends in psychological theory*. Pittsburgh, Pa.: Univer. Pittsburgh Press, 1961. (554)

ROSS, M. See Morrell.

ROSS, S., see Astin.

ROSS, S., and COLE, J. O. Psychopharmacology. *Annu. Rev. Psychol.*, 1960, **11**, 415–438. (559)

ROSVOLD, H. E., see Battig, Brush, Miles, Mishkin, Peters, Pribram.

ROSVOLD, H. E., and DELGADO, J. M. R. The effect of delayed-alternation test performance of stimulating or destroying electrically structures within the frontal lobes of the monkey's brain. *J. comp. physiol. Psychol.*, 1956, **49**, 365–372. (465)

ROSVOLD, H. E., MIRSKY, A. F., and PRIBRAM, K. H. Influence of amygdalectomy on social behavior in monkeys. *J. comp. physiol. Psychol.*, 1954, **47**, 173–178. (322)

ROSVOLD, H. E., SZWARCBART, M. K., MIRSKY, A. F., and MISHKIN, M. The effect of frontal-lobe damage on delayed-response performance in chimpanzees. *J. comp. physiol. Psychol.*, 1961, **54**, 368–374. (524, 528)

ROTH, J., GLICK, S. M., YALOW, R. S., and BERSON, S. A. Hypoglycemia: A potent stimulus to secretion of growth hormone. *Science*, 1963, **140**, 987–988. (93)

ROULE, L. *Fishes: their journeys and migrations.* New York: Norton, 1933. (437)

ROUSE, R. O., see Hull.

ROWAN, W. *The riddle of migration.* Baltimore: Williams & Wilkins, 1931. (438)

ROWAN W. Homing migration and instinct. *Science*, 1945, **102**, 210–211. (439)

ROWELL, T. E. On the retrieving of young and other behaviour in lactating golden hamsters. *Proc. Zool. Soc. Lond.*, 1960, 135, 265–282. (434)

ROWLAND, V. Differential electroencephalographic response to conditioned auditory stimuli in arousal from sleep. *EEG clin. Neurophysiol.*, 1957, **9**, 585–594. (472)

ROWLEY, J. D. A review of recent studies of chromosomes in mongolism. *Amer. J. ment. Defic.*, 1962, **66**, 529–532. (555)

ROZIN, P. N., and MAYER, J. Thermal reinforcement and thermoregulatory behavior in the goldfish, Carassius auratus. *Science*, 1961, **134**, 942–943. (393)

RUBEN, R. J., and SEKULA, J. Inhibition of central auditory response. *Science*, 1960, **131**, 163. (218)

RUCH, T. C. Cortical localization of somatic sensibility. The effect of precentral, postcentral, and posterior parietal lesions upon the performance of monkeys trained to discriminate weights. *Res. Publ. Ass. Res. Nerv. Ment. Dis.*, 1935, **15**, 289–330. (270, 486, 487)

RUCH, T. C., see Patton, Towe.

RUCH, T. C., reference given in text. (45)

RUCH, T. C., and FULTON, J. F., 1935, incorrectly cited, see Ruch, 1935 and Ruch, Fulton, and German, 1938. (488)

RUCH, T. C., and FULTON, J. F. (Eds.), *Medical physiology and biophysics.* 18th ed. Philadelphia: Saunders, 1960. (84, 89, 275, 277, 279, 283, 284, 286)

RUCH, T. C., FULTON, J. F., and GERMAN, W. J. Sensory discrimination in the mon-

key, chimpanzee, and man after lesions of the parietal lobe. *Arch. Neurol. Psychiat.*, Chicago, 1938, **39**, 919–937. (270, 271)

RUCH, T. C., and SHENKIN, H. A. The relation of area 13 of the orbital surface of the frontal lobe to hyperactivity and hyperphagia in monkeys. *J. Neurophysiol.*, 1943, **6**, 349–360. (359)

RUCKMICK, C. A. *The psychology of feeling and emotion.* New York: McGraw-Hill, 1936. (310)

RUPERT, A., see Galambos, Hubel, Simmons.

RUSHTON, W. A. H. Physical measurement of cone pigment in the living human eye. *Nature*, 1957, **179**, 571–573. (180)

RUSHTON, W. A. H. Dark adaptation and the regeneration of rhodopsin. *J. Physiol.*, 1961, **156**, 166–178. (180, 181)

RUSSELL, R. W. Effects of electroshock convulsions on learning and retention in rats as a function of difficulty of the task. *J. comp. physiol. Psychol.*, 1949, **42**, 137–142. (547)

RUSSELL, R. W., WATSON, R. H. J., and FRANKENHAEUSER, M. Effects of chronic reductions in brain cholinesterase activity on acquisition and extinction of a conditioned avoidance response. *Scand. J. Psychol.*, 1961, **2**, 21–29. (554)

RUSSELL, W., reference given in text. (571)

RUTLEDGE, L. T., see Doty.

SALGANICOFF, L., see de Robertis.

SAMET, S., see Stellar.

SAMUELS, I. Reticular mechanisms and behavior. *Psychol. Bull.*, 1959, **56**, 1–25. (350)

SANTIBANEZ-H. G., see Mancia.

SAWREY, W., CONGER, J., and TURRELL, E. An experimental investigation of the role of psychological factors in the production of gastric ulcers in rats. *J. comp. physiol. Psychol.*, 1956, **49**, 457–461. (338)

SAWREY, W., and WEISS, J. D. An experimental method of producing gastric ulcers. *J. comp. physiol. Psychol.*, 1956, **49**, 269–270. (338)

SCHERRER, H., see Hernández-Peón.

SCHLOSBERG, H. The relationship between success and the laws of conditioning. *Psychol. Rev.*, 1937, **44**, 379–394. (478)

SCHLOSBERG, H. Three dimensions of emotion. *Psychol. Rev.*, 1954, **61**, 81–88. (308)

SCHLOSBERG, H., see Woodworth.

SCHMIDT, E. C. H., see Richter.

SCHNEIDERMAN, N., see Gormezano.

SCHOENFELD, W. N., see Notterman.

SCHREINER, L., see Brady, Lindsley, Pechtel.

SCHREINER, L., and KLING, A. Behavioral

changes following rhinencephalic injury in cat. *J. Neurophysiol.*, 1953, **16**, 643–659. (419)

SCHREINER, L., and KLING, A. Effects of castration on hypersexual behavior induced by rhinencephalic injury in cat. *Arch. Neurol. Psychiat.*, 1954, **72**, 180–186. (419, 420)

SCHREINER, L., and KLING, A. Rhinencephalon and behavior. *Amer. J. Physiol.*, 1956, **184**, 486–490. (321)

SCHREINER, L., RIOCH, D., PECHTEL, C., and MASSERMAN, J. Behavioral changes following thalamic injury in cat. *J. Neurophysiol.*, 1953, **16**, 234–246. (318)

SCHUKNECHT, H. F. Lesions of the organ of Corti. *Trans. Amer. Acad. Ophthal. Otolaryngol.*, 1953, 366–383. (229)

SCHUKNECHT, H. F., and NEFF, W. D. Hearing losses after apical lesions in the cochlea. *Acta Oto-Lar.*, 1952, **42**, 263–274. (229)

SCHUKNECHT, H. F., and SUTTON, S. Hearing losses after experimental lesions in basal coil of cochlea. *AMA Arch. Otolaryngol.*, 1953, **58**, 129–142. (229, 230)

SCHUKNECHT, H. F., and WOELLNER, R. C. Hearing losses following partial section of the cochlear nerve. *Laryngoscope*, 1953, 63, 441–465. (232)

SCHULMAN, A., see Sidman.

SCHWARTZ, E., see Lansing.

SCHWARTZ, N. B., see Kling.

SCHWARTZBAUM, J. S. Response to changes in reinforcing conditions of bar pressing after ablation of the amygdaloid complex in monkeys. *Psychol. Rep.* 1960a, **6**, 215–221. (519)

SCHWARTZBAUM, J. S. Changes in reinforcing properties of stimuli following ablation of the amygdaloid complex in monkeys. *J. comp. physiol. Psychol.*, 1960b, **53**, 388–395. (519)

SCHWARTZBAUM, J. S., and PRIBRAM, K. H. The effects of amygdalectomy in monkeys on transposition along a brightness continuum. *J. comp. physiol. Psychol.*, 1960, **53**, 396–399. (504)

SCHWARTZBAUM, J. S., and WARD, H. P. An osmotic factor in the regulation of food intake in the rat. *J. comp. physiol. Psychol.*, 1958, **51**, 555–560. (373)

SCHWARTZKOPFF, J., see Galambos.

SCHWING, R. E., see Olds.

SCOTT, C. C., see Scott, W. W.

SCOTT, E. M. Self-selection of diet. I. Selection of purified components. *J. Nutrit.*, 1946, **31**, 397–406. (368)

SCOTT, E. M., and QUINT, ELEANOR. Self-selection of diet. III. Appetites for B vitamins. *J. Nutrit.*, 1946, **32**, 285–292. (368)

SCOTT, E. M., and QUINT, ELEANOR. Self-selection of diet. IV. Appetite for protein. *J. Nutrit.*, 1946, **32**, 293–302. (368)

SCOTT, E. M., and VERNEY, ETHEL L. Self-selection of diet. VI. The nature of appetites for B vitamins. *J. Nutrit.*, 1947, **34**, 471–480. (368)

SCOTT, J. P. Animal sexuality. In A. Ellis and A. Abarbanel (Eds.), *Encyclopedia of sexual behavior*. New York: Hawthorn Books, 1961. (396)

SCOTT, V. B., see Kellogg.

SCOTT, W. W., SCOTT, C. C., and LUCKHARDT, A. B. Observations in the blood sugar level before, during, and after hunger periods in humans. *Amer. J. Physiol.*, 1938, 123, 243–247. (375)

SCOW, R. O. The retarding effect of allyl thiourea and of partial thyroidectomy at birth upon learning in the rat. *J. comp. Psychol.*, 1946, **39**, 359–370. (559)

SECHZER, J. A., see Meikle.

SEGUNDO, J. P., ARANA, R., and FRENCH, J. D. Behavioral arousal by stimulation of the brain in the monkey. *J. Neurosurg.*, 1955, **12**, 601–613. (348)

SEKULA, J., see Ruben.

SELLS, S. B., see Haynes.

SELYE, H. *The physiology and pathology of exposure to stress*. Montreal: Acta, Inc., 1960. (336, 337)

SEM-JACOBSEN, C. W., and TORKILDSEN, A. In E. R. Ramey and D. S. O'Doherty (Eds.), *Electrical studies on the unanesthetized brain*. New York: Hoeber, 1960. Pp. 280–288. (330)

SEMMES, J., reference given in text. (570)

SEMMES, J., WEINSTEIN, S., GHENT, L., and TEUBER, H.-L. *Somatosensory changes after penetrating brain wounds in man*. Cambridge, Mass.: Harvard Univer. Press, 1960. (271)

SETTLAGE, P. H. The effect of occipital lesions on visually-guided behavior in the monkey: I. Influence of the lesions on final capacities in a variety of problem situations. *J. comp. Psychol.*, 1939, 27, 93–131. (498)

SETTLAGE, P. H., see Harlow, Meyer, Riopelle.

SEWARD, J. P. Studies on the reproductive activities of the guinea pig. III. The effect of androgenic hormone on sex drive in males and females. *J. comp. Psychol.*, 1940, **30**, 435–449. (407)

SHAGASS, C., see Jasper.

SHARMA, K. N., ANAND, B. D., DUA, S., and SINGH, B. Role of stomach in regulation of activities of hypothalamic feeding centers. *Amer. J. Physiol.*, 1961, **201**, 593–598. (381)

SHARPLESS, S. K., see Pearlman.

SHEARD, N. M., see Wiesner.

SHEATZ, G. C., see Galambos, Hearst.

SHEER, D. E., reference given in text. (571)

SHEFFIELD, F. D., see Campbell.

SHENKING, H. A., see Ruch.

SHERRINGTON, C. S. Experiments in the examination of the peripheral distribution of the fibres of the posterior roots of some spinal nerves. *Philos. Trans.*, 1893, **184B**, 641–763. (259)

SHERRINGTON, C. S. *The integrative action of the nervous system.* London: Constable, 1906. (71, 310)

SHERRINGTON, C. S., reference given in text. (292, 295)

SHUFORD, E. H., JR. Relative acceptability of sucrose and glucose solutions in the white rat. Doctoral thesis in Psychology, Univer. of Illinois, 1955. (372)

SHURRAGER, P. S., see Culler.

SHURRAGER, P. S., and CULLER, E. Conditioning in the spinal dog. *J. exp. Psychol.*, 1940, **26**, 133–159. (457)

SHURRAGER, P. S., and DYKMAN, R. A. Waling spinal carnivores. *J. comp. physiol. Psychol.*, 1951, 44, 252–262. (458)

SIDMAN, M., see Brady, Gelder.

SIDMAN, M., BRADY, J. V., BOREN, J. J., CONRAD, D. G., and SCHULMAN, A. Reward schedules and behavior maintained by intracranial self-stimulation. *Science*, 1955, **122**, 830–831. (329)

SILVERMAN, S. R., reference given in text. (570)

SIMMONS, F. B., GALAMBOS, R., and RUPERT, A. Conditioned response of middle ear muscles. *Amer. J. Physiol.*, 1959, **197**, 537–538. (227)

SIMON, A., reference given in text. (571)

SINCLAIR, J., see Olds.

SINGH, B., see Anand, Sharma.

SKINNER, B. R. Two types of conditioned reflex and a pseudo-type. *J. gen. Psychol.*, 1935, **12**, 66–77. (478)

SKINNER, B. F. *The behavior of organisms.* New York: Appleton-Century-Crofts, 1938. (445)

SKOGLUND, C. R., see Granit.

SMALLEY, R. L., and DRYER, R. L. Brown fat: thermogenic effect during arousal from hibernation in the bat. *Science,* 1963, **140**, 1333–1334. (440)

SMITH, A. H., see Anderson.

SMITH, C. J. Mass action and early environment in the rat. *J. comp. physiol. Psychol.*, 1959, **52**, 154–156. (515)

SMITH, D. E. Cerebral localization in somaesthetic discrimination in the rat. *J. comp. Psychol.*, 1939, **28**, 161–188. (269, 486)

SMITH, F. W., see Davis.

SMITH, K. U. The postoperative effects of removal of the striate cortex upon certain unlearned visually controlled reactions in the cat. *J. genet. Psychol.*, 1937, **50**, 137–156. (197)

SMITH, K. U. Visual discrimination in the cat: V. The postoperative effects of removal of the striate cortex upon intensity discrimination. *J. genet. Psychol.*, 1937, **51**, 329–369. (493)

SMITH, K. U. Visual discrimination in the cat. VI. The relation between pattern vision and visual acuity and the optic

projection centers of the nervous system. *J. genet. Psychol.*, 1938, **53**, 251–272. (194)

SMITH, K. U. Learning and the associative pathways of the human cerebral cortex. *Science*, 1951, **114**, 117–120. (536)

SMITH, K. U., see Bridgman, Wing.

SMITH, S. M., BROWN, H. D., TOMAN, J. E. P., and GOODMAN, L. S. The lack of cerebral effects of d-tubocurarine. *Anesthesiol.*, 1947, **8**, 1014. (477)

SMITH, W. K. Non-olfactory functions of the pyriform - amygdaloid - hippocampal complex. *Fed. Proc.*, 1950, **9**, 118. (321)

SOKOLOFF, L., see Weiss.

SOLLENBERGER, R. T., see Dennis.

SOLOMON, H. C., reference given in text. (570)

SOLOMON, R. L., see Black, Wynne.

SOLOMON, R. L., and TURNER, L. H. Discriminative classical conditioning in dogs paralyzed by curare can later control discriminative avoidance responses in the normal state. *Psychol. Rev.*, 1962, **69**, 202–219. (474, 477)

SOULAIRAC, A., SOULAIRAC, M.-L., and VAN STEENKISTE, J.-N. Dissociation experimentale entre l'action hypoglycemiante de l'insuline et ses effects sur le comportement alimentaire du rat. *J. Physiol.*, Paris, 1961, **53**, 474–475. (375)

SOULAIRAC, M.-L., see Soulairac, A.

SPAET, T., and HARLOW, H. F. Problem solution by monkeys following bilateral removal of the prefrontal areas: II. Delayed reaction problems involving use of the matching-from-sample method. *J. exp. Psychol.*, 1943, **32**, 424–434. (528)

SPECTOR, H., see Young, D. R.

SPENCER, S., see Kennard.

SPERLING, H. G., and JOLLIFFE, C. L. Chromatic response mechanisms in the human fovea as measured by threshold spectral sensitivity. *Science*, 1962, **136**, 317–318. (174, 176)

SPERRY, R. W. On the neural basis of the conditioned response. *Brit. J. anim. Behav.*, 1955, **3**, 41–44. (464)

SPERRY, R. W. Experiments on perceptual integration in animals. *Psychiat. Res. Rep.*, 1956, No. 6, 151–160. (505)

SPERRY, R. W. Cerebral organization and behavior. *Science*, 1961, **133**, 1749–1757. (504, 506, 508)

SPERRY, R. W., see Glickstein, Lashley, Myers, Stamm.

SPERRY, R. W., and MINER, N. Pattern perception following insertion of mica plates into visual cortex. *J. comp. physiol. Psychol.*, 1955, **48**, 463–469. (195)

SPERRY, R. W., MINER, N., and MYERS, R. E. Visual pattern perception following subpial slicing and tantalum wire implantations in the visual cortex. *J. comp. physiol. Psychol.*, 1955, **48**, 50–58. (195)

SPERRY, R. W., STAMM, J. S., and MINER, NANCY. Relearning tests for interocular transfer following division of the optic chiasma and corpus callosum in cats. *J. comp. physiol. Psychol.*, 1956, **49**, 529–533. (507)

SPONHOLZ, R. R., see Waisman.

SPORN, M. B., see Dingman.

STAGNER, R., see Harlow.

STAMM, J. S. Effects of cortical lesions on established hoarding activity in rats. *J. comp. physiol. Psychol.*, 1953, **46**, 299–304. (441)

STAMM, J. S. Control of hoarding activity in rats by the median cerebral cortex. *J. comp. physiol. Psychol.*, 1954, **47**, 21–27. (441)

STAMM, J. S., see Sperry, Wilson.

STAMM, J. S., and SPERRY, R. W. Function of corpus callosum in contralateral transfer of somesthetic discrimination in cats. *J. comp. physiol. Psychol.*, 1957, **50**, 138–143. (508)

STEGGERDA, F. R. Observations on the water intake in an adult man with dysfunctioning salivary glands. *Amer. J. Physiol.*, 1941, **132**, 517–521. (386)

STEIN, L. Anticholinergic drugs and the central control of thirst. *Science*, 1964, **139**, 46–48. (393)

STEIN, L., and RAY, O. S. Self regulation of brain-stimulating current intensity in the rat. *Science*, 1959, **130**, 570–572. (331)

STELLAR, E. The effect of epinephrine, insulin, and glucose upon hoarding in rats. *J. comp. Psychol.*, 1943, **36**, 21–31. (441)

STELLAR, E. The effect of experimental alterations of metabolism on the hoarding behavior of the rat. *J. comp. physiol. Psychol.*, 1951, **44**, 290–299. (441)

STELLAR, E. The physiology of motivation. *Psychol. Rev.*, 1954, **61**, 5–22. (423)

STELLAR, E., reference given in text. (423, 570)

STELLAR, E., see Dethier, Flexner, J. B., Morgan.

STELLAR, E., and HILL, J. H. The rat's rate of drinking as a function of water deprivation. *J. comp. physiol. Psychol.*, 1952, **45**, 96–102. (366)

STELLAR, E., HYMAN, R., and SAMET, S. Gastric factors controlling water- and salt-solution drinking. *J. comp. physiol. Psychol.*, 1954, **47**, 220–226. (371)

STELLAR, E., and MORGAN, C. T. The role of experience and deprivation in the onset of hoarding behavior in the rat. *J. comp. Psychol.*, 1943, **36**, 47–55. (440)

STERN, J. A. The effect of frontal cortical lesions on activity wheel and open-field behavior. *J. genet. Psychol.*, 1957, **90**, 203–212. (359)

STEVENS, S. S. (Ed.) *Handbook of experimental psychology.* New York: Wiley-InterScience, 1951. (164)

STEVENS, S. S., and DAVIS, H. *Hearing: Its psychology and physiology.* New York: Wiley, 1938. (226, 230, 233)

STEVENS, S. S., DAVIS, H., and LURIE, M. H. The localization of pitch perception on the basilar membrane. *J. gen. Psychol.*, 1935, **13**, 297–315. (228)

STEVENSON, J., see Miller.

STONE, C. P. Retention of copulatory ability in male rats following castration. *J. comp. physiol. Psychol.*, 1927, **7**, 369–387. (406)

STONE, C. P. Wildness and savageness in rats of different strains. In K. Lashley (Ed.), *Studies in the dynamics of behavior.* Chicago: Univer. Chicago Press, 1932. Pp. 3–55. (313)

STONE, C. P., and BARKER, R. G. Spontaneous activity, direct and indirect measures of sexual drive in adult male rats. *Proc. Soc. Exp. Biol.*, New York, 1934, **32**, 195–199. (356)

STONE, C. P., and KING, F. A. Effects of hypophysectomy on behavior in rats: I. Preliminary survey. *J. comp. physiol. Psychol.*, 1954, **47**, 213–219. (431)

STRAUS, R., reference given in text. (571)

STRÖHM, L., see Cohen.

STROMINGER, J. L., and BROBECK, J. R. A mechanism of regulation of food intake. *Yale J. Biol. Med.*, 1953, **25**, 383–390. (374)

STUMPF, P. K. ATP. *Scient. Amer.*, 1953, **188** (April), 85–92. (85)

SUMI, T., KATSUKI, Y., and UCHIYAMA, H. Cochlear nerve fibers. *Proc. Jap. Acad.*, 1956, **32**, 67–71. (223)

SUTTON, S., see Schuknecht.

SVAETICHIN, G. The cone action potential. *Acta Physiol. Scand.*, 1953, **29**, Suppl. 106, 565–600. (151)

SVAETICHIN, G., see MacNichol.

SVAETICHIN, G., and MAC NICHOL, E. F., JR. Retinal mechanisms for chromatic and achromatic vision. *Ann. N. Y. Acad. Sci.*, 1958, **74**, 404. (152)

SWANN, H. G. The function of the brain in olfaction. II. The results of destruction of olfactory and other nervous structures upon the discrimination of odors. *J. comp. Neurol.*, 1934, **59**, 175–201. (128)

SWEET, W. H. Pain. In J. Field, H. W. Magoun, and V. E. Hall (Eds.), *Handbook of physiology*, Vol. 1. Washington, D. C.: American Physiological Society, 1959. (255, 256)

SZWARCBART, M. K., see Rosvold.

TALBOT, S. A., see Thompson, J. M.

TARNECKI, R., see Wyrwicka.

TARSHES, E. L., see Reitan.

TASAKI, I. Nerve impulses in individual auditory nerve fibers of guinea pig. *J.*

Neurophysiol., 1954, **17**, 97–122. (219, 220)

TASAKI, I. Conduction of the nerve impulse. In J. Field, H. W. Magoun, and V. E. Hall (Eds.), *Handbook of physiology*, Vol. 1. Washington, D. C.: American Physiological Society, 1959. (71)

TASAKI, I., see Davis.

TASAKI, I., and CHANG, J. J. Electric responses of glia cells in cat brain. *Science*, 1958, **128**, 1209–1210. (21)

TASHIAN, R. E. Phenylpyruvic acid as a possible precursor of O-hydroxyphenyl-acetic acid man. *Science*, 1959, **129**, 1553. (556)

TAUB, E., see Knapp.

TAYLOR, N. B., see Best.

TEITELBAUM, P. Sensory control of hypothalamic hyperphagia. *J. comp. physiol. Psychol.*, 1955, **48**, 156–163. (378, 379)

TEITELBAUM, P. Random and food-directed activity in hyperphagic and normal rats. *J. comp. physiol. Psychol.*, 1957, **50**, 486–490. (378)

TEITELBAUM, P. Disturbances in feeding and drinking behavior after hypothalamic lesions. In *Nebraska symposium on motivation*. Lincoln, Nebr.: Univer. of Nebraska Press, 1961. (363, 375, 377–380)

TEITELBAUM, P., see Epstein, Hoebel, Williams.

TEITELBAUM, P., and CAMPBELL, B. A. Ingestion patterns in hyperphagic and normal rats. *J. comp. physiol. Psychol.*, 1958, **51**, 135–141. (379)

TEITELBAUM, P., and EPSTEIN, A. N. The lateral hypothalamic syndrome. *Psychol. Rev.*, 1962, **69**, 74–90. (382, 383)

TEPAS, D. I., see Williams.

TEPPERMAN, J., see Brobeck.

TERZUOLO, C. A., see Lowenstein.

TEUBER, H.-L. Perception. In J. Field, H. W. Magoun, and V. E. Hall (Eds.), *Handbook of physiology*, Vol. 3. Washington, D. C.: American Physiological Society, 1960. (192, 196, 200)

TEUBER, H.-L., reference given in text. (570)

TEUBER, H.-L., see Semmes, Weinstein.

TEUBER, H.-L., BATTERSBY, W. S., and BENDER, M. B. *Visual field defects after penetrating missile wounds of the brain.* Cambridge, Mass.: Harvard Univer. Press, 1960. (192, 193)

TEUBER, H.-L., and WEINSTEIN, S. Ability to discover hidden figures after cerebral lesions. *Arch. Neurol. Psychiat.*, 1956, **76**, 369–379. (195)

THERMAN, P. P., see Granit.

THOMAS, G. J., see Otis.

THOMAS, G. J., MOORE, R. Y., HARVEY, J. A., and HUNT, H. F. Relations between the behavioral syndrome produced by le-

sions in the septal region of the forebrain and maze learning of the rat. *J. comp. physiol. Psychol.*, 1959, **52**, 527–532. (517)

THOMAS, G. J., and OTIS, L. S. Effects of rhinencephalic lesions on conditioning of avoidance responses in the rat. *J. comp. physiol. Psychol.*, 1958, **51**, 130–134. (454, 517)

THOMPSON, A. F., and WALKER, A. E. Behavioral alterations following lesions of the medial surface. *AMA Arch. Neurol. Psychiat.*, 1951, **65**, 251–252. (321)

THOMPSON, J. M., WOOLSEY, C. N., and TALBOT, S. A. Visual areas I and II of cerebral cortex of rabbit. *J. Neurophysiol.*, 1950, **13**, 277–288. (161, 162)

THOMPSON, R. The comparative effects of anterior and posterior cortical lesions on maze retention. *J. comp. physiol. Psychol.*, 1959, **52**, 506–508. (451, 452, 516)

THOMPSON, R. Retention of a brightness discrimination following neocortical damage in the rat. *J. comp. physiol. Psychol.*, 1960, **53**, 212–215. (493, 494)

THOMPSON, R. Thalamic structures critical for retention of an avoidance conditioned response in rats. *J. comp. physiol. Psychol.*, 1963, **56**, 261–267. (455, 457)

THOMPSON, R., and MALIN, C. F. The effect of neocortical lesions on retention of a successive brightness discrimination in rats. *J. comp. physiol. Psychol.*, 1961, **54**, 326–328. (493)

THOMPSON, R., and MCCONNELL, J. V. Classical conditioning in the planarian, Dugesia dorotocephala. *J. comp. physiol. Psychol.*, 1955, **48**, 65–68. (552)

THOMPSON, R., and RICH, I. A discrete diencephalic pretectal area critical for retention of visual habits in the rat. *Exp. Neurol.*, 1961, **4**, 436–443. (201, 457, 495)

THOMPSON, R., and RICH, I. Differential effects of posterior thalamic lesions on retention of various visual habits. *J. comp. physiol. Psychol.*, 1963, **56**, 60–65. (495)

THOMPSON, R. L. Effects of lesions in the caudate nuclei and dorsofrontal cortex on conditioned avoidance behavior in cats. *J. comp. physiol. Psychol.*, 1959, **52**, 650–659. (451)

THORNDIKE, E. L. Animal intelligence; an experimental study of the associative processes in animals. *Psychol. Rev. Monogr.*, Suppl. II, 1898, 1, No. 8. (445)

THYSELL, T., see Forssman.

TINBERGEN, N. *The study of instinct.* London: Oxford Univer. Press, 1951. (421)

TOMAN, J. E. P., see Smith, S. M.

TOMITA, T. Electrical activity in the vertebrate retina. *J. Opt. Soc. Amer.*, 1963, **53**, 49–57. (151, 153)

TORKILDSEN, A., see Sem-Jacobsen.

TOWE, A. L., and RUCH, T. C., 1960, see Ruch and Fulton, 1960. (545)

TOWER, SARAH S. Pain: definition and properties of the unit for sensory reception. In *Pain*. Baltimore: Williams and Wilkins, 1943. Pp. 16–43. (253)

TOWNE, J. C., see Kling.

TRACY, W. H., and HARRISON, J. M. Aversive behavior following lesions of the septal region of the forebrain in the rat. *Amer. J. Psychol.*, 1956, **69**, 443–447. (453)

TRAVIS, R. P., see Olds.

TRYON, C. M., see Tryon, R. C.

TRYON, R. C. Genetic differences in maze learning in rats. In *National Society for the Study of Education, The thirty-ninth yearbook*. Bloomington, Ill.: Public School Publishing, 1940. (554)

TRYON, R. C., TRYON, C. M., and KUZNETS, G. Studies in individual differences in maze ability. X. Ratings and other measures of initial emotional responses of rats to novel inanimate objects. *J. comp. Psychol.*, 1941, **32**, 417–473. (313)

TSANG, Y. C. The functions of the visual areas of the cerebral cortex of the rat in the learning and retention of the maze. I. *Comp. Psychol. Monogr.*, 1934, **10**, 1–56. (514)

TSANG, Y. C. The functions of the visual areas of the cerebral cortex of the rat in the learning and retention of the maze. II. *Comp. Psychol. Monogr.*, 1936, **12**, No. 57. (514)

TSANG, Y. C. Hunger motivation in gastrectomized rats. *J. comp. Psychol.*, 1938, **26**, 1–17. (370)

TUNTURI, A. R. Further afferent connections to the acoustic cortex of the dog. *Amer. J. Physiol.*, 1945, **144**, 389–394. (490)

TURNER, L. H., see Solomon.

TURRELL, E., see Sawrey.

TWITTY, V. C. Migration and speciation in newts. *Science*, 1959, **130**, 1735–1743. (438)

UCHIYAMA, H., see Sumi.

UHLENHUTH, E. H., see Richter.

UHR, L., reference given in text. (572)

URSIN, H. The temporal lobe substrate of fear and anger. *Acta psychiat. neurol. Scand., Kbh.*, 1960, **35**, 378–396. (321)

VAES, G., see Brozek.

VALENSTEIN, E. S., see Hodos.

VANDER HOEVEN, T., see Woolley.

VAN DER WERFF TEN BOSCH, J. J., see Donovan.

VAN STEENKISTE, N.-N., see Soulairac, A.

VAUGHAN, E., and FISHER, A. E. Male sexual behavior induced by intracranial electrical stimulation. *Science*, 1962, **137**, 758–760. (418)

VERNEY, E. L., see Scott.

VERNIER, G. G., see Galambos.

VON BÉKÉSY, G. The variation of phase along the basilar membrane with sinusoidal vibrations. *J. Acoust. Soc. Amer.*, 1947, **19**, 452–460. (212)

VON BÉKÉSY, G. *Experiments in hearing.* New York: McGraw-Hill, 1960. (211)

VON BÉKÉSY, G. *Concerning the pleasures of observing, and the mechanics of the inner ear.* Stockholm: Nobel Lecture, 1962. (218)

VON BONIN, G., reference given in text. (570)

VON EULER, U. S. Autonomic neuroeffector transmission. In J. Field, H. W. Magoun, and V. E. Hall (Eds.), *Handbook of physiology*, Vol. 1. Washington, D. C.: American Physiological Society, 1959. (72, 75)

WADE, MARJORIE. The effect of sedatives upon delayed responses in monkeys following removal of the prefrontal lobes. *J. Neurophysiol.*, 1947, **10**, 57–61. (526)

WADE, M. Behavioral effects of prefrontal lobectomy, lobotomy, and circumsection in the monkey (Macaca mulatta). *J. comp. Neurol.*, 1952, **96**, 179–207. (525)

WAGNER, H. G., MACNICHOL, E. F., JR., and WOLBARSHT, M. L. The response properties of single ganglion cells in the goldfish retina. *J. gen. Physiol.*, 1960, **43**, 45–62. (149, 150)

WAGNER, H. G., MACNICHOL, E. F., JR., and WOLBARSHT, M. L. Functional basis for "on"-center and "off"-center receptive fields in the retina. *J. Opt. Soc. Amer.*, 1963, **53**, 66–70. (149, 150)

WAISMAN, H. A., WANG, H. L., HARLOW, H. F., and SPONHOLZ, R. R. Experimental phenylketonuria in the monkey. *Proc. Soc. Exp. Biol. Med.*, 1959, **101**, 864. (556)

WALD, G. Area and visual threshold. *J. gen. Physiol.*, 1938, **21**, 269–287. (181)

WALD, G. The photoreceptor process in vision. In J. Field, H. W. Magoun, and V. E. Hall (Eds.), *Handbook of physiology*, Vol. 1. Washington, D. C.: American Physiological Society, 1959. (137, 138, 179, 181)

WALD, G., and BROWN, P. K. Synthesis and bleaching of rhodopsin. *Nature*, London: 1956, **177**, 174–176. (145)

WALD, G., BROWN, P. K., and SMITH, P. H. Iodopsin. *J. gen. Physiol.*, 1955, **38**, 623–681. (141, 145, 167)

WALD, G., and JACKSON, B. Activity and nutritional deprivation. *Proc. Nat. Acad. Sci.*, 1944, **30**, 255–263. (357)

WALKER, A. E. *The primate thalamus.* Chicago: Univer. Chicago Press, 1938. (44, 45)

WALKER, A. E., see Halstead, Patton, Thompson, A. F.

WALLS, G. L. *The vertebrate eye and its adaptive radiation.* Bloomfield Hills,

Mich.: Cranbrook Institute of Science, 1942. (133, 134)

WALLS, G. L., reference given in text. (133)

WALSH, J., see Courville.

WALTER, W. G., reference given in text. (570)

WANG, G. H. The relation between "spontaneous" activity and estrous cycle in the white rat. Comp. Psychol. Monogr., 1923, 2, No. 6. (356)

WANG, H. L., see Waisman.

WANGENSTEEN, O. H., and CARLSON, A. J. Hunger sensations in a patient after total gastrectomy. Proc. Soc. exp. Biol. Med., 1931, 28, 545–547. (370)

WAPNER, S. The differential effects of cortical injury and retesting on equivalence reactions in the rat. Psychol. Monogr., 1944, 57, 1–59. (503)

WARD, H. P., see Schwartzbaum.

WARDEN, C. J., see Minnick.

WARR, W. B., see Harrison.

WARREN, H. C., reference given in text. (130)

WARREN, J. M., reference given in text. (571)

WARREN, J. M., and AKERT, K. (Eds.), The frontal granular cortex and behavior. New York: McGraw-Hill, 1964. (523)

WARREN, J. M., and HARLOW, H. F. Discrimination learning by normal and brain operated monkeys. J. genet. Psychol., 1952, 81, 45–52. (500)

WASHBURN, A. L., see Cannon.

WASHIZU, Y., see Lowenstein.

WASMAN, M., see Flynn.

WATERHOUSE, J. K. Effects of prefrontal lobotomy on conditioned fear and food responses in monkeys. J. comp. physiol. Psychol., 1957, 50, 81–88. (451, 452)

WATSON, R. H. J., see Russell.

WEDDELL, G. Receptors for somatic sensation. In M. A. B. Brazier (Ed.), Brain and Behavior, Vol. 1. Washington, D. C.: American Institute of Biological Sciences, 1961. Pp. 13–48. (247)

WEDDELL, G., see Lele, Woollard.

WEINSTEIN, S., reference given in text. (570)

WEINSTEIN, S., see Semmes, Teuber.

WEINSTEIN, S., and TEUBER, H.-L. Effects of penetrating brain injury on intelligence test scores. Science, 1957, 125, 1036–1037. (532)

WEISENBURG, T., and MCBRIDE, K. E. Aphasia. New York: Commonwealth Fund, 1935. (543)

WEISKRANTZ, L. Behavioral changes associated with ablation of the amygdaloid complex. Unpublished doctoral dissertation. Harvard Univer., 1953. (519)

WEISKRANTZ, L. Behavioral changes associated with ablation of the amygdaloid complex in monkeys. J. comp. physiol. Psychol., 1956, 49, 381–391. (453)

WEISKRANTZ, L., see Mishkin, Pribram.

WEISS, B. Thermal behavior of the subnourished and pantothenic-acid-deprived rat. J. comp. physiol. Psychol., 1957, 50, 481–485. (394)

WEISS, B., see Laties.

WEISS, J. D., see Sawrey.

WEISS, W. P., and SOKOLOFF, L. Reversal of thyroxine-induced hypermetabolism by puromycin. Science, 1963, 140, 1324–1326. (96)

WELD, H. P., see Boring.

WEPMAN, J. M., reference given in text. (571)

WESTCOTT, M. R., and HUTTENLOCHER, J. Cardiac conditioning: The effects and implications of controlled and uncontrolled respiration. J. exp. Psychol., 1961, 61, 353–359. (480)

WEVER, E. G. Theory of hearing. New York: Wiley, 1949. (213)

WEVER, E. G., see Lempert.

WEVER, E. G., and NEFF, W. D. A further study of the effects of partial section of the auditory nerve. J. comp. physiol. Psychol., 1947, 40, 217–226. (231)

WHALEN, R. E., and NADLER, R. D. Suppression of the development of female mating behavior by estrogen administered in infancy. Science, 1963, 141, 273–274. (410, 412)

WHEATLEY, M. D. The hypothalamus and affective behavior in cats: A study of the effects of experimental lesions, with anatomic correlations. Arch. Neurol. Psychiat., Chicago, 1944, 52, 296–316. (317)

WHITLOCK, D. G., see Nauta.

WHITLOCK, D. G., and NAUTA, W. J. H. Subcortical projections from the temporal neocortex in Macaca mulatta. J. comp. Neurol., 1956, 106, 183–212. (501)

WHITNEY, G. D., see Lindzey.

WICKELGREN, W. O., see Isaacson.

WIEMAN, H. L., reference given in text. (125)

WIESNER, B. P., and SHEARD, N. M. Sex behavior in hypophysectomized male rats. Nature, London: 1933, 132, 641. (433)

WIESSEL, T. N., see Hubel.

WIKLER, A., reference given in text. (572)

WILDER, C. E. Selection of rachitic and antirachitic diets in the rat. J. comp. Psychol., 1937, 24, 547–577. (368)

WILEY, L. E. A further investigation of auditory cerebral mechanisms. J. comp. Neurol., 1937, 66, 327–331. (490)

WILEY, L. E., see Lashley.

WILLIAMS, D. R., and TEITELBAUM, P. Some observations on the starvation resulting from lateral hypothalamic lesions. J. comp. physiol. Psychol., 1959, 52, 458–465. (383)

WILLIAMS, H. L., TEPAS, D. I., and MORLOCK, H. C. Evoked responses to clicks and electroencephalographic stages of sleep in man. *Science,* 1962, **138,** 685–686. (343)

WILLIAMS, K., see Hebb.

WILLIAMS, R. G., see Bazett.

WILLIAMS, R. J., reference given in text. (572)

WILLMER, E. N. Retinal structure and colour vision: A restatement and an hypothesis. Cambridge, England: Cambridge Univer. Press, 1946. (133)

WILSON, M., STAMM, J. S., and PRIBRAM, K. H. Deficits in roughness discrimination after posterior parietal lesions in monkeys. *J. comp. physiol. Psychol.,* 1960, **53,** 535–539. (270)

WILSON, W. A., and MISHKIN, M. Comparison of the effects of inferotemporal and lateral occipital lesions on visually guided behavior in monkeys. *J. comp. physiol. Psychol.,* 1959, **52,** 10–17. (501)

WINDLE, W. F., reference given in text. (571)

WING, K. G. The role of the optic cortex of the dog in the retention of learned responses to light: conditioning with light and shock. *Amer. J. Psychol.,* 1946, **59,** 583–612. (451)

WING, K. G. The role of the optic cortex of the dog in the retention of learned responses to light: conditioning with light and food. *Amer. J. Psychol.,* 1947, **60,** 30–67. (451)

WING, K. G., and SMITH, K. U. The role of the optic cortex in the dog in the determination of the functional properties of conditioned reactions to light. *J. exp. Psychol.,* 1942, **31,** 478–496. (451)

WINSTON, H. D., see Lindzey.

WITHERSPOON, Y. T. Brain weight and behavior. *Hum. Biol.,* 1960, **32,** 366–369. (60)

WOELLNER, R. C., see Schuknecht.

WOLBARSHT, M. L., see Wagner.

WOLF, E., see Crozier.

WOLF, H. A., reference given in text. (571)

WOLF, I. S., see Kellogg.

WOLFSON, A. Regulation of annual periodicity in the migration and reproduction of birds. *Cold Spring Harbor Symp. Quant. Biol.,* 1960, **25,** 507–514. (439)

WOLSTENHOLME, G. E. W., reference given in text. (570, 571)

WOOD, C. D. Behavioral changes following discrete lesions of temporal lobe structures. *Neurology,* 1958, **8,** 215–220. (419)

WOOD, W. M., see Morgan.

WOODWORTH, R. S., and SCHLOSBERG, H. *Experimental psychology* (Rev. ed.) New York: Holt, Rinehart and Winston, 1954. (113, 235, 236, 238, 242, 248)

WOOLDRIDGE, D. E., reference given in text. (570)

WOOLLARD, H. H., WEDDELL, G., and HARPMAN, J. A. Observations on the neurohistological basis of cutaneous pain. *J. Anat.,* 1940, **74,** 413–440. (245, 253)

WOOLLEY, D. W., and VAN DER HOEVEN, T. Alteration in learning ability caused by changes in cerebral serotonin and catechol amines. *Science,* 1963, **139,** 610–611. (559)

WOOLSEY, C. N. Patterns of sensory representation in the cerebral cortex. *Fed. Proc.,* 1947, **6,** 437–441. (59)

WOOLSEY, C. N. Patterns of localization in sensory and motor areas of the cerebral cortex. In Milbank Memorial Fund. 27th Annual Conference. *The biology of mental health and disease.* New York: Hoeber, 1952. (267, 268, 286)

WOOLSEY, C. N., reference given in text. (486, 570)

WOOLSEY, C. N., see Brady, Meyer, Rose, Thompson.

WORTIS, R. P., see Lehrman.

WOSKOW, M. H., see Gengerelli.

WRIGHT, W. D. The characteristics of tritanopia. *J. Opt. Soc. Amer.,* 1952, **42,** 509–521. (177)

WYNNE, L. C., and SOLOMON, R. L. Traumatic avoidance learning: Acquisition and extinction in dogs deprived of normal peripheral autonomic function. *Genet. Psychol. Monogr.,* 1955, **52,** 241–284. (478)

WYRWICKA, W., and DOBRZECKA, C. Relationship between feeding and satiation centers of the hypothalamus. *Science,* 1960, **123,** 805–806. (380)

WYRWICKA, W., DOBRZECKA, C., and TARNECKI, R. On the instrumental conditioned reaction evoked by electrical stimulation of the hypothalamus. *Science,* 1959, **130,** 336–337. (384)

YALOW, R. S., see Roth.

YANNET, H., see Darrow.

YASUKOCHI, G. Emotional responses elicited by electrical stimulation of the hypothalamus in cat. *Folia psychiat. neurol. Jap.,* 1960, **14,** 260–267. (316, 317)

YERKES, R. M., reference given in text. (443)

YOUNG, D. R., and SPECTOR, H. Physical performance capacity and nutriture: Evaluation of rations by animal experimentation. *Symposium on nutrition and behavior.* New York: National Vitamin Foundation, 1957. Pp. 27–38. (354, 558)

YOUNG, P. T. Studies of food preference, appetite, and dietary habit. I. Running activity and dietary habit of the rat in relation to food preference. *J. comp. Psychol.,* 1944, **37,** 327–370. (367)

YOUNG, P. T. Psychologic factors regulating the feeding process. In *Symposium on nutrition and behavior.* New York:

The National Vitamin Foundation, 1957. Pp. 52–59. (367, 372, 373)

YOUNG, P. T. Motivation and emotion: a survey of the determinants of human and animal activity. New York: Wiley, 1961. Pp. xxiv + 648. (310)

YOUNG, P. T., reference given in text. (571)

YOUNG, P. T., and CHAPLIN, J. P. Studies of food preference, appetite and dietary habit. III. Palatability and appetite in relation to body need. Comp. Psychol. Monogr., 1945, 18, No. 3, Pp. 45. (367)

YOUNG, W. C., reference given in text. (571)

YOUNG, W. C., see Boling, Phoenix.

YUWILER, A., and LOUTTIT, R. T. Effects of phenylalanine diet on brain serotonin in the rat. Science, 1961, 134, 831–832. (556)

ZANGWILL, O. L. Cerebral dominance and its relation to psychological function. Edinburgh, Scotland: Oliver and Boyd, 1960. (535, 543)

ZANGWILL, O. L. Speech. In J. Field, H. W. Magoun, and V. E. Hall (Eds.), Handbook of physiology, Vol. 3. Washington, D. C.: American Physiological Society, 1960. (535)

ZANGWILL, O. L., reference given in text. (571)

ZANGWILL, O. L., see McFie.

ZELIONY, G. P., see Poltyrew.

ZEWI, M., see Granit.

ZIEHER, L. M., see de Robertis.

ZOTTERMAN, Y. Special senses: Thermal receptors. Annu. Rev. Physiol., 1953, 15, 357–372. (251)

ZOTTERMAN, Y. Thermal sensations. In J. Field, H. W. Magoun, and V. E. Hall (Eds.), Handbook of physiology, Vol. 1. Washington, D. C.: American Physioogical Society, 1959. (251)

ZOTTERMAN, Y., see Cohen, Hensel.

ZUBEK, J. P. Recent electrophysiological studies of the cerebral cortex: Implications for localization of sensory functions. Canad. J. Psychol., 1951, 5, 110–121. (267, 269)

ZUBEK, J. P. Effects of cortical lesions upon hoarding behavior in rats. J. comp. physiol. Psychol., 1951, 44, 310–319. (441)

ZUBEK, J. P. Studies in somesthesis. I. Role of the somesthetic cortex in roughness discrimination in the rat. J. comp. physiol. Psychol., 1951, 44, 339–353. (269)

ZUBEK, J. P. Studies in somesthesis. II. Role of somatic sensory areas I and II in roughness discrimination. J. Neurophysiol., 1952, 15, 401–408. (269, 488)

ZUBEK, J. P. Studies in somesthesis. III. Role of somatic areas I and II in the acquisition of roughness discrimination in the rat. Canad. J. Psychol., 1952, 6, 183–193. (488)

ZUBEK, J. P., see Downer.

ZUBEK, J. P., and DELORENZO, A. J. The cerebral cortex and locomotor activity in rats. Canad. J. Psychol., 1952, 6, 55–70. (359)

Subject Index